Windows++

Windows++

Writing Reusable
Windows™ Code in C++

Paul DiLascia

Addison-Wesley Publishing Company
Reading, Massachusetts   Menlo Park, California   New York
Don Mills, Ontario   Wokingham, England   Amsterdam   Bonn
Sydney   Singapore   Tokyo   Madrid   San Juan
Paris   Seoul   Milan   Mexico City   Taipei

Many of the designations used by manufacturers and sellers to distinguish their products are claimed as trademarks. Where those designations appear in this book and Addison-Wesley was aware of a trademark claim, the designations have been printed in initial capital letters.

The authors and publishers have taken care in preparation of this book, but make no expressed or implied warranty of any kind and assume no responsibility for errors or omissions. No liability is assumed for incidental or consequential damages in connection with or arising out of the use of the information or programs contained herein.

Library of Congress Cataloging-in-Publication Data

DiLascia, Paul.
   Windows++ : writing reusable Windows code in C++ / Paul DiLascia.
      p. cm.
   Includes bibliographical references and index.
   ISBN 0-201-60891-X
   1. Windows (computer programs) 2. C++ (Computer program language)
   I. Title.
   QA76.76.W56D55 1992
   005.4'3--dc20   92-15872
                                              CIP

Managing Editor: Amorette Pedersen
Cover Design: Jean Seal
Set in 11-point Palatino

1 2 3 4 5 6 7 8 9-MW-9695949392
First Printing, June 1992

This book was created using Interleaf publishing software.

TABLE OF CONTENTS ■

PREFACE ∎

During the course of my consulting over the past few years, I now and then encountered opportunities to do Windows programming. Knowing little about Windows (I had programmed a bit in OS/2 PM), I turned these offers down—but the demand for Windows kept growing and growing. By early 1991, I decided that Windows was hot and it was time to become a Windows expert.

I'd heard that Windows was notorious for being difficult, so I figured I'd better get some of the commercial Windows programming tools I'd heard about. I spent a week or so investigating various products: code generators, high-level languages, user interface builders, class libraries, and sundry others. While each product I looked at had some merits, none struck me as especially wonderful. I was disappointed and wondered, "what should I buy?"

Suddenly it struck me that my predicament seemed rather odd. I thought, "Here I am, a professional software developer with years of experience—why am I perplexed about what software tool to buy to help me program Windows, instead of just *programming it myself?* How hard can it be?" Indeed, I wondered, why are there are so many products to assist Windows programming? Windows seems to have spawned an entire *industry* of programming tools. There's nothing like this for DOS (have you ever seen a DOS code generator?).

Is Windows programming really so difficult? If so, what's wrong with it?

I decided to find out. Instead of buying off-the-shelf tools, I resolved to build a system of my own. I figured even if my effort went bust, I'd at least learn a lot about Windows in the process. Since C++ is my language of choice, I decided to build a C++ class library, which I dubbed *Windows++* for obvious reasons.

Within about a month, I had built a system that was actually useful for writing "serious" applications. I was both surprised and delighted to discover that Windows programming isn't so dreadful after all; while Windows does have many quirks and flaws, they're easily overcome. It seems to me now that Windows' reputation for being "difficult" is something of a myth. It has more to do with the *way* most people program Windows than with Windows itself. I won't say any more here; you'll have to read the book to find out exactly what I mean.

Windows++, the book, is the story of how I built *Windows++*, the class library, and how you can build a similar library yourself. The book is essentially a recipe for building a C++ class library interface to Windows. Rather than teach you how to program Windows using commercially available class libraries, I'll show you how to build your own; one of my premises is that you can build your own system in the time it takes you to learn someone else's—and you're more likely to get what you want. I'll take you step-by-step through all the details, from humble beginnings to a full-blown library. Along the way, I'll teach you about object-oriented programming and C++, for I hope there are as many die-hard C programmers among my readers as there are born-again C++ fanatics.

In addition to *Windows++* itself, we'll implement several sample programs, ranging from the familiar "hello, world" program to a tic-tac-toe game; from a PEOPLE database to a Mandelbrot fractal generator and a DRAW program. While these programs are necessarily small enough to be described in a few pages or a chapter at most, they are nevertheless "real" programs, not toys that do no more than illustrate some simple concept (for example, a program that displays a dialog box with every kind of control in it). By choosing more realistic sample programs, I hope to lend credibility to my claim that *Windows++* makes Windows programming easier. More important: rather than simply illustrating how to use the library *post facto*, the applications guide its development. In most cases, we'll set out with a particular application in mind, and ask ourselves: what do we want it to look like when we're done? Then, we'll build the library support required to make it so.

While the primary aim of the book is to show how you can build reusable Windows code in C++, there's also a larger goal: the methods used to build *Windows++* have applicability beyond Windows. I hope this book will serve, by way of example, to illustrate the benefits and ease of object-oriented programming in general, and C++ in particular (not to mention several useful C++ "tricks"). Readers seeking to learn more about OOP and C++ should find the book educational.

Windows++ is a case history of object-oriented-programming in practice. As such, it reveals in general how to model complex systems such as Windows using object-oriented techniques. Often the best way to convey abstract concepts is through specific examples.

Caveats

Before proceeding any further, a few caveats are in order:

- Many of the ideas behind *Windows++* are described or implicit in other sources. A few programmers have developed libraries similar to *Windows++* on their own. Some are even commercially available. To implement *Windows++*, I've borrowed ideas and techniques from books, products, magazine articles, and whatever other sources I could find. I make no claim to have invented the idea of *Windows++*; on the contrary, I acknowledge my indebtedness to others. My contribution lies in being the first (as far as I know) to write down in one place how one goes about building such a system. (Of course, there are also a few tricks of my own invention which I'll share with you.)

- In the following pages, I will present an approach to Windows programming that differs from that described in the Microsoft *Software Development Kit* (hereafter abbreviated SDK) and other books on programming Windows. While I think my way is better (because it simplifies Windows programming and results in code that's reusable), my intention is not to denigrate other approaches, which are well-suited for many purposes.

- *Windows++* is not a comprehensive Windows guide; the book does not describe how to model all aspects of Windows. For example, color palettes, metafiles, and message filters are not covered. A complete treatment of Windows would necessarily require a much longer book, something I want to avoid, and would be beside the point anyway. My aim is not to model every aspect of Windows using C++, but rather to show *in general* how one goes about it. Readers who understand the basic principles can easily extend them to areas not covered in the book.

  That said, *Windows++* nevertheless encapsulates a sizable amount of Windows functionality, more than there is room to thoroughly explore in the book. I have myself used *Windows++* to build fairly sophisticated, "real" applications.

- Finally, as you may already have suspected, I'm an avid enthusiast of object-oriented programming and C++—but just in case you didn't, it's only fair that I state my bias from the outset. Don't worry, I have no desire to use my book as a pulpit from which to preach OOP gospel. Many books praise the benefits and wonders of OOP; my aim is to *show* them, in real life, honest-to-goodness programs. So I won't claim how great *polymorphism* is, but will simply point out where I use it and let you judge for yourself whether it has any merit. After all, the proof of the pudding is in the eating.

I should perhaps also mention a few words about my writing style. The book is a story, not a manual. I am most concerned with conveying a certain approach to programming Windows in C++, to showing you how I built *Windows++*, not just the finished product. So rather than simply describe *Windows++* in its final form (the way a programmer's manual would), I'll take you through its development step by step. We'll write some code, then go back and change it, then go back and change it again. As much as possible, I'll avoid simply stating flatly, "this is how it works," but will instead try to show you why it *must* work that way, and how you might have figured it out yourself. This approach is both more useful and true-to-life: it shows how large systems evolve gradually from smaller ones. Software development is in practice much more messy than you might guess from finished products. (Of course, there are some messy products, too.)

Prerequisites

In order to benefit from this book, you should be familiar with Windows and the C programming language. If you don't know C, you've bought the wrong book. If you don't know Windows, you may get by, but I urge you to consult either the Microsoft Windows *Guide to Programming*, or a book such as [Petzold 1990] before proceeding.

What about C++?

If you've had some exposure to C++, so much the better. If you're familiar with Windows, have read one C++ book such as [Stroustrup 1991], and want to learn how to put the two together, you're ideally prepared and have come to the right place.

If you're a C programmer who doesn't know C++, *don't go away!* One of my aims is to introduce C++ to C programmers, and show them the benefits of object-oriented programming through concrete examples. A mini-tour of C++ is given in Chapter 2, and I'll describe additional C++ features as we go. You should be able to glean a lot about C++ from reading along, enough to understand the text. Of course, this is not a comprehensive C++ treatise; if you want to learn more about C++, consult the bibliography. [Stroustrup 1991] is the official C++ bible.

Even if you don't intend to ever learn or use C++, astute C programmers should be able to adapt most of the techniques described to C. After all, there's nothing you can do in C++ that you can't do in C; "object-oriented" and *reusability* are really ways of programming, rather than properties inherent in one language or another. You can write object-oriented code in C, and you can write non-OO code in C++.

To actually build *Windows++* yourself, you'll need the following items:

- An IBM-compatible PC capable of running Windows 3.0 in protected (standard or 386 enhanced) mode. (I recommend at least a 386.)

- Microsoft Windows, version 3.0 or later. *Windows++* won't run in older versions.

- Either the Zortech (version 3.0r4 or later) or Borland (version 3.0 or later) C++ compiler. The Microsoft *Windows Software Development Kit* (SDK) is not required with either compiler, though I recommend that Windows programmers purchase the SDK documentation, which is available separately in bookstores. The Microsoft resource compiler (RC.EXE) is required, but this comes with both the Borland and Zortech compilers.

  I apologize that there's no mention of the Microsoft 7.0 C/C++ compiler. This compiler will be generally available by the time you read this, but it only became so as I was writing the final chapters; there simply wasn't enough time to cover it.

- To design dialog boxes interactively, you'll need a tool such as *Windows-Maker* (which comes with the Zortech compiler) or Borland's *Resource Workshop.*

Companion Disk

The source code for *Windows++* and the various sample programs are listed in Appendix A at the end of the book. If you don't particularly want to type in over a hundred pages of C++ code all by yourself (believe me, you don't), you can purchase the *Windows++* source disk directly from me for $25 (there's a coupon in the back of the book).

Both the listings in Appendix A and the code on the disk differ in minor ways from the samples shown in the text. The source code contains the latest last-minute revisions and bug-fixes, as well as compiler-specific directives that I've omitted in the text whenever it obscures the point I'm trying to make. Also, many of the code fragments that appear in the body of the book contain comments relating the code to the text; these comments don't actually appear in the source code.

Acknowledgments

I would like to thank the people who provided essential comments, suggestions, and other good ideas, and who took the time to read my early drafts. These include Tim Anderson, Ed Black, and Patrick Slaney. Patrick (Interleaf's "graphics wizard") helped me figure out the basic structure for Chapter 8, as well as providing many useful comments and suggestions, not to mention unyielding enthusiasm and encouragement.

I also want to thank the people at Benchmark Productions, in particular Amy Pedersen and Chris Williams. I'm especially indebted to Andrew Schulman, without whom this book would not be possible (it sounds cliché, but it's true). Andy not only provided numerous technical corrections and advice, but also went to bat for me at Benchmark. Many of Andy's ideas (and some of his code!) found their inexorable way into *Windows++*.

Finally, I thank Mara for making it possible, Jennifer for putting up with me, and Pandora for keeping me company.

CHAPTER ■ 1

Introducing *Windows++*

This book is about building a C++ class library (*Windows++*) that models Windows. Each chapter explores some different aspect of just what this means—but it seems natural to first ask: why is there any need to model Windows? Why not just use Windows as is?

There are many flaws in Windows, which I'll point out as we go, but they all boil down to essentially one thing: Windows is difficult to program. The main reason for building *Windows++* is to make Windows programming easier; the primary means by which it achieves this goal is *reusability*.

1.1 The Problem: How to Reuse Code?

Windows is notoriously difficult to program. Everyone has heard about the steep learning curve and how different Windows is from other systems, particularly DOS. Yet this should seem odd: since Windows does so much more than DOS, you'd expect it to make life easier, not more difficult! In fact, it does. So why is Windows known for being so difficult?

There are two major hurdles that confront would-be Windows programmers, one real and the other, I believe, imaginary.

Hurdle #1: The first hurdle (the "real" one) programmers must overcome is so-called event programming. The customary "procedural" way to write programs is to start by positing a top-level function, *do-the-right-thing,* and then divide it into smaller and smaller sub-tasks until each unit is small enough to implement as a single subroutine. In *event programming,* you instead write subroutines that respond to various "events," and then let your program wait until one of these events occurs. This wait-until-something-happens approach is characteristic of GUIs (Graphical User Interfaces) such as Windows, as well as of object-oriented programming in general. If you're used to programming procedurally, event

1

programming seems somewhat strange at first. It takes a little getting used to, but once you get the hang of it, it quickly becomes natural.[1]

Hurdle #2: The second hurdle (the imaginary one) is that you have to write lots of code to create a Windows application. Newcomers are dismayed when they first learn Windows that the famous "hello, world" program requires about 75 lines of code in its simplest form! The problem only gets worse as applications become more sophisticated: windows must be registered, then created; the *window procedure* (which not uncommonly runs for 20 pages) must be written—not to mention similarly lengthy *dialog procedures* for each dialog box. I have personally worked on large applications in which dialog and window procedures consumed literally thousands of source lines of "open" code: long sequences of program statements with no real structure and no subroutine calls. Such code is not only difficult to understand and maintain, it can result in needlessly enormous compiled programs.

The reason Windows programs require so much effort is that Windows fails to encapsulate enough functionality in subroutines. Instead, it leaves much grunt work for each application to perform. To make a hardware analogy: writing a program in Windows is like building a computer from individual resistors and transistors, when what's required are integrated circuit modules that perform high-level functions.

The solution to this problem is easy: just write the missing high-level subroutines. Yet few Windows programmers ever do so. Instead, they follow what I call the "copy-paste-edit" school of reusability: most Windows programmers write applications by first pasting an existing Windows application into their editor, and then modifying it to suit their purpose.

The reason this software engineering methodology (if it deserves to be called such) is so prevalent is that it's expounded by Microsoft. The SDK manual gives explicit instructions on how to do it: first you start with the "Generic" application, then you add a switch case to handle this and that message, a menu here, a dialog there, and so on until you're done:

> You can use Generic as a template to build your own applications. To do this, copy and rename the sources of an existing application, such as Generic, then change relevant function names, and insert new code. All sample applications in this guide have been created by copying and renaming Generic's

---

1   Interestingly, there are many aspects of lower-level DOS programming (device drivers, TSRs, interrupt handlers, and so on) that are event-driven rather than procedural. Event programming is nothing new; it's been around for a while—what's new is that it's exposed at a high level in GUIs like Windows. Event programming is in some sense inherently object-oriented partly because it's non-procedural.

source files, then modifying some of the function and resource names to make them unique to each new application.

Microsoft Windows SDK Guide to Programming, Chap. 2, p. 35.

Rather than *question* this copy-paste-edit philosophy of programming,[2] most Windows programming books have instead reinforced it. Even Charles Petzold's classic *Programming Windows* is filled with applications that contain the same code over and over again. There's a joke in the Windows folklore to the effect that only one Windows program was ever written, and every other Windows program is a copy of it. (This mythic program is of course the mother-of-all-Windows-programs.)

The similarities among Windows programs have not gone completely unnoticed, however. Among the many Windows programming tools whose stars have risen along with Windows' are the commercial *code generators*. These products let you design your application—windows, menus, dialog boxes, and all—interactively, on the screen. Press a button and *voilà!* The code generator actually writes the source code for you! If specialized processing is required, you simply insert your own code between the lines of generated code. The code generator even preserves your additions when you re-edit the application! Surely, code generators must be the greatest thing since sliced bread. (CASE zealots certainly think so.)

Yet, if you think about it, there's something peculiar about all this. If Windows code is so predictable that it can be copied from one source file to another, or even generated automatically by a program, then surely there must be some way to encapsulate its generic aspects into subroutines (remember them?) that can be called repeatedly. Has the subroutine gone out of style? Instead of recreating the same code for each new application, why not write it once, and be done with it?

That's precisely what this book shows you how to do.

1.2 A Solution: *Windows++*

Windows++ is one answer to the programming challenges of Windows. *Windows++* is a library of reusable Windows code, in the form of C++ object classes. I'll explain what classes are soon enough. By *reusable,* I mean that to write a new application, you write the application-specific parts of it, then compile and link your code with the *Windows++* library. The same object modules can be used, unchanged, in any *Windows++* application. The functions in the *Windows++*

---

2   This might be called "reusability at the source file level," but it's not, since the source files must be modified. It's really "reusability at the programmer level," since the same programmer is reused(!) to create each new application.

library are in this respect no different from the familiar *printf* and *strcpy* functions in the standard C runtime library.

Windows++ is more than just a collection of subroutines; it's an *application framework*. Rather than attempt to define this buzzword myself, let me simply quote Bjarne Stroustrup:

> An alternative, and sometimes more ambitious, approach to the support of design and re-use is to provide code that establishes a common framework into which the application builder fits application-specific code as building blocks. Such an approach is often called an application framework. . . . [Application frameworks] approximate the ideal of being complete applications, except that they don't do anything. The specific actions are supplied by the application programmer.

Stroustrup 1991, p. 455

Windows++ meets this definition quite well. As you'll see, *Windows++* does indeed provide a reusable framework into which programmers can insert application-specific code. *Windows++* is similar to *ObjectWindows*, which comes with the Borland C++ compiler (but *Windows++* is better!).

I must emphasize, however, that *Windows++* is *a* solution, not *the* solution to the problems of Windows programming. Here are some others:

- The cut-and-paste method described in the Windows SDK and elsewhere can be quite effective, though somewhat error-prone. Many sophisticated applications are written this way, and if you only plan to write *one* application, this is probably the quickest way to do it.

- Code generators are often useful for building prototypes quickly. Many of them even have an "animation mode" that lets you try out your user interface before generating the code. I've read many customer testimonials to the effect that "using XYZ code generator I put together a prototype in just two days and landed a big contract." What's more, I believe them. Most code generators fail, however, when you later attempt to add subtle features that go beyond simple command-response interaction. For example, it would be difficult, if not impossible, to implement direct manipulation using a code generator.

- High-level languages such as *Visual Basic, ObjectVision, Actor,* and others are extremely effective for many applications. Most are amazingly easy to learn and use, and while "hard core" C programmers sometimes scoff at them (What?—me program in *BASIC?!*), I think they should study some of these systems to learn just how easy programming can be. The primary disadvantage is that they're ill-suited for large applications, don't expose all Windows functionality, and generally produce slower programs than C does.

■ Class libraries similar to *Windows++* are commercially available. Borland provides *ObjectWindows* with its C++ compiler. *Zinc, Win++,* and *C++/Views* are commercial C++ class libraries similar in various respects to *Windows++*.

When confronted with the need to write Windows programs faster, I investigated all the options listed above and agonized for some time over which to choose. Finally, I decided to build my own C++ class library. Here are my reasons:

■ Because I needed to write many Windows applications, I stood to gain maximum leverage from a code library. Not only does the library approach make maximum use of existing code, the applications are easier to maintain: if there's a bug in the library, you fix it once for all applications. Likewise, if you add an enhancement to the library, you add it to all applications simultaneously. These benefits of reusable code are nothing new; programmers have been writing subroutines since ENIAC was built. What's surprising is that this established good-coding practice seems to have been forgotten in many Windows programs.

■ I wanted a system that provided access to *all* Windows functionality. I wanted the freedom to call any Windows API function, should the need arise.

■ I reasoned that by writing a system of my own, I would become a Windows expert. I mention this in all seriousness: if you want to become proficient in Windows, implementing a library like *Windows++* is an excellent way. While writing *Windows++*, I "got to know" the Windows API intimately.

■ I wanted a system that I understood completely, had total control over, and could modify at will. (This guaranteed that I would be writing it!)

Windows++ is not for everyone: it requires knowing or learning C++, which may alone be more trouble than many can afford. Even if you already know C++ (as I did), building *Windows++* requires a modest initial investment of time and effort. (Unless, of course, you decide to buy the disk. Then all you have to do is read the book!) *Windows++* is ideal for consultants and developers who write many applications and need total control over their programs.

On the other hand, I hope to show that building a system like *Windows++* is not that difficult, nor too time-consuming! If you're about to purchase a commercial Windows class library, you may want to reconsider after reading this. As I said in the Preface, it took me only about a month to get *Windows++* working to the point where it was actually useful for building applications! It often takes that much time (or more) to fully learn someone else's system, and even then you surely won't understand it as well as a system you've written yourself. (The vendors are really going to hate me now!)

Regardless of which Windows programming solution you choose, this book contains ample material to learn from. Most of the techniques used have wide applicability and can easily be adapted for other situations—so even if you don't plan to actually build *Windows++* yourself, read on!

1.2.1 Why C++?

The decision to write a library of reusable code and the decision to use object-oriented programming in C++ are *independent* decisions. One could develop a reusable library similar to *Windows++* in C or any other language. Making the code reusable requires identifying and implementing the appropriate subroutines, *not* programming in C++.

So why C++?

Long ago, I became convinced that object-oriented programming in general, and C++ in particular, offers a better way to program. So I really didn't give it a second thought. Nevertheless, some justification seems called for, so I will simply list the main reasons why I became so convinced, emphasizing aspects that are especially relevant to Windows:

- C++ provides a number of useful syntactic conveniences, such as function and operator overloading, default function arguments, and so on, that make programming easier.

- C++ is C. It therefore has all the benefits of C, including *performance, portability,* and *"closeness to the machine."* If C is the "lowest-level high-level language," C++ is the "lowest-level object-oriented language." C++ is the obvious object-oriented upgrade path from C. To abuse a tired cliché, C++ is evolutionary, not revolutionary. This is the main reason for choosing C++ over other object-oriented languages such as Smalltalk.

- The fact that C++ is C is crucial for Windows, since the Windows API is primarily designed for C. Since C++ *is* C, you can always call a Windows API function directly from the middle of your C++ program. No special effort is required to compile and link it.

- As we shall see, Windows is itself inherently object-oriented (though this fact is often obscured by its C interface and all the programming difficulties mentioned above), and is therefore naturally modeled by an object-oriented system. C++ offers the opportunity to expose Windows' latent object-orientedness through the medium of C++, which provides a much more precise and robust universe within which to play.

Underlying all these reasons is what I call the "cosmic" justification for OOP. The object-oriented paradigm of objects and operations fundamentally reflects the way human beings perceive reality, more closely and in more situations than the "procedural" paradigm. This is a metaphysical speculation we can leave for the philosophers and cognitive psychologists to debate. In my experience, OOP just works better. Of course, you can write object-oriented programs in any language, but with OOPLs such as C++, object-oriented features are *built in*, rather than merely possible.

1.2.2 Design Goals

Here's a brief list of goals for *Windows++*. I jotted down something more or less like this on a clean sheet of paper one afternoon before undertaking the project.

- *Reduce development time.* The primary goal is to make it easier to build Windows applications faster. The main vehicle for achieving this is *reusability*.

- *Support full Windows functionality.* The library should provide access to all Windows functionality. If you can do it in Windows, you should be able to do it in *Windows++*.

- *Maintain Windows look and feel.* It's possible to build a system that hides the Windows API entirely. Some commercial class libraries take this approach, but I chose not to. Instead, I've preserved the look and feel of Windows programming so that *Windows++* could easily be learned by programmers already familiar with Windows.

- *Lightweight. Windows++* does not build extensively on top of Windows but rather attempts to provide the "minimal C++ object-oriented programming interface to Windows." Exactly what this means is of course subject to debate. *Windows++* should not introduce unacceptable performance overhead; it should be a *minimal* layer above Windows.

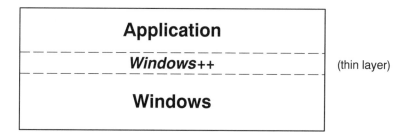

(thin layer)

- *Escape mechanism.* Just as you can always "pop out" of C++ and into C (perhaps violating all rules of tastefulness), you should be able to "pop out" of *Windows++* and into Windows. Naturally, the preferred way to program is through *Windows++*, but there should be a way to "escape"—for example, by getting the handle to your window.

There are two reasons for having an escape mechanism, both of them practical: First, while developing *Windows++*, it's often necessary to call Windows directly because a particular part of the library is not yet implemented. Second, a good programmer always knows when an expedient hack is called for. *Windows++* should not be confining, but let programmers break the rules, albeit at their own risk.

■ *Portability.* Finally, anyone building a library like *Windows++* must be aware that the OS/2 Presentation Manager is similar, but not quite identical to Windows. Other environments such as the MacIntosh and X Windows are less similar but share the overall spirit. In addition to this, a 32-bit version of Windows is expected soon from Microsoft. All of which means we should be concerned about portability. While absolute portability is *not* a goal (and not achieved), whenever it's easy and not too confusing, I've chosen the more portable approach when confronted with a design decision. For example, messages are passed in an event object rather that as *wParam* and *lParam*, the normal Windows message arguments.

1.3 Hello, *Windows++*

So far, the discussion has been fairly general and abstract, which is fine for an introduction, but I want to get down to earth as soon as possible, which is where I'll remain for most of the book. But first, I'd like to begin by showing you how easy it is to program in *Windows++*.

Unfortunately, there is a slight problem: even the most simple *Windows++* program (such as the infamous HELLO program) requires establishing a fair amount of infrastructure. So where do we begin? If you start (as I did) by building the infrastructure, you're likely to lose interest because it won't be at all clear where you're going or why. On the other hand, you can't build HELLO until you get at least a rudimentary version of *Windows++* working. This is the proverbial chicken-and-egg problem.

Fortunately, this is a book, where the beginning is written *after* the end—I can simply show you the finished HELLO program:

```
//////////////////////////////////////////////////////////////
// WINDOWS++ CLASS LIBRARY.  Copyright 1992 Paul DiLascia.
// FILE: HELLO.CPP
//
#include <wpp.h>

class HelloWin : public WPMainWin {
public:
    HelloWin() { createWin("Hello"); }
```

```
    void paint(WPPaintStruct &ps) {
        WPRect clientArea = this;
        ps.drawText(clientArea, "Hello, Windows++.",
            DT_SINGLELINE | DT_CENTER | DT_VCENTER);
    }
};
void WPApp::main()
{
    mainWin = new HelloWin;
    run();
}
```

This program is compiled and linked with the *Windows++* library. For the Borland C++ compiler, the command looks like this:

```
bcc -a -c -WE -WS hello.cpp wpp.lib
```

The HELLO program is, in a sense, our goal. To be precise, our goal is to design and implement the *Windows++* library (WPP.LIB) required to support the HELLO program as it appears above. This illustrates our first important principle: to build a library first imagine an *application* you want it to support, then build the *library* accordingly. While the library must logically precede the application, during design, the application comes first. This is no more than standard top-down programming, where you often find yourself calling subroutines that don't exist yet!

As you can see, HELLO is fairly small—23 lines, including comments. The same program in C (an example appears in Chapter 3) requires 72 lines—over three times bigger! I don't expect you to fully understand HELLO at this point, but Windows fans no doubt recognize some familiar elements. For example, the *drawText* function looks familiar (that's obviously where the message "Hello, Windows++" is displayed), and there's something to do with *PaintStruct,* which looks familiar too. But there's a lot of strange stuff going on: there's no window procedure, no switch statement, no window registration, just a few tiny functions—and where's *WinMain?*

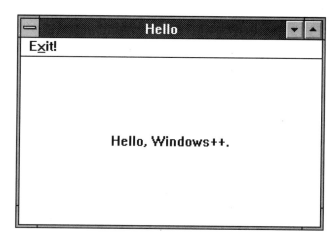

Furthermore, if you run HELLO, you'll discover that it has a menu bar with an Exit command that actually works, and when minimized, HELLO displays a smiley-face icon. Yet not a single line of code in HELLO deals with menus or icons!

I hope this little preview has piqued your curiosity enough to encourage you to read on, for it will take an entire lengthy chapter to fully explain how HELLO works. We'll start with a C version of HELLO and gradually transform it into the program above—but first, the next chapter provides a quick review of C++ for gurus and non-initiates alike.

CHAPTER ■ 2

Points, Rectangles, and a Quick Tour of C++

One of my goals in writing this book is to show non-C++ programmers why C++ is well-suited for programming Windows (C++ converts don't need convincing). Yet in order to understand the book, you need to know C++! Catch-22.

To include non-C++ gurus in my audience, I've provided this chapter, which is a sort of crash-course in C++. In this chapter, I'll teach you enough C++ to understand the rest of the book. C++ gurus should feel free to skim, but we'll use some of the examples later on, so don't skip it entirely. The chapter is *not* a comprehensive C++ guide; if you want to learn more, I recommend [Stroustrup 1991].

I originally conceived this chapter as a mini C++ tutorial, but after I'd written several pages, I realized they made dull reading. I could sense your eyes glazing over as I blandly enumerated features such as operator overloading, inheritance, virtual base classes, member functions, multiple inheritance, and so on.

So instead, I'll take this opportunity to introduce two *Windows++* structures used to model points and rectangles. The former, *WPPoint,* is an ordinary C *struct,* while the latter, *WPRect,* is our first example of a *class.* Besides playing an important role in *Windows++,* these objects serve to illustrate many aspects of C++. So as I describe *WPPoint* and *WPRect,* I'll explain C++ features as well, taking care to point out differences from C. I'll adopt the same strategy throughout the book, explaining new C++ features as we employ them in practice.

All along, we'll be making progress toward building *Windows++.*

C   *In future chapters, paragraphs like this one are used to describe how specific C++ techniques can be adapted for C. In this chapter, everything is pertinent to both C and C++.*

2.1 Points

Our first structure is called *WPPoint* (all the structure and class names in *Windows++* begin with the prefix *WP*). *WPPoint* is defined in a file called WPPOINT.H:

```
/////////////////////////////////////////////////////////////
// WINDOWS++ CLASS LIBRARY.
// Copyright 1991 Paul DiLascia. All Rights Reserved.
//
// Declarations for WPPoint structure.

#ifndef WPPOINT_H
#define WPPOINT_H

#include "wppdefs.h"

/////////////////////
// Used in place of Windows POINT structure.
// Must be declared identically to POINT so we can cast.
//
struct WPPoint {
    int x,y;                            // x,y coordinates

    WPPoint(int xx=0, int yy=0)         { set(xx,yy); }
    WPPoint(POINT p)                    { set(p); }

    void set(int xx=0, int yy=0)        { x=xx; y=yy; }
    void set(POINT p)                   { set(p.x, p.y); }

    BOOL operator==(WPPoint p)
        { return *((LONG*)this)==*((LONG*)&p); }
    BOOL operator!=(WPPoint p)
        { return *((LONG*)this)!=*((LONG*)&p); }

    WPPoint &operator++()               { ++x; ++y; return *this; }
    WPPoint& operator--()               { --x; --y; return *this; }

    WPPoint& operator+= (int n)         { x+=n; y+=n; return *this; }
    WPPoint& operator-= (int n)         { x-=n; y-=n; return *this; }

    WPPoint& operator+= (WPPoint p)     { x+=p.x; y+=p.y; return *this; }
    WPPoint& operator-= (WPPoint p)     { x-=p.x; y-=p.y; return *this; }

    WPPoint& operator*= (int m)         { x*=m; y*=m; return *this; }
    WPPoint& operator/= (int m)         { x/=m; y/=m; return *this; }

    WPPoint& operator*= (TEXTMETRIC &tm)
        { x*=tm.tmAveCharWidth; y*=tm.tmHeight; return *this; }

    WPPoint& operator= (POINT p)
        { set(p); return *this; }
    WPPoint& operator= (LONG l)
        { return *this = *((WPPoint*)&l); }
};

#endif
```

Wow! That's a lot of code for a measly point! Let's examine it slowly.

First of all, *WPPoint* is a *struct*. It contains two integers, *x* and *y*, which represent the coordinates of a point. The definition of *WPPoint* is thus identical to that of POINT, which is declared in WINDOWS.H as follows:

```
typedef struct tagPOINT
  {
    int   x;
    int   y;
  } POINT;
typedef POINT *PPOINT;
typedef POINT NEAR    *NPPOINT;
typedef POINT FAR     *LPPOINT;
```

This fact is crucial, since for performance efficiency, we will pass *WPPoint* structures to Windows functions by simply casting a pointer—for example:

```
WPPoint p;
.

.
ClientToScreen(hwnd, (LPPOINT)&p);
```

Despite all the functions defined for *WPPoint*, the size of a *WPPoint* object is the same as that of POINT; in other words:

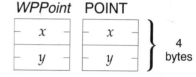

```
sizeof(WPPoint) == sizeof(POINT)
```

That is, both objects occupy the same amount (four bytes) of memory.

Note that in C++ you can use the *struct* name to declare variables; you don't have to invent another name (like *tagPOINT*) and use *typedef,* like you do with many C compilers. This is just one of C++'s many minor conveniences.

2.1.1 Member Functions

The first thing about *WPPoint* that's unfamiliar to C programmers is the list of what look like function definitions following the data members *x* and *y*. This is exactly what they are: in C++, a *struct* can have *member functions* as well as data members. In fact, If I had to explain OOP in a nutshell, I'd say something like this: "in object-oriented programming, data structures have functions as well as data, and each data structure defines what operations are allowed on it." This is an extreme simplification, but one that I think nevertheless captures the essence of object-oriented programming.[3]

---

3 Stroustrup describes the difference between procedural and object-oriented programming like this: *Procedural Programming Paradigm:* Decide which procedures you want; use the best algorithms you can find. *Object-oriented Programming Paradigm:* Decide which classes you want; provide a full set of operations for each class; make commonality explicit by using inheritance. He also describes "modular programming." See [Stroustrup 1991, p. 15 ff].

In C++, member functions are invoked using the same syntax that's used to reference data members (this looks a little strange at first):

```
WPPoint p, *pp;
.
.
p.set(1, 7);          // x=1, y=7
pp->set(1, 7);        // ditto
```

That is, using . or ->, depending on whether the reference is through an actual structure or a pointer. The function *set* is defined as follows.

```
void set(int xx=0, int yy=0)        { x=xx; y=yy; }
```

There are a few things worth noting about *set*. First, the arguments *xx* and *yy* are each declared to have *default values* of zero. In C++, functions arguments can have default values. Such arguments are *optional*, and may be omitted when calling the function. If so, the compiler supplies the default values:

```
p.set(4);      // equivalent to p.set(4,0)
p.set();       // equivalent to p.set(0,0)
```

If a function argument has a default value, so must all subsequent arguments:

```
void set(int x=0, int y)          // !#%$@! Not allowed: compiler error
```

This makes sense if you think about it: there's no way to omit x in a function invocation without also omitting y.

The second interesting thing about *set* is that it sets the data members x and y without referencing them through a structure. How does this work? To answer this question, we need to explore how C++ actually implements member functions.

Suppose for a minute that you were trying to build *WPPoint* in ordinary C. Instead of member functions (which are not supported in C), you would write a bunch of *extern* functions that all pass a *WPPoint** as their first argument. For example:

```
void PointSet(WPPoint* p, int x, int y)
{
    p->x = x;
    p->y = y;
}
```

To set the coordinates of a point, you'd write:

```
WPPoint *p;
.
.
PointSet(p, 4, 1);                 // set coords to (4, 1)
```

Before C++ was invented, many C programmers used this technique to build systems that followed the object-oriented paradigm. In fact, C++ does almost exactly the same thing! C++ implements member functions as ordinary C functions by combining the class name with the member function name and adding a special "hidden" argument called *this*, which is always a pointer to the object through which the member function was invoked. For example, if you define

```
class WPPoint {
    void set(int xx, int yy)        { x=xx; y=yy; }
};
```

C++ creates a function that looks something like this:

```
void WPPointset(WPPoint* this, int xx, int yy)
{
    this->x = xx;
    this->y = yy;
}
```

In fact, C++ was originally implemented as a pre-processor that converted C++ source code into C source code similar to that above. It's still implemented that way on some platforms.

While the *this* pointer does not appear in C++ member function definitions, it's available if you need to access it: *this* always points to the object through which the member function was invoked. For example, we could have written *set* like this:

```
struct WPPoint {
    void    set(int xx, int yy)        { this->x=xx; this->y=yy; }
};
```

Even though the variable *this* is not declared, it is implicitly of type *WPPoint** (pointer to *WPPoint*) and is automatically initialized by the compiler:

```
WPPoint p, *pp;
.
.
.
p.set(1, 7);      // "this" will be &p
pp->set(1, 7);    // "this" will be pp
```

Since it's tedious to type *this->foo* every time you want to access *foo*, C++ lets you reference the structure members directly, by name.

```
void set(int xx, int yy)
{
    x=xx;           // x is implicitly this->x
    y=yy;           // y is implicitly this->y
}
```

Within a member function, any reference to class (data or function) members is implicitly made through *this*. This makes sense, since there's no other *x* nor *y* you could have in mind. So when do you need to use *this?* Not often, but later on you'll see where it comes up.

2.1.2 Inline Functions

Not all member functions are defined within *struct* definitions—for example, we could rewrite *set* like this:

```
// Declaration is in WPPOINT.H:
struct WPPoint {
    void set(int, int);                // declaration only
};
// Definition is in WPPOINT.CPP
void WPPoint::set(int xx, int yy)      // Note syntax
{
    x = xx;
    y = yy;
}
```

That is, we could put the declaration in a header (.H) file and the implementation in a separate .CPP file. This is the normal C practice, where .H files contain prototypes for functions implemented in .C files. Note however, that when defining a C++ member function *outside* its structure definition, the structure name must be prepended to the function name, and separated from it by a double-colon (::). As we'll see in the next section, other structures may have *set* functions too, so the full name is required to tell the compiler which *set* function you mean.

You might wonder, what's the difference between defining a function inside the *struct* definition and defining it outside? When a member function like *set* is defined within a *struct* statement, it becomes an *inline function.*

In C++, ordinary (non-member) functions can be declared *inline*. For example,

```
inline int max(int a, int b)        { return a > b ? a : b; }
```

In C, this would be

```
#define max(a, b)                    ((a) > (b) ? (a) : (b))
```

An inline function is expanded wherever it's invoked. The compiler inserts the code for the function at the place it's invoked, rather than generating a function call. For this reason, inline functions are generally used only for small functions like *max*.

Inline functions have many advantages over C-style *#define* macros. For example, you don't have to type a back-slash (\) at the end of each line of a multi-line inline function. More important, while *#define* is a pre-processor directive that provides simple lexical substitution, *inline* functions are processed by the compiler. Not only can inline functions be more sophisticated, they eliminate the problems associated with evaluating arguments in *#define* macros. For example, consider what happens if you write:

```
max(x++, y++);
```

With *#define*, this expands using purely lexical substitution to

```
((x++) > (y++) ? (x++) : (y++));
```

which has the obvious problem that either *x* or *y* will be incremented twice, probably not what you intended. With inline functions, this won't happen. While the exact expansion of inline functions is compiler-dependent, you can be sure that however *max(x++, y++)* compiles, both *x* and *y* will be incremented exactly once, just as if *max* were a true function.

Most C++ compilers provide a command line switch to control whether or not inline functions are actually expanded. For example, in Zortech, you can specify *–C* to turn off inline function expansion; for Borland it's *–vi–*. You might want to turn inline expansion off while debugging, so you can trace your program's execution through "inline" functions as well as true functions—in fact, the Borland compiler automatically turns inline expansion off when you specify the debug switch, *–v*.

Back to structures: if a *member* function is *defined* (as well as *declared*) within a *struct* statement, it's automatically *inline*. This is the case for *set*. Thus

```
p.set(1, 7);
```

generates exactly the same code as

```
p.x = 1;
p.y = 7;
```

In fact, *all* the *WPPoint* member functions are inline, since they're all defined within the *struct* statement. None of them generates a function call when compiled! Hence there's no performance penalty incurred when using them.

2.1.3 Function Overloading

You may have noticed that there's another function called *set* defined for *WPPoint:*

```
void set(POINT p)    { set(p.x, p.y); }
```

This function sets a *WPPoint* from an ordinary Windows POINT, and it seems to call the first *set* to do this! C programmers are probably wondering: how can there be two *set* functions?! Will the real *set* please stand up!

In C++, you can use the same name for different functions, provided they take different arguments. This is called *function overloading.* This may seem bizarre at first, but it's extremely useful. Function overloading lets us write

```
WPPoint p;
POINT winPoint;
.
.
p.set(2, 5);        // set from x,y coords
p.set(winPoint);    // set from POINT
```

Even though the two *set* functions are really distinct, it's easier to call them by the same name, instead of inventing names like *setXY* and *setFromPOINT*. In C++, functions are implicitly qualified by their *signature* (arguments and return value) as well as by their *name.*

Given that function overloading is desirable, how is it possible? Let's examine how C++ does it. When C++ compiles a function, it modifies the function name by concatenating it with symbols that identify the function's arguments and return type. This is sometimes called *name mangling*. You can see the "mangled" names by examining the .MAP file produced by the linker. For example, the Zortech compiler produces the following symbols for the two *set* functions:[4]

```
_set__7WPPointN8tagPOINT
_set__7WPPointNii
```

These names encode the name of the function and its arguments as follows:

_	added to every function name;
set	name of function
__	separator
7	length of "WPPoint"
WPPoint	class name
N	near C++ function
8tagPOINT	1st arg is structure "tagPoint" (8 characters)
ii	1st and 2nd args are both integers

If these functions returned a value—say, an integer—the type would be appended at the end: *_set__7WPPointNii_i*. The Borland compiler uses a completely different name-mangling scheme. The actual method used to encode the function names is unimportant; what's important is that *in C++, a function's name effectively contains its declaration,* so the linker can be used to ensure that functions are always called with the appropriate arguments! This feature of C++ is called *type-safe linkage.* It eliminates an entire class of hard-to-find C bugs that arise when two modules accidentally "overload" a function by declaring it differently in several places.[5] For example, suppose you write a function called *foo* that takes two integers:

```
int foo(int x, int y)
{
    return (x+y)*y*x;
}
```

And suppose further that you call *foo* from a different module, where you mistakenly declare it to return a *long.*

```
extern long foo(int x, int y);
void MyFunc()
{
    int a, b;
    long c;
    .
    .
```

---

4   Actually, I cheated: there are no MAP symbols for either version of *set*, since they're both *inline*—but these are the symbols that would appear if you turn inline expansion off with the *–C* switch.

5   This kind of bug doesn't arise if all modules always include the function prototype from a common header file; it usually results from laziness.

```
   c = foo (a, b);
   .
   .
}
```

In C, your program will compile and link just fine, since all C cares about is that whatever arguments you pass to *foo* agree with whatever function prototype is in effect at the time, regardless of whether or not this prototype reflects the way *foo* is actually defined. Your program will either crash or at best behave erroneously when the "overloaded" function is called. In C++, the two *foo* functions produce different mangled names (something resembling, say, *foo_int* and *foo_long*); one will be undefined at link time, triggering a link error.

Name mangling has one drawback: if you want to call a C function from C++, the function must be declared as "C" or *_pascal*. This is the case with all the Windows API functions, since these functions were compiled into the Windows API libraries using C, not C++, linkage. The WINDOWS.H file that comes with most C++ compilers contains the following code:

```
#if defined( __cplusplus )
extern "C" {      /* tell compiler that following fns are C, not C++ */
#endif

/* Prototypes for Windows API functions. */
WORD    FAR PASCAL GetVersion(void);
WORD    FAR PASCAL GetNumTasks(void);
HANDLE FAR PASCAL GetCodeHandle(FARPROC);

.
. (More Windows API function prototypes.)
.

#if defined( __cplusplus )
}
#endif
```

The *extern "C"* tells the compiler to use C linkage (no name mangling) for the functions *GetVersion* and so on. The pre-processor symbol *_cplusplus* is defined when compiling C++, as opposed to C, files. By using this symbol, the same WINDOWS.H file can be used with either C or C++ programs.

Now that you understand how name mangling works, you can see how it's possible to overload functions. Since the mangled name encodes the arguments and return value, each overloaded version of the function actually has a different name. It's a different function! For member functions, the *struct* name is encoded as well, so you can also use the same names for member functions in different *structs*. For example, many *Windows++* structures besides *WPPoint* also have *set* functions.

2.1.4 *new* and *delete*

In C, if you wanted to allocate storage for a structure, you might write:[6]

```
POINT *pp = (POINT*)malloc(sizeof(POINT));
.
.
free(pp);
```

You might even write a general-purpose structure-allocation macro

```
#define ALLOC(foo)  (foo*)malloc(sizeof(foo));
```

to allocate a new instance of any kind of structure like so:

```
POINT *pp = ALLOC(POINT);
```

In C++, you'd write:

```
WPPoint *pp = new WPPoint;
.
.
delete pp;
```

The C++ operators *new* and *delete* are used to allocate and free storage, and should be used instead of *malloc* and *free*. Why? Because only then is the object properly initialized by its *constructor*.

2.1.5 Constructors

The first function defined for *WPPoint* has the same name as the structure itself (*WPPoint*), and has no return type:

```
struct WPPoint {
    WPPoint(int xx=0, int yy=0)    { set(xx,yy); }
};
```

This special function is called a *constructor*. *Constructors always have the same name as the class, and have no return type declaration.* The purpose of the constructor is to initialize the contents of a newly created structure instance: the compiler automatically generates a call to the constructor whenever an instance of the structure is created, either as an automatic variable on the stack or by allocating storage with *new.* The *WPPoint* constructor takes two (optional) arguments (default value = zero), and uses them to set *x* and *y*—in fact, it simply passes them to *set.* To create a point with initialized coordinates, you can use any of the following syntax styles:

```
WPPoint a(1, 7);                   // automatic, initialized to (1, 7)
WPPoint *p = new WPPoint(1, 7);    // allocated, initialized to (1, 7)

WPPoint a;                         // automatic, initialized to (0, 0)
WPPoint *p = new WPPoint;          // allocated, initialized to (0, 0)
```

---

6   Actually, you probably wouldn't do it for POINT since this structure is only four bytes and designed to fit in a *long*—so imagine a bigger structure.

```
WPPoint a(1);                     // automatic, initialized to (1, 0)
WPPoint *p = new WPPoint(1);      // allocated, initialized to (1, 0)
```

You can even create a nameless instance of a point on the stack—for example, as the return value of a function:

```
WPPoint MyFunc(...)
{
    .
    .
    return WPPoint(x, y);
}
```

In all these cases, the constructor is automatically invoked to initialize the object—for example, when *new* is invoked, the C++ compiler generates two function calls: first, a storage-allocation routine is called (perhaps even *malloc*—it depends on the compiler), then the constructor is invoked. Because the C++ compiler uses the *new* keyword as a clue that an object is being created, you should never create C++ structures by casting pointers returned from *malloc* (or any other storage-allocation function).

```
WPPoint *ppoint =
    (WPPoint*)malloc(sizeof(WPPoint));// WRONG! constructor not called
```

In the case of *WPPoint*, it probably wouldn't do any harm (especially if you immediately set *x* and *y*), but in general, structures may be more sophisticated (they may contain other objects that need to be initialized!) and should always be initialized by the appropriate constructor. Using *malloc* circumvents the constructors and is a definite no-no.

Constructors can be overloaded like any other function, provided of course the arguments are different for each overloaded version. In fact, *WPPoint* has another constructor:

```
WPPoint(POINT p)     { set(p); }
```

This one initializes the values of *x* and *y* from a Windows POINT structure. You can use it a number of different ways:

```
POINT P;
    .
    .
WPPoint  pt (P);                 // Create point on stack
WPPoint* ppt = new WPPoint(P);   // Create (allocate) point in memory
WPPoint  pt = P;                 // Same as first example, but using =
```

When a constructor has only one argument, you can use "=" to initialize an automatic variable (another C++ convenience). Of course, the right-hand side of the equal sign must be an expression that evaluates to an object of the proper type.

One constructor comes "built-in" with C++: the "copy" constructor. C++ knows how to initialize any object from an object of the same type:

```
WPPoint a;
WPPoint b = a;   // creates a (flat) copy of a
```

For Windows gurus, the constructor is much like the WM_CREATE message that's sent to a window when it's first created. This message gives the window a chance to initialize itself before the action starts. In the next chapter, we'll implement a *Windows++* class that makes this resemblance explicit.

2.1.6 The Destructor

Corresponding to the constructor is the *destructor*, which always has the name *~NameOfStruct* (that is, a tilde followed by the name of the class or structure). It has no arguments, and, like the constructor, has no return type. The destructor is called whenever an object instance is destroyed using *delete* or goes out of scope. "Going out of scope" means exiting the function or current block of code in curly braces ({}) for which the automatic variable is defined. Unlike constructors, you can't overload destructors; there can be only one for each type of structure. There might be several ways to initialize an object, but there's only one way to destroy it.[7]

WPPoint has no destructor, since there's nothing to do when a point is destroyed. In general, however, objects need to clean up after themselves—for example, the destructor for a *linkedList* might delete all the elements in the list. Later on, we'll see plenty of examples of destructors.

The Windows analog of the destructor is the WM_DESTROY message, which is sent to a window just before it's destroyed. In the next chapter, we'll make this analogy explicit.

2.1.7 Operator Overloading

We have seen how C++ lets you overload *functions;* it also lets you overload the standard C *operators* such as +, -, *, /, =, ==, !=, -=, ++, and so on. Wow!

To see how this works, let's see how *WPPoint* overloads the == and != operators:

```
BOOL operator==(WPPoint p)
    { return *((LONG*)this)==*((LONG*)&p); }
BOOL operator!=(WPPoint p)
    { return *((LONG*)this)!=*((LONG*)&p); }
```

These operators define what it means for two points to be equal or not. They let us write code like this:

```
WPPoint p1, p2;
.
.
.
if (p1 == p2) {
    .
    .
}
```

---

7   One could imagine having destructors with different arguments, but C++ doesn't allow it.

Furthermore, because of the way these operators are defined (inline, using casts), they generate compiled code equivalent to comparing two *longs*. In C, you'd have to write a function or *#define* macro to do this.

```
#define EqualPoint(p1, p2) ((*((LONG*)&p1)) == (*((LONG*)&p2)))
```

Then you'd have to invoke *EqualPoint* every time you wanted to compare two points. It sure is a lot easier and more natural to use ==.

Operator overloading is an extremely convenient and powerful feature. It lets you define the meaning of any C operator for structures of any kind. For example, I've defined various arithmetic operators for *WPPoints*:

```
struct WPPoint {
    .
    .
    // increment/decrement point
    WPPoint& operator++()            { ++x; ++y; return *this; }
    WPPoint& operator--()            { --x; --y; return *this; }

    // increment/decrement by any integer
    WPPoint& operator+= (int n)      { x+=n; y+=n; return *this; }
    WPPoint& operator-= (int n)      { x-=n; y-=n; return *this; }

    // add/subtract point
    WPPoint& operator+= (WPPoint p)  { x+=p.x; y+=p.y; return *this; }
    WPPoint& operator-= (WPPoint p)  { x-=p.x; y-=p.y; return *this; }

    // scale by integer factor
    WPPoint& operator*= (int m)      { x*=m; y*=m; return *this; }
    WPPoint& operator/= (int m)      { x/=m; y/=m; return *this; }
};
```

In C, you'd write ordinary functions or *#define* macros to get the same results, but it's easier and more natural to use operators:

```
WPPoint p1(1, -7), p2(17, 23), p;
    .
    .
++p1;               // p1 is now (2, -6)
p = p2;             // p is now (17, 23)
p -= p1;            // p is now (15, 29)
```

WPPoint even lets you multiply a point by a Windows TEXTMETRIC structure!

```
WPPoint& operator*= (TEXTMETRIC &tm)
    { x*=tm.tmAveCharWidth; y*=tm.tmHeight; return *this; }
```

This operator simply multiplies the *x* coordinate by the average character width and the *y* coordinate by the text height. This comes in handy when converting from text dimensions to pixels. For example:

```
TEXTMETRIC tm;
    .
    .
WPPoint p(5, 1);    // 5 characters in from left, one row down
p *= tm;            // ..convert to screen pixels
```

It's possible to go wild overloading operators, so caution is well advised. Unless it's obvious what a particular operator means, you're better off using ordinary functions with meaningful names. For example, *list->next()* is more readable than *list++*.

2.1.8 References

Non C++-ers have probably noticed the strange-looking *WPPoint&* return type declaration for all those overloaded operators:

```
WPPoint& operator++()                { ++x; ++y; return *this; }
WPPoint& operator--()                { --x; --y; return *this; }
```

Huh? What's & doing there?

In C, you usually pass pointers to structures, rather than the structures themselves, when calling functions. For example, to write a function that increments a point, you'd do something like this:

```
void IncPoint(WPPoint *p)
{
    ++(p->x);
    ++(p->y);
}
```

This function modifies the structure *p*, which is passed as a pointer. *IncPoint* is invoked like this:

```
void MyFunc()
{
    WPPoint p, *pp;
    .
    .
    IncPoint(&p);     // pass address of automatic variable
    IncPoint(pp);     // pass pointer
}
```

There are two main reasons for using pointers rather than entire structures:

- Passing whole structures requires copying them to the stack, which is inefficient, especially for large structures. A pointer is only two or four bytes (depending on whether it's *near* or *far*).

- By passing a pointer, the function can modify the caller's actual structure, not a copy of it.

In C++, you could write *IncPoint* exactly as above (C++ *is* C), but you could also do it like this:

```
void IncPoint(WPPoint& p)            // "reference" declaration
{
    ++(p.x);                         // note use of . instead of ->
    ++(p.y);
}
```

The funny declaration is called a *reference.* We say "*p* is a reference to a *WPPoint,*" just as in C we say "*p* is a pointer to a *WPPoint.*" C++ treats *p* syntactically as though it were an actual structure (which is why you use . instead of -> to access it), but in fact, the compiler passes *p* as a *pointer*, not a structure, and when *IncPoint* returns, the caller's point is modified! Syntactically, you invoke *IncPoint* as though you were passing the entire structure—but again, C++ really passes a pointer.

```
void MyFunc()
{
    WPPoint p, *pp;
    .
    .
    .
    IncPoint(p);     // & not required; p is modified
    IncPoint(*pp);   // * required; *pp is modified
}
```

A reference is in many respects no more than a syntactic sleight-of-hand (C++ is filled with them). The reference declaration (& following the type name) says, "treat the variable as though it were a whole structure, but pass it as a pointer." The two important things to remember about references are 1) they are always passed as pointers, not whole structures, and 2) when you modify a reference, you modify the actual structure it "references."

Back to *WPPoint.* Why do all the operators declare their return values as references (*WPPoint&*)?

```
WPPoint& operator++()        { ++x; ++y; return *this; }
WPPoint& operator--()        { --x; --y; return *this; }
```

Because a reference is a *modifiable value.* References are used so that we can chain expressions together:

```
++(++p)        // increment p twice
```

This works as follows: *operator++* first increments *x* and *y,* then returns **this.* Since *this* is a *pointer* to *WPPoint,* **this* is a *WPPoint,* which is syntactically equivalent to a reference to a *WPPoint.* So why not just return *WPPoint?* Because we don't want to return a *copy* of the point, but the point *itself.* If *operator++* returned *WPPoint* instead of *WPPoint&,* the second ++ operation above would increment a nameless copy of *p* returned on the stack, not *p* itself.[8]

If all this seems confusing, don't worry. Most C programmers find references strange at first. Part of the difficulty lies in the choice of & as the syntax. This makes

---

8   Starting in C++ Version 2.1, it's possible to differentiate between ++*p* and *p*++. As defined in the text, only the prefix-increment operator for *WPPoint* is defined, so *p*++ is not defined. The postfix-increment operator must be declared to take an integer. For example:

```
WPPoint& operator++(int foo)        { ++x; ++y; return *this; }
```

The integer *foo* is a dummy argument that's only used to distinguish *x*++ from ++*x.* It's supplied by the compiler and always has the value zero.

some sense when you think about it, but it's really just coincidental. To get used to references, you have to stop thinking of & as meaning *address-of*.

Think of it this way: a reference is just another name for a modifiable object—if you modify the reference, you modify the object it names.

C++ experts know I'm overlooking several subtle issues relating to references, but there's no space for a full presentation here. Consult one of the C++ books listed in the bibliography if you want more.

2.1.9 Overloading =

In *Windows++*, we don't often overload arithmetic operators such as + and * (what does it mean to add or multiply two windows?). However, one operator that's frequently overloaded is the *assignment operator (=)*. For example, *WPPoint* defines two versions:

```
WPPoint& operator= (POINT p)    { set(p); return *this; }
WPPoint& operator= (LONG l)     { return *this = *((WPPoint*)&l); }
```

These set the value of a point from a Windows POINT or a *long*.

```
WPPoint p1, p2; POINT P; long x;
.
.
.
p1 = P;          // assign from POINT
p2 = x;          // assign from long
```

The operators return *WPPoint&* for the same reason that *operator++* and *operator--* do: they return modifiable values so assignments can be strung together and combined with other operations.

```
p1 = p2 = x;     // p1 and p2 set from x
++(p1 = P);      // p1 is ++P; P is unchanged
```

It's common practice in C++ to have the assignment operator return a reference to the structure itself. The last line of such a function must always be

```
return *this;
```

This is one situation when you need to use *this*.

Just as with constructors, C++ knows how to assign $a = b$ when a and b are the same kind of structure: it's a flat copy from one structure to the other. A *flat* copy is one that copies only the structure itself and *not* secondary structures it might point to. A flat copy is accomplished in C by writing

```
memcpy(a, b, sizeof(a));
```

In most cases a flat copy will do, but if a and b contain fields that point to other structures that should be copied as well—that is, if you want a *deep* copy—all you have to do is write your own version of *operator=*.

You can see now how useful it is to overload functions. We can define as many different versions of = (or any other operator) as we like, to assign different kinds of data types to a structure. In C, you'd have to give each one a different name—it's much easier and more natural to simply write *a = b*.

2.2 Rectangles

Our next structure is actually a *class*. It's called *WPRect* and represents a rectangle. I'll describe what *classes* are in a moment, but first, let's look at the definition of *WPRect:*

```
////////////////////////////////////////////////////////////////
// WINDOWS++ CLASS LIBRARY.
// Copyright 1991 Paul DiLascia. All Rights Reserved.
// FILE: WPRECT.H
//
// Declarations for WPRect class.

#ifndef WPRECT_H
#define WPRECT_H

#include "wppoint.h"

//////
// This class must be defined exactly as a Windows RECT, because
// we need to cast it to a RECT when calling Windows.
//
class WPRect {
    WPPoint org;                        // origin of rectangle
    WPPoint end;                        // endpoint of rectangle
public:
    // Constructors
    WPRect() { }
    WPRect(WPPoint o, WPPoint e)   { set(org, end); }
    WPRect(int l, int t, int r, int b)       { set(l,t,r,b); }
    WPRect(RECT& rect)            { *this = rect; }
    WPRect(WPWin *win)            { *this = win; }
    WPRect(WPPaintStruct& ps)     { *this = ps; }

    void normalize();

    // Access
    int left()                   { return org.x; }
    int top()                    { return org.y; }
    int right()                  { return end.x; }
    int bottom()                 { return end.y; }

    // Set
    int left(int l)              { return org.x=l; }
    int top(int t)               { return org.y=t; }
    int right(int r)             { return end.x=r; }
    int bottom(int b)            { return end.y=b; }
```

```
void set(WPPoint o, WPPoint e)
    { origin(o); endpt(e); }
void set(int l, int t, int r, int b)
    { origin(l,t); endpt(r,b); }

// Width, height instead of top, bottom, etc.
int width()                     { return right()-left(); }
int height()                    { return bottom()-top(); }
int width(int w)                { right(left()+w); return width(); }
int height(int h)               { bottom(top()+h); return height();}

void origin(int x, int y)       { org.set(x,y); }
void endpt(int x, int y)        { end.set(x,y); }
void extent(int w, int h)       { width(w); height(h); }

// Get/set using points
WPPoint& origin()               { return org; }
WPPoint& endpt()                { return end; }
WPPoint& origin(WPPoint p)      { return org=p; }
WPPoint& endpt(WPPoint p)       { return end=p; }

// Miscellaneous
void setEmpty()   { org.set(0,0); end.set(0,0); }
BOOL isEmpty()
    { return IsRectEmpty((LPRECT)this); }
BOOL contains(WPPoint p)
    { return PtInRect((LPRECT)this, (POINT)p); }
void inflate(int w, int h)
    { InflateRect((LPRECT)this, w, h); }
void capture(WPPoint &p)
    {   p.x=min(max(p.x,left()),right()-1);
        p.y=min(max(p.y,top()),bottom()-1); }

void adjustWinRect(DWORD style, BOOL menu, DWORD exstyle=0)
    { AdjustWindowRectEx((LPRECT)this,style,menu,exstyle); }

// Assignment
WPRect& operator= (WPWin *win);
WPRect& operator= (WPPaintStruct& ps);
WPRect& operator= (RECT &rect)
    { return *this = *((WPRect*)&rect); }

// Other operators
BOOL operator==(WPRect& rect2)
    { return EqualRect((LPRECT)this, (LPRECT)&rect2); }

WPRect& operator+= (WPPoint p)
    { org+=p; end+=p; return *this; }
WPRect& operator-= (WPPoint p)
    { org-=p; end-=p; return *this; }
WPRect& operator*= (int m)
    { width(width()*m); height(height()*m); return *this; }
WPRect& operator/= (int m)
    { width(width()/m); height(height()/m); return *this; }

// grow/shrink
WPRect& operator+= (int n)      { org-=n; end+=n; return *this; }
WPRect& operator-= (int n)      { org+=n; end-=n; return *this; }
WPRect& operator++ ()           { --org; ++end; return *this; }
WPRect& operator-- ()           { ++org; --end; return *this; }
```

```
    WPRect& operator*= (TEXTMETRIC &tm)
        { org*=tm; end*=tm; return *this; }

    int operator&= (WPRect& rect2);
    int operator|= (WPRect& rect2);
};

/////////////////
// (Described below in Section 2.2.3)
//
class WPWindowRect : public WPRect {
public:
    WPWindowRect(WPWin *win)          { *this = win; }
    WPWindowRect& operator= (WPWin *win);
};

#endif
```

As you can see, it's even longer that *WPPoint!* Furthermore, that's not all. Some of the member functions are true functions (not inline), implemented in the source file WPRECT.CPP:

```
/////////////////////////////////////////////////////////////
// WINDOWS++ CLASS LIBRARY.
// Copyright 1991 Paul DiLascia. All Rights Reserved.
//
// WPRect implementation

#include "wprect.h"
#include "wpwin.h"
#include "wpgdi.h"

//////////////////
// Make sure that left <= right and top <= bottom.
//
void WPRect::normalize()
{
    if (left() > right()) {
        int r = right();
        right(left());
        left(r);
    }
    if (top() > bottom()) {
        int b = bottom();
        bottom(top());
        top(b);
    }
}

//////////////////
// Assignment to window: get the window's client area rectangle
//
WPRect& WPRect::operator=(WPWin *win)
{
    win->getClientRect(*this);
    return *this;
}
```

```
///////////////////
// Assign a WPRect to a paint struct: get the rectangle to be painted.
//
WPRect& WPRect::operator=(WPPaintStruct &ps)
{
    ps.getPaintRect(*this);
    return *this;
}


///////////////////
// Intersect rectangle with another rectangle.
//
BOOL WPRect::operator&= (WPRect& rect2)
{
    WPRect dest;
    BOOL nonempty =
        IntersectRect((LPRECT)&dest, (LPRECT)this, (LPRECT)&rect2);
    *this = dest;
    return nonempty;
}


///////////////////
// Union rectangle with another rectangle.
//
BOOL WPRect::operator|= (WPRect& rect2)
{
    WPRect dest;
    BOOL nonempty =
        UnionRect((LPRECT)&dest, (LPRECT)this, (LPRECT)&rect2);
    *this = dest;
    return nonempty;
}


///////////////
// WPWindowRect: get whole Window instead of client area.
// (Described below in Section 2.2.3)
//
WPWindowRect& WPWindowRect::operator=(WPWin *win)
{
    win->getWindowtRect(*this);
    return *this;
}
```

WPRect uses many of the same C++ features used by *WPPoint*. With what you now
know about C++, you should be able to understand most of *WPRect*. Here's a
quick summary:

- *WPRect* has two data members: *org* and *end,* which are both *WPPoints.* These
  represent the upper-left and lower-right corners of the rectangle. Thus
  WPRect mirrors exactly the definition of RECT in WINDOWS.H.

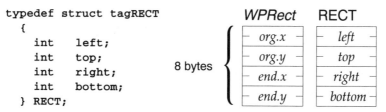

```
typedef struct tagRECT
  {
    int    left;
    int    top;
    int    right;
    int    bottom;
  } RECT;
```

In particular, *WPRect* occupies the same amount of storage (eight bytes) as RECT, despite all the code listed in the preceding pages. As with *WPPoint*, *WPRect* is deliberately defined this way, so we can cast:

```
BOOL isEmpty()       { return IsRectEmpty((LPRECT)this); }
```

■ *WPRect* defines the obvious functions to get and set the rectangle's coordinates—*left, right, top,* and *bottom*—as well as its *width* and *height*. These come in two overloaded flavors; one to get the datum, and one to set it:

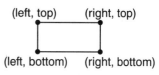

```
int r = rect.left();         // get left x-coordinate
rect.left(r);                // set left x-coordinate
```

■ Similar functions are defined to get and set the two corner points:

```
WPPoint& origin()            { return org; }
WPPoint& endpt()             { return end; }
WPPoint& origin(WPPoint p)   { return org=p; }
WPPoint& endpt(WPPoint p)    { return end=p; }
```

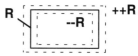

These return a *reference* to the internal point, which can then be modified. For example, to grow a rectangle outward by one pixel:

```
--rect.origin();
++rect.endpt();
```

This can be done more simply using *operator++*:

```
++rect;         // inflate rectangle one pixel
```

Likewise, *operator+=(int n)* lets you grow a rectangle by *n* in all directions:

```
rect += n;      // inflate rectangle n pixels
```

■ *WPRect* defines how to translate (move) a rectangle by a point.

```
void operator+= (WPPoint p)   { x+=p.x; y+=p.y; }
void operator-= (WPPoint p)   { x-=p.x; y-=p.y; }
```

Thus, for example, we can write:

```
WPRect rect; WPPoint p;
...
rect += p;
```

■ *WPRect* defines how to multiply a rectangle by a TEXTMETRIC: just multiply both corner points by it. This has the effect of converting character-based coordinates to display-based coordinates. For example

```
TEXTMETRIC tm;
WPRect rect;
    .
    .
    .
rect.origin(1,1);    // 1 char in from top left
rect.extent(40,10);  // 10 high x 40 wide characters
rect *= tm;          // ..convert to display coords
```

- *WPRect* overloads &= and | = to compute the intersection and union of two rectangles.

```
WPRect a,b;
...
WPRect i = a;
i &= b;
WPRect u = a;
u |= b;
```

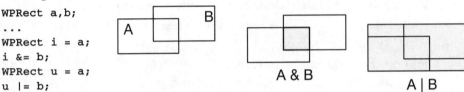

A & B

A | B

These operators simply call the Windows functions *IntersectRect* and *UnionRect*.

- *WPRect::capture* "captures" a point by forcing it to be inside the rectangle if it's not already. This is useful when confining the mouse or cursor to a particular rectangle.

R.capture(p)

- *WPRect* defines three versions of *operator=*:

```
WPRect& operator= (RECT &rect)    { *this = *((WPRect*)&rect); }
WPRect& operator= (WPWin *win);
WPRect& operator= (WPPaintStruct& ps);
```

These assign a RECT, window, or paint structure to a *WPRect*. The *WPWin* assignment operator is implemented as follows:

```
WPRect& WPRect::operator=(WPWin *win)
{
    win->getClientRect(*this);
    return *this;
}
```

WPWin is another class, described fully in the next chapter. For now, I'll just tell you that *WPWin* stores a window handle (HWND) and *getClientRect* stuffs the rectangle coordinates of the window's client area rectangle by calling *GetClientRect*. The upshot is that we can write

```
WPRect rect = mywin;
```

to get the coordinates of a window's client area rectangle. In C, you'd write:

```
RECT rect;
GetClientRect(hwnd, &rect);        // call API function
```

- *WPRect* has three constructors to match the preceding assignment operators, as well as three more that initialize the rectangle to zeros, or from four coordinates or two points.

2.2.1 Classes and Objects

Most of the C++ features we have so far been discussing (such as inline functions, function overloading, and default argument values) are syntactic enhancements that have nothing special to do with object-oriented programming. The only feature that's at all object-oriented is the notion of member functions for *structs*.

What really makes C++ object-oriented are *classes*.

While *WPPoint* is an ordinary *struct*, *WPRect* is our first example of a C++ *class*. A class is a special kind of *struct*. Like *structs*, classes have data and member functions—for example, *WPRect* contains two points, *org* and *end*, which represent the upper-left and lower-right corners of the rectangle. So what's special about classes? The answer is that while the members of a *struct* are always accessible anywhere within a program, the members (data and functions) of a class are *not*.

```
void MyFunc()                    // Some C++ function
{
    WPRect rect; int x;
    .
    .
    x = rect.org.x;              // NOT ALLOWED: gives compiler error
    x = rect.left();             // OK
}
```

C++ supports three *access levels* for class members:

- *Private* members can be accessed only by the class itself (that is, by its member functions).

- *Protected* members can be accessed only by the class itself or classes derived from it (derived classes are described shortly).

- *Public* members can be accessed by anyone.

You specify which access level a particular member has using the syntax:

```
class NameOfClass {
private:
    // private members
protected:
    // protected members
public:
    // public members
};
```

Members are *private* by default, so *private* may be omitted:

```
class NameOfClass {
    // private members (by default)
protected:
    // protected members
public:
    // public members
};
```

Classes are sometimes also called objects, but strictly speaking, a *class* is an abstract definition; an *object* is a particular instance of a class that resides in memory. This distinction is frequently blurred in everyday speech, where *class* and *object* are often used interchangeably. Also, while a *struct* is different from a *class*, instances of *structs* and *classes* are both called *objects*. Even instances of built-in C types such as *ints* and *chars* are considered "objects." In C++, anything that takes up storage is an object.

Windows also has a notion of classes, though it applies only to windows: whenever you create a window, you must create it as an instance of a some window *class*. Unless you use one of the built-in classes such as "edit" or "listbox", you must first *register* your class. When you register a window class, you specify the name of the class as well as various class properties, such as the style flags, menu name, icon, cursor, and background color. In the next chapter, we'll map the Windows notion of classes directly onto C++ classes. But first, let's explore C++ classes further.

Classes are the fundamental building blocks of object-oriented systems, and they're what make C++ an object-oriented programming language.

2.2.2 Encapsulation

Back to *WPRect*. Because *org* is declared *private*, to get the left *x* coordinate of a rectangle, you must call *left()* instead of accessing *org.x*:

```
WPRect rect; int x;
.
.
x = rect.org.x;     // NOT ALLOWED: gives compiler error
x = rect.left();    // OK, because left() is public
```

Why use *left* when you could just make *org* public and reference it directly?

Generally speaking, it's considered good object-oriented coding practice to use functions (inline or not) to access class data members, rather than making the data public. The purpose of this is to hide the implementation of a class from its callers. In the case of *WPRect*, this is probably unnecessary, since *WPRect* is constrained to match RECT exactly and therefore unlikely ever to change—yet one could imagine another universe in which *WPRect* were implemented like this:

```
class WPRect {
    WPPoint org;     // upper-left-hand corner
    int w,h;         // width, height instead of lower right corner
public:
    left()           { return org.x; }
    right()          { return org.x+w; }
    top()            { return y; }
    bottom()         { return org.y+h; }
};
```

In this universe, the width and height of the rectangle are stored instead of its lower-right-hand corner point. The implementations of *right* and *bottom* are changed accordingly. Because programs in our original universe access the data indirectly, by calling *right* and *bottom* instead of accessing *end.x* and *end.y*, they could nevertheless use this new version of *WPRect* without being modified! They would, of course, have to be recompiled, since *left* & co. are *inline*—but if they were true functions, even this would be unnecessary. Of course, the calls to Window functions would also have to be changed to work properly in our new universe, since *WPRect* would no longer match RECT.

Most classes keep their data private but provide public functions to manipulate them.[9] This general characteristic of object-oriented programming languages is called *data hiding* or *encapsulation*. We say, "the member functions *encapsulate* the class." In a philosophical sense, the member functions *are* the class, since the behavior of a class object and everything that can be done to it is completely determined by its member functions (in OOP jargon, *methods*). A C++ object is a "black box" that can only be manipulated through its member functions.[10]

One of the advantages of *inline* functions in C++ is that they let you eat your cake and have it too: you can force callers to access data members through inline "functions" without paying the performance penalty of a function call. It would be a waste of CPU cycles to call a true function just to get the *x* coordinate of the upper-left-hand corner of a rectangle; inline functions let you hide the data syntactically, without generating a function call. They're ideal for trivial functions like *left* that merely return a data member. (Many C programmers were doing the same sort of thing long before C++ came along, by using *#define* macros to access structure members.)

2.2.3 Derived Classes and Inheritance

Perhaps the most important feature of object-oriented programming languages such as C++ is the ability to *derive* new classes from old ones. For example, WPRECT.H defines a second class, *WPWindowRect*:

```
////////////////////
// This subclass is identical to WPRect in all respects except
// that the constructor and assignment for a WPWin pointer
// get the entire window rectangle rather than just the client area.
//
class WPWindowRect : public WPRect {
public:
    WPWindowRect(WPWin *win)        { *this = win; }
    WPWindowRect& operator= (WPWin *win);
};
```

---

9 In fact, some object-oriented programming languages don't even provide a way to make data members public, but *only* allow access through functions. Object-oriented purists sometimes criticize C++ for allowing *protected* and *public* members.

10 As long as we're in a philosophical frame of mind, it's interesting to observe that objects exhibit behaviorism: if an object walks like a duck, talks like a duck, acts like a duck—it's a duck!

WPWindowRect seems tiny compared with *WPRect*, but it has all the same functionality, since it's a kind of *WPRect*. The C++ syntax

```
class WPWindowRect : public WPRect {
    .
    .
    .
};
```

tells the compiler that *WPWindowRect* is *derived* from *WPRect*, and so should *inherit*
all the (data *and* function) members of *WPRect*. For example, *WPWindowRect* inherits *org* and *end*, as well as the functions *left, right, width,* and so on. In general,
anything you can do to a *WPRect* you can also do to a *WPWindowRect*.

```
WPWindowRect r;
TEXTMETRIC tm
r *= tm;
.
.
WPPoint p;
r += p;
.
. etc.
```

In C++ jargon, we say that *WPWindowRect* is the *derived class,* and *WPRect* is the
base class; we also say that *WPWindowRect* is a *subclass* of *WPRect*. This is because
WPWindowRect inherits all the properties of *WPRect*. So what's different about it?
The difference lies in just two functions: the constructor and *operator=* for a pointer
to *WPWin*. The constructor calls *operator=:*

```
//////////////////
// Get window rectangle instead of client area.
//
WPWindowRect& WPWindowRect::operator=(WPWin *win)
{
    win->getWindowRect(*this);
    return *this;
}
```

This function gets the entire window's bounding rectangle (in screen coordinates)
instead of the client area rectangle. Now we can write

```
WPWin *mywin;
.
.
WPRect clientRect = mywin;        // get client area rectangle
WPWindowRect winRect = mywin;     // get entire window rectangle
```

This is a common trick used throughout *Windows++:* When you want to overload a
constructor, but the overloaded versions would have the same arguments, invent
a derived class.

Another example of a subclass is *WPSquare,* which has a constructor that creates a
square rectangle with a given center and radius:

```
/////////////////////
// A square is a special kind of rectangle.
//
class WPSquare : public WPRect {
public:
    WPSquare(WPPoint p, int radius)   { set(p, radius); }
    void set(WPPoint p, int r)
        { origin(p.x-r, p.y-r); endpt(p.x+r, p.y+r)); }
};
```

Here's how *WPSquare* is used:

```
// Create square centered at p with side = 10
WPSquare sq(p, 5);
```

WPSquare reflects the fact that a square is a special kind of rectangle, one whose sides are the same length. Note, however, that while the *WPSquare* constructor and *set* function both create a square, there's nothing to prevent someone from writing

```
sq.width(10)
sq.height(17);        // sq is no longer square
```

WPSquare is not intended to *enforce* squareness, but rather to provide a convenient way of creating square rectangles (we'll use it in Chapter 8).

Earlier I mentioned that there are three access levels for class members: *private, protected,* and *public.* Because it's *private, WPWindowRect* cannot access *org* nor *end.* A derived class inherits, but cannot access, the private members of the class from which it is derived. It can, however, access *protected* members. Protected members are in-between: derived classes can access them; outside callers cannot.

Windows gurus are no doubt aware that Windows also provides a notion of "subclassing," but one based on a totally different mechanism. In Windows, you can "subclass" a window by replacing its window procedure with one of your own, one that gives the window a new behavior. You might wonder how Windows "subclassing" relates to C++ subclasses. In the next chapter, we'll build *Windows++* objects that make these two notions of subclassing coincide!

2.2.4 Class Hierarchies

Inheritance is a fundamental feature of all object-oriented programming languages. It provides a way to build entire *class hierarchies,* which is what we will do in *Windows++.* A class hierarchy is simply a collection of classes that are all derived from some common base class or ancestor. Class hierarchies occur all the time in the real world. For example, the following table shows part of an animal hierarchy:

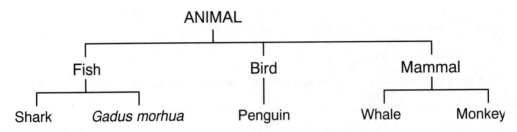

A similar diagram shows part of a window class hierarchy:[11]

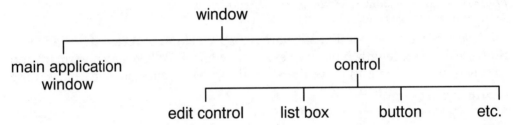

Each class in the tree is a *subclass of*, or *derived from*, the class above it. The class at the top of the tree is called the *base* class, but *base* is a relative term. For example, *window* might actually be derived some even more general class, *Object*, but it's useful to think of it as the base window class.

While *WPWindowRect* doesn't add any data members to *WPRect*, a derived class may in general do so. If so, the new data members are appended to the structure.

2.2.5 Inheritance *vs.* Membership

Inheritance should not be confused with *membership*. Objects of one class may contain objects of other classes as data members. For example:

```
class FooClass {

};

class BarClass {
    FooClass foo;              // instance of FooClass
    FooClass  *pFoo;           // pointer to instance of FooClass
};
```

In this case, we say that *FooClass* is a *member* of *BarClass*.

Inheritance and *membership* are fundamental notions of object-oriented programming, and correspond deeply to the way humans perceive and model reality. Whenever we group real-world objects into categories such as animal, mammal,

---

11 C++ actually lets you build non-tree hierarchies by using *multiple inheritance*. An example appears in Section 7.3.3.

primate, we're inventing classes and subclasses and invoking inheritance (a primate is *a kind of* mammal, which is is *a kind of* animal). Whenever we group objects into wholes and parts, we invoke *membership* (a mammal has two eyes and a nose, but mammals are not kinds of eyes and noses). This correspondence to human perception is what makes the object-oriented paradigm so well suited for modeling systems of all kinds.

The difference between inheritance and membership can be captured in the formal relationships *isa* (is a) and *hasa* (has a): a primate *isa* mammal (inheritance) and *hasa* nose (membership). The terms *member* and *membership* are perhaps unfortunate choices, since we also sometimes say in English "a primate is a member of the mammalian class," which evokes *inheritance.* Better terms might be *part* and *containment*—but alas, we're stuck with C++ the way it is.

The main challenge in designing any object-oriented system such as *Windows++* is identifying the proper classes and their inheritance and membership relationships. This entire book is essentially a solution to this challenge, where the system we are modeling is Windows itself, and the system we are building to model it is *Windows++.* Our challenge is thus to identify the meaningful objects (classes of objects) within Windows, and the proper relationships among them. For example, an edit control *isa* window, while a main window *hasa* menu.

For an excellent discussion of object-oriented analysis and design in general, see [Coad 1990] and/or [Stroustrup 1991].

2.3 Summary

Whew! If you're still with me, congratulations! This has been a very quick tour of C++ through the eyes of *WPPoint* and *WPRect.* I've waved my hands a lot, glossed over many details, and omitted others, but I hope I've covered at least enough for you to understand the rest of the book. If you didn't follow everything, don't worry, just keep reading. Many issues such as membership and inheritance will crop up again later.

Here's a summary of the important points.

- C++ functions can have *default argument values.*

- C++ functions and operators can be *overloaded.*

- A *reference* is another name for an object. Modifying the reference modifies the object it refers to. References are passed to functions as pointers.

- Classes and *structs* can have *member functions* as well as data members.

- Each class and *struct* can have one or more *constructors* and one *destructor.* The constructor is called to initialize an object instance; the destructor is called before destroying it.

- Class members are *private, protected,* or *public.* Only the class itself (i.e., its member functions) can access *private* members; only the class itself and classes derived from it can access *protected* members; anyone can access *public* members.

- New classes can be *derived* from old ones. The new class *inherits* all the properties of the old class.

- Inheritance is used to build *class hierarchies.*

And if your friends ask you to describe, in one sentence or less, what the difference is between object-oriented programming and "normal" programming, just tell them that *in object-oriented programming, data structures have functions as well as data, and each data structure specifies what actions can be performed on it.* In "normal" programming, data structures are *passive;* in object-oriented programming, they're *active.*

CHAPTER ∎ 3

Infrastructure

We're now ready (finally!) to begin building *Windows++*. In this chapter, we'll implement the basic infrastructure of *Windows++* by gradually transforming a C version of the HELLO program into the version shown on page 8. HELLO was chosen because it's one of the simplest programs we can write, has historical significance, and is a program everyone has come to know and love. (I suppose HELLO is the first program written in every new programming environment.) Our goal is not so much the transformation of HELLO, but rather the construction of *Windows++*; however, we'll go about it indirectly, by gradually incorporating the generic aspects of HELLO into reusable *Windows++* objects. This approach is fundamental throughout the book, and deserves to be elevated to the status of general principle: *The way we develop reusable code is by first implementing some particular application, then incorporating its general aspects into reusable object classes.*

In this chapter I'll guide you through all the programming details, including how to compile, create MAKE files, and so on; in later chapters I'll skip these details and explain only the code itself. In order to give you some idea how *Windows++* evolved historically from a few lines of code into a full-blown programming environment, each version of HELLO has its own self-contained version of the *Windows++* library. The final HELLO program uses the finished *Windows++* library in all its glory, as do all the other sample programs in the book.[12]

This is by far the most important chapter of the book, for this is where we'll construct the basic infrastructure of *Windows++*. It's also the most difficult chapter, because we have to bootstrap ourselves from nothing. For these reasons, it's essential that we take the time and care to get it right, so this chapter is necessarily long and detailed—but I promise that once we've laid a solid foundation, the rest will be smooth sailing as we reuse our library code again and again.

---

12 The source disk contains a separate version of the *Windows++* library for each HELLO program; however, only the final library is listed in Appendix A.

So find a comfortable spot, pop open a soda and put on your OOP cap, 'cause here we go.

3.1 HELLO: The C Version

As promised, we'll start with a "normal" C version of the HELLO program:

```
/*****************************************************/
/* This is the basic C version of the hello program. */
/*****************************************************/

#include <windows.h>

LONG FAR PASCAL WndProc(HWND hwnd, WORD msg, WORD wp, LONG lp);

int PASCAL WinMain(HANDLE hinst, HANDLE pinst, LPSTR cmdline, int show)
{
    HWND hwnd;
    MSG msg;

    if (pinst==NULL) {
        WNDCLASS wndcls;

        wndcls.style = CS_HREDRAW | CS_VREDRAW;
        wndcls.lpfnWndProc = WndProc;
        wndcls.cbClsExtra = 0;
        wndcls.cbWndExtra = 0;
        wndcls.hInstance = hinst;
        wndcls.hIcon = LoadIcon(hinst, "HELLOICON");
        wndcls.hCursor = LoadCursor(NULL, IDC_ARROW);
        wndcls.hbrBackground = GetStockObject(WHITE_BRUSH);
        wndcls.lpszMenuName = "HELLOMENU";
        wndcls.lpszClassName = "HELLOWIN";

        RegisterClass(&wndcls);
    }
    hwnd = CreateWindow("HELLOWIN",     /* class name */
        "HELLO--The C version",         /* title */
        WS_OVERLAPPEDWINDOW,            /* window style */
        CW_USEDEFAULT,                  /* x position */
        CW_USEDEFAULT,                  /* y position */
        CW_USEDEFAULT,                  /* width */
        CW_USEDEFAULT,                  /* height */
        NULL,                           /* parent */
        NULL,                           /* menu */
        hinst,                          /* module instance */
        NULL);                          /* create param */
    ShowWindow(hwnd, show);
    UpdateWindow(hwnd);
    while (GetMessage(&msg, NULL, 0, 0)) {
        TranslateMessage(&msg);
        DispatchMessage(&msg);
    }
    return msg.wParam;
}
```

```
LONG FAR PASCAL WndProc(HWND hwnd, WORD msg, WORD wp, LONG lp)
{
    PAINTSTRUCT ps;
    HDC hdc;
    RECT rect;

    switch(msg) {
    case WM_PAINT:
        hdc = BeginPaint(hwnd, &ps);
        GetClientRect(hwnd, &rect);
        DrawText(hdc, "Hello, world.", -1, &rect,
            DT_SINGLELINE | DT_CENTER | DT_VCENTER);
        EndPaint(hwnd, &ps);
        return 0;

    case WM_COMMAND:
        switch (wp) {
        case IDCANCEL:
            SendMessage(hwnd, WM_CLOSE, 0, 0);
            break;
        }
        return 0;

    case WM_DESTROY:
        PostQuitMessage(0);
        return 0;
    }
    return DefWindowProc(hwnd, msg, wp, lp);
}
```

I assume you're familiar enough with Windows to understand this program, so I won't explain how it works. If HELLO makes about as much sense to you as the Rosetta stone, then I suggest you go read a Windows book (such as the SDK *Guide to Programming* or [Petzold 1990]).

Just to make life interesting (and marginally more realistic), HELLO has a menu with an Exit command, as well as an application icon, which resembles a smiley-face. These are defined in the resource (.RC) file

```
#include "windows.h"

HELLOICON ICON hello.ico

HELLOMENU MENU {
    MENUITEM "&Exit!", IDCANCEL
}
```

HELLO.ICO

and the icon was created using Microsoft's SDKPAINT.

HELLO is a typical Windows program. It illustrates how much "set up" is required in Windows, even to do something as simple as display a message: the window class must be registered, then an instance created; the window must be "shown" and "updated"; messages must be translated, dispatched, and handled by a "window procedure". All this code, just to say "hello!" Furthermore, very little of the code has anything to do with HELLO *per se;* most of it is just the sort of generic stuff that Microsoft advises you to copy, paste, and edit every time you write a new program.

Well, copy-paste-edit is not for us. This is software engineering, not word processing! In this chapter we'll gradually encapsulate all of HELLO's generic aspects in reusable *object code.* Not reusable *files*, but honest-to-goodness linkable code that future applications can use over and over again, without any modification whatsoever. Remember *libraries?* Everything that one application has in common with another belongs in a library. What a concept!

3.2 HELLO1: *Windows++* Basics

3.2.1 Files, Files, Files

Our first C++ version of HELLO will be called HELLO1.CPP. The file extension .CPP is used for C++ files and cues the compiler that the file contains C++, not C, code.

Since we're about to write a lot of code, let's take care of a few organizational details before we actually begin. We'll create a header file called WPP.H for all our definitions. This file is the *Windows++* analog of WINDOWS.H and is the only file that any *Windows++* program need include. WPP.H in turn includes additional files (including WINDOWS.H). We'll keep adding to the list as the library grows. In general, we'll create a separate .H file for each new class or group of related classes.

```
/////////////////////////////////////////////////////////////
// WINDOWS++ CLASS LIBRARY. Copyright 1992 Paul DiLascia.
// FILE: WPP.H
//
// Main include file for Windows++ library.
// All it does is include all the other header files.

#ifndef WPP_H
#define WPP_H

#ifdef RC_INVOKED
#include "windows.h"
#else
#include "wppdefs.h"
#include "wprect.h"
#endif

#endif // WPP_H
```

RC_INVOKED is a symbol that's defined only when running the resource compiler, RC. The *#ifdef* is used so we don't include all the *Windows++* files when running the resource compiler. This is required because RC only recognizes C preprocessor directives such as *#define*, and not C and C++ statements like *struct*. WINDOWS.H uses the same trick.

One of the files included by WPP.H is WPPDEFS.H. This file includes yet more files and contains a few basic type definitions:

```
//////////////////////////////////////////////////
// WINDOWS++ CLASS LIBRARY. Copyright 1992 Paul DiLascia.
// FILE: WPPDEFS.H
//
// Basic Windows++ type definitions, constants, etc.

#ifndef WPPDEFS_H
#define WPPDEFS_H

#ifndef RC_INVOKED
#include <assert.h>
#include <string.h>
#include <stdlib.h>
#include <stdio.h>
#endif

typedef char* STR;
typedef const char* CSTR;
typedef const char FAR* LPCSTR;

class WPRect;    // Declared here so we can make forward references
class WPWin;     // ditto

#endif
```

The CSTR *typedef* is shorthand for *const char**. It's generally a good idea to declare all string function arguments as *const char**, rather than simply *char**, unless a function actually modifies the string. This helps avoid bugs and forces you to think about which functions change strings and which don't. Moreover, the compiler will enforce your decisions for you. If you declare a pointer as *const char**, the compiler will complain if you attempt to modify the string:

```
MyFunc(CSTR str)
{
    .
    .
    strcpy(str,"hello");                    // !#$%@! compiler error
}
```

The main drawback with *const* is that Windows declares all strings as LPSTR (*char far**), even if Windows doesn't actually modify the string. We must therefore explicitly cast CSTRs to LPSTRs when calling Windows functions. This cast is required *not* because LPSTR is a far pointer (the compiler will silently coerce a near pointer to a far one), but because CSTR is *const* and LPSTR is not. From the compiler's perspective, the Windows function can change your string, violating the *const* declaration. Of course, we must be careful not to use *const* for Windows functions that really do alter the string.

The other file included by WPP.H, WPRECT.H, contains the declarations for the *WPRect* class that was described in Chapter 2. *WPRect* represents a rectangle, and mirrors the Windows RECT structure.

3.2.2 The Base Window Class: *WPWin*

Now that we've created some files, where do we begin to build *Windows++*? The first step in designing any object-oriented system is to answer the question:

What are the objects?

Where do we find objects? Many books have been written to help software design-ers answer this seemingly simple question (an excellent one is [Coad 1990]). There are many techniques and guidelines, but the short answer is this: the first place to look for objects is in the "real world." For example, if we were modeling an airline reservation system, then planes, flights, pilots, baggage, and airports would be likely candidates for objects; if we wanted to write a chess program, the objects would surely include the board and chess pieces, of which there are several kinds: pawn, bishop, knight, rook, queen, and king.

Since we are modeling Windows, the "real world" is the Windows programming environment. All of the "things" (I almost said *objects!*) in Windows are candidates for objects in *Windows++*: windows, menus, dialog boxes, pens, brushes, and so on. In fact, these are indeed the objects (to be precise, the *classes* of objects) that comprise *Windows++*. Of these, the first and most basic class is the *window*, so let's begin there.

We ultimately want to have lots of different classes of windows—dialog boxes, edit controls, buttons, and so on. If we were to draw a map of all the different kinds of windows we expect to model, it might look something like this:

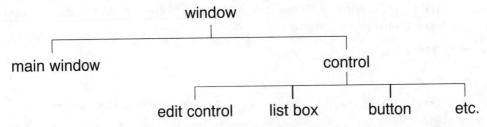

This map represents the window class hierarchy. Whatever the final hierarchy looks like, we need a common "root" window class (the one at the top of the tree) from which other window classes can be derived. Let's call this base window class *WPWin*. What data and function members should it have? Well, since the only way we can do anything with our window is by calling some Windows API function, and since all Windows functions identify windows by their handles (HWNDs), it seems certain that *WPWin* at the minimum needs to store a handle to the actual window, and provide a way of obtaining it.

```
/////////////////
// Base class for all window classes.
//
class WPWin {
   HWND hwnd;                             // Windows' handle to the window
public:
   HWND getHwnd()                         { return hwnd; }
   HWND operator()()                      { return hwnd; }
   static HWND GetHwnd(WPWin *win)        { return win ? win->hwnd : NULL }
};
```

In fact, this is essentially *all* that *WPWin* is: a handle to a window. There are three inline functions defined above:

■ *getHwnd* simply returns the window handle *hwnd*. Since we want applications using Windows++ to access Windows through our library, why make *getHwnd* public? Recall that one of the goals listed at the outset was an "escape mechanism." Well, here it is. If a program ever needs to access Windows directly, rather than through *Windows++*, it can always get the window's HWND.

■ The *operator()* is a special C++ operator called the *function operator*. The function operator lets you "invoke" an object using function notation, like so:

```
WPWin *win;
HWND hwnd = (*win)();                   // get window handle
```

which is equivalent to

```
HWND hwnd = win->getHwnd();             // get window handle
```

C++ lets you overload as many versions of the function operator as you like, as long as they all have different signatures (arguments and return values). Using function operators, you can "call" objects as if they were functions. Since this notation is somewhat confusing, most C++ programmers, including myself, avoid it. The one exception is *operator()()* (with no arguments), which usually returns "the obvious thing." In *Windows++*, it's always the underlying Windows handle to an object.

■ The last function, *GetHwnd*, is like *getHwnd*, but it's *static*. In C++, a *static* member function is called directly (rather than through an object instance), just like a ordinary C function. Thus we write

```
hwnd = GetHwnd(win);                    // get window's HWND
```

instead of

```
hwnd = win->getHwnd();                  // get window's HWND
```

The first example is more convenient if *win* is NULL, since the second example will crash in that situation.

```
hwnd = win->getHwnd();                    // !#@%! crashes if win==NULL
hwnd = GetHwnd(win);                      // returns NULL
```

In C++, you can't access data or function members through a NULL pointer. *GetHwnd* is really just shorthand for

```
return win ? win->getHwnd() : NULL;
```

Note that *GetHwnd* begins with a capital letter. This convention is used throughout *Windows++*: static member function names begin with capital letters; ordinary member functions begin with lower-case. This is intended to suggest that static class functions are "global," while ordinary member functions are "local."

The *WPWin* class definition is entered in a file called WPWIN.H, which is added to the list of files included in WPP.H. Generally, I'll use separate .H and .CPP files for each class or group of related classes. We want to have lots of little files rather than a few big ones, because we're building a library and want our applications to link only as much code as is actually required. If an application doesn't use a particular object, we don't want to link it. Having lots of small .H files also makes it possible to set up the appropriate MAKE dependencies so you recompile the smallest possible number of files when something changes. It also makes it easier for more than one person to work on a project, since it's less likely that they'll need to check out the same file at the same time. Of course, all this applies only to the modules *within* the *Windows++* library; applications that *use Windows++* should include WPP.H, which includes everything, just as Windows programs include WINDOWS.H.

What else should we put in our window class? Well, we know we'll need a way to show and update the window. We could just call

```
UpdateWindow(win->getHwnd());
```

which would certainly work (in fact, this is how Borland's *ObjectWindows* does it), but it leaves OO-programmers feeling somewhat cold because it "exposes" the internals of *WPWin* (*hwnd*) to arbitrary use. The whole idea of object-oriented programming is to manipulate objects through their *member functions* (also called *methods* in OO-terminology). Here's the C++ way to do it:

```
// Add show and update functions (In WPWIN.H)
class WPWin {
    HWND hwnd;
public:
    BOOL show(int how)          { return ShowWindow(hwnd, how); }
    void update()               { UpdateWindow(hwnd); }
};
```

The class member functions *show* and *update* correspond to the Windows functions *ShowWindow* and *UpdateWindow,* and are invoked like this:

```
win->show(how);
win->update();
```

Because these functions are *defined* (as well as *declared*) within the *class* declaration, they're *inline* functions, or macros. Thus the preceding two lines, when compiled, produce exactly the same code as

```
ShowWindow(win->hwnd, how);
UpdateWindow(win->hwnd);
```

(There are more important reasons for using *show* and *update* instead of *ShowWindow* and *UpdateWindow*—see Section 3.2.6.)

3.2.3 Creating the Window

So far, we have a basic window class with *show* and *update* functions—but how do we create a window? How do we get the *hwnd* field filled in with a real window handle? We have to somehow call the Windows API function *CreateWindow*. But first, we have to register the window class.

To register the window class, we need to fill in a special Windows structure called WNDCLASS, then invoke the Windows API function *RegisterClass*. Here's how a typical Windows program like HELLO.C does it:

```
WNDCLASS wndcls;

wndcls.style = CS_HREDRAW | CS_VREDRAW;
wndcls.lpfnWndProc = WndProc;
wndcls.cbClsExtra = 0;
wndcls.cbWndExtra = 0;
wndcls.hInstance = hinst;
wndcls.hIcon = LoadIcon(hinst, "HELLOICON");
wndcls.hCursor = LoadCursor(NULL, IDC_ARROW);
wndcls.hbrBackground = GetStockObject(WHITE_BRUSH);
wndcls.lpszMenuName = "HELLOMENU";
wndcls.lpszClassName = "HELLOWIN";

RegisterClass(&wndcls);
```

Once the class has been registered, we can create instances of it by invoking *CreateWindow*, which has several (!) arguments:

```
hwnd = CreateWindow("HELLOWIN",      /* class name */
    "HELLO--The C version",          /* title */
    WS_OVERLAPPEDWINDOW,             /* window style */
    CW_USEDEFAULT,                   /* x position */
    CW_USEDEFAULT,                   /* y position */
    CW_USEDEFAULT,                   /* width */
    CW_USEDEFAULT,                   /* height */
    NULL,                            /* parent */
    NULL,                            /* menu */
    hinst,                           /* module instance */
    NULL);                           /* create parameter */
```

We could of course write *WPWin* functions like *registerClass* and *createWindow* that mirror the API functions, but we have an opportunity to be more clever! Instead, let's write a *createWin* function that not only creates the window but registers it, too. This will free applications from ever again having to register window classes.

```
class WPWin {
    BOOL createWin( ??? );          // create window
};
```

We need to pass both the registration and creation arguments to *createWin*. To avoid passing twelve arguments on the stack (!), let's instead invent a structure similar to WNDCLASS:

```
//////////////////
// This structure is used to specify the Windows registration
// and creation arguments required to create the window.
//
struct WINCREATEARGS {
    WNDCLASS wndcls;                // Windows registration structure
    CSTR title;                     // window title
    DWORD style;                    // style (WS_OVERLAPPED, etc.)
    DWORD exstyle;                  // extended style (Windows 3.0)
    WPRect pos;                     // window position (x,y,w,h)
    WPWin* parent;                  // parent window
    HMENU hmenu;                    // menu handle
    long lParam;                    // generic parameter
};
```

As you can see, WINCREATEARGS contains an instance of WNDCLASS, as well as a number of other window creation parameters. For convenience, the coordinates and size of the window-to-be are stored in a *WPRect* object, rather than as four integers *x, y, width,* and *height*. There are no fields for the class name and module instance handle, since these items already appear in WNDCLASS. And since we're supporting Windows 3.0 (or later releases), there's a place for extended style flags.

For reasons that will soon become clear (in Section 3.2.5), it's convenient to provide an instance of WINCREATEARGS in *WPWin*, rather than making applications supply their own. We could just add it like this:

```
class WPWin {
    HWND hwnd;
    WINCREATEARGS createArgs;       // window creation arguments
};
```

but WINCREATEARGS is such a big structure, it's a waste of memory to add it to *every* window object, especially when *createArgs* are only needed when the window is created. C++ provides a feature that's ideal for this situation: *static data members*. This is what it looks like:

```
class WPWin {
public:
    static WINCREATEARGS createArgs;    // note "static" modifier
};
```

A *static* data member has only *one instance* for the entire class. You can think of it as a class-wide global. Since static data members like *createArgs* don't "live" in object instances, they must be explicitly instantiated, just like a static global in C:

```
// Instantiate createArgs (In WPWIN.CPP)
WINCREATEARGS WPWin::createArgs;
```

As with functions, the fully scoped symbol name (*className::memberName*) is required to instantiate *createArgs,* for there might be another class with a static member called *createArgs,* or even a global *createArgs.* Unless we specify the class name, the compiler has no way to tell which *createArgs* is being instantiated.

We'll worry about setting *createArgs* in a moment. Right now, let's just assume that *createArgs* has somehow been filled in. Given this, we can write *createWin:*

```
//////////////////
// Create window using current values in createArgs. (In WPWIN.CPP)
//
BOOL WPWin::createWin()                      // no arguments!
{
    LPSTR classnm = createArgs.wndcls.lpszClassName;
    assert(classnm);
    HANDLE hinst = createArgs.wndcls.hInstance;
    assert(hinst);
    WNDCLASS temp;

    // Register window class if it ain't already registered!
    if (!GetClassInfo(hinst, classnm, &temp) &&      // try module..
        !GetClassInfo(NULL, classnm, &temp)) {       // ..and built-in
        BOOL ret = RegisterClass(&createArgs.wndcls);
        assert(ret);
    }

    // Create window.
    // Since we're in Windows 3.0 or better, use CreateWindowEx.
    HWND newhwnd = CreateWindowEx(createArgs.exstyle,
        classnm,
        (LPSTR)createArgs.title,
        createArgs.style,
        createArgs.pos.left(),
        createArgs.pos.top(),
        createArgs.pos.width(),
        createArgs.pos.height(),
        GetHwnd(createArgs.parent),
        createArgs.hmenu,
        hinst,
        createArgs.lparam);

    assert(newhwnd);
    hwnd = newhwnd;
    return hwnd!=NULL;
}
```

Wow! That's a lot of code just to create a window!

Well, not really. It just seems like a lot because *CreateWindowEx* has so many arguments. In truth, *createWin* does only two things:

- First, it registers the window class if it's not already registered: *createWin* checks both the module instance and the "built-in" window classes that are preregistered by Windows (such as "Edit" and "ListBox"). If the class is not registered in either place, *createWin* registers it using whatever values are stored in *createArgs.wndcls*.

- Second, *createWin* creates the window using whatever values are stored in *createArgs*. The only interesting thing here is that *createWin* calls the Windows 3.0 function *CreateWindowEx* instead of the pre-3.0 *CreateWindow*. Since *Windows++* assumes Windows release 3.0 or greater, we should take advantage of 3.0 features. If *createArgs.exstyle* is zero, *CreateWindowEx* does the same thing as *CreateWindow*, but if *exstyle* is non-zero it creates a window with the desired extended window style. (*CreateWindowEx* was introduced in Windows 3.0 because Microsoft ran out of style bits; the old function had to be retained for backward compatibility, but we don't need it.)

The way *createWin* handles window registration may seem strange to Windows programmers. After all, practically every Windows program known to humankind registers all its window classes when the application is initialized, usually in *WinMain* (but sometimes in a function with a name like *InitApp*):

```
int PASCAL WinMain(HANDLE hinst, HANDLE pinst, LPSTR cmdline, int show)
{
    if (pinst==NULL) {
        WNDCLASS wndcls;
        .
        . fill in wndcls fields
        .
        RegisterClass(&wndcls);
        .
        . repeat for each window class
        .
}
```

Why invoke *GetClassInfo* instead of following the Traditional Windows Way? The short answer is: because it's more *reusable*. The code in *createWin* is totally generic; it works for absolutely any window class an application might ever create, so now there's no need for applications to ever again call *RegisterClass*! Instead, all a *Windows++* application has to do is call *createWin*, and the window class is automatically and invisibly registered. In fact, if you examine all of the programs and source code in Appendix A (good luck—it's over 100 pages), you'll see that there are only two places in the entire system where *RegisterClass* is invoked! (The other one has to do with MDI child windows—see Section 6.4.4.)

Performance misers may object that it's inefficient to invoke *GetClassInfo* every time a window is created, when we only need to register the window class once.

Hey, lighten up! We're living in the age of 33 MHz 486s! Besides, the extra function call only happens when a new window is created—hardly a performance-critical event. The benefit outweighs the cost: applications never again have to register window classes!

Before leaving *createWin*, let's enhance it slightly. (Programmers always love to make enhancements, especially ones that don't require much work!) Since it's sometimes useful to specify a window's title when it's created, let's add an overloaded *createWin* function that takes a title as argument:

```
// Add overloaded createWin with title argument
class WPWin {
public:
    BOOL createWin();                   // old createWin function
    BOOL createWin(CSTR title)          // new one sets title from argument
        { createArgs.title=title; return createWin(); }
};
```

This function simply sets *createArgs.title* and then calls the original *createWin*. This is a minor convenience, one I threw in partly just to give you another example of overloaded functions (and because we'll use it later).

3.2.4 A Few Words on *assert*

At this point, I should perhaps address an issue of coding style. I find it useful to sprinkle my programs liberally with *assert* statements in order to ensure that everything is how it should be and nothing is rotten in the state of Denmark. For example, *createWin* asserts that window registration and creation succeed. Recall that *assert* is a macro, defined in *<assert.h>*, which causes the program to exit with a message showing the source file name and code line number if the assertion fails—that is, if the expression passed to *assert* is FALSE (i.e., evaluates to zero). I find that *assert* saves a lot of time and effort tracking mysterious bugs, especially when I'm developing a new system. If a pointer is NULL, or some other anomalous situation occurs, I'd rather know right away than let the code hang five function calls later.

While the HELLO programs described in this chapter all use the built-in *assert* macro that comes with your compiler, the finished *Windows++* library provides its own *assert*, defined in WPPDEFS.H as follows.

```
//////////////////
// Roll our own assert macro for uniformity between compilers
//
#undef assert
#ifdef NODEBUG
#   define assert(ignore)        ((void) 0)
#else
#   define assert(x) ((void)((x) || (DoAssert(#x,__FILE__,__LINE__),1)))
#endif
```

The *assert* macro is written so it generates no code if the symbol NODEBUG is defined. You can thus effectively remove all *assert* statements by compiling with this symbol defined. In practice, people rarely do this, even in final ship code. I've worked at companies where customers report bugs such as "When I do such and such it says 'assertion failure in line 123....'" This information is extremely helpful in tracking down the bug, and better than hearing the complaint "it just hangs and I have to reboot." The performance cost of *assert* is usually negligible, but you probably wouldn't want to put one in a performance-critical loop.

If NODEBUG is undefined (the normal case), *assert* calls the function *DoAssert* with the expression text, source code line number, and file name. Since not everyone is a preprocessor jock, I should explain that __FILE__ and __LINE__ are predefined preprocessor symbols for the current source file name and line number, respectively; and that #*x* uses the "stringizing" operator, #, to place quotation marks around the argument *x*. The *assert* macro thus passes its argument as a string, along with the source file name and line number, to *DoAssert*:

```
// (In WPAPP.CPP, described later)
void DoAssert(CSTR msg, CSTR file, unsigned line)
{
    char buf[80];
    sprintf(buf,"at line %u in file %s: \"%s\"", line, file, msg);
    MessageBeep(0);
    if (MsgBox(buf,"ASSERTION FAILURE",
            MB_OKCANCEL|MB_ICONSTOP|MB_TASKMODAL)!=IDOK)
        exit(-1);
}
```

The upshot of all this is that when the *assert* expression is FALSE, *Windows++* displays a message similar to the one below.[13]

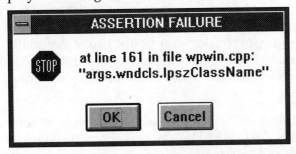

There are two reasons why I implemented my own *assert* rather than using the one that comes with the compiler: first, so that the message box looks the same for both the Borland and Zortech compilers (a minor nicety); and second, so I could provide both OK and CANCEL options. During debugging, it's sometimes possible

---

13 It might be more intelligible to name the buttons *Continue* and *Exit*, but there's no easy way to do so with *MessageBox*, and we don't want to create a dialog box just for *assert*. After all, if our program works properly, it will never be used.

to let your program continue running even after an assertion failure, and having the OK option comes in handy.

Despite my praise of *assert*, not all programmers like to use it, which is the only reason I've taken the time to discuss it. To each his own.

3.2.5 Filling in *createArgs:* The *WPWin* Constructor

Back to *Windows++*. So far, we have the base window class, *WPWin*, and a few member functions, including *createWin*, which actually creates the window using the arguments stored in the class global object *createArgs*. Before we create a window, we need to fill in *createArgs*. For example, we need to set the module instance handle and window procedure in the WNDCLASS member of *createArgs*.

```
createArgs.wndcls.hInstance = MyModuleInstance;
createArgs.wndcls.lpfnWndProc = MyWndProc;
```

Where should we do this? Any time before calling *createWin* will do, but preferably immediately beforehand, so there's no chance that *createArgs* will be altered in the meantime. It seems natural that creating a window should correspond to creating an object, so the window object constructor is a good place: the *WPWin* constructor seems like the logical place to initialize *createArgs*. Well, this is almost—but not quite—right: *WPWin* is only the *base* class, from which we expect each application will derive other window classes, such as our HELLO window:

```
class HelloWin : public WPWin {
public:
    HellowWin(HANDLE hinst);        // initialize hello window
};
```

In this case, there are actually *two* constructors where *createArgs* can be initialized: *WPWin::WPWin* and *HelloWin::HelloWin*. Remember, whenever a new object is created, C++ invokes not only that that object's constructor, but also the constructors for *all* classes in the inheritance chain from which it is derived. So which one should we use to initialize *createArgs? WPWin* or *HelloWin?* The answer is both!

Our strategy will be as follows: *WPWin* will initialize the fields that are generic to all applications, while *HelloWin* will set those that are HELLO-specific. For example, *WPWin* will initialize the cursor to the generic Windows arrow cursor, while *HelloWin* will set the menu name and icon to "HelloMenu" and "HelloIcon". In general, each new window class that we derive from *WPWin* will initialize some *createArgs* differently.

Let's start with *WPWin*.

```
// (In WPWIN.H)
class WPWin {
public:
    WPWin(CSTR classnm);            // constructor expects class name
};
```

```
// (In WPWIN.CPP)
WPWin::WPWin(CSTR classnm)
{
    hwnd = NULL;

    // set default window class registration args
    createArgs.wndcls.lpszClassName = classnm;
    createArgs.wndcls.style = CS_HREDRAW | CS_VREDRAW;
    createArgs.wndcls.lpfnWndProc = DefWindowProc;
    createArgs.wndcls.cbClsExtra = 0;
    createArgs.wndcls.cbWndExtra = 0;
    createArgs.wndcls.hInstance = NULL;
    createArgs.wndcls.hIcon = NULL;
    createArgs.wndcls.hCursor = LoadCursor(NULL, IDC_ARROW);
    createArgs.wndcls.hbrBackground = GetStockObject(WHITE_BRUSH);
    createArgs.wndcls.lpszMenuName = NULL;

    // set default window creation args
    createArgs.title = NULL;
    createArgs.style = createArgs.exstyle = 0;
    createArgs.pos.origin(CW_USEDEFAULT, CW_USEDEFAULT);
    createArgs.pos.extent(CW_USEDEFAULT, CW_USEDEFAULT);
    createArgs.hmenu = (HMENU)id;
    createArgs.parent = NULL;
    createArgs.lparam = NULL;
}
```

Since every (Windows) window class must have a name, we make this a required argument to *WPWin*; this ensures that we never attempt to create a Window class without giving it a name. The rest of *WPWin* simply initializes all the *createArgs* to reasonable defaults. For example, the default window coordinates are all CW_USEDEFAULT (which tells Windows to figure out where to put the window), and the default background brush is a solid white brush. Most fields simply default to zero or NULL. These values are only *defaults;* derived class constructors can always change them. For example:

```
HelloWin::HelloWin(HANDLE hinst) : WPWin("HELLOWIN")     // see below
{
    createArgs.wndcls.lpfnWndProc = WndProc;
    createArgs.wndcls.hInstance = hinst;
    createArgs.wndcls.lpszMenuName = "HelloMenu";
    createArgs.wndcls.hIcon = LoadIcon(hinst, "HelloIcon");
    createArgs.style = WS_OVERLAPPEDWINDOW;
    createWin("HELLO1--1st C++ version");
}
```

HelloWin overrides a number of the default values assigned by *WPWin:* it sets the window style to overlapped window and the menu name to "HelloMenu"; it sets the module instance handle from the argument *hinst.* After setting *createArgs,* *HelloWin* invokes *createWin* to actually create the window.

The funny-looking (to non-C++ gurus) initialization syntax

```
HelloWin::HelloWin(HANDLE hinst) : WPWin("HELLOWIN")
```

is used to specify the *classnm* argument required by the *WPWin* constructor. In C++, this syntax is required whenever a base class constructor expects arguments:

```
Derived::Derived(/* args */) : Base(/* base class args */)
{
    // Body of constructor
}
```

Just to see exactly how all this works in practice, let's examine carefully what happens when our program executes the statement

```
HelloWin *win = new HelloWin(MyModuleInstance);
```

The following chain of events is triggered:

- ■ C++ allocates enough storage for a *HelloWin* object instance and automatically invokes the *HelloWin* constructor with *MyModuleInstance* as argument. The first thing *HelloWin* does is call its base class (*WPWin*) constructor with "HELLOWIN" as the window class name (this call is automatically inserted by the compiler as the first line in the *HelloWin* constructor).

- ■ *WPWin* initializes default *createArgs*; for example, the cursor is set to IDC_ARROW (the normal Windows arrow cursor), the window coordinates are all set to CW_USEDEFAULT, and the menu name is set to NULL. When it's done, *WPWin* returns control to *HelloWin*.

- ■ *HelloWin* sets the HELLO-specific *createArgs*, overriding the values set by *WPWin*. It sets *wndcls.hInstance* to *MyModuleInstance*, as well as the window procedure, style, title, and menu and icon names. Finally, *HelloWin* calls *createWin* to actually register and create the window.

When all is said and done, our HELLO window has been created! Of course, it's not visible until we call *show*.

Now you can see why *createArgs* is more convenient than passing a plethora of arguments to *createWin*: each window class constructor sets default values for the fields in *createArgs* that are relevant to *it*; subsequent derived class constructors set additional fields and/or override the defaults. In general, each window class constructor in the hierarchy will contribute its two cents to *createArgs* before passing control to the next constructor. In this manner, the most generic creation parameters (such as *wndcls.cbClsExtra* and *wndcls.cbWndExtra*, which are always zero) can be initialized at a low level (in *WPWin*, which is part of the *library*), where applications never have to bother with them again, while creation parameters that are more likely to vary from one window class to another (such as the window style and menu) are initialized by more specialized subclasses.

For example, when we implement the edit control class, the constructor will look like this:

```
WPEdit::WPEdit() : WPWin("edit")
{
    createArgs.style |= WS_BORDER | ES_LEFT | ES_AUTOHSCROLL;
}
```

Only the style flags specific to an edit control need be set; all the other *createArgs* are simply inherited. The default *createArgs* can, of course, always be altered. If we should decide to give *HelloWin* a crosshairs cursor instead of an arrow, all we'd have to do is add the following line to its constructor:

```
createArgs.wndcls.hCursor = LoadCursor(NULL, IDC_CROSS);
```

The whole point of using constructors, *createArgs* and *createWin,* instead of *RegisterClass* and *CreateWindow(Ex)* is that it spreads the act of window creation between the (reusable) library and the applications that use it—the generic parts are done automatically by the library, while the application-specific stuff is left to the application itself. Doing it this way simplifies application development. In general, it's better to do as much work as possible up front, in the *library,* where we only have to write the code *once* for every application to use.

Some readers might wonder, why make *createArgs* a class-wide global? The more obvious thing would have been to store the creation arguments in the *WPWin* object itself (in fact, Borland's *ObjectWindows* does something like this).

Since *createArgs* are needed only when the window is created, and since all the information in *createArgs* can be obtained from Windows API functions, it's a waste of storage to carry these parameters around for the lifetime of the window. Because we made *createArgs* a static member, there's just one instance for the entire class, and our window object occupies only two bytes! Of course, we must be careful not to modify *createArgs* between the time the constructors set them and the time *createWin* is invoked (that's always the problem with globals). As a general rule, the constructor for the last derived subclass in the hierarchy should call *createWin* to actually create the window, immediately after setting *createArgs.* This ensures that the *createArgs* are not altered before calling *createWin.*[14]

If we agree to follow this rule (of calling *createWin* within the last object constructor), then our system has the following characteristic: creating a *(Windows++)*

---

14 Unfortunately, a derived window class can't always "know" when it's the last one in the inheritance chain. For example, we want to leave open the possibility that programmers may derive new edit control subclasses from *WPEdit,* so we don't want the constructor to call *createWin.* In this situation, callers must explicitly create the window immediately after creating the object:

```
WPEdit *editWin = new WPEdit;
editWin->createWin();
```

As you'll see in Chapter 7, this is not necessary for dialog boxes.

window object corresponds to creating the (Windows) window. This "feels right" and should give us some confidence that our design in on the right track.

3.2.6 Brainless Coding: Filling Out the *WPWin* Class

Our *WPWin* class so far has only a handful of functions, such as *show* and *update*, that simply invoke their Windows counterparts, passing the HWND stored in the object. It doesn't take a genius to see how these can be generalized. For example:

```
class WPWin {
    HWND hwnd;
public:
    int getText(char *buf, int len)
        { return GetWindowText(hwnd, buf, len); }
};
```

Once you get the hang of it, you can go wild implementing lots of *Windows++* code. It's the perfect thing for a rainy afternoon when your brain is fried from too much caffeine and assembly-language debugging, but you still want to be productive: why not reimplement the entire Windows interface in C++?

This is precisely what I did one rainy afternoon.

With a little help from my editor (Lugaru's *Epsilon*, which I cannot praise enough and must plug at least once), I even automated the process somewhat by starting from WINDOWS.H and applying the general formula

```
RETTYPE FAR PASCAL WindowsFunction(HWND, args . . .)
```

which becomes

```
RETTYPE windowsFunction(args . . .)
    { return WindowsFunction(hwnd, args); }
```

Within in a couple of hours I had written several pages of *Windows++* code:

```
class WPWin {
public:
    void destroyWin()                 { DestroyWindow(hwnd); }

    // properties
    HANDLE getProp(CSTR kwd)
        { return GetProp(hwnd, (LPSTR)kwd); }
    void setProp(CSTR kwd, HANDLE val)
        { SetProp(hwnd, (LPSTR)kwd, val); }
    void removeProp(CSTR kwd)
        { RemoveProp(hwnd, (LPSTR)kwd); }

    // rectangles
    void getClientRect(WPRect& rect)
        { GetClientRect(hwnd, (LPRECT)&rect); }
    void getWindowRect(WPRect& rect)
        { GetWindowRect(hwnd, (LPRECT)&rect); }
    BOOL getUpdateRect(WPRect& rect, BOOL erase=FALSE)
        { return GetUpdateRect(hwnd, (LPRECT)&rect, erase); }
    int getUpdateRgn(WPRegion& rgn, BOOL erase=FALSE);
```

```
// invalidate
void invalidate(BOOL erase=FALSE)
    { InvalidateRect(hwnd, NULL, erase); }
void invalidate(WPRect& rect, BOOL erase=FALSE)
    { InvalidateRect(hwnd, (LPRECT)&rect, erase); }
void invalidate(WPRegion& rgn, BOOL erase=FALSE);

// validate
void validate()
    { ValidateRect(hwnd, NULL); }
void validate(WPRect& rect)
    { ValidateRect(hwnd, (LPRECT)&rect); }
void validate(WPRegion& rgn);

// positioning
void setPos(int x, int y)
    { SetWindowPos(hwnd,NULL,x,y,0,0,SWP_NOSIZE|SWP_NOZORDER); }
void setSize(int w, int h)
    { SetWindowPos(hwnd,NULL,0,0,w,h,SWP_NOMOVE|SWP_NOZORDER); }

void setAfter(WPWin* after)
    { SetWindowPos(hwnd,GetHwnd(after),
        0,0,0,0,SWP_NOSIZE|SWP_NOMOVE);}
void bringToTop()
    { BringWindowToTop(hwnd); }
void bringToBottom()
    { SetWindowPos(hwnd,1,0,0,0,0,SWP_NOSIZE|SWP_NOMOVE); }

void moveWin(WPRect& box, BOOL repaint=TRUE)
    { MoveWindow(hwnd,
        box.left(), box.top(), box.width(), box.height(), repaint); }

// miscellaneous
void setFocus()                      { SetFocus(hwnd); }
void setReDraw(BOOL val)             { sendMsg(WM_SETREDRAW,val); }
void update()                        { UpdateWindow(hwnd); }
BOOL show(int how=SW_SHOW)           { return ShowWindow(hwnd, how); }
void showOwnedPopups(BOOL show)      { ShowOwnedPopups(hwnd, show); }

void setText(LPCSTR text)       { SetWindowText(hwnd,(LPSTR)text); }
int getText()                   { return GetWindowTextLength(hwnd); }
int getText(LPSTR buf, int buflen)
    { return GetWindowText(hwnd, buf, buflen); }

// timer
int setTimer(int id, int msec, FARPROC func=NULL)
    { return SetTimer(hwnd, id, msec, func); }
BOOL killTimer(int id)
    { return  KillTimer(hwnd, id); }

// coordinates
void clientToScreen(WPPoint &point)
    { ClientToScreen(hwnd, (LPPOINT)&point); }
void clientToScreen(WPRect &box)
    {  clientToScreen(box.origin()); clientToScreen(box.endpt()); }
void screenToClient(WPPoint &point)
    { ScreenToClient(hwnd, (LPPOINT)&point); }
void screenToClient(WPRect &box)
    { screenToClient(box.origin()); screenToClient(box.endpt()); }
```

```
// etc.
void close()                { sendMsg(WM_CLOSE); }
void minimize()             { CloseWindow(hwnd); }
void maximize()             { ShowWindow(hwnd, SW_SHOWMAXIMIZED);}
BOOL isMinimized()          { return IsIconic(hwnd); }
BOOL isMaximized()          { return IsZoomed(hwnd); }

BOOL openIcon()             { return OpenIcon(hwnd); }
BOOL isIconic()             { return IsIconic(hwnd); }
BOOL enableWin(BOOL b)      { return EnableWindow(hwnd, b); }
BOOL isEnabled()            { return IsWindowEnabled(hwnd); }
BOOL isVisible()            { return IsWindowVisible(hwnd); }
BOOL isZoomed()             { return IsZoomed(hwnd); }

BOOL flash(BOOL invert=TRUE)
    { return FlashWindow(hwnd, invert); }
int getClassName(LPSTR buf, int buflen)
    { return GetClassName(hwnd, buf, buflen); }

LONG style()
    { return GetWindowLong(hwnd, GWL_STYLE); }
LONG style(LONG style)
    { return SetWindowLong(hwnd, GWL_STYLE, style);}

void setMenu(HMENU hmenu)   { SetMenu(hwnd, hmenu); }
HMENU getMenu()             { return GetMenu(hwnd); }
void drawMenu()             { DrawMenuBar(hwnd); }
};
```

(I sure hope you didn't read all that!) Because virtually all of these functions are defined within the class declaration, they're *inline* functions, which means there's no performance penalty for calling them.

```
win->enableWin(TRUE)
```

generates exactly the same compiled code as

```
EnableWindow(win->hwnd, TRUE);
```

The only performance hit comes when you compile your program and have to load all those definitions in the *#include* files! (Actually, it's not too bad.)[15]

What do we gain with all these "brainless" functions?

As with *show* and *update*, they make our code more object-oriented by following the OO-dictum that only member functions should manipulate objects. This becomes more important as our system grows, for not all Windows functions are "allowed" in *Windows++* (for example, *CreateWindow* and *RegisterWindow* are now defunct). By providing "brainless" member functions, we in effect automatically document which operations are supported. Programmers need never wonder, "am I supposed to use *createWin* or *CreateWindow*?" The simple rule is *always use*

---

15 Note: I would have preferred to call the enable function simply *enable*, but this name conflicts with a Borland macro defined in *<dos.h>*. Sigh.

only the member functions supplied. This is the very essence of OOP: *objects are always and only manipulated through their methods (member functions).* In fact, true object-oriented programming languages don't even provide a notion of *extern* or "global" functions, only class methods. Global functions exist in C++ only because it evolved from, and maintains compatibility with, C.

Another benefit of "brainless" functions is *packaging:*

- Whenever a Windows function expects a quadruplet of integers representing a rectangle, the corresponding *Windows++* function uses a single *WPRect* structure. For example

  ```
  void moveWin(WPRect &box, BOOL repaint=TRUE)
      { MoveWindow(hwnd, box.left(), box.top(), box.width(),
          box.height(), repaint); }
  ```

  This is for convenience. (I hate typing and consider a function that requires more than four arguments to be unfriendly.)

- Wherever possible, I've exploited C++'s ability to specify default arguments. The preceding example illustrates this: the *repaint* flag is TRUE by default. Windows is full of functions with arguments that are NULL 90 percent of the time you use them. In *Windows++*, you can just omit them.

- Many functions have several overloaded versions. For example, *clientTo-Screen* has one version that converts a point and another that converts an entire rectangle.

- In very few cases, I renamed Windows functions outright when I thought doing so improved clarity and/or consistency. (This is the programmer's equivalent of poetic license.) For example, I changed *CloseWindow* to *minimize* and *IsZoomed* to *isMaximized*. The *close* function does what you'd expect; namely, close (not minimize) the window by sending it a WM_CLOSE message.

By repackaging the Windows API syntactically, we make it more consistent, easier to remember, and easier to use. In the process, we also transform it into the C++ paradigm, where all operations on objects are performed by member functions. Any Windows function that operates on an HWND should properly be thought of as a window "method" (OO-terminology for class member function). The "brainless" code makes this explicit using inline functions. Much of *Windows++* is just this sort of syntactic packaging, and while it may seem overly compulsive, it really makes programming a lot easier. Of course, *Windows++* is more than just repackaging (it's reusable!). Moreover, many *Windows++* functions actually *do* something (honest!). Nevertheless, the mundane things are often the most useful and frequently get overlooked.

If typing in a lot of trivial code bores you to tears, you have three options: 1) do it gradually—you don't have to implement each function until you actually need it;

2) you can always just call the Windows function directly, passing the HWND obtained from *getHwnd;* 3) buy the source disk.

In future chapters I won't describe each new *WPWin* function as I use it, especially if it's obvious from the name which Windows function it corresponds to. You can use the source listing in Appendix A to find out how any particular function is implemented.

3.2.7 HELLO1

We can now write HELLO1.CPP. In fact, we've practically done it already!

```
/////////////////////////////////////////////////
// HELLO1--The first C++ version of HELLO.
// Copyright 1992 Paul DiLascia.
//

#include "wpp.h"

LONG _export FAR PASCAL WndProc(HWND hwnd, WORD msg, WORD wp, LONG lp);

//////////////////
// This class represents the main hello window.
// It's derived from the base window class, WPWin.
//
class HelloWin : public WPWin {
public:
    HelloWin(HANDLE hinst);        // constructor takes module handle
};

//////////////////
// Initialize an instance of HelloWin:
// initialize createArgs, then create the window.
//
HelloWin::HelloWin(HANDLE hinst) : WPWin("HELLOWIN")
{
    createArgs.wndcls.lpfnWndProc = WndProc;
    createArgs.wndcls.hInstance = hinst;
    createArgs.wndcls.lpszMenuName = "HelloMenu";
    createArgs.wndcls.hIcon = LoadIcon(hinst, "HelloIcon");
    createArgs.style = WS_OVERLAPPEDWINDOW;
    createWin("HELLO1--1st C++ version");
}

//////////////////
// Program entry point
//
int PASCAL WinMain(HANDLE hinst, HANDLE pinst, LPSTR cmdline, int show)
{
    // Create HelloWin object (equiv to RegisterClass/CreateWindowEx).
    HelloWin *win = new HelloWin(hinst);

    win->show(show); // show it (=ShowWindow)
    win->update();   // update it (=UpdateWindow)
```

```
    // This a normal Windows message loop
    MSG msg;
    while (GetMessage(&msg, NULL, 0, 0)) {
        TranslateMessage(&msg);
        DispatchMessage(&msg);
    }

    delete win;      // destroy the window object
    return msg.wParam;
}

///////////////
// Here's the window procedure. It's unchanged from HELLO.C.
//
LONG _export FAR PASCAL WndProc(HWND hwnd, WORD msg, WORD wp, LONG lp)
{
    PAINTSTRUCT ps;
    HDC hdc;
    RECT rect;

    switch(msg) {
    case WM_PAINT:
        hdc = BeginPaint(hwnd, &ps);
        GetClientRect(hwnd, &rect);
        DrawText(hdc, "Goodbye, C. Hello C++.", -1, &rect,
            DT_SINGLELINE | DT_CENTER | DT_VCENTER);
        EndPaint(hwnd, &ps);
        return 0;

    case WM_COMMAND:
        switch (wp) {
        case IDCANCEL:
            SendMessage(hwnd, WM_CLOSE, 0, 0);
            break;
        }
        return 0;

    case WM_DESTROY:
        PostQuitMessage(0);
        return 0;
    }
    return DefWindowProc(hwnd, msg, wp, lp);
}
```

There's little that's new here; I've simply assembled the various pieces we've already discussed into a complete program. The derived window class *HelloWin* is implemented as shown in the preceding section. A few calls have been added to *WinMain* to create an instance of *HelloWin*, show it, update it, and destroy it before exiting. The rest, including *WndProc*, is unchanged from HELLO.C.

You may have noticed that *WndProc* in HELLO1 is declared with the *_export* modifier. This Windows-specific keyword tells the compiler that the function *WndProc* should be exported by the linker and makes it unnecessary to declare *WndProc* in the EXPORTS section of the module definition file. This is a major convenience: with *_export*, you never again need bother with EXPORTS. This will come in especially handy later, when we export C++ (as opposed to Pascal) functions, which have the mangled names described in the previous chapter, and again in Chapter 9, when we turn *Windows++* into a DLL.

We still have a long way to go, but already HELLO1 is an improvement over the original C program: we've encapsulated the entire window registration and creation sequence in a reusable library class, *WPWin*. In the following sections, we'll use similar techniques to encapsulate other generic aspects of HELLO.

HELLO1 illustrates a fundamental feature of *Windows++*: it uses the built-in library class *WPWin* to derive its own new window class, *HelloWin*. This is the primary means by which *Windows++* (and all object-oriented class libraries) supplies reusable code: *by providing "built-in" classes from which programs can derive application-specific subclasses.* This illustrates precisely what we mean by a "reusable class library." In general, the first thing you do when you write a *Windows++* program is derive some new window class (in this case, *HelloWin*) from one of the built-in classes. The built-in classes "encapsulate" generic Windows behavior (for example, window registration and creation), while the application's derived subclasses implement application-specific behavior (for example, displaying the message "Good-bye, C. Hello C++." Our goal throughout the book will be to encapsulate as much generic Windows behavior as possible in built-in classes, so that applications can simply inherit (reuse) it and only provide whatever behavior is unique to the application. Right now the only library class is *WPWin*, but we'll soon have more.

C   *In C, you could implement* WPWin *(and the other classes we are about to build) as window classes in the Windows sense; that is, you could provide library functions to register and create a window class called "WPWIN", as well as a window procedure that gives it the desired behavior.*

3.2.8 Compiling HELLO1

Before we can run HELLO1, we must compile and link it. This is straightforward, and most easily accomplished using a make file. Here's the Borland version:

```
# Makefile for HELLO1.CPP
#
.cpp.obj:
    bcc -c -WE -w-par $*

HELLO1.EXE: WPWIN.OBJ HELLO1.OBJ
    bcc -WE HELLO1.OBJ WPWIN.OBJ
    rc hello

HELLO1.obj : HELLO1.CPP
WPWIN.obj : wpwin.h wprect.h wppdefs.h WPWIN.CPP
```

The Zortech version is almost identical:

```
# Makefile for HELLO1.CPP
#
.cpp.obj:
    ztc -c -W2 $*

HELLO1.EXE: WPWIN.OBJ HELLO1.OBJ
    ztc -W2 HELLO1.OBJ WPWIN.OBJ
    zrc hello

HELLO1.obj : HELLO1.CPP
WPWIN.obj : wpwin.h wprect.h wppdefs.h WPWIN.CPP
```

The only thing of any particular interest is the use of the –WE (–W2 for Zortech) switch. What does it do?

Exported Windows functions require a special assembly-language prolog and epilog to set up the 80x86 DS (data segment) register appropriately. The normal Windows switch, –W, tells the compiler to generate the Windows prolog for all *far* functions; the –WE/–W2 switch tells the compiler to generate it only for *exported* functions (i.e., ones declared with _export). Since exported functions are the only functions that could be called from Windows, they're the only ones that need the special prolog and epilog. Using –WE saves some space and CPU cycles in functions that are *not* exported.[16]

3.3 HELLO2: The Application Class

So far, so good. We're well on our way to modeling Windows in C++: we have a base Window class, *WPWin,* that represents "any window." Where should we look for our next object to model? Once again, we look to the "real world," which for us is Windows. All Windows "objects" are prime candidates. In particular, anything that's represented by a HANDLE. But which one?

We don't just want to look for objects, we also want to look for objects and/or behavior that's *generic* to all applications. In general, if something appears in *every* application, then we should put it into our library, so it doesn't have to appear in *any* application!

What about the module instance handle? The *HelloWin* constructor contains the following line:

```
createArgs.wndcls.hInstance = hinst;
```

---

16 Since HELLO1 is compiled in the small model (by default), –W is equivalent to –WE; however, we will shortly compile under the medium and large models, where all functions are *far* by default. In this case, –WE/–W2 provides a real benefit.

Every Windows program has a module instance handle, and every program has to set *wndcls.hInstance*. This is generic behavior we should try to encapsulate. But what "thing" does the module instance handle represent? Why, the program itself. Since you have your OOP cap on (if not, put it on now!), a little light bulb should go on in your head that says application object!

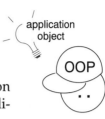

3.3.1 The Module Class: *WPModule*

Before attempting to model the application as an object, let's spend a few minutes observing that the application is really a special case of a more general windows object, the module. In Windows, the application is identified by its module instance handle; however, there can be other modules besides the application itself. For example, our program might load a DLL (dynamic link library) or even another program module. So the application is a special kind of module. Since we may want to deal with other modules later on, our design should reflect this observation: we will derive the application class from a more general module class:

```
///////////////////
// Class used to represent a Windows module.
// Essentially, it's just a module instance handle.
//
class WPModule {
protected:
    HANDLE hinst;                    // module handle
    LPCSTR cmdLine;                  // Windows cmd line (explained later)
public:
    WPModule(HANDLE h=NULL)          { hinst = h; }
    WPModule(CSTR name)              { hinst = GetModuleHandle(name); }

    HANDLE operator()()              { return hinst; }
    void getCmdLine(char *buf)       { lstrcpy(buf, (LPSTR)cmdLine); }
    int getFileName(char *buf, int buflen)
        { return GetModuleFileName(hinst, (LPSTR)buf, buflen); }

    HANDLE loadIcon(LPCSTR name)
        { return LoadIcon(HIWORD(name) ? hinst : NULL, (LPSTR)name); }
    HANDLE loadIcon(int id)
        { return LoadIcon(hinst, MAKEINTRESOURCE(id)); }
};
```

WPModule stores the module's instance handle and command line string. The function *operator()()* returns the Windows HANDLE (just as it does for *WPWin*). The member functions *getFileName* and *loadIcon* simply call their Windows equivalents, passing *hinst* to Windows.

Only *loadIcon* is non-trivial: it has two overloaded versions. The first takes a string, the second, an integer. Recall that in Windows, module resources are specified by name but also can be specified using a numeric ID. In the latter case, you pass a "fake" string pointer which contains the integer ID in the low-order word and zero in the high-order word. Windows provides a macro MAKEINTRESOURCE that creates such a pointer. In *Windows++*, we shield programmers from bothering with MAKEINTRESOURCE by providing an overloaded version of *loadIcon*:

```
HANDLE loadIcon(int id)
    { return LoadIcon(hinst, MAKEINTRESOURCE(id)); }
```

The other version looks like this:

```
HANDLE loadIcon(LPCSTR name)
    { return LoadIcon(HIWORD(name) ? hinst : NULL, (LPSTR)name); }
```

The reason this function passes NULL as the module handle if the high word of the string pointer is zero is that we might call *loadIcon* with one of the predefined Windows icons, which are defined in WINDOWS.H:

```
#define    IDI_APPLICATION        MAKEINTRESOURCE(32512)
#define    IDI_HAND               MAKEINTRESOURCE(32513)
#define    IDI_QUESTION           MAKEINTRESOURCE(32514)
#define    IDI_EXCLAMATION        MAKEINTRESOURCE(32515)
#define    IDI_ASTERISK           MAKEINTRESOURCE(32516)
```

To load these, you're supposed to pass a NULL module handle. *Windows++* assumes that the only "fake" string pointers are ones that come from WINDOWS.H. The upshot is, if you want to load resources by ID, don't use MAKEINT-RESOURCE! Use the integer version of loadIcon instead. This is easier anyway.

Thus, to load an icon by name, use

```
module->loadIcon("myIcon");
```

and to load by ID, use

```
module->loadIcon(17);
```

3.3.2 The Application Object: *App*

Now that we've implemented *WPModule*, we can implement the application class. This class represents the application itself—that is, our main program module. It's defined in WPAPP.H along with *WPModule* like this:

```
class WPApp : public WPModule {
    HANDLE pinst;                              // previous instance handle
    int cmdShow;                               // how to show window
    int exitCode;                              // returned from WinMain
    void init(HANDLE h, HANDLE p, LPSTR cmd, int show);
public:
    HANDLE getPrevInst()                       { return pinst; }
    BOOL first()                               { return pinst==NULL; }
};

extern WPApp App;                              // THE application
```

WPApp is derived from *WPModule*, reflecting our initial observation that the application is a special kind of module. It stores a few additional data members: *pinst*, *cmdShow,* and *exitCode.* WPAPP.H declares a global object, *App,* which represents the application. The reason for making *App* global is that it contains a number of items, such as the module instance handle, that any object or function might legitimately need. For example, we can immediately go back and rewrite the *WPWin* constructor as follows:

```
WPWin::WPWin(CSTR classnm)
{
    .
    .
    createArgs.wndcls.hInstance = App();
    .
    .
}
```

The function *WPApp::operator()* (inherited from *WPModule*) returns the module instance handle, *hinst* (also inherited from *WPModule*). Formerly, WPWin initialized the window's module instance handle to NULL, only because the application's instance handle was not readily available; now we can get it from the global *App* object. In fact, we never again need bother setting *createArgs.wndcls.hInstance.* Not in *HelloWin,* nor in any other window class our programs might derive. That's one more line of reusable code, one less thing to burden our programs with.

But how does *App* get initialized? In particular, how do *hinst* and *pinst* get set? *WinMain* does it:

```
int PASCAL WinMain(HANDLE hinst, HANDLE pinst, LPSTR cmd, int show)
{
    App.init(hinst, pinst, cmd, show);   // initialize app object
    .
    .
}
```

The *init* function is itself quite trivial: it just stores its arguments in the object:

```
/////////////////////
// Initialize application object. Called from WinMain.
//
void WPApp::init(HANDLE h, HANDLE p, LPSTR cmd, int show)
{
    hinst = h;
    pinst = p;
    cmdLine=cmd;
    cmdShow=show;
}
```

In order to guarantee that *WinMain* is the *only* place *init* is called, *init* is declared as a *private* member function, but *WinMain* is declared as a *friend* of *WPApp.*

```
class WPApp : public WPModule {
private:
    friend int PASCAL WinMain(HANDLE, HANDLE, LPSTR, int);
    void init(HANDLE h, HANDLE p, LPSTR cmd, int show);
};
```

In C++, if you declare that a particular function is a *friend* of a class, that function is allowed to access even the private (data *and* function) members of the class. Thus *WinMain* can call *WPApp::init* even though it's private. Of course, we could just make *init* public, but keeping it private helps make our library foolproof by guaranteeing that no one other than *WinMain* attempts to call *init*.[17]

3.3.3 Encapsulating the Message Loop

What else can we use *App* for? Don't forget that we're constantly on the lookout for generic code that we can move from HELLO into our library. Well, one obvious candidate is the message loop. How many times have you written the following lines of Windows code?

```
ShowWindow(hwnd, show);
UpdateWindow(hwnd);

MSG msg;
while (GetMessage(&msg, NULL, 0, 0)) {
    TranslateMessage(&msg);
    DispatchMessage(&msg);
}
```

Since every application needs a message loop, we should look for some way to encapsulate it. Since there's only one message loop for each application, *WPApp* is the logical place. All we have to do is introduce a new function—say, *WPApp::run*. The only application-specific items in the standard message loop shown above are the window handle and *show* flag; our *run* function will need to get these from somewhere. The *show* flag[18] is already stored in the application object as *cmdShow*, so that's no problem. What about the main window? Since most applications have a main window, it seems natural to add one to *WPApp*.

```
class WPApp {
private:
    WPWin *mainWin;                 // application's main window
public:
    void run();                     // run message loop
};
```

We can easily set *mainWin* from *WinMain*:

```
int PASCAL WinMain(HANDLE hinst,HANDLE pinst,LPSTR cmdline,int show)
{
    App.init(hinst, pinst);         // init THE application object
    App.mainWin = new HelloWin;     // create and set main window
    .
    .
    .
}
```

---

17 *WPApp::init* is analogous to the *InitApp* function that many Windows programmers write.

18 This Windows flag specifies how the window should be sized: normal, maximized, minimized, etc.

(Remember: *WinMain* is a *friend* of *WPApp,* so it can access *App.mainWin!*) Now that *mainWin* is hooked up, all we have to do to encapsulate the message loop is move our code from *WinMain* to *WPApp::run,* modifying it slightly to use the variables *mainWin* and *cmdShow:*

```
void WPApp::run()
{
    assert(mwinWin);
    mainWin->show(cmdShow);
    mainWin->update();

    MSG msg;
    while (GetMessage(&msg, NULL, 0, 0)) {
        TranslateMessage(&msg);
        DispatchMessage(&msg);
    }
    exitCode = msg.wParam;
}
```

Since we're letting *WPApp* handle the message loop, we need a function to terminate the loop while we're at it.

```
class WPApp {
public:
    void quit(int ret=0)            { PostQuitMessage(ret); }
};
```

Note the use of C++ default function arguments: *quit* takes a return code which, if unspecified, defaults to zero. This value will be returned by Windows as *msg.wParam,* which *WPApp::run* stores in the data member *WPApp::exitCode.* We'll return this value at the end of *WinMain,* so Windows can . . . ignore it! (Currently Windows does nothing with the *WinMain* return value, but we Windows programmers faithfully continue to return a meaningful code, probably for no other reason than compulsiveness.)

Now, instead of calling *PostQuitMessage* directly, HELLO calls *App.quit:*

```
LONG _export FAR PASCAL WndProc(HWND hwnd, WORD msg, WORD wp, LONG lp)
{
    switch(msg) {
        .
        .
    case WM_DESTROY:
        App.quit();
        return 0;
    }
    return DefWindowProc(hwnd, msg, wp, lp);
}
```

That's all there is to it! We've encapsulated the entire message loop in reusable code, in the function *WPApp::run.* We never have to write another one again!

"But wait a minute!," I hear the Windows gurus complaining, "your message loop is the simplest possible vanilla message loop, suitable only for dumb programs like HELLO. *Real* message loops translate accelerator keys, check for modeless dialog boxes—and what if you want to call *PeekMessage* instead of *GetMessage* in order to do background processing while the program is idle?"

No problem. All we have to do is enhance our modest message loop appropriately. Since you brought it up, let's add accelerators right now. This is hardly required for HELLO, but we have greater ambitions in mind.

3.3.4 Accelerators

To add accelerators to our message loop, all we need is a handle to the accelerator table and a way to set it, which we can easily add to *WPApp:*

```
class WPApp {
    HANDLE accel;      // handle to accelerator table
public:
    HANDLE findResource(CSTR nm, LPSTR type)
        { return FindResource(hinst, (LPSTR)nm, type); }
    HANDLE loadAccel(CSTR acname)
        { return accel = LoadAccelerators(hinst, (LPSTR)acname); }
};
```

Next, we modify the message loop:

```
int WPApp::run()
{
    .
    .
    while (GetMessage(&msg, NULL, 0, 0)) {
        if (!(accel &&
            TranslateAccelerator((*mainWin)(), accel, &msg))) {

            TranslateMessage(&msg);
            DispatchMessage(&msg);
        }
    }
    .
    .
}
```

Now all an application has to do to use an accelerator table is define it in the resource (.RC) file and then load it by calling

```
loadAccel("MyAccel");
```

We can even spare programs the trouble by doing it automatically in *WPApp::init:*

```
const char DFLTACCEL[] = "AppAccel";

void WPApp::init(HANDLE h, HANDLE p, LPSTR cmd, int show)
{
    .
    . (as before)
    .
    // Load default accelerator table if it exists
    if (findResource(DFLTACCEL, RT_ACCELERATOR))
        loadAccel(DFLTACCEL);
}
```

Now all our programs need do to specify accelerator keys is define them in the module's resource (.RC) file, using the predefined name "AppAccel". The rest is automatically taken care of by *Windows++*: the table is loaded, and the invisible message loop automatically handles the accelerator messages correctly! If no accelerator table called "AppAccel" exists, no harm is done, and if a program wants to use a different accelerator table, it can call *App.loadAccel* directly.[19]

Let's use this new *Window++* feature to add an accelerator table to our HELLO program; all we have to do is add a few lines to HELLO.RC:

```
APPACCEL ACCELERATORS
BEGIN
  "^X",    IDCANCEL
END
```

Now users can type *Control-X* to exit the HELLO program.

What we're really doing here is reusing(!) the resource name *AppAccel.* We'll employ this trick throughout *Windows++*, for menus, icons, controls, dialog boxes—anything we can. There's no reason reusability should be restricted to lines of C++ code!

Later (in Section 3.5.5) we'll enhance *run* again, to handle idle processing using *PeekMessage.* And in later chapters, we'll enhance it even further, until *run* eventually becomes a super-duper message loop capable of handling not only accelerator keys and *PeekMessage,* but modeless dialog boxes and MDI windows too. But no matter how complicated it gets, we'll reuse the same old message loop over and over again in every program we write. (Curious readers may want to peek at the final message loop in Appendix A. See also Sections 6.4.5 and 7.6.)

---

19 It would be more elegant to simply call *loadAccell*, rather than *findResource,* then *loadAccel,* but if you do, the DEBUG version of Windows will complain if *AppAccel* doesn't exist. Sigh.

3.3.5 Hiding *WinMain*

WinMain is shrinking to practically nothing! This is all that remains:

```
int PASCAL WinMain(HANDLE hinst,HANDLE pinst,LPSTR cmdline,int show)
{
    App.init(hinst, pinst);         // initialize global app object
    App.mainWin = new HelloWin;     // create a hello window instance
    App.run(show);                  // run the message loop
    delete mainWin;                 // delete the main window
    return App.exitCode;
}
```

Is there anything left that's generic enough to push into the library? Well, it seems unfriendly to require that *Windows++* programmers remember to call *App.init* every time they write *WinMain*, even if it is only one line of code. So let's get rid of it. In fact, let's get rid of *WinMain*!

What? How can you do that?!

It's easy. All we have to do is invent a new function, *WPApp::main*, which we agree should be the new entry point for every *Windows++* application, and modify *WinMain* to call it. We first declare *main* in the class definition for *WPApp*:

```
// (In WPAPP.H)
class WPApp {
private:
    void main();
};
```

(*main* is declared *private* because only *WinMain*—a *friend*—will call it.) Next, we implement *WinMain* in a file called WINMAIN.CPP as follows:

```
WPApp App;                               // instantiate global app object

int PASCAL WinMain(HANDLE hinst, HANDLE pinst, LPSTR cmd, int show)
{
    App.init(hinst, pinst, cmd, show);
    App.main();                          // call app entry-point
    return App.exitCode;
}
```

This function is entered in a file called WINMAIN.CPP, which becomes part of *Windows++*. This is also where *App* is instantiated. Now, instead of providing *WinMain*, HELLO provides *WPApp::main*:

```
////////////////
// Program entry point, called from internal WinMain.
//
void WPApp::main()
{
    mainWin = new HelloWin;         // create instance of HelloWin
    run();                          // run message loop
    delete mainWin;                 // delete window
}
```

How does all this work? It's really nothing complicated. *WinMain* is in the source file WINMAIN.CPP, which we'll compile along with all the other *Windows++* files that belong to the *Windows++* library. *WinMain* takes care of initialization, then calls *App.main,* which is *not* implemented in WPAPP.CPP. It's deliberately omitted, so the application (HELLO2.CPP) must supply it. There's no reason *WPApp::main* has to be in WPAPP.CPP. It can appear in any file whatsoever. But it must appear *somewhere,* or the linker will complain of an unresolved reference.

C   *All this has nothing to do with C++. You could do exactly the same thing in C: write a* WinMain *that calls* main *so that* main *is the program entry point. This sort of trick is sometimes used to build libraries that let you port DOS applications (which use* main) *unchanged to Windows.*

Some of you may be wondering why *main* doesn't have any arguments, Since *main* is a member of *WPApp,* it can access the private data members *hinst, pinst, cmdLine,* and *cmdShow.* If a program needs to use these for something, they're handy, so we needn't bother passing them to *main* as function arguments. For example, if we wanted HELLO to start as an icon for some reason, all we'd have to do is change *cmdShow* before calling *run:*

```
void WPApp::main()
{
    mainWin = new HelloWin;
    cmdShow = SW_SHOWMINNOACTIVE;       // show minimized (symbol is
    run();                              // defined in WINDOWS.H)
    delete mainWin;
}
```

3.3.6 The Main Window: *WPMainWin*

Our HELLO program is getting simpler and simpler all the time. *WinMain* has gone the way of the dodo, and so has the message loop. What's left that we can encapsulate into our code-hungry library? Well, currently the *HelloWin* constructor looks something like this:

```
HelloWin::HelloWin() : WPWin("HELLOWIN")
{
    createArgs.wndcls.lpfnWndProc = WndProc;
    createArgs.wndcls.lpszMenuName = "HelloMenu";
    createArgs.wndcls.hIcon = App.loadIcon("HelloIcon");
    createArgs.style = WS_OVERLAPPEDWINDOW;
    createWin("HELLO1--1st C++ version");
}
```

We've eliminated the need to set *wndcls.hInstance;* this datum is now filled in automatically by the *WPWin* constructor. What about the following line?

```
createArgs.style = WS_OVERLAPPEDWINDOW;
```

Most main windows use overlapped window as the style. In
fact, the notion of "main window" sounds like a special kind
of window, which makes OO programmers immediately
think *subclass*. Recall that the window class hierarchy we
sketched out earlier looked like this:

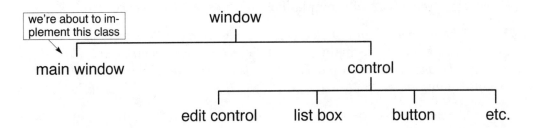

All Windows programs have a main window, which differs from other kinds of
windows in various ways. For example, the main window usually has a title,
menu bar, and icon; and destroying it normally terminates the application. Also,
there's only *one* main window. We've already implicitly recognized this fact by
making *mainWin* a member of *WPApp*, of which there is only one instance.

While setting the default window style does not alone justify introducing a new
class, these observations should convince us that we'll eventually want to model
the main window as a separate class. Now is the time to do it:

```
//////////////////
// Main application window. (In WPMAIN.H)
//
class WPMainWin : public WPWin {
public:
    WPMainWin(CSTR classnm = "MAINWIN");
};
```

WPMainWin is derived from *WPWin,* so it *inherits* all of the data and function
members of *WPWin*. For example, it inherits *hwnd*, as well as all the "brainless"
functions described in Section 3.2.6. The constructor looks like this:

```
WPMainWin::WPMainWin(CSTR classnm) : WPWin(classnm)
{
    createArgs.style = WS_OVERLAPPEDWINDOW;
}
```

The constructor initializes the window style as an overlapped window, the normal
style for main windows. The class name (which defaults to "MAINWIN" if unspecified), is simply passed along to *WPWin*. Since most applications don't give a
hoot what they call their main window class, why not automatically use some

generic name like "MAINWIN"?[20] Remember, this is merely a *default,* one that derived classes like *HelloWin* can always override by passing a different name:

```
HelloWin::HelloWin() : WPMainWin("HELLOWIN")
{
    ...
}
```

In most cases, "MAINWIN" is just fine, so we can write the constructor like so:

```
HelloWin::HelloWin()
{
    ...
}
```

To realize (inherit!) these defaults in our HELLO program, all we have to do is derive *HelloWin* from *WPMainWin* instead of *WPWin.*

```
class HelloWin : public WPMainWin {      // now derived from WPMainWin
public:
    HelloWin();
};
```

The constructor now looks like this:

```
HelloWin::HelloWin()                      // getting smaller all the time
{
    createArgs.wndcls.lpfnWndProc = WndProc;
    createArgs.wndcls.lpszMenuName = "HelloMenu";
    createArgs.wndcls.hIcon = App.loadIcon("HelloIcon");
    createWin("HELLO2--2nd C++ version");    // pass title
}
```

HelloWin no longer bothers with the window class name and style; it's content to use the *WPMainWin* defaults.

Our window class hierarchy now has two members: *WPWin* and *WPMainWin*

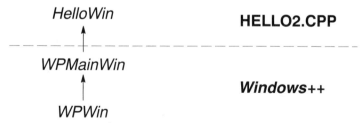

And when we create a new instance of *HelloWin*—

```
mainWin = new HelloWin;
```

—*three* constructors are now invoked:

---

20 There is one drawback to using "MAINWIN" as the default name: this name shows up in certain debugging utilities such as the Heap Walker and Spy. If you have lots of applications running at the same time that all use "MAINWIN" for the window class name, you won't be able to distinguish them. This is a minor problem, since it's trivial to specify a different name.

- First, *WPWin* initializes defaults for *createArgs*, including the module instance handle, which it gets from the global *App* object.

- Second, *WPMainWin* overrides the *createArgs* appropriate for a main window: it sets the class name to "MAINWIN" (by default) and window style to overlapped window.

- Third, *HelloWin* sets the window procedure in *createArgs* to *WndProc* and finally calls *createWin* (the one in *WPMainWin*, not the one in *WPWin*) with the window title as argument, to actually create the window.

Now that we have the main window class, we should go back and declare *WPApp::mainWin* as a main window:

```
class WPApp {
    WPMainWin *mainWin;              // application's main window
};
```

This will ensure that no one attempts to set *mainWin* to an object that's not derived from *WPMainWin*, just an added bit of bulletproofing.

3.3.7 Automatic Menus and Icons

What else can we push from HELLO into our library? What about the menu name and icon?

```
createArgs.wndcls.lpszMenuName = "HelloMenu";
createArgs.wndcls.hIcon = App.loadIcon("HelloIcon");
```

Like "HELLOWIN", these names seem HELLO-specific at first, but just as with the window class name, we don't really care *what* the menu and icon names are, so long as they match the names used in the resource (.RC) file. There's no particular reason to use "HelloMenu" and "HelloIcon." If we agree to use generic names such as "AppMenu" and "AppIcon," we can set these fields in *WPMainWin:*

```
WPMainWin::WPMainWin(CSTR classnm) : WPWin(classnm)
{
    createArgs.style = WS_OVERLAPPEDWINDOW;

    // Use "AppIcon" and "AppMenu"
    createArgs.wndcls.lpszMenuName = "AppMenu";
    createArgs.wndcls.hIcon = App.loadIcon("AppIcon");
    if (createArgs.wndcls.hIcon==NULL)
        createArgs.wndcls.hIcon = App.loadIcon(IDI_APPLICATION);
}
```

We're pulling the same trick here that we did with accelerators earlier: reusing predefined resource names to make programming easier. If no *AppIcon* exists, *WPMainWin* uses the Windows default, IDI_APPLICATION. If *AppMenu* doesn't exist, no harm is done; the window will simply have no menu. To specify a menu and/or icon, all an application has to do is add it to the resource (.RC) file, using predefined names. No code required! Of course, if you want to use different names, you can, but you must specify them in *createArgs* before calling *createWin*. If you stick with the predefined names, you don't have to do anything.

While we're on the subject of predefined symbols, let's add a few menu IDs for common Windows commands like Exit, New, and so on. Windows itself uses the predefined identifiers IDOK, IDCANCEL, IDYES, and so on for the OK, Cancel, and Yes buttons in dialog boxes; we can extend the idea by providing additional predefined IDs for commonly used menu commands:

```
///////////////
// IDs for built-in commands and controls. (In WPID.H)
//
#define WPPIDBASE              256
#define WPIDM_EXIT             (WPPIDBASE + 0)
#define WPIDM_NEW              (WPPIDBASE + 1)
#define WPIDM_OPEN             (WPPIDBASE + 2)
#define WPIDM_SAVE             (WPPIDBASE + 3)
...etc.
```

We'll add WPID.H to the list of files included by WPP.H:

```
#ifdef RC_INVOKED
#include "windows."
#include "wpid.h"                  // include IDs when running RC
#endif
```

Note that WPID.H is included even when running the resource compiler; this is because the symbols defined by WPID.H are commonly used in resource files:

```
// (HELLO2.RC)
#include "wpp.h"

// By calling the ICON "APPICON", it's automatically used.
APPICON ICON hello.ico

// By calling the MENU "APPMENU", it's automatically used.
APPMENU MENU {
    MENUITEM "&Exit!", WPIDM_EXIT
}
```

Once again, at the risk of belaboring the point, we are simply reusing resource names and menu IDs as well as code. You'll see just how useful this is when we implement HELLO3 in Section 3.4.

C   *As with the* WinMain, *you could do the reusable-resource-name and menu ID tricks just as easily in C as in C++. There's nothing object-oriented about them. Instead of loading the default resources in the object constructor, you'd do it in a C function—say,* AppLoadDfltResources.

3.3.8 HELLO2

We can now put all the pieces together to form HELLO2.CPP, our second C++ version of HELLO:

```
///////////////////////////////////////////////////
// HELLO2--The second C++ version of HELLO.
// Copyright 1991 Paul DiLascia.
//

#include "wpp.h"

LONG _export FAR PASCAL WndProc(HWND hwnd, WORD msg, WORD wp, LONG lp);

//////////////////
// This class represents the main hello window.
// Note that it's now derived from WPMainWin instead of WPWin.
//
class HelloWin : public WPMainWin {
public:
    HelloWin();        // constructor takes no args now
};

//////////////////
// Initialize an instance of HelloWin:
// it's much smaller now: only need to init window proc!
//
HelloWin::HelloWin()
{
    createArgs.wndcls.lpfnWndProc = WndProc;
    createWin("HELLO2--2nd C++ version");
}

//////////////////
// Program entry point, called from internal WinMain.
//
void WPApp::main()
{
    mainWin = new HelloWin;        // create instance of HelloWin
    run(show);                     // run message loop
    delete mainWin;                // delete window
}

//////////////////
// Here's the window procedure. The only difference from
// HELLO1 is that we now call App.quit instead of PostQuitMessage.
//
LONG _export FAR PASCAL WndProc(HWND hwnd, WORD msg, WORD wp, LONG lp)
{
    PAINTSTRUCT ps;
    HDC hdc;
    RECT rect;

    switch(msg) {
    case WM_PAINT:
        hdc = BeginPaint(hwnd, &ps);
        GetClientRect(hwnd, &rect);
        DrawText(hdc, "Two down, two to go.", -1, &rect,
            DT_SINGLELINE | DT_CENTER | DT_VCENTER);
        EndPaint(hwnd, &ps);
        return 0;
```

```
    case WM_COMMAND:
        switch (wp) {
        case WPIDM_EXIT:
            SendMessage(hwnd, WM_CLOSE, 0, 0);
            break;
        }
        return 0;
    case WM_DESTROY:
        App.quit(0);
        return 0;
    }
    return DefWindowProc(hwnd, msg, wp, lp);
}
```

The main differences between HELLO2.CPP and HELLO1 are highlighted below.

- ■ *WinMain* is gone, replaced by *WPApp::main. WinMain* is now part of *Windows++* and initializes *App* before calling *App.main,* the new entry point which every *Windows++* program must supply. *App::init* automatically loads the accelerator table *AppAccel* if there is one. The *WPWin* constructor sets the module instance handle in *createArgs* by getting it from *App.*

- ■ A new window class, *WPMainWin,* represents the application's main window. The constructor sets the window class name, style, menu name, and icon in *createArgs* appropriately for a main window, using the predefined names *AppMenu* and *AppIcon* for the menu and icon.

- ■ *HelloWin* is now derived from *WPMainWin.*

- ■ We've added predefined menu IDs such as WPIDM_EXIT for common commands.

- ■ The only things changed in *WndProc* are the call to *App.quit()* and the use of WPIDM_EXIT.

As before, only HELLO2 is shown in the text; the *Windows++* library source files are listed in Appendix A.

3.3.9 Making *Windows*++ a Library

Now that we've implemented lots of code in several files, it's time to turn *Windows++* into a library so we don't have to link HELLO2 and other applications with a long list of object modules. This requires no more than setting up an appropriate make file, which should be familiar to C programmers. Here's the Borland version.

```
# Makefile for HELLO2.CPP
#
CL=bcc
CFLAGS= -a -c -WE -w-par
LFLAGS= -WE
WPPOBJ = WPWIN.OBJ WPAPP.OBJ WPMAIN.OBJ WINMAIN.OBJ
```

```
.cpp.obj:
    $(CL) $(CFLAGS) $*
.obj.exe:
    $(CL) $(LFLAGS) $*.obj wpp.lib
    rc $*
hello2.exe: hello2.obj wpp.lib
wpp.lib: $(WPPOBJ)
    del wpp.lib
    tlib wpp.lib /C +WPWIN+WPAPP+WPMAIN+WINMAIN
```

The make file for Zortech is similar, but uses *ztc* and *zorlib* instead of *bcc* and *tlib*. The library WPP.LIB contains all the *Windows++* modules we've implemented so far: WPWIN, WPAPP, WPMAIN, and WINMAIN.

Note that at this point the library is an ordinary *static* link library; in Chapter 9, we'll convert it into a *dynamic* link library (DLL).

3.4 HELLO3: The Window Procedure

The next major challenge confronting us is figuring out how to incorporate the window procedure into our system. This will be a tricky affair, and I sense you may be growing tired, especially if you've been reading along continuously (this isn't exactly a suspense novel), so now's a good time to stop, get up, stretch your legs, and perhaps have another caffeine fix (but don't change the channel!).

Ok, back to work.

Here's the problem: we need a way for our *WPWin* objects to receive Windows messages such as WM_COMMAND and WM_KEYDOWN. We need a window procedure. The obvious ("brainless") way to write one is like this:

```
class WPWin {
    LONG msgProc(WORD msg, WORD wParam, LONG lParam);
};
```

This is almost, but not quite, what we'll do. But instead of using *msg, wParam,* and *lParam,* we'll invent a separate *event* object.

3.4.1 Events

The *Windows++* event object is defined in WPWIN.H:

```
struct WPEvent {
    WORD msg;        // the message
    WORD wp;         // word parameter
    LONG lp;         // long parameter
    LONG ret;        // return value
```

```
    WPEvent(WORD m, WORD w=0, LONG lg=0) { msg=m; wp=w; lp=lg; ret=0; }

    int cmd()          { return wp; }
    HMENU menu()       { return (HMENU)wp; }
    int childHwnd()    { return LOWORD(lp); }
    int childMsg()     { return HIWORD(lp); }
    int x()            { return LOWORD(lp); }
    int y()            { return HIWORD(lp); }
    int width()        { return LOWORD(lp); }
    int height()       { return HIWORD(lp); }
    char* text()       { return (char*)lp; }
    WPPoint point()    { return *((WPPoint *)&lp); }

    int key()          { return wp; }
    int keyRepeat()    { return LOWORD(lp); }
    int keyScan()      { return LOBYTE(HIWORD(lp)); }
    int keyFlags()     { return HIBYTE(HIWORD(lp)); }

    WPPoint screenPos()
        { return (WPPoint)GetMessagePos(); }
    DWORD time()       { return GetMessageTime(); }
};
```

As you can see, *WPEvent* is an ordinary C *struct*. All it does is bundle the message parameters into a single structure, just like the Windows MSG structure. There are several reasons for introducing *WPEvent*:

■ Conceptually, the Windows message ID and message parameters constitute a single entity, so it's natural to model them as a single object.

■ By implementing a few inline member functions, we spare ourselves the trouble of memorizing (or looking up) how Windows passes various arguments in *wParam* and *lParam*. For example, is the control notification message ID for WM_COMMAND in the high- or the low-order word of *lParam*? With *WPEvent*, you'll never have to remember, because you simply call *event.getChildMsg*. This is not only easier, it eliminates a common source of bugs and is excellent preparation for porting to Windows NT!

■ By using *WPEvent*, we leave open the possibility of passing other message parameters should we extend our system.

■ We only have to pass a single pointer on the stack when calling message functions, instead of three arguments.

WPEvent is declared as an ordinary C *struct* rather than a *class* because it's really just a collection of arguments, and there doesn't seem to be much benefit in hiding the data members.

3.4.2 Handling Events: *msgProc*

Now that we have *WPEvent*, our message procedure is declared like this:

```
class WPWin {
public:
    LONG msgProc(WPEvent& event);
};
```

Since we don't anticipate ever passing a NULL event (what would that mean?), *event* is declared as a reference rather than a pointer. How is *msgProc* implemented? Well, it depends on the window class. The simplest thing *msgProc* could do is pass the event right back to the Windows default window procedure:

```
LONG WPWin::msgProc(WPEvent &event)
{
    return DefWindowProc(hwnd, event.msg, event.wp, event.lp);
}
```

This *msgProc* is the *Windows++* equivalent of *DefWndowProc*. Of course, most windows want to process some messages. For example, the *msgProc* for *HelloWin* would go something like this:

```
LONG HelloWin::msgProc(WPEvent &event)
{
    switch (event.msg) {
    case WM_PAINT:
        .
        . // paint the screen
        .
        return 0;

    case WM_COMMAND:
        .
        . // handle menu command
        .
        return 0;
    }
    return WPWin::msgProc(event);       // pass to default msgProc
}
```

Note that *HelloWin::msgProc* passes unhandled events to its ancestor, *WPWin*. This lets *HelloWin* inherit any default message processing we might add to *WPWin*.

We have a *msgProc* for *WPWin*, and one for *HelloWin*. What about *WPMainWin*? Does it make sense for *WPMainWin* to have a message procedure? What would it mean? Well, the main window should process all events that are generic to main windows, such the Exit command and WM_DESTROY message. The processing required for these events is generic to all main windows, not just *HelloWin*, so it belongs in *WPMainWin:*

```
LONG WPMainWin::msgProc(WPEvent& event)
{
    switch (event.msg) {
    case WM_COMMAND:
```

```
        switch (event.cmd()) {
        case WPIDM_EXIT:
            close();
            return 0;
        case WM_DESTROY:
            App.quit();
            return 0;
        }
        break;
    }
    return WPWin::msgProc(event);
}
```

Now *HelloWin* should pass unhandled events to *WPMainWin*, not *WPWin*.

```
LONG HelloWin::msgProc(WPEvent &event)
{
    .
    .
    return WPMainWin::msgProc(event);
}
```

In general: each window class passes unhandled events to the *msgProc* of its immediate ancestor (that is, the base class from which it is derived) so that it inherits the ancestor's *msgProc* processing. This is exactly what happens when you *subclass* a window procedure in the Windows sense. What's emerging is a whole hierarchy of *msgProc*s; each class in the hierarchy handles some events by returning and passes the rest to its ancestor.

Window Class	Events Handled
WPWin	None (pass to *oldProc*, usually *DefWindowProc*)
WPMainWin	Exit command, WM_DESTROY message
HelloWin	WM_PAINT message

The advantage of this design is that we can maximize reusability by handling generic events at the lowest appropriate level in the window class hierarchy. For example, the Exit command and WM_DESTROY message are handled by *WPMainWin*, part of our library. *HelloWin* (and all other window classes derived from *WPMainWin*) needn't bother handling these events, since the appropriate behavior is automatically inherited (reused) simply because the class is derived from *WPMainWin*. All an application has to do is use the predefined menu IDs such as WPIDM_EXIT (I told you they'd come in handy) and remember to pass unhandled events to *WPMainWin*.

C   *Once again, you could accomplish the same thing in C using Windows' notion of subclassing: just define window classes for WPWIN, WPMAINWIN, etc., in your library, with window procedures that provide the proper behavior. Then have each one "subclass" its ancestor by hooking the window procedure and passing unhandled messages to the previous (ancestor) window procedure. Of course, the Windows mechanics are rather cumbersome (which is why few programmers would bother).*

There's just one problem I haven't addressed: how *HelloWin::msgProc* gets called. When Windows wants to send our window a message, it calls the registered window procedure (*WndProc*) with the usual arguments: *hwnd, msg, wParam,* and *lParam*. We want to intercept this, convert the arguments to a *WPEvent* object, and pass it to *msgProc*. Our window procedure will thus look something like this.

```
LONG _export FAR PASCAL WndProc(HWND hwnd, WORD msg, WORD wp, LONG lp)
{
    WPEvent event(msg, wp, lp);     // convert args to event
    WPWin *win = GetWin();          // GetWin how ???
    win->msgProc(event);            // call window's msgProc
}
```

The problem is, how do we write *GetWin*? We already have a way (*GetHwnd*, described in Section 3.2.3) to get the window handle (HWND) of the *Windows++* object; what we need is a way to go back. That is, given a window handle (HWND), how can we get its corresponding *Windows++* object?

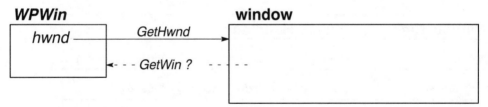

3.4.3 Linking the Window

Essentially, we need to somehow store our (*Windows++*) object pointer in the (Windows) window. There are several possible ways to do it:

- We could use *wndcls.cbWndExtra* to allocate extra space in the window to hold our object pointer, then retrieve it using *GetWindowWord* or *GetWindowLong*.

- We could use the Windows property mechanism to store our pointer in the window's property list. This general-purpose mechanism lets you associate a HANDLE with any character string. The string is considered a keyword that names the property. (The property mechanism is no doubt familiar to LISP programmers.)

■ We could implement some sort of global lookup table that associates an object pointer with each HWND handle.

The first approach would be ideal except that we will eventually want to create instances of built-in window classes, such as "listbox" and "button," but we can't allocate extra window bytes for these classes because they're already defined by Windows.[21] The last approach would require some sort of binary lookup or hash table, since we want to retrieve the object pointer quickly (we must retrieve it every time a message comes in). A hash table is too much bother right now (we're impatient). That leaves the property mechanism. To use it, we first choose a name for the property:

```
#define WP_WINPTR "w+"                    // name of window prop to store ptr
```

We can use any name we like for the window property, but it should be short so *GetProp* can find it quickly. Next, we'll write a function to set it:

```
///////////////////
// Link object to a real (Windows) window.
//
void WPWin::linkHwnd(HWND newhwnd)
{
    assert(hwnd==NULL);                  // better not be already linked!
    assert(IsWindow(newhwnd));           // better have a real HWND!
    hwnd = newhwnd;                      // store window handle
    setProp(WP_WINPTR, (HANDLE)this);    // store ourself in window
}
```

This is simple enough: first, *linkHwnd* asserts that the window isn't already linked and that the window handle is valid. This is just a little extra bullet-proofing to keep the code honest. After this, *linkHwnd* stores the window handle and calls *setProp* to set the WP_WINPTR property to the object pointer, *this*. (*setProp* is one of the "brainless" functions described in Section 3.2.6; it just calls the Windows API equivalent, *SetProp*.)

(Astute readers may have detected a slight flaw in *linkHwnd*: the property mechanism only lets us store a handle, which is 16 bits. What if our object pointer were a 32-bit *far* pointer? Our code would fail miserably when *GetWin* returned our object pointer missing half its bits! Never fear, we'll fix this in Chapter 4. For now, all our HELLO programs are compiled under the small model, so the issue is moot.)

---

21 Actually, it *is* possible to change the window structure size for built-in windows classes. You could call *GetClassInfo* to get the WNDCLASS structure for a window class, then examine *wndcls.cbWndExtra*, add to it, and change it by calling *SetClassWord*. Any window subsequently created would presumably have the added bytes (I never actually tried it). This method could be made to work but requires creating a window instance of each built-in class in order to call *SetClassLong* (why this function requires an *hwnd* is a mystery to me—it sets *class* properties, which have nothing to do with a particular window instance). Furthermore, what about windows created before *Windows++* is loaded? Using the property mechanism is more straightforward.

To link our window objects to their windows, all we have to do is invoke *linkHwnd* immediately after creating the window:

```
BOOL WPWin::createWin()
{
    .
    .
    .
    HWND newhwnd = CreateWindowEx(...);
    linkHwnd(newhwnd);                  // <<<<<<<<< call linkHwnd
    return hwnd!=NULL;
}
```

Now whenever we create a window, it's linked in both directions automatically! With the object pointer safely tucked away in the window's property list, it's a simple matter to write our sorely-needed *GetWin* function, which *retrieves* it.

```
class WPWin {
public:
    static WPWin* GetWin(HWND hwnd);
};
WPWin* WPWin::GetWin(HWND hwnd)
{
    if (hwnd==NULL)
        return NULL;
    assert(IsWindow(hwnd));
    return (WPWin*)GetProp(hwnd, WP_WINPTR);
}
```

GetWin returns NULL if the window handle is NULL, but otherwise asserts that the window handle is valid (more foolproofing). If so, *GetWin* simply retrieves the pointer stored in the WP_WINPTR property. If this property was for some reason never set (perhaps the window handle identifies a window which was not created by *Windows++*, such as the desktop window, or one that belongs to another application), *getProp* returns zero, so *GetWin* returns a NULL pointer. *GetWin* is declared *public* so anyone can use it; it's declared *static* because it's not a member function: it's not invoked through a *WPWin* object instance but called like a normal C *extern* function. (The whole purpose of *GetWin* is to get the object instance!)

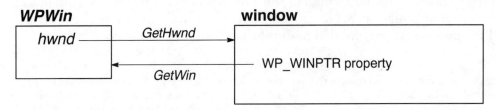

3.4.4 Unlinking the Window

Before leaving *linkHwnd*, we may as well write *unLinkHwnd*, since we'll eventually need it (every operation has its inverse):

```
void WPWin::unLinkHwnd()
{
    if (hwnd) {                         // if linked:
        assert(GetWin(hwnd)==this);     // double-check for safety
        removeProp(WP_WINPTR);          // free up window property
        hwnd = NULL;                    // goodbye window handle!
    }
}
```

This is fairly self-explanatory: *unLinkHwnd* simply undoes what *linkHwnd* did. When should we call *unLinkHwnd?* Keep reading, you'll find out shortly. For now, just note that the entire linking mechanism is localized to only three functions: *linkHwnd, unLinkHwnd,* and *GetWin.* Should we ever decide to implement that hash table after all, these are the only functions we need change. This is the whole point (and benefit) of encapsulation.

You may have forgotten exactly where we are in this tangled plot, so I'll remind you: we're trying to get messages sent to *HelloWin*'s *msgProc* function, which is why we had to link the window and write *GetWin.* We've written a window procedure that seems like it should work:

```
long _export FAR PASCAL WndProc(HWND hwnd, WORD msg, WORD wp, LONG lp)
{
    WPWin *win = WPWin::GetWin(hwnd); // get ptr to window object
    assert(win);
    WPEvent event(msg, wp, lp);       // create event object
    return win->msgProc(event);       // call message proc
}
```

GetWin seems to do the trick: it returns the window object pointer that was automatically stored in the window when we created *HelloWin,* so *win* will actually point to our *HelloWin.*

So what's wrong?

There is in fact a slight problem: when *WndProc* executes the statement

```
return win->msgProc(event);
```

which *msgProc* is called? *WPWin::msgProc, WPMainWin::msgProc,* or *HelloWin:: msgProc?* We *want* to call the *HelloWin* version, but the way the code is written, *win* is declared as *WPWin*,* so the compiler calls *WPWin::msgProc.*

Sigh.

We could solve this problem by simply declaring *win* to be of type *HelloWin,* but then we would have to write a *WndProc* for every application. So far, the code in *WndProc* is general. We should try to keep it that way.

Fortunately, C++ provides a better way to solve the problem: *virtual functions.*

3.4.5 Virtual Function Magic

One of the most important features of C++, and of object-oriented programming languages in general, is *virtual functions*. Since this is such an important concept, I'm going to take a little detour to explain it (C++ gurus, feel free to skip ahead).

In order to understand virtual functions, let's consider a hypothetical graphics system with two classes of objects: *Rectangle* and *Circle*. (In Chapter 8 we'll implement just such a system.) Both of these classes are derived from a generic *Shape* class, which defines a virtual function called *area*.

```
class Shape {
    virtual long area() = 0;        // get shape's area
};
```

This function is implemented differently for each object:

```
class Rectangle : public Shape {
    long width, height;
public:
    long area()   { return width*height; }
};
class Circle : public Shape {
    long radius;
public:
    long area()   { return radius*radius*PI; }
}
```

Whenever the area of a shape is required, it can be obtained as follows.

```
Shape *obj;
long a = obj->area();              // get area of object
```

Because *area* is declared as a *virtual* function, C++ calls the appropriate *area* function for whatever kind of object *obj* really is: if it's a rectangle, C++ calls *Rectangle::area*; if it's a circle, C++ calls *Circle::area*. C++ does not call *Shape::area*, even though *obj* is declared to be of type *Shape*. In fact, there is no *area* function for *Shape*. The "= 0" following the declaration of *Shape::area* tells C++ that there is no *area* function for *Shape*; this function must be supplied by classes such as *Rectangle* and *Circle* that are derived from *Shape*. Such a virtual function is called a "pure" virtual function, and a class that contains a pure virtual function is called an "abstract class," because such a class is not allowed to have any instances.

```
Shape *s = new Shape;              // NOT ALLOWED! compiler error
```

This makes sense when you think about it: our graphics system comprises different kinds of shapes (circles and rectangles), but there's no shape called "shape." What would it be? *Shape* is an abstract class (also called *abstract data type* or ADT). Abstract classes arise all the time in the real world. For example, *mammal* is an abstract class—there is no animal called "mammal," only various kinds of mammals, such as monkeys, whales, and humans. *Mammal* and *Shape* are abstract classes, in both the technical/OOP and human/metaphysical senses of the word.

How does C++ "know" which *area* function to call when *obj->area()* is invoked? The actual implementation is up to the specific compiler, but usually C++ stores a hidden type code within each object; the code identifies the object's true class. When C++ compiles the call to *obj->area()*, it does not produce a normal function call but rather code that uses the type code to fetch the address of *area* from a table of virtual functions for whatever class *obj* really is (circle or rectangle). C++ creates this table somewhere handy, usually in your program's data segment.[22] Thus C++ does not actually determine which function to call until the program runs. This is called "late binding," because the function is not "bound" to the object until run-time. Non-virtual functions are bound at compile time ("early binding").

To Windows gurus, virtual function tables are somewhat similar to so-called instance thunks, while the concept of late binding is analogous to dynamic linking used in DLLs.

Virtual functions are a fundamental and extremely powerful feature of object-oriented programming languages. They allow different objects to respond differently to the same function, depending on the actual class of the object, regardless of what class type the reference or pointer is declared to be. This feature is called *polymorphism.* This fancy term is no more than multi-syllabic OOP-jargon for the idea that different classes of objects can respond differently to the same function. Polymorphism means that you can write code that calls some generic virtual function (such as *area*), without knowing in advance which function will actually receive control—in fact, the function might not even be written yet! For example, we could later add *Ellipse* to our hypothetical graphics system. All we'd have to do is provide an *area* function to compute the area of the ellipse and then add it to the system. Anywhere that *obj->area()* is called, *Ellipse::area* will then be called if *obj* is really an *Ellipse*, despite the fact that the original graphics system had no conception of ellipse.

You may already have guessed how virtual functions solve our *Windows++* problem of which *msgProc* is called from *WndProc*—all we have to do is make *msgProc* a virtual function:

```
class WPWin {
protected:
    virtual LONG msgProc(WPEvent& event);
};
```

Simply by adding the keyword *virtual* before *msgProc*, we guarantee that when *WndProc* executes the line

```
return win->msgProc(event);
```

---

22 The Borland compiler provides a number of switches that let you control how virtual function tables are implemented. For example, *-Vf* causes all virtual function pointers to be *far* and locates the tables in the program's code segment rather than the data segment.

C++ calls the version of *msgProc* for whichever class *win* actually is, no matter how many layers of derived classes with *msgProc*'s might sit between *WPWin* and the final subclass. In our HELLO program, *WndProc* will call *HelloWin::msgProc* because *win* is actually an instance of the *HelloWin* class.

3.4.6 The Window Procedure

Now, here's the kicker: *WndProc* is the only window procedure we'll ever write! Every application *Windows++* program, no matter how complex, no matter how many different kinds of window classes it registers, uses the same window procedure. In fact, let's rename it to *WPWndProc* and put it in the library, to be reused by all programs. This is the only window procedure that Windows ever sees, the only one we'll ever _*export*! Our programs no longer "do" window procedures. How is this possible? What if we want a different kind of window to do something else?

If we want a different kind of window to do something else, we write a different *msgProc* for it. This the whole point of virtual functions and the meaning of polymorphism: different classes respond differently to the same function! Writing *msgProc* for a new kind of window is just like writing *area* for a new kind of shape.

Thus the same *WPWndProc* works for all windows, since the C++ virtual function mechanism effectively dispatches the *msgProc* call to the appropriate *msgProc* for whatever class the window object really is. If *win* is really a *HelloWin*, *WPWndProc* calls *HelloWin::msgProc*; if it's some other window class—say, a text editor window—*WPWndProc* calls the *msgProc* for the text editor. No matter how many different window classes with different *msgProc*s we create, the same window procedure works for all. In effect, we're using the C++ virtual function tables, rather than Windows, to store the "real" window procedure.

Since there's only one window procedure in the entire system, we may as well install it automatically whenever we create a window. To do this, we modify *WPWin*, *linkHwnd,* and *unLinkHwnd* as follows.

```
// (In WPWIN.H)
class WPWin {
private:
    FARPROC oldProc; // add a place to store original window proc
};

// (In WPWIN.CPP)
void WPWin::linkHwnd(HWND newhwnd)
{

    .
    .
    // save old window proc, then replace with system proc
    oldProc = (FARPROC)GetWindowLong(hwnd, GWL_WNDPROC);
    SetWindowLong(hwnd, GWL_WNDPROC, (LONG)WPWndProc);
}
```

```
void WPWin::unLinkHwnd()
{
    if (hwnd) {
        // restore original window proc
        SetWindowLong(hwnd, GWL_WNDPROC, (LONG)oldProc);
        .
        .
        .
    }
}
```

linkHwnd now replaces the window's window procedure with the generic window procedure *WPWndProc,* saving the old one in *oldProc; unLinkHwnd* reverses the operation.[23] Next, we have to modify *WPWin::msgProc* so it calls *oldProc* instead of *DefWindowProc:*

```
LONG WPWin::msgProc(WPEvent &e)
{
    assert(oldProc); // safety-check
    return CallWindowProc(oldProc,hwnd, e.gmsg, e.wp, e.lp);
}
```

Finally, in order to make sure that any window we actually register and create has a window procedure, we modify the *WPWin* constructor.

```
WPWin::WPWin(CSTR classnm)
{
    .
    .
    .
    createArgs.wndcls.lpfnWndProc = DefWindowProc;
    .
    .
    .
}
```

Now there's no need for applications to set *lpfnWndProc,* or even to supply a window procedure. Not in HELLO, nor in any other *Windows++* program. In fact, our programs no longer bother with window procedures at all—the entire event-handling mechanism has been replaced with C++ virtual functions. Our *HelloWin* constructor has achieved its ultimate simplicity. It specifies the only remaining window datum that's application-specific, namely, the window title.

```
HelloWin::HelloWin()
{
    createWin("HELLO3--3rd C++ version");
}
```

Some of you may be wondering, why not just set *lpfnWndProc* to *WPWndProc* in the *WPWin* constructor, instead of doing it in *linkHwnd?* While this would work

---

23 Astute Windows programmers may wonder how we can get by setting the window procedure to *WPWndProc* directly, without first calling *MakeProcInstance.* Well, both the Borland and Zortech compilers support so-called smart callbacks. By specifying the appropriate compiler switch (–WS for Borland; –W2 for Zortech), the compiler produces code to load the DS (data segment) register from SS (stack segment) upon entry to any exported function, obviating the need for *MakeProcInstance.*

fine for HELLO, later on we'll want to create instances of built-in Windows classes such as list boxes, buttons, and so on; since these classes are already registered by Windows, we can only change their window procedures with *SetWindowLong*. Furthermore, the default procedure for these windows is not *DefWindowProc*, but some other procedure known only to Windows, so we must save the original window procedure in *oldProc* so we can invoke it as the handler-of-last-resort. In short, the approach taken is more general, since it works whether the window class is one that our program registered, or one of Windows' built-in window classes.

Just in case you're totally confused (and who wouldn't be?), let's take a careful look at exactly how all this works, starting from when *HelloWin* is created:

```
mainWin = new HelloWin;
```

This seemingly innocent statement triggers several events (that's C++ for you):

- A new instance of *HelloWin* is created.

- The base class constructor, *WPWin*, sets *wndcls.lpfnWndProc* to *DefWindowProc*, along with all the other default *createArgs*.

- *WPMainWin* supplies additional default *createArgs* appropriate for main windows: the style is set to overlapped and the menu name to *AppMenu*.

- *HelloWin* invokes *createWin*, which registers and creates the window. In the process, *createWin* links the window: its object pointer is stored in the window's property list, and the window procedure is changed to *WPWndProc* after the old one (*DefWindowProc*) is saved as *oldProc*. Windows now directs all messages for our window to *WPWndProc*.

When *WPWndProc* receives a message, it first calls *GetWin* to retrieve the window object from its HWND, then transforms the message parameters into a *WPEvent* object and passes it to the window object's *msgProc* function. Because this function is *virtual*, C++ ensures that the correct *msgProc* is called for whichever class the window object really is—in our case, *HelloWin::msgProc*. Whew! *HelloWin* finally got the message! If the event is a WM_PAINT message, *HelloWin* processes it and returns zero; otherwise, it passes the event along to *WPMainWin::msgProc*, which processes a couple of additional events: the Exit command and WM_DESTROY. If the event is not one of these, *WPMainWin* passes it to *WPWin::msgProc*, which simply calls *oldProc*, which is (whaddaya know!) *DefWindowProc*. Everything is hunky-dory, and peace and harmony reign in our world.

The following figure illustrates the message flow:

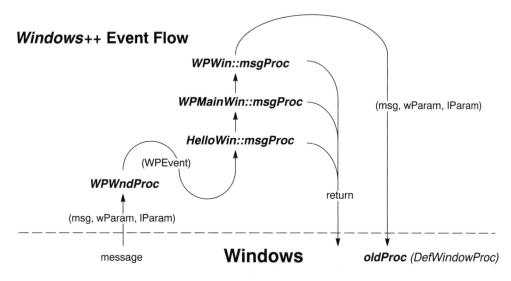

Windows++ **Event Flow**

All this may seem convoluted, but the beauty is that it's totally general, which means: reusable. As we'll see later, this basic mechanism works for all windows: modal and modeless dialog boxes, control windows—even MDI windows!

Windows gurus will recognize that what we've done in *linkHwnd* is *subclass* the window. This is official Windows jargon for replacing the original window procedure with one of our own. In *Windows++* every window is subclassed! This observation, makes added sense of the event flow shown in the diagram above—each class passes unhandled events to its immediate ancestor, which is precisely how "subclassing" in the Windows sense is supposed to work. Each new class "installs" its own message procedure and passes unhandled messages to its predecessor. Conceptually, we're doing the same thing in *Windows++*, but we're using C++ instead of Windows. In short, we have exposed Windows' inherent object-orientedness by transforming its notion of subclassing into the more explicit and general C++ notion of derived subclasses.

3.4.7 Destroying the Window

Now that we have created and linked our window, and our message procedure is hooked up, we can provide an automatic way to destroy the window. (Pity our poor window: only just born and now we're trying to destroy it.) Until now, we've been doing it in *WPApp::main:*

```
void WPApp::main()
{
    mainWin = new HelloWin;
    .

    .
    delete mainWin;
}
```

But there's a more elegant way. Before actually destroying a window, Windows first sends it the WM_DESTROY message. Wouldn't it be nice if we could somehow take this opportunity to automatically *delete* our window object? No problem; a few lines in *WPWndProc* do the trick.

```
long _export FAR PASCAL WPWndProc(HWND hwnd,WORD msg,WORD wp,LONG lp)
{
    WPWin *win = WPWin::GetWin(hwnd);
    assert(win);

    if (msg==WM_DESTROY) {          // got WM_DESTROY:
        delete win;                 // destroy object..
        return 0;                   // and return to Windows
    }
    WPEvent event(msg, wp, lp);
    return win->msgProc(event);
}
```

We have the same problem here as we did with *msgProc*. When C++ deletes an object, it first calls the object's destructor function before freeing its storage. But which one? ~*WPWin* or ~*HelloWin*? To ensure that the proper destructor is called, all we have to do is make the destructor *virtual*, just like *msgProc*.

```
class WPWin {
public:
    virtual ~WPWin()                { unLinkHwnd(); }
};
```

The implementation of ~*WPWin* is trivial—it just unlinks the window (careful readers may have been wondering when I was going to unlink it). Our window is now automatically unlinked and deleted whenever WM_DESTROY is received. We never again need remember to delete a window object! In fact, our window now never even receives WM_DESTROY, since *WPWndProc* intercepts this message and returns without passing it to *msgProc*. But what if you need to perform some cleanup when your window is destroyed? For example, currently *WPMainWin* calls *App.quit* to terminate the message loop:

```
LONG WPMainWin::msgProc(WPEvent& event)
{
    switch(event.msg) {
    case WM_DESTROY:
        App.quit();
        return 0;
        .
        .
    }
    return WPWin::msgProc(event);
}
```

With our latest change to *WPWndProc*, *WPMainWin* will never get a WM_DE-STROY message. To fix this, we can simply move the code to the destructor:

```
WPMainWin::~WPMainWin()
{
    App.quit();
}
```

In this case, the *WPMainWin* destructor is part of the library. If *Windows++* didn't go the extra yard by putting *App.quit* in *WPMainWin*, applications such as HELLO would have to do it in their own window class destructors (e.g., in ~*HelloWin*).

In general, anything that would formerly have been done in response to WM_DE-STROY should now be done in the destructor.

When *WPWndProc* executes the simple statement

```
delete win;
```

the following events take place:

- Since the *WPWin* destructor is declared virtual, C++ first calls the destructor for the class that *win* actually is (the one for *HelloWin*). In this case, there's no destructor for *HelloWin* (to be precise, it's inherited from *WPMainWin*).

- C++ thus calls ~*WPMainWin*. This function posts a quit message by calling *App.quit().*[24] The last line in ~*WPMainWin* is a call (inserted automatically by the C++ compiler) to ~*WPWin*, its base class destructor.

- ~*WPWin* unlinks the window: the window procedure is restored to *oldProc*, and the WP_WINPTR property is removed.

- Finally, C++ frees the storage occupied by the window object.

All this happens automatically, in one reusable place, without HELLO having to do anything. The mechanism is totally general and works for all windows. Even window objects for built-in window classes (e.g., edit controls) will automatically be deleted this fashion, since we'll still use *WPWndProc* as the window procedure.

You may have noticed that window objects never receive WM_CREATE either, since this message is sent by Windows as soon as *CreateWindowEx* is called, before our window is even linked. (The message goes to *DefWindowProc*, which ignores it.) There is no need to receive WM_CREATE, since the window object constructor can perform any initialization it needs before or after calling *createWin*.

This important design principle deserves highlighting. *In Windows++, the window class constructors and destructor play the role that WM_CREATE and WM_DESTROY do in Windows.* Window objects never receive WM_CREATE or WM_DESTROY

---

24 If you want to call *App.quit* with a return code other than zero (the default), you can do so in your window class destructor (e.g., ~*HelloWin*). The first WM_QUIT message posted is the one that ends the message loop; the extra WM_QUIT posted by ~*WPMainWin* is harmless, since windows flushes the message queue before destroying a window. Of course, the point is moot, since Windows doesn't do anything with the return code from *WinMain* anyway.

messages; initialization and termination are instead performed in the class constructors and destructor.

Once again, we have transformed Windows' implicit object-orientedness into the explicit C++ model. This feels right and should inspire confidence that our design is sound. Of course, it's no accident: I designed *Windows++* with the deliberate intention that construction and destruction should correspond to WM_CREATE and WM_DESTROY messages.

3.4.8 Differentiating Between Stack and Memory Objects

One unfortunate consequence of the way we destroy windows automatically in *WPWndProc* is that *delete* will fail miserably if the window object was created on the stack. So far this isn't a problem, since we've been using *new* to create window objects:

```
mainWin = new HelloWin;
```

But what happens if we attempt to create a *HelloWin* on the stack?

```
HelloWin mywin;
mainWin = &mywin;
```

If we did so, everything would work fine until the window is destroyed, and *WPWndProc* attempts to execute the line

```
delete win;
```

This is like trying to free a stack object. Even if our program somehow survived the bad call to *delete,* it would have another good chance to crash when the destructor for *win* is called twice: once in *WPWndProc* and again when it goes out of scope from whatever function it was created in.

We could of course simply outlaw allocating window objects from the stack and say, "thou shalt not create window objects on the stack in *Windows++.*" But who are we to be so imperious? Some programmer might have a good reason to create a stack object (in fact, we'll do it with dialog boxes in Chapter 7).

What we need is some way to distinguish between a *WPWin* that was allocated by *new* and one that was created on the stack. We'd like some sort of flag that tells whether the object is deletable, so we could rewrite *WPWndProc* as follows.

```
if (win->deletable)
    delete win;
else
    win->unLinkHwnd();
```

(Even if the window object is not deletable, we still want to unlink it when the window is destroyed.) How can we initialize *deletable* appropriately? This boils down to the more general question, how can we differentiate memory objects from stack objects in C++?

Amazing as it may seem, it is in fact possible to do so! The solution lies in our ability to overload the *new* and *delete* operators for *WPWin*.

```
class WPWin {
public:
    void *operator new(size_t size);
    void delete(void *ptr);
};
```

In C++, *new* and *delete* are operators, just like +, -, =, and all the rest. In particular, they can be overloaded for a particular class. All we have to do is use the proper declarations shown above. Simply by defining our own versions of *new* and *delete* for *WPWin*, we automatically invoke them whenever a function allocates or destroys a *WPWin* object (or an object of any class derived from *WPWin*). Since C++ does not invoke *new* and *delete* for stack objects, we can distinguish them from memory objects.

At first, we might try something like this:

```
class WPWin {
    BOOL deletable;                         // OK to delete object
public:
    void *operator new(size_t size);
};
void* WPWin::operator new(size_t size)
{
    WPWin *win = (WPWin*)new char [size];   // allocate using global new
    if (win)
        win->deletable = TRUE;              // mark as deletable
    return win;
}
```

The overloaded *new* operator simply allocates *size* bytes (a character array of length *size*) and then sets *deletable* to TRUE. What could be more simple?

Unfortunately, this doesn't work because when a *WPWin* object is created on the stack, our overloaded *new* is not invoked, so *deletable* is not initialized. Instead, *deletable* will have a quite easily non-zero garbage value. Sigh. We could perhaps improve the situation by making *deletable* a *long* and storing some improbable quantity in it like 0x1234ABCD—but even then, there's still a one in 2^{32} chance that the stack will just happen to have 0x1234ABCD in the wrong place. While this might be good enough for all practical purposes, it's not perfect—here's a surefire solution:

```
// (In WPWIN.H)
class WPWin {
    static WPWin* NewWin;        // global: WPWin in creation
    BOOL deletable;              // OK to delete
public:
    void *operator new(size_t size);
    void delete(void *win);
};
```

```
// (In WPWIN.CPP)
WPWin *WPWin::NewWin = NULL;

void* WPWin::operator new(size_t size)
{
    // Set NewWin to new object allocated.
    return NewWin = (WPWin*)new char [size];
}
void WPWin::operator delete(void* ptr)
{
    assert(((WPWIN*)ptr)->deletable); // safety-check
    delete ptr;
}
WPWin::WPWin(CSTR classnm)
{
    deletable = (this==NewWin);          // set flag and..
    NewWin = NULL;                       // ..invalidate NewWin
    .
    .
}
```

The trick is to introduce a static class global, *NewWin,* which is set to the newly created window every time *new* is invoked. The constructor then sets *deletable* to TRUE if and only if the window constructed is the same as *NewWin.* If the window was created on the stack, it can never have the same address as *NewWin,* since *NewWin* is always either NULL or the address of some window object that was actually allocated from memory. For added bullet-proofing, the *delete* operator *asserts* that the object is deletable before deleting it.

This solves our *WPWndProc* problem. The solution is general; you can use it any time you need to distinguish between stack and memory objects.

3.4.9 HELLO3

We can now write HELLO3. As usual, we've already done all the work.

```
//////////////////////////////////////////////////////
// HELLO3--The third C++ version of HELLO.
// Copyright 1991 Paul DiLascia.
//

#include <wpp.h>

/////////////////////
// Hello window class. The only new thing is msgProc.
//
class HelloWin : public WPMainWin {
public:
    HelloWin()    { createWin("HELLO3--3rd C++ version"); }
    LONG msgProc(WPEvent &event);
};
```

```
///////////////////
// Main program entry point, called from internal WinMain
//
void WPApp::main(LPSTR cmdline, int show)
{
    mainWin = new HelloWin;         // We never explicitly delete it!
    run(show);
}

///////////////////
// This is the Windows++ virtual message procedure, called
// from the internal window procedure, WPWndProc.
//
LONG HelloWin::msgProc(WPEvent &event)
{
    switch(event.msg) {
    case WM_PAINT:
        PAINTSTRUCT ps;
        HDC hdc = BeginPaint(getHwnd(), &ps);
        RECT rect;
        GetClientRect(getHwnd(), &rect);
        DrawText(hdc, "Almost there.", -1, &rect,
            DT_SINGLELINE | DT_CENTER | DT_VCENTER);
        EndPaint(getHwnd(), &ps);
        return 0;
    }
    return WPMainWin::msgProc(event);
}
```

Here are HELLO3's main improvements over HELLO2:

■ We've incorporated the window procedure into our system. *WndProc* is gone, replaced by the library function *WPWndProc*, which can be reused for every window we ever create. Instead of *WndProc*, window classes now provide *msgProc* to handle specific windows messages. *HelloWin::msgProc* processes only WM_PAINT (it passes all other messages to its ancestor, *WPMainWin*).

■ The *HelloWin* constructor is down to just one line of code since it no longer has to bother setting *lpfnWndProc*.

■ Window destruction (WM_DESTROY) and the Exit command are handled automatically by *WPMainWin*.

As for compiling HELLO3, the only difference from compiling HELLO2 is that we use the "smart callbacks" compiler option (–WS for Borland; –W2 for Zortech). This option tells the compiler to load the DS (data segment) register from SS (stack segment) upon entry to any *exported* function (e.g., *WPWndProc*), thereby obviating the need to use *MakeProcInstance* before we set our window procedure in *linkHwnd* (see footnote 23).

If you've made it this far, congratulations! We're really on the home stretch now. The next version of HELLO will be our last.

3.5 The Final HELLO: "Virtualizing" Window Messages

3.5.1 The 14-Page Switch Statement

A common feature of most Windows programs is a window procedure that runs for several pages. Window and dialog procedures are a frequent point of accumulation for so-called open code, long sequences of statements with no real structure and no attempt to group common sequences into subroutines.

Extremely long functions like this are not only difficult to read and understand, they create a number of difficulties. Many compilers don't optimize them properly, and if you're working on a project with other people, everyone wants to modify the window procedure at the same time. So far, our event handling mechanism shares this unfortunate drawback, since all we've done is pass messages to a new virtual function, *msgProc*, which resembles a typical window procedure.

```
LONG MyWindowClass::msgProc(WPEvent& event)
{
    switch (event.msg) {
    case WM_PAINT:

        .
        . (14 pages of code)
        .

    }
    return WPMainWin::msgProc();
}
```

We should look for some way to break this function up into smaller functional pieces.

3.5.2 Message = Virtual Function

In the preceding section, I described virtual functions and the notion of *polymorphism*, by which different classes of objects respond differently to the same virtual function (for example, *area* or *msgProc*). Windows itself provides a kind of polymorphism—the window procedure. By implementing its own window procedure, each window class can respond differently to predefined Windows messages such as WM_PAINT and WM_KEYDOWN. Thus Windows messages and virtual functions are two ways to provide polymorphism. In fact, object-oriented programmers commonly think of function calls (particularly virtual function calls) as *messages*. If *foo* is a member function, we think of a call to *obj->foo()* as "sending the *foo* message to *obj*."

A natural question thus arises: is there some way we can make the Windows messages (WM_PAINT, etc.) correspond to messages in the C++ sense?

For example, instead of sending WM_PAINT to *msgProc*, why not call a virtual *paint* function? This function could be passed whatever arguments are required for painting—for example, a PAINTSTRUCT. Then, to paint a window, instead of writing a *switch* case in *msgProc*, we would write a *paint* function:

```
void HelloWin::paint(PAINTSTRUCT& ps)
{
    RECT rect;
    GetClientRect(getHwnd(), &rect);
    DrawText(ps.hdc, "Hellow, Windows++.", -1, &rect,
        DT_SINGLELINE | DT_CENTER | DT_VCENTER);
}
```

This would not only eliminate the humongous *msgProc* but also means that applications don't have to extract event arguments from *WPEvent*. Instead they get them served up on a platter, ready-to-eat. We can even make the library call *Begin-Paint* and *EndPaint*.

How can we implement something like this? Well, one way is to simply write a big switch statement that dispatches each WM_ message to the appropriate virtual function after extracting the appropriate arguments from *WPEvent*. We would want to do this at a low level in the class hierarchy, namely, in *WPWin*.

```
long WPWin::msgProc(WPEvent& event)
{
    switch (event.msg) {
    case WM_PAINT:
        PAINTSTRUCT ps;
        BeginPaint(hwnd, &ps);
        paint(ps);                    // call virtual paint function
        EndPaint();
        return 0;

    case WM_COMMAND:
        command(event.wp);            // call virtual command function
        return 0;
        .
        .
    }
    CallWindowProc(oldProc, event.msg, event.lp, event.wp);
}
```

Other messages are handled similarly by other virtual functions. The *paint* and other functions must be virtual so C++ calls the version for whichever derived class the window actually is, not *WPWin::paint*.

This technique (I call it "virtualizing" the Windows messages) is used in most commercial C++ Windows class libraries (including Borland's *ObjectWindows*), and has a number of benefits:

■ Instead of writing one long message procedure, you write several small functions, one for each message you want to handle.

■ The virtual functions are called with the proper arguments already extracted from the event. This is my own invention; most commercial libraries, including *ObjectWindows*, pass an event object to each virtual function, without extracting the arguments.

■ If message-specific initialization is called for (for example, *BeginPaint*), it can be done at a low level before calling the message function.

■ Using virtual functions is somewhat more portable to other environments such as the MacIntosh or X Windows, since the application program need not reference WM_ symbols.

Using virtual functions also has a "cosmic" benefit: it transforms the Windows flavor of polymorphism (using window procedures and WM_ messages) into true C++ polymorphism using virtual functions.

3.5.3 How Many Functions?

So far, this approach looks promising—but before we write lots of code, let's think it through a little further.

There are around 130 or so documented Windows messages (and growing). Do we really want to implement virtual functions for all of them? Granted, any particular application need only implement functions for those messages it intends to process, but somewhere in *Windows++* we would have to declare the names and arguments for all possible virtual functions and write the central dispatch switch that routes each message to the proper one—not to mention default implementations for each, even if most of them do nothing. This seems like a lot of work, especially since most of these 130 messages are rarely used. When's the last time you wrote code to handle WM_NCCREATE or WM_SIZECLIPBOARD?

Furthermore, we have to start worrying about the size of virtual function tables. C++ stores the addresses of all the virtual functions defined for a class in a table associated with that class. Currently, we've been working in the small model, where function pointers are only two bytes, but we'll soon switch to the medium and large models, which use four-byte *far* pointers. Say we have 130 functions, times four bytes each—that's 520 bytes. No big deal. But we will eventually have around 20 or 25 window classes. Dialog boxes, edit controls, buttons, scroll bars, plus special dialog boxes for About, File Open, Print Setup, and so on. Twenty classes times 520 is over 10K of nothing but function tables—this is starting to become significant. Since most messages are rarely processed, this seems like a waste of storage. Surely we can be more efficient.

In order to reduce the total number of virtual functions, we'll adopt the following strategy.

■ We'll provide virtual functions for commonly used messages such as WM_PAINT, WM_SIZE, and so on.

- Keyboard and mouse messages are condensed into two groups, corresponding to the virtual functions *kbd* and *mouse.*

- Everything else is passed to a catch-all *other* function.

What exactly constitutes the "commonly used" messages is, of course, subject to debate. Here's my list:

General:
WM_PAINT
WM_ACTIVATE
WM_ENABLE
WM_GETMINMAXINFO
WM_SETFOCUS
WM_KILLFOCUS
WM_HSCROLL
WM_VSCROLL
WM_CLOSE
WM_DESTROY
WM_MOVE

WM_SIZE
WM_COMMAND
WM_INITMENU
WM_MENUSELECT
WM_QUERYENDSESSION
WM_QUERYOPEN
WM_TIMER
Keyboard:
WM_KEYDOWN
WM_KEYUP
WM_CHAR
WM_DEADCHAR

Mouse:
WM_MOUSEMOVE
WM_LBUTTONDOWN
WM_LBUTTONUP
WM_LBUTTONDBLCLK
WM_RBUTTONDOWN
WM_RBUTTONUP
WM_RBUTTONDBLCLK
WM_MBUTTONDOWN
WM_MBUTTONUP
WM_MBUTTONDBLCLK

Obviously, there is no "correct" list (except perhaps the list containing *all* messages). It all depends on your needs. For me, the above are the most common messages. If your favorite message is missing, you can easily add it using the techniques described in the next section or simply handle it in *other.*

3.5.4 Implementing the Virtual Message Functions

Now that we have a plan, we can implement virtual message functions. The first thing we have to do is define a virtual *WPWin* function for each message we've decided to handle.

```
class WPWin {
protected:
    // message procedure
    virtual LONG msgProc(WPEvent& e);
    LONG dfltMsgProc(WPEvent& e)
        { return CallWindowProc(oldProc, hwnd, e.msg, e.wp, e.lp); }

    // virtual message functions
    virtual BOOL activated(WORD state, BOOL iconic) { return FALSE; }
    virtual BOOL closed()                           { return FALSE; }
    virtual BOOL command(int id, WORD msg)          { return FALSE; }
    virtual BOOL enabled(BOOL state)                { return FALSE; }
    virtual BOOL getMinMaxInfo(LPMINMAXINFO m)      { return FALSE; }
    virtual BOOL gotFocus(WPWin *prev)              { return FALSE; }
    virtual BOOL kbd(WPEvent& event)                { return FALSE; }
    virtual BOOL killedFocus(WPWin *next)           { return FALSE; }
    virtual BOOL menuInit(WPMenu &menu)             { return FALSE; }
    virtual BOOL menuSelected(int id, WORD f)       { return FALSE; }
    virtual BOOL mouse(int, WPPoint, WORD)          { return FALSE; }
    virtual BOOL moved(int x, int y)                { return FALSE; }
    virtual BOOL paint()                            { return FALSE; }
```

```
    virtual BOOL queryEnd()                    { return TRUE; }
    virtual BOOL queryOpen()                   { return TRUE; }
    virtual BOOL scrolled(int, int ,int)       { return FALSE; }
    virtual BOOL sized(WPRect &box, WORD how)  { return FALSE; }
    virtual BOOL timer(int id)                 { return FALSE; }
    virtual BOOL other(WPEvent &event)         { return FALSE; }
};
```

Each function has arguments appropriate for the particular message it represents
and returns a BOOL. If the event was handled, the function should return TRUE;
otherwise it should return FALSE. Most of the default functions return FALSE (the
exceptions are *queryEnd* and *queryOpen*, which return TRUE because their return
values have a different meaning). There are 19 functions in all, far fewer than the
total number of 130 Windows messages.

We next modify *msgProc* to call our virtual functions:

```
LONG WPWin::msgProc(WPEvent &event)
{
    switch (event.msg) {
    case WM_QUERYENDSESSION:        // Special case: return value for
        return queryEnd();          // these messages has a different
    case WM_QUERYOPEN:              // meaning: allow end or open, not
        return queryMaximize();     // whether event was handled.
    }
    return dispatchEvent(event) ? event.ret : dfltMsgProc(event);
}

///////////////////
// Dispatch message to appropriate virtual function
//
BOOL WPWin::dispatchEvent(WPEvent &event)
{
    switch (event.msg) {
    case WM_PAINT:
        return paint();

    case WM_GETMINMAXINFO:
        return getMinMaxInfo((LPMINMAXINFO)event.lp);
    case WM_ACTIVATE:
        return activated(event.wp, HIWORD(event.lp));
    case WM_ENABLE:
        return enabled(event.wp);
    case WM_SETFOCUS:
        return gotFocus(GetWin(event.focusHwnd()));
    case WM_KILLFOCUS:
        return killedFocus(GetWin(event.focusHwnd()));

    case WM_HSCROLL:
    case WM_VSCROLL:
        HWND sbhwnd = HIWORD(event.lp);
        int id = sbhwnd ? GetDlgCtrlID(sbhwnd) :
            event.msg==WM_VSCROLL ? WPIDSB_VERT : WPIDSB_HORZ;
        return scrolled(event.wp, id, LOWORD(event.lp));

    case WM_KEYDOWN: case WM_KEYUP: case WM_CHAR: case WM_DEADCHAR:
        return kbd(event);
```

```
case WM_MOUSEMOVE:
case WM_LBUTTONDOWN: case WM_LBUTTONUP: case WM_LBUTTONDBLCLK:
case WM_RBUTTONDOWN: case WM_RBUTTONUP: case WM_RBUTTONDBLCLK:
case WM_MBUTTONDOWN: case WM_MBUTTONUP: case WM_MBUTTONDBLCLK:
    return mouse(event.msg, event.point(), event.wp);

case WM_MOVE:
    return moved(event.x(), event.y());
case WM_SIZE:
    WPRect box=this;
    box.extent(event.width() ,event.height());
    return sized(box, event.wp);

case WM_COMMAND:
    return command(event.cmd(), event.childMsg());
case WM_SYSCOMMAND:
    return command(event.cmd(), 0);
case WM_INITMENU:
    WPMenu menu = (HMENU)event.wp;
    return menuInit(menu);
case WM_MENUSELECT:
    return menuSelected(event.wp, LOWORD(event.lp));

case WM_CLOSE:
    return closed();
case WM_TIMER:
    return timer(event.wp);
}
    return other(event);
}
```

Basically, *msgProc* is just a giant switch statement (the only one we'll ever write) that forks each message to the appropriate virtual function.[25] I've broken out a separate function, *dispatchEvent,* to do the actual dispatching (this is because later on, in Chapter 7, we'll use *dispatchEvent* to handle dialog messages as well): if the message is handled, *dispatchEvent* returns TRUE, and *msgProc* returns *event.ret;* otherwise *msgProc* passes the event to *dfltMsgProc,* which in turn simply invokes the original window procedure stored in *oldProc* (e.g., *DefWindowProc*). The WM_QUERY messages are handled separately because their return values have a different meaning.

The only thing we have to watch out for in *dispatchEvent* is performance. Few compilers do a great job compiling switch statements. Unless the *case* values fall into a range of consecutive integers, most compilers simply generate *if* statements:

```
if (msg==WM_GETMINMAXINFO) {

} else if (msg == WM_ACTIVATE) {

} else if // ...etc.
```

---

25 Borland's *ObjectWindows* uses Borland's home-grown "dynamic dispatch virtual tables" rather than a switch statement. This convenient mechanism lets you assign a virtual function to an integer ID such as a WM_ message, but it's non-standard C++, so I've avoided it.

We could improve on the *switch* statement by storing function pointers in an array indexed by the WM_ message, perhaps with a base offset for the first WM_MESSAGE. The reason I chose not to do this is that it requires that the arguments to each function be homogenous; that is, all the functions in the table must have the same *signature* (arguments and return value). This would make it impossible to do all the useful argument packaging that *Windows++* provides.

I have not found performance to be a major issue with the approach I've taken (but then, my applications tend to run on fast machines like 33MHz 386s at the minimum). My philosophy is that when choosing between ease of programming (clarity, legibility) and performance, ease of programming always wins. You can always make it go faster if performance is a problem.[26]

We'll explore how many of the individual virtual message functions work in later chapters, so I won't elaborate here, but only list a few highlights:

- The *queryEnd* and *queryOpen* functions return a BOOL indicating whether the window may be closed or maximized, respectively; by default, these operations are allowed.

- All keyboard messages are passed to a single function, *kbd*; likewise, all mouse messages are sent to *mouse*. It's up to the specific *kbd* or *mouse* function to differentiate messages. This has some drawbacks (for example, it's less portable, since applications must use WM_ symbols), but it's expedient. Some readers might prefer to use a separate function for each mouse event: *lButtonDown, mouseMove,* and so on.

- WM_SYSCOMMAND messages are sent through as ordinary *command*s. Our programs can thus add their own commands to the system menu, and handle them in *command*; if the command is a genuine system command, *command* should return FALSE, which sends it back to Windows.

- Any message that has no corresponding virtual function is sent to *other*; to handle one of these "rare" messages, all a window class has to do is provide an *other* function:

```
BOOL MyWinClass::other(WPEvent& event)
{
    switch (event.msg) {
    case WM_RARELY_HANDLED_MESSAGE:
         .
         .
```

---

26 For example, the approach taken here could be speeded up as follows. First use a function table to dispatch to one of several homogenous functions, then from there do the argument packaging and invoke to the appropriate virtual function. Note, however, that only *WPWin* would have to be modified. This is the beauty of encapsulation: if we *do* decide to improve performance, we only have to do it in *one place* in order for all applications to benefit.

```
            event.ret = rare_message_return_value;
            return TRUE; // handled
        }
        return WPWin::other(event);
    }
```

The details of each function are not important at this point. What's important is the overall idea of using virtual functions instead of messages or *msgProc*—in fact, *msgProc* is now gone from our applications' vocabulary. It's still there in the bowels of *Windows++*, as part of *WPWin*, but applications never use it to handle messages. Instead, they provide the corresponding virtual functions. For example, instead of *msgProc*, *WPMainWin* now provides *command:*

```
class WPMainWin {
public:
    command(int id, WORD msg);
};

BOOL WPMainWin::command(int id, WORD msg)
{
    if (id==WPIDM_EXIT) {
        close();
        return TRUE;
    }
    return WPWin::command(id, msg);
}
```

Just like the old *msgProc,* a virtual message function should always pass unhandled messages back to its ancestor. This gives each class in the window class hierarchy a crack at the message. For example, suppose we add a command to HELLO.

```
HelloWin::command(int id, WORD msg)
{
    if (id==ID_MY_HELLO_COMMAND)
        // do it
        return TRUE;
    }
    return WPMainWin::command(id, msg);
}
```

HelloWin::command must pass unhandled menu IDs to *WPMainWin* in order to inherit all the (reusable) behavior of *WPMainWin,* such as closing the window when the user selects the Exit command.

We can use our new virtual message functions to add more generic "main window" behavior to *WPMainWin.* For example, most main windows destroy themselves in response to a WM_CLOSE message, which is sent when the user selects the CLOSE command from the window ventilator (system) menu (that's the menu that pops up when you click the "close" icon in the upper-left-hand corner).

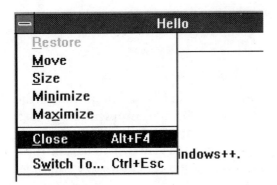

In our old system, we'd add a *switch* case for WM_CLOSE; now instead we write a *closed* function:

```
class WPMainWin : public WPWin {
protected:
   BOOL closed();
};
BOOL WPMainWin::closed()
{
   // Automatically destroy window when close message is received.
   if (queryEnd())
      destroyWin();
   return TRUE;
}
```

With *closed* implemented for *WPMainWin,* applications such as HELLO needn't bother providing it (unless they want to respond to the *closed* event in a non-standard manner). Once again, by encapsulating functionality common to *all* Windows applications in the library, *no* applications have to provide it.

What does HELLO look like now? Well, *msgProc* is defunct; instead we have *paint.*

```
BOOL HelloWin::paint()
{
   WPPaintStruct ps = this;       // see below
   WPRect clientArea = this;
   ps.drawText(clientArea, "Hello, Windows++.",
      DT_SINGLELINE | DT_CENTER | DT_VCENTER);
   return TRUE;
}
```

I'll explain what *WPPaintStruct* is all about in a moment. Right now, let's examine what happens when Windows sends a WM_PAINT message:

- *WPWndProc* receives the message, calls *GetWin* to obtain the window object pointer, and then invokes that object's virtual *msgProc* function.

- There is no *msgProc* defined for *HelloWin* nor *WPMainWin,* so *HelloWin* inherits *msgProc* from *WPWin. WPWin::msgProc* receives control.

- The giant switch statement in *WPWin::msgProc* dispatches the message to the virtual *paint* function. Since the window object is actually an instance of *HelloWin*, control passes to *HelloWin::paint*, which paints the window's client area.

Our programs no longer use *msgProc* to handle events. Instead, they simply provide the appropriate virtual functions. To process WM_PAINT, all our HELLO program does is provide a *paint* function. Just by "being there," *paint* is automatically invoked whenever the window receives a WM_PAINT message. If *paint* were not defined for *HelloWin*, the message would go to *WPWin::paint*, which does nothing. Just as with *msgProc*, this magic is possible only because virtual functions are not bound until run time.

The following figure depicts the flow of events in our new system.

Revised Event Flow

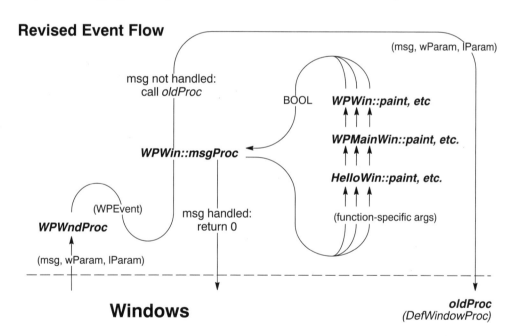

The switch statement in *WPWin::msgProc* inserts a giant loop in the event flow. This loop is the main difference between the new diagram and the one on page 95.

C *To implement something like this in C, you could use an array of function pointers indexed by the WM_ message ID or a sparse lookup table that stored only the functions your program processes. You could then write a generic* MsgDispatch *routine to invoke the proper function from this table, with the message arguments already extracted. In general, any C++ virtual function scheme can be implemented in C as a function array. After all, that's how C++ does it (see Chapter 2).*

To recap, we've converted the Windows model of polymorphism, which uses message IDs and window procedures, into the C++ model of polymorphism, which uses virtual functions. In the process, we've eliminated *msgProc* and the 14-page switch statement, which was one of the reasons we undertook this virtual message function project in the first place. While *msgProc* remains, our applications no longer use it. Instead of one giant function, our programs now provide separate virtual functions for each particular event they wish to handle. Applications don't have to "do" anything else; simply by *providing* the appropriate virtual function, the function receives control whenever the corresponding event occurs.

3.5.5 A Brief Digression: *PeekMessage* and *doIdle*

There's no reason to restrict virtual functions to handling Windows messages; we can add whatever other virtual functions we want as place-holders for additional functionality.

To see what this means, consider the standard Windows way of doing idle processing: you modify your message loop so that it calls *PeekMessage* instead of *GetMessage,* and invokes a "do idle" subroutine whenever there's no message in the queue.

Instead of rewriting the message loop to call *PeekMessage*, it sure would be a lot easier to simply tell the system, "here's my idle function. Call it whenever there are no messages waiting." Well, virtual functions provide just the ticket: all we have to do is introduce a generic *doIdle* virtual function. Since only main windows are associated with the message loop, we add it to *WPMainWin:*

```
// Add doIdle function to WPMainWin
class WPMainWin : public WPWin {
public:
    virtual BOOL doIdle()          { return FALSE; }
};
```

Next, we modify the central message loop as follows:

```
void WPApp::run()
{
    MSG msg
    BOOL peek=TRUE;

    while (peek || GetMessage(&msg, NULL, 0, 0)) {
        if (peek) {
            // Use PeekMessage instead of GetMessage
            if (!PeekMessage(&msg, NULL, 0, 0, PM_REMOVE)) {
                peek = mainWin->doIdle();      // <<< call idle function!
                continue;
            }
            if (msg.message==WM_QUIT)
                break;
        }
```

```
    // The rest is the same as before
    if (!(accel &&
        TranslateAccelerator((*mainWin)(),accel,&msg))) {
            TranslateMessage(&msg);
            DispatchMessage(&msg);
        }
    }
}
```

The first time the message loop executes, the variable *peek* is TRUE, so *run* calls *PeekMessage* instead of *GetMessage*. If *PeekMessage* returns FALSE (no message waiting), the message loop invokes *doIdle*. The default *doIdle* function (the one defined for *WPMainWin*) returns FALSE, in which case *run* goes back to using *GetMessage* and never calls *doIdle* again. But if a specialized main window class defines its own *doIdle* function that returns TRUE, *run* will continue to call it during idle moments.

```
BOOL MyWinClass::doIdle()
{
    .
    . Compute prime numbers during my spare time
    .
    return TRUE;      // must return TRUE to "activate"
};
```

The upshot is that when you (as application programmer) want your application to perform idle processing, all you have to do is provide a *doIdle* function that returns TRUE. That's it. No *PeekMessage*, no messing with the message loop—it all happens through the wonders of C++ virtual functions, just because *doIdle* exists!

C   *You could achieve the same effect in C by setting up a function pointer somewhere, say as a global variable* DoIdle *that defaults to NULL. If this variable is set, the message loop calls it during idle moments, in a manner similar to* WPApp::run. *All the application then has to do is set* DoIdle.

This example offers another way to think of virtual functions. *WPMainWin::doIdle* is a place-holder for functionality that some application *might* provide. You can also think of *doIdle* it as adding a new Windows message: WM_DOIDLE. In fact, you even implement such a message in C!

The RANDRECT and MANDEL programs described in Sections 8.2.6 and 8.2.7 provide concrete examples of applications that use *doIdle*.

3.5.6 Drawing on the Screen: A Peek at GDI

Our HELLO program is almost complete. The *msgProc* is gone, replaced with *paint*, and the Exit command and WM_DESTROY events are automatically and invisibly handled by *WPMainWin*. The only thing I still owe you is an explanation of *WPPaintStruct*. The GDI (Graphics Device Interface) is discussed more fully in Chapter 8, but let's take a peek here so we can finish HELLO.

In Windows, the primary object used to draw on the screen, printer, or any other output device is something called a *device context*. This object stores all sorts of information about the actual device. Windows provides a device-independent (well, almost) interface of API functions that lets you draw on the device. The device context is identified by a handle declared as HDC ("handle to device context"). In *Windows++*, the corresponding object class is *WPDevContext*, which as usual just stores the HDC and provides a number of member functions corresponding to all the Windows GDI functions.

```
class WPDevContext {
protected:
    HDC hdc;                         // handle to device context
    WPWin *win;                      // window whose HDC it is (if any)
public:
    WPDevContext(WPWin *win);
    ~WPDevContext();

    HDC operator()()                 { return hdc; }
    int getDeviceCaps(int cap)       { return GetDeviceCaps(hdc, cap); }

    int drawText(WPRect& rect, CSTR text, WORD format=0, int len=-1)
        { return DrawText(hdc,(LPSTR)text,len,(LPRECT)&rect,format); }

    BOOL rectangle(WPRect &box)
        { return Rectangle(hdc,box.left(),box.top(),
            box.right(),box.bottom()); }

    .
    . etc. (more of the same)
    .
}
```

Most of these functions are of the "brainless" sort described in Section 3.2.6., the benefits of which are the same as described there (see also Chapter 8). Thus, for example, *DrawText* becomes

```
int drawText(WPRect& rect, CSTR text, WORD format=0, int len=-1)
    {   return DrawText(hdc,(LPSTR)text,len,(LPRECT)&rect,format); }
```

As before, we make use of C++ default arguments wherever possible to make programming easier—in this case, the default format and length are zero and –1, respectively.

As you'll see later, there are several different kinds of device contexts, all implemented as derived classes from *WPDevContext*. One of them is *WPPaintStruct*. Recall that the Windows PAINTSTRUCT structure is used to paint a window. Essentially, PAINTSTRUCT is just a handle to a device context (HDC), plus a few additional pieces of information such as the update rectangle and an erase flag. It's defined in WINDOWS.H:

```
typedef struct tagPAINTSTRUCT
 {
  HDC  hdc;
  BOOL fErase;
  RECT rcPaint;
  BOOL fRestore;
  BOOL fIncUpdate;
  BYTE rgbReserved[16];
 } PAINTSTRUCT;
```

The normal programming sequence for using PAINTSTRUCT goes like this:

```
LONG MyWndProc(HWND hwnd, WORD msg, WORD wp, LONG lp)
{
    PAINTSTRUCT ps;
    HDC hdc;

    switch (msg) {
    case WM_PAINT:
        hdc = BeginPaint(hwnd &ps);
        .
        . (draw on hdc)
        .
        EndPaint(hwnd, &ps);
        return 0;
    }
}
```

When part of a window becomes invalid (say, because it was obscured by another window), Windows adds the invalid area to the window's "update region." Eventually, Windows sends a WM_PAINT message requesting that the window paint itself. The window procedure is expected to call *BeginPaint* and *EndPaint*, even if nothing is painted. This is because one of the things *EndPaint* does is re-validate the update region; if you don't call *EndPaint*, Windows will keep sending WM_PAINT messages forever.

If you examine the default window procedure, *DefWindowProc* (the source code is provided with the Microsoft SDK), you'll see that it handles WM_PAINT like this:

```
PAINTSTRUCT ps;
switch (message)
{
    case WM_PAINT:
        BeginPaint(hwnd, (LPPAINTSTRUCT)&ps);
        EndPaint(hwnd, (LPPAINTSTRUCT)&ps);
        break;
}
```

DefWindowProc just calls *BeginPaint*, then *EndPaint;* the net result is that the update region is validated.

How should we model all this in *Windows++?* Well, since *BeginPaint* and *EndPaint* must always be called, we should put these calls somewhere in our reusable library. Any generic processing we can do for our applications, we should. As for modeling PAINTSTRUCT, while *hdc* is a *member* of PAINTSTRUCT, it's more convenient to think of PAINTSTRUCT as a special kind of device context:

```
// (In WPGDI.H)
class WPPaintStruct : public WPDevContext {
    PAINTSTRUCT ps;                       // PAINTSTRUCT is a data member
public:
    WPPaintStruct(WPWin *win);
    ~WPPaintStruct();
    BOOL bkRedrawn()                   { return ps.fErase; }
    void getPaintRect(WPRect &box)     { box = ps.rcPaint; }
};
```

WPPaintStruct stores a Windows PAINTSTRUCT, in addition to the window pointer and HDC inherited from *WPDevContext*. The constructor initializes the object as follows:

```
WPPaintStruct::WPPaintStruct(WPWin *w)
{
    hdc = BeginPaint((*w)(), &ps);     // (*w)() is window's HWND
    win = w;                           // store window ptr
}
```

The constructor simply calls *BeginPaint* to initialize painting and fill in the PAINTSTRUCT, then stores the HDC returned and *WPWin* pointer argument. The destructor does the reverse: it calls *EndPaint*.

```
WPPaintStruct::~WPPaintStruct()
{
    EndPaint((*win)(), &ps);
    hdc = NULL;
    win = NULL;
}
```

Because ~*WPPaintStruct* sets *win* to NULL, ~*WPDevContext* won't attempt to call *ReleaseDC*, which would be a definite no-no (the SDK documentation warns you never to release a device context obtained from *BeginPaint*) (see Chapter 8).

We can now write *HelloWin::paint* (we already did back on page 110, but it probably didn't make sense at the time):

```
BOOL HelloWin::paint()
{
    WPPaintStruct ps = this;        // (this == this HelloWin)
    WPRect clientArea = this;
    ps.drawText(clientArea, "Hello, Windows++.",
        DT_SINGLELINE | DT_CENTER | DT_VCENTER);
    return TRUE;
}
```

First, *paint* creates a *WPPaintStruct* object on the stack, initialized from the *HelloWin* pointer *this* (the constructor automatically calls *BeginPaint*). Then it "draws" on the paint structure, using the "brainless" GDI functions that *WPPaintStruct* inherits from *WPDevContext*. It first gets the window's client area coordinates (using the overloaded *WPRect::operator=(WPWin* w)* from Chapter 2), then invokes *drawText* to display the "hello" message centered in this rectangle. Finally, *paint* returns TRUE to indicate that it handled the *paint* event.

What about *EndPaint?* When *paint* terminates, the automatic variable *ps* goes out of scope, which triggers a call to the destructor *~WPPaintStruct*, which calls *EndPaint*. HELLO doesn't have to do anything.

While it's perhaps excessive to go to this extreme, we can simplify *paint* even further with just a little extra work. Since every *paint* function needs a *WPaintStruct* to paint on, why not have *Windows++* automatically set one up and pass it to *paint* as an argument? This is easy to do, but we have to be a little careful—we don't want to do it for any window, only windows that we plan to paint ourselves, such as the main window. Other windows, such as the built-in controls "listbox" and "button", should have WM_PAINT messages passed on to the original window procedure. So we'll make the change in *WPMainWin* instead of *WPWin:*

```
class WPMainWin {
protected:
    // paint function called from WPWin::msgProc
    BOOL paint();

    // new paint function for main windows
    virtual void paint(WPPaintStruct& ps) { }
};
BOOL WPMainWin:::paint()
{
    WPPaintStruct ps = this;
    paint(ps);
    return TRUE;
}
```

When the window receives a WM_PAINT message, control passes to *WPMainWin::paint* (the first version), which simply sets up a paint structure and invokes a new (overloaded) virtual *paint* function. *HelloWin* now uses the second overloaded version of *paint*.

```
void HelloWin::paint(WPPaintStruct& ps)
{
    WPRect clientArea = this;
    ps.drawText(clientArea, "Hello, Windows++.",
        DT_SINGLELINE | DT_CENTER | DT_VCENTER);
}
```

That's two fewer lines in *HelloWin::paint* and every program we write! This mechanism even works if the derived class doesn't supply a *paint* function, because the default *paint* function for *WPMainWin* does nothing, so the net effect is to call *BeginPaint*, then *EndPaint* immediately after, which simply validates the update region, exactly as *DefWindowProc* would do.

3.5.7 HELLO: The Final Version

Believe it or not, HELLO is finally complete! Here's the finished program, in its full simplicity, the same program shown in the introduction.

```
/////////////////////////////////////////////////////////
// WINDOWS++ CLASS LIBRARY. Copyright 1992 Paul DiLascia.
// FILE: HELLO.CPP
//

#include <wpp.h>

class HelloWin : public WPMainWin {
public:
    HelloWin() { createWin("Hello"); }
    void paint(WPPaintStruct &ps) {
        WPRect clientArea = this;
        ps.drawText(clientArea, "Hello, Windows++.",
            DT_SINGLELINE | DT_CENTER | DT_VCENTER);
    }
};

void WPApp::main()
{
    mainWin = new HelloWin;
    run();
}
```

The main improvement over HELLO3 is that we've dumped *msgProc* for virtual message functions such as *paint*.

While HELLO is only 23 lines, if you actually compile it using the full *Windows++* library, you'll find that the executable file is around 36K, over four times the size of the original C version! Furthermore, it's taken almost 80 pages just to describe it. You might well wonder what's so great about *Windows++*?

What's great is that all of the code we've written is *reusable*. While the source for HELLO.CPP is smaller and simpler than HELLO.C, our goal is not primarily to shrink HELLO to as few lines of code as possible (we could make it *one* line by implementing HELLO as part of *Windows++*). Obviously, no one would build *Windows++* just for the sake of HELLO. But all the *Windows++* code we've written is completely general and can therefore be reused in application after application. The first application (in this case, HELLO) is necessarily the hardest, since we've had to "bootstrap" ourselves from nothing in order to get the basic infrastructure working. But as you'll soon see, each new program we write requires less effort as it reuses code that's already written.

As for the executable size, 36K is small—many commercial C++ libraries compile HELLO at around 150K! 36K is nothing to worry about (I must admit 150K would disturb me somewhat). Even the simplest program necessarily brings in a good many of the *Windows++* library object files. 36K represents the minimal *Windows++* overhead. More sophisticated programs are not proportionately inflated, but generally add only as much code as is contained in the application itself. In other words, the overhead is fixed. In fact, very large applications compile to executables that are smaller than their C counterparts, because the same class subroutines are invoked repeatedly within the program instead of being replicated as "open code" throughout.

3.6 Looking Back

It's been a long chapter (I warned you), but we've accomplished a lot. The basic infrastructure for *Windows++* is established. We've written a lot of code, but all of it is totally general and therefore reusable. Now is a good time to stop, plant one foot on the crest of the hill, and survey the valley below to see where we've just been.

Here's a summary of the main features of *Windows++* at this point.

- The *WPApp* class represents the application and has exactly one instance: the program-wide global variable *App*. Among other things, it stores the module name and instance handle and encapsulates the main message loop in the function *WPApp::run*.

- *WinMain* is hidden and replaced with *WPApp::main*, which must be supplied by each *Windows++* application.

- The base class *WPWin* is used to represent a window. It's essentially no more than a window handle (HWND). It provides a class global *createArgs* that derived classes use to set window registration and creation parameters, and a member function *createWin* to actually create the window. Each derived class constructor sets default *createArgs* depending on what kind of window it represents. For example, *WPMainWin* sets the style to overlapped window and the menu name to *AppMenu*. Subsequent constructors can override these defaults. The last derived class in the inheritance chain is supposed to call *createWin* from its constructor, immediately after setting *createArgs*.

- The *WPWin* class provides "brainless" functions that mirror and repackage their Windows API counterparts.

- The derived class *WPMainWin* represents the application's main window. Classes derived from *WPMainWin* automatically inherit generic main window behavior. For example, the Exit command closes the window, and a WM_QUIT message is automatically posted when the main window is destroyed.

- *Windows++* uses predefined resource names and menu IDs to provide reusable behavior. If a program's resource file has a menu called *AppMenu*, an icon called *AppIcon*, or an accelerator table called *AppAccel*, it's automatically used. To inherit generic command behavior, resource menus must use predefined menu IDs such as WPIDM_EXIT.

■ There is a single window procedure, *WPWndProc*, for the entire system.

■ Window objects never receive WM_CREATE or WM_DESTROY messages. Window object initialization and termination are instead performed by the class constructors and destructors.

■ *Windows++* programs handle specific events by supplying virtual functions such as *paint* and *command* instead of a window procedure or *msgProc*. The base window class, *WPWin*, takes care of dispatching each WM_ message to the appropriate virtual function. Only the commonly used messages have virtual functions; the rest are passed to *other*.

■ Drawing is accomplished in *Windows++* using the *WPDevContext* class, which provides "brainless" functions that mirror the Windows GDI. A special kind of device context, *WPPaintStruct*, is used to paint windows and is automatically passed to the *paint* function for main windows.

■ Window objects are *delete*d automatically whenever WM_DESTROY is received. *Windows++* programs should never *delete* window objects.

Speaking of *delete*, it's time to worry about an often overlooked but crucial aspect of Windows programming: memory management.

CHAPTER ■ 4

Memory Management

In all of the HELLO programs described in the preceding chapter we used the *new* operator to create our *HelloWin* object.

```
mainWin = new HelloWin;
```

In the interest of getting our foundation built, I neglected an interesting and important question: where does the storage come from?

The answer depends on the compiler implementation, but usually *new* does no more than call *malloc*, which is also compiler-specific but in Windows usually allocates memory from the program's local heap.[27] The local heap is a portion of the program's data segment (which also includes the program's static data and stack) managed by Windows. The total size of this segment (heap plus static data plus stack) is limited to 64K, the maximum size of any segment in the 80x86 architecture. This just won't do for large programs.

All the HELLO programs in the preceding chapter were compiled in the small memory model by default, since we didn't specify which model to use. This is fine for small programs such as HELLO, but sooner or later (probably sooner) our programs will grow as they inevitably do, and the small model will be too small.

All of which means it's time to worry about *memory management*.

Memory management is a topic that many programmers dread, something akin to programming a 6502 in assembly language. After all, memory management is so mundane! Do I really have to mess with blocks and locks and heaps and free chains and all that low-level stuff?! Yecch!! The operating system is supposed to do that; OO programmers don't *do* memory management!

Unfortunately, memory management is *extremely* important, especially in Windows, where there's no more 640K memory barrier (Windows is a DOS extender,

---

27 In the large and compact models, *malloc* usually calls *GlobalAlloc*, which has its own problems (see Section 4.2.3).

too) and programs can potentially access gobs of RAM. If you don't take memory management seriously, it will definitely get you, when you least expect it. When it does, your fears will be realized, then transformed to guilt, as you regret not having done it right from the outset.

Don't worry, help is here. Memory management isn't all that difficult, just a little tedious. Once you take the time to do it right (as we will now do together), you can forget all about it and sleep easily knowing that your programs are making efficient use of all those megabytes of RAM you just dropped six bills for and delicately installed with tweezers somewhere in the bowels of your motherboard, with one hand strapped by grounding cable to the radiator pipes.

So if you tremble when memory management is mentioned, consider this chapter as therapy. After reading it, not only will your code purr like a well-tuned engine, but your inner fears will be exorcized in the process. Now, without further ado, here we go again . . .

4.1 Preliminaries

4.1.1 Windows Modes

Before choosing a memory management scheme, we need to decide which Windows modes we plan to run in. Windows 3.0 supports three modes of operation: real, standard, and 386 enhanced.

- *Real mode* provides maximum compatibility with earlier *(2.x)* versions of Windows. It's the only mode available for computers with less than 1MB of memory and runs in the 80x86 processor's "real" mode. Real mode was phased out in Windows 3.1 and can for all practical purposes be considered a relic from the past.

- *Standard mode* is the, well, standard operating mode for Windows 3.0. It provides access to extended memory and runs in 80286 *protected mode*, which provides virtual memory management.

- *386 enhanced mode* is for 80386 (and higher) systems, runs in 80386 protected mode (which provides virtual memory as well as "virtual DOS boxes"), and supports a number of other features unique to the Intel 80386 processor. In 386 enhanced mode, Windows pages memory to disk and can obtain more megabytes of virtual memory that there is physical memory installed in your computer.

Since both standard and 386 enhanced modes run in (80286 or 80386) protected mode, I sometimes use the phrase "protected mode" for either of them, even though protected mode is, strictly speaking, a property of Intel processors, not Windows.

One of the things about Windows programming that scares many programmers away is its use of "handles" instead of pointers, and all the associated convolutions required to "lock" and "unlock" memory blocks. This is an artifact of 2.x versions of Windows, which run in real mode on small machines with little memory and, fortunately, is much ado about nothing when you run in protected mode. In protected mode, programs can lock their memory without really locking it! This will be described in more detail shortly.

Because programming is so vastly simplified in protected mode, and because real mode is not terribly useful anyway, I made the decision *not* to support real mode in *Windows++*: *Windows++ is designed to run in protected mode only.* To ensure this, all our programs are compiled with the *–t* resource compiler switch, which causes Windows to display the following message if anyone attempts to run the program in real mode.

Since most large applications can only realistically run on machines capable of supporting protected mode anyway, this is hardly a significant limitation.

4.1.2 Memory Models

Windows programs can be written for any of the normal DOS memory models: small, medium, compact, and large. Recall that in the segmented architecture of the 80x86 processors, code and data segments can use either near (16-bit) or far (32-bit) pointers. This results in four possible memory configurations or *models*, as shown in the following table:

Windows Memory Models

| | | **Data** | |
		near (16 bit) pointer	far (32 bit) pointer
Code	near	small	compact
	far	medium	large

Actually, *all* pointers are really 32 bits wide; it's just that *near* pointers are assumed to be relative to the program segment (for code) or data segment (for data), whose address is at all times stored in the CS (code) or DS (data) register. All this should be more or less familiar to DOS and Windows programmers alike, so I won't go into any further detail.

Which memory model should we use for *Windows++*? The large model would seem to be the obvious choice for large applications, since it allows more than 64K of data; however, in Windows the large model has the following restrictions:

- In large model programs, the data segment must be declared FIXED in the module definition (.DEF) file.[28]

- You cannot run more than one instance of a large model program at the same time. (As we'll see, this isn't quite true).

For these reasons, most Windows programmers avoid the large model and choose the medium model instead. Actually, most Windows programs are "mixed" model programs, because that way they can use explicit *far* declarations to gain access to more than 64K of data. For example:

```
char FAR * p = farmalloc(4096);
```

This tells the compiler to use a full 32-bit pointer for *p*, even when compiling under the medium model (*farmalloc* is like *malloc*, but allocates far memory). In fact, virtually all Windows API functions declare their pointer arguments as *far*, so you can pass structures back and forth that were allocated from any segment, not just *near* pointers to memory in the program's data segment. So it looks like we should use the mixed-medium model.

Unfortunately, there are a number of special C++ issues that make mixed-model programming a little tricky.

There are two basic problems. The first arises from the fact that in C++, the *new* operator must be declared as follows:

```
void *operator new (size_t sz);
```

You can't declare *new* to return *void FAR* * (this is just a rule of C++). Thus there's no way to allocate *far* objects in C++ unless you use the large model. In C, you'd simply allocate *far* memory (using *farmalloc* or *GlobalAlloc*, which is described shortly) and then cast the far pointer to whatever type of structure you want. But in C++ you should never create an object in this manner, because the constructor won't get called. In C++, you must use *new* to allocate objects, and *new* returns whatever kind of pointer (*near* or *far*) is the default for the model you're using.

---

28 This is required because Windows cannot distinguish between any old transient pointer in your program (such as an automatic variable that's a *char**) and one that's persistent across function calls and therefore cannot be moved; the only safe course is to lock the entire data segment.

Even if you could get *new* to return a far pointer, you'd still face the second problem. As mentioned in Chapter 2, all C++ class member functions have a hidden *this* pointer as their first argument. For example, *WPWin::createWin()* is implemented in C++ as an ordinary C function with a mangled name something like

```
BOOL _xxx_WPWin_createWin_yyy(WPWin* this);
```

The *this* argument is added by the C++ compiler. If we expect to invoke *createWin* through a far object, then *this* must be declared *far:*

```
BOOL _xxx_WPWin_createWin_yyy(WPWin FAR* this);
```

But how can we do this if the *this* pointer is hidden? All *this* pointers are automatically *near* if we compile under the medium model and *far* under the large model; there's no way to declare them otherwise.[29]

The upshot is that we can't use mixed-model programming to get more than 64K of objects, the way C programs do; we can only allocate more than than 64K worth of objects using the large model. This is because object pointers in the medium model must be *near*, and the amount of memory available to our program for creating objects is thus limited to a maximum of 64K.

Therefore, *Windows++* supports *both* the medium and large models.

What about the two large model restrictions mentioned above? Well, fortunately, the first one (fixed data segment) disappears in protected mode, where the processor provides movable memory at the hardware level. In protected mode, all memory addresses are mapped through a transfer table (called the *descriptor table*); this lets Windows move memory around without changing the pointers in our programs. Thus even though the data segment must be FIXED in large model programs, in protected mode it's really movable! (There's no space for a full discussion of how Windows uses 80x86 virtual memory; for an excellent explanation, see [Yao 1990].)

As for the other restriction (only one instance), it turns out that despite what the Microsoft manual says,[30] "only one instance" applies *only* to large model programs that have *multiple* data segments. Neither the Borland nor Zortech compilers normally produce large model programs with multiple data segments, so as long as we don't have more than 64K of static data, the restriction doesn't apply.

---

29 Actually, the Borland compiler provides a way to do this by declaring classes as *huge,* but Zortech doesn't allow it, so I won't use it. See Chapter 9 for more information. In general, Borland does a better job at supporting mixed-model C++ programming by letting you use the *far* and *huge* modifiers with classes as well as functions.

30 Here's the direct quote, from the *Guide to Programming*, Chapter 16, page 35: "...if a module is compiled with the large memory model, its data segments are always fixed in real mode, and *in all modes Windows will be able to load only one instance of the module*" (my italics). This is true only when using the Microsoft compiler. In the large model, it generates multiple data segments even when there's less than 64K of static data. (This may have been corrected in C 7.0.)

(Borland doesn't even allow multiple data segments in the large model; you have to use the "huge" memory model to get multiple data segments and more than 64K of static data.) Most programs don't need more than 64K of static data anyway, and for those that do, there are ways to get around it. For example, you can store static data in the resource file and load it when your program starts up.[31]

Of course, large model programs still incur the slight performance penalty associated with far functions and data; however, I've rarely seen programs where this was a significant issue. When it is, the relevant functions and arguments can always be declared explicitly as *near* or otherwise sped up.

One of the many unfortunate historical consequences of real mode Windows programming is that it's given the large model a bum rap. Many Windows programming books are filled with dire warnings about what evil things will happen if you use the large model, but many readers don't realize that most of the objections to using the large model simply don't apply any longer. At a time when 386 processors are virtually standard, with 50MHz 486 chips at the high end, it seems odd that programmers should still use the medium model for large programs.

4.1.3 A Review of Windows Memory Management

So much for memory models. Now let's review how Windows manages memory. Windows provides two basic mechanisms for allocating memory: the *local heap* and the *global heap*.

Each program has its very own private local heap; this storage comes from the program's data segment. Because memory allocated from the local heap comes from the program's data segment, it can be addressed using a *near* pointer. Near pointers are relative to the program's data segment, which is at all times stored in the DS register. Windows provides functions *LocalAlloc* and *LocalFree* to allocate and free memory from the local heap. The standard sequence goes like this:

```
HANDLE h = LocalAlloc(LMEM_ZEROINIT|LMEM_FIXED, size);
char NEAR * ptr = LocalLock(h);
strcpy(ptr, "hello, world.");        // use the memory
LocalUnlock(ptr);
LocallFree(h);
```

Locking local memory locks it *within* the local heap; the entire data segment itself is movable in protected mode.

---

31 If a program contains *far* data, the compiler will normally place it in a separate data segment, which results in multiple data segments; however, in Borland, you can overcome this problem by using the following compiler switches:

```
bcc -zE_DATA -zHDGROUP -zFDATA ...
```

This tells the compiler to locate *far* data in the program's data segment (DGROUP), just like any other static data. You can even put the switches in your code your code as follows:

```
#pragma option -zE_DATA -zHDGROUP -zFDATA
```

This line appears in WPPDEFS.H.

In addition to all the programs' local heaps, Windows manages a single *global heap,* which is shared among all applications. Global memory comes from the general pool of system memory that Windows manages, not the program's data segment. Global memory may come from any segment; for this reason, a full 32-bit *far* pointer is required to address global memory. The far pointer contains the segment selector in the high word, and a segment byte offset in the low word (*seg:offset*). The Windows functions *GlobalAlloc, GlobalLock, GlobalUnlock,* and *GlobalFree* mirror the *Local* versions (there are others, but these are the primary ones), and the standard calling sequence is basically the same:

```
HANDLE h = GlobalAlloc(GMEM_ZEROINIT|GMEM_MOVEABLE, size);
char FAR * ptr = GlobalLock(h);
lstrcpy(ptr, "hello, world.");              // use the memory
GlobalUnlock(h);
GlobalFree(h);
```

This material should be familiar to Windows programmers, so I won't go into any further detail. If you want to learn more about Windows memory management, you should consult your compiler documentation, the SDK manuals, or a good Windows book.

4.2 *Windows*++ Memory Management

Now we're ready to do some memory management. We've decided to run in protected mode, and to support both the medium and large models.

In C++, it's easy to implement whatever memory management scheme you want simply by overriding the *new* and *delete* operators. These operators are just like any other functions, so if we write our own versions, they'll be compiled and linked instead of the standard C++ versions. Our memory management strategy goes like this: we'll provide our own home-grown *new* and *delete* operators to allocate and free memory from the *local* heap if we're compiling in the *medium* model, and the *global* heap if we're compiling for the *large* model.

```
// (In WPPDEFS.H)
void *operator new (size_t sz);
void operator delete (void *p);

///////////////////////
// (In WINMAIN.CPP)
// System-wide global new and delete operators.
// For large model, allocate objects from far (global) memory;
// for medium model, allocate from the local heap.
//
void * operator new(size_t size)
{
#ifdef __LARGE__
    return App.farAlloc(size);
```

```
#else
    return App.localAlloc(size);
#endif
}
void operator delete(void *ptr)
{
    if (ptr)
#ifdef __LARGE__
        App.farFree(ptr);
#else
        App.localFree(ptr);
#endif
}
```

(The predefined compiler symbol __LARGE__ is defined only when compiling for the large model.) As you can see, *new* and *delete* simply invoke four yet-to-be-written *WPApp* functions:

```
// (In WPAPP.H)
class WPApp {
public:
    void FAR * farAlloc(DWORD size);
    void farFree(void FAR* ptr);
    void *localAlloc(WORD size);
    void localFree(void* ptr);
};
```

We'll implement these functions shortly. But first, why declare them as part of *WPApp?* Why not just do the work inside *new* and *delete?*

The reason for breaking the memory allocation function out as a separate functions, rather than simply doing the work in *new* and *delete,* is that these functions are useful in their own right. While our programs should never use *farAlloc* to allocate objects (remember, we must use *new* and *delete* to allocate objects, so the constructor and destructor are called), it's perfectly OK, and even desirable, to use *farAlloc* to allocate large character arrays and other unstructured memory, even in the medium model. By exposing *farAlloc* as a separate function, we give medium model programs a way to allocate large chunks of (non-object) storage. For example, a text editor could use *farAlloc* to allocate a large character buffer to read a file:

```
char FAR * bigbuf = App.farAlloc(size);
ReadFileIntoBuffer(bigbuf, fileid);
    .
    .
App.farFree(bigbuf);
```

In this manner, medium model programs can use *App.farAlloc* to allocate more than 64K of far memory. Likewise, large model programs can call *localAlloc* and *localFree* to allocate storage from the local heap. As we'll soon see, there are times when large model programs must explicitly allocate memory from the local heap.

As for making *farAlloc* and the others member functions of *WPApp,* the reason for this won't become fully clear until we turn *Windows++* into a dynamic link library

(DLL) in Chapter 9, but the basic idea is that we want all memory to "belong" to the application that allocates it. Also, we'll keep statistics on memory usage, and the *App* object is a convenient place to store them.

The following table summarizes how *Windows++* allocates memory in the medium and large models.

Windows++ **Memory Usage**	objects (*new/delete*)	unstructured FAR memory
medium	*new* uses local heap (*App.localAlloc*) 64K total limit	can use *App.farAlloc* no limit
large	*new* uses global heap (*App.farAlloc*) no limit	can use *new* or *App.farAlloc* no limit

Memory Model (medium / large)

4.2.1 The First Cut

So much for the overview; now let's get down to the nitty-gritty. Our memory-management problem is reduced to writing four *WPApp* functions: *farAlloc, farFree, localAlloc,* and *localFree.* As a first cut, these functions simply call the appropriate Windows functions. For example, *farAlloc* goes like this:

```
void FAR * WPApp::farAlloc(DWORD size)
{
    HANDLE h = GlobalAlloc(GMEM_MOVEABLE | GMEM_ZEROINIT, size);
    if (h==NULL)
        return NULL;
    return (void FAR *)GlobalLock(h);
}
```

WPApp::farAlloc simply allocates a zero-filled chunk of global memory and immediately locks it, returning a pointer to the memory. But wait a minute! Some of you may be wondering why the global memory is always locked. Didn't your mother tell you never to lock your blocks?

In the old days of Windows 2.x and real mode, it was essential to lock memory *only* when you used it, and to unlock it immediately afterwards; the rest of the time, the memory was supposed to be unlocked so Windows would be free to move it.

But remember, we're in protected mode! In protected mode, locked memory is not all that locked, since the processor maps all segment addresses through the descriptor table. This lets Windows move memory around simply by changing the entries in the table, without modifying our program's pointers. In protected mode, even if you lock a memory block, it's still movable! There's only one catch: you must allocate the memory as GMEM_MOVEABLE (before you lock it), not

GMEM_FIXED; if you use GMEM_FIXED, it's really fixed (this observation was made in [Schulman 1991b]).

Thanks to 286/386 protected mode, we can lock our blocks with impunity, which sure makes life a lot simpler. In fact, this is precisely why we *only* support protected mode—so we can lock our blocks and let our programs deal with pointers instead of handles.

Back to work. We're done with *farAlloc;* so let's write *farFree:*

```
void WPApp::farFree(void FAR* ptr)
{
    if (ptr) {
        HANDLE h = GlobalHandle(FP_SEG(ptr));
        GlobalUnlock(h);
        GlobalFree(h);
    }
}
```

This simply undoes what *farAlloc* did. It first calls *GlobalHandle* to obtain the memory block's handle, then unlocks and frees it (FP_SEG is a macro in *<dos.h>* that obtains a pointer's segment selector). Note that *farFree* does nothing when called with a NULL pointer. C++ stipulates that *delete*ing the NULL pointer is allowed, but doing so should have no affect.

Two down, two to go: *localAlloc* and *localFree:*

```
void* WPApp::localAlloc(WORD size)
{
    HANDLE h = LocalAlloc(LMEM_FIXED | LMEM_ZEROINIT, size);
    return h ? (void *)LocalLock(h) : NULL;
}
void WPApp::localFree(void* ptr)
{
    if (ptr) {
        LocalUnlock((HANDLE)ptr);
        LocalFree((WORD)ptr);
    }
}
```

As you can see, they're almost identical to their *far* counterparts.

4.2.2 Handling the Out-of-Memory Condition

If Windows can't meet our memory request, *farAlloc* and *localAlloc* return NULL. Since it's tedious to check for a NULL pointer every time we call *new, farAlloc,* or *localAlloc* (and since many programmers refuse to do it), it's a good idea to provide a more invisible and automatic way to handle the situation when the system runs out of memory.

We can take as our model C++ itself, which already provides such a mechanism. C++ has a built-in global variable, *_new_handler,* which points to a function to call when *new* is out of memory. We could use this pointer, but it's more convenient to add our own, since we'll declare the function slightly differently.

```
typedef BOOL (* NOMEMHANDLER)(WORD);

class WPApp {
private:
    NOMEMHANDLER noMemHandler;      // fn to call when no memory left
    int inNoMemHandler;
    BOOL callNoMemHandler(WORD size);
public:
    NOMEMHANDLER setNoMemHandler(NOMEMHANDLER fn);
};
```

A NOMEMHANDLER is an application-supplied function that we'll call when we run out of memory. The function pointer itself is private; to set it, you must call *setNoMemHandler*, which returns the old handler:

```
///////////////////
// Set the "no-memory" handler; returns old handler. Applications
// can use this to trap the "out of memory" condition. The function
// should return TRUE if we're supposed to retry the allocation.
//
NOMEMHANDLER WPApp::setNoMemHandler(NOMEMHANDLER fn)
{
    NOMEMHANDLER oldFn = noMemHandler;
    noMemHandler = fn;
    return oldFn;
}
```

Next, we make *farAlloc* call the no-memory handler when memory is exhausted:

```
// (In WPAPP.H)
class WPApp {
public:
    void FAR * farAlloc(DWORD size, BOOL useHandler = TRUE);
};

// (In WPAPP.CPP)
void FAR * WPApp::farAlloc(DWORD size, BOOL useHandler)
{
    do {
        HANDLE h = GlobalAlloc(GMEM_MOVEABLE | GMEM_ZEROINIT, size);
        if (h) {
            void FAR * ptr = (void FAR *)GlobalLock(h);
            if (ptr)
                return ptr;
        }
    } while (useHandler && callNoMemHandler(size));
    return NULL;
}

///////////////////
// Call the "no memory" handler, if any. Returns BOOL indicating
// whether or not to retry the allocation that failed.
//
BOOL WPApp::callNoMemHandler(WORD size)
{
```

```
    BOOL ret = FALSE;
    if (noMemHandler && !inNoMemHandler) {
        inNoMemHandler++;                       // prevent infinite recursion
        ret = (*noMemHandler)(size);
        inNoMemHandler--;
    }
    return ret;
}
```

The no-memory handler is passed the size of the request that failed and is expected to return a BOOL indicating whether or not we should retry the allocation. If it returns TRUE, we'll try again; otherwise, we'll just return NULL, as before.

A small detail: since some programs may prefer to check for NULL themselves, rather than using the no-memory handler, I've added a flag (*useHandler*, default = TRUE) to ignore the handler on a per-call basis:

```
void FAR *ptr = App.farAlloc(32000, FALSE);
if (ptr == NULL)
    error("file too big.");
```

The no-memory handler is a standard memory management technique. It provides an easy way for applications to do something other than crash when the system runs out of memory, without checking for NULL after every allocation. The handler is especially useful in multi-tasking environments such as Windows, where it's often possible to reclaim large amounts of memory simply by closing other applications or windows that may be running concurrently. A simple no-memory handler could prompt the user to close other applications, then retry. In fact, we may as well write a default no-memory handler that does just that, since the benefits of our extra effort will be multiplied by the number of applications we later write.

```
// (In WPAPP.H)
class WPApp : public WPModule {
private:
    static BOOL DfltNoMemHandler(WORD size);
public:
    WPApp::WPApp()    {  noMemHandler = WPApp::DfltNoMemHandler; }
};


BOOL WPApp::DfltNoMemHandler(WORD size)
{
    if (MsgBox("The system has run out of memory. You may be able to
reclaim some memory by closing other applications; if so, close them
now and then press 'Retry'; otherwise, press 'Cancel' to terminate this
application", "ATTENTION", MB_ICONSTOP|MB_RETRYCANCEL)==IDRETRY)
        return TRUE;
    exit(-1);          // goodbye!
    return FALSE;      // to make compiler happy
}
```

The constructor initializes *noMemHandler* to the default, so now every *Windows++* program we write gets it. Other programs can provide different no-memory handlers if they like. A multi-window text editor might provide a no-memory handler that successively prompts the user to save and close each open file. Of course, if there's really no more memory, the user will have no choice but to Cancel. We can't work miracles.

4.2.3 The LDT Problem

At this point, everything seems hunky-dory. We've implemented a few memory allocation functions, we've written *new* and *delete* operators that use them, and we've even added a mechanism to handle out-of-memory conditions, which is icing on the cake.

So why do you have the feeling that something ominous is looming around the corner?

Your suspicions are correct; there is indeed a problem with *farAlloc*. There's no way that you could possibly know it unless you either are a Windows guru, or read the article by Andrew Schulman (that's where I learned about it), for it has to do with the way Windows allocates global memory.

The problems is that while *GlobalAlloc* is great for allocating large blocks of memory, it doesn't work well when allocating small blocks. There are two reasons for this. The first is that the smallest block you can allocate with *GlobalAlloc* is 32 bytes. OK, so this is a bit wasteful, but we might be able to tolerate it. It's the second problem that's the real killer: Windows imposes a maximum limit on the *total number of blocks* it can allocate from global memory. This is because Windows creates an eight-byte "descriptor" for each global memory block it allocates (four bytes in 386 enhanced mode). These descriptors are allocated from a segment called the "local descriptor table" (LDT), which, like any other 80x86 data segment, is limited to 64K (even in 32-bit protected mode, because the the segment registers are only 16 bits). A quick application of second-grade mathematics (64 ÷ 8 = 8) shows that Windows cannot allocate more than 8K (that's 8192) global memory blocks.[32] This limit applies not just to a single application, but to *all of Windows*, since Windows uses a single LDT for the entire system.

Even if a single program got all 8000 blocks, it's not enough! (Our memory demands are insatiable.) Many programs may need more than 8000 objects. Consider, for example, a text editor that uses an eight-byte structure to represent each line of text: 8 x 8K is 64K, only a fraction of the memory available on a four- or eight-megabyte machine. The editor should not be restricted to 8000 lines of text just because Windows can't handle it. Even ordinary old real mode DOS programs can allocate more objects that!

---

32 In standard mode, it's even worse—you only get 4096 blocks, because Windows needs *two* descriptors for each block—one for its own housekeeping and another for your program's data.

4.2.4 Fixing the LDT Problem: *MemHeap*

Unfortunately, fixing the problem requires a bit of work. The basic idea comes from [Schulman 1991b]; I've just adapted it to C++. Conceptually, the idea is simple: rather than call *GlobalAlloc* for each object, we'll call it to allocate big chunks of memory—say, 8K at a time—and then "suballocate" small objects from the big chunks. We'll do this for small blocks only; we'll still allocate large blocks with *GlobalAlloc*, as before. To suballocate the little blocks, we need some kind of heap allocation scheme. Fortunately, Windows provides just the ticket: *LocalAlloc*, *LocalFree* & co. can manage a heap of memory in any chunk of global storage, not just the local heap; once a local heap is initialized (by calling *LocalInit*) in some chunk of memory, we can suballocate smaller, object-sized blocks from it using *LocalAlloc*.

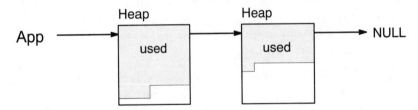

The basis for all of this is (what else?) a new class: *MemHeap*. This class represents a heap of storage and is used by the *WPApp* memory functions. In fact, since these are the only functions that need use *MemHeaps*, *MemHeap* has no public members. Instead, *WPApp* is declared as a *friend* of *MemHeap*. In C++, an entire class, as well as an individual function, can be a *friend* of a class.

```
//////////////////////
// Memory heap. This class is used by the application object ONLY.
// It manages a chunk of Windows global memory as a "local" heap.
// The heap is identified by its data segment.
//
class MemHeap {
protected:
    MemHeap* next;     // next heap in list (see Section 4.2.6)
    long numBytes;     // total num bytes ever allocated from this heap
    int numObj;        // number of extant objects
    WORD seg;          // segment selector for this heap

    void NEAR * alloc(WORD size);
    void free (void NEAR* ptr);
    void FAR * makeFarPtr(void NEAR * np)
        { return (void FAR*) MK_FP(seg, (WORD)np); }
    WORD blockSize(void NEAR* ptr);

    MemHeap() { }      // for local heap, described later
    MemHeap(WORD sz);
    ~MemHeap();

    friend WPApp;
};
```

```
const HEAPSIZE = 8192;              // smallest heap size
```

Let's go through this slowly. *MemHeap* stores four data members: a *next* pointer, the total number of objects and bytes allocated from the heap, and the heap's segment selector. The *next* pointer will be used to link all the heaps in a list; the second two items are for bookkeeping purposes; and the last item, *seg,* identifies the block of global memory that the *MemHeap* manages. It's initialized in the constructor:

```
/////////////////////
// Initialize a new heap: allocate memory from Windows' global
// heap, and store its data segment.
//
MemHeap::MemHeap(WORD hpsz)
{
    assert(hpsz > 0);
    hpsz = max(hpsz, HEAPSIZE);
    HANDLE h = GlobalAlloc(GMEM_MOVEABLE|GMEM_ZEROINIT, hpsz);
    if (h) {
        void FAR* ptr = GlobalLock(h);
        if (ptr) {
            seg = FP_SEG(ptr);
            if (LocalInit(seg, 0, hpsz-1)==0) {
                GlobalUnlock(h);
                GlobalFree(h);
                seg = 0;
            }
        } else
            GlobalFree(h);
    }
}
```

When a new heap is created, the constructor allocates a chunk of global memory big enough to meet the request, but at least HEAPSIZE (8K) bytes. HEAPSIZE specifies the "granularity" of our heaps. You can easily change it if you like (8K seems like a nice round number). The global memory chunk is locked (in protected mode it's still movable), and its segment selector is stored in *seg,* unless the memory could not be allocated, in which case *seg* remains zero. The segment selector uniquely identifies each heap, since Windows allocates each block of global memory from a different segment. Next, the constructor calls *LocalInit* to initialize a Windows "local" heap in the global memory chunk. Once the heap is initialized, we can use *LocalAlloc* and *LocalFree* to suballocate small objects:

```
#ifdef __BORLANDC__                // Borland:

#define    SWAPDS(val)             asm { push ds; mov ds, val; pop val; }
#define    GETDS(var)              asm { mov ax, ds; mov var, ax; }

#elif __ZTC__                      // Zortech:

extern "C" WORD setDS(WORD seg);
#define    SWAPDS(val)             (val = setDS(val))
#define    GETDS(var)              (var = (unsigned short)asm(0x8C,0xD8))

#endif
```

```
/////////////////
// Allocate a block of memory from heap.
// Returns near pointer, relative to heap's data segment, or NULL.
//
void NEAR* MemHeap::alloc(WORD size)
{
    WORD dsval = seg;
    SWAPDS(dsval);
    HANDLE h = LocalAlloc(LMEM_FIXED | LMEM_ZEROINIT, size);
    void NEAR *np = h ? (void NEAR*)LocalLock(h) : NULL;
    size = LocalSize((HANDLE)np);
    SWAPDS(dsval);

    if (np) {
        numObj++;
        numBytes+=size;
    }
    return np;
}
/////////////////
// Return a block of memory to heap.
// Complain if more objects freed than allocated.
//
void MemHeap::free(void NEAR* ptr)
{
    if (numObj-- > 0) {
        WORD dsval = seg;
        SWAPDS(dsval);
        WORD size = LocalSize((HANDLE)ptr);
        LocalUnlock((HANDLE)ptr);
        LocalFree((WORD)ptr);
        SWAPDS(dsval);
        numBytes -= size;
    } else
        ErrBox("Extra object freed!\nsegment: %x\toffset: %x.",
            seg, ptr);
}
```

The key trick here is that we use SWAPDS to set and restore the DS register to the heap's segment selector immediately before and after the call to *LocalAlloc* or *Local-Free*. This trick (described in [Yao 1990]) "fakes out" *LocalAlloc* and *LocalFree* into allocating the memory from the *MemHeap*'s segment rather than the program's data segment. SWAPDS is defined differently depending on which compiler we're using. Borland allows in-line assembly language, while Zortech only allows hex machine instructions (the Zortech version calls a separate assembly language function, *setDS*, which is listed in Appendix A).

Note also that *alloc* and *free* perform rudimentary storage bookkeeping: they keep track of the total number of objects and bytes outstanding. We'll use this information a little later on.

The destructor for *MemHeap* simply frees the global memory chunk that the con-structor allocated:

```
/////////////////
// Destroy local heap: return its global memory to windows.
//
MemHeap::~MemHeap()
{
    if (seg) {
        HANDLE h = GlobalHandle(seg);
        assert(h);
        GlobalUnlock(h);          // undo our lock
        GlobalUnlock(h);          // undo LocalInit's lock
        GlobalFree(h);            // free global memory
    }
}
```

GlobalUnlock must be called twice because *LocalInit* locks the block once and we lock it again (to get the memory pointer).

Before leaving *MemHeaps,* let me point out that our decision to use *LocalInit* is purely a matter of convenience; we could use any other heap allocation scheme. We could borrow one from a reference book on buffering algorithms; we might decide that it's more efficient to keep free chains for objects of frequently-used small sizes. Anything is possible, for once we allocate a chunk of global memory, we can slice it up any way we like. All we'd have to do is rewrite a few *MemHeap* functions. Our entire suballocation mechanism is localized to *MemHeaps.* This is another good example of what's meant by *encapsulation.*

4.2.5 The Local Heap

Our *MemHeaps* create a "local" heap in a chunk of global memory. But what about the real local heap? (The one in the program's data segment.) How can we allocate memory from *it?* Well, the "real" local heap is just a special kind of *MemHeap* (with your OOP cap on, you should immediately think *subclass*), namely, the one whose segment selector is the same as the program's data segment. To model it, we derive a new class:

```
/////////////////
// Special subclass models the application's "real" local heap.
// --I.e., the one whose data segment is the app's data segment.
//
class MemLocalHeap : public MemHeap {
public:
    MemLocalHeap();
};
```

The only difference between *MemLocalHeap* and *MemHeap* lies in the constructor:

```
/////////////////
// Constructor for local heap, a subclass of the general heap.
// Instead of allocating global memory, the true local heap gets its
// segment from the application's data segment.
//
MemLocalHeap::MemLocalHeap()
```

```
{
    WORD dsval;
    GETDS(dsval);
    seg = dsval;
}
```

This constructor invokes the *MemHeap* constructor with no arguments (by default) and, instead of allocating a chunk of global memory, sets *seg* from the current value of DS, which is the segment selector for the program's data segment. We must also modify ~*MemHeap* so it doesn't attempt to free the local heap:

```
//////////////////
// Destroy local heap: return its global memory to
// windows, unless it happens to be the real local heap.
//
MemHeap::~MemHeap()
{
    WORD dsval;
    GETDS(dsval);
    if (seg && dsval != seg) {      // (if not local heap)
        .
        . (as before)
        .
    }
}
```

Since *MemLocalHeap* is derived from *MemHeap*, it inherits *alloc, free,* and all the other *MemHeap* functions. Furthermore, these work exactly as desired, since SWAPDS will effectively set DS to itself, because for a *MemLocalHeap, seg* = DS.

Since there is exactly one local heap for each application, it makes sense to add an instance of *MemLocalHeap* to the application object (of which there is also exactly one instance):

```
class WPApp {
    MemLocalHeap localHeap;        // THE local heap
};
```

We can now rewrite *localAlloc* and *localFree:*

```
void * WPApp::localAlloc(WORD size, BOOL useHandler)
{
    void NEAR * np;
    do {
        np = localHeap.alloc(size);
    } while (np==NULL && useHandler && callNoMemHandler(size));

    return (void*)np;
}
void WPApp::localFree(void *ptr)
{
    if (ptr)
        localHeap.free((void NEAR *)ptr);
}
```

These functions simply allocate or free memory from the *localHeap* object, which in turn allocates or frees memory from the program's "real" local heap.

4.2.6 Using the Heaps

So far, so good. We have a *MemHeap* class that manages a chunk of global memory as a heap, with a subclass *MemLocalHeap* for the "real" local heap. We even have an instance (the only one we'll ever create) of *MemLocalHeap* stored in the application object, and we've rewritten *localAlloc* and *localFree* to use it. All that remains is to use our *MemHeaps* when allocating *far* memory. In other words, we have to rewrite *farAlloc* and *farFree*.

Allocating local memory was easy because there's only one local heap; but for far memory, we expect to use several heaps, as many as are required to meet the program's memory demands. The application object must therefore manage a *list* of *MemHeaps:* whenever the program requests some memory, we'll try to allocate it from one of the heaps; if no heap can meet the request, we'll create a new one. First, we need a few more items in *WPApp:*

```
class WPApp : public WPModule {
private:
    MemHeap * firstHeap;              // first heap in chain
    MemHeap * mruHeap;               // most recently used heap

    long   nBigObjBytes;             // number of bytes in "big" blocks
    int nBigObj;                     // number of "big" blocks allocated

    MemHeap* addHeap(WORD size);     // add new heap to chain
    MemHeap *findHeap(WORD seg);     // find heap w/given data segment
    void delHeap(MemHeap *heap);     // delete and remove from chain
};
```

The data member *firstHeap* points to a list of *MemHeaps; mruHeap* points to the one most recently used; *nBigObjBytes* and *nBigObj* count the number of big objects and bytes allocated. All these are described in more detail later. The three private functions *addHeap, findHeap,* and *delHeap* are used to add a new heap to the list, find the heap with a given data segment, or remove a heap. Here's *addHeap:*

```
/////////////////////
// Allocate another heap.
//
MemHeap * WPApp::addHeap(WORD size)
{
    MemHeap *heap = new MemHeap(size);
    if (heap==NULL || heap->seg==0) {
        delete heap;
        return NULL;
    }
    heap->next = firstHeap;              // add heap to list
    firstHeap = mruHeap = heap;          // ...and set MRU heap
    return heap;
}
```

It simply allocates a new heap of the required size and, if successful, adds the heap to the list pointed to by *firstHeap.* This function is used by *farAlloc,* which we can now write as

```
//////////////////
// Allocate far memory
//
void FAR * WPApp::farAlloc(DWORD size, BOOL useHandler)
{
    do {
        if (size >= HEAPSIZE) {
            HANDLE h = GlobalAlloc(GMEM_MOVEABLE | GMEM_ZEROINIT, size);
            if (h) {
                nBigObj++;
                nBigObjBytes += GlobalSize(h);
                return (void FAR *)GlobalLock(h);
            }
        } else {
            void NEAR* np;
            // first try most recently used heap
            MemHeap *heap = mruHeap;
            if (heap && ((np = heap->alloc(size)) != NULL))
                return heap->makeFarPtr(np);
            // try other heaps
            for (heap = firstHeap; heap; heap=heap->next) {
                if (heap != mruHeap && (np = heap->alloc(size)) != NULL) {
                    mruHeap = heap;
                    return heap->makeFarPtr(np);
                }
            }
            // still no memory: try creating a new heap
            heap = addHeap(size);
            if (heap) {
                if ((np = heap->alloc(size))!=NULL)
                    return heap->makeFarPtr(np);
                delHeap(heap);
            }
            // We are really out of memory: try calling no-memory
            // handler to let app free some memory if possible.
        }
    } while (useHandler && callNoMemHandler(size));
    return NULL; // all efforts failed (sob, sob): return NULL
}
```

If the size requested is larger than HEAPSIZE, *farAlloc* simply allocates global memory as before, incrementing *nBigObj* and *nBigObjBytes* before returning the pointer. Remember, we only need to use the heap mechanism for small objects. Using it for big ones is a waste of time and memory (there's some overhead associated with each *MemHeap*).

For small objects, *farAlloc* first tries to allocate the memory block from one of the heaps already allocated (starting with *mruHeap* for performance's sake); if the block could not be allocated from one of the existing heaps, *farAlloc* creates a new heap and allocates the block from it. If this too fails, *farAlloc* calls the no-memory handler (if there is one) and will attempt the whole process over again if the handler returns TRUE.

Far memory is de-allocated by *farFree*.

```
void WPApp::farFree(void FAR* ptr)
{
    if (ptr==NULL)
        return;

    WORD seg = FP_SEG(ptr);                 // get data segment..
    WORD off = FP_OFF(ptr);                 // ..and seg-relative offset

    if (off==0)   {                         // big block with no heap
        HANDLE h  = GlobalHandle(seg);
        nBigObj--;
        nBigObjBytes -= GlobalSize(h);
        GlobalUnlock(h);
        GlobalFree(h);
    } else {
        MemHeap *heap = findHeap(seg);      // find heap the mem belongs to
        heap->free((void NEAR*)off);        // free it
        if (heap->numObj==0)                // if that was the last object:
            delHeap(heap);                  // free the whole heap
    }
}
```

If the block to be freed is one of the "big" blocks allocated directly from global memory, without using a heap, its offset will always be zero. This is an undocumented fact that's a consequence of the way Windows allocates memory (see [Schulman 1991a] and [Yao 1990]); *farFree* uses it to distinguish between big blocks and little ones. The former are freed using *GlobalFree*; the latter are freed using *WPApp::findHeap* and then *MemHeap::free*. Here's *findHeap*:

```
///////////////////
// Find heap with given data segment.
// Uses MRU algorithm to improve performance (see below).
//
MemHeap * WPApp::findHeap(WORD seg)
{
    if (mruHeap && mruHeap->seg==seg)
        return mruHeap;

    // Not MRU heap: search the list.
    //
    for (MemHeap *heap=firstHeap; heap; heap=heap->next) {
        if (heap->seg == seg)
            return mruHeap = heap;
    }
    assert(FALSE);    // should never get here!
    return NULL;
}
```

Once it finds the right heap, *farFree* calls *MemHeap::free* to return the block to that heap. If the block freed was the last outstanding block allocated from that heap, *farFree* frees the entire heap itself, by calling *delHeap*, which looks like this:

```
////////////////////
// Delete (free) a heap: remove from chain, and delete it.
//
void WPApp::delHeap(MemHeap *heap)
{
    if (heap==firstHeap)
        firstHeap = heap->next;

    else {
        for (MemHeap *h=firstHeap; h; h=h->next) {
            if (h->next == heap) {
                h->next = heap->next;
                break;
            }
        }
    }

    if (heap==mruHeap)
        mruHeap = NULL;
    delete heap;
}
```

Throughout all these operations, the variable *mruHeap* is maintained so that it always points to the most recently used heap. This buffering algorithm improves performance significantly (I first wrote the code without *mruHeap*), since whenever an object is allocated or freed, the likelihood is great that the next object allocated or freed will come from the same heap.

Just in case you've forgotten where we are in this lurid story (I have), we're trying to overcome the LDT problem, which limits programs to a maximum of 8192 individual memory blocks. To solve the problem, we first implemented *MemHeaps*; now we've just written *farAlloc* and *farFree* to use them. So let's see what happens when a program allocates a *far* block of memory, either by calling *farAlloc* explicitly, or by calling *new* in the large model:

- If the size requested is larger than the heap size, the block is allocated directly from global memory.

- Otherwise (that is, for small objects), *farAlloc* tries to allocate the block from one of the existing heaps; if successful, it returns a pointer to the block.

- If the block cannot be allocated from one of the existing heaps (for example, the first time a block is allocated, the list is empty), *farAlloc* creates a new heap and allocates the block from it.

- If a new heap could not be allocated (we are *really* out of memory), *farAlloc* makes one last-ditch effort by calling the no-memory handler, which gives the application a chance to free some memory. If it can, the handler is supposed to return TRUE, in which case *farAlloc* will try again.

Everything works fine, except for one little problem: the first time a program calls *farAlloc*, the heap list will be empty (*firstHeap* = NULL), so *farAlloc* will call *addHeap* to create a new heap; *addHeap* in turn calls *new* to create a new *MemHeap*. But in the large model, *new* calls *farAlloc*, and our program will go into an infinite loop!

Sigh.

4.2.7 Overloading *new* and *delete*

Never fear, this one is easy to fix. We'll *overload* the *new* and *delete* operators for *MemHeap*, like we did for *WPWin* in Section 3.4.8:

```
/////////////////////
// Overloaded new and delete operators always allocate storage
// for MemHeap objects from the application's local heap.
//
void *MemHeap::operator new(size_t size)
{
    return App.localAlloc(size);
}
void MemHeap::operator delete(void *heap)
{
    App.localFree((void NEAR*)heap);
}
```

Now the *MemHeaps* themselves are always allocated from the local heap. This fixes our infinite loop problem, since now when *farAlloc* creates a new *MemHeap*, *MemHeap::new* is invoked (which calls *localAlloc*), instead of the global *new* operator (which calls *farAlloc* again).

That's it. Our memory management scheme is now essentially finished. No more bugs, I promise. There are a few improvements we'll make, but the basic mechanism is in place. We've implemented *new* and *delete*, which call *farAlloc* and *farFree* (large model) or *localAlloc* and *localFree* (medium model). The *far* functions allocate global memory either directly or from *MemHeaps*, while the *local* functions allocate memory from the program's local heap.

There are other memory functions I didn't show you (they're listed in Appendix A). For example, *WPApp::memSize* returns the size of a memory block. It's straightforward if you understand what we've done so far. There are also some functions I should have implemented, such as a *realloc* function, but didn't, only because I never needed them.

4.2.8 Force-Allocating Global Memory

If the amount of memory requested of *farAlloc* is larger than HEAPSIZE, the memory is allocated directly from global memory, rather than being suballocated from a heap. Sometimes, it's necessary to do the same thing for smaller blocks of memory, because a particular Windows function wants a handle to a block of global memory. For example, in Chapter 7 we'll use the function *DialogBoxIndirectParam* to create dialog boxes on the fly. This function is declared in WINDOWS.H:

```
int   FAR PASCAL
DialogBoxIndirectParam(HANDLE, HANDLE, HWND, FARPROC, LONG);
```

The second HANDLE argument is supposed to be the handle to a global block of memory that contains a data structure called DLGTEMPLATE that describes how to build the dialog box. We would like to use this as follows.

```
DLGTEMPLATE *p = (DLGTEMPLATE *)farAlloc(size);
    .
    .
DialogBoxIndirectParam( hinst, GlobalHandle(FP_SEG(p)), . . .);
```

The dialog details are unimportant; what matters is that the above code will fail because unless *size* is greater than HEAPSIZE, *farAlloc* will suballocate the memory block from some *MemHeap*, and *GlobalHandle* won't recognize it as global memory. (I know. I tried it.) What we need is a way to request that the memory be allocated as its own global block, even if the size is smaller than HEAPSIZE.

Well, this is trivial: all we have to do is add a flag, something programmers have been doing ever since God invented BOOL:

```
class WPApp : public WPModule {
public:
    void FAR * farAlloc(DWORD size, BOOL usHandler=TRUE,
        BOOL useGlobal=FALSE);      // new flag
};
void FAR * WPApp::farAlloc(DWORD size, BOOL useHandler, BOOL useGlobal)
{
    do {
        if (size >= HEAPSIZE || useGlobal) {
            HANDLE h = GlobalAlloc(GMEM_MOVEABLE | GMEM_ZEROINIT, size);
            .
            .
    (as before)
}
```

The *useGlobal* flag directs *farAlloc* to bypass the heap mechanism and allocate the block directly from global memory. C++ default function arguments sure come in handy here. Since *useGlobal* is FALSE by default, callers needn't bother with this nonsense unless they want to force the allocation from global memory, which is rarely done.

4.2.9 Fixing *GetWin*

You've probably forgotten it by now, but I'll remind you of an outstanding problem in our *GetWin* function. Recall that we implemented *GetWin* in Section 3.4, along with *linkHwnd* and *unLinkHwnd,* when we "linked" our window object to its (Windows) window by storing the object pointer in the window's property list. I pointed out then that the property list only lets us store a 16-bit word, whereas in the large model, our window object pointer is a 32-bit *far* pointer. Now that we're officially supporting the large model, it's time to fix *GetWin.*

There are a couple of ways to go. We could store both the high- and low-order words of the object pointer in two separate properties, but this would introduce a performance hit (*GetProp* is relatively slow because it must match a particular string in the property list). Since *WPWndProc* calls *GetWin* every time it receives a message from Windows (which is a lot), using two properties is a bad idea.

Besides, there's a better way. Under our new memory-management scheme, all far memory is allocated from some *MemHeap,* which is identified by its data segment selector. All *far* pointers to memory allocated from a particular heap have the same segment selector in their high-order word. If we could somehow guarantee that all window objects were allocated from the same heap, they would all have the same segment selector, and we could easily reconstruct the 32-bit far pointers from this (fixed) segment selector and the 16-bit offsets stored in the window property. The most obvious heap to use is the *local* heap, since we can always get its data segment selector from the DS register.

How can we ensure that all window objects are allocated from the local heap? It's easy—we already overloaded the *new* and *delete* operators for *WPWin* (back in Section 3.4.8). All we have to do is modify them to use the same trick as *MemHeap,* namely, to allocate the objects from the local heap!

```
/////////////////
// Always allocate from local heap so we can store
// 16-bit offset in window property list
//
void* WPWin::operator new(size_t size)
{
    return NewWin = (WPWin*)App.localAlloc(size);
}

void WPWin::operator delete(void* ptr)
{
    assert(((WPWin*)ptr)->deletable);
    App.localFree(ptr);
}
```

Now, whenever an instance of *WPWin* is allocated (including an instance of any class derived from *WPWin*), it comes from the local heap. We can now fix *GetWin:*

```
///////////////////
// Get window object from window handle (HWND)
//
WPWin* WPWin::GetWin(HWND hwnd)
{
    .
    .
    .
    HANDLE winptr = GetProp(hwnd, WP_WINPTR);
#ifdef __MEDIUM__
    return (WPWin*)winptr;          // in medium model, just cast to ptr
#else
    WORD appds;
    GETDS(appds);                   // get data segment selector
    return (WPWin*)MK_FP(appds, winptr);
#endif
}
```

In the medium model, where all pointers are *near* by default, we simply return *winptr* as before. But in the large model, we build a *far* pointer from the application's data segment selector (DS register) and the offset stored in the window property.

Of course, there is one minor drawback: the total number of window objects we can allocate (including the *MemHeaps* themselves) is now limited by the size of the program's local heap, which is 64K minus the size of the program's stack, static data, *MemHeaps,* and other local objects. In practice, I've never bumped into this limit (but then, I've never written a program that creates an unusually large number of windows).[33]

4.2.10 Returning Memory to Windows

One advantage of our centralized memory management scheme is that we can guarantee that when an application terminates, it returns all its memory to Windows. The following lines in the *WPApp* destructor do the trick:

```
WPApp::~WPApp()
{
    // Free all the app's memory heaps.
    long numObj = nBigObj;
    while (firstHeap) {
        numObj += firstHeap->numObj;
        delHeap(firstHeap);
    }
```

---

33 The limitation could be overcome easily enough. We don't really need to use the local heap for window objects; we could use *any* heap, so long it's the same one for all window objects. It would be a simple matter to implement a special heap, the "window heap," reserved for window objects, from which *WPWin::new* would allocate storage (in the large model only). *GetWin* would then build a pointer with this heap's segment selector instead of DS.

```
    if (numObj != 0)
        ErrBox("%ld objects remaining!", numObj);
}
```

The destructor simply frees each heap in the heap chain and displays a warning message if any objects are outstanding. If a program forgets to free one or more objects, a message box will appear when the program terminates:

Recall that *App* is a static global object, instantiated in WINMAIN.CPP. Just like any other object, *App* is initialized by its constructor and "terminated" by its destructor. But when are these called? *App* is not an automatic stack variable declared inside some function, but a static global object, instantiated *outside* of any function.

One of the many responsibilities of the C++ compiler is to keep track of all static objects and to call their constructors before your program receives control and their destructors after it terminates. To understand exactly how this works, consider the following simple program:

```
////////////////////////////////////////////////////////////////
// Program to demonstrate static initialization of C++ objects
//
#include <windows.h>
class FOO {
public:
    FOO()      { MessageBox(NULL, "Hello", "", MB_OK); }
    ~FOO()     { MessageBox(NULL, "Goodbye", "", MB_OK); }
} fooInstance;

int PASCAL WinMain(HANDLE hinst, HANDLE pinst, LPSTR cmdline, int show)
{
    return 0;
}
```

If you compile and run this program, you'll see two message boxes appear: first, one that says "Hello," and then one that says "Goodbye." When you compile this program, the C++ compiler notes the object *fooInstance* and says, "Aha! A static object—I need to initialize that," and adds the object to a list of other static objects. This list is stored somewhere accessible by the start-up code. All compilers provide some sort of start-up code that runs before your program actually receives control. For example, typical C start-up code initializes the standard i/o streams such as *stdin* and *stdout* before calling *main*. C++ does the same thing, only it has an additional chore to perform: it must initialize static objects by calling their constructors. Likewise, it must call the corresponding destructors (if any) before terminating the program (this is usually done in the *exit* routine).[34]

The upshot is that in C++, you can easily perform system initialization or termination before and after the main entry point receives control! This is often extremely convenient. For example, our *App* destructor is guaranteed to be called after our program terminates, by which point, all memory should have been freed by the program. If not, it's a bug (but one our *App* object will spot and report). In any event, *App* will return all the memory to Windows.

4.2.11 Reporting on Memory Usage

It's often useful to know how much memory our programs use, so let's write a function that reports some informative statistics:

```
////////////////////
// Display application statistics in a message box.
//
int WPApp::showStats(BOOL cancel)
{
    char *s=scratch; // use scratch pad to build message string
    // Show number and size of "big" objects
    s += sprintf(s,"BIG OBJECTS:\t%d obj\t%ld bytes\n",
                                    nBigObj,nBigObjBytes);
    // First show stats for local heap
    long nObj = localHeap.numObj;
    long nBytes = localHeap.numBytes;
    s += sprintf(s, "LOCAL HEAP:\t%ld obj\t%ld bytes\n", nObj, nBytes);
    // Now show stats for other heaps, up to ten of them.
    MemHeap *h, *next;
    int nHeaps;
    for (h=firstHeap, nHeaps=0; h; h=h->next,nHeaps++) {
        if (nHeaps < 10)
            s += sprintf(s, "HEAP [%x]:\t%d obj\t%ld bytes\n",
                    h->seg, h->numObj, h->numBytes);
        else if (nHeaps==10)
            s += sprintf(s,". . .");
        nObj += h->numObj;
        nBytes += h->numBytes;
    }
    if (nHeaps)
        sprintf(s, "\nTotals: %d heaps, %ld objects, %ld bytes.",
            nHeaps, nObj, nBytes);
    return MsgBox(scratch, getName(), cancel ? MB_OKCANCEL : MB_OK);
}
```

---

34 Unfortunately, not all compilers get it right. In particular, the Zortech version 3.0 compiler does not implement its C++ start-up code correctly. It calls the static constructors *before* calling the Windows task initialization functions, and your program will crash if it attempts to display a message box from within a static object constructor or destructor. Fortunately, Zortech provides the source for the start-up code, and I've provided a fix in Appendix A.

This function is fairly straightforward, so I won't explain it in any detail. The only new thing here is the data member *scratch*, which I added to the application object.

```
class WPApp {
public:
    char scratch[1024];                 // transient buffer anyone can use
};
```

Scratch is just a 1K character buffer that any program can use whenever it needs a transient place to build a string, such as a *printf* message. It's comforting to know you always have a 1K "scratch pad," even if you're in the midst of running out of memory. (By the way, this is a useful thing to add to C programs as well.) Our *showStats* function builds a message in *scratch* that lists how much memory has been allocated from global memory, the local heap, and up to ten *MemHeap*s. The message is then displayed using *MsgBox*.

To use *showStats*, we'll add another built-in command ID and three lines of code to *WPMainWin*:

```
// (in WPID.H)
#define WPID_MEMSTATS    21


// (in WPMAIN.CPP)
BOOL WPMainWin::command(int id, WORD msg)
{
    switch (id) {
    .
    .
    case WPIDM_MEMSTATS:
        App.showStats();
        return TRUE;
    }
    return WPWin::command(id, msg);
}
```

Now all an application has to do to provide a "memory statistics" command is add it somewhere in the resource (.RC) file. For example, we can add an accelerator key to HELLO:

```
// (In HELLO.RC)
AppAccel ACCELERATORS
BEGIN
    "^X",  WPIDM_EXIT
    "^Z",  WPIDM_MEMSTATS                /* add MEMSTATS command */
END
```

Now if you type *Control-Z* at the HELLO program, you'll get a message like this:

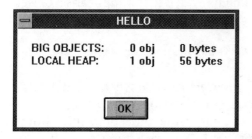

The only object HELLO creates is its *HelloWin,* which is 56 bytes. All the sample programs described in this book use *Control-Z* as an accelerator key for MEMSTATS, so you can examine how any of them use memory by simply pressing this key. This also shows how easy it is to add a generic command to all *Windows++* programs in one fell swoop. Since the MEMSTATS command is implemented in the library class *WPMainWin,* programs need only add the command to their resource file and inherit the class to get the command for free. No code required! That's what I call reusability.

4.3 MEMTEST

The MEMSTATS command is useful for inspecting a program's memory usage, but the only way to know how much memory is *available* is to see how much we can allocate. So let's write a simple program called MEMTEST that does no more than allocate memory blocks until memory is exhausted:

```
///////////////////////////////////////////////////////
// WINDOWS++ CLASS LIBRARY.  Copyright 1992 Paul DiLascia.
// FILE: MEMTEST.CPP
//
// "Memory Hog" program demonstrates Windows++ memory management.

#include <wpp.h>

// A typical small C++ object.
class memBlock {
   char str[32];
public:
   memBlock* next;
   memBlock()  { strcpy(str, "hello, world"); }
};

const BIGOBJSIZE = 20000;               // a large chunk of storage

static memBlock * firstBlock = NULL;    // first small block in list
static long objSize = 0;                // size of current obj to alloc
static long numObj = 0;                 // number of objects allocated
```

```
/////////////////
// Show how many objects we allocated and memory stats too.
//
void ShowTestResults()
{
    sprintf(App.scratch,
        "Allocated %ld %ld-byte objects.",numObj,objSize);
    MsgBox(App.scratch,"MEMTEST");
    App.showStats();
}
/////////////////
// No memory handler just displays a message.
//
BOOL NoMemHandler(WORD size)
{
    MsgBox("Ran out of memory!", "MEMTEST");
    return FALSE;
}
/////////////////
// Program entry point
//
void WPApp::main()
{
    if (MsgBox("Start small object test?\n
        (It may take a minute or two).",
        "MEMTEST", MB_YESNO)!=IDYES)
        return;

    HCURSOR save = Cursor = IDC_WAIT;        // set cursor to wait icon
    App.setNoMemHandler(NoMemHandler);       // set our handler

    // Allocate as many little objects as we can.
    // Stop at 40,000 (otherwise it will take all day!).
    // The point is to prove that we can allocate many more than
    // 8K objects (the LDT limit).
    //
    memBlock *mb;
    objSize = sizeof(memBlock);
    for (numObj=0; numObj <= 40000; numObj++) {
        if ( numObj >= 40000 )
            break;
        mb = new memBlock;                   // alloc new block
        if (mb==NULL)
            break;
        mb->next = firstBlock;               // chain it..
        firstBlock = mb;                     // ..to the list
    }
    ShowTestResults();

    // Free all small blocks
    while ((mb = firstBlock) != NULL) {
        firstBlock = mb->next;
        delete mb;
    }

    // Tell user we're about to start big obj test, but give him/her
    // a chance to cancel if we're in 386 enhanced mode.
```

```
    //
    strcpy(App.scratch, "Starting big object test.");
    int buttons = MB_OK;
    DWORD winflags = GetWinFlags();
    if (winflags & WF_ENHANCED) {
        strcat(App.scratch, "\nWARNING: this may take several minutes!");
        buttons = MB_OKCANCEL;
    }
    if (MsgBox(App.scratch,"MEMTEST", buttons)==IDCANCEL)
        return;

    // OK, start the big object test.
    //
    objSize = BIGOBJSIZE;
    for (numObj = 0; numObj <= 1000; numObj++) {
        char FAR* p = (char FAR*)App.farAlloc(BIGOBJSIZE);
        if (p==NULL)
            break;

        // actually write into all of memory
        for (int i=0; i<BIGOBJSIZE; i++)
            *p++ = 'X';
    }
    ShowTestResults();

    Cursor = save;      // restore cursor
}
```

MEMTEST performs two tests: a small object test and a big object test. First, it allocates as many *memBlock* objects as it can, until it either runs out of memory or allocates 40,000 objects. In the large model, it's easy to allocate more than 40,000 little objects if you have several megabytes of memory installed in your computer, but it will take a long time, so why bother? We don't really care how many blocks can be allocated; the main thing is to prove that we can get more than the 8K LDT limit imposed by Windows. If Windows runs out of memory before allocating 40,000 objects, the *NoMemHandler* displays a message. Whatever the results, when the test is over (it may take a minute or two), MEMTEST displays a message box telling how many objects were allocated, then shows the memory statistics, which look something like this:

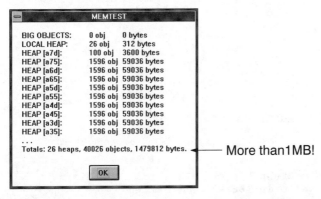

These statistics show what a memory hog MEMTEST is. There sure are a lot more heaps allocated than for HELLO!

After showing the test results, MEMTEST frees all the little objects it allocated and starts the second, "big object," test. This test is similar to the first, but allocates chunks of 20K, rather that 36 bytes. In 386 enhanced mode, we give the user a chance to abort, for it's truly amazing how long Windows can continue to allocate blocks in 386 enhanced mode, which uses disk-swapping to gain extra memory. Even in 386 enhanced mode, MEMTEST stops at 1000 objects—that's 20MB! (If you really want to see how much memory you can get on a 386, you can delete this check, but be prepared to wait a long, long time.) When it either runs out of memory or reaches 1000 blocks, MEMTEST again displays the memory statistics, but this time makes no attempt to free the blocks before terminating. When it does, ~WPApp catches our error and displays a message:

This confirms that our ever-vigilant memory police are alert, ready to catch us attempting to steal even a single byte of memory.

4.4 Summary

I hope this exploration of Windows memory management has been therapeutic—if not for you, then certainly for your programs. If you implement a system like the one described here, you will be one of the few kids on the block to do Windows memory management correctly, and your programs will have gobs and gobs of memory to play with.

Here's a quick summary of memory management under *Windows++*.

- *Windows++* runs in protected mode (standard or 386 enhanced) *only*. This lets us lock all memory blocks as soon as they're allocated, so our programs always deal with pointers instead of handles. It also lets us support the large model without really locking the data segment.

- *Windows++* supports both the medium and large memory models.

- In the medium model, all objects are allocated from the local heap (near memory); in the large model, they are allocated from Windows' global heap (far memory). This is accomplished by providing our own *new* and *delete* operators. In either model, programs may explicitly allocate either *far* or *local* memory.

■ In order to overcome the 8K total object limit imposed by the Windows Local Descriptor Table (LDT), *Windows++* employs a heap-based memory management scheme. Global memory is allocated in 8K chunks, from which smaller blocks are suballocated using *LocalAlloc*. The heaps are implemented by the class *MemHeap*.

■ *Windows++* provides a mechanism for programs to supply their own no-memory handlers, as well as a default handler that displays a message box prompting the user to close other applications.

■ *Windows++* performs storage bookkeeping, and the memory statistics can be displayed at any time by calling *App.showStats*. *Windows++* provides a built-in command ID for this, so programs need only add the ID (WPIDM_MEMSTATS) to their .RC files in order to use this command. All the sample programs in this book use *Control-Z* to show memory statistics.

■ When an application terminates, *Windows++* automatically checks that all objects have been freed; if not, it displays an error box and returns the memory to Windows anyway.

■ All window objects (*WPWin* and its descendants) are allocated from the local heap, even in the large model, so we can reconstruct their 32-bit far pointers from the data segment selector (DS register) and the 16-bit offset stored in the window property list.

CHAPTER ▪ 5

Global Objects and TOE

Now that we've built the basic core of *Windows++* and bitten the memory-management bullet (it wasn't *that* bad, was it?), it's time for some fun. In this chapter we'll actually write some programs (amazing). You'll get a chance to see how the virtual functions described in Section 3.5 work in practice. In the process, I'll show you how to model shared Windows resources such as the mouse, keyboard, and cursor as global objects.

We'll start by implementing a simple program, MKC, which illustrates how the mouse, keyboard, cursor work in *Windows++*. Then we'll apply the same techniques to a more interesting program: a game that "learns" how to play tic-tac-toe.

5.1 The MKC Program

MKC reports basic information about the state of the mouse and CAPS, NUM, and SCROLL-lock keys, as well as the cursor position, which is continuously updated as the user moves the mouse about the window's client area. The cursor can also be moved with the arrow keys, so the program works even when there's no mouse. Finally, just to show how it's done, MKC uses its own X-shaped cursor instead of the normal Windows arrow. The main purpose

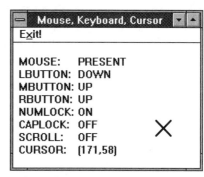

of MKC is to illustrate how *Windows++* programs handle mouse and keyboard events, and manipulate the cursor.

As with all *Windows++* programs, MKC starts off by deriving a new window class from *WPMainWin*:

```
class MKCWin : public WPMainWin {
    TEXTMETRIC tm;                          // text metrics
    int button[3];                          // button states
    int repeat;                             // keyboard repeat count
public:
    MKCWin();
    void paint(WPPaintStruct &ps);
    BOOL mouse(int msg, WPPoint p, WORD flags);
    BOOL kbd(WPEvent& event);
    BOOL activated(WORD state, BOOL minimized);
};
```

MKCWin stores the window text metrics, the state of each mouse button, and the keyboard repeat rate as data members. *MKCWin* processes four events by implementing the four virtual functions *paint, mouse, kbd,* and *activated*. Recall that these "virtualized" message functions are called (as described in Section 3.5) from *WPWin::msgProc* whenever the corresponding event occurs.

Here's the constructor:

```
int TABS[] = { 12, 25, };            // tab stops, in text coords

MKCWin::MKCWin()
{
    createArgs.wndcls.hCursor = App.loadCursor("XCURSOR");
    createWin("Mouse, Keyboard, Cursor");

    // Convert tab stops from text to pixel coordinates
    WPDevContext dc = this;
    dc.textMetrics(tm);
    TABS[0] *= tm.tmAveCharWidth;
    TABS[1] *= tm.tmAveCharWidth;
}
```

The constructor sets the window class cursor in *createArgs*, creates the window, and then converts the tab stops in the integer array TABS from text-dimensions to pixels. XCURSOR is defined in the resource file, MKC.RC, along with the menu and accelerator keys:

```
// (In MKC.RC)
#include "wpp.h"

xcursor CURSOR mkc.cur

AppMenu MENU {
    MENUITEM "E&xit!",                      WPIDM_EXIT
}

AppAccel ACCELERATORS
BEGIN
    "^X", WPIDM_EXIT
    "^Z", WPIDM_MEMSTATS
END
```

MKC.CUR is a cursor designed with SDKPAINT to resemble an "X".

5.1.1 The Mouse

The way *MKCWin* receives mouse input is by implementing the virtual *mouse* function. If this function exists, *Windows++* calls it whenever a mouse event occurs, as described in Section 3.5. For MKC, the processing is very simple: it simply records the state of the mouse buttons then invalidates its client area so it'll get repainted:

```
///////////////////
// Handle mouse message.
// Record button state and always invalidate the client area.
//
BOOL MKCWin::mouse(int msg, WPPoint p, WORD flags)
{
    switch(msg) {
    case WM_LBUTTONDOWN:
    case WM_LBUTTONUP:
        button[0] = (msg==WM_LBUTTONDOWN);
        break;
    case WM_MBUTTONDOWN:
    case WM_MBUTTONUP:
        button[1] = (msg==WM_MBUTTONDOWN);
        break;
    case WM_RBUTTONDOWN:
    case WM_RBUTTONUP:
        button[2] = (msg==WM_RBUTTONDOWN);
    }
    invalidate();
    return TRUE;
}
```

The window is invalidated even for other messages such as WM_MOUSEMOVE, since *MKCWin* must also display the cursor position in real time. (The *invalidate* function is one of the "brainless" *WPWin* functions: it simply calls *InvalidateRect* with a NULL rectangle in order to invalidate the entire client area; another overloaded version invalidates a specific rectangle.)

One of the pieces of information displayed in the MKC window is whether or not a mouse is present. The customary Windows way to test for the existence of the mouse is to call *GetSystemMetrics*. This is easy enough, but there are a handful of other mouse-related functions that programs might use:

```
GetSystemMetrics(SM_MOUSEPRESENT)
GetSystemMetrics(SM_SWAPBUTTON)
GetCapture
GetDoubleClickTime
ReleaseCapture
SetCapture
SetDoubleClickTime
SwapMouseButton
```

We could call these functions directly; however, it would be nice to group them together somehow. With our OOP caps on, we should look for an object to attach them to. Well, what other object is there but the mouse itself? After all, the basic object-oriented rule is: look for objects in the real world. The mouse is an ideal candidate: it has a physical existence (you can touch it!), unlike the abstract objects we've been modeling, such as windows and applications. So let's implement a mouse object, with "brainless" functions for the above Windows API functions:

```
class WPMouse {
public:
    WPMouse() { }

    WPWin* capture()
        { return WPWin::GetWin(GetCapture()); }
    WPWin* capture(WPWin *win)
        { return WPWin::GetWin(SetCapture((*win)())); }

    void release()                  { ReleaseCapture(); }
    WORD getDoubleClickTime()       { return GetDoubleClickTime(); }
    void setDoubleClickTime(WORD msec)
        { SetDoubleClickTime(msec); }
    BOOL swapButtons(BOOL swap)     { return SwapMouseButton(swap); }
    BOOL swapButtons()
        { return GetSystemMetrics(SM_SWAPBUTTON); }
    BOOL present()
        { return GetSystemMetrics(SM_MOUSEPRESENT); }
};
extern WPMouse Mouse;
```

These definitions are entered in a new file, WPGLOB.H. Like *App*, there is exactly one mouse object, the global variable *Mouse*, which (also like *App*) is instantiated in WINMAIN.CPP:

```
WPMouse Mouse;   // THE mouse
```

Now, to test if a mouse is present, we can write

```
if (Mouse.present())
    ...
```

and to capture the mouse, we can write

```
Mouse.capture(mywin);
```

All we've really done is repackage the Windows mouse functions, but our repackaging helps make our code easier to read and write.

Back to MKC. We're ready to write the *paint* function:

```
void MKCWin::paint(WPPaintStruct &ps)
{
    ps.setTabs(TABS);

    WPPoint pt(tm.tmAveCharWidth, tm.tmHeight);

    ps.printF(pt, "MOUSE:\t%sPRESENT\t",
        Mouse.present() ? "" : "NOT ");
    pt.y += tm.tmHeight;                    // move down one line
```

```
    for (int i=0; i<3; i++) {
        ps.printF(pt, "%cBUTTON:\t%s\t",
            "LMR"[i], button[i] ? "DOWN" : "UP");
        pt.y += tm.tmHeight;
    }
}
```

The first thing *paint* does is set the tab stops for the paint structure device context (the same *TABS* that were initialized in the constructor). Tabbed text is described in more detail in Chapter 8; for now, all you need to know is that *Windows++* supports the tabbed text feature, which lets you define tab stops at specific pixel locations. Once you set tab stops for a particular device context, they're used in all subsequent text operations such as *textOut* and *printF*. These functions are also described in Chapter 8, but I'll simply tell you here that *textOut* is a brainless equivalent of *TextOut*, and *printF* invokes *texOut* after converting its *printf*-style arguments to a single string:

```
/////////////////////
// printf-like function for device context.
//
long WPDevContext::printF(WPPoint p, CSTR format, ...)
{
    char buf[128];

    va_list argptr;
    va_start(argptr, format);
    int len = vsprintf(buf, format, argptr);
    va_end(argptr);
    return textOut(p.x, p.y, buf, len);
}
```

(*va_list*, etc., are defined in *<stdargs.h>*, part of the C runtime library.)

If you take my word for it that tabbed text and *printF* work properly, then it's obvious how *paint* works: it just displays whether or not the mouse is present, as well as the state of each button. It uses the TEXTMETRICs stored in *tm* (loaded when the window was created) to position the text properly.

5.1.2 The Keyboard

MKC handles keyboard events in a similar manner, by implementing a *kbd* function. The implementation is again straightforward. If the user presses the CAPS, NUM, or SCROLL lock keys, we invalidate the window.

```
const VK_SCROLLLOCK = 0x91;        // scan code for scroll lock

void MKCWin::kbd(WPEvent& event)
{
    switch (event.key()) {
    case VK_NUMLOCK:                // for any of these...
    case VK_CAPITAL:
    case VK_SCROLLLOCK:
        invalidate();               // repaint window
```

```
        return;
    }
    WPMainWin::kbd(event);          // default handler
}
```

We don't care whether the message is WM_KEYUP or WM_KEYDOWN, only what key was pressed or released. To paint the status of the three lock keys, we need to call the Windows function *GetKeyState*. But instead of calling it directly, we can more conveniently model the keyboard as a global object, just like we did for *Mouse*. The technique is the same—find all the Windows functions that have anything to do with the keyboard, then encapsulate them in a new class:

```
class WPKeyboard {
public:
    int codePage()                          { return GetKBCodePage(); }
    int type()                              { return GetKeyboardType(0); }
    int subType()                           { return GetKeyboardType(1); }
    int numFnKeys()                         { return GetKeyboardType(2); }
    int keyName(LONG lparam, char *buf, int buflen)
        { return GetKeyNameText(lparam, buf, buflen); }

    int state(int vkey)                     { return GetKeyState(vkey); }
    void getState(BYTE* buf)                { GetKeyboardState(buf); }
    void setState(BYTE* buf)                { SetKeyboardState(buf); }
    BOOL isArrowKey(int key);
};

extern WPKeyboard Keyboard;
```

The only non-inline function, *isArrowKey*, is in WPGLOB.CPP:

```
static char ArrowKeys[] = { VK_UP, VK_DOWN, VK_LEFT, VK_RIGHT, 0 };

BOOL WPKeyboard::isArrowKey(int key)
{
    return strchr(ArrowKeys, key) != NULL;
}
```

Back to MKC. We can now add a few lines in *paint* to display the states of the NUM, CAP, and SCROLL-lock keys:

```
void MKCWin::paint(WPPaintStruct &ps)
{
    .
    . (paint mouse state as before)
    .
    ps.printF(pt, "NUMLOCK:\t%s\t",
        Keyboard.state(VK_NUMLOCK) ? "ON" : "OFF");
    pt.y += tm.tmHeight;

    ps.printF(pt, "CAPLOCK:\t%s\t",
        Keyboard.state(VK_CAPITAL) ? "ON" : "OFF");
    pt.y += tm.tmHeight;
```

```
ps.printF(pt, "SCROLL:\t%s\t",
    Keyboard.state(VK_SCROLLLOCK) ? "ON" : "OFF");
pt.y += tm.tmHeight;
}
```

5.1.3 The Cursor

All that remains to finish MKC is to deal with the cursor. In particular, we want to display the cursor position as it moves and allow it to be moved using the arrow keys as well as the mouse. Windows 3.0 provides eight cursor-related functions:

```
ClipCursor
CreateCursor
DestroyCursor
GetCursorPos
LoadCursor
SetCursor
SetCursorPos
ShowCursor
```

Of these, only three are involved in creating new cursor shapes: *LoadCursor, CreateCursor,* and *DestroyCursor.* The last two are new for 3.0 and rarely used (*CreateCursor* creates a cursor with specified dimensions and bit planes; *DestroyCursor* destroys such a cursor), so we won't bother modeling them in *Windows++* (they can always be called directly). Most programmers create cursors with SDKPAINT or some other editor, then load them by calling *LoadCursor.* We already have a *Windows++* function (*WPModule::loadCursor*) to load cursors, so *LoadCursor* is taken care of.

The five remaining cursor functions manipulate the system cursor, which is a shared resource just like the mouse and keyboard. It therefore makes sense to model it as a global object too:

```
class WPCursor : public WPObj {
public:
    HCURSOR operator= (HCURSOR hc){ return SetCursor(hc); }
    HCURSOR operator= (LPCSTR name)
        { return *this = App.loadCursor(name); }
    HCURSOR operator= (int id)
        { return *this = App.loadCursor(id); }

    void setPos(int x, int y)      { SetCursorPos(x, y); }
    void getPos(WPPoint& p)        { GetCursorPos((LPPOINT)&p); }

    WPPoint operator()()
        { WPPoint p; getPos(p); return p; }
    WPPoint operator= (WPPoint p)
        { SetCursorPos(p.x, p.y); return p; }

    void clip(WPRect &rect)        { ClipCursor((LPRECT)&rect); }
    void unClip()                  { ClipCursor(NULL); }
    void show(BOOL val)            { ShowCursor(val); }
};

extern WPCursor Cursor;
```

WPCursor is used to represent *the* system cursor, not individual cursor shapes, which are identified by handles (HCURSORs). *WPCursor* provides more packaging. For example, it lets us write

```
Cursor = IDC_WAIT;                // set cursor to hourglass
Cursor = "XCURSOR";               // load cursor from named resource

WPPoint p = Cursor();             // get current cursor position
Cursor = p;                       // move cursor

WPRect clientArea = myWin;        // get client area rectangle
Cursor.clip(clientArea);          // restrict cursor to client area
Cursor.unClip();                  // let go of cursor
```

Using the assignment operator to move and change the cursor is both easier and more natural than invoking Windows functions like *SetCursor* and *LoadCursor*.

We can use *WPCursor* to finish writing *paint*. All that's left is to show the cursor position:

```
void MKCWin::paint(WPPaintStruct &ps)
{
    .
    . (as before)
    .
    WPPoint crs = Cursor();
    screenToClient(crs);
    ps.printF(pt, "CURSOR:\t(%d,%d)\t", crs.x, crs.y);
}
```

Next, we have to make MKC handle arrow keys. Chapter 6 of the Microsoft Windows *Guide to Programming* describes the proper way of doing it. I've simply transliterated the Windows code into *Windows++* and added it to our *kbd* function:

```
void MKCWin::kbd(WPEvent& event)
{
    .
    . (check for CAPLOCK, etc., as before)
    .
    switch (event.getMsg()) {
    case WM_KEYDOWN:
        if (Keyboard.isArrowKey(event.key())) {
            // Got arrow key: move cursor
            WPPoint pt = Cursor();
            screenToClient(pt);            // convert to client coords
            repeat += event.keyRepeat();   // bump repeat count

            switch (event.key()) {
            case VK_LEFT:  pt.x -= repeat; break;
            case VK_RIGHT: pt.x += repeat; break;
            case VK_UP:    pt.y -= repeat; break;
            case VK_DOWN:  pt.y += repeat; break;
            }
```

```
                // Don't move cursor outside our window's client area
                WPClientRect rect = this;
                rect.capture(pt);           // WPRect function does the trick
                clientToScreen(pt);         // convert back to screen coords
                Cursor = pt;                // move it!
                return;
            }
        break;

    case WM_KEYUP:
        repeat = 1;                         // reset repeat count
        break;
    }
    WPMainWin::kbd(event);
}
```

The keyboard *repeat* count is stored as a data member in *MKCWin*, not as a static variable, as would be done in most Windows programs written in C. In *Windows++*, there's never a need to use static globals for such things, since every *Windows++* window has a C++ object associated with it; this object provides a natural place to store whatever information you want to associate with the window.

The fruits of our labor are starting to appear in *kbd*. Look how easy it is to manipulate points and the cursor using various overloaded operators: we get the cursor position simply by assigning *pt = Cursor;* we get the window's client area rectangle by assigning *rect = this;* we keep the cursor in this rectangle using *rect.capture;* and finally, we move the cursor using yet another assignment, *Cursor = pt*. These assignments, so simple and natural in C++, would require several functions calls and arithmetic calculations in C. The best you could do in C would be to bundle each operation into a subroutine.

The last thing we must take care of is showing the cursor if the mouse is not present. As described in the Microsoft manual, this must be done whenever the window is activated—that is, whenever the window receives a WM_ACTIVATED message, which, in *Windows++*, invokes the *activated* function:

```
BOOL MKCWin::activated(WORD state, BOOL minimized)
{
    if (!Mouse.present() && !minimized)
        Cursor.show(state);
    return WPMainWin::activated(state, minimized);
}
```

Once again, the code is transliterated from the SDK manual. *MKCWin* passes the activated event back to its ancestor (*WPMainWin*), so it will eventually find its way through *Windows++* back to *DefWindowProc*, which responds by setting the focus to the window activated.

5.1.4 The WAIT Cursor

We're done with MKC, but before leaving the cursor, and while we're still open to Chapter 6 of the SDK *Guide to Programming*, I want to show you a clever way to change the cursor to an hourglass icon. Whenever a Windows application has to do some lengthy processing during which the system is "locked," the application is supposed to capture the mouse and change the cursor to an hourglass by setting it to IDC_WAIT. Here's the approved C calling sequence, straight from the Microsoft manual:

```
HCURSOR hSaveCursor;
HCURSOR hHourGlass;
hHourGlass = LoadCursor(NULL, IDC_WAIT);
.
.
SetCapture(hWnd);
hSaveCursor = SetCursor(hHourGlass);
.
. /* Lengthy operation */
.
SetCursor(hSaveCursor);
ReleaseCapture();
```

We can encapsulate this entire calling sequence in a single object:

```
class WPWaitCursor : public WPObj {
    HCURSOR save;
public:
    WPWaitCursor(WPWin *win)
        { Mouse.capture(win); save = Cursor = IDC_WAIT; }
    ~WPWaitCursor()
        { Cursor = save; Mouse.release(); }
};
```

Now, whenever we want to display an hourglass, we can write

```
WPWaitCursor wait = myWin;
.
. (lengthy operation)
.
```

Through the magic of C++, when *wait* is instantiated, C++ calls the *WPWaitCursor* constructor, which captures the mouse and changes the cursor to an hourglass, saving the old cursor as it does so. And before *wait* goes out of scope (ithat is, before control passes out of the function or code block in curly braces), C++ invokes the destructor ~*WPWaitCursor*, which releases the mouse and restores the cursor.

5.1.5 Encapsulating What's Generic in MKC

Before moving on, let's stop for a minute to ask whether there is anything we've implemented for MKC that's generic to *all* Windows applications. After all, our mission is to write reusable code.

Well, there are a couple of things:

■ The *MKCWin* constructor loads the window's TEXTMETRICs immediately after calling *createWin*. Since most applications need to get the text metrics sooner or later, why not have *createWin* do it automatically? We don't want to add *tm* to every window object (it's 31 bytes), but we could make *tm* a static class global, just like *createArgs*, and fill it in every time we create a new window. Of course, this bashes the previous value of *tm*, but *tm* is often only needed during initialization. If you need to save *tm*, you should copy it somewhere else.

■ The way MKC handles the arrow keys and cursor when there's no mouse is also totally generic; moreover, it's something that all applications *should* do (but which is boring to program and therefore often neglected). This functionality is a perfect candidate for the reusable code library. All we have to do is move the relevant code to *WPMainWin*.

Consider it done: the final implementations of *WPWin* and *WPMainWin* listed in Appendix A contain these two suggestions. The text metrics and cursor functionality are henceforth automatically inherited by all *Windows++* applications.

This illustrates one of the main themes of the book: reusable *code is produced gradually, by incorporating the generic aspects of each new application into the class library.* This build-as-you go strategy is ideal for a couple of reasons. First, it spreads the time and effort required to build *Windows++* out over an extended period, during which you also produce "real" applications; and second, by expanding the library when a particular need arises, you're much more likely to end up with the "right" solution. It's easier to know what's called for when you have a particular application in mind than it is to dream up needs in a vacuum.

5.2 Other Global Objects

While all it really amounts to is a syntactic transformation modeling the mouse, keyboard, and cursor as global objects is natural and convenient. It's easier to manipulate them using overloaded C++ operators than it is to call Windows API functions. *Windows++* extends this basic technique to a number of other objects: the caret, WIN.INI, and the clipboard. I won't cover these in gory detail, but only relate the highlights.

5.2.1 The Caret

The caret is similar to the cursor in many respects. But whereas the cursor marks the mouse location, the caret marks a place where a user may enter text. There's only one caret, which is shared by all Windows applications.

```
//////////////////
// Global Caret resource, similar to cursor.
//
class WPCaret {
public:
    void create(WPWin *win, WPBitmap& bm)
        { CreateCaret((*win)(), bm(), 0, 0); }
    void create(WPWin *win, int w, int h, BOOL gray=FALSE)
        { CreateCaret((*win)(), gray==TRUE, w, h); }

    void hide(WPWin *win)          { HideCaret((*win)()); }
    void show(WPWin *win)          { ShowCaret((*win)()); }
    void getPos(WPPoint& p)        { GetCaretPos((LPPOINT)&p); }
    void setPos(int x, int y)      { SetCaretPos(x, y); }
    void setBlinkTime(WORD msec)   { SetCaretBlinkTime(msec); }
    WORD getBlinkTime()            { return GetCaretBlinkTime(); }
    void destroy()                 { DestroyCaret(); }

    WPPoint operator()()           { WPPoint p; getPos(p); return p; }
    WPPoint operator= (WPPoint p)  { SetCaretPos(p.x, p.y); return p; }
};

extern WPCaret Caret;
```

The implementation is similar to *WPCursor*. The usual overloaded operators let us write

```
WPPoint p = Caret();       // get caret pos
Caret = p;                 // set caret pos
```

to get and set the position of the caret. The remaining functions are "brainless" transliterations of Windows caret functions. *CreateCaret* is modeled as two different *create* methods: one to create a block caret; the other to create the caret from a bitmap (see Section 8.2.7).[35]

5.2.2 WIN.INI

The Windows API provides two functions to read from and write to the Windows initialization file, WIN.INI. Applications can use this file to store their own initialization information. WINI.INI is an ASCII file with entries like this:

```
[topic]
keyword = value
 .
 .
```

Windows++ provides access to WIN.INI through another global object: *WinIni*.

---

35 My proofreader points out an interesting bit of etymological trivia: the word *caret* is derived from a Latin root meaning "there is something missing." If you remember this, you'll never get it confused with *cursor*.

```
///////////////////
// This global object represents the WIN.INI file.
// Use it to read/write from WIN.INI.
//
class WPWinIni {
public:
    int get(CSTR app, CSTR key, char *buf, int buflen, CSTR dflt="")
        { return GetProfileString((LPSTR)app,
           key ? (LPSTR)key : NULL, (LPSTR)dflt, (LPSTR)buf, buflen); }
    int get(CSTR app, CSTR key, int dflt=0)
        { return GetProfileInt((LPSTR)app, (LPSTR)key, dflt); }

    int getPrinterName(char* buf, int len);

    BOOL set(CSTR app, CSTR key, CSTR val)
       {return WriteProfileString((LPSTR)app,(LPSTR)key,(LPSTR)val);}
    BOOL set(CSTR app, CSTR key, int val)
        { char buf[16]; itoa(val, buf, 10);
        return WriteProfileString((LPSTR)app,(LPSTR)key,(LPSTR)buf); }

    int getKeys(CSTR app, char *buf, int buflen)
        { return GetProfileString((LPSTR)app,NULL,"",
                                  (LPSTR)buf,buflen); }
};
extern WPWinIni WinIni;
```

The *get* and *set* functions are the primary means of accessing WIN.INI. Overloaded versions let you get and set strings or integers.

```
// get integer key
int x = WinIni.get("appname", "intkeyname")
```

```
// get string key
int len = WinIni.get("appname", "charkeyname", buf, sizeof(buf));
```

The function *getKeys* gets a string of all the keys, and a special function *getPrinterName* gets the name of the default printer:

```
int WPWinIni::getPrinterName(char* buf, int len)
{
    int ret = get("windows", "device", buf, len);
    strtok(buf,",");
    return ret;
}
```

Recall that the default printer is stored in the "[windows]" section of WIN.INI under the key name "device" as follows:

```
[windows]
.
.
.
device=HP LaserJet III,HPPCL5A,LPT2:
```

All *getPrinterName* does is copy this string into the caller's buffer, truncating the text following the first comma; in this example, *getPrinterName* returns "HP LaserJet III".

The same technique could be used to retrieve other information besides the printer name; I singled out the printer name as an example to illustrate the technique.

5.2.3 The Clipboard

Another global object in *Windows++* is the Clipboard. It's modeled, like all the other global objects, using a class (*WPClipboard*) and a static global instance (*Clipboard*). Programs can open, close, read, and write clipboard data using the member functions. The class is implemented in WPGLOB.H and WPGLOB.CPP; the full source code is in Appendix A.

5.3 TOE

Watching the MKC screen change when you press a mouse button or the CAPS LOCK key is hardly exciting. While MKC shows how the cursor, keyboard, and mouse work in *Windows++*, as a program it's pretty useless. I promised you we'd have some fun, so let's use *Windows++* to build a tic-tac-toe game, a program someone might actually use.[36]

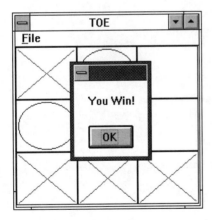

Here's a brief specification of the TOE program.

- TOE initially displays an empty tic-tac-toe board. The user moves first, selecting a square by clicking it with the mouse, whereupon TOE paints an "X" in the chosen square, then responds with its own move, painting an "O" in

---

36 Just in case anyone doesn't know what tic-tac-toe is, it's a two-player game played on a three-by-three grid of squares in which each player alternately puts his or her mark—usually an X or an O—in any free square. The goal is to mark three squares in a row, either horizontally, vertically, or diagonally. Getting three in a row is called "tic-tac-toe." English readers know this game as *naughts and crosses*.

some other square. The game proceeds this way until either the user or the program wins, or there are no more free squares (a draw).

■ As the user moves the mouse, the cursor changes shape depending on whether or not the square is free. If the square is free, the cursor resembles an X, indicating that the user may place an X in this square; otherwise the cursor is the normal Windows arrow.

■ Users may move the cursor using the arrow keys as well as the mouse, and press the space bar to put an X in a free square. Pressing an arrow key should move the cursor to the next square in the direction of the arrow pressed.

The above items describe the user interface. Here's the playing strategy:

■ The program first looks for a winning move (one that makes tic-tac-toe). This is called a *win* move.

■ If there's no winning move, TOE next looks to block the user from winning on the next move. This is called a *block* move.

■ If there's no win or block, TOE selects the best move from a history of previous games it has played during the current session. As games are played, TOE records each game and its outcome. To make its move, TOE considers all historical games that match the current position, and selects the best one (i.e., the one that wins or draws the most number of times).

It's fun to watch TOE gradually figure out how to play by learning from its past experience. Eventually, it always learns to draw against a perfect opponent. You can experiment with different "teaching" strategies: for example, you can fool it by letting it win when it makes a poor move, or encourage it by doing so when it makes a good one. TOE is not very sophisticated. It doesn't apply symmetry to recognize when a particular board configuration is a rotation or reflection of a previous one. Those who are so inclined can no doubt improve the program or even program it with a winning strategy.

To implement TOE, we'll create two window classes: *ToeBoard* and *Square*. *ToeBoard* is the main window and contains nine child *Square* windows. But wait a minute—what are child windows? We haven't discussed them yet!

5.3.1 Child Windows

Before implementing the tic-tac-toe game, we'll need a way to create *child windows*. Recall that in Windows you can make a particular window a *child* of another window by simply specifying a parent window handle (HWND) when you call *CreateWindow*. In this case, Windows interprets the menu handle (HMENU) passed to *CreateWindowEx* as an integer ID that identifies the child, rather than as a real menu handle (child windows can't have menus). I glossed over all this in the discussion of *createWin* (in Section 3.2.3), which simply passes *createArgs* to *CreateWindowEx:*

```
BOOL WPWin::createWin()
{
    .
    .
    HWND newhwnd = CreateWindowEx(createArgs.exstyle,
        /* ..more args.. */
        GetHwnd(createArgs.parent),     // parent window's HWND
        createArgs.hmenu,               // hmenu = child id
        /* etc.*/);
```

It should be obvious from the above code that all we have to do to create a child window is set *createArgs.parent* and *createArgs.hmenu*. Since any window can potentially be a child window, we should do it at the lowest possible level, namely, in *WPWin*. All we have to do is modify the constructor slightly:

```
class WPWin : public WPObj {
public:
    WPWin(CSTR classnm, WPWin *pwin=NULL, int id=0);
};

WPWin::WPWin(CSTR classnm, WPWin *pwin, int id)
{
    .
    . (same as before)
    .
    createArgs.parent = pwin;
    createArgs.hmenu = (HMENU)id;
    if (pwin)
        // parent specified: this is a child window
        createArgs.style = WS_CHILDWINDOW | WS_VISIBLE;
}
```

WPWin now takes two optional arguments: a pointer to the parent window and the child window ID (defaults: NULL and zero). For a normal window, *pwin* is NULL and *id* is zero, so *WPWin* works exactly as before. If, however, *pwin* and *id* are specified, the constructor sets *createArgs* appropriately and also, just to be friendly, sets the default window style to be a visible child window. (Remember, derived classes can always override the default *createArgs*.) To navigate the child windows, we'll implement a new class:

```
//////////////////////
// Class used to navigate the child windows of a window.
//
class WPChildWinList {
private:
    WPWin *pwin; // parent window;
    WPWin *cwin; // current child
    WPWin *nextWPWin(HWND hwnd);
public:
    WPChildWinList(WPWin *p)          { pwin=p; cwin=NULL; }
```

```
    WPWin * first();
    WPWin * next()
        { return cwin = nextWPWin(WPWin::GetHwnd(cwin)); }
};
//////////////////////
// Go to first child window.
//
WPWin * WPChildWinList::first()
{
    HWND hwnd = GetWindow((*pwin)(), GW_CHILD);
    cwin = WPWin::GetWin(hwnd);
    return cwin ? cwin : nextWPWin(hwnd);
}
//////////////////////
// Get next Windows++ sibling window.
// (Skip windows w/no WPWin object.)
//
WPWin * WPChildWinList::nextWPWin(HWND hwnd)
{
    while (hwnd) {
        hwnd = GetWindow(hwnd, GW_HWNDNEXT);
        if ((cwin = WPWin::GetWin(hwnd))!=NULL)
            return cwin;
    }
    return NULL;
}
```

The implementation is straightforward; this class uses the Windows API function *GetWindow* to get the child and sibling windows and skips over child windows that have no *WPWin* object attached to them (this can happen in dialogs, as we'll see in Chapter 7). Applications can use *WPChildWinList* to navigate the children of a window as follows:

```
MyWin::memberFn()
{
    WPChildWinList children = this;
    for (WPWin *child=children.first(); child; child=children.next())
        // do something
}
```

Classes like *WPChildWinList* are sometimes called *iterators* and are quite common in C++ class libraries. For example a *ListIterator* might be used to navigate the entries in a generic *List*. Many C++ libraries define various kinds of *set* or *collection* classes, such as *lists, bags, arrays, queues,* etc., with iterators to navigate them. The advantage of iterator objects is that they hide (encapsulate) the true implementation of the collection. If we later decide to keep our own list of child windows (say, for performance reasons), we need only modify *WPChildWinList* appropriately.

We can make navigation even easier by defining a macro:

```
#define forEachChildWin(pwin, cwin) \
    WPChildWinList _children = pwin; \
    for (WPWin *cwin=_children.first(); cwin; cwin=_children.next())
```

Now, *Windows++* programmers can write

```
MyWin::memberFn()
{
    forEachChildWin(this, child)
        child->doSomething();
}
```

Most C++ iterators provide *forEach* iterators as *member functions*, in which case you must pass an "enumerator" function to *forEach*. This approach is problematic, because the arguments to the enumerator function must be declared somehow; most enumerator functions simply use *void**, which is not type-safe (just like the Windows API function *EnumChildWindows* and other Windows *Enum* functions). I prefer the macro, because it lets me do anything to the iteratee, in a type-safe manner, and also because it more resembles the familiar C *for* and *while* statements.

[C] *A* forEachChild *macro could easily be written for C; there's nothing object-oriented about it. Just call* GetWindow *directly, without using* WPChildWinList.

Now we're ready to create child windows. The general formula goes like this:

```
// Hypothetical child window class
class ChildWin : public WPWin {
public:
    ChildWin(WPWin *pwin, int id) : WPWin("childwin", pwin, id) { }
};

// Hypothetical parent window class derived from WPMainWin
class ParentWin : public WPMainWin {
public:
    ParentWin();
}

// Initialize parent window: create parent and child.
ParentWin::ParentWin()
{
    createWin();                        // create parent win
    new ChildWin(this, MY_CHILD_ID);    // create child
}
```

Note that, as with the main window, there's no need to delete child windows, since Windows automatically destroys all child windows whenever a parent window is destroyed. Windows sends a WM_DESTROY message to each child window before actually destroying it, whereupon the child window object is deleted in the same fashion as the main application window (see Section 3.4.7).

The *WPWin* object provides a few "brainless" functions to deal with child windows. For example, *getChild* retrieves a child window from its ID:

```
class WPWin : public WPObj {
    WPWin *getChild(int id)
        { return id>0 ? GetWin(GetDlgItem(hwnd, id)) : NULL; }
};
```

Note that *getChild* always returns NULL if the child ID is negative. This is a *Windows++* convention adopted primarily because –1 is usually used as the ID for dialog controls that are never accessed (for example, static text and icons). The moral is, don't use negative IDs for child windows that you need to retrieve by ID.

5.3.2 TOE Squares

Now that we can create child windows, we're ready to build TOE. We'll implement each square of the TOE board as a child window, *Square*, of the the main window, *ToeBoard*. Each *Square* stores its own state (X, O, or free), paints itself, and handles mouse events. When the user clicks on a *Square*, it either beeps if the square is taken or notifies its parent window, *ToeBoard*. Here's the definition for *Square*, from TOE.CPP:

```
const SQM_CHECKED = 1;          // message sent to parent

enum SQSTATE {
    SQFREE= 1,                  // square is free
    SQOOO = 3,                  // square is O
    SQXXX = 5,                  // square is X
};

//////////////////
// Window class for a board square
//
class Square : public WPWin {
    SQSTATE state;                    // state of square: free, X or O
public:
    Square(WPWin *pwin, int id);

    BOOL paint();
    BOOL mouse(int msg, WPPoint p, WORD flags);

    SQSTATE operator()()            { return state; }
    void set(SQSTATE newstate);
};
```

I'll describe each function, one by one. The *paint* function is straightforward. It paints either an X, O or nothing, depending on the *state* of the square:

```
BOOL Square::paint()
{
    WPPaintStruct ps = this;    // get paint strcuture
    WPClientRect box = this;    // get client area rectangle
    box -=2;                    // ..shrink 2 pixels
    switch (state) {
    case SQOOO:
        ps.setPen(COLOR_BLUE);  // (see Chapter 8)
        ps.ellipse(box);        // draw circle
        break;
```

```
    case SQXXX:
        ps.setPen(COLOR_RED);        // (see Chapter 8)
        // draw "X"
        ps.line( box.origin(),      box.endpt() );
        ps.line( box.topRight(),    box.bottomLeft() );
        break;
    }
    return TRUE;
}
```

Note how easy it is to shrink the client area rectangle by two pixels using -=. This improves the appearance of the X's and O's by drawing them fully inside the square, rather than letting them touch its borders.

The *mouse* function is equally simple:

```
BOOL Square::mouse(int msg, WPPoint p, WORD flags)
{
    switch (msg) {
    case WM_LBUTTONDOWN:
        if (state!=SQFREE)
            MsgBeep();                    // square is taken: beep
        else
            notifyParent(SQM_CHECKED); // tell main window
        break;
    case WM_MOUSEMOVE:
        Cursor = state==SQFREE ? "XCURSOR" : IDC_ARROW;
        break;
    }
    return TRUE;
}
```

If the user clicks the mouse in a square that already has an X or O in it, the square beeps; otherwise it sends a child window message (SQM_CHECKED) to the parent (main) window, *ToeBoard*, by calling *notifyParent*:

```
class WPWin {
public:
    void notifyParent(int msg)          // send WM_COMMAND msg to parent
        { if (getParent())
            getParent()->sendMsg(WM_COMMAND,
                getID(), MAKELONG(hwnd, msg)); }
};
```

This function simply sends the appropriately coded WM_COMMAND message to the parent window. *Square* uses the same mechanism that built-in control windows such as *button* and *listbox* use to communicate with their parents. For example, button windows send a BN_CLICKED notification when the user clicks the mouse on the button. *Square* does practically the same thing (in fact, *Square* could have been modeled as an owner-draw button).

We'll see what *ToeBoard* does with this message in a moment. For now, let's finish *Square*. The only other thing that *mouse* does is set the cursor whenever the mouse is moved. If the square is free, the cursor is set to "XCURSOR" (the same one used in MKC); otherwise the normal Windows arrow cursor (IDC_ARROW) is used. The *Square* constructor sets the window class cursor to NULL, which is the officially documented correct Windows incantation to utter whenever your program sets the cursor manually with every mouse movement.

```
Square::Square(WPWin *pwin, int id) : WPWin("square", pwin, id)
{
    state = SQFREE;                      // square is free to start
    createArgs.wndcls.hCursor = NULL;    // we'll set cursor manually
    createArgs.style |= WS_BORDER;       // draw a border around it
    createWin();                         // create the window
}
```

The constructor also initializes the base class *WPWin* instance with the class name "square" and the parent window and child window ID passed to it. The last thing the constructor does before actually creating the window is give it a border. Note that *Square* leaves most *createArgs* as they are, since the built-in *Windows++* defaults inherited from *WPWin* are acceptable. For example, the default child window style is WS_CHILD | WS_VISIBLE. To preserve these defaults, *Square* ORs the style with WS_BORDER, rather than setting it directly.

The only *Square* functions left is *set*, which changes the square's *state*:

```
void Square::set(SQSTATE newstate)
{
    state = newstate;
    invalidate(TRUE);
    Cursor = state==SQFREE ? "XCURSOR" : IDC_ARROW;
}
```

Square::set invalidates the client area (with the *erase* flag set), so the square will get repainted, then changes the cursor to the appropriate shape.

5.3.3 *ToeBoard*

The main application window is represented by the class *ToeBoard*. This class is quite a bit more complicated than *Square*, but most of the code implements the playing strategy as outlined above. This is exactly as it should be. The main programming effort should always be implementing the application itself, not programming Windows; however, since the main subject of the book is *Windows++*, I'll focus primarily on the Windows-related part and merely highlight the TOE-specific details. TOE enthusiasts can figure out how TOE works by reading the source (it's not really that complicated), while those who couldn't care less will be spared this misery.

First, TOE defines a few basic structures and symbols primarily used to maintain the game history:

```
///////////////
// This structure is used to save the result of a game.
//
struct GAME {
    char moves[9];              // the game
    int nmoves;                 // number of moves
    int result;                 // whether I won, lost or drew
};
const NHISTORY = 50;            // save this many games
const NSQUARES = 9;             // nine squares in board
enum RESULT { LOSE=-1, DRAW=0, WIN=2 };
```

A game is represented as a sequence of up to nine integers. The n*th* integer is the number of the square that was filled on the n*th* move, the squares being numbered as shown at the right. The *ToeBoard* class definition is given below.

0	1	2
3	4	5
6	7	8

```
///////////////////
// This is the main tic-tac-toe window.
//
class ToeBoard : public WPMainWin {
    Square *squares[NSQUARES];  // the board = 9 child squares
    GAME history[NHISTORY];     // history of past games
    int histLen;                // number of games played
    int curGame;                // current game number
    int curMove;                // current nove number
    int win,block;              // hint: move to win or block

    // these are all special toe functions
    SQSTATE operator[](int x)       { return (*squares[x%NSQUARES])(); }
    BOOL tictactoe();                   // test if tic-tac-toe
    BOOL tictactoe(int i,int j,int k);  // ditto
    BOOL computeValue(int move);        // compute value of move
    void newGame(int result);           // start a new game
    int computeMove();                  // figure out next move
    void think();                       // pretend to "think"
    void setSquare(int move, SQSTATE which);

    // Here are the virtual message functions
    void sized(WPRect &box, WORD how);  // re-size window
    void command(int id, int msg);      // handle child message
    void kbd(WPEvent& event);
public:
    ToeBoard();
};
```

Most of the data and function members implement tic-tac-toe strategy. The only functions that are Windows-related are *sized, command, kbd,* and the constructor:

```
///////////////////
// Create tic-tac-toe board
//
ToeBoard::ToeBoard()
{
    // compute default size of toe board from screen size
```

```
int cx = GetSystemMetrics(SM_CXSCREEN);
int cy = GetSystemMetrics(SM_CYSCREEN);
int side = min(cx,cy)/2;
createArgs.pos.origin((cx-side)/2, (cy-side)/2);
createArgs.pos.extent(side, side);
createWin();                       // create window
histLen = curGame = 0;             // no games played yet

// create child window for each square
for (int i=0; i<NSQUARES; i++)
    squares[i] = new Square(this, i);
}
```

Before creating the main *ToeBoard* window, the constructor first computes the desired screen dimensions in *createArgs.pos*. These dimensions are calculated to yield a square whose side is half the shortest screen dimension. After creating itself, *ToeBoard* next creates nine child *Square*s, storing them in the pointer array *squares*. Each square is assigned its board number as its child ID.

5.3.4 A Trick with Constructors and Destructors

How do our tic-tac-toe *Square*s get positioned? Whenever a new window is created, Windows sends a flurry of messages to it, one of which is WM_SIZE, which signals that the size of the window has changed. This message is passed by *WPWin* to the virtual *sized* function, as described in Section 3.5.4. To process WM_SIZE, all *ToeBoard* has to do is implement *sized*.

We could use *WPWin::move* to position the squares, but just for fun, we'll use a new Windows feature to do it. Windows 3.0 provides three functions that let you change the sizes and positions of several Windows, deferring the screen update until all the windows have been positioned:

```
BeginDeferWindowPos             // start deferred positioning
DeferWindowPos                  // move one window
EndDeferWindowPos               // end deferred positioning
```

They work like this: first, you call *BeginDeferWindowPos;* then you call *DeferWindowPos* repeatedly for each window you want to move; finally, you call *EndDeferWindowPos* to update the display. In C, it goes something like this:

```
HANDE posInfo = BeginDeferWindowPos(9);
for (int i=0; i<9; i++) {
    posInfo =
        DeferWindowPos(posInfo,hwnd[i],NULL,x[i],y[i],w[i],h[i],0);
}
EndDeferWindowPos(posInfo);
```

Throughout the operation, Windows uses a handle (*posInfo* in the example) to keep track of the deferred positions. This handle points to a data structure which, because it can be reallocated without warning, must be reassigned after each call to *DeferWindowPos*.

How should we model this in *Windows++?* The obvious way to do it is using our standard "brainless" translation formula (described in Section 3.2.6), with three *WPWin* member functions corresponding to the three Windows functions. This would certainly work, but, lest you infer that *Windows++* could have been implemented by chimpanzees at typewriters, let me show you how to do it more elegantly with a new class:

```
class WPDeferWinPos : public WPObj {
    HANDLE posInfo;
public:
    WPDeferWinPos(int nWins=10)
        { posInfo = BeginDeferWindowPos(nWins); }
    ~WPDeferWinPos()
        { EndDeferWindowPos(posInfo); }

    void move(WPWin* win, WPRect& pos,
        WORD flags=SWP_NOZORDER|SWP_NOREDRAW, WPWin *after=NULL)
        { posInfo = DeferWindowPos(posInfo, win->getHwnd(),
                after ? after->getHwnd() : NULL,
                pos.left(),pos.top(),pos.width(),pos.height(),flags); }
};
```

The constructor takes the initial number of windows (default = 10) and calls *Begin-DeferWindowPos,* setting the private data member *posInfo* to the handle returned. The destructor calls *EndDeferWindowPos* with this same handle. The public member function *move* calls *DeferWindowPos,* updating *posInfo* with the handle returned by Windows.

Now, to position several windows in *Windows++,* we can write

```
WPDeferWinPos deferPos = 9;
for (int i=0; i<9; i++)
    deferPos.move(wpwin1, pos[i]);
```

Notice that there's no need to explicitly call *EndDeferWindowPos,* since the compiler automatically invokes *~WPDeferWinPos* (which calls *EndDeferWindowPos*) when the automatic variable *deferPos* goes out of scope. Thus the initialization, termination, and handling of *posInfo* are completely hidden (but automatically performed) by *WPDeferWinPos.* All the application has to do is create an object instance and move the windows.

This technique is quite general and can be used whenever the Windows API (or any other system) calls for a calling sequence of the form

```
PrologFunction(initArgs);
DoSomething(args);
EpilogFunction();
```

This calling sequence is encapsulated by implementing a C++ class:

```
class foo {
public:
    foo(initArgs)                  { PrologFunction(initArgs); }
    ~foo()                         { EpilogFunction(); }
    doSomething(args)              { DoSomething(args); }
};
```

If intermediate results like *posInfo* must be maintained throughout the operation, they can be stored (and hidden) as private data members. (We used this trick once before, in *WPWaitCursor.*)

The technique exploits the fact that C++ automatically calls the appropriate constructor when an automatic variable is instantiated, and the destructor when it goes out of scope. This lets us encapsulate the prolog-epilog calling sequence, so we never have to remember it again. We're using C++ to ensure that the appropriate functions are called in the correct order (assuming that we've implemented the class correctly, which we only have to do *once*).

Windows is full of calling sequences that must be performed in a specific order. For example, in the GDI, display objects must first be deselected, then deleted after they're used. As we build *Windows++*, we should be on the lookout for such calling sequences. If some group of two or three functions are always called in the same order in a certain way, we should encapsulate the sequence in a new object or function. Our goal is to make programming as foolproof as possible. If we can use C++ to prevent ourselves from accidentally committing an error, we should do so.

We can now write our *sized* function for *Square:*

```
///////////////////
// Resize all the squares to fit the window.
//
void ToeBoard::sized(WPRect &pos WORD how)
{
    pos /= 3;                          // shrink by 1/3
    WPPoint moveRight(pos.width());    // moves rectangle right 1 square
    WPPoint moveDown(0,pos.height()); // moves rect down 1 square

    // Now reposition each square (child window)
    int s = 0;
    WPDeferWinPos defer = NSQUARES;
    for (int i=0; i<3; i++) {
        WPRect box = pos;              // position of 1st square in row
        for (int j=0; j<3; j++) {
            defer.move(squares[s++],box); // move the window
            box += moveRight;          // move box right one
        }
        pos += moveDown;               // move down one row
    }
}
```

The implementation of *sized* is an exercise in point and rectangle arithmetic—but see how easy it is using the operators we defined back in Chapter 2! For example, we "divide" the main window client area by three to compute the size of each square and "add" a point to the rectangle to translate it to the right or down. The *sized* function uses the deferred window positioning mechanism described in the preceding section to actually position the squares.

5.3.5 Keyboard Events

The next Windows-related *ToeBoard* function is the keyboard handler, *kbd*.

```
void ToeBoard::kbd(WPEvent& event)
{
    Square *sq;

    switch (event.getMsg()) {
    case WM_CHAR:
        if (event.key() == ' ' || event.key() == '\r') {
            sq = (Square*)WinFromPoint(Cursor());
            assert(sq);
            sq->mouse(WM_LBUTTONDOWN, Cursor(), 0);
        }
        return;

    case WM_KEYDOWN:
        if (Keyboard.isArrowKey(event.key())) {

            // Got arrow key: move cursor
            sq = (Square*)WinFromPoint(Cursor());
            assert(sq);
            WPRect winRect = sq;

            int id = sq->getID();
            switch (event.key()) {
            case VK_LEFT:           id--;   break;
            case VK_RIGHT:          id++;   break;
            case VK_UP:             id-=3;  break;
            case VK_DOWN:           id+=3;  break;
            }
            id = (id+NSQUARES) % NSQUARES;// new square

            winRect = squares[id];          // new square's rectangle
            winRect /= 2;                    // ..halve it
            Cursor = winRect.endpt();        // curs --> center of square
            return;
        }
        break;
    }
    WPMainWin::kbd(event);
}
```

This is fairly straightforward. The first half responds when the user presses the space bar or ENTER key; *kbd* gets the square that contains the cursor and sends a WM_LBUTTONDOWN message directly to it, through the virtual message function *mouse*, simulating a mouse click. The second half of *kbd* handles the arrow keys in much the same fashion as MKC, the main difference being that, instead of moving one or several pixels, the unit of motion is one board square. This is accomplished using arithmetic modulo nine and the observation that adding or subtracting three from the square number yields the square above or below. Once again, overloaded rectangle operators make the calculations a snap.

5.3.6 Handling Child Messages

The last Windows-related *ToeBoard* function is *command*. It handles notifications from child windows, as well as menu commands (it's the virtual function equivalent of WM_COMMAND). Thus *command* is called when the child *Squares* send SQM_CHECKED, which happens when the user makes his or her move by clicking the mouse on a free square. *ToeBoard* processes the message as follows:

```
///////////////////
// Process message from child square.
//
void ToeBoard::command(int id, int msg)
{
    if (id >= NSQUARES)
        return WPMainWin::command(id, msg);  // (must be menu command)

    // Must be child message
    switch (msg) {
    case SQM_CHECKED:
        setSquare(id, SQXXX);                // put X where user clicked
        if (tictactoe())                     // user got three in a row?
            newGame(LOSE);                   // too bad, I lose
        else {
            int mymove = computeMove();      // figure out my move
            if (mymove >= 0) {               // got a move:
                think();                     // pretend to think
                setSquare(mymove, SQOOO);    // put O in my square
                if (tictactoe())             // three in a row?
                    newGame(WIN);            // hooray, I win!
            } else
                newGame(DRAW);               // no possible move: draw
        }
        break;
    }
    return TRUE;
}
```

If the message is from one of the child squares, *command* responds by calling *setSquare*, which stores the move in the history buffer and changes the square; otherwise, the command is passed to *WPMainWin*. The rest of *command* is a lot of TOE-related strategy that I won't describe in detail, except the function *think*, which uses the wait cursor described earlier in this chapter:

```
///////////////////
// Simulate thinking by waiting 2 seconds.
//
void ToeBoard::think()
{
```

```
WPWaitCursor wait = this;          // change cursor to wait icon
    time_t t;
    t = time(NULL)+2;
    while (time(NULL) < t)
        ;
}
```

When *wait* is initialized (by calling its constructor), the cursor is changed to an hourglass. Next, the *while* loop makes the program do nothing for two seconds in order to create the illusion that it's "thinking" about its next move and thus to temporally differentiate the user's move from the computer's response (it would be simpler to call the C runtime library function *sleep*, but while Zortech allows this in Windows, Borland does not). As control passes out of *think*, C++ automatically calls the destructor for *wait*, which restores the cursor to its original shape.

The rest of TOE is in Appendix A. As I said, I won't describe it, since it's not strictly related to *Windows++*.

5.4 Summary

In this chapter, we built on the infrastructure established in earlier chapters and wrote two sample programs: MKC and TOE. In particular,

- We modeled the mouse, keyboard, and cursor as global objects, and used "brainless" functions and operator overloading to package them in a way that makes programming easier and more natural.

- We saw how several virtual message functions work in action: *mouse*, *kbd*, *activated*, *sized*, and *command*.

- We used C++ classes to encapsulate standard Windows calling sequences in constructors and destructors. For example, *WPWaitCursor* encapsulates the calls to set up an hourglass cursor, while *WPDeferWinPos* encapsulates the calls to do deferred window positioning.

- We saw a few more GDI functions, *textOut* and *printF*, and how to display tabbed text.

- We implemented logic in MKC to detect when there's no mouse, and, if so, use the arrow keys to move the cursor. We then moved the code into *WPMainWin* so all applications can inherit it.

The last item is of special interest. By moving the arrow key logic to *WPMainWin*, we have essentially taken a generic user interface feature (use arrow keys when there's no mouse) and encapsulated it in our library, where all applications inherit it without doing anything. You might wonder whether we can do the same for other user interface behavior.

We can. In the next chapter, I'll show you how.

CHAPTER ■ 6

User Interface

In this chapter we'll address yet another frequent source of headaches for Windows programmers: the interface. Have you ever had fits trying to gray your menus properly or getting the File Open dialog to work? Or figuring out which window handles which messages in an MDI (Multiple Document Interface) application? Yes? Then read on. If not, read on anyway—it's amusing.

In this chapter, we'll incorporate some useful and generic user interface behavior into our growing *Windows++* library. As our "guiding application,"we'll build a simple text editor (WINEDIT) that's similar to Windows' own Notepad program, the POPPAD program in [Petzold 1990] and EDITFILE (one of the sample programs that comes with the Windows SDK). While WINEDIT is admittedly somewhat dull and predictable (practically every Windows programming book does "the editor"), it serves to illustrate a number of user interface issues that frequently boggle Windows programmers (but not us!).

WINEDIT also illustrates the practical benefits of reusability. While it's similar in behavior to its C siblings POPPAD and EDITFILE, WINEDIT is over four times smaller than POPPAD, and *ten times* smaller than EDITFILE—and WINEDIT has more functionality to boot!

After we're done with WINEDIT, we'll transform it into an MDI application (MEDIT) similar to the SDK MULTIPAD program. We'll encapsulate all the generic MDI behavior in *Windows++*, so that MEDIT itself becomes almost trivial.

Sounds pretty good, no?

And, as always, the benefits accrue not only to WINEDIT and MEDIT, but to *all* applications. By the end of the chapter, we'll have implemented an object-oriented GUI framework (OO-ey GUI?) that encapsulates a good deal of generic, CUA-compliant, UI behavior into reusable *Windows++* objects.

Huh? What's CUA?

6.1 The Windows GUI

6.1.1 CUA: GUI Guidelines Galore

Along with every graphical user interface (GUI) comes a complete set of vendor-approved guidelines on how to be a good UI-citizen. While vendors vary in their degree of GUI-religiosity (Apple has been the most flagrantly evangelical), every GUI has its own "correct" way of doing things. For Windows (and OS/2), the rules are spelled out in IBM's *Common User Access (CUA) Advanced Interface Design Guide* [IBM 1989], which comes with the Windows SDK. The CUA manual covers practically every aspect of a program's user interface, from the correct name and placement of menu items to which accelerator to use, and from audible feedback and mouse buttons to work space layout, foreign language translation, and multiple document applications. It's all spelled out in excruciating detail. While the CUA guide is a bit out of date, most of the material in it still applies to today's programs, so, like it or not, you should be familiar with CUA, or at least be aware that it exists, so you can consult it when necessary and knowingly ignore it when not.[37]

The main justification for user interface conventions is that they make it easier for users to learn new programs, the central idea being that if you know one program, you know 'em all. While this philosophy doesn't always hold (more complex applications necessarily have more complex user interfaces), it is nevertheless desirable that whenever programs do the same thing, they do them in the same way. Thus in Windows the "File Open" command should always be used to open a file (rather than Open File or File Load or GetThat DarnedFile). Similarly, the standard CUA command to transfer a selected thing to the clipboard is Edit Cut.

Unfortunately for us programmers, what's easy for users has (until now) been our nightmare—while software developers are encouraged to follow GUI guidelines, vendors do little to help. Microsoft's strategy is to dump the CUA manual in your lap. ("Here, Fred, read this!") You might think that CUA behavior ought to be somehow embedded in Windows itself, so your programs get it automatically, without having to do anything. But no! You have to implement the entire user interface all by your lonesome self. Moreover, if you follow the traditional Windows Way (the copy-paste-edit school of "reusability"), you have to do it over and over again for every program you write.

You know where this is leading, don't you?

In the next couple of sections, we'll *Windows++*-ify two of the most generic CUA commands: File and Edit. By the time we're done, just using *Windows++* will guarantee that these commands are CUA-compliant! (Sounds like getting FDA

---

37 Microsoft is expected to release its own updated guidelines soon, making CUA old hat. This is no doubt part of the ongoing Microsoft/IBM war.

approval or something.) While File and Edit represent just a small portion of a typical program's overall user interface, we'll develop a general notion of an "abstract windows app" that can be extended using the same techniques to build a complete CUA-compliant GUI-in-a-box. Later on in the chapter we'll apply the same techniques to tackle the dreaded MDI.

To see just what it is I'm talking about, let's look at the specification for WINEDIT. Pretend that your boss, teacher, mentor, or other scary super-ego figure has just handed this down from above, with a yellow Post-It note attached: "I need this ASAP!!" (in thick red ink):

6.1.2 Specification of WINEDIT

WINEDIT is a simple text editor, similar to Windows' NOTEPAD, that lets users edit ASCII files. The main window displays the contents of the file, which can be edited by simply typing into the window and/or by using any of the special editing keys BACKSPACE, DELETE, INSERT, HOME, END, and so on.

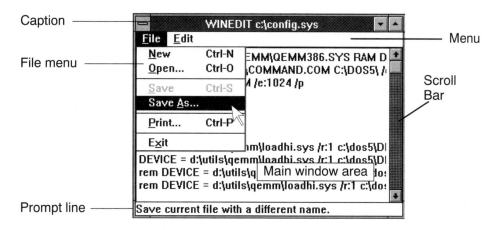

WINEDIT provides two menu commands, File and Edit, which work as follows:

- The File menu contains commands to create a New file, Open an existing one, Save the current file (or Save As another name), Print the file, and Exit the program. Open and Save As display a dialog box from which the user may select or enter the name of the desired file; likewise, Print displays the usual dialog to set various print properties, including which printer to use.

- The Edit menu contains commands to Cut, Copy, and Delete selected (highlighted) text, and a Paste command to insert the contents of the clipboard at the current cursor location. Delete is like Cut, but doesn't transfer the deleted material to the clipboard.

- WINEDIT displays a prompt line along the bottom of its main window. This line displays a one-sentence description of each menu item as the user highlights it.

Not all of these commands are available at all times. If a command is not allowed, it's disabled by graying its name in the menu:

- If no file is open (perhaps the user just invoked File New), File Save, Save As, and Print are grayed.

- If the current file has not been modified, File Save is grayed.

- If no text is selected, Edit Cut, Copy, and Delete are grayed.

- Edit Paste is grayed if there's nothing in the clipboard to Paste.

WINEDIT also provides the following additional features:

- A file name may be specified on the command line, when the program is invoked, like so:

```
WINEDIT myfile.txt
```

- If the user attempts to Exit the program, Open another file, or create a New one when the current file has been modified, but not saved, the program should prompt him or her to save the file before continuing.

- At all times, the name of the current file is displayed as the window caption, preceded by the word WINEDIT.

In short, WINEDIT is your typical well-behaved (CUA-compliant) Windows program, one that exhibits the normal user-friendliness you'd expect.

That's how WINEDIT works. Now let's think about how we're going to implement it. (You might simply rename NOTEPAD.EXE to WINEDIT.EXE and hand it to your boss, but that would be cheating! Besides, you could be sued.) In the following pages, we'll implement WINEDIT as specified; however, in so doing, I'll rely on two *Windows++* features that aren't fully explained until the next chapter:

- the control classes *WPMultiEdit* and *WPStatic*, which represent multi-line edit controls and static text controls; and

- the *Windows++* built-in dialogs for File Open, Save As, and Print.

We'll use *WPMultiEdit* for the main window, and *WPStatic* for the prompt line; and we obviously need the dialogs to make the File commands work properly. At this point you don't have to understand *how WPMultiEdit* and the file dialogs work, only *that* they work. In this chapter, I will simply *use* them, with a brief explanation of what they do, and ask that you suspend your disbelief until Chapter 7 (which you now have an added incentive to read). If this bothers you terribly, feel free to jump ahead—or look at it this way: we're engaging in top-down design. If *WPMultiEdit* and *WPstatic* didn't exist, we'd invent them now.

6.1.3 Brainstorming WINEDIT

How are we going to implement WINEDIT?

Let's start with the main window. We'll use the aforementioned-but-not-yet-fully-explained *WPMultiEdit* control class to create a multi-line edit control that occupies the entire main window. We'll have to write a *sized* function to keep it that way when the user resizes the main window. We've already seen how *sized* works (in the TOE program), so this part will be easy. Obviously, we'll also have to write some code to load and save the contents of the edit control from or to a disk file, but that too seems straightforward: all we have to do is pull out the Windows manual to see what the proper file i/o calls are.

The only other thing in WINEDIT that we haven't dealt with before is the menu. It's a simple matter to make the menu commands appear; all we have to do is add them to the resource file:

```
// (In WINEDIT.RC)
AppMenu MENU {
    POPUP "&File" {
        MENUITEM "&New\tCtrl-N",        WPIDM_FILENEW
        MENUITEM "&Open...\tCtrl-O",    WPIDM_FILEOPEN
        MENUITEM SEPARATOR
        MENUITEM "&Save\tCtrl-S",       WPIDM_FILESAVE
          .
          .
          .
    }
    POPUP "&Edit" {
          .
          .
          .
}
```

But there's more to File and Edit than just adding resource statements! We have to write a *command* function to actually handle (perform) the commands. Confirmations must be obtained, dialogs must be run—and what about graying and ungraying the menu items? Here's a to-do list for the File command:

■ We have to prompt the user to save the current file before Exiting the program or opening or creating a new file, if it's been modified but not saved. We'll have to maintain the current file's *modified* status.

■ We have to run the appropriate dialogs for File Open and File Save. Fortunately, we can use the file dialogs from the next chapter.

■ We have to disable (gray) Save, Save As and Print when there's no current file, and Save when the current file isn't modified. To gray the menus, we'll have to handle WM_INITMENU messages, which we haven't done before.

■ Finally, we have to worry about the prompt line. We'll need to handle WM_MENUSELECT, which is also something new.

These chores are hardly rocket science, but they're the UI bread and butter of Windows applications.

And generic!

If you look at the list carefully, you'll see that there's nothing in it that has anything in particular to do with WINEDIT. Every Windows program that uses files exhibits the same behavior (or should). Since it's generic, we should try to encapsulate this stuff in low-level library objects.

We've already built some UI behavior into *Windows++*: in Chapter 5 we added code to move the cursor with arrow keys when there's no mouse (CUA-approved), and in Section 3.5.4 we added code to *WPMainWin::command* that handles the Exit command, so that simply adding Exit to a program's resource file suffices to make Exit actually work.

Why not try to do the same thing with the File commands? Obviously, they're more complicated than Exit, but let's ask a radical question: why *shouldn't* just adding the File commands to the resource file be sufficient to make them actually work? Or, to put it another way, what prevents us from implementing File Open and so forth entirely in *WPMainWin*, just like Exit?

The only thing that differs from one application to another is what actually happens when one of these commands is invoked. For example, when the user issues File Open, WINEDIT opens the selected file and loads its contents into a multi-line edit control. Another program (a database, say) might do something else totally different. But the grueling UI mechanics of graying menu items, running dialogs, obtaining overwrite confirmation, and so on are the same for all applications.

Furthermore, application programmers shouldn't have to bother with that stuff. As far as they're concerned, it's just a lot of boring UI minutiae. What application programmers really want is to somehow tell the system (*Windows++*), "my program uses files, so do all that File menu garbage and just let me know when I have to open or save the darned file!"

6.1.4 Abstract Windows Apps

To satisfy our demanding application programmers (we try to please), we must somehow separate the application-generic aspects of File (menu graying, confirmation, dialogs) from the application-specific stuff. This is the very essence of object-oriented programming. (Actually, it's the essence of *good* programming; the OOP bandwagon has merely elevated the practice to the status of a guiding principle.)

But how can we do it?

Hint: think virtual.

I hope by now that I've drummed the following lesson into your head: whenever different kinds of things (programs, windows, applications, objects) perform the same action (operation, event, message, function) in different ways, the action can be expressed as a virtual function. In this case, the thing is the program's main window, and the action is a particular menu command, such as File Open. So we should make *fileOpen* a virtual function:

```
class WPMainWin : public WPWin {
public:
    virtual BOOL fileOpen(CSTR fname) { return FALSE; }
};
```

The boolean return value is intended to signify whether the command was performed successfully. By making *fileOpen* virtual, we can put all the low-level, generic File Open UI stuff in *WPMainWin,*

```
// In Windows++ (WPMAIN.CPP)
BOOL WPMainWin::command(int id, WORD msg)
{
    switch (id)
    case WPIDM_FILEOPEN:
        .
        . Do save confirmation, run dialog to obtain file name, etc.
        .
        fileOpen(filename);          // << call virtual fn to really do it!
        return TRUE;
    .
    .
    .
}
```

while letting the *application* actually *do* the command. Since *fileOpen* is virtual, *WPMainWin* invokes the *fileOpen* for whatever class of window the main window really is. For example, *EditWin::fileOpen* becomes

```
// (In WINEDIT.CPP)
BOOL EditWin:fileOpen(CSTR fname)
{
    .
    . Open file, read contents and copy to edit control.
    .
    return TRUE;
}
```

We can introduce similar functions for all the other commands:

```
class WPMainWin : public WPWin {
public:
    // Virtual functions to perform File commands.
    virtual BOOL fileSave(CSTR fname)    { return FALSE; }
    virtual BOOL fileOpen(CSTR fname)    { return FALSE; }
    virtual BOOL fileNew()               { return FALSE; }
```

```
// Virtual functions to perform Edit commands.
virtual BOOL editCut()                { return FALSE; }
virtual BOOL editCopy()               { return FALSE; }
virtual BOOL editPaste()              { return FALSE; }
virtual BOOL editDelete()             { return FALSE; }
virtual BOOL editUndo()               { return FALSE; }
};
```

What we're essentially doing here is defining an abstract windows application. By declaring these functions for *WPMainWin*, we're saying, "a main window is a window that 'knows' how to open, save, and 'new' a file, and how to edit, cut, copy, paste, and delete things." The implementations in *WPMainWin* are trivial, since specific main window classes that support File and Edit are expected to provide the "real" implementations. Each such class will in general implement these functions differently, but every main window has them.

C   *In C, you could store (pointers to) these functions in a table similar to the one used for handling WM_ messages. The table could be indexed by the menu ID, normalized to some starting base value. Or you could implement them as new window messages: WM_FILE_NEW, etc.*

Another way to think of these functions is as "virtual command functions," similar to the virtual message functions *paint* and so forth. introduced in Section 3.5.4. In fact, all we've really done is broken the command event into a finer granularity (for main windows). Instead of a shotgun blast (WM_COMMAND), now each File and Edit command has its own virtual function. We think of *fileOpen* as the function that handles the "File Open" event.

Command Event Flow

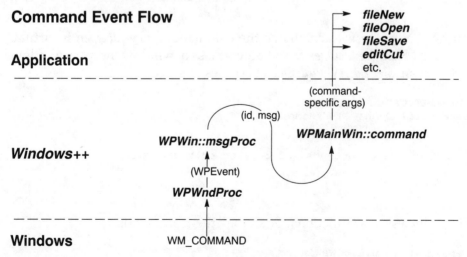

In the same way that *WPMainWin* does some set-up before invoking the virtual *paint* function, we can make it run the appropriate confirmations and dialogs before invoking *fileOpen*. We can make *WPMainWin* handle other low-level UI events as well—for example, menu graying.

In general, we want *Windows++* (e.g., *WPMainWin*) do as much of the user interface grunt work as possible, so application programmers are free to focus on their
applications, not the tedious and error-prone Windows mechanics of graying menus, creating dialogs, and so on. To implement a program that has a File Open
command, all an application programmer should have to do is

- ■ add the command to the resource file and

- ■ write a *fileOpen* function to actually open the file.

In the following pages, we'll flesh these ideas out into working code. But, as usual,
we first need to build a little more infrastructure (not much, I promise).

6.2 Menu Basics

Since we're obviously going to be working with menus, we have to bring them
into the *Windows++* fold. This means implementing a menu class, so we can manipulate menus as C++ objects instead of through Windows handles (HMENUs).
Instead of writing

```
WPWin *mywin;
 .
 .
HMENU hmenu = GetMenu(mywin->getHwnd());
EnableMenuItem(hmenu, IDM_FILESAVE, MF_DISABLED);
```

we'd like to write

```
WPWin *mywin;
 .
 .
WPMenu menu = mywin;
menu.enableItem(IDM_FILESAVE, FALSE);
```

Besides being more OOP-ish, this eliminates the need to remember (or even know)
all the MF_ flags defined in WINDOWS.H.

6.2.1 *WPMenu*

To model menus in *Windows++*, all we have to do is invent a new class that's essentially just a menu handle, then add "brainless" functions as described in Section
3.2.6. This process should be so familiar by now that you could do it in your sleep.

```
/////////////////
// Class to represent a menu. (In WPMENU.H)
//
class WPMenu {
protected:
    HMENU hmenu;
```

```
public:
    WPMenu(HMENU h)                     { hmenu=h; }
    WPMenu(WPWin *win);                 { hmenu = GetMenu(win->getHwnd()); }

    void destroy()                      { DestroyMenu(hmenu); }
    HMENU operator()()                  { return hmenu; }
    WPMenu& operator=(HMENU h)          { hmenu=h; return *this; }

    int count()                         { return GetMenuItemCount(hmenu); }
    int itemID(int pos)                 { return GetMenuItemID(hmenu, pos); }
    BOOL checkItem(int id, BOOL chk, WORD how=MF_BYCOMMAND)
        { return CheckMenuItem(hmenu, id,
            chk ? (how|MF_CHECKED) : (how|MF_UNCHECKED)); }
    BOOL enableItem(int id, BOOL enab, WORD how=MF_BYCOMMAND)
        { return EnableMenuItem(hmenu, id,
            enab ? (how|MF_ENABLED) : (how|MF_GRAYED)); }
    BOOL append(int id, CSTR text, WORD flags=0)
        { return AppendMenu(hmenu, MF_STRING|flags, id, (LPSTR)text); }
    BOOL appendSep()
        { return AppendMenu(hmenu, MF_SEPARATOR, 0, NULL); }
    .
    . etc.
};
```

The complete definition is a bit longer, but it's just more of the same, so I've omitted it here (see Appendix A), and will simply list the highlights:

- One constructor initializes a menu object directly from a menu handle (HMENU); another initializes it from a window (by invoking the Windows API function *GetMenu*).

- Many functions (*checkItem, enableItem*, etc.) have an argument that specifies whether the menu item is referenced by command ID (the default) or by the item's relative position within the menu (for this, you have to specify MF_BYPOSITION, just like in C).

```
menu.enableItem(ID_FOO,FALSE);          // disable "foo" command
menu.enableItem(0, TRUE, MF_BYPOSITION);// enable 1st menu item
```

- A subclass is defined for submenus:

```
class WPSubMenu : public WPMenu {
public:
    WPSubMenu(WPMenu& menu, int pos)
        : WPMenu(GetSubMenu(menu(), pos)) { }
};
```

The following code fragment shows how to enable a submenu item:

```
WPMenu menu = mywin;                // get window's menu
WPSubMenu submenu(menu, 0);        // get submenu for 1st item
submenu.enableItem(ID_FOO, TRUE); // enable submenu item "Foo"..
```

- Another subclass represents the system menu—you know, the one that pops up when you click the close icon in the upper left hand corner of a window.

```
class WPSysMenu : public WPMenu {
   WPWin *win;
public:
   WPSysMenu(WPWin *w) : WPMenu(GetSystemMenu((*w)(), FALSE)) { }
   void revert(WPWin *w)
      { hmenu = GetSystemMenu((*w)(), TRUE); }
};
```

This class makes it easy to add commands to the system menu, like so:

```
// Add "About" command to system menu.
WPSysMenu sm = mywin;
sm.appendSep();
sm.append(WPIDM_ABOUT, "About");
```

An example of this appears in the LAUNCH program (see Appendix A).[38]

Once again, the benefits of using *WPMenu* (instead of calling Windows directly) and "brainless" functions are the same as those described in Section 3.2.6: the C++ functions are more type-safe, provide helpful default arguments wherever possible, require you to remember less, are self-documenting, and expose the inherent class hierarchy among menus, submenus, and the system menu. *WPMenu* is "just" packaging, but packaging matters.

6.2.2 Menu Messages

Among the many messages that Windows sends to programs are two menu-related messages:[39]

- WM_INITMENU is sent when Windows is about to display the main menu, so programs have a chance to initialize their menus before they're displayed. This usually involves enabling or disabling (graying) menu items, checking them (putting ✔ next to the name), and so on.

- WM_MENUSELECT is sent whenever the user selects a new menu item, whether by dragging the mouse over it or by highlighting it with the arrow keys. WM_MENUSELECT is usually used to implement prompt lines such as the one specified for WINEDIT, and that's just what we'll do.

Among the many virtual message functions introduced (and glossed over) in Section 3.5.4 were two functions for handling these menu messages: *menuInit* and *menuSelected*.

---

38 Since *WPWin::dispatchEvent* passes both WM_COMMAND *and* WM_SYSCOMMAND messages to the *command* function, programs can handle system commands like ordinary menu commands. Just make sure you return FALSE if the command is not one of yours, so that Windows can process standard system commands like Close, Restore, and Move.

39 Two other messages, WM_INITMENUPOPUP and WM_MENUCHAR, are not supported as virtual functions. Programs that need to handle these messages should do so in the catch-all *other* function (see Section 3.5.4).

```
class WPWwin {
public:
    virtual BOOL menuInit(WPMenu &menu)              { return FALSE; }
    virtual BOOL menuSelected(int id, WORD flags)    { return FALSE; }
};
```

Our central event dispatcher, *WPWin::dispatchEvent*, routes messages to these functions as follows:

```
BOOL WPWin::dispatchEvent(WPEvent &event)
{
    switch (event.msg) {
    case WM_INITMENU:
        WPMenu menu = (HMENU)event.wp;
        return menuInit(menu);
    case WM_MENUSELECT:
        return menuSelected(event.wp, LOWORD(event.lp));
        .
        .
        .
}
```

As with all the other virtual message functions, all a program has to do to handle menu messages is provide the corresponding virtual function. To initialize its menus, WINEDIT need only provide *menuInit*:

```
BOOL EditWin::menuInit(WPMenu &menu)
{
    BOOL gotFile = filename[0]!=0;
    menu.enableItem(WPIDM_FILESAVE, gotFile && fileIsModified());
    .
    . etc.
    return TRUE;
}
```

Likewise, we'll write *menuSelected* to handle the prompt line, but not yet. We'll come back to it later. Right now, we're just setting the stage.

6.3 Implementing WINEDIT

So much for menu basics. (Not all infrastructure is overwhelming.) Now that menus are part of our *Windows++* vocabulary, we can start implementing WINEDIT. We will proceed by implementing the application (WINEDIT) and the library (*Windows++*) hand-in-hand: we'll first figure out what we want WINEDIT to look like, then we'll implement *Windows++* accordingly.

And awaaaay we go!

6.3.1 The Main Window

The first thing we need is a main window. Let's define one:

```
/////////////////
// Main window class for WINEDIT.
//
class EditWin : public WPMainWin {
   WPMultiEdit *editCtl;            // multi-line edit control
public:
   EditWin(CSTR fname=NULL);
};
```

The constructor takes an initial file name (default = none) and stores a pointer to a multi-line edit control that's used to hold the file. This control is created in the constructor, along with the main window:

```
/////////////////
// Initialize main WINEDIT window.
//
EditWin::EditWin(CSTR fname)
{
   createWin();                              // create main window

   // Create edit control
   editCtl = new WPMultiEdit(this, ID_EDITWIN); // create object,
   createArgs.style |= WS_VSCROLL;           // add vert scroll bar,
   editCtl->createWin("WINEDIT");            // ..and create window
}
```

As explained earlier, edit controls aren't fully described until the next chapter, so please just believe me when I tell you that *WPMultiEdit* is a *Windows++* class that represents a multi-line edit control, and when *EditWin* invokes *editCtl->createWin*, the edit control is created using *createArgs*, just like we've been doing all along.

We'll worry about what to do with *fname* in a moment. Right now, let's write *WPApp::main*, the *Windows++* analog of *WinMain*, which every program must supply. We have to pass the file name from the command line to the constructor, like so:

```
/////////////////
// Main entry point. Command line argument is name of file to open.
//
void WPApp::main()
{
   char fname[80];
   getCmdLine(fname);                   // get file name from command line,
   mainWin = new WinEdit(fname);        // create main window,
   run();                               // ..and run message loop
}
```

(In case you forgot: *WPApp::getCmdLine* copies the command line into a buffer.)

We'll also need a *sized* function to maintain the edit control at the same size as the main window every time Windows sends a WM_SIZED message, and we need to set the focus to the edit control whenever the main window receives focus.

```
class EditWin : public WPMainWin {
public:
    BOOL sized(WPRect &box, WORD how)
        { editCtl->moveWin(box); return TRUE; }
    BOOL gotFocus(WPWin *prev)
        { editCtl->setFocus(); return TRUE; }
};
```

We don't have to do anything to destroy *editCtl* because Windows automatically destroys child windows along with their parents, and our reliable *Windows++* infrastructure (specifically, *WPWndProc*) automatically deletes window objects whenever Windows sends a WM_DESTROY message.

6.3.2 Adding File Names to *WPMainWin*

We still haven't figured out what to do with the file name argument in the *EditWin* constructor, but it's safe to bet that we'll need to store it somewhere, along with the file's *modified* status. The obvious place to put them is in *EditWin*—but since practically all main windows have a "current file", why not put them in *WPMainWin*, where they can be reused? What a good idea! In general, *always add generic features at the lowest possible level (closest to the root) in the class hierarchy,* where they can be most reused. We wouldn't want to add the file name to *WPWin*, since not all windows have a file name, only main windows.

```
// Add file name and modified flag to WPMainWin (in WPMAIN.H)
class WPMainWin : public WPWin {
private:
    char    filename[MAXFILENAMELEN];
    BOOL    modified;

public:
    void    fileName(CSTR fname);            // set file name (see below)
    CSTR    fileName()                       { return filename; }
    virtual BOOL fileIsModified()            { return modified; }
    virtual void fileIsModified(BOOL m)      { modified=m; }
};
```

The functions to access the modified flag are virtual because programs may store the modified flag elsewhere. For example, edit controls store their own modified status, so we'll write *EditWin* like so:

```
class EditWin : public WPMainWin {
    WPMultiEdit *editCtl;          // multi-line edit control
public:
    BOOL fileIsModified()          { return editCtl->isModified(); }
    void fileIsModified(BOOL m)    { editCtl->setModified(m); }
};
```

The only function not defined above is *fileName:*

```
// Set main window file name (in WPMAIN.CPP)
void WPMainWin::fileName(CSTR fname)
{
    if (fname && *fname)
        strcpy(filename, fname);
    else
        filename[0]=0;
    fileIsModified(FALSE);           // <<< clear modified status
}
```

While we're adding generic file name stuff to *WPMainWin,* is there anything else you can think of that we should throw in?

Hint: What's something most programs do when the file name changes?

Answer: Update the window title!

So let's do it, in *WPMainWin.* Remember, every line of generic code we put in the library is a line eliminated from every application we write. To handle the caption, all we have to do is add a *caption* string and a way of setting it. Then we can automatically update the window caption whenever the file name is changed, like so:

```
void WPMainWin::fileName(CSTR fname)
{
    .
    . (as above)
    .
    if (caption) {
        char *buf = App.scratch;
        sprintf(buf, "%s %s", caption,
            filename[0] ? filename : "(untitled)");
        setText(buf); // set window caption in title bar
    }
}
```

We can even display the filename as "(untitled)" if the file doesn't have a name. More CUA behavior-in-a-box.

Our use of *fileName* illustrates another benefit of data hiding: the only way the file name can be altered is through *fileName,* which also updates the window caption and clears the modified flag. There's no way a programmer can accidentally forget to update the caption when he or she changes the file name, as would be the case in C, where we'd have to expose the *filename* string for anyone to mung. By making *filename* private and providing a function to set it, we ensure that the appropriate side effects (updating the window caption) always take place.

C   *In C, you could write a similar function to set the file name, but you'd have to rely on programmers using it since there's no way in C to hide the members of a struct.*

Here are the changes to add *caption:*

```
// Add caption (to WPMAIN.H).
class WPMainWin : public WPWin {
private:
    CSTR caption;                    // window caption
public:
    CSTR fileCaption()               { return caption; }
    void fileCaption(CSTR cap)       { caption = cap; }
};
```

The only thing we have to be careful about whenever we add new features to low-level objects is that we don't force anything on applications. In this case, if there's no *caption*, none of the file-name-caption behavior occurs, so applications that want to manage the window caption themselves can, while applications that use the typical "APPNAME *filename*" header can simply set the *caption*, and let *Windows++* maintain it whenever the file name changes.

Now that we have a place to store the file name and caption, we can finish the *EditWin* constructor:

```
EditWin::EditWin(CSTR fname)
{
    .
    .
    fileCaption("WINEDIT");          // set caption to "WINEDIT"
    if (fname && *fname)             // if file name specified:
        fileOpen(fname);             // ..open it (decsribed later)
    fileName(fname);                 // ..and set file name
}
```

This four-line sequence is so generic-looking, I can't resist bundling it into a subroutine:

```
// (In WPMAIN.H)
class WPMainWin : public WPWin {
public:
    void fileInit(CSTR fname, CSTR cap=NULL);   // default = no caption
};
// (In WPMAIN.CPP)
void WPMainWin::fileInit(CSTR fname, CSTR cap)
{
    fileCaption(cap);
    if (fname && *fname)
        fileOpen(fname);
    fileName(fname);
}
```

Now the *EditWin* constructor (and every future application-specific main window constructor) is even simpler:

```
EditWin::EditWin(CSTR fname)
{
    .
    .
    fileInit(fname, "WINEDIT");
}
```

6.3.3 The File Commands

With the file name and modified status tucked away in *WPMainWin*, let's next tackle the File commands. In the opening section we sketched a plan for implementing them as virtual functions:

```
class WPMainWin : public WPWin {
public:
    // Virtual functions to perform File commands.
    virtual BOOL fileSave(CSTR fname)    { return FALSE; }
    virtual BOOL fileOpen(CSTR fname)    { return FALSE; }
    virtual BOOL fileNew()               { return FALSE; }
};
```

All we have to do to make this scheme work is modify *WPMainWin* to do all the Windows UI gruntwork and then call the proper virtual function when it's time to actually perform the command. We'll tackle command separately, starting with an easy one, File New.

When the user invokes File New, we want to perform the following actions:

■ First, we'll check to see whether the current file is modified, but not saved. If so, we'll prompt the user to save it.

■ Next, we'll invoke *fileNew* to actually create a new file.

■ Finally, if *fileNew* succeeds, we can clear the *filename,* which automatically clears the *modified* flag and updates the window caption as well.

Here's the code:

```
BOOL WPMainWin::command(int id, WORD msg)
{
    switch (id) {
    case WPIDM_FILENEW:
        if (fileKillConfirm() && fileNew())
            fileName("");
        return TRUE;
        .
        .
        .
}
```

I've added several command IDs to WPID.H, for all the built-in menu commands:

```
#define WPIDM_FILENEW         (WPPIDBASE + 1)
#define WPIDM_FILEOPEN        (WPPIDBASE + 2)
#define WPIDM_FILESAVE        (WPPIDBASE + 3)
.
. etc. (Edit commands too!)
```

I've also introduced a new (private) function, *fileKillConfirm,* which does the proper file-overwrite-confirmation:

```
BOOL WPMainWin::fileKillConfirm()
{
    if (!fileIsModified())
        return TRUE;
    CSTR fname = fileName();
```

```
char buf[MAXFILENAMELEN+40]="Save changes";
if (fname[0]) {
    strcat(buf," to ");
    strcat(buf, fname);
}
strcat(buf,"?");
MsgBeep();
int answer = MsgBox(buf, caption, MB_YESNOCANCEL | MB_ICONQUESTION);
if (answer==IDYES) {
    char temp[MAXFILENAMELEN];
    if (fname[0]==0) {
        WPDlgFileSaveAs saveDlg(this, temp);
        saveDlg.setFilter(fnFilter);
        if (!saveDlg.run())
            return FALSE;
        fname = temp;
    }
    return fileSave(fname);
}
return answer==IDNO;
}
```

If the current file is modified, but not saved, *fileKillConfirm* beeps and displays the following message box:

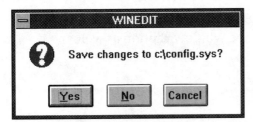

If the user answers *Yes*, the file is saved (*fileSave* and the dialog are described later in this section). Whatever the user's response, *fileKillConfirm* returns either TRUE to indicate that the operation should proceed, or FALSE if it should not.

While *fileKillConfirm* is on our minds, we can (re)use it in *queryEnd*, the virtual message function that handles WM_QUERYENDSESSION:

```
class WPMainWin : public WPWin {
public:
    BOOL queryEnd()  { return fileKillConfirm(); }
};
```

WPMainWin responds to the Exit command by closing the window, but *close* is only carried out if *queryEnd* returns TRUE (see Section 3.5.4). So now our main windows are automatically Exit-proof. If a user attempts to Exit the program (or Windows), he or she will first get a chance to save any outstanding changes.

So much for *fileKillConfirm* and *WPMainWin*. To make File New actually *work*, all we have to do now is implement *fileNew* for WINEDIT:

```
// WINEDIT.CPP
class WinEdit : public WPMainWin {
   WPMultiEdit *editCtl;
public:
   BOOL fileNew() { editCtl->setSel(); editCtl->clear(); return TRUE; }
};
```

The implementation is trivial: *fileNew* invokes two *WPEdit* functions; *setSel* selects the entire contents of the edit control (it sends an EM_SETSEL message); and *clear* deletes the selected text (it sends WM_CLEAR). These functions are more fully described in Section 7.3.2, but take my word for it, they work as claimed.

To see how all this works in practice, let's examine what happens when the user invokes File New from the menu:

- Windows sends a WM_COMMAND message with WPIDM_FILENEW as the menu ID.

- *Windows++* routes the message via *WPWndProc, WPWin::msgProc* and *WPWin::dispatchEvent* to the virtual *command* function. *EditWin* has no *command* function, so it inherits the one from *WPMainWin*.

- *WPMainWin::command* handles WPDIM_FILENEW by first prompting the user to save the current file if necessary, then invokes *fileNew,* which is defined for *EditWin*.

- *EditWin::fileNew* clears the contents of the edit control and returns TRUE.

- *WPMainWin::command* clears the file name, which has the side-effects of clearing the *modified* flag and updating the window caption to read "WINEDIT (untitled)".

Pretty good, eh? All WINEDIT has to do is provide *fileNew,* which is practically trivial and, in any case, application-specific. *Windows++* does everything else.

What about the other File commands? Well, they're almost as easy. Here they are:

```
BOOL WPMainWin::command(int id, WORD msg)
{
   char temp[MAXFILENAMELEN];
   switch (id) {
   case WPIDM_FILEOPEN:
      if (fileKillConfirm()) {
         WPDlgFileOpen openDlg(this, temp);    // described below
         openDlg.setFilter(fnFilter);          // ditto
         if (openDlg.run() && fileOpen(temp))
            fileName(temp);
      }
      return TRUE;
```

```
case WPIDM_FILESAVE:
    if (filename[0]) {
        if (fileSave(filename))
            fileIsModified(FALSE);
        return TRUE;
    }
    // no filename: fall through
case WPIDM_FILESAVEAS:
    WPDlgFileSaveAs saveDlg(this, temp);
    saveDlg.setFilter(fnFilter);
    if (saveDlg.run() && fileSave(temp))
        fileName(temp);
    return TRUE;
case WPIDM_FILEPRINT:
    WPDlgPrint pdlg = this;       // explained below
    if (pdlg.run())
        filePrint(pdlg);
    return TRUE;
    .
    .
    .
}
```

Note that File Save and Save As both use the same *fileSave* function, the difference being that Save uses the current file name, while Save As invokes a dialog to get the file name. The main thing that's new here are the dialogs, which I've already asked you to take my word for. They're described fully in the next chapter, but I'll describe them briefly here. Consider the following sequence of code from *WPMainWin::command*:

```
WPDlgFileOpen openDlg(this, temp);    // create file open dialog
openDlg.setFilter(fnFilter);          // set filename "filter"
if (openDlg.run() && fileOpen(temp))
    fileName(temp);
return TRUE;
```

The first line creates an instance of *WPDlgFileOpen*, which is the file open dialog. Next, *WPMainWin* sets the file name "filter" (described below) from a private data member. Next *WPMainWin* runs the dialog, after which *temp* contains the name of the file that the user selected or entered. Finally, *WPMainWin* invokes *fileOpen* to actually open the file. If this is successful, it sets the file name to *temp* (which also clears the *modified* flag and updates the window caption).

The filename "filter" is a string that's used in the file dialogs to specify which files should be displayed in the dialog—for example, *.TXT or *.EXE. The default is *.* (all files). *WPMainWin* stores the filter as a new data member:

```
class WPMainWin : public WPWin {
private:
    CSTR fnFilter;                        // file name filter
public:
    void fileNameFilter(CSTR filt)        { fnFilter = filt; }
    CSTR fileNameFilter()                 { return fnFilter; }
};
```

Applications may set the filename filter once, when the main window is created, then forget about it. WINEDIT doesn't ever set it, since the default *.* is OK.

The only other unexplained code in *WPMainWin* is the case that handles File Print:

```
WPDlgPrint pdlg = this;          // create print dialog
if (pdlg.run())                  // run dialog
    filePrint(pdlg);             // call virtual print function
return TRUE;
```

WPMainWin runs another reusable dialog from Chapter 7, then passes it to the virtual function *filePrint*, which can interpret the dialog results however it likes. We've thus encapsulated more GUI behavior-in-a-box. The only thing missing that you might want to add is a "hook" to alter the print dialog before running it. For example, you could add another main window virtual function, *initPrintDialog*, then modify *WPMainWin* to invoke it before running the dialog:

```
WPDlgPrint pdlg = this;
initPrintDialog(pdlg);           // do app-specific initialization
if (pdlg.run())
    filePrint(printer);
return TRUE;
```

This would give applications a chance to hide or show various dialog controls, such as the range of pages to print or a *Collate* option. The general technique is to introduce virtual functions wherever application-specific processing is required. (Note: the print dialog is described in Section 7.5.4; printing is covered in Section 8.5.)

With all this code in *WPMainWin*, applications need never again bother intercepting File command IDs, creating file dialogs, checking or setting *modified* flags, graying menus, updating the window caption, or any of the other tedious UI mechanics. *WPMainWin* does it all. The only thing *WPMainWin doesn't* do is actually Open, Save, or "New" the file.

The following table shows how the task of performing the File commands split between the application (WINEDIT) and the library *(Windows++)*.

Windows++	**App (e.g., WINEDIT)**
Obtain overwrite confirmation, run dialogs. Invoke app-specific virtual function. ———▶	
	Open, Save, or create a New file.
Update file name, modified status, ◀——— and window caption.	

6.3.4 File Open and Save: Enhancing *WPMultiEdit*

In case you've forgotten where we are, we're implementing the File commands for WINEDIT. So far, we've only done File New, but we've encapsulated a lot of generic command behavior in *WPMainWin* and defined virtual functions for all the commands. All we have to do is implement them for WINEDIT. We'll tackle *fileOpen* and *fileSave* here; we'll do printing in the next section.

To open a file in WINEDIT, we have to open the file, read it into a buffer, and then copy the contents to the edit control. Saving a file is just the opposite. The obvious thing would be to put the code in *fileOpen* and *fileSave*, like so:

```
BOOL EditWin::fileOpen(CSTR fname)
{
        .
      . Open the file, read it, copy to edit control.
        .
}
```

But if we stop to think for a moment, we'll realize that these functions might be useful in other programs besides WINEDIT. Loading and dumping the contents of edit controls is a common thing to do. So instead of implementing these operations in *EditWin*, let's add them to *WPMultiEdit*. (Technically, we haven't even implemented *WPMultiEdit* yet, but we know we need these functions, so let's write them now. This is no more than good top-down software engineering.)

Since *WPMultiEdit* is derived from *WPWin* (believe me), it inherits *getText* and *setText*, which get and set the contents of the edit control. All we have to do is add *load* and *save* functions:

```
// Add load and save functions (in WPEDIT.H)
class WPMultiEdit : public WPEdit {
public:
    BOOL load(CSTR fname);        // load contents from disk file
    BOOL save(CSTR fname);        // save contents to disk file
};
```

Here's the code for *load* (from WPCTRL.CPP):

```
#include <sys\stat.h>              // for "stat" fn, to get file size

/////////////////////
// Load contents of file into edit control.
//
BOOL WPMultiEdit::load(CSTR fname)
{
    int ret = FALSE;

    struct stat temp;
    if (stat((char*)fname, &temp) >= 0) {
        DWORD len = temp.st_size;
        LPSTR buf = (LPSTR)App.farAlloc(len+1, FALSE);
        if (buf) {
            OFSTRUCT of;
```

```
            int fd = OpenFile((LPSTR)fname, (LPOFSTRUCT)&of, OF_READ);
            if (fd!=-1) {
                _lread(fd, buf, len);
                _lclose(fd);
                buf[len] = 0;
                setText(buf);
                ret = TRUE;
            } else
                ErrBox("Unable to open file '%s'.", fname);
            App.farFree(buf);

        } else
            ErrBox("File too big.");
    }
    return ret;
}
```

The implementation is straightforward—*load* first obtains the file size from *stat* (a standard C i/o library function), then allocates a buffer to hold it, reads the file into this buffer using the normal Windows file i/o functions *OpenFile, _lread* and so forth, and finally copies the buffer to the edit control (by calling *setText*). If any of these operations fails, *load* returns FALSE; otherwise it returns TRUE to indicate success.

WPMultiEdit::save is equally straightforward:

```
///////////////////
// Write contents of edit control to file.
//
BOOL WPMultiEdit::save(CSTR fname)
{
    assert(*fname);
    DWORD len = getText();
    LPSTR buf = (LPSTR)App.farAlloc(len, FALSE);
    if (buf) {
        OFSTRUCT of;

        getText(buf, len);
        int fd = OpenFile((LPSTR)fname, (LPOFSTRUCT)&of, OF_CREATE);
        if (fd!=-1) {
            _lwrite(fd, buf, len);
            _lclose(fd);

        } else
            ErrBox("Unable to open file '%s'.", fname);

        App.farFree(buf);
        return TRUE;

    } else
        ErrBox("File too big.");
    return FALSE;
}
```

That's two more useful functions we'll never write again. They make the open and save operations for *EditWin* completely trivial:

```
class EditWin : public WPMainWin {
    WPMultiEdit *editCtl;            // main edit window
public:
    // File command functions
    BOOL fileOpen(CSTR fname)        { return editCtl->load(fname); }
    BOOL fileSave(CSTR fname)        { return editCtl->save(fname); }
};
```

6.3.5 File Print

Technically, we don't know how to print yet, but if we did, this is more or less how we'd like to write *filePrint*:

```
////////////////////
// Print the file (i.e., contents of the edit control).
//
BOOL EditWin::filePrint(WPDlgPrint &pdlg)
{
    char *line = App.scratch;
    int nlines = editCtl->numLines();

    WPLinePrinter p = pdlg;          // line printer class (see below)
    p.doAbortDlg(this);              // tell printer to do the abort dialog
    p.startDoc(fileName());          // start printing

    // Loop: print each line
    for (int i=0; i < nlines && !p.aborted(); i++) {
        int len = editCtl->getLine(i, line, 256);
        p.outLine(line, len);
    }
    p.endDoc();                      // end printing
    return TRUE;
}
```

In fact, this exactly how *EditWin::filePrint* is implemented (what did you expect?). Those of you who have ever attempted to print in Windows will no doubt be amazed at how simple it is. To understand how it works, you'll just have to read Section 8.5 (I bet the suspense is killing you).

6.3.6 The Edit Commands

We can employ the same techniques to implement the Edit commands. Since they don't require confirmations, dialog boxes, or any of the other stuff we had to do for File, they're a lot simpler. First, we define virtual functions for all the commands:

```
class WPMainWin : public WPWin {
public:
    // Virtual functions to perform Edit commands.
    virtual BOOL editCut()           { return FALSE; }
    virtual BOOL editCopy()          { return FALSE; }
    virtual BOOL editPaste()         { return FALSE; }
    virtual BOOL editDelete()        { return FALSE; }
    virtual BOOL editUndo()          { return FALSE; }
};
```

Next, we make *WPMainWin* call them in response to the appropriate WM_COM-
MAND events:

```
BOOL WPMainWin::command(int id, WORD msg)
{
    switch (id) {
    case WPIDM_EDITCUT:             return editCut();
    case WPIDM_EDITCOPY:            return editCopy();
    case WPIDM_EDITPASTE:           return editPaste();
    case WPIDM_EDITDELETE:          return editDelete();
    case WPIDM_EDITUNDO:            return editUndo();

        .
        .
        .
}
```

To finish the job, we have to write *editCut* and so forth for *EditWin:*

```
class EditWin : public WPMainWin {
    WPMultiEdit *editCtl;           // main edit window
public:
    // Edit command functions
    BOOL editCut()                  { editCtl->cut(); return TRUE; }
    BOOL editCopy()                 { editCtl->copy(); return TRUE; }
    BOOL editPaste()                { editCtl->paste(); return TRUE; }
    BOOL editDelete()               { editCtl->clear(); return TRUE; }
    BOOL editUndo()                 { editCtl->undo(); return TRUE; }
};
```

The edit control functions *cut, copy,* and the rest simply send the corresponding
Windows message to the edit control:

```
class WPEdit {
public:
    void cut()       { sendMsg(WM_CUT); }
    void copy()      { sendMsg(WM_COPY); }
    void clear()     { sendMsg(WM_CLEAR); }
    void paste()     // more substantial, but straightforward
    BOOL undo()      { return sendMsg(EM_UNDO); }
    BOOL canUndo()   { return sendMsg(EM_CANUNDO); }
};
```

Boy, that sure was easy! Now all the Edit commands work!

This is one place where *Windows* provides the reusability (hooray for Windows!).
The edit control does the work for Cut, Copy, Paste, and the rest, and handles the
other basic editing functions such as typing in text, selecting with the mouse,
BACKSPACE, DELETE, INSERT, and so on.

6.3.7 Menu Graying

At this point, all the WINEDIT commands work. File Open displays a dialog and
then actually opens the selected file; Edit Cut transfers the selected text to the clipboard. All the other commands do what they're supposed to.

Now we have to worry about *graying* the menu items. All we have to do is write a *menuInit* function somewhere. Our strategy is to implement whatever we can in *WPMainWin*, so let's do it there.

```
///////////////////
// Handle WM_MENUINIT: gray menus according to current state.
// (In WPMAIN.CPP)
BOOL WPMainWin::menuInit(WPMenu &menu)
{
    WPMenu mainMenu = this;
    if (menu == mainMenu) {
        BOOL gotFile = filename[0]!=0;
        menu.enableItem(WPIDM_FILESAVE, gotFile && fileIsModified());

        BOOL any = anySelected();                        // anySelected ??
        menu.enableItem(WPIDM_EDITCUT, any);
        menu.enableItem(WPIDM_EDITCOPY, any);
        menu.enableItem(WPIDM_EDITDELETE, any);
        menu.enableItem(WPIDM_EDITPASTE, canPaste());    // canPaste ??
        menu.enableItem(WPIDM_EDITUNDO, canUndo());      // canUndo ??
        return TRUE;
    }
    return FALSE;
}
```

For the File menu, *WPMainWin* has all the information it needs to gray the menu items correctly (the filename and its *modified* status). But for Edit we need to know some additional information, namely, whether there's anything in the clipboard that can be pasted, whether anything is selected, and whether an Undo operation can be performed.

Where are we going to get this information? Why, from the application, of course. Information about what's selected and so on is clearly application-dependent (WINEDIT selects and pastes *text,* but a paint program would probably have a completely different notion of selection and should be able to paste graphics as well as text). Anything that's application-dependent can be left out of *WPMainWin* by introducing more virtual functions:

```
class WPMainWin : public WPWin {
public:
    virtual BOOL canPaste()                 { return FALSE; }
    virtual BOOL canUndo()                  { return FALSE; }
    virtual BOOL anySelected()              { return FALSE; }
};
```

Of course, this is a burden on our applications, which must provide these functions if they want the menus to gray properly. There's no getting around this, since there's no generic way to tell if something is selected, or whether there's something Paste-able in the clipboard.

Here's how WINEDIT implements the new functions:

```
class EditWin : public WPMainWin {
    WPMultiEdit *editCtl;              // main edit window
public:
    BOOL canPaste()   { return Clipboard.available(CF_TEXT); }
    BOOL canUndo()    { return editCtl->canUndo(); }
    BOOL anySelected()
        { int beg,end; return editCtl->getSel(beg, end); }
};
```

EditWin simply obtains the information from other objects. *Clipboard.available* returns true if the specified format (in this case, text) is available for pasting (see Section 5.2.3); *WPEdit::canUndo* sends WM_CANUNDO to the edit control; and *WPEdit::getSel* returns TRUE only if something is selected (these functions are implemented in *WPEdit*, the base class for *WPMultiEdit*; see Section 7.3.2).

6.3.8 The Prompt Line

The last major item remaining for WINEDIT is the prompt line. We want to create a line at the bottom of the main window that displays a short sentence describing each command. We'll store the prompts themselves in a string table:

```
// (In WINEDIT.RC)
STRINGTABLE {
    WPIDM_FILENEW, "Create a new file."
    WPIDM_FILEOPEN, "Open an existing file."
    WPIDM_FILESAVE, "Save current file on disk."
    WPIDM_FILESAVEAS, "Save current file with a different name."
        .
        .
        .
}
```

We'll load these as needed from the application object, like so:

```
char buf[80];
int len = App.loadString(id, buf, sizeof(buf)));
```

To display each prompt as the user selects different menu items, we'll implement a *menuSelected* function (the virtual function for WM_MENUSELECT). Assuming that *promptWin* points to the prompt line window, *menuSelected* goes like this:

```
///////////////////
// Handle WM_MENUSELECT message: update prompt line.
//
BOOL EditWin::menuSelected(int id, WORD flags)
{
    char buf[80]="";
    App.loadString(id, buf, sizeof(buf));      // load from string table
    promptWin->invalidate(TRUE)                // erase previous prompt
    promptWin->setText(buf);                   // set prompt
    return TRUE;
}
```

Now all we have to do is create *promptWin*. For this I'll pull my last rabbit out of my hat, another control class from the next chapter: *WPStatic*. This class represents a static text control.

```
// Add prompt line and height to WINEDIT main window class
// (in WPEDIT.CPP).
class EditWin : public WPMainWin {
   WPStatic *promptWin;          // prompt line window
   int pmtHeight;                // hieght of prompt line
};
// Create prompt line in window constructor.
EditWin::EditWin(CSTR fname)
{
     .
     .
   promptWin = new WPStatic(this,ID_PROMPTWIN);      // create object
   promptWin->createWin();          // create window
   pmtHeight = tm.tmHeight;         // save text height
}
```

Recall that *WPWin::tm* is a static global that's stuffed with the window's TEXT-METRICs after creating a window (see Section 5.1.5). The reason for saving the height of the prompt line is that we need to resize it along with the main window in our *sized* function:

```
//////////////////////
// Got WM_SIZED message: adjust edit control and prompt line.
//
BOOL EditWin::sized(WPRect &box, WORD how)
{
   box.height(box.height()-pmtHeight);       // subtract ht of pmt line
   editCtl->moveWin(box);                    // ..adjust edit control

   WPRect pmtbox;
   pmtbox.origin(0, box.height());           // y = bottom of edit ctl
   pmtbox.extent(box.width(),pmtHeight);     // wid=same, ht=pmtHeight
   promptWin->moveWin(pmtbox);               // ..adjust prompt line

   return TRUE;
}
```

The edit control is now a little smaller. We have to subtract the height of the prompt line from its former height; but look how easy the resizing is with *WPRect!*

That's it for the prompt line. Before we move on, is there anything generic we can move to *WPMainWin*? (It's feeding time for *Windows++* again.)

Well, not *all* Windows programs have prompt lines, but many *do*, so why not move the prompt line functionality to *WPMainWin*? The only things that are application-dependent are the prompt window itself and the actual prompts. The mechanics of *menuSelected* are generic. So let's move *promptWin* to *WPMainWin*, add a virtual function to get the prompt for each menu ID, and rewrite the whole thing:

```
// (In WPMAIN.H)
const MAXPROMPTLEN = 80;

class WPMainWin : public WPWin {
protected:
   WPWin *promptWin;                // menu prompt window
```

```
public:
   virtual int getMenuPrompt(char* buf, int id, WORD flags)
       { return 0; }
};
// (In WPMAIN.CPP)
BOOL WPMainWin::menuSelected(int id, WORD flags)
{
   if (promptWin) {
       char* buf = App.scratch;
       *buf=0;
       getMenuPrompt(buf, id, flags);          // get prompt from app
       promptWin->invalidate(TRUE);            // erase previous prompt
       promptWin->setText(buf);                // set new one
   }
   return TRUE;
}
```

Now the *menuSelected* function is in *WPMainWin*. It invokes a new virtual function, *getMenuPrompt*, to obtain the prompt. The *promptWin* has also been moved to *WPMainWin*, but it's protected, so applications like WINEDIT can set it if they want (otherwise the "prompt" functionality is turned off).

This eliminates a few more lines of code from WINEDIT (and every other application we write): now all WINEDIT has to do is create and set *promptWin*, size it, and provide a function to get the prompt for a particular menu command:

```
// (In WINEDIT.CPP)
class EditWin : public WPMainWin {
public:
   int getMenuPrompt(char* buf, int id, WORD flags)
       { return id ? App.loadString(id, buf, MAXPROMPTLEN) : 0; }
};
```

In summary, to create a prompt line, an application must do just three things:

- Create and set the prompt window (*promptWin*) when the main window is initialized (usually in the constructor).

- Handle the *sized* event to reposition the prompt line when the main window is resized.

- Provide a *getMenuPrompt* function to stuff prompt messages into a buffer.

See? User interface coding is getting easier and easier. Pretty soon there won't be anything left to do but write applications!

6.3.9 Resource Coding Made Simple

It's time for a little surprise quiz (closed-book; no peeking at the CUA manual!).

1. What's the accelerator key for the Edit Cut command?
   A. *Control-Delete*   B. *Shift–Delete*   C. *Delete*

2. What's the accelerator key for Edit Copy?

3. What about Edit Undo?

4. What's the proper menu mnemonic for Cut?
   A. Cut   B. Cut   C. Cut?

5. What's the proper menu mnemonic for Delete?

Answers: *Who remembers this stuff?!*

If you follow the Traditional Windows Way (of reinventing every Windows program from scratch), you have to pull out your CUA manual when it comes time to code the resource file. Why bother remembering, when you can write the code once and never again?!

Take a look at this resource file fragment, from WINEDIT.RC:

```
#include "wpp.h"

AppMenu MENU {
    POPUP "&File" {
        MENUITEM FileNew
        MENUITEM FileOpen
        MENUITEM SEPARATOR
        MENUITEM FileSave
        MENUITEM FileSaveAs
        MENUITEM SEPARATOR
        MENUITEM FilePrint
        MENUITEM SEPARATOR
        MENUITEM Exit
    }
    POPUP "&Edit" {
        MENUITEM EditCut
        MENUITEM EditCopy
        MENUITEM EditPaste
        MENUITEM SEPARATOR
        MENUITEM EditDelete
    }
}
```

It doesn't look like a normal resource file, does it?

All I did to get the clean (and reusable) look was *#define* a few handy macros in WPID.H:

```
#ifdef RC_INVOKED    // defined when running the resource compiler (RC).
/////////////////////
// Resource macros to define CUA-compliant menus.
//
// File Menu
#define    FileNew    "&New\tCtrl-N",     WPIDM_FILENEW
#define    FileOpen   "&Open...\tCtrl-O", WPIDM_FILEOPEN
    .
    .
```

```
// Edit menu
#define    EditUndo    "&Undo\tAlt+Backspace",WPIDM_EDITUNDO
#define    EditCut     "Cu&t\tShift+Del",  WPIDM_EDITCUT
.
.
#endif // RC_INVOKED
```

The macros are defined *only* when running the resource compiler, to reduce the chance of the symbols *FileNew* and so forth conflicting with other program symbols. WPID.H defines similar macros for accelerator keys:

```
// CUA accelerators
#define    AccFileNew    "^N"
#define    AccFileOpen   "^O"
.
.
#define    AccEditCut    VK_DELETE, WPIDM_EDITCUT,   SHIFT,    VIRTKEY
#define    AccEditCopy   VK_INSERT, WPIDM_EDITCOPY,  CONTROL,  VIRTKEY
.
.
```

(I know, I know, *Control*-O and *Control*-N are not officially CUA, but they're common and useful enough to include anyway). The accelerator key macros are used in WINEDIT.RC like so:

```
// WINEDIT.RC
AppAccel ACCELERATORS
BEGIN
    AccFileNew
    AccFileOpen
    AccFilePrint
    AccFileSave
    AccEditUndo
    AccEditCut
    AccEditCopy
    AccEditPaste
END
```

No more remembering accelerator keys or command mnemonics! All you have to remember is the command name. The macros make resource coding easy, clean and neat, not to mention reliable. Programs that use them are guaranteed to be CUA-compliant.

The individual menu item macros could be combined into macros that generate entire popup menus, like so:

```
// WPID.H
#define    FilePopup \
    POPUP "&File" { \
        MENUITEM FileNew \
        MENUITEM FileOpen \
        MENUITEM SEPARATOR \
        MENUITEM FileSave \
        MENUITEM FileSaveAs \
        MENUITEM SEPARATOR \
```

```
        MENUITEM FilePrint \
        MENUITEM SEPARATOR \
        MENUITEM Exit \
    }

#define AccFile \
    AccFileNew \
    AccFileOpen \
    AccFilePrint \
    AccFileSave
```

With these, WINEDIT.RC is even simpler:

```
// WINEDIT.RC
AppMenu MENU {
    FilePopup
    EditPopup
}

AppAccel ACCELERATORS
BEGIN
    AccFile
    AccEdit
END
```

FilePopup and the rest even generate menu separators in the right places!

I chose not to implement *FilePopup* because not all programs have the same commands. For example, not all programs have an Undo command, and most programs have additional, application-specific File and Edit commands. Having separate macros for each command requires a bit more typing but gives applications the flexibility to include commands individually rather than *en masse*.

C *These resource macros are pure C. There's nothing object-oriented about them. (They couldn't be, because they're only defined for the resource compiler, which doesn't know diddly about C++.)*

While the macros are trivial to implement, they greatly reduce the chore of resource-coding. Furthermore, they are a form of reusable code. There's no reason reusability has to be restricted to C++ objects! Most important, though, the macros, like everything else we've done in this chapter, help enforce the CUA guidelines automatically, without programmers having to do anything.

6.3.10 Small is Beautiful

So far, I've only shown you snippets of WINEDIT at a time. The complete program is shown in Appendix A. It's about 112 lines, including comments. That may seem like a lot of code, but it's not. POPPAD is over 600 lines, and EDITFILE is over 1000!

The table below shows the relative sizes and functionality of different incarnations of "the editor," and just how reusable *Windows++* really is:

	source lines	Edit Undo, Cut, etc?	prompt line?
WINEDIT	˜112	Yes	Yes
POPPAD (with printing)	˜600	Yes	No
EDITFILE	˜1000	No	No

Skeptics will say, "sure, WINEDIT is smaller. All you did is move all the code into the library. You still had to write the same amount of code!" To which I reply, "Ah, but I only had to write it *once!*"

Indeed, we did move all the code into the library. That's precisely the point! In doing so, we made the code generic, so not only WINEDIT is smaller, but so too every other application we write from now on. We'll never again bother with any of the user interface details of File and Edit: graying menus, displaying dialogs, checking the file's *modified* status, and so on. Future applications need only add these commands to the resource file (using our foolproof macros) and provide the functions that actually do something; all the normal CUA menu dynamics happen automatically. (I wonder how many hours Windows programmers have spent getting their menus grayed properly.)

And don't forget all the other Windows gruntwork we've encapsulated in previous chapters, such as the message loop, window registration and creation, and window procedures. That's why WINEDIT is so small. We're reaping the benefits of the infrastructure we built in previous chapters.

6.4 Modeling MDI

(If MDI is not your bag, feel free to skip this section.)

Just so you don't get the idea that *Windows++* is only good for "little" things like the File and Edit menus, let me show you how the same basic techniques can be applied to encapsulate something "big", something many programmers dread even more than memory management: the Multiple Document Interface (MDI). In this section, we'll turn WINEDIT into MEDIT, a multiple-file editor similar to MULTIPAD (one of the sample programs that comes with the SDK)—only the *Windows++* version is *twenty-size times smaller!*

The MDI specification (in the CUA guide, where else?) describes the "correct" user interface for applications that let users work with several open files at a time.

The basic idea is to turn the main window into a mini-desktop, within which files may be opened in their own windows. These windows, called *MDI child windows*, are like main windows: they can be moved, sized, and even minimized to icons. The only constraint is that they must remain inside the main window.

The implementation of MDI is perhaps one of the biggest kludges in all of Windows. Window creation, destruction, message handling and numerous other things all work differently for MDI. This is one reason programmers hate it. Oh well, *c'est la vie.* Difficult or not, MDI is an important feature of Windows, one that many commercial applications such a Excel and TaxCut use. We really should deal with it.

Fortunately, with all the infrastructure we've already built, stuffing MDI under our belts is a small incremental effort. We've already done most of the work. In fact, one of my reasons for including it here is to show how easy it is using the system we've already built.[40] That, plus the fact that MDI provides a good example of something messy, confusing, and dreadful in Windows but easy and simple in *Windows++.*

A few caveats before we begin. Since MDI is fully explained elsewhere (for example, in the SDK *Guide to Programming*, and in [Petzold 1990]), I'll assume that you already know how MDI works in Windows and merely explain the *Windows++* side of it. Furthermore, I won't go into the same level of detail I've been using up to now but will sketch the highlights. Between the brief explanations here and the source code in Appendix A, MDI enthusiasts (should any exist) should have no trouble figuring out what's going on. I apologize for dumping all this in your lap without building up the motivation, but we have to cover a lot of ground rapidly. Besides, I have to prepare you for the next chapter, where the pace picks up.

6.4.1 Three New Window Classes

MDI applications are implemented around three kinds of windows:

- The *frame* window is the main application window. It contains the menu bar, receives WM_COMMAND messages, and owns the client window.

- The *client* window is basically just a blank workspace, sort of like a mini-desktop, within which *child* windows can be created, moved, and sized. The child windows are constrained to appear entirely within the client window. The client window handles most MDI-specific messages.

- Each *child* window represents an open file. MDI child windows are like normal main windows, except that they don't have their own menus, but

---

40 One criteria by which to judge complex systems (class libraries, application frameworks, operating systems) such as *Windows++* is how easily it can accommodate new things.

instead use the frame window's menu. At any given time, one child is the *active* child window, the one that has the focus, and upon which the menu commands operate.

The following picture is perhaps worth more than the words above:

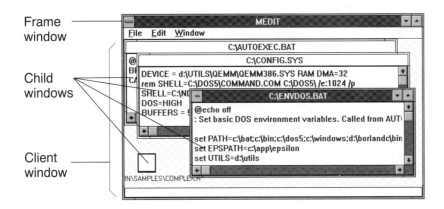

As is typical of Windows, everything works differently in MDI-land. For example, instead of calling *CreateWindow* to create an MDI child window, you must first fill out a special MDICREATESTRUCT then send it as a WM_MDICREATE message to the client window. Most of the *Windows++* MDI infrastructure I'm about to describe is devoted to hiding Windows' numerous inconsistencies behind the uniform interface presented by *Windows++*, where, for example, *createWin* is always used to create a window, no matter what kind of window is created.

Windows++ provides three C++ classes corresponding to the MDI windows. *WPMDIClient* is derived from *WPWin; WPMDIFrame* and *WPMDIChild* are subclasses of *WPMainWin:*

Let's examine each class separately.

6.4.2 *WPMDIClient*

The simplest class is *WPMDIClient.* Here's the complete implementation (all MDI objects are implemented in WPMDI.H and WPMDI.CPP):

```
///////////////////
// MDI client window. (In WPMDI.H)
//
class WPMDIClient : public WPWin {
private:
    WPMDIClient(WPMDIFrame *pwin);
    ~WPMDIClient();
    WPMDIChild* activeWin()
        { return (WPMDIChild*)GetWin(LOWORD(sendMsg(WM_MDIGETACTIVE))); }
    friend WPMDIFrame;
};

///////////////////
// (In WPMDI.CPP)
// Initialize client window object.
// Note that the constructor actually creates the window too.
//
WPMDIClient::WPMDIClient(WPMDIFrame *frm) : WPWin("MDICLIENT", frm, 1)
{
    createArgs.style = WS_CHILD | WS_CLIPCHILDREN | WS_VISIBLE;

    // Get Window popup menu
    WPMenu menu=frame;
    WPSubMenu submenu(menu, frame->winMenuPos);

    // Set up weird windows structure.
    CLIENTCREATESTRUCT ccs;
    ccs.hWindowMenu = submenu();
    ccs.idFirstChild = 1;
    createArgs.lparam = (LPSTR)&ccs;

    createWin();      // actually create window

    // Tell app to translate accelerator keys (explained below).
    App.mdiClientHwnd = getHwnd();
}

///////////////////
// Destroy client window: Tell app to stop translating accelerators.
//
WPMDIClient::~WPMDIClient()
{
    App.mdiClientHwnd = NULL;
}
```

The constructor initializes a special Windows *struct* (CLIENTCREATESTRUCT), which is passed to Windows as the *lParam* argument to *CreateWindow.* The structure contains the menu handle of the "Window" menu (the one with Tile, Arrange, etc.) and the ID of the first child window, which is always set to one. Since *WPMDI- Client* is only used by *WPMDIFrame*, all its functions (all three of them) are private, and *WPMDIFrame* is declared as a friend.

The constructor also stores the window handle of the client window in the application object, *App*, which has been modified to accept it. This is so the application can translate accelerator keys (a full explanation appears below, in Section 6.4.5). The destructor restores *App.mdiClientHwnd* to NULL. These details are part of the internals of *Windows++*; applications never see them.

6.4.3 *WPMDIFrame*

The frame window is the most complicated class. It's derived from *WPMainWin*, and thus inherits all the command-handling, code we wrote in the preceding sections for the File and Edit commands. Here's the class definition:

```
///////////////////
// MDI Frame window.
//
class WPMDIFrame : public WPMainWin {
    WPMDIClient *client;            // ptr to client window
    int winMenuPos;                 // relative pos of "Window" menu
    friend WPMDIClient;
    friend WPMDIChild;
public:
    WPMDIFrame(int winMenu, CSTR classnm = "MDIFRAME");
    ~WPMDIFrame();

    WPMDIClient* clientWin()        { return client; }
    WPMDIChild* activeWin()         { return client->activeWin(); }

    BOOL createWin();

    // Brainless functions
    void cascade()                  { client->sendMsg(WM_MDICASCADE); }
    void tile()                     { client->sendMsg(WM_MDITILE); }
    void arrangeIcons()             { client->sendMsg(WM_MDIICONARRANGE);}
    void nextWin()                  { client->sendMsg(WM_MDINEXT); }
    BOOL closeAll(BOOL force=FALSE);

    // Virtual message functions
    BOOL menuInit(WPMenu &menu);
    BOOL command(int id, WORD msg);
    BOOL queryEnd();
};
```

Most of it is straightforward:

■ The constructor initializes *createArgs* appropriately for a frame window:

```
///////////////////
// Initialize frame window.
// Argument is relative position in menu of "Window" popup.
//
WPMDIFrame::WPMDIFrame(int winMenu, CSTR classnm)
    : WPMainWin(classnm)
{
    createArgs.wndcls.lpfnWndProc = CASTWNDPROC WPDefFrameProc;
    createArgs.wndcls.hbrBackground = COLOR_APPWORKSPACE+1;
    createArgs.style |= WS_CLIPCHILDREN;
    client = NULL;
    winMenuPos = winMenu;
}
```

The only interesting thing is that the window procedure is set to *WPDef-FrameProc*:

```
LONG _export FAR PASCAL
WPDefFrameProc(HWND hwnd, WORD msg, WORD wp, LONG lp)
{
    HWND clientHwnd = GetWindow(hwnd, GW_CHILD);
    return DefFrameProc(hwnd, clientHwnd, msg, wp, lp);
}
```

For some reason, the default window procedure (*DefFrameProc*) that Windows provides for MDI frame windows requires five arguments instead of the usual four. *Windows++* overcomes this inconsistency by providing a window procedure with normal arguments that simply extracts the fifth argument (the client window's handle) and passes it along with the other four to *DefFrameProc*. Why Windows uses an aberrant frame-window procedure is beyond my ken.

■ The constructor requires as its only argument an integer, the relative position in the menu of the "Window" menu. Part of this menu is maintained by Windows as child windows are created and destroyed.

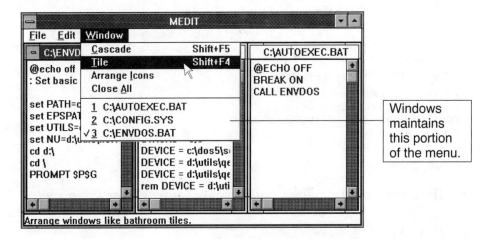

■ *WPMDIFrame* stores a pointer to its *client* window. The client window is created in the frame window's own *createWin* function, which is now virtual (see Section 7.2.1):

```
BOOL WPMDIFrame::createWin()
{
    if (WPMainWin::createWin()) {         // create frame window
        client = new WPMDIClient(this);   // create client window
        assert(client);
        return TRUE;
    }
    return FALSE;
}
```

■ *WPMDIFrame* provides a few "brainless" functions to *cascade* and *tile* the MDI Windows, go to the next window, and so on.

■ *WPMDIFrame* provides a few virtual message functions. For example, *queryEnd* simply checks *queryEnd* for all child windows:

```
BOOL WPMDIFrame::queryEnd()
{
    forEachChildWin(client, cwin) {
        if (!cwin->queryEnd())
            return FALSE;
    }
    return TRUE;
}
```

Note how easy it is to navigate the child windows with *forEachChildWin* (See Section 5.3.1.). Now every MDI application we ever write is Exit-proof.

■ A member function, *closeAll,* is provided to close all the MDI child windows. This function takes a boolean argument: whether to force the windows closed or not.

```
BOOL WPMDIFrame::closeAll(BOOL force)
{
    WPChildWinList children = client;
    WPWin *nextwin;
    for (WPWin *cwin=children.first(); cwin; cwin=nextwin) {
        nextwin = children.next();
        if (force || cwin->queryEnd())
            cwin->destroyWin();
        else
            return FALSE;
    }
    return TRUE;
}
```

The destructor invokes *closeAll* like so:

```
WPMDIFrame::~WPMDIFrame()
{
    closeAll(TRUE);
}
```

■ The *command* function handles a few generic MDI commands, such as Window Tile and Close All. The rest are passed either to the base class *WPMainWin* or sent to the currently active child window.

```
BOOL WPMDIFrame::command(int id, WORD msg)
{
    WPMDIChild *active = activeWin();
```

```
    switch (id) {
    case WPIDM_WINCASCADE:      cascade();          return TRUE;
    case WPIDM_WINTILE:         tile();             return TRUE;
    case WPIDM_WINARRANGE:      arrangeIcons();     return TRUE;
    case WPIDM_WINNEXT:         nextWin();          return TRUE;
    case WPIDM_WINCLOSEALL:     closeAll();         return TRUE;

    // Some File commands stay here; others go to child
    case WPIDM_FILEOPEN:        // These go up the inheritance..
    case WPIDM_FILENEW:         // ..chain to WPMainWin.
    case WPIDM_EXIT:            // ..More inherited behavior!
        break;

    case WPIDM_FILECLOSE:
        if (active)
            active->close();
        return TRUE;

    default:
        // By default, pass menu commands to child window.
        if (active && active->command(id, msg))
            return TRUE;
    }
    return WPMainWin::command(id, msg);  // Let WPMainWin do it.
}
```

By default, *command* sends all command messages to the currently active
MDI child window. For example, all the Edit commands are routed to the
child window, so applications don't have to do anything to get messages
sent to their child windows. *Windows++* takes care of it.

■ *WPMDIFrame::menuInit* initializes the File, Edit, and Window menu items:

```
BOOL WPMDIFrame::menuInit(WPMenu &menu)
{
    WPMenu mainMenu = this;
    if (menu==mainMenu) {
        WPMDIChild *active = activeWin();

        // Initialize File menu
        BOOL gotFile = active && active->fileName()[0]!=0;
        menu.enableItem(WPIDM_FILESAVE,
            gotFile && active->fileIsModified());
        menu.enableItem(WPIDM_FILEPSAVEAS, active!=NULL);
        menu.enableItem(WPIDM_FILEPRINT, active!=NULL);
        menu.enableItem(WPIDM_FILECLOSE, active!=NULL);

        // Initialize Edit menu
        BOOL any = active && active->anySelected();
        menu.enableItem(WPIDM_EDITPASTE,
            active && active->canPaste());
        menu.enableItem(WPIDM_EDITCUT, any);
        menu.enableItem(WPIDM_EDITCOPY, any);
        menu.enableItem(WPIDM_EDITDELETE, any);
```

```
        menu.enableItem(WPIDM_EDITUNDO,
            active && active->canUndo());

        // Initialize "Window" menu
        for (int id = WPIDM_WINTILE; id <= WPIDM_WINCLOSEALL; id++)
            menu.enableItem(id, active!=NULL);
        return TRUE;
    }
    return FALSE;
}
```

The File and Edit commands are initialized slightly differently than for a normal main window. The file name, *modified* status, current selection, and so on are obtained from the currently active child window rather than from the frame window itself.

Most of the code is pretty straightforward, once you learn the magic Windows incantations, which, believe me, isn't easy. That's why reusability is so important: once you figure out the correct voodoo, you simply encapsulate it in subroutines and forget about it.

6.4.4 *WPMDIChild*

The last MDI window class, *WPMDIChild*, is also derived from *WPMainWin*, since it behaves like a main window in more respects than it may at first appear to do. For example, MDI child windows have a file name, *modified* status, and current selection, so we want them to inherit all the File and Edit command logic from *WPMainWin*.

```
///////////////////
// MDI Child window.
//
class WPMDIChild : public WPMainWin {
    WPMDIClient* client;              // client window
public:
    WPMDIChild(CSTR classnm, WPMDIFrame *frame);
    BOOL createWin();
    void destroyWin()
        { client->sendMsg(WM_MDIDESTROY, getHwnd()); }
    void maximize()  { client->sendMsg(WM_MDIMAXIMIZE, getHwnd()); }
    void restore()   { client->sendMsg(WM_MDIRESTORE, getHwnd()); }
    void activate()  { client->sendMsg(WM_MDIACTIVATE, getHwnd()); }
};
```

Here's the quick summary:

■ The constructor sets up the appropriate *createArgs*, including setting the window procedure to the Windows default (*DefMDIChildProc*):

```
/////////////////
// Initialize MDI child window.
//
WPMDIChild::WPMDIChild(CSTR classnm, WPMDIFrame *frame) :
WPMainWin(classnm)
{
    createArgs.parent = frame->clientWin();
    createArgs.wndcls.lpfnWndProc = DefMDIChildProc;
    createArgs.wndcls.lpszMenuName = NULL;
    createArgs.title = NULL;
    createArgs.style = 0;
    noAppQuit=TRUE;  // hack so WPMainWin won't post WM_QUIT msg
}
```

There's just one little hack (OK, I admit it) required for child windows: Normally, the *WPMainWin* destructor invokes *App.quit* (since destroying a main window ends the application). But we don't want this behavior for MDI child windows, so I introduced a flag *appNoQuit* that's normally FALSE, but set to TRUE for MDI child windows. When this flag is set, ˜*WPMainWin* doesn't invoke *App.quit*.[41]

■ MDI Child windows have their own *createWin* and *destroyWin* functions, which have been altered in *WPWin* to be virtual (see Section 7.2.1). These functions hide the inconsistent way Windows has of creating MDI child windows. The destroy function is brainless: it just sends WM_MDI-DESTROY to the client window; *createWin* is a little more substantial:

```
/////////////////
// Create child window: do weird Windows incantations.
//
BOOL WPMDIChild::createWin()
{
    MDICREATESTRUCT cs;     // another unecessary Windows structure
    cs.szClass = (char*)createArgs.wndcls.lpszClassName;
    cs.szTitle = (char*)createArgs.title;
    cs.hOwner = createArgs.wndcls.hInstance;
    cs.x  = createArgs.pos.left();
    cs.y  = createArgs.pos.top();
    cs.cx = createArgs.pos.width();
    cs.cy = createArgs.pos.height();
```

---

41 This is just the sort of compromise that occurs in real systems. An MDI child window is not really a main window (the frame window is), but there's so much useful code in *WPMainWin* that I couldn't resist using *WPMainWin* for MDI child windows, which after all act very much like main windows. It seemed more expedient to introduce *appNoQuit*, since this turns out to be the only main window behavior that we don't want for MDI child windows.

This illustrates one advantage of building your own library: when you're both application *and* system programmer, you have the privilege of modifying the system to suit your application needs. *Don't abuse it!*

```
    cs.style = createArgs.style;
    cs.lParam = NULL;

    // Register window class if it ain't already registered!
    WNDCLASS temp;
    if (!GetClassInfo(cs.hOwner, cs.szClass, &temp)) {
        BOOL ret = RegisterClass(&createArgs.wndcls);
        assert(ret);
    }
    // Now create the child window.
    client = (WPMDIClient*)createArgs.parent;
    assert(client);
    HWND newhwnd = (HWND)(client->sendMsg(WM_MDICREATE, 0, &cs));
    linkHwnd(newhwnd);
    return hwnd!=NULL;
}
```

After setting up the special MDICREATESTRUCT, *createWin* sends the magic Windows WM_MDICREATE message to the client window, then links the window object to its handle; *createWin* even registers the window class if necessary (this is exactly the same thing we did back in Section 3.2.3).

▪ *WPMDIChild* provides a few MDI-specific brainless functions such as *restore* and *activate*.

6.4.5 Modifying the Main Message Loop

There's only one modification required in our basic infrastructure to make MDI fly. We have to modify the main message loop in *WPApp::run* (remember?) to translate MDI accelerator keys. Say what? Never mind, it's just more Windows voodoo that's described in the SDK *Guide To Programming*. Just do it:[42]

```
// Add MDI client window to application object.
// (In WPAPP.H)
class WPApp : public WPModule {
private:
    HWND mdiClientHwnd;                  // MDI client win, if any
    friend WPMDIClient;
};
// Modify message loop to translate MDI accelerator keys
// (In WPAPP.CPP).
void WPApp::run()
{
```

---

42 Some readers may tire of my continual jabbing at Windows. So be it. One reason Windows is so difficult to program is that the API is disorganized. Once you realize this, you can deal with it using either the techniques described in this book or your own. Too many programmers simply accept Windows as gospel, thinking "well, I guess it *has* to be complicated to do all that." Wrong. Don't make the mistake of thinking that just because a system is *successful* (and therefore worth programming for), it must be *right*. Another example of this is *dBase*.

```
      .
      .
   while (GetMessage(&msg, NULL, 0, 0)) {
      if (mdiClientHwnd && TranslateMDISysAccel(mdiClientHwnd, &msg))
         continue;
      .
      .
}
```

WPMDIClient sets *App.mdiClientHwnd* when the client window is created and re-stores it to NULL when the client window is destroyed. It's allowed to do this be-cause it's declared as a *friend* of *WPApp*. By modifying *WPApp::run*, application programmers no longer need even know that anything special is required to make MDI accelerator keys work. *Windows++* takes care of them invisibly.

Way back in Section 3.3.4 I told you we'd gradually enhance the main message loop until it was capable of handling everything. See? I didn't lie.

6.4.6 MDI Resource Macros

Using the same techniques described in Section 6.3.9, I've added a few MDI-re-lated resource file macros to WPID.H:

```
// Built-in command IDs for Window commands
#define WPIDM_WINTILE            (WPPIDBASE + 30)
#define WPIDM_WINCASCADE         (WPPIDBASE + 31)
#define WPIDM_WINARRANGE         (WPPIDBASE + 32)
#define WPIDM_WINCLOSEALL        (WPPIDBASE + 33)
#define WPIDM_WINNEXT            (WPPIDBASE + 34)

// Window menu items
#define   WindowCascade  "&Cascade\tShift+F5", WPIDM_WINCASCADE
#define   WindowTile     "&Tile\tShift+F4",    WPIDM_WINTILE
#define   WindowArrange  "Arrange &Icons",     WPIDM_WINARRANGE
#define   WindowCloseAll "Close &All",         WPIDM_WINCLOSEALL

// Window accelerator keys
#define   AccWinCascade VK_F5, WPIDM_WINCASCADE, SHIFT, VIRTKEY
#define   AccWinTile    VK_F4, WPIDM_WINTILE, SHIFT, VIRTKEY
#define   AccWinNext    VK_F6, WPIDM_WINNEXT, CONTROL, VIRTKEY
```

Now we'll never have to remember the exact names, mnemonics, or accelerator keys for the various Window commands. Here's the cleaned-up resource file for MEDIT:

```
// (From MEDIT.RC)
AppMenu MENU {
   .
   . (File, Edit commands just like WINEDIT)
   .
   POPUP "&Window" {
      MENUITEM  WindowCascade
      MENUITEM  WindowTile
      MENUITEM  WindowArrange
      MENUITEM  WindowCloseAll
```

```
    }
}

AppAccel ACCELERATORS
BEGIN
    . (File, Edit accelerators)
    .
    AccWinCascade
    AccWinTile
    AccWinNext
END
```

6.4.7 MEDIT

The main purpose of the MDI classes described above is to make writing MDI applications easy. Almost every line of code in *WPMDIClient, WPMDIFrame,* and *WPMDIChild* exists for one of two reasons:

■ Either the code encapsulates some useful MDI user interface behavior, such as graying menus or handling standard MDI commands (the Window commands); or

■ the code hides the grueling and error-prone Windows API mechanics required to make MDI work. For example, *createWin* and *destroyWin* make MDI child windows look to the programmer like any other kind of window; the code we added to *WPApp::run* hides the strangeness with MDI accelerator keys; and *WPMDIFrame* hides the client window entirely.

To see how what we might call *MDI++* works in practice, let's examine MEDIT. Once again, in the interests of completing the book within a reasonable number of pages, I'll simply show you the program, and provide a bulleted summary.

```
/////////////////////////////////////////////////////////////
// WINDOWS++ CLASS LIBRARY. Copyright 1992 Paul DiLascia.
// FILE: MEDIT.CPP
//
// Multi-file editor.

#include <wpp.h>

////////////////////
// Main edit window class--almost identical to WINEDIT.
//
class EditWin : public WPMDIChild {
    static BOOL first;              // first edit window created?
    WPMultiEdit *editCtl;           // main edit window
protected:
    BOOL gotFocus(WPWin *prev)
        { editCtl->setFocus(); return FALSE; }
public:
    EditWin(WPMDIFrame *frame, CSTR fname=NULL);
    BOOL sized(WPRect &box, WORD how)
        { editCtl->moveWin(box); return FALSE; }
```

```
    // File command functions
    BOOL fileIsModified()        { return editCtl->isModified(); }
    void fileIsModified(BOOL m)  { editCtl->setModified(m); }
    BOOL fileOpen(CSTR fname)    { return editCtl->load(fname); }
    BOOL fileSave(CSTR fname)    { return editCtl->save(fname); }
    BOOL fileNew()
        { editCtl->setSel(); editCtl->clear(); return TRUE; }

    // Edit command functions
    BOOL editCut()               { editCtl->cut(); return TRUE; }
    BOOL editCopy()              { editCtl->copy(); return TRUE; }
    BOOL editPaste()             { editCtl->paste(); return TRUE; }
    BOOL editDelete()            { editCtl->clear(); return TRUE; }
    BOOL editUndo()              { editCtl->undo(); return TRUE; }
    BOOL canUndo()               { return editCtl->canUndo(); }
    BOOL canPaste()              {return Clipboard.available(CF_TEXT);}
    BOOL anySelected()
        { int beg,end; return editCtl->getSel(beg, end); }
};

BOOL EditWin::first = TRUE;

//////////////////
// Create new edit window (as MDI child).
//
EditWin::EditWin(WPMDIFrame *pwin, CSTR fname)
    : WPMDIChild("EDITWIN", pwin)
{
    createWin();                        // create this window

    // Create multi-line edit control
    editCtl = new WPMultiEdit(this, -1);
    createArgs.pos = this;
    createArgs.style |=
        ES_AUTOVSCROLL | ES_AUTOHSCROLL | WS_VSCROLL | WS_HSCROLL;
    editCtl->createWin();

    fileInit(fname, "");
    setFocus();
    if (first) {
        maximize();
        first = FALSE;
    }
}

//////////////////
// Main (MDI Frame) window class.
//
class EditFrame : public WPMDIFrame {
    int pmtHeight;                      // height of prompt line
public:
    EditFrame(CSTR fname=NULL);
    BOOL sized(WPRect &box, WORD how);
    BOOL fileOpen(CSTR fname)
        { new EditWin(this, fname); return TRUE; }
    BOOL fileNew()
        { new EditWin(this); return TRUE; }
    int getMenuPrompt(char* buf, int id, WORD flags)
```

```
        { return id ? App.loadString(id, buf, MAXPROMPTLEN) : 0; }
};
///////////////////
// Initialize main window.
//
EditFrame::EditFrame(CSTR fname) : WPMDIFrame(2 /* "Window" menu pos*/)
{
    createArgs.style |= CS_DBLCLKS;
    WPWin::createWin("MEDIT");      // create main window

    // Create prompt line
    promptWin = new WPStatic(this, -1);
    createArgs.style |= WS_BORDER;
    promptWin->createWin();
    pmtHeight = tm.tmHeight;

    if (fname && *fname)
        fileOpen(fname);
}
///////////////////
// Re-size frame window.
//
BOOL EditFrame::sized(WPRect &box, WORD how)
{
    // Adjust client window
    box.height(box.height()-pmtHeight);
    clientWin()->moveWin(box);

    // Adjust prompt line
    WPRect pmtbox;
    pmtbox.origin(0, box.height());
    pmtbox.extent(box.width(), pmtHeight);
    promptWin->moveWin(pmtbox);
    return TRUE;
}
///////////////////
// Program entry point.
//
void WPApp::main()
{
    char fname[80];
    getCmdLine(fname);
    mainWin = new EditFrame(fname);
    run();
}
```

I didn't bother listing the resource (.RC) file (it's in Appendix A). Here are the highlights:

■ MEDIT defines two window classes: *EditWin*, which is used for each open file, and *EditFrame*, which is the main (MDI frame) window.

■ The frame window, *EditFrame*, is derived from *WPMDIFrame*, and so inherits all our MDI infrastructure, such as client window creation, the Window commands, and so on. *EditFrame* handles File Open and File New by providing *fileNew* and *fileOpen*, which create a new child (*EditWin*) window, either empty or initialized with a particular file.

- *EditWin* is almost identical to the *EditWin* in WINEDIT. The main differences are that it's derived from *WPMDIChild* instead of *WPMainWin* and no longer has a prompt line (the prompt line is now owned by the frame window). *EditWin* inherits all the File and Edit command logic from *WPMainWin*.

- The prompt line works exactly as before, but now it's handled in *EditFrame* instead of *EditWin* (and of course, there are additional prompts for the new Window commands). The *sized* function is slightly different: *EditFrame* shrinks the client window to allow room for the prompt line.

- *EditWin* uses a static class global (*first*) to maximize the first child window created. Subsequent windows are created using Windows' default size (the size of a cascaded window).

Most of the code in MEDIT is identical to that in WINEDIT. The main difference is that where everything in WINEDIT is done by a single window class (*EditWin*), the work in MEDIT is split between the frame and child windows. All the grueling MDI mechanics are inherited from *Windows++* objects. Aside from the lines that derive *EditFrame* and *EditWin* from *WPMDIFrame* and *WPMDIChild*, there's not a single line of code in MEDIT that has anything to do with MDI!

Who says MDI applications have to be difficult?

Most important, look how small MEDIT is! With all the API mechanics (not just MDI) encapsulated in library objects, MEDIT is hardly bigger than WINEDIT (145 lines *vs.* 112 at last count). Compare this with MULTIPAD, which requires several files that add up to well over 2500 lines! Granted, the Microsoft program contains lots of comments, does searching, and has a few error messages as well, but even taking all this into account, MEDIT is at least an order of magnitude smaller.

See? This reusability stuff really works!

6.5 Summary

We've encapsulated a good deal of low-level, generic, CUA-compliant user interface behavior in *Windows++* library objects, where any application can now inherit it for free. We added code in *WPMainWin* to handle the details of the File and Edit commands (overwrite confirmation, dialogs, menu graying), and we implemented three new classes that do all the gruntwork required for MDI applications.

The same techniques could be applied to "boxify" other CUA behavior. The approach can be generalized in the form of two basic rules:

Reusability Rules

■ Put anything and everything that's application-generic in the library.

■ If necessary, introduce virtual functions as place-holders to perform operations that are application-specific.

Just so "reusability" doesn't become a tired expression that only becomes a substitute for Goodness, Truth, and Apple Pie, let me reiterate once again its practical benefits:

■ By reusing library code, applications are smaller, which means simpler and easier to write. WINEDIT and MEDIT are dramatically smaller than their C counterparts.

■ By reducing the burden of UI coding, we set application programmers free to focus their energies on applications, without having to worry about a lot of trivial nonsense like graying menus and running dialog boxes.

■ Applications are more reliable for two reasons: 1) they are smaller (every line of code is a potential bug); and 2) they inherit our tried-and-proven, bug-free (of course) library code, instead of reinventing it anew each time. Our approach is immeasurably more reliable than copy-paste-editing the code from another application (as Microsoft would have you do), since bugs are always introduced in that process. And if (heaven forbid) someone should discover a bug in our library, you only have to fix it once, for all applications.

■ Applications are more consistent. By encapsulating low-level user interface behavior in one reusable place, we've eliminated the possibility that application programmers might stray from the CUA guidelines, whether out of error, ignorance or just plain laziness. Just using *Windows++* guarantees that an application is CUA-compliant.

Practically every OOP book lists the magic buzzwords *reusability, consistency, reliability,* and so on, but their significance often gets lost in abstractions. I've tried to show you the benefits, in real life, honest-to-goodness Windows programs.

[C] *The same techniques can be applied in C. Any C++ member function that you see here can be implemented as an ordinary C subroutine. For example, you could write subroutines that do all the File and Edit commands, including graying the menus and running the prompt line. Of course, you can't simply inherit the behavior by deriving a subclass; you have to call the subroutines explicitly, but that's still a lot easier than reinventing the code each time you write a new application. Virtual functions can always be mimicked in C using function pointers.*

There's just one drawback with adding all this reusable functionality to *Windows++*: code bloat. Every *Windows++* program now brings in more object modules when it's
linked. While the MDI code (WPMDI.OBJ) is only linked if
the program actually uses it, the dialog modules (WPCTRL,
WPDLG, WPDLFILE, etc.) from the next chapter are now
brought in by *WPMainWin*, even if the program doesn't have
File or Edit commands or even use dialogs. For example, HELLO.EXE is now several kilobytes larger. Yet this is a small price to pay for the benefits listed above.
Besides, while *Windows++* makes even small programs like HELLO much easier
to write, its benefits shine brightest in large programs, which stand to reuse more
code. Such programs almost certainly have File commands and dialog boxes. We
shouldn't design *Windows++* around dopey programs like HELLO.

## CHAPTER 7

Dialogs

One of the fundamental user interface building blocks in Windows is the *dialog box*, or *dialog* for short. A dialog is a special kind of window that's used to get information from the user. Sometimes, an entire application is little more than a dialog.[43] While dialogs are an essential element of Windows programs, coding them is notoriously laborious—unnecessarily so, as you'll soon see, for in this chapter, I'll show you how to make dialog coding a snap.

As always, we'll design our system around a concrete application: a rolodex database that manages a list of names and addresses. The PEOPLE program contains a number of dialogs typical of Windows applications, such as "File Open" and "File Save", as well as an "Edit Person" dialog that lets users edit the information about a particular person. PEOPLE also provides an example showing how controls can be created on the fly, outside of dialogs. It uses a list box to display the list of names in its main window.

Throughout the chapter we'll alternate between building the PEOPLE program and *Windows++* itself. We'll use PEOPLE to guide the design of our dialog system, through a process of wishful thinking: first, we'll put ourselves in the shoes of someone writing the PEOPLE program, and ask, "how should *Windows++* look from this point of view?" Then, we'll surrender our roles as application programmers, don our *Windows++* system-architect caps, and proceed to fulfill the wishes of our former selves. PEOPLE will thus lead the development of *Windows++*, illustrating once again one of my main themes: build the application first, then ecapsulate its generic aspects in reusable library code.

I should warn you at the outset that 1) this is the longest chapter in the book and 2) the pace picks up a bit. I won't go into the same level of detail as I've been doing all

---

43 Examples of this are Charles Petzold's HEXCALC program (see [Petzold 1990], and my own LAUNCH program, which in the interests of keeping the chapter size down, is not described but merely listed in Appendix A.

along but will assume you're starting to get the hang of things by now. So if you need a breather, now's the time to take it.

The reason the chapter is so long is that we have so much to cover. First, we have to build the usual *Windows++* infrastructure to model dialogs and controls. Next, we'll implement "object-oriented" dialogs. Then we'll use them to build specific, reusable dialogs based on the dialogs in COMMDLG, a DLL that comes with Windows 3.1 (but runs under 3.0 as well). Finally, we'll wind out the chapter with a discussion of modeless dialogs. That's a lot to cover in one chapter!

While the chapter is long, the results are well worth it. By the time we're finished, we'll have built a totally reusable, table-driven dialog system that renders dialog procedures practically obsolete!

Let's begin by reviewing how dialogs work in Windows, and why you'd want to get rid of dialog procedures in the first place.

7.1 The Problem with Dialogs

To implement a dialog in Windows, you must complete two tasks:

- You must create a *dialog template* in the program's resource (.RC) file.

- You must write a *dialog procedure* to handle messages from the dialog.

Then to run the dialog, you invoke one of the Windows dialog-creation functions such as *DialogBox* or *CreateDialog*, passing it the name of the resource template and address of your dialog procedure. Which function you use depends on what kind of dialog you want to create. Windows distinguishes between *modal* and *modeless* dialogs. Modal dialogs prevent users from doing anything else until completing the dialog; modeless dialogs let users continue to do things in the main window.

Let's examine each of the above two steps in a little more detail.

7.1.1 The Resource Template

The resource template specifies the appearance of the dialog. The About dialog for the PEOPLE program is a typical example:

```
DLGABOUT DIALOG  72,13,124,70
STYLE DS_MODALFRAME | WS_POPUP | WS_CLIPSIBLINGS
BEGIN
    CONTROL "OK",IDOK,"Button",BS_DEFPUSHBUTTON | WS_TABSTOP |
        WS_CHILD | WS_VISIBLE,32,50,30,14
    CONTROL "Written using the Windows++ Class Library by
        Paul DiLascia",-1,"static",WS_CHILD | SS_LEFT,32,18,88,28
    CONTROL "AppIcon",IDSI_ABOUTICON,"static",
        SS_ICON | WS_CHILD,7,22,16,16
    CONTROL "People Database",-1,"static",WS_CHILD | SS_LEFT,32,5,80,8
END
```

These statements specify the size, position, and contents of several child windows called *controls*. A control is a special window class that's used to present a particular kind of information such as a string or list. The About box for PEOPLE contains four controls: three "static" controls and an OK button.

It's possible to "clean up" the resource file to make it look nicer (not to mention easier to read), but in practice few people edit the resource file directly, except to make minor modifications. Most programmers use one of the interactive dialog design tools provided with most compilers (Borland provides its *Resource Workshop*; Zortech comes with a subset of Blue Sky's *WindowsMaker*). These tools let you edit dialogs interactively, on the screen, then generate the resource file.

There's no real reason (or way) to improve on this aspect of dialog coding, since one way or another, you simply have to specify what the dialog looks like. One could imagine some sort of algorithm for designing dialogs (try to line things up, space controls evenly, etc.), but there's no substitute for the human eye. Besides, using an interactive dialog designer not only works well, it's fun!

It's the dialog procedure that, as you'll soon see, provides ample grist for the reusability mill.

7.1.2 The Dialog Procedure

The dialog procedure is similar to the window procedure used for windows. Its job is to process messages sent by Windows when things "happen" in the dialog, like when the user clicks a button or types something. Most Windows programs contain many long dialog procedures, each replete with the 14-page switch statement that seems to be the hallmark of Windows programming. Much of the effort in dialog procedures is spent mired in the cumbersome and mundane Windows API mechanics of copying information back and forth between controls and the program's internal data structures, not actually doing anything.

```
BOOL FAR PASCAL MyDlgProc(HWND hdlg, WORD msg, WORD wp, LONG lp)
{
    switch (msg) {
    case IDOK:
        // copy everything from controls to data structure
        GeWindowtText(hwndEditName, person.name, sizeof(person.name);
        GetWindowText(hwndEditAddr, person.addr, sizeof(person.addr);
        person.retired = (BOOL)SendMessage(hwndButnRetired, BM_GETCHECK);
        ...etc.
        EndDialog(hdlg, 0);
        break;
        .
        .
        .
}
```

This requires storing handles to all the controls (*hwndEditName*, etc.) and invoking strange Windows functions to access their contents. This chore is an annoying and unnecessary burden on programmers, who should be free to focus their energies on applications, not dialog mechanics.

While dialog procedures are almost identical to window procedures, they do have a couple of annoying differences. For example, the return value is BOOL instead of LONG, and there's at least one message unique to dialogs, WM_INITDIALOG.

To make matters even worse, dialogs have a window procedure also! This raises the obvious question: should you handle a given message in the dialog procedure or in the window procedure? Answer: most "vanilla" Windows applications use the dialog procedure. But vanilla isn't good enough for us (we want chocolate and strawberry too). Our basic *Windows++* infrastructure is based on subclassing (in the Windows sense, of replacing the window procedure) every window. Why should dialogs be different?

In fact, you might well wonder why Windows even has a dialog procedure. Why not just use the window procedure to handle dialog messages? That's a good question, but sadly, a moot one, since we have to live with Windows the way it is.

One solution to the problem of dialog coding is to use a commercial code generator. These after-market products devote a significant portion of their energies to fabricating dialog procedures from programmers' specifications. In a typical code generator, you design the dialog interactively on the screen, just as you would for the resource template, but then you specify additional information about what goes where in your program, for example, that the contents of a particular edit control should be copied to a variable called *Address*. Click a button and—*presto!* Instant dialog procedure.

As with window procedures, this should make you suspicious. The fact that dialog procedures can be generated in such an automated fashion belies their fundamental sameness. It seems reasonable to wonder, if it's possible to generate a dialog procedure from a specification of the dialog, why not just write one dialog procedure with variable parameters, and *reuse* it in every program?

Why not, indeed!

Of course, while all dialogs are more or less similar, they're *not* identical; it's precisely in the "more or less" that things get tricky (if it were trivial, someone would have done it already). Our job will be to isolate the identical aspects of *all* dialogs and encapsulate them in reusable code. This is the very essence of object-oriented programming: *grouping the common features of disparate entities into single components that can be reused.*

7.1.3 Wishful Thinking: Object-Oriented Dialogs

Now let's forget about what Windows does and think about how dialogs *should* work, from the point of view of an application such as the PEOPLE program. Are you ready? OK, forget everything you just read, and instead consider the Edit Person dialog:

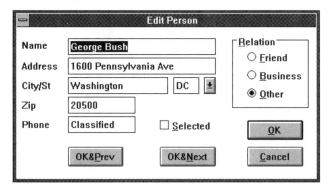

This dialog lets users edit information about a particular person in the database. The information is stored within the program as an instance of the class *Person:*

```
enum STATUS { STFRIEND=0, STBUSINESS, STOTHER, NSTATUS };

class Person {
    char    name[50]; // person's name
    char    addr[50]; // address
    char    city[30]; // ...and so on
    char    state[3];
    char    zip[10];
    STATUS status;
public:
    Person()        { clear(); }
    void clear()    { memset(this, 0, sizeof(Person); }
};
```

There's an obvious correspondence between the data members of *Person* and the controls in the dialog:

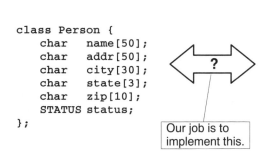

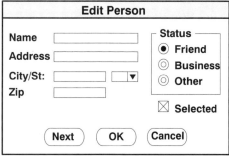

Object   **User Interface**

Each control lets the user edit a particular data member; the entire dialog lets the user edit the whole *Person*. In other words, a dialog box is just a user interface to an object. Dialogs are thus naturally object-oriented. Pursuing the idea further, we can think of "running the dialog box" as "editing the object." We can make this idea explicit by positing an *edit* operation:

```
class Person {
public:
    BOOL edit();       // run dialog box
};
```

The *edit* function is supposed to create the appropriate dialog box, initialize it with the object's contents, let the user edit them, and (if the user presses OK) copy the changes back to the object. The boolean return value is intended to indicate whether the object was modified or not. With this definition, creating a dialog to edit a *Person* is a simple as

```
Person *p;
if (p->edit()) {
    // modified: do something
}
```

Now that looks easy! If I were writing the PEOPLE program (and I am), that's how I'd want it to work.

As long as we're indulging in wishful thinking, what else might we (as application programmers) want from our pie-in-the-sky dialog system? Well, sooner or later we'll want to manipulate the contents of the dialog. In Windows, this requires storing handles to controls, then sending them all sorts of bizarre messages like BM_SETCHECK and LB_GETCURSEL. It sure would be nice if we didn't have to bother with all that, but could instead manipulate the underlying object directly. For example, to clear the dialog, instead of writing

```
SetWindowText(hCtlName, "");
SetWindowText(hCtlAddr, "");
SetWindowText(hCtlCity, "");
SetWindowText(hCtlState, "");
SetWindowText(hCtlZip, "");
SendMessage(hCtlSelected, BM_SETCHECK, FALSE, 0L);
```

I'd like to write

```
Person p;
dlg->somehowConnectObjectToDialog(&p);
p.clear();                          // does memset(p, 0, sizeof(Person);
```

and have the dialog automatically reflect the changes. It's easier and more natural to manipulate data objects directly, rather than having to invoke API functions to copy information back and forth between controls. In fact, if we could figure out how to do it, this would eliminate the need to deal with controls entirely.

More importantly, by thinking of dialogs as user interfaces to objects, we have a powerful model to guide us, one that provides a fundamental clarity to what we're doing. While every dialog doesn't necessarily match some internal data structure, it probably should. Having a user interface that reflects a program's internal organization is a healthy thing, since it eliminates the need for complicated and bug-prone UI code that maps the internal model to the external one. In any case, a dialog can always be made to represent an object class, simply by inventing a new class that mirrors the dialog.

Of course, dialogs are more than just passive collections of independent controls; they often contain active components. Push buttons may execute commands such as OK and CANCEL, and controls may interact. Editing one item may affect another. For example, dragging a scroll bar might continuously display its numeric value in an edit control. Selecting a check box might even create a new edit control in the dialog. In short, dialogs possess a dynamic aspect, over and above their static nature as a collection of controls.

While it's possible to imagine a system that encapsulates even the dynamics of dialogs in some high-level formulation,[44] doing so goes beyond the scope of this book. We will be content to capture the static aspect of dialogs, plus the most generic dynamics such as OK and CANCEL. As you'll see, this modest goal alleviates most of the burden of dialog coding. For sophisticated dialogs with interacting controls, we'll simply assume from the outset that some application-specific code must be written. But if programmers can manipulate the underlying object instead of the dialog, just imagine how easy it'll be!

7.1.4 Plan of Attack

In this chapter, we will in fact implement object-oriented dialogs as just outlined. The effort will be long and complex, but I think you'll agree when we're done that the results are well worth it. The preceding section was intended not only to explain where we're going, but to whet your appetite and provide some motivation to sustain you through the next three sections, which are long and detailed.

The task that looms ahead seems daunting from our current vantage. Where do we even begin?

As Bjarne Stroustrup says, "There is only one basic way of dealing with complexity: Divide and conquer." ([Stroustrup 1991], p. 364.) We can break the work into three main pieces:

---

44 For example, it might be possible to link control attributes such as *isEnabled* and *isVisible* to the states of other controls using some sort of table mechanism such as the one described in Section 7.4.1. Sophisticated dynamics can also often be encapsulated in specialized controls. For example, a scroll bar and edit control could be combined into a new, "complex" control (*ScrollEdit?*), which would manage the interaction between the two and which, once implemented, could be reused. A combo box is just such a complex control: it's an amalgam of a list box and an edit control. Some examples of specialized controls are the US States combo box described in Section 7.3.5 and the "alternating icon" described in Section 7.5.1.

1. First, we'll implement the basic infrastructure required to create and destroy dialogs, and handle dialog events. This is necessary because, as we've already noted, Windows does things differently for dialogs. If dialogs worked the same way as normal windows, we'd simply inherit everything from *WPWin*.

2. Next, we'll implement a number of *Windows++* classes to model controls such as edit controls and list boxes. This process will be a more or less easy and straightforward application of the "brainless" techniques described in Section 3.2.6. Along the way, we'll add a couple of specialized controls of our own: an edit control for zip codes and a combo box for US States.

3. Finally, we'll implement object-oriented dialogs as sketched in the preceding section. We'll replace the question mark in the figure on page 237 with working code.

These tasks suffice to build our dialog system, but the dialog story doesn't end there. As soon as our shiny new dialog system is working, we'll immediately put it to work in the PEOPLE program and in reusable dialogs for future applications to inherit. Finally, the chapter concludes with a discussion of modeless dialogs.

7.2 *Windows++* Dialog Mechanics

In this section, we'll implement the basic infrastructure required to create and destroy dialogs and handle dialog events. You might be wondering, "we already have ways to create and destroy windows, and we have a whole collection of virtual functions to handle events, so why do we have to do anything?"

Indeed, we'd like to use all the code we've already written; we'd like to use the same virtual message function mechanism to handle dialog events. For example, to handle WM_COMMAND, we'd like to simply write a *command* function:

```
DlgEditPerson::command(int id, WORD msg)
{
    switch (id) {
    case IOK:
        // handle OK button
        return TRUE;

      .
      .
}
```

So what's stopping us?

The problem is that Windows does many things differently for dialogs. For example, instead of *CreateWindow*, Windows provides eight functions to create dialogs:

```
CreateDialog
CreateDialogParam
CreateDialogIndirect
CreateDialogIndirectParam
DialogBox
DialogBoxParam
DialogBoxIndirect
DialogBoxIndirectParam
```

Which function you use depends on what kind of dialog you want to create and what arguments you have.[45] Dialogs are also destroyed differently from normal windows, and they use a slightly different mechanism to handle messages. Thus dialogs are not automatically "hooked up" to our wonderful infrastructure; we can't simply inherit everything from *WPWin*.

What we *can* do, and what we *will* do, is write code that makes dialogs work like any other kind of window and thereby present a more consistent interface to applications. From the perspective of a *Windows++* programmer writing the PEOPLE or any other application, dialogs will seem no different than any other kind of window. All the dialog-specific code will be hidden within *Windows++*.

We'll start, as always, by defining a new class:

```
class WPDialog : public WPWin {

};
```

Since dialogs are a special kind of window, they're derived from *WPWin*. We can even go one step further—we can *class*ify dialogs as either modal or modeless:

```
class WPDialogModal : public WPDialog {

};
class WPDialogModeless : public WPDialog {

};
```

As we implement dialogs, any property or behavior that's common to both modal and modeless dialogs will be implemented as part of *WPDialog*; functionality that's specific to modal or modeless dialogs will be implemented in the corresponding subclass. Modal dialogs are more common, so we'll restrict our attention to them for a while. (Modeless dialogs are covered in Section 7.6.)

As with windows, these classes will become the basis from which applications may derive application-specific dialogs. For example, the "Edit Person" dialog in the PEOPLE program is a kind of modal dialog:

---

45 The *CreateDialog* functions all create modeless dialogs; the *DialogBox* functions create modal dialogs. The *Param* functions pass an arbitrary 32-bit parameter to the dialog; the *Indirect* versions create the dialog from a memory-resident data structure, rather than a resource template.

```
class DlgEditPerson : public WPDialogModal {

};
```

OK, now that we have a class, what next? Since we want dialogs to work just like any other kind of window, let's try to follow our established conventions for manipulating window objects. Since you may not remember all the details, I'll review them briefly here (consult Chapter 3 for further explanation).

- The base class constructors (e.g., *WPWin, WPMainWin, HelloWin*) initialize the window creation arguments in *createArgs*, and perform any additional application-specific initialization that may be required. The last constructor (e.g., *HelloWin*) calls *createWin* to actually create the window.

- After creating the window, *createWin* invokes *linkHwnd* to link the window's HWND to the *Windows++* window object: *linkHwnd* stores the object pointer in the window's property list, and also also replaces the default window procedure with our universal window procedure, *WPWndProc*.

- Once the window is linked, messages are routed via *WPWndProc* and *msgProc* to the appropriate virtual message function (e.g., *paint,* etc.). Establishing the link in *linkHwnd* is crucial, since otherwise *WPWndProc* doesn't know which object to pass events to.

- The window object is automatically destroyed by *WPWndProc*, when Windows sends the WM_DESTROY message.

We'll do essentially the same thing for dialogs: we'll write a *createWin* function that creates and links the dialog, and a universal dialog procedure, *WPDlgProc*, that routes events to the proper virtual message function.

7.2.1 Creating Dialogs

To create a dialog object, we need a constructor. To write the constructor, we need to know what dialog creation arguments Windows requires. The most basic dialog creation functions are *DialogBox* (for modal dialogs) and *CreateDialog* (for modeless dialogs), both of which have the same "signature" (arguments and return value):

```
int  FAR PASCAL DialogBox(HANDLE, LPSTR, HWND, FARPROC);
int  FAR PASCAL CreateDialog(HANDLE, LPSTR, HWND, FARPROC);
```

The four arguments are the program's module instance handle, the name of the resource template, the handle of the parent window, and a pointer to the dialog procedure. The return value is –1 if the dialog could not be loaded; otherwise it's whatever value is specified when the dialog is terminated (we'll deal with ending the dialog in a moment).

We have to get the four arguments from somewhere. The module instance handle is readily available from our global *App* object, and the dialog procedure will always be *WPDlgProc* (described in the next section). That leaves the parent window and resource template name. Since these are application-specific, we'll pass them as arguments to the constructor.

```
class WPDialog : public WPWin {
protected:
    CSTR templateName;                 // resource file template name
public:
    WPDialog(CSTR resname, WPWin *pwin) : WPWin(NULL, pwin)
        { templateName = resname; }
};
```

The template name is stored in a data member, *templateName,* that's protected (so derived subclasses can access it).[46] The parent window pointer is simply passed along to *WPWin,* along with a NULL class name (class names aren't normally used for dialogs). Since *DialogBox* and *CreateDialog* have the same signature, so do the constructors for *WPDialogModal* and *WPDialogModeless:*

```
class WPDialogModal : public WPDialog {
public:
    WPDialogModal(CSTR resname, WPWin *pwin)
        : WPDialog(resname, pwin) { }
};
class WPDialogModeless : public WPDialog {
public:
    WPDialogModeless(CSTR resname, WPWin *pwin)
        : WPDialog(resname, pwin) { }
};
```

So far so good. The creation arguments are tucked away, ready to go. Now to actually create the dialog. Normally, we'd call *createWin,* but we don't want the one we wrote for *WPWin* (which calls *CreateWindowEx*), we want a new one that calls *DialogBox.* No problem, we can write a different *createWin* function for dialogs. But first, we must go back to *WPWin* and make *createWin* virtual:

```
class WPWin {
public:
    virtual BOOL createWin();        // same as before, but virtual
};
```

This is required so that *win->createWin()* invokes the proper *createWin* function for whichever class of object *win* really is: if it's a *WPWin, WPWin::createWin* is invoked; if it's a dialog, *WPDialog::createWin.*

Now that *createWin* is virtual, we can implement it for dialogs. All we have to do is invoke *DialogBox* with the creation arguments:

---

46 We could make *templateName* a static global, like *createArgs,* to save a little space in *WPDialog,* but this is hardly worth it since, unlike windows, most applications rarely have more than a few dialogs running at the same time.

```
// (In WPDLG.H)
class WPDialog : public WPWin {
protected
    int result;                         // dialog return code
public:
    int returnCode()                    { return result; }
};

class WPDialogModal : public WPDialog {
public:
    BOOL createWin();
};

// (In WPDLG.CPP)
BOOL WPDialogModal::createWin()
{
    result = DialogBox(App(),           // program's instance handle
        templateName,                   // name of resource template
        GetHwnd(createArgs.parent),     // parent window handle
        WPDlgProc);                     // dialog proc (described later)
    assert(result!=-1);                 // should always succeed
    return (result != -1);
}
```

(The parent window pointer was stored in *createArgs.parent* by the *WPWin* constructor.) The return code from *DialogBox* is stored in a new data member, *result*, in case it's needed later, and *createWin* returns TRUE only if the dialog was successfully created. Since the *result* is generic to both modal and modeless dialogs, I added it to *WPDialog*; on the other hand, *DialogBox* creates only modal dialogs, so *createWin* is a member of *WPDialogModal*.

To finish *createWin*, we must invoke *linkHwnd* to store the window handle in the window's property list. This will have to wait until after the next section, because we'll use the dialog procedure to do it.

It's worth taking time out for a moment to consider what we've just done. By making *createWin* virtual, with a different implementation for dialogs, we provide consistency to *Windows++* where none exists in Windows. In Windows, the function used to create windows is different from those used to create dialogs. But in *Windows++*, the same virtual function *createWin* is used for both. There's no need to scratch your head wondering, "which function do I use?" It's always *createWin*. (If the designers of Windows had followed this practice, there'd be a lot fewer functions in the API.)

We can elevate this observation to a general design principle: *wherever Windows provides different ways to accomplish the same thing, we should seek to hide the disparity behind a uniform interface.* This not only makes programming easier (there's less trivia to remember), it lets us write reusable code. Virtual functions are essential. They provide the way to expose disparate entities through a uniform interface.

Back to dialogs. Since it's sometimes more natural to think of "running" a dialog rather than "creating" it, let's add a *run* function that simply invokes *createWin*, and returns the result from *DialogBox*.

```
class WPDialog : public WPWin {
    int run()          { createWin(); return result; }
};
```

We can also add a *modified* flag: since most dialogs need to keep track of whether or not their contents have been altered, why not add the flag at a low level, where it can be reused?

```
class WPDialog : public WPWin {
    BOOL modified;
public:
    BOOL isModified()                { return modified; }
    void isModified(BOOL b)          { modified = b; }
};
```

7.2.2 The Dialog Procedure

With the dialog created, the next thing we have to do is handle dialog events. Once again, we want dialogs to look just like windows. In other words, we want to use the virtual message functions, such as *command*, to handle dialog events. To do this, all we have to do is implement a universal dialog procedure, *WPDlgProc*, that essentially mimics *WPWndProc*:

```
// This is THE dialog procedure used for all Windows++ dialog boxes.
//
BOOL _export FAR PASCAL
WPDlgProc(HWND hdlg, WORD msg, WORD wp, LONG lp)
{
    WPDialog *dlg = (WPDialog*)WPWin::GetWin(hdlg);
    if (dlg==NULL)
        return FALSE;
    WPEvent event(msg, wp, lp);
    return dlg->dispatchEvent(event);     // call virtual dialog proc
}
```

Like *WPWndProc*, *WPDlgProc* is *_exported*, since it's passed to Windows as a callback function (it's one of the arguments passed to *DialogBox*), and so that when we use the appropriate compiler switch, *WPDlgProc* gets the "smart" function prolog that obviates the need for *MakeProcInstance*. *WPDlgProc* is almost identical to *WPWndProc*. It first obtains the window object by calling *GetWin* (we haven't linked the dialog to its HWND yet; we'll do it shortly), then invokes *dispatchEvent* to route the message (in the form of an event) to the appropriate virtual function.

Remember *dispatchEvent*? We implemented it way back in Section 3.5.4. It's basically just a giant switch statement:

```
BOOL WPWin::dispatchEvent(WPEvent &event)
{
    switch (event.msg) {
    case WM_PAINT:
        return paint();
    case WM_GETMINMAXINFO:
        return getMinMaxInfo((LPMINMAXINFO)event.lp);
    case WM_ACTIVATE:
        return activated(event.wp, HIWORD(event.lp));
    .
    . etc.
}
```

The only reason for breaking *dispatchEvent* out as a separate function was so we can now use it in dialogs. We can't use *msgProc* because it returns a LONG; *dispatchEvent* returns the BOOL that Windows expects from a dialog procedure. There'd be no justification for *dispatchEvent* if window and dialog procedures had the same signature.

But there's a problem (you'd never know it until your code crashed like mine did when I first built this stuff): dialogs have a window procedure *and* a dialog procedure. In fact, the way Windows routes messages to our dialog procedure is via the window procedure. To see this, all you have to do is examine Windows' default window procedure for dialogs, *DefDlgProc*, the source code for which is provided with the SDK. In pseudo-code, it looks more or less like this:

```
LONG DefDlgProc(HWND hDlg, wMsg, wParam, lParam)
{
    if ( callDialogProcedure(hDlg, wMsg, wParam, lParam) )
        return 0;
    switch (wMsg) {
        .
        . default message handling
        .
    }
    return result
}
```

The default window procedure simply invokes the dialog procedure: if the dialog procedure handled the message (that is, if it returns TRUE), *DefDlgProc* returns; otherwise it goes on to process various messages.

Currently, our low-level window object (*WPWin*) subclasses every window we create by replacing the window procedure with *WPWndProc*. This is done by *linkHwnd*. We still haven't linked our dialog object yet, but when we do (in the next section), the window procedure will get replaced with *WPWndProc*, which passes messages to *msgProc*, which invokes *dispatchEvent*. In other words, every message will get processed twice. First by the *window* procedure and again by the *dialog* procedure. Sigh.

To fix this, all we have to do is short-circuit *msgProc* for dialogs:

```
class WPDialog : public WPWin {
   LONG msgProc(WPEvent &event) { return dfltMsgProc(event); }
};
```

Since *msgProc* is already virtual, all we have to do is write a different one for dialogs: instead of invoking *dispatchEvent*, as *WPWin::msgProc* does, the dialog version sends all events back to *DefDlgProc*, which will call our dialog procedure. (In case you forgot: *dfltMsgProc* sends the message back to whatever window procedure the window had before we subclassed it, the one stored in *oldProc*, which for dialogs is *DefDlgProc*.)

7.2.3 Linking the Dialog

There's one crucial detail that was postponed when we implemented *createWin*: we didn't link the dialog to its window. Recall from Chapter 3 (and from the opening review) that the way we connect *Windows++* window objects to their underlying window handle (HWND) is by storing the object pointer in the window's property list. This is required so *WPDlgProc* and *WPWndProc* have a way to obtain the object instance that should receive the event:

```
BOOL _export FAR PASCAL
WPDlgProc(HWND hdlg, WORD msg, WORD wp, LONG lp)
{
   WPDialog *dlg = (WPDialog*)WPWin::GetWin(hdlg);
   .
   .
   .
}
```

GetWin simply calls *getProp* to retrieve the object pointer from the property list. The crucial link between (*Windows++*) window objects and their (Windows) HWNDs is established by *WPWin::linkHwnd*, which is normally invoked when the window is created, in *WPWin::createWin*:

```
BOOL WPWin::createWin()
{
   .
   .
   HWND newhwnd = CreateWindowEx(...);
   linkHwnd(newhwnd);            // <<< establish link
   return hwnd!=NULL;
}
```

But we just wrote a different *createWin* for dialogs, and we didn't call *linkHwnd*. Until we link the dialog, there's no way for *WPDlgProc* to know which dialog object to pass events to—*GetWin* won't work.

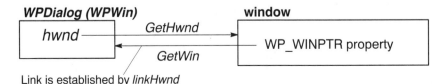

Link is established by *linkHwnd*

You might think we could simply call *linkHwnd* from within *createWin,* as we do for *WPWin,* like so:

```
BOOL WPDialog::createWin(CSTR title)
{
    result = DialogBox(App(),
        templateName,
        GetHwnd(parent),
        WPDlgProc);
    linkHwnd( ??? );                        // where's the HWND ?
    assert(result!=-1);
    return (result != -1);
}
```

Unfortunately, this won't work because the dialog is launched as soon as we invoke *DialogBox.* Control doesn't return to *createWin* until the dialog ends. Once we invoke *DialogBox,* the only code of ours that will ever receive control again is the dialog procedure, *WPDlgProc.* But that's just where we need the missing object pointer.

Fortunately, Windows provides a solution. The *DialogBoxParam* API function is like *DialogBox* except that it lets us pass an arbitrary 32-bit DWORD parameter to the dialog procedure as the *lParam* of the WM_INITDIALOG message. We can use it to pass our object pointer to the dialog procedure as follows:

```
BOOL WPDialogModal::createWin()
{
    result = DialogBoxParam(App(),      // <<<< use Param variety
        templateName,
        GetHwnd(createArgs.parent),
        WPDlgProc,
        (DWORD)this);                   // <<<< pass object pointer
    assert(result!=-1);
    return result != -1;
}
```

Now *WPDlgProc* can grab this pointer and link the dialog:

```
BOOL _export FAR PASCAL
WPDlgProc(HWND hdlg, WORD msg, WORD wp, LONG lp)
{
    WPDialog *dlg;

    if (msg == WM_INITDIALOG) {
        dlg = (WPDialog*)lp;            // passed from DialogBoxParam
        assert(dlg);                    // safety-check
        dlg->linkHwnd(hdlg);            // link to window
    }
    .
    . (as before)
    .
}
```

Our dialog object is now automatically linked to its window as soon as the (Windows) dialog is created. The same solution even works for modeless dialogs, since Windows provides a *CreateDialogParam* analog to *CreateDialog*.

Unfortunately, there's one situation when using *lParam* won't work.

A little later on (in Section 7.5.3), we'll use COMMDLG, which contains a number of essential dialogs. This DLL was introduced in Windows version 3.1 (but works in 3.0 too). As so often happens when systems are enhanced, consistency was thrown out the Windows: the designers of Windows 3.1 neglected to provide *Param* versions of the common dialogs supported in COMMDLG.DLL. In fact, the common dialogs use the WM_INITDIALOG parameter for their own purposes. Which means we can't use it for ours. Common dialogs provide a totally different mechanism to set the application-specific DWORD. Having so many different ways to accomplish the same result is just the sort of thing that makes programmers prematurely bald. Since we want *WPDlgProc* to work for all dialogs (without it "knowing" whether the dialog is a common dialog or any other particular type of dialog), we can't use *DialogBoxParam*.

So how can we link our dialog, *in a generic, dialog-independent way?* It's simple—we can use an inelegant but expedient device to which all programmers resort sooner or later, namely, a global. (A programmer friend of mine once blurted out in the middle of a design session, "I can't program without globals!" He now works at Microsoft.) We'll introduce a static class global, *NewDialog*, and set it whenever a dialog object is created. (We introduced a similar global in Section 3.4.8, *NewWin*, to distinguish between stack and memory-resident window objects.)

```
// (In WPDLG.H)
class WPDialog : public WPWin {
private:
    static WPDialog* NewDialog;    // global: dialog being initialized
};

// (in WPDLG.CPP)
WPDialog * WPDialog::NewDialog = NULL;

WPDialog::WPDialog(CSTR resname, WPWin *pwin) : WPWin(NULL, pwin)
{
    NewDialog = this;              // <<<< so WPDlgProc will link me
    .
    .
}
```

To link our dialogs, we now get the object from *NewDialog* instead of from *lParam*.

```
BOOL _export FAR PASCAL
WPDlgProc(HWND hdlg, WORD msg, WORD wp, LONG lp)
{
    WPDialog *dlg;
```

```
    if (msg == WM_INITDIALOG) {
        dlg = WPDialog::NewDialog;        // dialog obj passed as global
        assert(dlg);                      // it better be defined!
        WPDialog::NewDialog = NULL;       // don't re-init!
        dlg->linkHwnd(hdlg);              // link to window
    }
    .
    .
    . (as before)
}
```

Experience shows that this solution works well in practice. Once again, the global *NewDialog* is required only because the common dialogs introduced in Windows 3.1 already use the WM_INITDIALOG parameter.

7.2.4 Dialog Initialization

While WM_INITDIALOG can be used to pass an argument to the dialog, its main purpose is to provide an opportunity for dialogs to initialize themselves before passing control to the user. WM_INITDIALOG is the dialog equivalent of WM_CREATE. If you recall from Chapter 3, our window objects don't process (or even receive) the WM_CREATE message, since we initialize objects in the class constructor either before or after calling *createWin* to actually create the window.

We'd like to do the same thing for dialogs; namely, ignore WM_INITDIALOG, and let the dialog constructors do the initialization. Unfortunately, this won't work for modal dialogs, where *createWin* doesn't return until the dialog is over. For modal dialogs, the constructor must complete its initialization before invoking *createWin*. But most dialogs can only initialize their contents after all the controls have been created.

To give application-specific modal dialogs a way to initialize themselves, we must somehow pass along the WM_INITDIALOG event. All we have to do is introduce a new virtual function:

```
class WPDialogModal : public WPWin {
protected:
    virtual BOOL initDlg();
};
```

We can invoke it from *WPDlgProc*, like so:

```
BOOL _export FAR PASCL WPDlgProc(HWND hdlg, WORD msg, WORD wp, LONG lp)
{
    WPDialog *dlg;
    if (msg == WM_INITDIALOG) {
        .
        . (link dialog as before)
        .
        return dlg->initDlg();        // call virtual init function
    }
    .
    .
    .
}
```

The return value from WM_INITDIALOG has a different meaning from that of all other dialog messages: if it's TRUE, Windows will initialize the focus to the first control in the dialog's tab order; otherwise, Windows assumes that the application has set the focus and does nothing.[47]

Rather than force *Windows++* programmers to remember whether they're supposed to return TRUE or FALSE, we can provide a simpler mechanism set the focus. We'll add a protected data member, *focusID*, that application-specific subclasses can set to specify which control should receive initial focus, and a low-level initialization function, *init*, that's called before the application gets a crack at WM_INITDIALOG.

```
class WPDialog : public WPWin
private:
    BOOL init();                    // private init fn for Windows++
protected:
    int focusID;                    // ID of control to get focus
    virtual void initDlg();         // public virtual init fn for apps
};
BOOL WPDialog::init()
{
    modified = FALSE;               // clear modified flag
    initDlg();                      // call app-specific init function

    // Now set initial focus from focusID
    WPWin *cwin = getChild(focusID);
    if (cwin) {
        cwin->setFocus();
        return FALSE;
    }
    return TRUE;
}
```

Now *initDlg* returns *void*, and all a programmer has to do to set the initial focus is set *focusID*, either in the constructor or in *initDlg*. What could be simpler?

```
void DlgEditPerson::initDlg()
{
    .
    .
    focusID = IDED_NAME;            // set initial focus to person's name
}
```

In general, *initDlg* might do practically anything. Setting the initial focus is only one minor chore, but a *generic* one that we should make as easy and trouble-free as possible. It's the little things like this that add up to make programming easier.

---

47 For non-Windows initiates: at any given time, one control has the *focus*; this is the control that the user may edit. The controls in a dialog have a "tab order" that determines in which sequence the controls are navigated when the user presses the TAB key. The tab order is specified by the order in which the controls appear in the resource file, and whether or not the control has the WS_TABSTOP style flag set.

Having a private initialization function (*init*) for *WPDialog* will be useful later, when we build object-oriented dialogs. It provides a way for *Windows++* to perform low-level dialog initialization even if the application-specific derived dialog class doesn't provide an *initDlg* function. Moreover, the low-level initialization can be done either before or after invoking *initDlg*. Of course, we have to modify *WPDlgProc* to call *init* instead of *initDlg*. (Consider it done.)

The following figure illustrates how *Windows++* dialogs are initialized when Windows sends the WM_INITDIALOG message.

Event flow for WM_INITDIALOG.

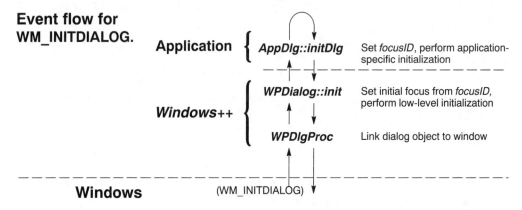

This may seem like a lot of trouble just to handle WM_INITDIALOG, but remember that we do the extra work in the library to avoid having to repeat it in each application. Our goal is to make programming easier. It always takes a little effort to implement something in a generic way, but the payoff comes later when we write applications. (Being a good programmer requires delaying gratification.)

7.2.5 Ending the Dialog

There's only one item left as far as dialog mechanics are concerned: destroying the dialog. Windows are normally destroyed by invoking *destroyWin*, which simply calls *DestroyWindow*. But once again, modal dialogs have their own way of doing it: the official Windows way to end a modal dialog is by calling *EndDialog* (*DestroyWindow* is still used for modeless dialogs). The "reason" for this is that you can only end a modal dialog from within its dialog procedure. Since *DialogBox* doesn't return until the dialog is over, there's no way to get "outside" the dialog procedure to call *DestroyWindow*. Rather than make *DestroyWindow* work correctly even in this situation, the designers of Windows introduced a new function, *EndDialog*, which sets a flag inside the dialog that tells it to terminate as soon as the dialog procedure returns.

Despite this peculiarity of modal dialogs, we should still think of ending a modal dialog as destroying it and simply implement *destroyWin* appropriately, just like we did with *createWin*. This function is already defined for *WPWin*, but as with *createWin*, we must first go back to *WPWin* and make it virtual:

```
class WPWin {
public:
    // as before, but make it virtual
    virtual void destroyWin()        { DestroyWindow(hwnd); }
};
```

Once it's virtual, we can write a different version for modal dialogs:

```
class WPDialogModal : public WPDialog {
protected:
    void destroyWin()                { EndDialog(getHwnd(), result); }
};
```

For those who like the feel of Windows, or who are so used to *EndDialog* that they don't perceive it as an inconsistent kludge, we can provide an *endDlg* function that sets the return code and ends the dialog in a single stroke, just like *EndDialog*:

```
class WPDialog : public WPWin {
    int result;                      //  return code, as before
public:
    void endDlg(int code)            { result=code; destroyWin(); }
};
```

Since *endDlg* invokes *destroyWin* (which is virtual), it works for both modal and modeless dialogs, and is therefore implemented as part of *WPDialog*. On the other hand, invoking *EndDialog* to end the dialog is unique to modal dialogs and therefore implemented as part of *WPDialogModal*.

Now that we have a way to end the dialog, what about unlinking and deleting the dialog object? For window objects, this happens automatically in *WPWndProc*:

```
LONG _export FAR PASCAL WPWndProc(HWND hwnd,WORD msg,WORD wp,LONG lp)
{
    .
    .
    .
    if (msg==WM_DESTROY) {           // got WM_DESTROY:
        if (win->deletable)          // if deletable (memory-resident):
            delete win;              // bye-bye window!
        else                         // not deletable (stack-resident):
            win->unLinkHwnd();       // just unlink
        return 0;
    }
    .
    .
    .
    return win->msgProc(event);      // call object to handle event
}
```

How does this work for dialogs? Well, while we've short-circuited *msgProc* so it returns all messages right back to Windows, WM_DESTROY is handled by *WPWndProc*, not *msgProc*. In other words, we don't have to do anything. Dialog objects are destroyed automatically, using the same mechanism as for non-dialog windows. *WPWndProc* even does the right thing if the dialog lives on the stack.

7.2.6 Summary

That's it as far as dialog mechanics are concerned. Before moving on, let's review how it all works, from the perspective of the PEOPLE program (put your application-programmer caps on again). Here's what the Edit Person dialog looks like, using what we've written so far.

```
/////////////////
// Edit Person dialog
//
class DlgEditPerson : public WPDialogModal {
public:
    DlgEditPerson(WPWin *pwin) : WPDialogModal("DlgEditPerson", pwin)
        { createWin(); }
    void initDlg()    {   focusID = IDED_NAME; }
    void command(int id, WORD msg)
        { if (id==IDOK || id = IDCANCEL) endDlg(id); }
};
```

The name of the resource template, "DlgEditPerson", is hard-wired into the constructor, which invokes *createWin,* just like a normal window object. All *initDlg* does is set *focusID* to the control ID of the person's name. (This could be done in the constructor, before calling *createWin,* since it doesn't require that the dialog exist, but wanted to show you how to use *initDlg.*) When the user selects the Edit Person command, the event is passed to the *command* function, which creates the dialog:

```
// Handle command (WM_COMMAND message).
//
void PeopleWin::command(int id, WORD msg)
{
    switch (id) {
    case IDM_EDIT:
        DlgEditPerson dlg(this);                // create & run dialog
        if (dlg.isModified()) {
            // dialog modified: do something
        }
        .
        .
}
```

The dialog is created on the stack, rather than being allocated from storage with *new.* Using the stack for modal dialogs is convenient, since they're transient objects. Modal dialogs live only long enough to obtain the user's input; afterwards, they get thrown in the trash heap. (You may recall that in Section 3.4.8, we went out of our way to overload *new* and *delete* for *WPWin* objects, just so we could distinguish between stack and memory-resident window objects.)

Let's take a careful look at what happens when the following line is executed:

```
DlgEditPerson dlg(this);
```

- The resource name ("DlgEditPerson") and parent window (*this*) are passed down to the base class constructors for *WPDialog* and *WPWin,* which store them in *templateName* and *createArgs.parent*. *WPDialog* also sets the class global *NewDialog* to point to the new object just created.

■ The last constructor, *DlgEditPerson* invokes *createWin* to actually create the dialog: *createWin* (the one for *WPDialogModal*) in turn simply calls *DialogBox* with the proper creation arguments, including our universal dialog procedure, *WPDlgProc*. Control now passes to Windows; *DialogBox* doesn't return until the dialog is over.

■ The first message Windows sends to *WPDlgProc* is WM_INITDIALOG. *WPDlgProc* responds by first linking the dialog (it gets the object from *NewDialog*), then invoking *WPDialog::init*.

■ *WPDialog::init* invokes the virtual function *initDlg*, which is defined for *DlgEditPerson*. It simply sets *focusID* to IDED_NAME. When *initDlg* returns, *init* actually sets the focus and returns FALSE to Windows.

■ The dialog runs until the user clicks either the OK or CANCEL button.

■ When this happens, the event is passed via *WPDlgProc* and *dispatchEvent* to *DlgEditPerson::command*, which responds by invoking *endDlg* to end the dialog: *endDlg* in turn invokes *destroyWin*, which is virtual, with a version for *WPDialogModal* that simply calls *EndDialog*.

■ As Windows destroys the dialog, it sends a WM_DESTROY message to the *window* procedure (not the *dialog* procedure). This message is intercepted by *WPWndProc*, which unlinks the dialog (it doesn't delete it, since the magic from Section 3.4.8 detects that the dialog resides on the stack).

■ Finally, control returns to *PeopleWin::command*.

All this happens invisibly as far as application programmers are concerned. To them, dialogs are just like any other kind of window object. They're created and destroyed using the same functions, and events are handled using the same virtual message functions, such as *command*. There are just two anomalies: *initDlg* and the behavior of *createWin* for modal dialogs (it doesn't return until the dialog is over). Both of these are direct and unavoidable consequences of the modality of modal dialogs.

As in Chapter 3, our infrastructure seems convoluted, but the benefit is that it's entirely generic and therefore *reusable*. Moreover, it only appears convoluted from the inside: to applications programmers, *Windows++* appears clean and neat. In fact, practically all our efforts have been directed at hiding Windows' kludginess; most of the code we've written (*WPDlgProc*, *createWin*, the subterfuge of short-circuiting *msgProc*, and so on) is required only because Windows uses totally different mechanisms for dialogs than it does for non-dialog windows. If Windows were more consistent, everything could simply have been inherited from *WPWin*. (But then authors like me would have nothing to write about.)

What we've done is essentially reshape Windows' inconsistencies to fit a uniform mold. We've buried all the grueling API mechanics deep within our library and presented *Windows++* programmers with a more consistent interface. With the mechanics buried, we can forget about Windows and proceed to more interesting things (like writing applications), confident that our dialog code will silently but reliably continue to perform its ever-important job of making *Windows++* dialogs hum.

7.3 Controls

We've now taken care of the basic mechanics for dialogs. The next thing on our agenda is modeling *controls*. Controls are specialized window classes that let users edit a particular particular kind of information. For example, an *edit control* represents a character string, while a *list box* displays a list of choices. We'd like to manipulate controls using *Windows++*. For example, we'd like to set the person's name in our Edit Person dialog using *setText*:

```
WPEdit *edName;
edName->setText(person.name);
```

Likewise, instead of writing

```
char *item;
SendMessage(hwndListBox, LB_APPENDSTRING, 0, (LONG)(LPSTR)textitem);
```

as you would in C, we'd rather write

```
char *item;
listbox->append(textitem);
```

This not only obviates the need to know what parameters each message requires, it's also *type-safe*. Providing an *append* function like the one above requires no more than writing a brainless function:

```
void append(CSTR item) { sendMsg(LB_APPENDSTRING, 0, (LPSTR)item); }
```

There's just one slight problem: we have no class to put this function in. We've implemented *WPDialog* for dialogs, but no classes for the controls they contain. In fact, you may have been wondering, when *initDlg* sets the initial focus

```
WPWin *cwin = getChild(focusID);
if (cwin) {
    cwin->setFocus();
    .
    .
```

where does *cwin* come from? Well, to be honest, this was a bit of foreshadowing, because we hadn't gotten to controls yet. Now we have.

7.3.1 Control Basics

OK, we need a class for controls. So let's invent one:

```
class WPControl : public WPWin {

};
```

Because *WPControl* derives from *WPWin*, controls automatically inherit all the properties (data and functions) of windows. We can thus write

```
WPControl *ctl;                    // some control
ctl->setText("Hello");             // set text to "hello"
ctl->setSize(15, 40);              // set width, height to 15, 40
WPRect clientBox = ctl;            // get client area rectangle
.
. etc.
```

This is just one of many situations where the power of inheritance is evident. *WPControl inherits* all the properties of windows "for free." We'll use *WPControl* as the base class from which to derive specific kinds of controls:

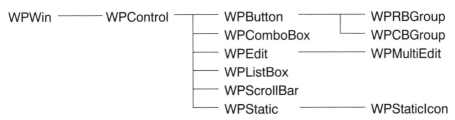

Before building all these classes, our first question should be, what can we say about controls in general? In other words, what properties and operations do list boxes, buttons, and all controls have in common? Object-oriented design is a continual process of categorization. Objects are grouped according to their properties; whenever objects have common properties, a base class is invented from which to derive them.

Let's start with control creation. The creation arguments are the same as for a normal window: the window class name, parent window, and control ID. As always, creation arguments are initialized in the constructor:

```
// (In WPCTRL.H)
class WPControl : public WPWin {
public:
    WPControl(CSTR  classnm, WPWin *pwin, int id)
        : WPWin(classnm, pwin, id) { }
};
```

Unlike normal windows, *pwin* and *id* are required for controls, since we want programmers to give every control a parent window and ID. As for actually creating the window, controls present an interesting problem. They can be created either on the fly, like any other kind of window, or as part of a dialog.

- To create a control on the fly, we can use the standard *createWin* function (the one for *WPWin*, the one that calls *CreateWindow*).

- If the control belongs to a dialog, its window is created automatically by Windows when the dialog is loaded; in this case, we need only invoke *link-Hwnd* to link the dialog to its HWND, as described in Sections 3.4.3 and 7.4.1.

Naturally, we want to hide this difference; programmers shouldn't have to do anything different in these two situations, but simply invoke *createWin*, as always. Here's the code to do it:

```
class WPControl : public WPWin {
private:
    BOOL tryLink();                  // try to link to pre-existing window
public:
    BOOL createWin()
        { return tryLink() ? TRUE : WPWin::createWin(); }
};
```

If *createWin* can link the control to a pre-existing window, it does so and returns TRUE; otherwise, it creates the window using the normal *WPWin* function. Here's *tryLink:*

```
///////////////////
// Try to link control to pre-existing window (i.e., dialog control).
//
BOOL WPControl::tryLink()
{
    if (getHwnd())
        return TRUE;                        // (already linked)
    HWND hwndParent = GetHwnd(createArgs.parent);
    if (hwndParent) {
        HWND hwndChild = GetDlgItem(hwndParent, createArgs.id());
        if (hwndChild) {
            linkHwnd(hwndChild);             // <<<< link it!
            return TRUE;
        }
    }
    return FALSE;
}
```

Note that *tryLink* uses window handles (HWNDs) instead of window objects, since the window isn't linked yet (that's what we're trying to do). It gets the parent HWND from *createArgs.parent* and the control ID from *createArgs.id()*, which is an inline function that simply returns *createArgs.hmenu*. Recall that the *parent* and *id* fields in *createArgs* are set by the *WPWin* constructor.

To see how creating controls works in practice, let's consider two examples from the PEOPLE program: creating a list box for the PEOPLE main window and creating an edit control for the Edit Person dialog.

Here's the list box example:

```
// Main PEOPLE window (In PEOPLE.CPP)
class PeopleWin : public WPMainWin {
    WPListBox *lbPeople;            // list box of people
public:
    PeopleWin();
};
// Create main PEOPLE window
PeopleWin::PeopleWin()
{
    // Create main window
    createWin("People Database");

    // Create list box
    lbPeople = new WPListBox(this, IDLB_PEOPLE);
    createArgs.pos = this;
    createArgs.style &= ~WS_BORDER;
    lbPeople->createWin();
}
```

We haven't implemented *WPListBox* yet, but you don't need to know the details to follow what's going on. After creating its own main window, the *PeopleWin* constructor creates a new list box object, sets additional *createArgs* (to set the size of the list box and remove its border), then invokes *createWin* to actually create the list box window. Since *createWin* is virtual and *WPListBox* is derived from *WPControl* (trust me), control passes to *WPControl::createWin,* which first tries to link the control and then, when *tryLink* fails (since there's no pre-existing child window), calls the normal *WPWin::createWin* function, which creates the window. *Voilà!* List box.

Now the second case: creating an edit control in the Edit Person dialog. This modal dialog contains edit controls for the person's name, address, city, state, and zip:

```
// Edit Person Dialog
class DlgEditPerson : public WPDialogModal {
    Person *p;                      // Person to edit
    WPEdit *edName;                 // edit control for person's name
    WPEdit *edAddr;                 // .. address, etc.
    WPEdit *edCity;
    WPEdit *edState;
    WPEdit *edZip;
public:
    DlgEditPerson(WPWin *pwin)      // constructor
    void initDlg();                 // handler for WM_INITDIALOG
};
```

Where should we create all the edit controls? If we mimicked *PeopleWin,* we'd do it in the constructor:

```
DlgEditPerson::DlgEditPerson(WPWin *pwin)
    : WPDialogModal("DLGEDITPERSON", pwin)
{
    createWin();                            // create the dialog
    edName = new WPEdit(this, IDED_NAME);
    edName->createWin();
    edName->setText(p->name);
```

```
        .
        .
        .
}
```

But this won't work, because the *WPDialogModal::createWin* doesn't return until the dialog is over. So instead, we create the controls in *initDlg*. This is a general rule: controls for modal dialogs must be created in the *initDlg* function, not in the dialog constructor. This unfortunate peculiarity is a direct consequence of the "modality" of modal dialogs. In general, modal dialog objects are initialized in *initDlg* rather than the class constructor. OK, so we create the controls in *initDlg*:

```
// Initialize dialog: create control object for each control.
void DlgEditPerson::initDlg()
{
    edName = new WPEdit(this, IDED_NAME);
    edName->createWin();
    edName->setText(p->name);

    edAddr = new WPEdit(this, IDED_ADDRESS);
    edAddr->createWin();
    edAddr->setText(p->addr);

    .
    . ditto for city, state, zip
    .
}
```

Now what happens when *createWin* is invoked? This time, the edit controls already exist (they were created by Windows when it loaded the dialog, in *DialogBox*), so *tryLink* succeeds without invoking *WPWin::createWin*. The net result is the same as in the list box example—the window is created and linked.

The code in *initDlg* looks rather tedious. It seems unfriendly to make *Windows++* programmers call *createWin* every time they create a dialog control, especially when the window already exists! All that's required is to link the control object to its HWND, which *Windows++* can do automatically, in the constructor, when the control *object* is created:

```
// (In WPCTRL.H)
class WPControl : public WPWin {
protected:
   WPControl(CSTR  classnm, WPWin *pwin, int id)
       : WPWin(classnm, pwin, id) { tryLink(); }
};
```

Now there's no need to call *createWin*. (But if a programmer does call it, no harm is done.) We can rewrite *initDlg* more simply, like so:

```
void DlgEditPerson::intDlg()
{
    // No more createWin!
    edName = new WPEdit(this, IDED_NAME);
    edName->setText(p->name);

    edAddr = new WPEdit(this, IDED_ADDRESS);
    edAddr->setText(p->addr);
```

```
    .
    . ditto for city, state, zip
    .
}
```

Eventually, we'll get rid of this code, too.

The rules for creating controls are important enough to reiterate briefly:

- *On-the-fly* controls are created in the normal fashion, just like any other child window. First, you invoke *new* to create the object, then *createWin* to create its window. Between these calls, you may set *createArgs* to set the control's size, position, style flags, and other creation arguments.

- *Dialog* controls are created in *initDlg*, not in the dialog constructor. There's no need to call *createWin*, since the window already exists and is automatically linked by the *WPControl* constructor.

So much for creating controls. What about destroying them? Do we have to write a special *destroyWin* function for controls?

Well, when our control is linked (in *linkHwnd*), it's hooked to our old reliable *WPWndProc* function. As with any other kind of window, the control object is automatically deleted when Windows sends the WM_DESTROY message (you may want to review Section 3.4.7 to recall how this works). Windows automatically destroys child windows along with their parent, so we don't have to do anything special. *WPControl* objects are destroyed automatically through the normal channels. In short, no, we don't have to write a special function to destroy controls.

Once again, this illustrates the power of inheritance. Since *WPControl* is derived from *WPWin*, it inherits all the infrastructure we established in Chapter 3. It pays to build infrastructure.

That's about it for *WPControl* (we'll return to controls in Section 7.4.). We're now ready to model specific subclasses such as *WPEdit* and *WPListBox*. In the following pages, I'll show you how; however, my goal is not to exhaustively explore every kind of Windows control, but to advance a general approach for modeling them. You'd bore rather quickly if I were to explain each control class in excruciating detail, especially since they're all pretty much the same. Instead, I'll describe *WPEdit* and *WPListBox*, then wave my hands and refer you to the complete source listing in Appendix A for the rest.

7.3.2 A Typical Control: *WPEdit*

Perhaps the most utilitarian control is the *edit* control, which lets users edit a string of text. Edit controls can be single- or multi-line, left- or right-justified, scrollable, or possess any of a variety of other properties specified in the edit control's style flags. To model edit controls, we'll begin, as always, by deriving a new class.

```
#define ES_DEFAULT   (WS_BORDER | ES_LEFT | ES_AUTOHSCROLL)

///////////////////
// Your basic edit control.
//
class WPEdit : public WPControl {
public:
    WPEdit(WPWin *pwin, int id, long style=ES_DEFAULT)
        : WPControl("Edit", pwin, id, style) { }

};
```

Since controls make frequent use of style flags, I've added a new *style* argument to the *WPControl* constructor. The *style* is ORed with *createArgs.style*:

```
class WPControl : public WPWin {
protected:
    WPControl(CSTR classnm, WPWin *pwin, int id, long style=0);
};

WPControl::WPControl(CSTR classnm, WPWin *pwin, int id, long style)
    : WPWin(classnm, pwin, id)
{
    createArgs.style |= style;    // OR style flags w/defaults
    tryLink();                    // (as before)
}
```

C++ default function arguments are used here: if *style* isn't specified, it defaults to zero. The style flags are used only for controls created on the fly, since the styles of dialog controls are determined by the resource template.

To create an edit control, we now write

```
WPEdit *editCtl = new WPEdit(mywin, ID_MYEDIT, ES_CENTER);

// The following lines apply to on-the-fly controls ONLY
createArgs.pos.origin(0,0);        // set screen position
createArgs.pos.extent(100,200);    // ...
editCtl->createWin();              // create window
```

Setting *createArgs* and invoking *createWin* are necessary only for edit controls created on the fly; in a dialog, the style, position, and other creation arguments are all initialized from the resource template when the dialog is loaded.

To set and get the contents of an edit control, Windows uses the functions *SetWindowText* and *GetWindowText*, for which we already have "brainless" equivalents inherited from *WPWin*. Thus we can write

```
edName->setText("Paul");
edName->getText(p->name, sizeof(p->name));
..etc.
```

But edit controls have several additional operations that apply only to them. These operations are invoked by sending special messages that only edit controls respond to. The messages are defined in WINDOWS.H and documented in the SDK *Reference, Volume 1*. Here's the complete list:

EM_GETSEL	EM_SETMODIFY	EM_UNDO
EM_SETSEL	EM_GETLINECOUNT	EM_FMTLINES
EM_GETRECT	EM_LINEINDEX	EM_LINEFROMCHAR
EM_SETRECT	EM_LINELENGTH	EM_SETWORDBREAK
EM_SETRECTNP	EM_REPLACESEL	EM_SETTABSTOPS
EM_SCROLL	EM_GETLINE	EM_SETPASSWORDCHAR
EM_LINESCROLL	EM_LIMITTEXT	EM_EMPTYUNDOBUFFER
EM_GETMODIFY	EM_CANUNDO	EM_MSGMAX

To use these, we could of course simply write

```
BOOL canUndo = (BOOL)edCtl->sendMsg(EM_CANUNDO);
```

but, as we've seen, it's more convenient to write "brainless" functions:

```
class WPEdit : public WPControl {
    // Windows-related functions
    BOOL canUndo()                  { return sendMsg(EM_CANUNDO); }
    BOOL undo()                     { return sendMsg(EM_UNDO); }
    void emptyUndo()                { sendMsg(EM_EMPTYUNDOBUFFER); }
    BOOL modified()                 { return sendMsg(EM_GETMODIFY); }
    BOOL modified(BOOL m)           { sendMsg(EM_SETMODIFY,m);return m;}
    void getRect(WPRect &r)         { sendMsg(EM_GETRECT, 0, (LONG)&r); }
    void setPasswordChar(char c)    { sendMsg(EM_SETPASSWORDCHAR, c); }
    void replaceSel(char *text)     { sendMsg(EM_REPLACESEL, 0, text); }
    void setMaxLen(int len)         { sendMsg(EM_LIMITTEXT, len); }

    LONG getSel() { return sendMsg(EM_GETSEL); }
    LONG getSel(int& beg, int& end)
        { LONG x = getSel(); beg=LOWORD(x); end=HIWORD(x); return x; }
    void setSel(int beg=0, int end=MAXINT)
        { sendMsg(EM_SETSEL, 0, MAKELONG(beg, end)); }
};
```

so we can write:

```
BOOL canUndo = edCtl->canUndo();
```

Using brainless functions instead of *sendMsg* is easier, since you don't have to re-member what arguments go with each message; they're documented in the func-tion prototype (and type-safe). Moreover, the functions clearly define what operations are and and are not supported by *Windows++*. As always, "brainless" functions incur no performance penalty since they're *inline*.

Careful readers may have noticed that not all the EM_ messages are supported by *WPEdit*. Only those that apply for single-line edit controls are supported. Multi-line edit controls (ones that have the ES_MULTILINE style) are represented in *Windows++* as a separate class.

```
#define ES_DEFAULTMULTI (ES_DEFAULT|ES_MULTILINE|ES_AUTOVSCROLL)
///////////////////
// Multi-line edit control.
//
DLLCLASS WPMultiEdit : public WPEdit {
public:
    WPMultiEdit(WPWin *pwin, int id, long sty=ES_DEFAULTMULTI)
        : WPEdit(pwin, id, sty) { }
```

```
    // Windows functions for multi-edit controls only
    int numLines()                    { return sendMsg(EM_GETLINECOUNT); }
    int getLine(int nLine, char *buf, int len)
        { *((WORD*)buf) = len; return sendMsg(EM_GETLINE, nLine, buf); }
    int lineFromChar(int pos)
        { return sendMsg(EM_LINEFROMCHAR,pos); }
    int linePos(int nLine)
        { return sendMsg(EM_LINEINDEX, nLine); }
    int lineLenFromPos(int pos)
        { return sendMsg(EM_LINELENGTH, pos); }
    int lineLen(int nLine)
        { return lineLenFromPos(linePos(nLine)); }
    void lineScroll(int h, int v)
        { sendMsg(EM_LINESCROLL, 0, MAKELONG(v,h)); }
    void setRect(WPRect &rect, BOOL repaint=TRUE)
        { sendMsg(repaint ? EM_SETRECT : EM_SETRECTNP, 0, (LONG)&rect); }
    BOOL format(BOOL crlf)            { return sendMsg(EM_FMTLINES, crlf); }
};
```

We already used *WPMultiEdit* back in Chapter 6, in WINEDIT. Why make *WPMultiLine* a separate class? Because by doing so, we make a distinction that's implicit in Windows explicit in *Windows++*. Since many of the EM_ messages apply only to multi-line edit controls, why allow them for single-line edit controls?

In general, there's no reason our class hierarchy need exactly match Windows'! If a multi-line edit control is really a different beast from a single-line edit control, we can model it as such. We'll do the same thing for buttons. Where Windows uses the style flags to create essentially different kinds of buttons, we'll introduce different subclasses of buttons. In other words, *sometimes we bury the details of Windows; other times we expose them.* We don't have to take the Windows API as *fait accompli*.

What else can we do with *WPEdit*? Well, we can take the opportunity to add a little reusable functionality. In a dialog box, when you TAB to a new edit control, the text contents are normally highlighted. Unfortunately, this behavior does not occur if your program manually sets the focus to an edit control. We can fix this by implementing the *gotFocus* virtual message function for edit controls:

```
class WPEdit : public WPControl {
public:
    BOOL gotFocus(WPWin *prev)
        { setSel(); return WPControl::gotFocus(prev); }
};
```

Remember, controls are just another kind of window object (*WPWin*), so they inherit all the work we did in Chapter 3—in particular, the virtual message functions such as *gotFocus*. Simply by writing *gotFocus* for edit controls, we ensure that it's automatically invoked whenever Windows sends WM_SETFOCUS to the control. Now our edit controls always highlight their contents whenever they receive focus, not just as a result of pressing the TAB key in a dialog box.

In general, virtual functions can be used to implement specialized control classes. For example, we can easily implement an edit control for zip codes:

```
/////////////////////
// Special edit control lets user type digits only.
// (In PEOPLE.CPP)
//
class EditZip : public WPEdit {
public:
    EditZip(WPWin *pwin, int id) : WPEdit(pwin, id) { }
    BOOL kbd(WPEvent& event);
};
BOOL EditZip::kbd(WPEvent& event)
{
    char c = event.key();
    if ( event.msg==WM_CHAR &&
            ( isprint(c) && !(isdigit(c) || c=='-')) ) {
        MsgBeep();
        return TRUE;
    }
    return WPEdit::kbd(event);
}
```

This control intercepts WM_CHAR messages and beeps if the user types anything but a digit or hyphen. Once again, the power of inheritance is exploited. All the routine edit control stuff is simply inherited from *WPEdit*, for free. Only the behavior unique to zip codes need be implemented, namely, beeping if the user types a character that's not a digit.

Consider for a moment what you'd have to do to accomplish the same result in Windows. The normal practice is to handle the EN_UPDATE notification in the dialog procedure, but that's poor design, because the specialized behavior (beeping in response to a non-digit) is really a property of the control, not the dialog. Doing it in the dialog is not reusable. To implement *EditZip* correctly in Windows, you'd have to "subclass" the normal Windows edit control by writing a different window procedure for it (one that handled WM_CHAR) and install the procedure with *SetWindowLong*. In *Windows++*, these mechanical details are performed automatically and invisibly. All that application programmers need do is implement the virtual message functions that do something different. In this case, the only one is *kbd*.

As it stands, *EditZip* is part of the PEOPLE program. We could easily add it to the library (we'd have to give it a *WP* prefix). In fact, we could add a whole slew of edit controls for various kinds of information such as zip codes, numbers, and so on. Better yet, we could just add a new member to *WPEdit* that lets programmers specify an arbitrary string of permissible characters:

```
class WPEdit : public WPControl {
private:
    CSTR legalChars;                    // user can only type these
```

```
public:
    setLegalChars(CSTR s)           { legalChars = s; }
    BOOL kbd(WPEvent &event);
};
BOOL WPEdit::kbd(WPEvent& event)
{
    if (legalChars) {
        char c = event.key();
        if ( event.msg==WM_CHAR &&
                ( isprint(c) && strchr(legalChars, c)==NULL ) {
            MsgBeep();
            return TRUE;
        }
    }
    return WPControl::kbd(event); // default processing
}
```

EditZip can now be implemented trivially like so:

```
class EditZip : public WPEdit {
public:
    EditZip(WPWin *pwin, int id) : WPEdit(pwin, id)
        { setLegalChars("0123456789-"); }
};
```

By adding just one extra reusable property to edit controls, we've greatly enhanced them. The *legalChars* feature is especially valuable in applications that deal
with forms management and data entry (which includes a lot of applications). If
it's more convenient to specify the illegal characters, just add another string to
WPEdit.

So much for *WPEdit*. Before we move on, let's take a moment to generalize what
we've done, since the same techniques apply to all controls. *WPEdit* provides us
with a cookbook recipe for modeling a control in *Windows++:*

Paul's Object-Oriented Controls

INGREDIENTS:

1 listing of Windows messages for *Foo* controls, from the SDK *Reference*
   Volume 1, or WINDOWS.H

1 *Windows++ WPFooControl* class, derived from *WPControl*

DIRECTIONS:

1. Write constructor for *WPFooControl;* set appropriate default *style* flags.

2. Translate Windows messages into "brainless" *WPFooControl* member
   functions. (Think of something else while you do it.)

3. If Windows uses the style flags to specify controls that are really
   fundamentally different, model each different style as a separate class.

7.3.3 List Boxes

If we apply the recipe to list boxes, this is what we get:

```
#define LBS_DEFAULT (WS_BORDER|LBS_NOTIFY|LBS_USETABSTOPS|WS_VSCROLL)
class WPListBox : public WPControl {
public:
    WPListBox(WPWin *pwin, int id, long sty=LBS_DEFAULT)
        : WPControl("ListBox", pwin, id, sty) { }

    // Brainless functions
    int count()                     { return sendMsg(LB_GETCOUNT); }
    void reset()                    { sendMsg(LB_RESETCONTENT); }
    void delItem(int index)         { sendMsg(LB_DELETESTRING, index); }
    void append(CSTR text)          { sendMsg(LB_ADDSTRING, 0, text); }
    void insert(CSTR text, int where)
        { sendMsg(LB_INSERTSTRING, where, text); }

    int getSel()                    { return sendMsg(LB_GETCURSEL); }
    void setSel(int sel)            { sendMsg(LB_SETCURSEL, sel); }
    int setSel(CSTR text, int start=-1)
        { return sendMsg(LB_SELECTSTRING, start, text); }
    int getSel(char *buf)
        { return (int)sendMsg(LB_GETTEXT, getSel(), buf); }
};
```

We could stop here, but why not go a little further? When you create a list box, it's empty. To add contents to the list, programmers must invoke the *append* or *insert* functions to manually add each item to the list. For example, to initialize its main window, PEOPLE would do something like this.

```
for (Person *p=firstPerson; p; p=p->next)
    lbPeople->append(p->name);
```

This seems rather tiresome, especially since it's so generic. Every program that contains a list box needs to set its contents. (What good is an empty list box?) As an application programmer, I'd like to simply hand the list box a list of items and let it do the rest.

```
lbPeople->setList(list_of_people);
```

The only problem is, what's a list? In other words, how do we declare *setList*? To answer this question, we'll introduce (you guessed it) another class.

```
/////////////////
// Generic list data.
//
class WPListData {
public:
    virtual BOOL firstItem() = 0;
    virtual BOOL nextItem() = 0;
    virtual void getItemText(char *buf, int len) = 0;
};
```

This class represents a generic list, from the point of view of a list box. It has two pure virtual functions to navigate the list (*firstItem* and *nextItem*), and another to get the current item's text (*getItemText*). By making the virtual functions *pure* (by setting them to zero), we make *WPListData* an abstract class, one that can have no instances and can only be used to derive subclasses. In effect, we're saying, "a list is something that has *first* and *next* operations, and a way to get a text string." We've said nothing about how the list is actually implemented; the "list" might really be an array:

```
char *strings[] = { "one", "two", "three" };
const NITEMS = 3;

class MyListData : public WPListData {
    int current;
public:
    BOOL firstItem() { current=0; return TRUE; }
    BOOL nextItem()  { return current < NITEMS-1 ? ++current : FALSE; }
    void getItemText(char* buf, int len)
        { strcpy(buf, strings[current]); }
};
```

or it might be a linked list:

```
struct Item {
    Item *next;      // next item
    char *text;      // this item's text
};

class MyListData : public WPListData {
    Item    *head;    // first item
    Item    *current; // current item
public:
    BOOL firstItem() { return (current=head) != NULL; }
    BOOL nextItem()  { return (current=current->next) != NULL; }
    void getItemText(char* buf, int len)
        { strcpy(buf, current->text); }
};
```

From the perspective of the list box, the implementation is irrelevant; all that matters is that it can navigate the list and get each item's text. A list is anything that behaves this way; *WPListData* thus captures the "essence of listness" for a list box.

With *WPListData* defined, we can now write *setList*:

```
class WPListBox : public WPControl {
public:
    void setList(WPListData *ld, int selected=0, BOOL redraw=TRUE);
};

void WPListBox::setList(WPListData *ld, int selected, BOOL redraw)
{
    if ((list = ld) != NULL) {
        reset();                          // delete all contents
        if (list->firstItem()) {
            char buf[80];
            setReDraw(FALSE);

            // add items 2 through N
            while (list->nextItem()) {
```

```
                list->getItemText(buf, sizeof(buf));
                append(buf);
            }
            if (redraw)
                setReDraw(TRUE);
            // Now insert 1st item
            list->firstItem();
            list->getItemText(buf, sizeof(buf));
            insert(buf, 0);
        }
    }
    setSel(selected);
}
```

I've thrown in a couple of extra useful arguments: *selected* specifies which list item should be highlighted (default = zero, the first item); the *redraw* flag specifies whether or not to actually draw the list (default=TRUE). The implementation of *setList* is straightforward. It follows the SDK-recommended practice of setting *ReDraw* to FALSE as each item is added to the list, then turning it on again for the last item. This avoids the flicker that would otherwise occur if the list were redrawn for each item.

C   *If you were doing this in C, you could use a struct for WPListData, but then you'd have to decide whether to implement lists as arrays or linked lists, since C doesn't support virtual functions. If you wanted to get fancy, you could pass the three list-navigation functions as pointers. That's all WPListData really is anyway: a place-holder for three function pointers.*

To see how *WPListData* works in practice, let's examine the PEOPLE program, which creates a list of people in its main window. Each person is represented by a *Person* object:

```
// Class used to represent a person.
class Person {
    char    name[50];
    char    addr[50];
    char    city[30];
    char    state[3];
    char    zip[10];
public:
    int format(char *buf, int len)
        { return sprintf(buf,"%s\t%s", name, addr); }
};
```

The *format* function copies the person's name and phone number, separated by a TAB, into the caller's buffer. This will be used to set the contents of the list box in the main PEOPLE window:

```
// Main PEOPLE window (In PEOPLE.CPP)
class PeopleWin : public WPMainWin, public WPListData {
    WPListBox *lbPeople;        // list box
    Person    *firstPerson;     // first person in database
    Person    *curPerson;       // current person
```

```
public:
    PeopleWin();
    ~PeopleWin();

    // These are the WPListData methods.
    BOOL firstItem()
        { return (curPerson=firstPerson) != NULL; }
    BOOL nextItem()
        { if (curPerson)
            curPerson=curPerson->next; return curPerson!=NULL; }
    void getItemText(char *buf, int len)
        { if (curPerson) curPerson->format(buf, len); else *buf = 0; }
};
```

PeopleWin is derived from *WPMainWin* and *WPListData!* This powerful C++ feature is called *multiple inheritance*. We are in effect saying that a *PeopleWin* is a kind of main window, *and* a kind of list. This situation arises all the time in the real world, where things don't always fall into purely hierarchical classifications. For example, a bird is an animal, but it also belongs to the class of things that fly, which contains other non-animal objects such as airplanes.

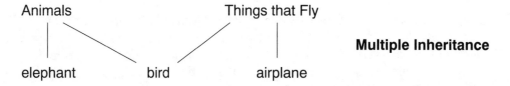

C++ lets you derive classes from more than one base class, in which case the derived class inherits the data and function members of all base classes. The syntax is

```
class derived : public base1, public base1, . . . public baseN {

};
```

To see how multiple inheritance works in practice, let's look at the *PeopleWin* constructor.

```
PeopleWin::PeopleWin()
{
    createWin();
    lbPeople = new WPListBox(this,1);
    createArgs.pos = this;
    createArgs.style &= ~WS_BORDER;
    lbPeople->createWin();
    lbPeople->setList(this);              // <<<< set list to myself !!
}
```

Most of what's in the constructor is old hat. The interesting thing is that *PeopleWin* sets the list box's list to itself! This is valid because *PeopleWin* is not only a *WPMainWin*, it's also a *WPListData* (it provides the requisite list-navigation functions). After invoking *setList*, the main window displays the list of people:

If *PeopleWin* were not derived from *WPListData*, we'd have to invent another structure to hold the list of people. It's more convenient to let *PeopleWin* itself "be" the list.

7.3.4 Other Built-in Controls

What about all the other controls—buttons, scroll bars, combo boxes, and so on? To model these, all we (you) have to do is apply the cookbook formula at the end of Section 7.3.2. Are you ready? OK, go do it.

Are you finished yet?

(If you're having trouble, you can peek at the source code in Appendix A.)

Seriously folks, you don't really want me to go through all that. As promised, this is where I wave my hands and point to Appendix A, which contains the full source code for all controls. There's really not much of any special interest, just more of the same sort of stuff we've seen with edit controls and list boxes. Here are a few highlights:

■ *WPStatic* represents static text; *WPStaticIcon* represents a static icon. (We already used *WPStatic* in Chapter 6, in the WINEDIT program.)

■ *WPButton* represents a button, either a push button, check box, or radio button. Two subclasses, *WPRBGroup* and *WPCBGroup* represent a group of radio buttons and a group of check boxes. These classes provide functions to set or get a value from the button group as a whole. For example, *WPRBGroup* (which is used for the "Relation" field in the Edit Person dialog in the PEOPLE program) gets a single integer representing which option is selected: zero for the first, one for the second, and so on. In the example shown, *WPRBGroup::getSel* returns zero, since the first option (Friend) is selected.

■ *WPCBGroup* is similar, but stuffs an array of BOOLs with the on/off values of each check box in the group. In the pizza order form shown at left, *WPCBGroup::getSel* stuffs an array of BOOLS with 010100, indicating which toppings are checked.

```
┌─ Toppings ──────────────────────┐
│                                 │
│   ☐ Anchovies   ☒ Mushrooms     │
│                                 │
│   ☒ Pepperoni   ☐ Sausage       │
│                                 │
│   ☐ Peppers     ☐ Jelly         │
│                                 │
└─────────────────────────────────┘
```

A radio button group typically lets users choose from mutually exclusive options; a check box group is used when any combination of options is allowed.

■ *WPScrollBar* represents a scroll bar. The derived classes *WPHScrollBar* and *WPVScrollBar* represent not controls, but the horizontal and vertical scroll bars in a main application window.

■ *WPListBox* only supports single-selection list boxes; multiple-selection list boxes should be supported by a separate class, say *WPMultiListBox*, but I never had a need for it, so I never implemented it.

■ *WPComboBox* is similar to *WPListBox* and also uses *WPListData*.

If you want more, read the source code.

7.3.5 Specialized Controls

As with all the classes defined in *Windows++*, the basic control classes are intended to be used by applications to derive more specialized controls. We've already seen one example of this: *EditZip*. Just for fun, let's do another. We'll derive a new kind of combo box, *CBUSStates*, that lets users choose from among the abbreviations of the 50 States in the USA, plus Washington, DC. (Non-US readers can no doubt think of similar combo box applications.)

```
/////////////////////
// Special combo box for US States (in PEOPLE.CPP).
//
class CBUSStates : public WPComboBox, public WPListData {
    static CSTR States[];
    int curState;
public:
    CBUSStates(WPWin *pwin, int id) : WPComboBox(pwin, id)
        { setList(this); }

    BOOL firstItem() { return curState = 1; }
    BOOL nextItem()  { return States[curState] ? ++curState : 0; }
    int getItemText(char *buf, int len)
        { strcpy(buf, States[curState-1]); return 2; }
};
```

```
CSTR CBUSStates::States[] = {
    "AL","AK","AZ","AR","CA","CO","CN","DC","DE","FL","GA","HI","ID",
    "IL","IN","IA","KS","KY","LA","ME","MD","MA","MI","MN","MO","MS",
    "MT","NE","NV","NH","NJ","NM","NY","NC","ND","OH","OK","OR","PA",
    "RI","SC","SD","TN","TX","UT","VT","VA","WA","WV","WI","WY",NULL
};
```

CBUSStates is multiply derived, just like *PeopleWin*. It's both a *WPComboBox* and a *WPListData*. The constructor sets the combo box list to itself, just like *PeopleWin* does. The virtual *WPListData* functions navigate the list of states, the abbreviations for which are stored in the class global *States*.

That's all there is to it. *CBUSStates* can now be used whenever the abbreviation for a state is called for. All we have to do is create the control:

```
void DlgEditPerson::initDlg()
{
    .
    .
    cbState = new CBUSStates(this, IDCB_STATES);
}
```

(Here, and throughout this chapter, control IDs like IDCB_STATES are defined in the module's .H file and are not shown in the text. This ID must correspond to an actual combo box control in the dialog, as defined in the resource file.) When this line is executed, the usual C++ events are set in motion: storage is allocated and all the base class constructors are invoked. The last one, *CBUSStates*, calls *setList* to set the combo box list: *setList* in turn invokes *firstItem*, *nextItem*, and *getItemText* to fill the combo box. The result is that when the user clicks the "drop-down" button, a list of states appears:

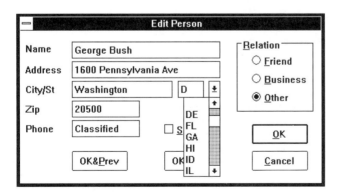

This simple example shows how the basic controls provided by *Windows++* can be reused to derive more specialized controls, which are themselves reusable! *CBUSStates* was implemented for PEOPLE, but all you'd have to do to use it in other programs is compile it as a separate module.

7.4 Object-Oriented Dialogs

Two down, one to go. We've implemented the basic dialog mechanics and, with a little hand waving, built *Windows++* objects for all the standard Windows controls. The last item on our dialog agenda is *object-oriented dialogs.* Now for the fun part.

In the opening pages of this chapter, we spent some time daydreaming about what we'd like the ideal dialog system to look like and came up with the idea of object-oriented dialogs, which view a dialog as a user interface to some underlying object. We wistfully observed how easy dialog coding would be if we could manipulate dialogs by manipulating the underlying objects they represent, instead of invoking Windows to copy information back and forth between the dialog and our programs' data structures.

In this section, we'll turn our pinings into reality.

Just to refresh your memory, let's review for a moment what's required to write the Edit Person dialog, using what we have so far. Recall that this dialog lets users edit the information stored in a *Person* object.

```
class Person {
    char    name[50];
    char    addr[50];
    char    city[30];
    char    state[3];
    char    zip[10];
};
```

First, we have to code the resource template. Go do it.

OK, you're back. Next, we derive a new class:

```
/////////////////////
// Edit person dialog (in PEOPLE.CPP)
//
class DlgEditPerson : public WPDialogModal {
    Person *p;                      // Person to edit
    WPEdit *edName;                 // edit control for person's name
    WPEdit *edAddr;                 // ..address
    WPEdit *edCity;                 // ..city
    CBUSStates*cbState;             // ..state (special combo box)
    EditZip    *edZip;              // ..zip (special edit control)
protected:
    void initDlg();                 // initialize dialog
public:
    DlgEditPerson(WPWin *pwin, Person *pp)
        : WPDialogModal("DlgEditPerson", pwin) { p = pp; createWin(); }
};
```

The constructor takes the parent window and a pointer to a *Person* to edit and actually creates the dialog. The name of the dialog resource template is hard-wired to "DlgEditPerson". In addition to the *Person*, the dialog also stores pointers to all the control objects, which are created and initialized in *initDlg*:

```
// Initialize dialog: create and initialize all the control objects
void DlgEditPerson::initDlg()
{
    edName = new WPEdit(this, IDED_NAME);
    ed->setText(p->name);

    edAddr = new WPEdit(this, IDED_ADDR);
    ed->setText(p->addr);

    edCity = new WPEdit(this, IDED_CITY);
    ed->setText(p->city);

    cbState = new CBUSStates(this, IDCB_STATE);
    ed->setText(p->state);

    edZip = new WPEdit(this, IDED_ZIP);
    ed->setText(p->zip);
}
```

Already this is becoming quite tedious; *initDlg* is starting to resemble the typical sort of "open" code (long sequences of repeated statements without any structure or subroutine calls) found in most Windows programs—just the thing we want to avoid. But suppose we plod onward, and create all the controls. Then what? At a minimum, we'll need to process the OK and CANCEL commands.

```
// Virtual message function to handle WM_COMMAND message.
DlgEditPerson::command(int id, WORD msg)
{
    switch (id) {
    case IDOK:
    case IDCANCEL:
        if  (id==IDOK) {
            // copy everything from dialog to Person object (p).
            edName->getText(p->name, sizeof(p->name));
            edAddr->getText(p->addr, sizeof(p->addr));
            edCity->getText(p->city, sizeof(p->city));
            cbState->getText(p->state, sizeof(p->state));
            edZip->getText(p->zip, sizeof(p->zip));
        }
        endDlg(id);
        return TRUE;
    }
    return WPDialogModal::command(id, msg);
}
```

More open code. Moreover, code that's generic: every dialog box responds to OK and CANCEL in more or less the same way: OK copies a bunch of information from the dialog to the underlying object, then quits; CANCEL just quits without copying anything.

So much for what we *have*; now let's consider what we *want*.

What we want is some way to "link" an object to a dialog, so we can manipulate the object instead of the dialog. Once "linked," we want the contents of the dialog to reflect the object, and *vice versa*. How might we implement something like this?

Well, suppose we posit the existence of a function that does what we want, then see where it leads us. Let's assume for a moment that we have a function to "link" the *Person* object:

```
void DlgEditPerson::initDlg()
{
    .
    .
    linkObject(p);                    // magic
}
```

We don't know how, but *p* is now "linked" to the dialog. What should this mean? It should mean that each control is linked to the appropriate data member, for example, that *p->name* is linked to IDED_NAME. But what does it mean for a control to be "linked?" If it means anything, it should mean that once linked, the control "knows" how to copy information back and forth between the object and the control.

In other words, linking a dialog means being able to perform two basic operations:

- *update the screen:* that is, copy the information from the underlying object to the controls in the dialog; and

- *update the object:* that is, copy the information displayed in the control to the underlying object (assuming the user has clicked OK rather than Cancel).

We can translate this observation into the following code:

```
class WPDialog : public WPWin {
public:
    void updateScreen();            // copy object ==> screen
    void updateObject();            // copy screen ==> object
};
```

These functions give meaning to the question mark in the figure on page 237:

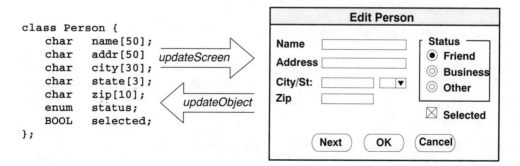

Since updating the dialog is simply a matter of updating each control, we can even implement the functions now:

```
void WPDialog::updateScreen()
{
    forEachChildWin(this, cwin) {
        ((WPControl*)cwin)->updateScreen();
        if (cwin->getID()==focusID)      // no charge for extra feature:
            cwin->setFocus();            // set focus too
    }
}
void WPDialog::updateObject()
{
    modified = TRUE;
    forEachChildWin(this, cwin)
        ((WPControl*)cwin)->updateObject();
}
```

(As added bonuses, *updateScreen* sets the focus from *focusID*, and *updateObject* sets the *modified* flag in *WPDialog*.) We've now reduced the problem to updating controls:

```
class WPControl : public WPWin {
public:
    virtual void updateScreen();         // how to implement ??
    virtual void updateObject();         // ??
};
```

We don't yet know how to implement these functions, but suppose for a minute that they work as claimed. What have we accomplished? Well, *updateScreen* and *updateObject* are precisely what's required to manipulate dialogs through their objects. If we had *updateObject* and *updateScreen*, we could write:

```
void MyDialog::doSomethingSpecial
{
    updateObject();  // copy dialog ==> object
    // manipulate underlying object in any way whatsoever; for example,
    // convert name to upper case
    strupr(p->name);
    updateScreen();  // copy object ==> dialog
}
```

And that's not all—we can use *updateScreen* to initialize the contents of any dialog, like so:

```
// Low-level dialog init fn introduced in Section 7.2.4
BOOL WPDialog::init(WPEvent &event)
{
    modified = FALSE;              // ..
    initDlg();                     // .. (as before)
    updateScreen();                // <<<< copy object to screen!
      .
      .
      .
}
```

We don't know how, but after invoking *updateScreen,* the person's name, address, etc. appear on the screen. This eliminates half the code in *DlgEditPerson::initDlg,* and every other application-specific *initDlg* function. (The other half is still required to create all the control objects. I'll get to that soon enough.) Because the *update* functions are general, they lets us write reusable code. Not just dialog initialization, but other behavior as well. For example, we can use *updateObject* to implement OK in a totally generic fashion:

```
BOOL WPDialog::command(int id, WORD msg)
{
    switch (id) {

    case IDCANCEL:

    case IDOK:
        if (id==IDOK)
            updateObject();             // copy screen ==> object
        endDlg(id);
        return TRUE;
    }
    WPWin::command(id, msg);
}
```

When the user clicks OK, *WPDialog* automatically copies the dialog's contents to the underlying object, then quits (if the user presses CANCEL, *WPDialog* just quits without copying). Again, we don't know how, but *updateObject* performs the magic. It copies whatever changes the user made into the underlying *Person* object, which is mysteriously "linked" to the dialog. If the user changed the city or zip, the changes are automatically copied into *Person.city* and *Person.zip* along with the other fields.

The beauty of this is that we can now initialize dialog contents and handle OK and CANCEL at the lowest level in our dialog class hierarchy, namely, in *WPDialog*. The code is totally generic; there's no mention of *p* or *Person* anywhere.

Granted that all this is totally wonderful, how do we implement it? To convert our wistful dialog musings into C++ reality, we must solve two problems:

- First, we must figure out how to "link" an object to a dialog. We'll break this problem into two pieces: 1) linking individual controls; and 2) linking the whole dialog.

- Second, we have to implement *updateObject* and *updateScreen* for controls.

To these, we can add a third wish-item, which, though not strictly required, would sure make life a lot easier for application programmers:

- We'd like some way to create all the control objects automatically.

Divide and conquer!

7.4.1 Linking Control Objects

Our first problem is figuring how to link an arbitrary object such as *Person* to a dialog. Earlier, we postulated the existence of a function to do this:

```
editDialog->linkObject(p);
```

Now we have to implement it. How? What we want is some generic way to tell the dialog that *p->name* should be "linked" to the edit control whose ID is IDED_NAME, that *p->addr* goes with IDED_ADDR, and so on. In general, we want to link each data member to a particular control in the dialog. So clearly, before we can link the whole dialog, we must first figure out how to link individual controls to individual data members.

So let's postulate another function, one to link controls (it's always fun to postulate functions that, in the immortal words of Spike Lee, do the right thing).

```
class WPControl : public WPWin {
    void linkObject( ??? );
};
```

The declaration is missing because we don't know what kind of object a particular control can be linked to unless we know what kind of control it is. As we've observed, each control class represents a different kind of information. A button represents a boolean quantity; an edit control represents a text string. Here's a complete list:

Control	Object	Meaning
WPButton	BOOL	on/off state
WPEdit	char *	text
WPComboBox	char *	text
WPListBox	int	selected item
WPScrollBar	int	thumb position
WPStatic	char*	text
WPStaticIcon	HICON	icon

(It may seem strange to think of *int* and BOOL as objects, but technically speaking, they are.) Even though each control represents a different kind of object, we can represent a pointer to any object as a *void**, together with its size.

```
class WPControl : public WPWin {
private:
    void linkObject(void *obj, int siz)        { object=obj; objsiz=siz; }
    friend WPDialog;
protected:
    void *object;      // ptr to unknown object
    int objsiz;        // size of object
};
```

It's generally unwise to use *void**, since it defeats the purpose and benefits of type-safe languages such as C++. A better idea is to let each specific control class provide its own *linkObject* function with type-safe arguments. In fact, we will do this also. For example, *WPEdit* links a string:

```
class WPEdit : public WPControl {
public:
    void linkObject(char *buf, int len)  { object=buf; objsiz=len; }
};
```

while *WPButton* links a boolean quantity:

```
class WPButton : public WPControl {
public:
    void linkObject(BOOL *pbool)  { data = pbool; }
};
```

(Since a BOOL always has a fixed length, there's no need to specify it.) In the same manner, we can go down the list of control classes and write *linkObject* functions for each one. This is straightforward, so I'll spare you the details. Just consider it done.

If each control class has its own *linkObject*, why have a generic one with *void** for *WPControls*? The full justification won't become clear for a few pages yet, but the basic idea is that it lets us link different controls in a uniform way. For now, just note that while the class-specific *linkObject* functions are for public consumption, the *void* version for *WPControl* is private, and will only be used internally (by *WPDialog,* which I've declared a *friend* of *WPControl*).[48]

We can now use the *linkObject* functions to link our *Person* object, like so:

```
void DlgEditPerson::initDlg()
{
    edName = new WPEdit(this, IDED_NAME);
    ed->linkObject(p->name, sizeof(p->name));
    edAddr = new WPEdit(this, IDED_ADDR);
    ed->linkObject(p->addr, sizeof(p->addr));
    ...etc.
}
```

This still has the stink of "open" code, but we're getting closer. All we have to do is figure out how to link the controls in a more generic manner. I'll come back to this shortly. Right now we have enough to implement the two *update* operations, so let's do it.

---

48 Note also that, while using *void** is nothing to be proud of, it nevertheless illustrates feature of C++ that distinguishes it from other OOPLs. It lets programmers make the choice between doing things the "correct" OO way and using an expedient "hack" instead. Other so-called pure OOPLs don't have any notion like *void*, nor any of the other non-object-oriented features C++ has inherited from C. Critics say, "yes, C++ gives you the rope to hang yourself." True, but sometimes you just have to break the rules.

7.4.2 Updating Controls

If you recall, we reduced the problem of updating the whole dialog to that of updating each control. All we have to do is implement *updateObject* and *updateScreen* for *WPControl* objects. But clearly, each kind (class) of control behaves differently. Updating a list box is different from updating a button or edit control. So how can we write *updateScreen* and *updateObject?*

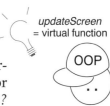

updateScreen
= virtual function

OOP

Simple: whenever different classes of objects respond differently to the same function, the function must be *virtual*.

```
class WPControl : public WPWin {
    virtual void updateObject() = 0;
    virtual void updateScreen() = 0;
};
```

By setting *updateObject* and *updateScreen* to zero, we make them pure virtual functions, and *WPControl* an abstract class. This means that *WPControl* cannot have any instances; it can only be used to derive subclasses, which must provide *updateObject* and *updateScreen*. This also jibes well with reality (Windows), where there's no such thing as a "control" by itself, only specific kinds of controls. The situation is entirely similar to the hypothetical *Shapes* described in Section 3.4.5.

So now we've reduced the problem still further, to implementing *updateScreen* and *updateObject* for specific control classes, such as *WPEdit* and *WPButton*. But now that the controls are linked to their underlying objects, this is trivial:

```
class WPEdit : public WPControl {
public:
    void updateObject()
        { if (object) getText((char*)object, objsiz); }
    void updateScreen()
        { if (object) { setText((char*)object); setMaxLen(objsiz-1); } }
};
```

We simply invoke the appropriate "brainless" function to set or get the text from or to *object*, which is (for edit controls) really a string. In addition, *updateScreen* sets the maximum text length, so Windows won't let users type too many characters.

WPEdit

| object | • | → "George" |
| objsiz | 6 |

updateObject =gsetText ⟵

updateScreen = setText ⟶

edit control

| George |

Here's *WPListBox:*

```
class WPListBox : public WPControl {
public:
    void updateScreen()  { if (object) setSel(*((int*)object)); }
    void updateObject()  { if (object) *((int*)object) = getSel(); }
};
```

In this case, the object is really an integer (the index of the selected item), and *WPListBox* invokes *setSel* or *getSel* (which send LB_SETCURSEL or LB_GETCUR-SEL) to set or get the selected list item.

The other controls are just as trivial, so I won't bother going through them all, but only mention a few highlights.

- Since users can't alter static controls, there's no need for *updateObject*, so it's implemented as an empty function (it must still be defined, since it's de-clared pure for *WPControl*).

```
class WPStatic : public WPControl {
public:
    void updateScreen() { if (data) setText((char*)data); }
    void updateObject() { /* static is read-only */ }
};
```

  On the other hand, programs often modify static controls internally, so *updateScreen* is provided.

- The *objsiz* doesn't always represent the size of the object in *bytes;* it is rather a general-purpose "size" parameter that individual control classes are free to interpret as they choose. For example, *WPRBGroup* and *WPCBGroup* inter-pret *objsiz* as the number of buttons in the group.

- Some classes don't have update operations, but inherit them from their ancestor(s). For example, *EditZip* and *CBUSStates* inherit their update func-tions from *WPEdit* and *WPComboBox*.

In all cases, *updateScreen* and *updateObject* do nothing if the control is not linked to any object—that is, if *object* is NULL.

7.4.3 Linking the Whole Dialog

Having detoured to implement *updateScreen* and *updateObject*, we can now return to the problem of linking the whole dialog. We've already solved the micro prob-lem of linking controls; what remains is the macro one of linking an entire object to the dialog. Using what we have so far, the only way to do it is manually, like so:

```
void DlgEditPerson::initDlg()
{
    edName = new WPEdit(this, IDED_NAME);
    ed->linkObject(p->name, sizeof(p->name));
    edAddr = new WPEdit(this, IDED_ADDR);
    ed->linkObject(p->addr, sizeof(p->addr));
    ...etc.
}
```

This isn't much of an improvement as far as the number of lines of code is con-cerned. All we've done is replace the calls to *setText* with calls to *linkObject*. But notice that we have eliminated the need to handle the OK message, since *WPDialog::command* does it by invoking *updateObject* (which now works).

How can we make *WPDialog* link the controls to their data objects *in some generic way*—that is, without referencing *name, addr,* or any of the other *Person* fields? We want to somehow iterate over all the controls in the dialog, and invoke *linkObject* for each one, passing it the address and length of the appropriate data member. But how does *WPDialog* know which data member to link without knowing anything about *Person?*

Essentially, we want to describe the object, in a generic way. For example, we want to say, "the first data member is a string that's 50 bytes long; next comes another string that's also 50 bytes," and so on. We must also tell the dialog which of these data members goes with which control. How can we do this?

There's an old software aphorism that says, *one table is worth a thousand lines of code.*

We can describe our *Person* object (or any other object) in a table. Each entry in the table describes one control/data member pair: the control's ID and the offset (from the start of the object) and size of the data member it goes with.

Control ID	Offset	Length
IDED_NAME	0	50
IDED_ADDR	50	50
IDED_CITY	100	30
etc...		
0	0	0

Control Map

Table makes dialogs *data-driven!*

The last entry is all zeroes, to indicate the end of the table. To implement this table, all we need is an ordinary C *struct:*

```
// (In WPDLG.H)
struct WPControlMap {
    int id;         // control ID
    int offset;     // offset of data member
    int len;        // length of data
};
```

We can use *WPControlMap* in the PEOPLE program to build a static table that completely describes *Person:*

```
static WPControlMap ControlMap[] = {
    { IDED_NAME,  0,   50  },      // offset 0,  size 50
    { IDED_ADDR,  50,  50  },      // offset 50, size 50
    { IDED_CITY,  100, 30  },      // etc..
    { IDCB_STATE, 130, 3   },
    { IDED_ZIP,   134, 10 },
    { 0, 0, 0 }                    // last entry ends the table
};
```

Back in our *Windows++* library, we'll add places in *WPDialog* to store the table and object, and new constructor arguments to initialize them.

```
class WPDialog : public WPWin {
private:
    WPControlMap *ctlmap;            // control map
    void *object;                    // underlying data object
public:
    WPDialog(CSTR resname, WPWin *pwin=NULL,
        WPControlMap *map=NULL, void* obj=NULL);

    void linkObject(void *obj);      // TBW (To Be Written)
    void* getObject()                { return object; }
};
```

The constructor simply sets *object* and *ctlmap* from its arguments, in addition to whatever else it did before.

```
WPDialog::WPDialog(CSTR resname, WPWin *pwin,
    WPControlMap *map, void *obj) : WPWin(NULL, pwin)
{
    ctlmap = map;
    object = obj;
    .
    . (as before)
}
```

(The same arguments are also added to *WPDialogModal* and *WPDialogModeless*.) Now, to finally link the object, all we have to do is run down the control map, linking each control as we go:

```
//////////////////////
// Link object to dialog. ctlmap specifies structure of the object,
// and which control is linked to which data member.
//
void WPDialog::linkObject(void *obj)
{
    object = obj;
    if (ctlmap==NULL)
        return;
    for (WPControlMap* map = ctlmap; map->id; map++) {
        ctl = (WPControl*)getChild(map->id);
        if (ctl==NULL) {
            ErrBox("Error: ID %d is in control map but not dialog!", id);
            continue;
        }
        if (object)
            ctl->linkObject((char*)object + map->offset, map->len);
        else
            ctl->linkObject(NULL, 0);
    }
}
```

The implementation is straightforward: *linkObject* navigates the table, linking each control to the appropriate data member, as specified by the *offset* and *len* in the control map. If no control object exists for a particular *id*, *linkObject* displays an error message (this should never happen, but the error message is a nicer way than *assert* to inform programmers of their mistakes)—*linkObject* even works properly if the object is NULL; it links each control to NULL.

You can now understand why I chose to represent each control's underlying object as a *void** and integer *objsiz*—so *WPDialog::linkObject* can treat each control in the same way. That is, generically, regardless of what kind (class) of control it is. *WPDialog::linkObject* doesn't need to know anything about the type of each control and its object, it just blindly passes the information from the control map to the controls. It's up to each control to interpret its *object* and *objsiz*. By using *void**, we're able to describe the controls and their data members in a single table with homogeneous entries.

7.4.4 Creating the Controls

We're almost home. We've figured out how to link a dialog to any object, and we have generic functions to update the object and screen. The only task remaining is our last wish-list item. We want *WPDialog* to create all the control objects automatically, so we don't have to bother with this chore in applications like PEOPLE. Currently, the *initDlg* function for our Edit Person dialog looks like this:

```
// Initialize dialog: all that's left is creating the controls objects.
void DlgEditPerson::initDlg()
{
    new WPEdit(this, IDED_NAME);
    new WPEdit(this, IDED_ADDR);
    new WPEdit(this, IDED_CITY);
    new CBUSStates(this, IDCB_STATE);
    new WPEdit(this, IDED_ZIP);
    linkObject(p);
}
```

We've eliminated all the calls to *linkObject*; linking is now done automatically using the control map. In fact, since we no longer have any need to reference them, there's no need to save pointers to all the controls in *edName*, etc. Yet all those tedious, repetitive calls to *new* still remain. They look so appetizing all alone like that, just waiting to be gobbled up by our library!

Creating the controls automatically seems like it should be easy enough. We already have the perfect place to do it, namely, in *WPDialog::linkObject*. As it grovels down the control map, linking each control, *linkObject* has the perfect opportunity to create the controls. It already detects when a control doesn't exist; all we have to do is make it respond by creating the control instead of reporting an error:

```
void WPDialog::linkObject(void *obj)
{
    for (WPControlMap* map = ctlmap; map->id; map++) {
        .

        .
        if ((ctl=(WPControl*)getChild(map->id))==NULL)
            ctl = new what ????
    .
    .
}
```

This sounds pretty good in theory, but there's a slight problem: how does *WPDialog* know what kind (class) of control to create? For example, whether to create an instance of *WPEdit* or *WPListBox?* We could perhaps determine the answer by examining the class name of the control's Window:

```
char classname[40];
GetClassName(hwndCtl, classname, 40);
if (strcmp(classname, "Edit")==0)
    ctl = new WPEdit(this, map->id);
else if  (strcmp(classname, "ListBox")==0)
    ctl = new WPListBox(this, map->id);
else if . . .
```

But what about specialized application control classes such as *EditZip* and *CBUSS-tates?* The window class names are still "Edit" and "ListBox", but we want to create specialized control objects for them, not the vanilla *Windows++* objects *WPEdit* and *WPListBox*. In general, *WPDialog* has no *a priori* idea what bizarre classes applications may use, so how can it possibly create the control?

Well, *WPDialog* doesn't really need to know what kind of control object to create, only how to create it. You may think I'm playing semantic games, but there *is* a difference. The application can tell the dialog how to create the control by passing it a function. All we have to do is add another entry to the control map, a pointer to a function that creates the desired control.

```
typedef WPControl* pWPControl;
typedef pWPControl (*NEWCTLFN) (WPWin*, int);

struct WPControlMap {
    NEWCTLFN newfn;                     // <<< function to create control obj
    int id;
    int offset;
    int len;
};
```

The *newfn* is supposed to create the control object given its parent window and ID. We can easily write such functions for all the built-in controls:

```
class WPEdit {
public:
    static WPControl *New(WPWin *pwin, int id)
        { return new WPEdit(int, id); }
};
```

```
class WPButton {
public:
    static WPControl *New(WPWin *pwin, int id)
        { return new WPButton(int, id); }
};
```

...etc. for each control subclass

I've used the name *New* with a capital *N* because these functions are sort of like the *new* operator. The *New* functions are static because they're invoked like an ordinary old *extern*, not through object instances (their whole purpose is to create the instances). Applications that implement their own specialized control classes must also provide *New* functions for them:

```
class EditZip {
public:
    static WPControl *New(WPWin *pwin, int id)
        { return new EditZip(int, id); }
};

class CBUSStates {
public:
    static WPControl *New(WPWin *pwin, int id)
        { return new CBUSStates(int, id); }
};
```

These functions are used along with the built-in (*Windows++*) functions to initialize control maps, like so:

```
static WPControlMap ControlMap[] = {
    { WPEdit::New,    IDED_NAME,   0,   50  },
    { WPEdit::New,    IDED_ADDR,   50,  50  },
    { WPEdit::New,    IDED_CITY,   100, 30, },
    { CBUSStates::New,IDED_STATE,  130, 3   },
    ...etc.
    { NULL, IDED_NAME, 0 }          // last entry ends the table
};
```

With the control-object-creation function specified in the control map, *WPDialog* now knows how to create each control (but not what class it is), and we can rewrite *linkObject*:

```
void WPDialog::linkObject(void *obj, BOOL redisplay)
{
    .
    .
    .
    for (WPControlMap* map = ctlmap; map->newfn; map++) {
        int id = map->id;
        HWND chwnd = GetDlgItem(getHwnd(), id);
        if (chwnd==NULL) {
            // Control window doesn't exist in dialog: complain
            ErrBox("Error: ID %d is in control map but not dialog!", id);
            continue;
        }
```

```
        WPControl *ctl = (WPControl*)GetWin(chwnd);
        if (ctl==NULL)
            // control obj doesn't exist: invoke map->newfn to create it!
            ctl = (*map->newfn)(this, id);
        assert(ctl);                    // bulletproofing
        .
        .
        .

    }
    // Bonus feature explained below
    focusID = map->id;                  // last id = initial focus
    if (redisplay)                      // redisplay requested:
        updateScreen();                 // update all the controls on screen
}
```

As an extra bonus, I've added a couple of enhancements: first, a boolean flag that says whether or not to update the screen after linking the object (default = TRUE); and second, the last entry in the control map is now used to specify the *focusID* (if you recall, *updateScreen* uses *focusID* to set the focus).

Back in the PEOPLE program, there's hardly anything left in *initDlg:*

```
void DlgEditPerson::initDlg()
{
    linkObject(p);
}
```

Even this is generic and so can be eliminated, simply by moving it to *WPDialog*:

```
// Low-level dialog init function.
BOOL WPDialog::init()
{
    modified = FALSE;
    linkObject(object, FALSE);    // <<<< link the object!
    initDlg();
    updateScreen();
    return focusID==0;
}
```

(We call *linkObject* with *redisplay* = FALSE, because the screen will be displayed when *updateScreen* is invoked right after calling *initDlg*.) Back to PEOPLE again. With all the controls created automatically, this is what Edit Person now looks like:

```
class DlgEditPerson : public WPDialogModal {
    static WPControlMap ControlMap;
public:
    DlgEditPerson(WPWin *pwin, Person *p)
        : WPDialogModal("DlgEditPerson", pwin, ControlMap, p)
    { createWin(); }
};
static WPControlMap ControlMap[] = {
    { WPEdit::New,     IDED_NAME,   0,   50  },
    { WPEdit::New,     IDED_ADDR,   50,  50  },
    { WPEdit::New,     IDED_CITY,   100, 30, },
    { CBUSStates::New, IDED_STATE,  130, 3   },
    { WPEdit::New,     IDED_ZIP,    134, 10  },
```

```
    { NULL, IDED_NAME, 0 }          // last entry ends the table
};
```

There's nothing left. *There's no code!* (Well, just one line in the constructor.) The entire dialog is specified in the *ControlMap*. Now do you believe in the power of tables?

That's it. We're done. The dialog is linked, *updateScreen* and *updateObject* work, and the controls are created. There's no more code left in *DlgEditPerson;* the whole thing is table-driven. You can go home now.

But why not stick around for more fun?

7.4.5 Some Useful Macros

Our dialog system is complete. In just a moment, I'll review it from the perspective of the PEOPLE program. But first, let's add a few macros to make creating the control map easier. Currently, our control map for *DlgEditPerson* Person looks like this:

```
static WPControlMap ControlMap[] = {
    { WPEdit::New,     IDED_NAME,    0,    50   },
    { WPEdit::New,     IDED_ADDR,    50,   50   },
    { WPEdit::New,     IDED_CITY,    100,  30,  },
    { CBUSStates::New, IDED_STATE,   130,  3    },
    { WPEdit::New,     IDED_ZIP,     134,  10  },

    .
    . etc.
    .
    { NULL, IDED_NAME, 0 }          // last entry ends the table
};
```

All those hard-wired numbers sure look disgusting. More important, they're subject to becoming out-of-whack at the slightest change to *Person*. What if we decide to allow 60 characters instead of 50 for the name? And how do we reliably specify each field's *offset,* taking into account whether the compiler is set to use 1-, 2-, or 4-byte alignment?! What we need are some macros to make building control maps easier and more reliable:

```
//////////////////
// Macros used to initialize static control maps (in WPDLG.H).
//
#define offsetof(typ,mbr) \
    ((size_t)((char *)&((typ *)0)->mbr - (char *)0))
#define cmCust(fn, id, typ, mbr) \
    { fn,id,offsetof(typ,mbr),sizeof(((typ *)0)->mbr) },

#define cmEdit(id, typ, mbr)       cmCust(WPEdit::New, id, typ, mbr)
#define cmButn(id, typ, mbr)       cmCust(WPButton::New, id, typ, mbr)
#define cmCmbo(id, typ, mbr)       cmCust(WPComboBox::New,id, typ, mbr)
#define cmList(id, typ, mbr)       cmCust(WPListBox::New,id, typ, mbr)
#define cmSbar(id, typ, mbr)       cmCust(WPScrollBar::New, id, typ, mbr)
#define cmRBgp(id, typ, mbr, n) \
```

```
    { WPRBGroup::New, id, offsetof(typ, mbr), n },
#define cmCBgp(id, typ, mbr, n) \
    { WPCBGroup::New, id, offsetof(typ,mbr), n },

#define cmPush(id)                   { WPButton::New, id, NULL, 0 },
#define cmEnd(id)                    { NULL, id }
```

To see how these work in practice, let's look at the final control map in PEOPLE.CPP:

```
WPControlMap DlgEditPerson::ControlMap[] = {
    cmEdit( IDED_NAME,                Person,   name )
    cmEdit( IDED_ADDR,                Person,   addr )
    cmEdit( IDED_CITY,                Person,   city )
    cmCust( CBUSStates::New,IDCB_STATE,       Person,    state )
    cmEdit( IDED_PHONE,               Person,   phone )
    cmRBgp( IDRBG_STATUS,             Person,   status,   NSTATUS )
    cmCust( EditZip::New,             IDED_ZIP, Person,   zip )
    cmButn( IDB_SELECTED,             Person,   selected )
    cmPush( IDM_OKNEXT)
    cmPush( IDM_OKPREV)
    cmEnd(IDED_NAME)
};
```

This is not only more legible, it's more reliable. The basic idea behind the macros is to use *offsetof* and *sizeof* to determine the offset and size of each data member. Thus

```
cmCust( EditZip::New, IDED_ZIP, Person, zip )
```

expands to

```
{ EditZip::New, IDED_ZIP,
    offsetof(Person, name), sizeof(((Person*)0)->zip) },
```

The *offset* term is further expanded to

```
((size_t)((char *)&((Person *)0)->zip - (char *)0))
```

Other macros have the control-creation function hard-wired for common built-in control objects. For example,

```
cmEdit( IDED_NAME, Person, name )
```

expands to

```
cmCust( WPEDIT::New, IDED_NAME, Person, name )
```

which is further expanded as above. Some macros require an explicit *objsiz*. For example, a radio or check box button group interprets *objsiz* as the number of buttons in the group. Since push buttons have no data, *cmPush* takes only an ID. The macro *cmEnd* ends the table with a NULL entry and the desired focus control ID.

While the macros are a big improvement, *WPControlMap* tables are not foolproof. For example, it's possible to link incompatible controls: what if ID_STATES is not really a combo box (in the dialog template), but an edit control? Most likely, the program will crash. The fundamental problem lies in the fact that the control map is not *type-safe*.[49] We could of course provide additional checks; for example, we could add a virtual function, *WPControl::getCompatibleClass,* that returns the name of the Windows class that goes with the control object (*WPListBox* would return "ListBox", while *WPScrollBar* would return "ScrollBar"), then have *linkObject* check this against the actual window class name. I chose not to do this only because I judged that it wasn't worth the effort. My experience shows that, using the macros, the process of creating control maps is reliable enough. Every now and then I accidentally code the map incorrectly, but it's usually obvious what the problem is when my program crashes. Once I fix the table, it tends to stay fixed.

7.4.6 Putting It All Together: *DlgEditPerson*

To review what we've just done, let's take a look at the final Edit Person dialog in the PEOPLE program. Here's the entire implementation:

```
// (In PEOPLE.CPP)
class DlgEditPerson : public WPDialogModal {
    static WPControlMap ControlMap[];
public:
    DlgEditPerson(WPWin *pwin, Person *p)
        : WPDialogModal("DLGEDITPERSON", pwin, ControlMap, p)
            { createWin(); }

    BOOL command(int id, WORD msg);
    void updateScreen();
};

WPControlMap DlgEditPerson::ControlMap[] = {
    cmEdit( IDED_NAME,              Person,    name )
    cmEdit( IDED_ADDR,              Person,    addr )
    cmEdit( IDED_CITY,              Person,    city )
    cmCust( CBUSStates::New, IDCB_STATE,       Person,    state )
    cmEdit( IDED_PHONE,             Person,    phone )
    cmRBgp( IDRBG_STATUS,           Person,    status,    NSTATUS )
    cmCust( EditZip::New,           IDED_ZIP, Person,    zip )
    cmButn( IDB_SELECTED,           Person,    selected )
    cmPush( IDM_OKNEXT)
    cmPush( IDM_OKPREV)
    cmEnd(IDED_NAME)
};
////////////////////
// Handle OK&Next and OK&Prev pushbutton commands.
//
BOOL DlgEditPerson::command(int id, WORD msg)
{
    switch (id) {
```

<hr/>

49 This raises an interesting issue. There is often a direct conflict between table-driven, generic structures on the one hand, and type-safeness on the other. There's no "correct" trade-off; as with most things, it's a matter of judgment. You have to weigh the pros and cons in each situation, then decide. In this case, the benefits of table-driven dialogs justify the sacrifice of type-safeness.

```
    case IDM_OKNEXT:                // OK&Next pushbutton:
    case IDM_OKPREV:                // OK&Prev pushbutton:
        updateObject();             // update current object
        Person *p = (Person*)getObject();
        p = id==IDM_OKNEXT ? p->next : p->prev;
        assert(p);                  // (should always find p)
        linkObject(p);              // link new obj (& update screen!)
        return TRUE;
    }
    return WPDialogModal::command(id, msg);
}

/////////////////////
// Specialized updateScreen function enables/disables
// pushbuttons before doing normal updateScreen.
//
void DlgEditPerson::updateScreen()
{
    Person *p = (Person*)getObject();
    getChild(IDM_OKNEXT)->enableWin(p->next != NULL);
    getChild(IDM_OKPREV)->enableWin(p->prev != NULL);
    WPDialogModal::updateScreen();
}
```

As you can see, it's quite simple compared to what things looked like in the first few pages of this section (7.4), before we implemented object-oriented dialogs (not to mention what it would look like in Windows) Practically the entire implementation is specified in the control map. One table really is worth a thousand lines of code. (If not for PEOPLE, then certainly for all the other unborn applications) And not just source lines, but executable code.[50]

As you can see, I lied earlier. There is *some* code in *DlgEditPerson*. But it all of it deals with the OK&Next and OK&Prev buttons (dynamics), which accept the user's input then move to the next or previous person in the list. But just look how simple this code is, now that we have the *update* operations: *command* responds to OK&NEXT by invoking *updateObject*, which copies everything in the dialog to the current *Person* object then links the dialog to the next person in the list. Since *linkObject* also updates the screen, there's nothing else to do!

The only other interesting thing is *updateScreen*, which grays the push buttons appropriately (more dynamics). If there's no next person, OK&Next is disabled; likewise, OK&Prev is disabled if there's no previous person. After adjusting the buttons, *updateScreen* calls the standard *updateScreen* for *WPDialogModal* (inherited from *WPDialog*), which copies all the information in the underlying *Person* object to the controls in the dialog. In order to let applications such as PEOPLE provide different behavior, the *update* functions have been made virtual.

---

50 I once worked on a software project where dialog boxes comprised almost a megabyte of executable code, most of it just the sort of open code that our system eliminates.

With *DlgEditPerson* complete, we can write the *edit* function we postulated at the start of this long journey.

```
/////////////////
// Edit person object: piece o'cake!
//
BOOL Person::edit(WPWin *pwin)
{
    DlgEditPerson dlg(pwin, this);
    return dlg.isModified();
}
```

Here's how to use *edit:*

```
Person paul = { "Paul DiLascia","1 Windows Way",...};
paul.edit(mywin);
```

Let's take a careful look at what happens when *paul.edit* is invoked:

■ *Person::edit* creates an instance of *DlgEditPerson* on the stack. *DlgEditPerson* sets *object* to *&paul* and *ctlmap* to *ControlMap*, and passes "DlgEditPerson" and *mywin* along to *WPDialog* via *WPDialogModal* ("DlgEditPerson" and *ControlMap* are hard-wired into the *DlgEditPerson* constructor).

■ The last constructor, ˜*DlgEditPerson*, invokes *createWin*, which loads, creates, and runs the dialog. The dialog is automatically hooked up to all the Windows++ infrastructure, so that messages are now routed via *WPDlgProc* and *dispatchEvent* to the appropriate virtual message function.

■ Windows sends a WM_INITDIALOG message, whence *WPDlgProc* invokes *WPDialog::init*, which first clears the *modified* flag then invokes *linkObject,* which in turn iterates over the *ControlMap*, creating and linking each control as it goes. For example, it creates a *WPEdit* control for the *name* field, and links it to *paul.name*. It even creates PEOPLE-specific controls like *CBUSStates* and *EditZip*, since the create function is given in the *ControlMap*.

■ When *linkObject* returns, *init* next invokes *initDlg*, which doesn't exist for *DlgEditPerson* (it inherits an empty *initDlg* function from *WPDialog*). Nothing happens.

■ Finally, *init* calls *updateScreen* to update the dialog window. This function is virtual, and *DlgEditPerson* has its own version, so control passes there. *DlgEditPerson::updateScreen* enables or disables the OK&Next and OK&Prev buttons, then invokes *WPDialogModal::updateScreen,* which copies the contents of *paul* to the dialog. Presto! The dialog is filled with information (*updateScreen* even sets the focus):

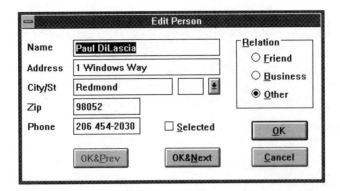

- When the user finishes editing and presses OK, the event works its way past *DlgEditPerson::command* to *WPDialog::command*, which invokes *updateObject* before ending the dialog; *updateObject* sets the *modified* flag and copies the contents of the dialog to the underlying object (*paul*).

The only code in *DlgEditPerson* deals with the dynamics of graying the OK&Next and OK&Prev buttons. Everything else is done by *WPDialog*: it copies information from the object to the screen when the dialog is initialized, and back again when the user says OK. At the heart of our dialog system is the control map. This table describes an arbitrary object in abstract, generic terms our dialog object can understand.

C   *It would be easy to implement a similar system in C (I once did). In fact, the control map is very C-ish. The table itself is not object-oriented; the object-orientedness comes from the fact that we model dialogs as user interfaces to objects. In C, you'd use an ordinary* struct.

We can now rest, proud of our shiny new dialog system. We've eliminated all the open code we set out to. Our object-oriented dialog system dramatically reduces the amount of code required to write dialogs. And best of all, it's reusable.

7.5 Reusable Dialogs

Now that we've built a powerful dialog system, let's put it to work. In this section, we'll build a number of common dialog boxes that we can use in our applications, including dialogs for File Open and File Save. It will be the first and last time we ever do.

7.5.1 About

The simplest kind of dialog box most applications deal with is the About dialog. According to the CUA (Common User Access; see the introduction to Chapter 6) guidelines, this dialog is supposed to display the program's logo and other information about the program, such as who wrote it. Generally, the dialog contains an icon, some text, and an OK button. I've already shown you the resource template and dialog itself for the PEOPLE About box (in Section 7.1.1); to display it, all we have to do is add a few lines to *command*:

```
// (In PEOPLE.CPP)
BOOL PeopleWin::command(int id, WORD msg)
{
    switch (id) {
    case ID_ABOUT:
        WPDialogModal about("DLGABOUT", this);
        about.createWin();
        break;
    .
    .
}
```

That's it. When *about.createWin* is invoked, the dialog is loaded, created, and displayed. Control doesn't return until the user clicks OK.

But wait! This code is almost entirely generic. The only PEOPLE-specific variable is the name of the resource template ("DLGABOUT") and menu ID (ID_ABOUT). In Section 3.3.7, I showed you how to reuse resource names. Remember? We used "AppMenu" and "AppIcon" as the default application menu and icon names. Why not do the same for About? All we have to do is add another built-in menu ID in WPID.H and move the code from *PeopleWin* to *WPMainWin*:

```
BOOL WPMainWin::command(int id, WORD msg)
{
    switch (id) {
    case WPIDM_ABOUT:
        WPDialogModal aboutBox(this,"DLGABOUT");
        if (aboutBox.run()==-1)
            MsgBeep();                    // couldn't load it: beep
        return TRUE;
    .
    .
}
```

By adding the above lines to our library, we provide one more little bit of reusable functionality for *Windows++* programs. To add an About dialog to a *Windows++* program, all a programmer has to do is define the dialog box in the resource file with the name "DLGABOUT" and add a menu command with WPIDM_ABOUT as the ID. There's no code to write; the dialog is completely data-driven!

In fact, if you run the TOE program from Chapter 5, you'll see that it has an About command that displays a dialog like this:

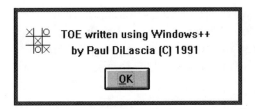

Yet if you look at the code for TOE, you won't find anything having to do with About. The only place the word "about" even appears is in the resource file.

As with menus and icons, WPID_ABOUT and "DLGABOUT" are only the default, most-reusable conventions; if you want to do something special with the About dialog, you can always handle the command yourself. Just for the fun of it, let's add an animated About dialog to our PEOPLE program. After all, the About dialog is supposed to be a place to show your stuff by doing something fancy.

The About box for PEOPLE uses the same wimpy smiley-face icon as the HELLO program. Let's make the smiley-face stick out its tongue every now and then. We'll do this by implementing a new type of control, called *AltIcon*, that alternately draws two icons over the smiley face: one that contains a red tongue sticking out, and another that has a yellow tongue (which effectively erases the red one). We'll set a timer to control the animation.

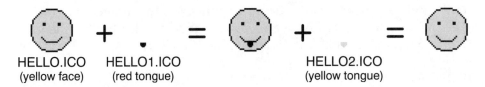

HELLO.ICO   HELLO1.ICO   HELLO2.ICO
(yellow face)   (red tongue)   (yellow tongue)

Here's the class definition:

```
////////////////////
// Alternating icon is special kind of static icon.
//
class AltIcon : public WPStaticIcon {
    HICON icon1;
    HICON icon2;
    HICON whichIcon;
    int nclicks;
protected:
    BOOL timer(int id);
public:
    AltIcon(WPWin *pwin, int id, CSTR name1, CSTR name2);
    ~AltIcon() { killTimer(1); }
};
```

AltIcon is derived from the *Windows++* built-in class *WPStaticIcon*, which represents a Windows "static" control with the SS_ICON style flag. The only non-inline functions are the the constructor and *timer.*

```
//////////////////
// Constructor: create alternating icon.
//
AltIcon::AltIcon(WPWin *pwin, int id, CSTR name1, CSTR name2)
    : WPStaticIcon(pwin, id)
{
    whichIcon = icon1 = App.loadIcon(name1);
    icon2 = App.loadIcon(name2);
    nclicks=0;
    setTimer(1, 200);
    createWin();
}
```

The constructor loads the two icons and stores their handles in *icon1* and *icon2*. It also sets a timer to go off every 200 milliseconds (1/5 of a second). (The destructor destroys this timer, which isn't really necessary, since Windows does so automatically when the window is destroyed). When the timer goes off, Windows sends a WM_TIMER message, which goes to the virtual *timer* function.

```
//////////////////
// Handle timer message: swap icons
//
BOOL AltIcon::timer(int id)
{
    if (++nclicks > 5) {
        linkObject(whichIcon = whichIcon==icon1 ? icon2 : icon1);
        updateScreen();
        if (nclicks > 6)
            nclicks=0;
    }
    return TRUE;
}
```

The *timer* function responds by changing the icon and updating the screen every five "clicks," then back again on the sixth click (the timer ID, used to distinguish multiple timers, is ignored). Note how *AltIcon* simply uses *linkObject* and *updateScreen* to actually change the icon.[51] The end result is that the smiley-face sticks out its tongue for 1/5 of a second, every second.

---

51 The implementation of *WPStaticIcon::updateScreen* uses GDI functionality that we won't get to until the next chapter (it basically just calls the Windows API function *DrawIcon* to draw the icon).

AltIcon illustrates the power of inheritance. Most of *AltIcon* is inherited from its base class ancestors *WPStaticIcon, WPControl,* and *WPWin.* Only the behavior that's unique to *AltIcon* requires additional code. This is the whole point of inheritance. Furthermore, while *AltIcon* is not part of *Windows++,* it's nevertheless reusable, just like *EditZip* and *CBUSStates.* All that would be required to use *AltIcon* in other programs is to compile it as a separate module. There's no reason to confine reusability to *Windows++;* application developers should feel encouraged to build additional reusable objects on *top* of *Windows++.*

To finish the About box, all we have to do is create the dialog with an instance of *AltIcon.* This requires deriving a special dialog class and writing a small amount of *Windows++* code:

```
/////////////////////
// Special animated About box for PEOPLE program
//
class AboutPeople : public WPDialogModal {
public:
    AboutPeople(WPWin *pwin) : WPDialogModal("DLGABOUT", pwin)
        { createWin(); }
    void initDlg()
        { new AltIcon(this, IDSI_ABOUTICON, "Hello1","Hello2"); }
};
```

This class is even simpler than *AltIcon.* The constructor invokes *createWin* to actually create the dialog; the only other function, *initDlg,* simply creates an instance of *AltIcon* with "hello1" and "hello2" as the names of the icons to use. The icons are defined in the resource file:

```
// (In PEOPLE.RC)
Hello1 ICON hello1.ico              // (Icon files drawn with SDKPAINT)
Hello2 ICON hello2.ico
```

With *AboutPeople* defined, all that remains is to use it:

```
BOOL PeopleWin::command(int id, WORD msg)
{
    switch (id) {
    case WPIDM_ABOUT:
        AboutPeople about(this);
        return TRUE;
        .
        .
        .
}
```

PeopleWin::command intercepts the About command, processes it, and returns TRUE without passing the command to *WPMainWin.* (Otherwise, *WPMainWin* would handle About by creating a "vanilla" About dialog, not our fancy animated one.) Since the *AboutPeople* constructor invokes *createWin,* the dialog runs as soon as it's instantiated: The dialog is loaded, created, and displayed. Every now and then the smiley-face sticks out its impish tongue at unsuspecting users.

have a
nice day

7.5.2 String Input

For our next trick, let's implement a missing Windows function.

Windows programmers frequently use the old reliable workhorse function *MessageBox* to display a message. This function actually creates a simple dialog box that contains static text and up to three buttons, depending on what flags you call it with. For example, the call

```
MessageBox(NULL,
    "Do you like green eggs and ham?", "Question:", MB_YESNO);
```

displays the following dialog:

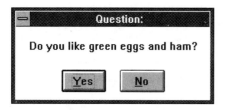

It would be nice if there were a similar function to *get* a string of text from the user. In almost every other programming language or system, there's some easy way to do this. In C, you'd use *gets*:

```
char name[50];
printf("What's your name? ");
gets(name);
```

Languages such as BASIC, FORTRAN, and Pascal all have ways to do the same thing. But not Windows. In Windows, you have to first design a dialog box (either interactively, using a resource editor, or manually, by editing the resource file directly), then write a dialog procedure to handle messages from the dialog box. At a minimum, you'd have to handle WM_INITDIALOG and WM_COMMAND (to handle OK). Needless to say, that's a lot of work just to get a lousy string from the user.

To correct this omission on Windows' part, let's use our killer dialog system to implement a generic "string" dialog that does more or less what *gets* does. As programmers, we'd like to be able to write something like this:

```
char name[50];
input("What's your name? ", name, sizeof(name));
```

This is almost a good idea. The only problem is that it introduces the symbol *input* into the global name space.[52] Besides, with our OOP caps on, we should think of string dialogs as special kinds of dialogs, so we'll do the normal object-oriented thing: introduce a new class (what else?). Instead of calling *input*, we'll write

```
char name[50];
WPDlgString dlg(pwin, name, sizeof(name), "What's your name?",
"HELLO");
```

The constructor accepts a parent window, a buffer to stuff with the user's input, the length of this buffer, a prompt, and a caption. The constructor actually displays the dialog box (there's no need to call *createWin* or *run*), so when the next line of code is executed, *name* is filled with the user's input.

How do we implement *WPDlgString?* One way would be to simply load a resource template with a predefined name such as "DLGSTRING" but that would force programmers to design the resource template, which is what we're trying to avoid. We could provide the resource template as part of *Windows++*, say in a file called STRING.DLG (Borland's *ObjectWindows* does this)—but then our programmer would still have to type

```
#include "string.dlg"
```

in the .RC file. This isn't so bad, but we can do even better. We can create the dialog from scratch, on the fly, without a resource template. Windows provides the function *DialogBoxIndirect* for just this purpose. It lets you create a dialog box from a data structure instead of a named resource. Using it is simple in theory but messy in practice, since the data structure is somewhat baroque—it comprises a header, followed by separate structures for each control. The structure is illustrated in the following figure:

DLGTEMPLATE structure	} header
DLGITEMTEMPLATE structure	
DLGITEMTEMPLATE structure	} controls
DLGITEMTEMPLATE structure	
· ·	

DLGTEMPLATE and DLGITEMTEMPLATE are not defined in WINDOWS.H (they're documented in the SDK *Reference, Volume 2*), so we'll have to define our own *struct*s for them. You'd probably never go to this trouble in an application, but

---

52 As a general rule, when designing a library it's a bad idea to introduce common English words like *input* into the name space, since they're likely to conflict with the programmer's symbols or even those in other libraries. Who knows what other libraries *Windows++* will be linked with? Furthermore, it's difficult to tell where such names come from.

the effort is well worth it for library code that can be reused. As always, a little time
and effort spent on the library saves a lot when it comes time to write applications.

```
///////////////////
// Dialog template structure, from the SDK Reference Manual, Volume 2.
// (In WPDLSTR.CPP)
//
struct DLGTEMPLATE {
    long style;                    // dialog style flags
    BYTE nItems;                   // total number of items (controls)
    int  x,y,cx,cy;                // position, size
    char menuName[1];              // actual length is variable
    char className[1];             // ditto
    char caption[1];               // ditto
    struct DLGITEMTEMPLATE * setCaption(CSTR text);
};
///////////////////
// Dialog ITEM template structure, from SDK Reference Manual, Vol. 2
//
struct DLGITEMTEMPLATE {
    int x,y,cx,cy;                 // position, size of control
    int id;                        // child window ID
    long style;                    // style flags
    char className[15];            // actual length is variable
// char text[];                    // these are filled in..
// BYTE extraBytes;                // by setText
    DLGITEMTEMPLATE * setText(CSTR text);
};
```

One advantage of rolling our own structures is that we're free to add member
functions. I've added one to set the dialog caption, and one to set an item's text.
The first function, *DLGTEMPLATE::setCaption,* simply copies the caption into the
appropriate place and returns a pointer to the end of the header, where the first
item structure begins:

```
///////////////////
// Set caption in dialog template, and return ptr to end
// of header, which is first item template structure.
//
DLGITEMTEMPLATE * DLGTEMPLATE::setCaption(CSTR text)
{
    if (text)
        strcpy(caption, text);
    else
        caption[0]=0;
    return (DLGITEMTEMPLATE *)(caption + strlen(caption)+1);
}
```

The other function, *DLGITEMTEMPLATE::setText,* sets the text for a dialog item
and returns a pointer to the next item:

```
///////////////////
// Set item text. Returns pointer to next item following this one.
//
DLGITEMTEMPLATE * DLGITEMTEMPLATE::setText(CSTR text)
```

```
{
    char *p = className + strlen(className)+1;
    if (text) {
        strcpy(p, text);                    // append text to structure
        p += strlen(p)+1;                   // ...
    } else
        *p++ = 0;
    *p++ = 0;                               // length of extra info = zero
    return (DLGITEMTEMPLATE *)p;
}
```

One thing we must be aware of (I found out the hard way) is that these structures must be compiled with *byte alignment*, since that's what Windows expects. To ensure this, we add the following lines at the beginning of WPDLSTR.CPP:

```
/////////////////
// Use byte-alignment when compiling this
// module--required for DLGTEMPLATE & co.
//
#ifdef __BORLANDC__
#pragma option -a-
#elif __ZTC__
#pragma ZTC align 1
#endif
```

The *#pragma* preprocessor directive is a general "escape mechanism" that lets you pass compiler-specific commands to the compiler. For Borland, the command is *option -a-*; for Zortech, it's *ZTC align 1*.

With these structures defined, we're ready to build *WPDlgString*. The first thing we have to do is write the constructor, which is straightforward (but ugly). It just builds the DLGTEMPLATE and DLGITEMTEMPLATE structures. We need a header and four controls: static text for the prompt, an edit control for the user's input, and OK and Cancel buttons. Since most of the information in these structures is constant (only the prompt, caption, and screen position are variable), let's start with some static objects:

```
//////
// Static definition of dialog box.
// These structures are copied and filled in with
// the necessary variables, e.g., prompt and width, etc.
//

// First, a few constants to make the code more legible
const CXBUTTON = 30;                // width of button
const CXEDIT = 150;                 // width of edit control
const CYITEM = 13;                  // height of button or edit control
const CYSPACE = 5;                  // interline space
const XMARGIN = 5;

// Here are the static structures.  Ugh!
static  DLGTEMPLATE DlgTemplate = {
    WS_POPUPWINDOW|DS_MODALFRAME|WS_DLGFRAME,4,40,80,0,55,0,0,0
};
```

```
static DLGITEMTEMPLATE ItemPrompt = {
    XMARGIN,CYSPACE,0,8,-1,
    WS_VISIBLE|WS_CHILD|SS_LEFT,"Static"
};

static DLGITEMTEMPLATE ItemInput = {
    XMARGIN,16,CXEDIT,CYITEM,WPIDED_STRING,
    WS_VISIBLE|WS_CHILD|WS_TABSTOP|WS_BORDER|ES_LEFT|ES_AUTOHSCROLL,
    "Edit"
};

static DLGITEMTEMPLATE ItemOK = {
    0,35,CXBUTTON,CYITEM,IDOK,
    WS_VISIBLE|WS_CHILD|WS_TABSTOP|BS_DEFPUSHBUTTON,"Button"
};

static DLGITEMTEMPLATE ItemCancel = {
    0,35,CXBUTTON,CYITEM,IDCANCEL,
    WS_VISIBLE|WS_CHILD|WS_TABSTOP|BS_PUSHBUTTON,"Button"
};
```

(All this static data reminds me of BASIC programs with pages of DATA statements.) I got the default values by designing the dialog interactively in *WindowsMaker* and copying the results from the .RC file produced. With these structures instantiated, we can now write the rest of *WPDlgString*. Here's the full class definition:

```
class WPDlgString : public WPDialogModal {
    LPSTR memTemplate;              // memory-resident dialog template
    char *strBuf;                   // caller's buffer..
    int strLen;                     // ..and its length
public:
    WPDlgString(WPWin *pwin, char *buf, int len,
        CSTR prompt, CSTR caption);
    ~WPDlgString()                  { App.farFree(memTemplate); }
    BOOL createWin();
    void initDlg();
};
```

And here's the constructor:

```
/////////////////////
// Create string dialog and run it.
// caller's buffer will be stuffed w/user's input.
// Create dialog box on the fly (Probably the most disgusting
// function in all of Windows++!).
//
WPDlgString::WPDlgString(WPWin *pwin, char *buf, int len,
    CSTR pmt, CSTR cap) : WPDialogModal(NULL, pwin)
{
    assert(buf && pmt);
    strBuf = buf;
    strLen = len;
    if (cap==NULL)
        cap = "";
```

```
    // Create dialog template header.  Build it in App.scratch.
    DLGTEMPLATE *hdr = (DLGTEMPLATE *)App.scratch;
    *hdr = DlgTemplate;

    WPRect box = pmt;                   // get text dimensions of prompt
    int pmtHt = 8*box.height();    // convert height to dialog units

    // Compute size and position of dialog box.
    hdr->cx = max(4*box.width(), CXEDIT) + 2*XMARGIN;
    hdr->cy = 3*CYITEM + CYSPACE + pmtHt;

    // Center dialog box in parent window
    box = pwin;                         // dimensions of parent window
    hdr->x = (2*box.width())/LOWORD(GetDialogBaseUnits())  -(hdr->cx)/2;
    hdr->y = (4*box.height())/HIWORD(GetDialogBaseUnits()) -(hdr->cy)/2;

    // Create static text control for prompt.
    DLGITEMTEMPLATE *item = hdr->setCaption(cap);
    *item = ItemPrompt;
    item->cx = hdr->cx-XMARGIN;
    item->cy = pmtHt;
    item = item->setText(pmt);

    // Create edit control for input.
    *item = ItemInput;
    item->y = pmtHt + 2*CYSPACE;
    item = item->setText(NULL);

    // Create OK button.
    *item = ItemOK;
    int xOK = (hdr->cx - 3*CXBUTTON)/2;
    item->x = xOK;
    item->y = pmtHt + CYITEM + 3*CYSPACE;
    item = item->setText("&OK");

    // Create Cancel button.
    *item = ItemCancel;
    item->x = xOK + 2*CXBUTTON;
    item->y = pmtHt + CYITEM + 3*CYSPACE;
    item = item->setText("&Cancel");

    // Now we know how much storage is required; allocate it from
    // GLOBAL memory. This is required because DialogBoxIndirect
    // expects a handle to global memory.
    //
    int size = ((char*)item) - App.scratch;
    memTemplate = (LPSTR)App.farAlloc(size,TRUE,TRUE);
    char *src = App.scratch;            // copy from scratch..
    LPSTR dst = memTemplate;            // ..to global memory block
    while (size-->0)
        *dst++ = *src++;
    createWin();                        // run the dialog!
}
```

(I told you it would be messy.) Most of the code deals with building the dialog template. The template is built in the scratch buffer *App.scratch*. First, we copy the static objects, then "fill in the blanks" by copying the prompt and caption strings to the appropriate places and doing a little arithmetic to position the controls. Most of this is straightforward, so I'll spare you the gory details. The only interesting thing is that we use an overloaded *operator=* for *WPRect* that gets the dimensions of a text string in characters:

```
WPRect box = pmt;    // get text dimensions of prompt
```

This function was not described in Chapter 2, but it's in Appendix A. *WPDlgString* uses it to compute the size of the dialog box.

Once the template has been created in *scratch*, a global memory block is allocated for it, and stored as *memTemplate*. This memory is passed to *DialogBoxIndirect* when the dialog is created (in *createWin*, as follows). It would be nice to simply pass the *memTemplate* pointer directly to Windows, but unfortunately the dialog-creation function we want to use, *DialogBoxIndirect,* requires a handle to global memory, not a pointer.[53] Way back in Chapter 4, we added an optional global flag to direct *App.farAlloc* to allocate the memory as a separate block of global memory, rather than suballocating it from a heap as would normally be done. This flag was added precisely so we can now use it for *DialogBoxIndirect.*

The last thing the constructor does is invoke *createWin* to actually create the dialog. Since we want to use *DialogBoxIndirect,* we need a special *createWin* function:

```
//////////////////
// Create string dialog. Use DialogBoxIndirect instead of DialogBox.
//
BOOL WPDlgString::createWin()
{
    // Run the dialog!
    result = DialogBoxIndirect(App(),
        GlobalHandle(FP_SEG(memTemplate)),
        GetHwnd(createArgs.parent),
        App.getDlgProc());
    assert(result!=-1);
    return result != -1;
}
```

OK, the dialog is created. Next, we have to link our caller's buffer to the edit control, so we can inherit all the generic dialog behavior (OK, CANCEL, initialization) we implemented earlier. We can either build a control map or link it manually. Since there's only one control, the latter is easier:

```
void WPDlgString::initDlg()
{
    WPEdit * ed = new WPEdit(this, WPIDED_STRING);
    ed->linkObject(strBuf, strLen);
}
```

We're done. Never again will *Windows++* programmers have to design a dialog and write a dialog procedure just to get a string from the user. To get a string from the user, we can now write

---

53 I wonder why the *DialogBoxIndirect* functions require a handle when the corresponding *CreateDialogIndirect* functions for modeless dialog boxes use pointers. If you know, write me.

```
char name[50] = "Type your name here";
WPDlgString dlg(this, name, sizeof(name),
    "What's your name?", "HELLO");
```

whereupon the following dialog appears:

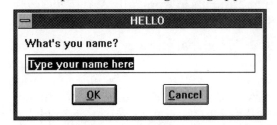

So much for *WPDlgString*. But wait, there's more!

While we're at it, we may as well add another little feature (we programmers can't resist adding features). Just in case someone wants to do something fancy like display an icon in the string dialog, let's provide another constructor that lets programmers specify a *resource* template:

```
class WPDlgString : public WPDialogModal {
public:
    WPDlgString(WPWin *pwin, char *buf, int len, CSTR resname)
    : WPDialogModal(resname, pwin) { memTemplate=NULL; createWin(); }
};
```

This requires modifying *createWin* ever so slightly, to use *DialogBoxIndirect* only if *memTemplate* is set:

```
BOOL WPDlgString::createWin()
{
    if (memTemplate) {
        .
        . (as before)
        .
    }
    return WPDialogModal::createWin();
}
```

Now if a programmer wants to use a resource template for string input, he or she can. The only requirement is that the template must use the predefined control ID WPIDED_STRING for the edit control that receives the string.

C   *C programmers could easily borrow the code for* WPDlgString, *since it makes little use of C++. Since C doesn't allow function overloading, you'd need two separate functions for each version—say* GetString *to create the dialog on the fly, and* GetStringResource *to get it using a resource dialog. In either case, you could reuse control IDs like* WPIDED_STRING, *just as* Windows++ *does.*

7.5.3 File Dialogs

Practically every Windows program, including PEOPLE, contains commands to open or save a file, and corresponding dialogs to get the file name from the user. In the old days of Windows 3.0, programmers were left to write these dialogs themselves, with little help from Windows beyond the API function *DlgDirList,* which stuffs a list box with file and/or directory names. With Windows 3.1, Microsoft has introduced a new dynamic link library, COMMDLG.DLL, that contains a number of prefabricated, reusable (hooray for Microsoft!) dialogs—something they should have done all along, but better late than never. The dialogs actually work in Windows 3.0; all you need is the DLL, which is provided with the *Windows++* source disk. Developers may redistribute this DLL with their applications.

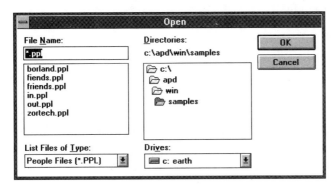

File Open dialog from COMMDLG

Let's bring these dialogs into the *Windows++* fold, starting with File Open.

COMMDLG.DLL contains a function called *GetOpenFileName,* which runs the File Open dialog. You pass it a special structure that contains a number of creation parameters. This structure is defined in COMMDLG.H, which is part of the Windows 3.1 SDK. Since not all of you may have this, I've rekeyed the declaration into WPDLFILE.H (and by so doing, may pass it on to you):

```
extern "C" {
////////////////
// The following definitions were re-keyed from COMMDLG.H,
// in the Micrsoft Windows 3.1 SDK.
//
struct OPENFILENAME {
    DWORD    lStructSize;           // size of this structure
    HWND     hwndOwner;            // owner window
    HANDLE   hInstance;            // module instance
    LPSTR    lpstrFilter;          // filename "filter" e.g., *.TXT
    LPSTR    lpstrCustomFilter;    // custom filter
    DWORD    nMaxCustFilter;       // ..size
    DWORD    nFilterIndex;         // index of filter to display
    LPSTR    lpstrFile;            // file name
    DWORD    nMaxFile;             // ..
    LPSTR    lpstrFileTitle;       // file title
    DWORD    nMaxFileTitle;        // ..
    LPSTR    lpstrInitialDir;      // name of initial directory
    LPSTR    lpstrTitle;           // dialog title
    DWORD    Flags;                // see below
    WORD     nFileOffset;          // used internally ??
```

```
    WORD     nFileExtension;          // size of extension
    LPSTR    lpstrDefExt;             // default extension
    DWORD    lCustData;               // custom data
    FARPROC  lpfnHook;                // dialog procedure, if hooked
    LPSTR    lpTemplateName;
};
typedef OPENFILENAME FAR * LPOPENFILENAME;

// DLL functions to run file dialogs.
BOOL    FAR PASCAL GetOpenFileName(LPOPENFILENAME);
BOOL    FAR PASCAL GetSaveFileName(LPOPENFILENAME);
short   FAR PASCAL GetFileTitle(LPSTR, LPSTR, WORD);

#define OFN_READONLY              0x00000001
#define OFN_OVERWRITEPROMPT       0x00000002
#define OFN_HIDEREADONLY          0x00000004
#define OFN_NOCHANGEDIR           0x00000008
...etc (many more flags)
} // extern "C"
```

The entire sequence is enclosed within the declaration *extern "C" { ... }*, which tells the compiler that any functions declared within the braces should be compiled as C functions, without the type-safe name mangling used for C++ functions (see Section 2.1.3). WINDOWS.H does the same thing. This is required because, like the rest of Windows, COMMDLG.DLL was compiled for C.

I've also divined the resource IDs for the controls in the file dialog (which are not defined in COMMDLG.H) and added them to WPID.H (you're welcome):

```
//////////////////////
// IDs for COMMDLG controls. (From WPID.H)
//
#define IDOFN_EDFILENAME          1152
#define IDOFN_LBFILENAME          1120
#define IDOFN_SSPATHNAME          1088
#define IDOFN_PBHELP              1038
#define IDOFN_CBREADONLY          1040
```

So much for definitions. Here's the Microsoft-approved way to run the File Open dialog using C:

```
OPENFILENAME ofn;
ofn.lStructSize = sizeof(OPENFILENAME);
ofn.hwndOwner = myHwnd;
ofn.lpstrFile = mybuf;
ofn.nMaxFile = sizeof(mybuf);
.
. initialize more fields
.
if (GetOpenFileName(&ofn)) {
    // do something
    // mybuf now contains the name of the file selected
} else
    // error
```

First, you initialize OPENFILENAME, then you invoke *GetOpenFileName*.

We could, of course, simply call *GetOpenFileName* directly from the PEOPLE program, but it's more natural to model File Open as a special class of dialog:

```
// (In WPDLFILE.H)
class WPDlgFfileOpen : public WPDialogModal {
protected:
    OPENFILENAME ofn;                  // open structure
    char tempbuf[MAXFILENAMELEN];      // buffer to hold file name
    char *filename;                    // caller's buffer
public:
    WPDlgFileOpen(WPWin *pwin, char* fname, CSTR title=NULL);

    BOOL createWin();
    void destroyWin() { sendMsg(WM_COMMAND, IDABORT, result); }
    BOOL command(int id, WORD msg){ return FALSE; }

    void setFilter(CSTR filt)
        { if (filt) ofn.lpstrFilter=(LPSTR)filt; }
    void setDir(CSTR dir)
        { ofn.lpstrInitialDir=(LPSTR)dir; }
};
```

Most of the code is fairly straightforward. The biggest function is the constructor:

```
// Default flags
const OFN_DEFAULT =
    OFN_ENABLEHOOK | OFN_PATHMUSTEXIST | OFN_HIDEREADONLY;
const OFN_OPENDEFAULT = OFN_DEFAULT | OFN_FILEMUSTEXIST;

// Default filter
const char DEFAULTFILT[] = "Any File (*.*)\0*.*\0";

WPDlgFileOpen::WPDlgFileOpen(WPWin *pwin, char* fname, CSTR title)
    : WPDialogModal(NULL, pwin)
{
    filename = fname;                  // caller's buffer to get filename
    tempbuf[0]=0;
    memset(&ofn, 0, sizeof(ofn));      // clear Windows open struct
    ofn.lStructSize=sizeof(ofn);       // set size,
    ofn.hwndOwner = GetHwnd(pwin);     // parent window handle,
    ofn.lpstrFile=tempbuf;             // file name,
    ofn.nMaxFile=sizeof(tempbuf);      // its length,
    ofn.lpstrTitle= (LPSTR)title;      // dialog title,
    ofn.Flags= OFN_OPENDEFAULT;        // flags,
    ofn.lpfnHook = WPDlgProc;          // dialog proc,
    ofn.nFilterIndex=1;                // use first filename filter,
    setFilter(DEFAULTFILT);            // and set default filename filter
}
```

It initializes various OPENFILENAME fields, such as the filename *filter*, which defaults to *.* (any file). Applications may change the default using *setFilter*; PEOPLE sets it to *.PPL. The dialog procedure (*lpfnHook*) is set to our universal dialog procedure, *WPDlgProc*, since we want to route messages through our virtual message functions. The filename itself is retrieved in a temporary area, *tempbuf*, and then copied to the caller's buffer only if the dialog runs successfully.

WPDlgFileOpen has its own *createWin* function, which invokes *GetOpenFileName* to run the dialog (this should seem old hat by now):

```
BOOL WPDlgFileOpen::createWin()
{
    if ((result = GetOpenFileName(&ofn))!=0 && filename)
        strcpy(filename, tempbuf);
    return result != -1;
}
```

It also has its own *destroyWin*, since the Microsoft-approved way to end a common dialog is by sending it the IDABORT command, not by calling *EndDialog*:

```
class WPDlgFileOpen : public WPDialogModal {
public:
    void destroyWin() { sendMsg(WM_COMMAND, IDABORT, result); }
};
```

Once again, we hide this annoying inconsistency behind the uniform interface of *destroyWin*. In *Windows++*, you always use *destroyWin* to destroy a window.

That's all there is to File Open. The File Save dialog is almost identical, so I won't bother describing it, except to say that it's modeled using a class, *WPDlgFileSave*, which is listed in Appendix A. The finished dialogs are the same ones we used back in Chapter 6 to implement the File commands in *WPMainWin*.

The same techniques can be applied to all the other common dialogs provided in COMMDLG.DLL. As with controls, we can generalize from *WPDlgFileOpen* to a cookbook formula for common dialogs:

Common Dialogs à la *Windows*++

INGREDIENTS:
1   copy of COMMDLG.H
1   common-dialog-specific FOODLGSTRUCT, as defined in COMMDLG.H
1   *Windows++ WPDlgFoo* class derived from *WPDialogModal*

DIRECTIONS:
1. Add instance of FOODLGSTRUCT to *WPDlgFoo*.
2. Initialize FOODLGSTRUCT in *WPDlgFoo* constructor. Provide member functions to initialize "interesting" fields.
3. Write *createWin* and *destroyWin* functions: *createWin* should call whatever DLL function runs the dialog (declared in COMMDLG.DLL); *destroyWin* usually just sends an IDABORT command.
4. Add other interesting dialog-specific functions, if any.

For another example of a program that uses the File Open dialog, see the LAUNCH program in Appendix A. LAUNCH is no more than a modified File

Open dialog (it has no main window) that launches other programs, either normally or under your favorite debugger. I use it all the time to run programs I write. It renames the HELP button to DEBUG, and uses *WPDlgString* to set the name of the debugger, a command for which is added to the system menu. LAUNCH also saves its state in WIN.INI, so it always starts up in the same state you last left it.

7.5.4 The Print Dialog

Let's use the recipe to implement one more reusable common dialog: the Print dialog. This dialog lets users select a printer and various printing options, such as how many copies to print, which pages, and so on. The dialog even has a button to run the Setup dialog (which is provided by the device driver):

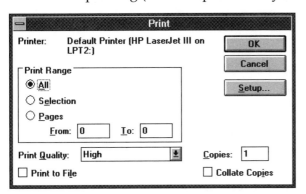

Print dialog from COMMDLG

The corresponding COMMDLG structure is PRINTDLG:

```
///////////////
// (In WPDLPRT.H, from COMMDLG.H in the Micrsoft Windows 3.1 SDK.)
//
struct PRINTDLG {
    DWORD    lStructSize;
    HWND     hwndOwner;
    HANDLE   hDevMode;
    HANDLE   hDevNames;
    HDC      hDC;
    DWORD    Flags;
    WORD     nFromPage;
    WORD     nToPage;
    WORD     nMinPage;
    WORD     nMaxPage;
    WORD     nCopies;
    HANDLE   hInstance;
    DWORD    lCustData;
    FARPROC  lpfnPrintHook;
    FARPROC  lpfnSetupHook;
    LPSTR    lpPrintTemplateName;
    LPSTR    lpSetupTemplateName;
    HANDLE   hPrintTemplate;
    HANDLE   hSetupTemplate;
};
```

Following our recipe, we define a new class, *WPDlgPrint*, with an instance of PRINTDLG as a member, and a constructor to initialize it:

```
///////////////////
// Standard print dialog from Windows COMMDLG.DLL. (In WPDLPRT.H)
//
class WPDlgPrint : public WPDialogModal {
    PRINTDLG pdlg;                  // Windows COMMDLG structore
public:
    WPDlgPrint(WPWin *pwin);
    ~WPDlgPrint();
};

// Default flags for print dialog: get printer DC.
const DWORD PD_DEFAULT = PD_RETURNDC;

///////////////////
// Create print dialog: initialize pdlg. (In WPDLPRT.CPP)
//
WPDlgPrint::WPDlgPrint(WPWin *pwin) : WPDialogModal(NULL, pwin)
{
    memset(&pdlg, 0, sizeof(pdlg));   // clear to all zeroes
    pdlg.lStructSize=sizeof(pdlg);    // set struct size
    pdlg.hwndOwner = GetHwnd(pwin);   // owner = parent window
    pdlg.Flags = PD_DEFAULT;          // default flags
}
```

The only thing interesting here is that we use the default flag PD_RETURNDC, which tells Windows to return a handle to the printer device context in *pdlg.hdc*. We'll use *hdc* Section 8.5 to actually print. As per the official Windows SDK instructions, we must delete this device context when we're done using it. The most natural place to do it is in the destructor:

```
WPDlgPrint::~WPDlgPrint()
{
    if (pdlg.hDC)
        DeleteDC(pdlg.hDC);
}
```

Still following the recipe, we next write *createWin* and *destroyWin* functions:

```
class WPDlgPrint : public WPDialogModal {
    void destroyWin()            { sendMsg(WM_COMMAND, IDABORT); }
    BOOL createWin()             { return result = PrintDlg(&pdlg); }
};
```

In this case, *createWin* calls *PrintDlg*, which is the COMMDLG function to run the print dialog; *destroyWin* sends an abort command, just like in the File dialogs.

Finally, we add "other interesting dialog-specific functions":

```
class WPDlgPrint : public WPDialogModal {
    HDC getHDC()                  { return pdlg.hdc; }
    friend WPPrinter;             // see below
```

```
public:
    // Brainless Functions to get results from PRINTDLG structure.
    DWORD   flags()             { return pdlg.Flags; }
    void    flags(DWORD f)      { pdlg.flags = f; }
    WORD    nCopies()           { return pdlg.nCopies; }
    void    nCopies(WORD n)     { pdlg.nCopies = n; }
    // etc..
};
```

These "brainless" functions are completely straightforward. For example, there are overloaded versions of *nCopies* to get and set the number of copies to print. But note once again the benefit of packaging: since *getHDC* should only be used to create a *WPPrinter* object (see Section 8.5), it's private; and since it can only be gotten, never set, there's no *setHDC* function. This makes programming more foolproof: there's no way anyone can mess with *hdc*.

To run the print dialog, all an application has to do is

```
WPDlgPrint printDialog;
if (printDialog.run()) {
    // print
}
```

Even this is unnecessary, since *WPMainWin::command* automatically runs the print dialog before invoking *filePrint* (see Section 6.3.3):

```
BOOL WPMainWin::command(int id, WORD msg)
{
    switch (id) {
    case WPIDM_FILEPRINT:
        WPDlgPrint pdlg = this;
        if (pdlg.run())
            filePrint(pdlg);
        return TRUE;
    .
    .
    .
}
```

All the application has to do is implement *filePrint*.

So much for the print dialog. The same recipe could be used to implement the other COMMDLG dialogs; I never did, only because I never had a need for them. My motto is *implement it when you need it*.

7.6 Modeless Dialogs

In this final section, we'll implement modeless dialogs. There's really not that much to do; there are only three differences between modal and modeless dialogs that we must address:

- Modeless dialogs are created using *CreateDialog* instead of *DialogBox*.

- Modeless dialogs are destroyed using *DestroyWindow*.

- Messages for modeless dialogs are sent via the main message queue and must be routed manually to the dialog using the Windows API function *IsDialogMessage*.

The first two items present no particular difficulty. All we have to do is write *createWin* and *destroyWin* appropriately. In fact, since *WPWin::destroyWin* normally invokes *DestroyWindow*, we don't even have to write *destroyWin* for modeless dialogs, but can simply inherit it from *WPWin*. Consider it done.

The only challenge is the last item: routing messages to modeless dialogs. Naturally, we want to do it automatically and invisibly, so applications never see a difference between modal and modeless dialogs. Why should they be different? The message routing is just more Windows kludginess—but kludginess we can hide. All we have to do is modify our application object (*WPApp*) to keep track of modeless dialogs and route their messages in the main message loop (*WPApp::run*).

First, we'll add a *next* pointer to *WPDialogModeless* and make *WPApp* a friend:

```
class WPDialogModeless : public WPDialog {
private:
   WPDialogModeless* next;        // next modeless dlg in app
   friend WPApp;
};
```

Next, we add a few members to *WPApp,* to maintain the list of dialogs:

```
class WPApp : public WPModule {
private:
   WPDialogModeless *dialogs; // list of modeless dialogs
public:
   void addDialog(WPDialogModeless *dlg);
   void removeDialog(WPDialogModeless *dlg);
};
////////////////
// Add modeless dialog to application's list.
//
void WPApp::addDialog(WPDialogModeless *dlg)
{
   dlg->next = dialogs;
   dialogs = dlg;
}
////////////////
// Remove modeless dialog from application's list
//
void WPApp::removeDialog(WPDialogModeless *dlg)
{
   if (dlg==dialogs)
      dialogs=dlg->next;
```

```
    else {
        for (WPDialogModeless *d=dialogs; d; d=d->next) {
            if (d->next == dlg) {
                d->next = dlg->next;
                break;
            }
        }
        assert(d);
    }
}
```

These functions are trivial, a textbook exercise in list manipulation. Now whenever a modeless dialog is created, we'll add it to the application; conversely, when one is destroyed, we'll remove it. The perfect places to do this are in the constructor and destructor for modeless dialogs:

```
WPDialogModeless::WPDialogModeless(CSTR resname, WPWin *pwin,
    WPControlMap *map, void *obj) : WPDialog(resname, pwin, map, obj)
{
    App.addDialog(this);
}

WPDialogModeless::~WPDialogModeless()
{
    App.removeDialog(this);
}
```

Now the application object is automatically informed whenever a modeless dialog is created or destroyed. The only thing left to do is route the messages. For this, we simply modify the main message loop in *WPApp::run*, as per Microsoft's instructions (SDK *Guide to Programming*, Chapter 9, page 3):

```
void WPApp::run()
{
    .
    .
    while (GetMessage(&msg, NULL, 0, 0)) {
        .
        .
        BOOL dlgmsg = FALSE;
        for (WPDialogModeless *dlg=dialogs; dlg; dlg=dlg->next) {
            if (dlg->getHwnd() && IsDialogMessage(dlg->getHwnd(),&msg)) {
                dlgmsg=TRUE;
                break;
            }
        }

        if (dlgmsg)
            continue;

        TranslateMessage(&msg);
        DispatchMessage(&msg);
    }
}
```

The only twist is that instead of just one modeless dialog, we have a whole list to check. If the *msg* is destined for one of our dialogs, *IsDialogMessage* passes it to the dialog and returns TRUE; otherwise it just returns FALSE.[54]

For an example of a modeless dialog, see the Print Abort dialog in Section 8.5.3.

7.7 Summary

It's been a long chapter, I know. But we've done a lot! Now's the time to sit back proudly and review our dialog accomplishments:

- We implemented basic infrastructure to make dialogs work just like any other kind of window. Our infrastructure hides Windows' numerous inconsistencies behind our own more rational programming interface.

- We implemented a number of basic control objects, plus a few specialized controls for zip codes, US States and "alternating" icons.

- Our greatest achievement is object-oriented dialogs, which encapsulate a significant portion of the dialog code in a static table, the control map. Object-oriented dialogs make the model of dialog-as-user-interface-to-object explicit and easy. In many cases, the entire dialog is reduced to a single table. The Edit Person dialog in the PEOPLE program is almost totally codeless.

- We added a number of reusable dialogs to *Windows++*. About dialogs are handled automatically in *WPMainWin*, and we built reusable dialogs for getting string input and for File Open, File Save, and File Print.

- Finally, we encapsulated (hid) the Windows weirdness associated with modeless dialogs, so applications need never suspect that they're any different from modal ones (we, however, can smile knowingly).

I never showed you the complete PEOPLE program. Sorry, but it's too long to include here, so I refer you to Appendix A.

We're really on a roll. Now that we've successfully tamed dialogs, a major Windows programming bottleneck, we're ready to move on: in the next chapter, we'll tackle another Windows programming bugaboo: graphics.

---

54 One can't help but wonder why, if Windows (*IsDialogMessage*) knows the message is for the dialog, it doesn't just send it there in the first place.

CHAPTER ■ 8

Graphics

Graphics programming is another notoriously difficult area of Windows programming, one which few commercial Windows add-on products have addressed. Even commercial class libraries such as Borland's *ObjectWindows* provide little or no additional support in this area, but simply leave you to call the Windows API directly.[55]

Graphics programming in Windows is based on the infamous *GDI* (that's Graphics Device Interface). The basic goal of GDI is laudable: to provide a *device-independent* graphics programming interface. Whether you're drawing on a VGA screen, printer, plotter, or ball point pen (just kidding), you call the same API functions to "draw" on the device.

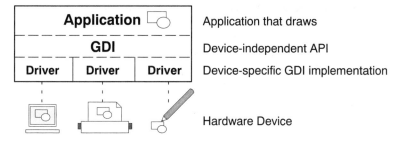

As with any API, the benefits are reaped on both sides of the interface: GDI not only aids application programmers, it also gives device vendors a target to aim for. If *Acme Devices, Inc.* should ever decide to implement that ball point pen, all it has to do is write a device "driver" that supports all the GDI functions (good luck). Nowadays, even the hardware itself is sometimes built to the GDI specification.

Unfortunately, things never work in practice as well as they sound in theory. GDI is not so easy to program, and it's not always so device-independent either.

---

55 At the time of this writing, a C++ Windows graphics class library called *ObjectGraphics* was just introduced by the Whitewater Group.

Nevertheless, it *is* a big improvement over the graphics API that DOS provides (what API?), and a vital part of Windows. It just needs a little repackaging—which we are only too willing, ready, and able to provide.

In this chapter, we'll apply our standard C++ tricks to make GDI programming easier and more foolproof. We'll also build an object-oriented graphics library on top of *Windows++*, one modeled loosely after the *shapes* described in [Stroustrup 1991]. Along the way, we'll write a couple of small programs: a program that draws random rectangles and another that lets users explore the Mandelbrot set. But the *pièce de résistance* is DRAW, a mini object-oriented drawing program.

Throughout the chapter, I'll assume that you're more or less familiar with basic GDI concepts, such as device contexts, pens, bitmaps, and so on, or that you know enough about other graphics programming environments to understand what's going on. If GDI and graphics programming are totally unfamiliar to you, I suggest you first read either the Microsoft Windows SDK manual, or a good book on Windows programming such as [Petzold 1990]. If you want to learn more about the theory behind graphics programming, I recommend [Foley & Van Dam 1982].

8.1 Two Areas of Improvement

Our graphics efforts will target two main areas:

- First, we'll use our standard techniques to improve the GDI itself, where the usual sort of Windows madness impedes programming.

- Second, we'll build an object-oriented graphics library as a layer above the GDI (one that Windows should have provided).

8.1.1 Problems with GDI

The GDI is filled with numerous idiosyncrasies, inconsistencies, and headache-causing nuisances that are characteristic of Windows. To wit:

- As with dialogs and MDI windows, GDI provides many different ways of doing the same thing. For example, to get a device context you call *GetDC*. Or *GetWinDC*. Or *BeginPaint*. Or *CreateDC*. To free a device context you call *ReleaseDC*, except when you call *DeleteDC*. Other times it's *EndPaint*. Still other times you don't do anything because Windows frees it for you. As with dialogs, we'll hide these inconsistencies behind a consistent C++ API.

- Unlike most memory objects (such as menus and resources) that programs use, GDI objects are not automatically freed by Windows when an application terminates. Ill-behaved programs can thus permanently steal valuable memory. We'll fix this.

- GDI contains many programming rules that are not explicit in the API, but which you must simply know from reading the SDK manuals or a Windows programming book (or, more likely, from bitter experience). For example, you must "de-select" display objects before destroying them. Another example is that not all GDI functions are allowed for all device contexts. We will encapsulate these rules in objects, so that just using *Windows++* guarantees that they're enforced.

- Many of the GDI functions are cumbersome to use. They frequently require many arguments, most of which are usually NULL. We'll use our standard tricks (brainless functions, default arguments, *WPPoint* and *WPRect*, etc.) to repackage GDI in a way that simplifies programming and reduces typing.

- GDI is missing some useful functions, which we will provide. For example, we'll add a function to draw a bitmap on a device context and a *printF* function that draws text using *printf*-style arguments.

- The GDI is implicitly object-oriented, though this fact is obscured (and to some extent, murdered) by C. By modeling GDI in C++, we will expose the inherent differences among various GDI objects.

- Printing is a major Windows bugaboo, one that drives many programmers crazy. Printing is something that most programs need, but that every programmer hates (like cough medicine). In Section 8.5, I'll show you how *Windows++* makes printing painless.

8.1.2 Object-Oriented Graphics

Our second major effort will be building a small object-oriented graphics system on top of GDI. A full-featured graphics system is beyond the scope of a single chapter, but the basic design described here could, with a little effort, be extended to a more complete graphics package.

But first, why does Windows need a graphics package? What's wrong with GDI?

It's not so much that GDI is wrong as that it's incomplete. Any well-designed graphics system would have a device-independent layer that, like GDI, provides functions to draw various shapes on a device. But while this layer is essential to providing device independence, it's too klunky: it leaves too much work to applications.

To see why this is so, let's examine how a typical Windows program draws on the screen.

Whenever Windows determines that all or part of your application's window must be redrawn (for example, when it's resized or brought to the fore from behind some other window that previously obscured it), it sends a WM_PAINT message to the window procedure, which is expected to paint the window. In *Windows++*, this message is passed to the virtual *paint*. How each application implements *paint* depends of course on what the application does, but in general, applications must manage their own data structures for painting. For example, if your main window contained a bunch of rectangles, you might keep a list of RECT structures in memory, to store the positions and sizes of the rectangles.

The data structures are required because GDI provides no notion of memory-persistent graphics objects.[56] In Windows, *Rectangle* is not an object but a fleeting operation; once drawn, rectangles are gone forever.

Programs that use graphics should be able to simply create rectangles, ellipses, and so on, then forget about them. As long as the objects exist, there should be no need for applications to repaint them manually every time something happens to the window; instead, the system should automatically take care of this. What's needed is a level of graphics API above GDI, one that provides memory-persistent graphics objects. To reiterate, we want to model shapes as objects, not operations.

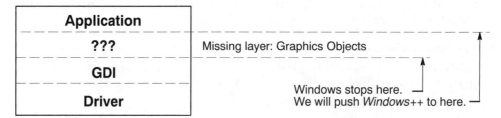

In Section 8.3, we'll build such a layer. But before we extend GDI, let's clean it up.

8.2 Repackaging GDI

As always, we begin by identifying objects. The most fundamental object in GDI is the *device context*. A device context is, loosely speaking, "something to draw on." It's represented in C by the type HDC (Handle to Device Context), defined in WINDOWS.H; in *Windows++*, we'll use a class (as always).

```
// (In WPGDI.H).
class WPDevContext {
    HDC hdc;                          // Windows handle to device context.
public:
    HDC operator()()                  { return hdc; }
};
```

---

56 To be fair, Windows does provide a notion of *regions*, which can be built from rectangles, polygons, and ellipses, but they aren't terribly useful.

To this, we can add the obvious "brainless" functions:

```
class WPDevContext {
public:
    BOOL rectangle(WPRect &box)
        { return Rectangle(hdc,
            box.left(), box.top(), box.right(), box.bottom()); }
    long textOut(int x, int y, LPCSTR text, int len)
        { return TextOut(hdc, x, y, (LPSTR)text, len); }
    // etc.
};
```

But before we go writing lots of code, let's take the time to think things through.

8.2.1 A Device Context for Every Occasion

Windows supports many different kinds of device contexts. There are window device contexts, memory device contexts, *information* contexts, and so on. Some GDI functions are allowed only for certain kinds of device contexts. For example, an information context only supports functions, like *GetDeviceCaps,* that get information about the device context, not functions that actually draw on the device. This should immediately make you think subclasses.

different kinds of device contexts = *subclasses*

OOP

In fact, a device context is really a kind of information context, namely, one that you can also draw on. This can be expressed in C++ like so:

```
// Information context
class WPDevInfo {
protected:
    HDC hdc;                          // Windows handle
public:
    HDC operator()()                  { return hdc; }
};
// Device context is now derived from information context.
class WPDevContext : public WPDevInfo {

};
```

This may seem strange at first, because information contexts are less common, so we naturally think of them as the aberration, or specialization (subclass); but actually, information contexts are more general, since anything you can do with an information context you can also do with a device context, but not *vice versa.* Thus *WPDevInfo* is the base class and *WPDevContext* the derived subclass.

But why bother to make *WPDevInfo* a separate class at all? Because we can now put the functions that are allowed for information contexts in *WPDevInfo:*

```
class WPDevInfo {
public:
    // Get device capability identified by "cap"
```

```
    int getCap(int cap)            { return GetDeviceCaps(hdc, cap); }
    int getDRIVERVERSION()         { return getCap(DRIVERVERSION); }
    int getTECHNOLOGY()            { return getCap(TECHNOLOGY); }
    int getHORZSIZE()              { return getCap(HORZSIZE); }
    int getVERTSIZE()              { return getCap(VERTSIZE); }
    int getHORZRES()               { return getCap(HORZRES); }

    .
    . (etc. for all device capabilities)
};
```

while those that are allowed only for device contexts go in *WPDevContext:*

```
class WPDevContext : public WPDevInfo {
public:
    BOOL rectangle(WPRect &box)    // Draw rectangle on device
        { return Rectangle(hdc,
            box.left(), box.top(), box.right(), box.bottom()); }
};
```

Now there's no way a programmer could accidentally attempt to draw a rectangle on an information context; the function to do it simply doesn't exist. In Windows, there's nothing to stop you from calling *Rectangle* for an information context, since both device contexts and information contexts are declared HDC in C. There's no way to distinguish an HDC that's really an information context from one that isn't; this is precisely what C++ provides with the notion of subclasses.

It doesn't take much imagination to leap from information contexts to a full-blown class hierarchy of device contexts:

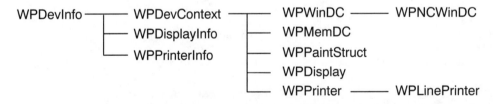

We'll explore some of these classes in more detail shortly. Right now, the important thing is to understand why *Windows++* models different kinds of device contexts as subclasses: to expose the differences among them and thereby make the implicit rules for programming GDI *explicit*. A general principle of good software design is: design the API in such a way that the programming rules are automatically enforced, rather than requiring programmers to learn and remember them.

C   *Sorry, C die-hards, but there's no easy way to do this in C. There's just no way to distinguish among different kinds of HDCs. If a function expects an argument of type HDC, you can only pass it an argument of that type. Only C++ has the notion of subclasses, where if HDCA is a subclass of HDC, you can use HDCA anywhere that HDC is expected.*

8.2.2 Creating and Destroying Device Contexts

Having identified several classes, we next have to worry about creating and destroying instances of them. There are many (and I mean many) ways to get hold of an HDC in Windows. Most HDCs come from one of the following API functions:

```
CreateIC      // Create information context
CreateDC      // Create device context
GetDC         // Get window DC
GetWindowDC   // Get window DC including non-client area
BeginPaint    // Get window DC and initialize window for painting
```

In addition to these, Windows sometimes hands you the HDC as a structure member. (This happens with the common printer dialog described in Section 7.5.4.)

Once you've gotten hold of a device context, you can draw on it (provided it's not really an information context) using GDI functions like *Rectangle* and *TextOut*. When you're done using the device context, you're supposed to "terminate" it by calling the proper function. If the device context was created with *CreateIC* or *CreateDC*, you call *DeleteDC*; if it was obtained using *GetDC* or *GetWindowDC*, you call *ReleaseDC*; if the device came from *BeginPaint*, you call *EndPaint*; if it came from the print dialog (in COMMDLG), it's *DeleteDC* again.

Aaaargh!! Who can remember all this stuff?!

Fortunately, C++ provides the perfect mechanism to hide all these annoying idiosyncrasies: we can encapsulate them in constructors and destructors. Once we do so, we can forget all about them. Let's start with the base class, *WPDevInfo*.

```
// (In WPGDI.H)
class WPDevInfo {
   HDC hdc;
public:
   WPDevInfo(CSTR devname, CSTR driver, CSTR output, CSTR init)
      { hdc = CreateDC((LPSTR)driver, (LPSTR)devname,
         (LPSTR)output, (LPSTR)init); assert(hdc); }
   virtual ~WPDevInfo();
      { if (hdc) { BOOL ret = DeleteDC(hdc); assert(ret); } }
};
```

The constructor just brainlessly passes its arguments to *CreateIC*, which creates the information context, and the destructor deletes it.

So much for *WPDevInfo*. *WPDevContext* is similar:

```
class WPDevContext : public WPDevInfo {
public:
   WPDevContext(CSTR devname, CSTR driver, CSTR output, CSTR init)
      { hdc = CreateIC((LPSTR)driver, (LPSTR)devname,
         (LPSTR)output, (LPSTR)init); assert(hdc); }
};
```

This time, the constructor calls *CreateDC* instead of *CreateIC*. There is no destructor, since the one for *WPDevInfo* is fine. Device contexts are destroyed using *DeleteDC*, just like information contexts.

Now lets bring a third subclass, *WPWinDC,* into the picture.

```
/////////////////////
// Class to represent window (client area) device context
//
class WPWinDC : public WPDevContext {    // DC for window
protected:
    WPWin *win;                          // the window
public:
    WPWinDC(WPWin *w);
    ~WPWinDC();
};
```

Now the constructor gets *hdc* from the GDI function *GetDC:*

```
WPWinDC::WPWinDC(WPWin *w)
{
    assert(w);
    win = w;                         // save for later use
    hdc = GetDC((*w)());             // (*w)() = w's HWND
    assert(hdc);
}
```

and the destructor releases it:

```
WPWinDC::~WPWinDC()
{
    BOOL ret = ReleaseDC((*win)());
    assert(ret);
    hdc = NULL;
}
```

This time, the destructor invokes *ReleaseDC* instead of *DeleteDC,* as per the certified Windows voodoo. The only trick is that it also sets *hdc* to NULL before returning, so the base class destructor *~WPDevInfo* won't attempt to delete it. (*~WPDevInfo* only calls *DeleteDC* if *hdc* is non-NULL.) Remember, when C++ invokes a destructor, all the base class destructors are invoked too.

The upshot (and purpose) of all this is that we can now write code like this (we'll deal with device names shortly):

```
WPDevInfo *ic = new WPDevInfo("MyDevname", "MyDriverName", NULL);
WPDevInfo *dc = new WPDevContext("MyDevname", "MyDriverName", NULL);
WPDevInfo *wc = new WPWinDC(myWin);
.
.

delete ic;
delete dc;
delete wc;
```

In all cases, the same operator (*delete*) is used to destroy the device context. In practice, it's often more convenient to create device contexts on the stack:

```
WPWinDC dc(args);    // get window dc
dc.rectangle(rect);  // draw on window
.
.
```

Then there's no need to invoke *delete*, since C++ automatically invokes the proper destructor when *dc* goes out of scope. Stack DCs are more convenient because most Windows programs get a DC, draw on it, then immediately release it, all within a single function. It's generally bad practice to leave an "open" device context hanging around, since device contexts are scarce resources (one exception to this is memory device contexts, described in Section 8.2.7).

The same basic technique is used with all the other device contexts. Here's a table that shows how some of the other device contexts are created and destroyed:

Class	Constructor calls:	Destructor calls:
WPDevInfo	CreateIC	DeleteDC
WPWinDC	GetDC	ReleaseDC
WPNCWinDC	GetWindowDC	ReleaseDC
WPMemDC	CreateCompatableDC	DeleteDC
WPPaintStruct	BeginPaint	EndPaint
WPDisplayInfo	CreateIC	DeleteDC
WPDisplay	CreateDC	DeleteDC

This is not a complete list, but most of the other kinds of device contexts are straightforward. I won't bother to explain all of them, since they're fairly obvious. For example, *WPNCWinDC* gets the entire window DC, including the non-client area, and *WPDisplayInfo* and *WPDisplay* are information and device contexts for the display. I've already explained *WPPaintStruct* in Section 3.5.6.

8.2.3 Device Names

One of the many little nuisances in Windows is dealing with device names. From the user's perspective, a device is identified by a name. For example, "HP LaserJet III" or "PostScript Printer." This name can be anything the user wants; it's specified in WIN.INI like so:

```
; Printer devices (fragment of WIN.INI)
[devices]
HP LaserJet III=HPPCL5A,LPT2:
PostScript Printer=PSCRIPT,None
    .
    .
```

The WIN.INI file makes the connection between the device name and its *driver* and *output file* name. In the example above, the driver name for "HP LaserJet III" is *HPPCL5A* and the output file is *LPT2;* these parameters are required by *CreateDC:*

```
HDC hdc = CreateDC("HPPCL5A", "HP LaserJet III", "LPT2", NULL);
```

The arguments would seem to be redundant. Since the driver and output file names can be derived from WIN.INI, why does *CreateDC* require them? Why not just write

```
HDC hdc = CreateDC("HP LaserJet III");
```

Alas, the question is moot, since that's just the way Windows does it, and every application that messes with printers contains code to parse the names from WIN.INI before calling *CreateDC*. This is just the sort of boring detail that's grist for the reusability mill.

To make parsing device names a snap, we can introduce a new structure:

```
//////////////////
// Structure used to parse the driver and output names
// from WIN.INI, given a device name.  Makes it easier to create
// device contexts for printers and other devices.
//
struct WPDEVNAME {
    char namebuf[50];           // name buffer
    char* driverName;           // parsed driver name
    char* outputName;           // output file (e.g., LPT1:)
    WPDEVNAME(CSTR devname=NULL);
};
```

Since WPDEVNAME is so simple, it hardly seems worth the trouble of making it a class just to hide its data members, so I made it an ordinary *struct*. The only function is the constructor:

```
// Parse device name.  If devname is NULL, get printer info.
WPDEVNAME::WPDEVNAME(CSTR devname)
{
    char buf[50];
    if (devname==NULL) {
        // Use default device as defined in WIN.INI (the printer).
        WinIni.get("windows", "device", buf, sizeof(buf));
        devname = strtok(buf,",");
    }
    WinIni.get("devices", devname, namebuf, sizeof(namebuf));
    driverName = strtok(namebuf,",");
    outputName = strtok(NULL,",");
}
```

It simply parses the driver and output names from WIN.INI (using the global *WinIni* object from Chapter 5). The purpose of WPDEVNAME is to let us write

```
WPDEVNAME dv = "HP LaserJet II";
```

after which *dv.driverName* is *"HPPCL5A"* and *dv.outputName* is *"LPT2"*. With WPDEVNAME defined, we can now add constructors for *WPDevInfo* and *WPDevContext*:

```
// (In WPGDI.H)
class WPDevInfo {
public:
```

```
    WPDevInfo(char* devname)        // <<<<< new constructor
        {   WPDEVNAME dv = devname;
            hdc = CreateIC(dv.driverName,devname,dv.outputName,NULL); }
};
class WPDevContext : public WPDevInfo {
public:
    WPDevContext(char* devname)     // <<<<< new constructor
        {   WPDEVNAME dv = devname;
            hdc = CreateDC(dv.driverName,devname,dv.outputName,NULL); }
};
```

These constructors let application programs create information and device contexts directly from the device name, without translating them through WIN.INI.

```
WPDevInfo ic =   "HP LaserJet III";     // Get printer info
WPDevContext dc = "HP LaserJet III";    // Get real DC
```

8.2.4 Brainless GDI functions

While the root of the device context class hierarchy is *WPDevInfo*, most of the action is in *WPDevContext*, since this is the base class for device contexts that you can actually draw on (as opposed to mere *information* contexts). Most of the functions defined for *WPDevContext* are of the "brainless" variety: inline functions that simply call their Windows counterparts after packaging the arguments suitably. Here are the highlights (as always, the full source is in Appendix A):

■ Wherever possible and/or useful, *WPPoint* and *WPRect* are used as arguments instead of *x, y, w, h*, etc. For example

```
BOOL rectangle(WPRect &box)
    { return Rectangle(hdc,
        box.left(), box.top(), box.right(), box.bottom()); }
BOOL arc(WPRect& box, WPPoint beg, WPPoint end)
    { return Arc(hdc, box.left(), box.top(), box.right(),
        box.bottom(), beg.x, beg.y, end.x, end.y); }
```

This not only reduces typing, it gives the system a more "geometric" feel.

■ *WPDevContext* supplies overloaded coordinate-conversion functions:

```
// Functions to convert between logical and device coordinates
BOOL DP2LP(WPPoint *pts, int nPoints)
    { return DPtoLP(hdc, (LPPOINT)pts, nPoints); }
BOOL LP2DP(WPPoint *pts, int nPoints)
    { return LPtoDP(hdc, (LPPOINT)pts, nPoints); }
BOOL DP2LP(WPPoint& p)          { return DP2LP(&p,1); }
BOOL LP2DP(WPPoint& p)          { return LP2DP(&p,1); }
BOOL DP2LP(WPRect& r)           { return DP2LP((WPPoint*)&r,2); }
BOOL LP2DP(WPRect& r)           { return LP2DP((WPPoint*)&r,2); }
```

For example, to convert a rectangle from device to logical coordinates:

```
WPRect rect = win;              // get window client rectangle
dc.DP2LP(rect);                 // convert to logical coords
```

- *WPDevContext* provides functions to quickly fill a rectangle white or black:

```
void whiteOut(WPRect rect)        { patBlt(rect, WHITENESS); }
void blackOut(WPRect rect)        { patBlt(rect, BLACKNESS); }
```

  These use *PatBlt*, which is slightly more efficient than selecting a white or black brush and then calling *FillRect*.

- *Windows++* also makes it easier to deal with tabbed text. Windows supports tabbed text using a function called *TabbedTextOut*, which draws a text string with tabs expanded as specified in an array of integers that you pass as an argument.[57] Unfortunately, you have to specify the tabs every time you call it. Instead, *Windows++* lets you set the tabs once, for the device context, whereupon all subsequent text operations are implicitly tabbed. To draw a string of tabbed text on a device context *dc,* you'd write

```
const int TABS = {40,80,120};
const NTABS = 3;

dc.setTabs(TABS, NTABS);
dc.textOut(0, 0, "one\ttwo\tthree\tfour");
dc.textOut(0, 9, "five\tsize\tseve\teight");
```

  The tabs still have to be set every time you load the device context, since there's no way to save them in Windows. The implementation of *setTabs* and *textOut* is straightforward—they're in Appendix A.

- On the subject of text, *WPDevContext* provides a function *printF* that is like *textOut*, but accepts arguments in *printf* format. For example

```
dc.printF(x, y, "Happy Birthday, %s", myName);
```

Of course, there are also several brain*ful* functions in *WPDevContext*, but I'll describe those in more detail.

8.2.5 Pens, Brushes, and All That Rot

GDI has a notion of *drawing tools* or *drawing objects*. These tools control how various shapes are drawn. For example, a *pen* is used to draw lines, while a *brush* us used to fill the interior of two-dimensional shapes such as rectangles and ellipses. GDI supports six kinds of drawing objects: pens, brushes, fonts, bitmaps, regions, and palettes. Each is represented in C as a HANDLE, but in C++ it's more natural to model them as subclasses of a generic "drawing tool" class:

---

57 The internal Windows name for this function is *TabTheTextOutForWimps* (see [Schulman 1992]). Sadly, this reveals the attitude that Windows developers have toward their users: anyone wanting higher-level functionality is a wimp and probably eats quiche and wears purple shirts. *Real* programmers write system software. This attitude would not be so annoying if the system software they wrote were good.

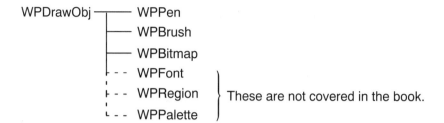

In the interests of keeping the chapter short, I'll only discuss pens, brushes, and bitmaps; the same techniques could be applied to handle fonts, regions, and palettes. Pens and brushes are discussed in this section; bitmaps are covered along with memory device contexts in Section 8.2.7.

Drawing objects are created using any one of a number of Windows API functions:

```
CreatePen            // create pen w/given color, width and style
CreatePenIndirect    // create pen from LOGPEN structure
CreateBrushIndirect  // create brush from LOGBRUSH structure
CreateHatchBrush     // create brush w/given hatch pattern
CreatePatternBrush   // create brush w/given bitmap pattern
CreateSolidBrush     // create solid brush w/given color
 .
 . etc.
```

Windows also provides "stock" objects, commonly used pens, brushes, and other drawing tools that are identified by integer IDs defined in WINDOWS.H. To use them, you call *GetStockObject:*

```
HANDLE hpen = GetStockObject(BLACK_PEN);      // solid black pen
HANDLE hbrush = GetStockObject(WHITE_BRUSH);  // solid white brush
```

Once created, drawing objects can be *selected* into a device context by invoking *SelectObject* (*SelectPalette* for palettes). Only one object of a given type (pen, brush, etc.) can be selected for a given device context. Once selected, the drawing tool becomes the default tool of its type for future drawing operations. For example, if you select a dashed pen, then all lines are drawn using dashes until you select another pen. Drawing objects are destroyed by invoking *DeleteObject*.

Windows imposes a number of not-so-obvious rules governing the use of drawing tools:

- Stock objects must not be destroyed.

- A drawing object must be de-selected before it's destroyed.

- Generally, programs should restore the original selection before releasing a device context; to facilitate this, *SelectObject* returns the handle of the previously selected object:

```
HANDLE hOldPen = SelectObject(hdc, hNewPen);
    .
    .
    .
SelectObject(hdc, hOldPen);
ReleaseDC(hdc);
```

■ Drawing objects are allocated from GDI's local heap, so you should create them judiciously. Windows does not automatically destroy GDI objects when an application terminates, so programs must be careful about cleaning up after themselves, since it's possible to permanently steal memory from Windows.

■ A bitmap can only be selected for a *memory* device context.

■ A bitmap cannot be selected in more than one device context at a time.

Our goal will be to encapsulate as many of these rules as possible in *Windows++* objects, so they're automatically enforced, just by using the objects. While the rules are not exactly rocket science, they are a potential source of bugs (since they're easy to forget). Furthermore, they make for cumbersome coding. Just look at what's required to draw a red rectangle:

```
HDC hdc = GetDC(hwnd);
HBRUSH hRedBrush = CreateSolidBrush(COLOR_RED);
HBRUSH hOldBrush = SelectObject(hdc, hRedBrush);
Rectangle(hdc, x, y, w, h);
SelectObject(hdc, hOldBrush);
DeleteObject(hRedBrush);
ReleaseDC(hdc);
```

Once we've experienced the joy of getting the GDI calls just right, we should encapsulate them, so we only have to write the code once. The usual calling sequence is too tedious; what we'd like to write instead is

```
WPWinDC dc = this;
dc.setBrush(COLOR_RED);
dc.rectangle(myRect);
```

The *setBrush* function should automatically and invisibly invoke the proper Windows voodoo to create a red brush on the fly and select it; and the destructor for *WPDevContext* should delete the red brush and restore the original one.

Let's do it.

The first thing we have to do is implement the base class for drawing tools:

```
//////////////////
// Base class for all drawing objects (pen, brush, etc.)
//
class WPDrawObj {
protected:
    HANDLE hobj;                    // Windows handle
    BOOL del;                       // whether to delete
```

```
    void set(int h, BOOL d)              { hobj=h; del =d; }
    void destroy();
    WPDrawObj(int h, BOOL d)             { set(h, d); }
    ~WPDrawObj()                         { destroy(); }
    friend WPDevContext;
public:
    HANDLE operator()()                  { return hobj; }
};
```

The reason for implementing separately callable *set* and *destroy* functions, rather than putting the code directly in the constructor and destructor, will be explained shortly. *WPDrawObj* stores two data members: the Windows handle to the drawing object and a boolean flag that indicates whether this handle should be deleted. These are initialized by the constructor and can also be *set*. The constructor is protected, since we'll never create an instance of *WPDrawObj* directly, but only instances of specific kinds of subclasses. *(WPDevContext is conceptually an abstract class, even though it has no pure virtual functions.)*

The destructor calls a protected *destroy* function to delete the drawing tool:

```
void WPDrawObj::destroy()
{
    if (hobj && del) {                   // only delete if flag says so
        BOOL res=DeleteObject(hobj);
        assert(res);
    }
    hobj=NULL;
}
```

While each subclass of *WPDrawObj* will have its own constructors, we'll use the same destructor for all. There are many ways to create a drawing tool, but only one way to destroy it.

Speaking of subclasses, here's our *pen* class:

```
class WPPen : public WPDrawObj {
public:
    // Constructors
    WPPen(int id) : WPDrawObj(GetStockObject(id), FALSE) { }
    WPPen(LPLOGPEN data) : WPDrawObj(CreatePenIndirect(data), TRUE) { }
    WPPen(COLORREF color, int style=PS_SOLID, int wid=1 )
        : WPDrawObj(CreatePen(style, wid, color), TRUE) { }
};
```

That's all. *WPPen* provides constructors corresponding to the various Windows *Create* functions for pens. The constructors initialize the delete flag appropriately. For stock objects, the flag is FALSE; otherwise, it's TRUE. All this magic with the delete flag is, of course, invisible to application programmers; to create a colored pen, all they have to do is write

```
WPPen *pen = new WPPen(myColor, PS_DASHDOTDOT, myWidth);
.
.
delete pen;
```

To create a stock pen, it's

```
WPPen *pen = new WPPen(BLACK_PEN);
.
.
delete pen;
```

In either case, *delete* does the right thing. *DeleteObject* is invoked if and only if the object is not a stock object. In most cases, we'll create pens on the stack, so *delete* is unnecessary (it's implicitly invoked when the stack variable goes out of scope):

```
WPPen pen = BLACK_PEN;
.
.
```

Brushes are similar. Where Windows has five different functions, we have five overloaded constructors with different arguments:

```
class WPBrush : public WPDrawObj {
public:
    // Constructors
    WPBrush(int id) : WPDrawObj(GetStockObject(id), FALSE) { }
    WPBrush(COLORREF color)
        : WPDrawObj(CreateSolidBrush(color), TRUE) { }
    WPBrush(COLORREF c, int h)
        : WPDrawObj(CreateHatchBrush(h, c), TRUE) { }
    WPBrush(LPLOGBRUSH data)
        : WPDrawObj(CreateBrushIndirect(data), TRUE) { }
    WPBrush(GLOBALHANDLE dib, WORD usage)
        : WPDrawObj(CreateDIBPatternBrush(dib, usage), TRUE) { }
};
```

(Since there's nothing to initialize, all the constructors are empty.) As an added bonus, simply by using C++ objects (instead of HANDLEs) to represent pens and brushes, we automatically bring them under the watchful aegis of our memory-management system. If an application fails to delete a pen or brush, *Windows++* will spot and report the error using the mechanisms described in Chapter 4.

By breaking *SelectObject* into separate functions, we're doing the same sort of thing we did in Section 7.3.2, when we implemented single- and multi-line edit controls as separate classes. Once again, sometimes we hide diversity in Windows; other times we expose it. Generally, if the diversity is idiosyncratic (e.g., all the rules for creating and deleting pens and brushes) we hide it; but if the diversity is fundamental, we expose it.

So much for creating pens and brushes. Now we have to worry about selecting them. Let me remind you where we are in this story: We're trying to implement the library in such a way that we can write

```
WPWinDC dc = this;
dc.setBrush(COLOR_RED);
dc.rectangle(myRect);
```

The first thing we can observe from this wishful code fragment is that, whereas Windows uses a single *SelectObject* function to select any kind of drawing tool, we need separate functions *setBrush, setPen,* and so on. This makes more sense for a couple of reasons. First, *SelectObject* isn't really universal, since it doesn't work for palettes (there's a separate *SelectPalette* function); and second, you can't select a bitmap into any old device context, only into a memory device context. To expose this rule, we'll implement *setBitmap* for *WPMemDC,* not *WPDevContext* (see Section 8.2.7).

To implement *setBrush,* all we have to do is create the brush and select it. Of course, we must keep track of a few things. First of all, we must to save the handle of the originally selected brush, so we can restore it later (in the destructor for *WPDevContext*). We also may need to destroy the old brush. For example, if someone writes

```
WPWinDC dc = this;
dc.setBrush(COLOR_RED);        // creates red brush on the fly
dc.setBrush(COLOR_BLUE);       // creates blue brush on the fly
```

we want to destroy the red brush after creating and selecting the blue one; otherwise, the brush will never be destroyed. We will not push this problem onto the programmer (as Windows does).

To keep track of the drawing tools we'll introduce two arrays as data members in *WPDevContext:* an array of *WPDrawObj* objects to hold the currently selected drawing tools, and an array of HANDLEs to hold the originally selected drawing tools. Each array has six entries, one for each kind of drawing tool. An *enum* variable is used to index them:

```
///////////////////
// Each type of drawing object has an ID, used as table offset
// Used internally by Windows++ ONLY.
//
enum WHICHOBJ { DPEN=0,DBRUSH,DBITMAP,DFONT,DRGN,DPALETTE,NDRAWOBJ };
class WPDevContext : public WPDevInfo {
   WPDrawObj drawObj[NDRAWOBJ];   // current selected drawing objects
   HANDLE originalObj[NDRAWOBJ];  // original drawing objects
protected:
   BOOL anySelected;             // whether any new tool was selected

   void restoreSelection();      // restore original selection

   HANDLE select(WHICHOBJ which, int h, BOOL d);
   HANDLE select(WHICHOBJ which, WPDrawObj *obj)
      { return select(which, obj->hobj, FALSE); }
};
```

To initialize the *drawObj* array, we need another constructor:

```
class WPDrawObj {
public:
   WPDrawObj()   { hobj=NULL; del=FALSE; }
};
```

The drawing objects all start out with NULL handles and are set when a new drawing object is selected:

```
const MAXSTOCKOBJ = 32;

////////////////////
// Internal method to select a display object. Destroys old selected
// object if required. "which" specifies whether object is a pen,
// brush, etc. "del" specifies whether to delete the object.
// If handle is small integer, assume it's a stock object.
//
HANDLE WPDevContext::select(WHICHOBJ which, int h, BOOL del)
{
    if ((HANDLE)h < MAXSTOCKOBJ) {
        h = GetStockObject(h);
        del = FALSE;                        // never delete stock object!
    }
    assert(h);
    HANDLE old = SelectObject(hdc, (HANDLE)h);
    assert(old);
    WPDrawObj& obj = drawObj[which];
    assert(obj.hobj==NULL || obj.hobj==old);
    obj.destroy();                          // delete old drawing tool
    obj.set((HANDLE)h, del);                // select new one
    if (originalObj[which]==NULL)
        originalObj[which]=old;
    anySelected=TRUE;
    return old;
}
```

This function performs the following magic:

- If the "handle" is really a stock object, the stock object is loaded to retrieve its handle, and the delete flag is set to FALSE so the object won't be deleted.

- The new drawing tool is selected.

- The currently selected *which* tool is set to the new handle. Now you see why *WPDrawObj::set* is a separate function.

- The old drawing object is destroyed. Of course, if the old object has its delete flag set to FALSE, it's not really destroyed. This is why *WPDrawObj::destroy* is a separate function.[58]

- If this is the first time a tool of *which* type has been selected, the old tool's handle is saved in the *originalObj* array.

Next, we modify the destructor like so:

---

58 It's possible to invoke destructors explicitly, like any other function, but for some reason I don't like this. One reason is that the syntax differs among compilers. With some you need the fully scoped name; with others you don't.

```
WPDevContext::~WPDevContext()
{
    if (hdc && anySelected)
        restoreSelection();          // described below
}
```

When the device context is destroyed, all the original handles are restored by invoking the function *restoreSelection*, provided *anySelected* is TRUE. That is, provided at least one new object has been selected since the device context was created. The *anySelected* flag is a performance improvement—there's no need to call *restoreSelection* if the drawing tools haven't been changed.

We must take care here that we also invoke *restoreSelection* from other destructors. For example, in ~*WPWinDC*

```
WPWinDC::~WPWinDC()
{
    if (anySelected)
        restoreSelection();
    BOOL ret = ReleaseDC((*win)(), hdc);
    assert(ret);
    hdc=NULL;
}
```

This is required because ~*WPWinDC* invokes *ReleaseDC* before the base class destructor (~*WPDevContext*) receives control. Naturally, we have to restore the selection before releasing the device context. The same goes for *WPPaintStruct*, and any other device context that has a specialized deletion function.

As for *restoreSelection*, it looks like this:

```
void WPDevContext::restoreSelection()
{
    assert(hdc);
    if (anySelected) {
        for (int i=0; i < NDRAWOBJ; i++) {
            if (originalObj[i]) {
                SelectObject(hdc, originalObj[i]);
                originalObj[i]=NULL;    // don't restore twice!
                drawObj[i].destroy();
            }
        }
    }
}
```

It just restores each handle in *originalObj*. Now (finally) we can implement our long-awaited *setBrush* and *setPen* functions:

```
class WPDevContext : public WPDevInfo {
public:
    // Pen
    HANDLE setPen(WPPen *pen)            { return select(DPEN, pen); }
    HANDLE setPen(int h)                 { return select(DPEN, h, FALSE); }
    HANDLE setPen(COLORREF color, int style=PS_SOLID, int wid=1)
        { return select(DPEN, CreatePen(style, wid, color), TRUE); }
```

```
    // Brush
    HANDLE setBrush(WPBrush* brush)    { return select(DBRUSH, brush); }
    HANDLE setBrush(int h)             { return select(DBRUSH,h,FALSE); }
    HANDLE setBrush(COLORREF color)
        { return select(DBRUSH, CreateSolidBrush(color), TRUE); }
};
```

Each function simply selects the appropriate drawing tool, creating it on the fly if necessary. To see how all this wonderful code actually works, let's take a look at what happens when we write

```
WPWinDC dc = this;
dc.setBrush(COLOR_RED);
dc.rectangle(myRect);
```

Several things happen:

- A window device context is created on the stack (from *GetDC*).

- Next, *setBrush* invisibly creates a new solid brush, then selects it. The original brush handle is saved in *originalObj*, and the current one in *drawObj*.

- The application draws a rectangle. (GDI uses the brush we selected.)

- When the variable *dc* goes out of scope, ~*WPWinDC* is invoked; the destructor in turn calls *restoreSelection*, which restores the original brush.

- As part of the normal destruction sequence, C++ also invokes the destructors for each element of the array *drawObj*, which takes care of destroying the red brush that we created on the fly.

If all this seems somewhat convoluted and mysterious, it is. The only way to convince yourself that the code really works is to carefully trace what happens in several different cases; I'll leave it up to you to perform this exercise on your own. The main point is that you only have to do it once. Once you've figured out all the proper Windows voodoo, you can simply encapsulate it, as I've done, in the appropriate C++ classes, then forget about it forever.

That's more or less the end of the story as far as drawing objects are concerned. We haven't encapsulated all the GDI rules; for example, there's nothing to prevent an application programmer from writing

```
WPPen *pen = new WPPen(COLOR_RED);    // create new pen
dc.setPen(pen);                       // select it
delete pen;                           // !$#&% delete while selected!
```

If we wanted to catch this error, we'd have to store and maintain a list of device contexts in which each drawing tool is selected. It's just not worth the trouble. Encapsulating creation/selection/deletion is worth it because it not only enforces GDI rules, it also makes programming easier.

8.2.6 RANDRECT

We've written a lot of code without actually using it (which is dangerous), so it's about time we wrote a simple program, if only to see how our code works. To this end, I've implemented the RANDRECT program from [Petzold 1990] in *Windows++*, partly to show how much smaller it is (34 lines *vs.* 100), but mainly because it's simple. This program draws random rectangles until you terminate it. Petzold uses this program to illustrate the use of *PeekMessage* to do idle processing; it serves the same purpose in *Windows++*, but all we have to do is provide a *doIdle* function (see Section 3.5.5).

Here's RANDRECT:

```
//////////////////////////////////////////////////////////
// WINDOWS++ CLASS LIBRARY.  Copyright 1992 Paul DiLascia.
// FILE: RANDRECT.CPP
//
// RANDRECT adapted for Windows++ from orignal program by
// Charles Petzold in "Porgramming Windows" Chapter 12.
#include <wpp.h>
class RandRect : public WPMainWin {
public:
    RandRect()        { createWin("Windows++ Random Rectangles"); }
    BOOL doIdle();    // virtual function called during idle loop
};
void WPApp::main()
{
    mainWin = new RandRect;        // create main window
    run();                         // and run message loop
}
BOOL RandRect::doIdle()
{
    WPRect win = this;
    WPRect box(  rand() % win.width(), rand() % win.height(),
                 rand() % win.width(), rand() % win.height());
    box.normalize();

    WPWinDC dc = this;
    dc.settBrush(RGB(rand()&255, rand()&255, rand()&255));
    dc.rectangle(box);

    return TRUE;
}
```

The main window class is *RandRect*. The only non-trivial function it provides is *doIdle*, which simply draws a random-sized rectangle filled with a random brush every time it's invoked. The following lines are of special interest:

```
WPWinDC dc = this;
dc.setBrush(RGB(rand()&255, rand()&255, rand()&255));
dc.rectangle(box);
```

The brush is never explicitly created, de-selected, nor destroyed, nor is the device context explicitly released. The classes we've built do all the Windows voodoo automatically and invisibly. By hiding the details in C++ objects, we not only make application programming easier, we make it more foolproof. By encapsulating the magic create/select/destroy calling sequences, we guarantee that they're performed correctly every time.

Just to remind you how much we've simplified things, here's what the equivalent of *doIdle* looks like in C (from [Petzold 1990] p. 603):

```
void DrawRectangle(HWND hwnd)
    {
    HBRUSH   hBrush  ;
    HDC      hdc ;
    short    xLeft, xRight, yTop, yBottom, nRed, nGreen, nBlue ;

    xLeft   = rand () % cxClient ;
    xRight  = rand () % cxClient ;
    yTop    = rand () % cyClient ;
    yBottom = rand () % cyClient ;
    nRed    = rand () % 255 ;
    nBlue   = rand () % 255 ;
    nGreen  = rand () % 255 ;

    hdc = GetDC(hwnd) ;
    hBrush = CreateSolidBrush (RGB (nRed, nGreen, nBlue)) ;
    SelectObject(hdc, hBrush);

    Rectangle (hdc,  min (xLeft, xRight), min (yTop, yBottom),
                     max (xLeft, xRight), max (yTop, yBottom)) ;

    ReleaseDC (hwnd, hdc) ;
    DeleteObject(hBrush) ;
    }
```

The code savings comes not only from *WPDevContext* and *setBrush*, but also from all the other infrastructure we've built. In particular, drawing and manipulating rectangles is much easier using *WPRect*.

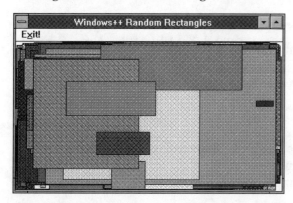

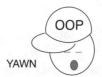

8.2.7 Bitmaps, Memory Device Contexts, and MANDEL

This is my hand-waving section (I figure I'm allowed at least one per chapter). The highlight is a program called MANDEL that displays the Mandelbrot set. A full explanation of MANDEL would consume too many pages, so I'll simply tell you how it works and highlight some of the implementation details. The main purpose of MANDEL is to illustrate the use of bitmaps and memory device contexts in *Windows++*.

If you've gotten the hang of pens and brushes, bitmaps are easy. In Windows terminology, a bitmap is just another kind of drawing tool.

```
class WPBitmap : public WPDrawObj {
public:
    WPBitmap(CSTR name) : WPDrawObj(App.loadBitmap(name), TRUE) { }
    WPBitmap(int id) : WPDrawObj(App.loadBitmap(id), TRUE) { }
    WPBitmap(WPDevContext* dc, int w, int h);

    // Brainless functions
    DWORD getBits(LPSTR buf,int len)
        { return GetBitmapBits(hobj,len,buf); }
    LONG  setBits(LPSTR buf,int len)
        { return SetBitmapBits(hobj,len,buf); }
    DWORD extent()
        { return GetBitmapDimension(hobj); }
    DWORD extent(int w, int h)
        { return SetBitmapDimension(hobj,w,h); }
};
```

WPBitmap provides "brainless" functions to get and set the actual bits and bitmap dimensions, as well as constructors to create a bitmap from a resource file name or ID, or from another device context:

```
WPBitmap::WPBitmap(WPDevContext* dc, int w, int h)
{
    assert(dc);
    hobj = CreateCompatibleBitmap((*dc)(), w, h);
    assert(hobj);
    del = TRUE;
}
```

One difference between bitmaps and other drawing tools is that a bitmap can only be selected for a memory device context, which in *Windows++* is represented by the subclass *WPMemDC*:

```
class WPMemDC : public WPDevContext {
public:
    WPMemDC(WPDevContext* dc, WPBitmap *bm);
    WPMemDC(WPDevContext* dc, WPRect &winRect, BOOL mono=FALSE);

    // setBitmap implemented for WPMemDC, not WPDevContext
    HANDLE setBitmap(WPBitmap *bm) { return select(DBITMAP, bm); }
};
```

Memory device contexts are always created from some real (non-memory) device context. For example, you can create a memory device context to represent the display or printer. There are two *WPMemDC* constructors. One initializes the DC from a bitmap:

```
WPMemDC::WPMemDC(WPDevContext *dc, WPBitmap *bm)
{
    hdc = CreateCompatibleDC(GetHDC(dc));
    assert(hdc);
    if (bm)
        setBitmap(bm);
    if (dc)
        mapMode(dc->mapMode());
}
```

The other creates a blank bitmap as a specified "window" on the original device context:

```
//////////////////
// Create memory DC compatible w/existing DC.
// Rectangle says which window in primary DC to map;
// "mono" flags creates monochrome bitmap.
//
WPMemDC::WPMemDC(WPDevContext *dc, WPRect& winRect, BOOL mono)
{
    hdc = CreateCompatibleDC(GetHDC(dc));
    assert(hdc);

    // Get bitmap dimensions: convert window rect to device coords.
    WPPoint p = winRect.extent();
    if (dc) {
        dc->LP2DP(&p, 1);
        mapMode(dc->mapMode());
    }
    HBITMAP h =
        CreateCompatibleBitmap((dc && !mono) ? (*dc)() : hdc, p.x, p.y);
    assert(h);
    select(DBITMAP, h, TRUE);
    windowOrg(winRect.origin()); // set window origin
}
```

The constructors primarily just call the corresponding Windows *Create* function. However, they also do some of the obvious things that Windows should do but doesn't. For example, the mapping mode is copied from the original device context, and the window origin is set properly.[59] Rather than take you through all the tedious details of bitmaps and memory device contexts (most of which you can figure out on your own), let's see how they're used in MANDEL.

The MANDEL program lets users explore the Mandelbrot set. This set, named after the mathematician Benoit Mandelbrot, exhibits fractal geometry. The Mandelbrot set is closely tied to computer science, since it's only with the aid of a computer that people can see what it looks like. For this reason, Mandelbrot programs (as they are called) are something of a cult among computer enthusiasts, and many

---

59 If these terms are unfamiliar to you, consult a Windows book. Briefly, the *window origin* speci-fies the logical origin of the device context; the *mapping mode* specifies on of several predefined logical coordinate sizes. For example, in MM_LOMETRIC, one unit = .1 millimeter.

readers are no doubt already familiar with them. For those that aren't, I'll provide a quick review. For a full treatment, see [R. Stevens 1989] or [Mandelbrot 1982].

To describe the Mandelbrot set, you need to understand the mathematical notion of *complex numbers*. Complex numbers are numbers of the form $z = x + iy$, where x and y are real numbers and i is the imaginary square root of -1. We say, "x is the real part of z, and y is the imaginary part." Complex numbers are manipulated using the normal rules of algebra, with the added rule that $i^2 = -1$. For example

$$(a + ib) * (c + id) = ac + iad + ibc + i^2bd = (ac - bd) + i(bc + ad)$$

These definitions are purely formal (algebraic); where geometry and graphics come is that complex numbers can be represented as points in a two-dimensional plane by representing the complex number $x + iy$ as the point (x, y):

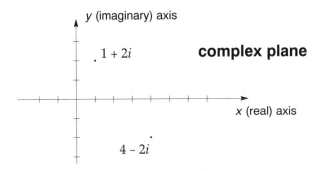

The Mandelbrot set is a region in the complex plane defined in the following roundabout way: Consider the sequence of complex numbers $\{z_n\}$ defined by the equations

$$z_{n+1} = z_n^2 + c;$$
$$z_0 = 0.$$

That is, pick a complex number c, then, starting with the number zero, square each number and add c to get the next number. For example, if $c = 0$

$$z_0 = z_1 = \ldots = z_n = 0 \text{ for all } n.$$

Likewise, if $c = 1$, all the z's are also 1, and if c is any real number less than one, the z's converge to zero as n increases. For an arbitrary c, it's not obvious what happens to the sequence $\{z_n\}$, but it will either converge to some value or it won't

Now, the Mandelbrot set is defined like this: for each point c in the complex plane, c is *in* the Mandelbrot set if the sequence $\{z_n\}$ converges for c; otherwise, it's *out*. This is a fairly complex (no pun intended) definition, but then the Mandelbrot set is a complex set. Here's what it looks like:

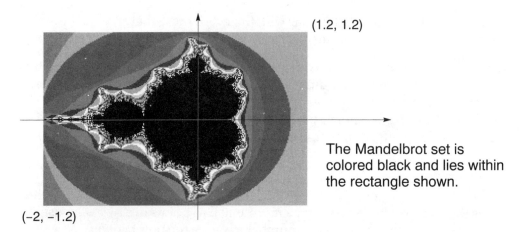

(1.2, 1.2)

(−2, −1.2)

The Mandelbrot set is colored black and lies within the rectangle shown.

The Mandelbrot set has many interesting properties, but its most essential feature is that its boundary is "infinitely ragged": no matter how closely you examine (magnify) the boundary, it's never smooth. Mathematicians had historically avoided such "weird" sets until the advent of computers, which made it possible to explore them. While such a task would quickly bore even the most persistent human, computers are perfectly happy to multiply complex numbers all day long, and they do it a lot faster and more reliably than you or I.

Most Mandelbrot programs color the points that converge (i.e., that are in the Mandelbrot set) black, while the points outside are colored differently, depending on how "fast" they diverge. Points that diverge slowly are colored red (say), while ones that diverge a little faster are colored purple, and so on. "Slow" and "fast" can be given precise mathematical meaning in terms of how long (how many iterations) it takes for $|z_n|$ to exceed some specified value.

Our own MANDEL program works like this:

- When MANDEL starts up, it begins computing the Mandelbrot set in the rectangular region with corners at (−2, −1.2) and (1.2, 1.2).

- MANDEL uses however many colors are available on the display, up to a maximum of 64 colors. When the program starts (and every time File New is invoked), a random color is assigned to each iteration. For example, if 1 = red and 2 = blue, then points that diverge after one iteration will be painted red, while points that diverge after two iterations will appear blue.

- The user may suspend the program at any time by invoking a *Pause* command, whereupon this command changes to *Continue*, which can be invoked to resume operation.

- At any time, the user may drag the mouse to zoom in on any part of the Mandelbrot set. This is done by holding the left button down while moving the mouse over the desired region. When the mouse button is released, MAN-DEL computes the Mandelbrot set in the smaller rectangle, enlarged to fit in the whole window and thus show more detail.

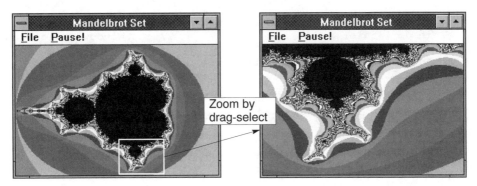

- The File New command clears the window, selects a new set of colors, and starts all over again.

The full MANDEL program is too long (about 400 lines) to explain in detail, so I'll just summarize the highlights.

The central algorithm for computing points goes something like this:

```
for (each complex number c in the region we are computing) {
    complex z = 0;
    for (int i = 0; i < MAXITERATIONS; i++) {
        z = z*z + c;
        if (abs(z) > DIVERGE)
            break;
    }
    if (n >= MAXITERATIONS)
        point c converged: color it black;
    else
        point c diverged after i iterations: use ith color;
}
```

Most Mandelbrot programs use this generic algorithm, but the exact details are always more complicated, primarily because various tricks are added to improve performance. In MANDEL, the algorithm is implemented in the function *compute-Pixel* (described a couple of pages later).

As for the Windows mechanics, MANDEL's basic strategy goes like this: it first creates a memory device context that mirrors its main window. The DC is saved in the class member *memdc:*

```
void Mandelbrot::init()
{
   clientBox = this;                             // get client rectangle
   .
   .
   // Create memory bitmap and initialize it to all white
   WPWin dc = this;                              // get Window device context
   delete memdc;                                 // delete memory dc, if any
   memdc = new WPMemDC(&dc,clientBox);           // create memory DC
   memdc->whiteOut(clientBox);                   // paint all white
}
```

MANDEL uses a memory device context to improve performance. Rather than display each pixel as it's computed, MANDEL computes several pixels at a time, in memory, then blasts them to the screen in one fell swoop. The memory bitmap is also used to paint the screen, like so:

```
/////////////////////
// Paint: just blast the bitmap to the screen.
//
void Mandelbrot::paint(WPPaintStruct& ps)
{
   WPRect dst = this;
   ps.stretchBlt(dst, *memdc, clientBox);
}
```

The *stretchBlt* function is equivalent to Windows' *StretchBlt*, which transfers a rectangle of bits from one device context to another, possibly stretching them.

The *doIdle* function computes the colors of individual pixels in this memory bitmap, then blasts them to the screen when it's done. In order to avoid locking the system for long periods of time, MANDEL divides the main window into a series of smaller rectangles and computes them one at time, from left to right, top to bottom. Each invocation of *doIdle* computes the pixels within one such rectangle, then blasts them to the screen and yields control so other applications can get a crack at the message queue. When a "little" rectangle is computed, it's blasted to the screen like so:

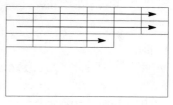

```
// Now blast the result to window
WPWinDC dc = this;
dc.windowOrg(clientBox.origin());
WPRect box = drawBox;                            // drawBox = "little" rectangle
dc.bitBlt(box, *memdc, box.origin());           // copy memory to window
```

bitBlt is another brainless function, equivalent to *BitBlt*. It's like *stretchBlt,* but assumes that no stretching is required; that is, that the source and destination rectangles have the same dimensions.

The function that actually computes pixels is *computePixel* (what else?):

```
//////////////////
// Compute color of pixel and set it in the bitmap. Returns color.
//
COLORREF Mandelbrot::computePixel(WPPoint p, complex &c)
{
    COLORREF color = memdc->pixel(p);
    if (color == COLOR_WHITE) {              // pixel not done yet:
        complex z;

        for (int n = 0; n<MAXITERATIONS; n++) {
            REAL zrr = z.real() * z.real();  // zrr = real part, squared
            REAL zii = z.imag() * z.imag();  // zii = imag part, squared
            REAL zir2 = 2 * z.real() * z.imag();
            if (zrr + zii >= DIVERGE)
                break;
            z.real(zrr-zii + c.real());
            z.imag(zir2 + c.imag());
        }
        color = n>=MAXITERATIONS ? COLOR_BLACK : colors[n % ncolors];
        memdc->pixel(p, color);

        if (clientBox.top() != 0) {
            p.y = -p.y;                       // use symmetry to set..
            memdc->pixel(p, color);           //..mirror image
        }
    }
    return color;
}
```

In determining whether the series diverges for a particular value of *c*, MANDEL uses the following algorithm. If the absolute value of z_n ever reaches 2 or more, the series diverges; if after MAXITERATIONS iterations, $|z_n|$ is still less than 2, the series is assumed to converge. Obviously, this isn't mathematically correct, but we can't keep calculating all day. You can experiment values of MAXITERATIONS. Smaller values make the program run faster, but with less accuracy; larger values have the opposite effect. In practice, 128 is a decent compromise for generating pretty displays.

You may have noticed the automatic variable

```
complex z;
```

Complex numbers are defined in the file COMPLEX.H, like so:

```
typedef float REAL;                  // could be float

class complex
{
private:
    REAL re;                         // real part
    REAL im;                         // imaginary part
public:
    complex()                        { re=0; im=0; }
    complex(REAL r, REAL i)          { set(r,i); }
```

```
void set(REAL r, REAL i)        { re=r; im=i; }
REAL& real()                    { return re; }
REAL& imag()                    { return im; }
void real(REAL r)               { re=r; }
void imag(REAL i)               { im=i; }
REAL abs2()                     { return re*re + im*im; }
friend complex operator+ (const complex &c1, const complex &c2)
    { return complex(c1.re + c2.re, c1.im + c2.im); }
friend complex operator- (const complex &c1, const complex &c2)
    { return  complex( c1.re - c2.re, c1.im - c2.im ); }
friend complex operator* (const complex &c1, const complex &c2)
    { return  complex( c1.re*c2.re - c1.im*c2.im,
        c1.re*c2.im + c1.im*c2.re ); }
friend int operator== (const complex &c1, const complex &c2)
    { return c1.re == c2.re && c1.im==c2.im; }
friend int operator!= (const complex &c1, const complex & c2)
    { return c1==c2 ? 0 : 1; }
};
```

This class is hardly required for MANDEL, which only does a few complex calculations, but I threw it in to show how powerful C++ is for such things. The *complex* class is tiny compared to what a real math package might supply; it provides
only a few functions and operators. Complex numbers are based on REAL numbers; if you want more precision, just change REAL from *float* to *double*.[60]

Here are a few additional items of interest:

- The colors are stored in an array that's initialized like so

```
// Allocate array of colors
WPWinDC dc = this;
ncolors = min(dc.getNUMCOLORS(), MAXNCOLORS);
colors = new COLORREF [ncolors];
for (int i=0; i<ncolors; i++)
    colors[i] = dc.nearestColor(RGB(5+rand()%250,
        5+rand()%250, 5+rand()%250));
```

Adding 5 to the random RGB values ensures that black is not used for points
outside the Mandelbrot set (black is reserved for the points inside it).

- MANDEL uses two mathematical tricks to speed things up. First, it makes
use of symmetry: if the point $a + ib$ is in the Mandelbrot set, then so is $a - ib$.
Second, it makes use of the fact that the colored conversion regions are connected: if all the points along the boundary of a rectangle have the same col-
or, then so do all the points inside the rectangle.

- Mandel displays an About dialog that contains a bitmap. The bitmap is implemented as an owner-draw button. You can figure out how this works
from examining the source code in Appendix A.

---

60 This could be handled more elegantly using C++ *templates*.

- The drag-zoom function is straightforward. MANDEL uses *drawFocusRect*, a brainless equivalent to the Windows function *DrawFocusRect*, to indicate the zoom region while dragging.

- The Pause/Continue commands are also totally straightforward.

I'll leave the rest up to Mandelbrot fans to explore on their own. MANDEL is not the fastest Mandelbrot program ever written, but it's not bad.[61] More important, *Windows++* makes it much easier to write.

Tip for MANDEL users: If you want to explore some region of the plane quickly, first resize your window so that it's small. The smaller the window, the faster MANDEL paints it. Then zoom (perhaps several times) to the region you want and when you're there, make the window big again and zoom one more time to see all the detail.

8.3 Object-Oriented Graphics

That's it for repackaging the GDI. Now let's have some real fun! In this section, we'll move beyond the basics of GDI to build an object-oriented graphics system. We'll implement the "missing layer" suggested at the outset (on page 320), in the form of a *Windows++* graphics library.

Application
GPP
GDI
Driver

Missing layer: Graphics Objects
("Graphics Plus Plus")

8.3.1 DRAW

We'll design our graphics system with a particular application in mind: a simple DRAW program. DRAW is not to be confused with the numerous paint programs written for Windows. Paint programs mirror the GDI, where *Rectangle, Ellipse,* and *Line(To)* are not objects, but bit-blasting operations. Paint programs work the same way. Once you paint a rectangle, it's gone. You can't move it, size it, or perform any other operation on it *qua* rectangle, since it only exists as a configuration of bits.

Drawing programs, on the other hand, let you manipulate shapes *as* shapes. You can move a rectangle from one location to another, size it, delete it, or change any

---

61 The best way to speed up MANDEL would be to use fixed-point math instead of *float*s.

of its properties, such as its fill pattern or line color. The easiest way to tell a paint program from a drawing program is to see if you can select a shape by clicking the mouse on it. Selected shapes are usually indicated by the appearance of *size handles* around the shape:

Ellipse   **Selected Ellipse**

Once selected, a shape can be sized by dragging one of the size handles. This is how we'll do it in DRAW. Here's a rough specification of the full program:

■ DRAW supports three shapes: lines, rectangles, and ellipses.

■ The position and extent of each shape are stored in logical units (as opposed to pixels). In particular, DRAW uses the Windows mapping mode MM_LO-METRIC, where each logical unit corresponds to .1 mm. (Other modes could easily be supported or even left as a user option.)

■ Each shape has two properties, an edge color and a fill color, both of which can be black, white, red, green, blue, random, or none. A shape that has a fill color is said to be *filled.*

■ The shapes are arranged from back to front, bottom to top. Each shape obscures the shapes behind it.

■ Clicking the mouse anywhere in the window selects the topmost shape under the mouse cursor, if any. To select a shape, the cursor must be "close" to the shape's edge, or, if the shape is filled, anywhere within its interior.

■ The selected shape is indicated by the appearance of size handles at the four corners of the rectangle defining the shape, except for lines, where the size handles appear only at the endpoints.

■ Shapes may be moved by dragging, that is, by moving the mouse while holding the left button down. This operation is called *drag move.* As long as the left button is down, the cursor appears as a crosshairs, and the shape moves with it (only its outline, not the filled interior). Throughout this operation, the original shape and size handles remain visible, until the mouse button is released, whereupon the shape disappears from its original position and is redrawn at the new location, still selected.

■ After a shape has been selected, it can be sized by dragging one of the size handles. This operation is called *drag size.* As with drag move, the shape follows the mouse, and the original shape remains visible until the mouse button is released; however, while *moving* can be initiated with the same click action that selects the shape, *sizing* cannot. The shape must already be selected to size it. (This feature reduces the likelihood of accidental sizing.)

drag size

■ DRAW supports two mouse "chords." If the *Shift* key is held down during drag-move or drag-size, the mouse motion is constrained to be either horizontal or vertical, as determined by the initial motion. If the *Control* key is held down during drag-size, the shape's aspect ratio is maintained as it's sized.

Shift

Control

■ DRAW has two menus: File and Edit. The File menu has New, Print, About and Exit commands, which do the expected things; Edit is described below.

Edit New creates a new line, rectangle, or ellipse. New rectangles are created

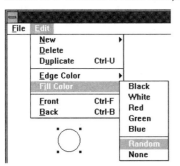

as squares, and new ellipses as circles. This provides a way of creating squares and circles. (Once created, they can of course be resized.)

Delete deletes the selected shape.

Duplicate creates a copy of the selected shape at its current position (without copying it to the clipboard).

Edge and Fill change the edge and fill color. The color is selected from a pop-up submenu. If Random is selected as the color, DRAW picks a random color for the edge or fill.

Finally, Front and Back move the selected shape to the front or back of the drawing.

That's a lot of functionality for a sample program. While DRAW is a mere toy compared to commercial drawing packages such as Adobe *Illustrator, Corel-DRAW!* and others, it nevertheless exhibits many of their basic properties.

We have our work cut out for us.

8.3.2 The GPP Library

We could, of course, just start building DRAW, but since graphics are useful in many applications, we'll do better to first build a graphics layer that provides general services for DRAW and other potential graphics applications. So that's what we'll do—we'll build a graphics library called GPP (Graphics Plus Plus?) on top of (that is, using) *Windows++*. Conceptually, GPP is separate from *Windows++*, but for practical reasons (to use the same memory management, *App* object and DLL magic described in the next chapter), it's part of the same library (WPP.LIB).

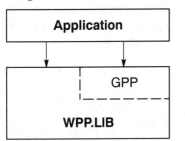

GPP is logically separate from *Windows++*, but part of the same physical library.

The graphics definitions are in a separate header file, GPP.H.

8.3.3 Shapes

So much for file names. What should GPP provide?

Essentially, anything that a graphics program might need. In particular, it needs to support the notion of *shapes* implicit in the description of DRAW. Thus GPP should provide a general shape class, with subclasses for lines, rectangles, and ellipses.[62] It should provide functions to do the obvious things like create and destroy shapes, paint them, move and size them, and so on.

Let's begin building GPP by defining an abstract shape class:

```
//////////////////
// Generic shape, an abstract class
//
class GPShape {
    COLORREF edge;                    // edge color
    COLORREF fill;                    // interior color
    WPRect extent;                    // extent (position, size) of shape
    void init();                      { edge=COLOR_BLACK; fill=COLOR_NONE; }
public:
    GPShape()                         { init(); }
    GPShape(WPRect& r)                { init(); setExtent(r); }
    virtual ~GPShape()                { }

    // Data access
    COLORREF edgeColor()              { return edge; }
    COLORREF edgeColor(COLORREF c){ return edge=c; }
    COLORREF fillColor()              { return fill; }
    COLORREF fillColor(COLORREF c){ return fill=c; }

    void getExtent(WPRect& e)         { e = extent; }
    void setExtent(WPRect& e)         { extent = e; }
};
```

---

62 I took the basic idea for the *Shapes* class from [Stroustrup 1991], but he didn't invent it. I don't know who did. The notion is so basic it's part of the general graphics programming wisdom.

Since all shapes have an extent and edge and fill colors, this information is stored in *GPShape*, which serves as the base class from which we will derive specific shapes, such as lines and rectangles:

```
class GPLine : public GPShape {
public:
    GPLine(WPRect& r) : GPShape(r){ }
};
class GPRect : public GPShape {
public:
    GPRect(WPRect &r) : GPShape(r){ }
};
class GPEllipse : public GPShape {
public:
    GPEllipse(WPRect &r) : GPShape(r) { }
};
```

The constructors for these shapes all invoke the same *GPShape* constructor to initialize the extent from a given rectangle.

So far, every shape seems the same. How do we express the differences among them? Why, in virtual functions of course. For every operation we need, we simply invent a virtual function. For example, we obviously need a function to draw shapes. Since each shape draws itself differently, this function must be virtual:

```
class GPShape {
public:
    virtual void draw(WPDevContext &dc);
    virtual void drawShape(WPDevContext &dc) = 0;
};
```

As you can see, there are actually two drawing functions. The first is *draw*, which invokes the second drawing function, *drawShape*, which is pure:

```
//////////////////////
// Draw shape. Calls shape-dependent drawing method.
//
void GPShape::draw(WPDevContext &dc)
{
    if (edgeColor()==COLOR_NONE)
        dc.setPen(NULL_PEN);
    else
        dc.setPen(edgeColor());

    if (fillColor()==COLOR_NONE)
        dc.setBrush(NULL_BRUSH);
    else
        dc.setBrush(fillColor());

    drawShape(dc);                    // <<<<< draw the shape
}
```

Since every shape needs to set the pen and brush, these operations are performed in *GPShape::draw*, so we don't have to repeat them in each *draw* function. All each shape has to do is actually draw itself:

```
class GPRect : public GPShape {
public:
    void drawShape(WPDevContext &dc)        { dc.rectangle(extent); }
};
class GPEllipse : public GPShape {
public:
    void drawShape(WPDevContext &dc)        { dc.ellipse(extent); }
};
class GPLine : public GPShape {
public:
    void drawShape(WPDevContext &dc)
        { dc.line(extent.origin(), extent.endpt()); }
};
```

Having a separate *drawShape* function has another benefit: it provides a way to draw a shape without setting the pen and brush. This will come in handy for dragging operations in DRAW, where we'll need to draw the shape in XOR mode (explained later) instead of using its normal pen:

```
dc.setPen(WHITE_PEN);                   // use white pen
dc.setBrush(NULL_BRUSH);                // ..and no brush
dc.rop2(R2_XORPEN);                     // use XOR raster operation
shp->drawShape(dc);                     // draw the shape
```

8.3.4 Bounds

Another property of a shape is its *bounds*, which can be defined as the smallest rectangle that completely contains the shape. This is slightly different from the shape's extent. For example, a horizontal line would 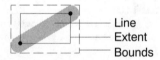 have an *extent* rectangle with zero height; however, the bounding rectangle is as high as the pen width. While a mathematical line has zero thickness, any line that's drawn has a finite thickness, which must be taken into account when computing the bounding rectangle.

To get the bounds of a shape, we need a new function:

```
const MINBOUNDS = 4;
void GPShape::getBounds(WPRect& r)
{
    r = extent;
    r.normalize();
    if (r.width()<MINBOUNDS || r.height() < MINBOUNDS)
        r += MINBOUNDS/2;                // a poor hack, but it works
}
```

To get the bounds, we simply increase the extent rectangle by a small amount, if necessary, in order to guarantee that the bounds are never empty. Graphics gurus might hold their noses in the vicinity of this casual implementation; a more accurate one would compute the bounds exactly, using the pen width and other factors. However, this implementation is good enough for our purposes, since GPP doesn't support different pen weights anyway. If it did, we'd have to modify *getBounds* appropriately.

Some of you may be wondering why bounds are important. Because they're used to paint shapes incrementally. Suppose for example, that a DRAW user deletes an ellipse. To reflect the change, we have to draw all the shapes that may have been obscured by the ellipse. We don't want to update the whole window (that would be inefficient overkill), just the area formerly containing the now defunct ellipse— that is, its bounding rectangle.

In fact, invalidating shapes is so common that it deserves its own function:

```
///////////////////
// Invalidate shape; i.e., invalidate its bounding rectangle.
//
void GPShape::invalidate(WPWin *win, BOOL erase)
{
    WPRect rect;
    getBounds(rect);              // get bounding rectangle
    WPWinDC dc = win;             // get device context
    dc.LP2DP(rect);               // convert logical to screen coords
    win->invalidate(rect, erase); // invalidate rectangle
}
```

Now, whenever a shape is deleted, all an application has to do to repaint it is

```
shape->invalidate(mywin);        // invalidate rect containing shape
mywin->update();                 // force repaint
```

Recall that *WPWin::update* invokes the Windows *UpdateWindow* function, which sends a WM_PAINT message to the window.

8.3.5 Clipping

When Windows sends a WM_PAINT message, only a portion of the window may need painting, not the whole client area. The PAINTSTRUCT contains a RECT that identifies the rectangle that needs painting. Programs can improve performance by only painting the contents of this rectangle. (If you paint the whole screen, Windows will do the "clipping" anyway; if you paint outside the update region, Windows suppresses the final bits from reaching the screen. This eliminates unnecessary bit-copying, but your program still incurs the performance penalty of invoking GDI.)

This is the perfect sort of tedious but useful thing for us to encapsulate in our graphics library. We only have to implement the clipping logic once, then reuse it in all our applications. A few minor modifications do the trick:

```
// (In GPP.H)
class GPShape {
protected:
    static WPRect ClipRect;          // globals: clipping rectangle
    static BOOL DoClip;              // ..and whether to clip
public:
    static void Clip(WPRect* r);     // set clipping rectangle
};


// (In GPP.CPP)
WPRect GPShape::ClipRect;             // instantiate clip rectangle
BOOL   GPShape::DoClip=FALSE;         // ..and flag

//////////////////////
// Set clipping rectangle from WPRect
//
void GPShape::Clip(WPRect *rect)
{
    DoClip = rect != NULL;
    if (rect) {
        ClipRect = *rect;
        ClipRect.normalize();
    }
}

void GPShape::draw(WPDevContext &dc)
{
    if (DoClip) {      // Only draw if shape intesects clipping rectangle.
        WPRect temp;
        getBounds(temp);
        temp &= ClipRect;
        if (temp.isEmpty())
            return
    }
    ...(draw as before)

}
```

The *draw* function actually does the clipping. If the shape (that is, its bounds) lies totally outside the clipped rectangle, it's not drawn. Now all applications have to do is set the clip region before painting, like so:

```
void DrawWin::paint(WPPaintStruct &ps)
{
    WPRect clip;
    ps.getPaintRect(clip);
    GPShape::Clip(&clip);
    myShape->draw(ps);
}
```

In Section 8.3.6, we'll simplify this even further.

8.3.6 Shape Lists

One thing we definitely need in DRAW is the ability to deal with more than one shape. We want to create lots of shapes. To do so, we need a list class:

```
// (In GPP.H)
// Add next pointer to GPShape and make GPShapeList a friend
//
class GPShapeList {
    GPShape *next;                  // next in list
    friend GPShapeList;
};

// List of shapes.  List is implicitly ordered from bottom to top,
// so drawing can be done in list order.
//
class GPShapeList {
    GPShape *firstShape;            // first in list
    GPShape *current;              // current for list navigation
public:
    GPShapeList()                  { firstShape = current = NULL; }
    ~GPShapeList()                 { deleteAll(); }

    void deleteAll();

    // Navigation methods
    GPShape *operator()()          { return current; }
    GPShape *first()               { return current=firstShape; }
    GPShape *next()
        { return current ? current=current->next : NULL; }

    // Add/remove etc.
    GPShape *add(GPShape *obj);
    GPShape *remove(GPShape *obj);
    GPShape *front(GPShape *obj)   { return add(remove(obj)); }
    GPShape *back(GPShape *obj)
        { remove(obj); obj->next = firstShape; return firstShape = obj; }

    void draw(WPDevContext& dc);
    void paint(WPPaintStruct& ps);
};

#define forEachGPShape(list, s) \
    GPShape *s; \
    for (s = (list).first(); s; s=(list).next())
```

The implementation of *GPShapeList* is mostly a trivial exercise in list manipulation. For example, to add a new shape to the list we write

```
/////////////////
// Add shape to end of list (front, top).
//
GPShape *GPShapeList::add(GPShape *shp)
{
    if (firstShape==NULL)
        firstShape=shp;
```

```
        else {
            GPShape *s;
            for (s = firstShape; s->next; s=s->next)
                ;   // (run to end of list)
            s->next = shp;
        }
        shp->next = NULL;
        return shp;
}
```

The other functions are similar, so I won't bore you with them here. The only interesting ones are *draw* and *paint*:

```
//////////////////////
// Draw each shape in list
//
void GPShapeList::draw(WPDevContext& dc)
{
    forEachGPShape(*this, s)
        s->draw(dc);
}

//////////////////////
// Paint shapes in list. Like draw, but do clipping.
//
void GPShapeList::paint(WPPaintStruct& ps)
{
    ps.getPaintRect(GPShape::ClipRect);
    GPShape::ClipRect.normalize();
    BOOL save = GPShape::DoClip;
    GPShape::DoClip = TRUE;
    draw(ps);
    GPShape::DoClip = save;
}
```

The *paint* function makes it easy to paint a list of shapes in one fell swoop. DRAW uses it to paint its main window:

```
class DrawWin : public WPMainWin {   // Main window class for DRAW
    GPShapeList shapes;               // list of all the shapes
public:
    void paint(WPPaintStruct& ps)     { shapes.paint(ps); }
};
```

GPShapeList::paint makes painting trivial, and it even does clipping properly, without applications having to do anything!

8.3.7 Hit Detection

Another operation that's required for DRAW is a way to determine whether a particular point "hits" a shape. When the user clicks the mouse somewhere in the drawing, we need to figure out whether there's a shape at that mouse location.

This determination is called *hit-detection*. There are a number of ways to do it. For some shapes, such as rectangles, it's fairly easy; for others, like ellipses, it's not so easy. In general, hit-detection is a complex problem, one that usually requires resurrecting sophisticated mathematical algorithms from your favorite geometry textbook.

Windows provides several functions to assist in this. These involve first creating a *region* (from a rectangle, ellipse, or other shape), then invoking the *PtInRegion*:

```
HREGION r = CreateEllipticRegion(x1, y1, x2, y2);
BOOL hit = PtInRegion(r, px, py);
DeleteObject(r);
```

Unfortunately, *PtInRegion* only tests whether a point lies within the region, not *on* it (that is, on its boundary). Furthermore, it can only be used for rectangles, ellipses, and polygons. If we ever add Bezier curves to GPP, we're out of luck.

Fortunately, there's yet another way to do it—the one we'll use. This technique may be slower (I'm not really sure, never having conducted a scientific comparison), but it's completely general. It works for any shape: line, rectangle, ellipse, arc, Bezier curve, or squiggle.

Suppose we want to know whether a particular point *p* "hits" a given shape. The meaning of *hit* is specified by an integer radius *r*: if any part of the shape passes through the box with radius *r* centered at *p*, the point hits the shape; otherwise, it does not. To make this determination, we'll create a monochrome memory device context (i.e., a bitmap) for the hit box, initialize all its pixels to white, render the shape into it, then see if any pixel is on. This operation is cheap if the hit box is small, and we can avoid it entirely if the hit box lies totally outside the shape's bounds.

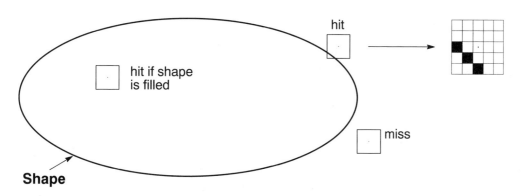

Here's the code that does it:

```
//////////////////
// Test whether object "touches" specified point.
// Algorithm:
//      First, try to eliminate by testing bounds; if can't eliminate,
//      render shape into little square and see if any pixels are on.
//
BOOL GPShape::hitTest(WPPoint p, int radius)
{
    WPSquare hit(p,radius);             // create hit box
    WPRect temp;
    getBounds(temp);                    // get bounds
    temp &= hit;                        // intersect them
    if (temp.isEmpty())                 // if intersection is empty:
        return FALSE;                   // ..miss

    // Possible hit: explore further
    WPMemDC dc(NULL, hit);              // screen-compatible DC
    dc.whiteOut(hit);                   // set all pixels white
    dc.setBrush(fillColor()==COLOR_NONE ? NULL_BRUSH : BLACK_BRUSH);
    drawShape(dc);                      // render into square
    // Test each pixel
    for (int x=hit.left(); x<hit.right(); x++) {
        for (int y=hit.top(); y<hit.bottom(); y++) {
            if (dc.pixel(x, y)==0)
                return TRUE;
        }
    }
    return FALSE;
}
```

Through the magic of virtual functions, this is merely the *default* method of performing hit detection; specific subclasses can provide their own version of *hitTest*. For example, it's easy to compute hit-detection rectangles just by comparing coordinates. I didn't bother because I was lazy, and I never noticed any performance problems with the above algorithm.[63]

8.3.8 Hilite Shapes

At this point we have an interesting design choice to make. We know that the DRAW program requires a notion of "size handles" that are used to indicate (highlight) a selected shape. Since the size operation is based on selecting one of the handles and dragging it, we need to do hit-detection on the size handles. And since we already have a means of doing hit-detection for shapes, we should implement the size handles as a special kind of shape:

---

63 There are other ways to improve hit-detection. For example, instead of testing each *pixel* individually, we could load the pixels into a byte array and test them eight at a time. Once again, I didn't bother because I haven't had performance problems. But then, I use a 33MHz 486.

```
class Hilite : public GPShape {

};
```

Now, the interesting question is, should *Hilite* be implemented as part of the generic GPP library, or should it be implemented as part of DRAW? Logically, the highlighting feature is a property of the DRAW program, and *Hilite* seems like a DRAW-specific shape. One might imagine, for example, a different draw program that highlighted shapes differently—say, by making it blink.

On the other hand, the location of the size handles is intimately related to the shape itself. Rectangles and ellipses have handles at all four corners of their extent, whereas lines have handles only at their endpoints. If we implement *Hilite* in DRAW, we'll need some way to find out whether the shape is a rectangle or line:

```
Hilite *hilite;
switch (shape->getType()) {
case GPLINE:
    hilite = // create highlight w/two endpoints
default:
    hilite = // create highlight w/all four corners
}
```

In general, "knowing" about the type of a library class in an application that uses the library is an OO no-no. A better way is to encapsulate the creation of *Hilite* shapes within each specific kind of shape, as a virtual function:

```
Hilite *hilite = shape->createHilite();
```

The whole point of OOP is to express the differences among different kinds of objects *within the objects themselves.* As soon as outside programs distinguish among different classes (for example, in *switch* statements) extensibility goes out the window. If we later decide to add *GPPolygon,* or some other shape with a different constellation of size handles, we'll have to add another *switch* case in DRAW. Ugh! One of the reasons for using OOP is to avoid precisely this situation. We want the ability to add new shapes to the library without having to modify existing applications. This is only possible if all shape-dependent behavior is implemented in GPP.[64]

Thus, we'll implement *GPHilite* as part of the library. But first, let's introduce another virtual function that gets a shape's handles:

```
class GPShape {
public:
    virtual int getHandles(WPPoint *buf);
};
```

---

64 As a general rule, any time you think you need to add some kind of type code or other way to "find out" the true type of a class within a class hierarchy, you should immediately suspect that your design is flawed. There's always a way to do it without type codes (usually by using virtual functions). Unfortunately, type codes are so familiar to C programmers that they're often hard to resist.

```
/////////////////
// Get list of handles. Default: get four corners of extent.
//
int GPShape::getHandles(WPPoint* pts)
{
    pts[0]=extent.origin();
    pts[1]=extent.topRight();
    pts[2]=extent.endpt();
    pts[3]=extent.bottomLeft();
    return 4;
}

/////////////////
// For lines, handles are at endpoints only
//
int GPLine::getHandles(WPPoint* pts)
{
    pts[0]=extent.origin();
    pts[1]=extent.endpt();
    return 2;
}
```

By adding *getHandles*, we encapsulate (hide) the information about the location of handles within each shape. If we ever add polygons, all we have to do is write *GPPolygon::getHandles* appropriately.

Now let's implement *GPHilite*. The constructor invokes *getHandles* to get the highlighted shape's size handles:

```
// (In GPP.H)
class GPHilite : public GPShape {
    GPShape *hishape;                  // hilighted shape
    WPPoint handles[4];                // size handles
    int nhandles;                      // number of handles
    int radius;                        // handle radius
public:
    GPHilite(GPShape *obj, int r);
    GPShape *shape()                   { return hishape; }
    WPPoint anchor(WPPoint p);
};

/////////////////
// Create "hilite" shape from given shape.
//
GPHilite::GPHilite(GPShape *shp, int r)
{
    assert(shp);
    hishape = shp;
    nhandles = shp->getHandles(handles);
    radius = r;
    shp->getExtent(extent);            // extent same as shape
    fillColor(COLOR_BLACK);            // handles are solid black
}
```

GPShape assumes that there are never more than four handles. If this assumption later becomes untrue (for example, if we add polygons), *GPHilite* would have to be modified. This presents no architectural problem, since *GPHilite* is part of the GPP library. To draw a hilite shape, we draw a little square centered at each handle:

```
void GPHilite::drawShape(WPDevContext &dc)
{
    for (int i=0; i<nhandles; i++) {
        WPPoint p = handles[i];             // center of handle
        dc.LP2DP(p);                        // convert to pixel coords
        WPSquare handle(p, radius);         // create square
        int old = dc.mapMode(MM_TEXT);      // make logical coords = pixels
        dc.rectangle(handle);               // draw recctangle
        dc.mapMode(old);                    // restore original map mode
    }
}
```

In order to ensure that the handles are in fact square, the radius is interpreted in *device* coordinates (pixels) and the rectangle is draw in MM_TEXT mode, where logical units are pixels. If this were not done, rounding errors would cause the handles to appear rectangular, (as opposed to square), depending on where they lie (I know because I found out the hard way).

Now, to highlight a selected shape in the DRAW program, all we have to do is write:

```
GPHilite *hilite = new GPHilite(shape, HANDLE_RAIDUS);
hilite->draw(dc);
```

HANDLE_RADIUS is a constant that specifies the radius of the size handles in pixels. The very same lines of code would work if we should ever decide to add polygons or Bezier curves to our graphics library.

There are other *GPHilite* functions besides the ones I've shown. For example, *GPHilite invalidate*s itself like so:

```
///////////////////
// Invalidate hilite: invalidate each size anchor
//
void GPHilite::invalidate(WPWin *win, BOOL erase)
{
    WPWinDC dc = win;
    for (int i=0; i<nhandles; i++) {
        WPPoint p = handles[i];
        dc.LP2DP(p);
        WPSquare handle(p, radius);
        win->invalidate(handle, erase);        // invalidate size handle
    }
}
```

Invalidating each handle results in less screen flicker, since if an application erases a hilite shape, only the size handles themselves are erased, not the entire bounding rectangle. This is illustrated in the following diagram:

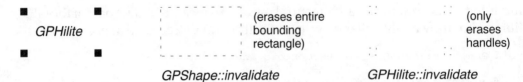

GPShape::invalidate   GPHilite::invalidate

GPHilite also provides a *hitTest* function that's more efficient. It's straightforward, so I refer you to Appendix A for the source code.

In general, the whole point (and beauty) of virtual functions is that they let different subclasses respond to the same function (method, message) differently. If *GPHilite* needs a more clever *invalidate* algorithm, virtual functions provide the way to do it.

8.4 Implementing DRAW

With GPP implemented, DRAW is fairly straightforward. GPP provides the basic functionality required to create and manipulate lines, rectangles, and ellipses; all we have to do for DRAW is write a user interface that invokes them. Most of the work is in implementing the menu commands and mouse action.

8.4.1 The Main Window

As always, the first thing we do to write a new application is derive a new main window class:

```
///////////////////
// Main DRAW window class.
//
classS DrawWin : public WPMainWin {
    static WPRect DfltSize;       // default size for new objects
    GPShapeList shapes;           // list of shapes
    GPHilite* hilite;             // current hilite (selected) shape
    GPShape* newShape;            // pending new shape
    .
    .
public:
    DrawWin();
    ~DrawWin();

    // Virtual message functions
    BOOL menuInit(WPMenu &menu);
    void paint(WPPaintStruct &ps);
    BOOL mouse(int msg, WPPoint p, WORD flags);
    BOOL command(int id, WORD msg);
    BOOL anySelected()            { return hilite!=NULL; }
    BOOL fileNew();
    BOOL filePrint(WPDlgPrint &pdlg);
};
```

DrawWin contains a number of data members to keep track of things: for example, a list of shapes, the currently selected (highlighted) shape, and a "new" shape. It also provides a number of virtual message functions, such as *menuInit* and *paint*. The constructor is fairly straightforward; the only interesting thing is that it sets the window class flag CS_OWNDC:

```
DrawWin::DrawWin() : WPMainWin("DRAWWIN")
{
    createArgs.wndcls.hCursor = NULL;
    createArgs.wndcls.style |= CS_OWNDC; // <<< create my own DC
    createWin("Windows++ DRAW");
    WPWinDC dc = this;
    dc.mapMode(MM_LOMETRIC);              // (1 logical unit = .1 mm)
    fileNew();
}
```

This flag tells Windows to give the window its own permanent device context, as opposed to creating one on the fly each time *GetDC* is called. The purpose of this is so we can set the mapping mode (MM_LOMETRIC) once and have it be remembered until the window is destroyed; otherwise, we'd have to set the mapping mode every time we obtain the device context. (Windows with their OWNDC also retain other device context properties besides the mapping mode.)

8.4.2 Creating Shapes

Let's start with something easy: the Edit New commands. There are three choices in the pop-up: Line, Rectangle, and Ellipse.

```
/////////////////
// Handle menu command.
//
BOOL DrawWin::command(int id, WORD msg)
{
    switch (id) {
    case ID_NEWLINE:
        setNewShape(new GPLine(DfltSize));
        return TRUE;
    case ID_NEWRECT:
        setNewShape(new GPRect(DfltSize));
        return TRUE;
    case ID_NEWELLIPSE:
        setNewShape(new GPEllipse(DfltSize));
        return TRUE;
    .
    .
}
```

When the user invokes one of these commands, DRAW creates a new shape of the appropriate type, using the static global *DfltSize*, an instance of *WPRect*.

```
// Default size for new shapes = 100 square units (= 1 sq. centimeter)
WPRect DrawWin::DfltSize(0,0,100,-100);
```

Once created, the new shape is placed in temporary "limbo" by *setNewShape:*

```
/////////////////
// Set the new shape: destroy old one, change cursor.
//
GPShape* DrawWin::setNewShape(GPShape *shp)
{
    delete newShape;                    // delete previous new shape, if any
    if (shp)
        Cursor = "CrsNew";              // change cursor
    return newShape = shp;
}
```

The cursor is changed as a way of reminding the user that he or she is now creating
a new shape and should click the mouse to deposit it on the drawing. That done,
the virtual *mouse* function responds:

```
BOOL DrawWin::mouse(int msg, WPPoint p, WORD flags)
{
    .
    .
    switch(msg) {
    case WM_LBUTTONDOWN:
        if (newShape) {
            // New shape pending: drop it at mouse location
            WPRect extent;
            shp = newShape;
            shp->getExtent(extent);         // get extent of new shape
            extent += p-extent.endpt();     // move to mouse location
            shp->setExtent(extent);         // ..and set
            shapes.add(shp);                // add new shape to shape list
            shp->draw(dc);                  // ..and draw it
            newShape = NULL;
        }
        .
        .
}
```

8.4.3 Selection and Dragging

A good portion of the code in DRAW deals with the logic for implementing drag-
move and drag-size, all of which resides in the virtual *mouse* function. Everything
begins when the user presses the left mouse button.

```
BOOL DrawWin::mouse(int msg, WPPoint p, WORD flags)
{
    GPShape *shp;
    WPWinDC dc = this;                  // get window DC..
    dc.DP2LP(p);                        // convert mouse to logical coords
    switch(msg) {
    case WM_LBUTTONDOWN:
        if (newShape) {
            shp = newShape;
            .
            . (as shown above)
            .
```

```
    } else
        shp = shapes.hitText(p, HIT_RADIUS);
    if (setHilite(shp)) {              // if hit succeeded:
        Cursor = "CrsDrag";            // change cursor to cross
        Cursor.clip(this);             // restrict cursor to window
        prevPt = orgPt = p;            // save mouse points
        shp->getBounds(orgBounds);     // ..and bounds
        anchorPt = hilite->anchor(p);  // get anchor in case drag-size

        // Now go into appropriate mode and XOR shape.
        if (shp==hilite) {
            dragging = DRAGSIZE;
            shp=hilite->shape();
        } else
            dragging = DRAGMOVE;
        XORShape(dc, shp);
    }
    break;
```

Assuming that we're not creating a new shape, the *mouse* function first invokes *hitTest* to find the shape selected and invokes *setHilite* to highlight it:

```
/////////////////////
// Select new shape. De-select previous one, if any.
//
GPHilite* DrawWin::setHilite(GPShape *shp)
{
    if (shp != hilite) {
        if (hilite) {
            if (hilite->shape()==shp)
                return hilite;
            // Invalidate previous selection
            hilite->invalidate(this,TRUE);
            delete shapes.remove(hilite);
            hilite = NULL;
            update();
        }
        if (shp) {
            // Hilite new object
            hilite = new GPHilite(shp, HANDLE_RADIUS);
            hilite->invalidate(this);
            shapes.add(hilite);
            update();
        }
    }
    return hilite;
}
```

This function takes care of creating a *GPHilite* shape for the selected shape, and updating the window appropriately to remove the old hilite (if any) and add the new one (if any). Note that it works correctly even when the previous or new selection is NULL.

To finish up, *mouse* changes the cursor to a crosshairs and clips (confines) it to the window's client area, then sets a few state variables, including *dragging*, which indicates whether we're doing drag-move or drag-size. The last thing *mouse* does is invoke *XORShape* to draw the shape in XOR mode:

```
void DrawWin::XORShape(WPDevContext& dc, GPShape *shp)
{
    dc.setPen(WHITE_PEN);
    dc.setBrush(NULL_BRUSH);
    dc.rop2(R2_XORPEN);
    shp->drawShape(dc);
    dc.rop2(R2_COPYPEN);
}
```

The XOR raster operation (ROP) is a standard graphics trick. Whenever you draw a rectangle, ellipse, or other shape in Windows, the color of each pixel painted is a combination of the new (pen or brush) color and the old one, as determined by the current ROP. Normally, the ROP is COPYPEN, which simply copies the pen or brush color to the window. However, if the ROP is XOR, the resulting color is obtained by XORing the bits of the pen or brush with those in the window. When the pen is white (all ones), this has the effect of negating the area painted. Once negated, the pixels can be restored to their original color by negating them again. In other words, if you draw a shape twice in XOR mode, the net effect is nil. XOR is thus used to make a shape appear to "move" by successively XORing the shape from one location to the next.

That's a lot of work for a measly mouse down event!

Here's what happens when the mouse is *moved:*

```
case WM_MOUSEMOVE:
    Cursor = newShape ? "CrsNew" : (dragging ? "CrsDrag" : IDC_ARROW);
    if (dragging && p != prevPt) {
        shp = hilite->shape();           // get selected shape
        XORShape(dc,shp);                // XOR (erase) at old location

        WPRect extent;                   // get shape's extent
        shp->getExtent(extent);          // ...
        if (dragging==DRAGMOVE)          // drag-move:
            extent += p-prevPt;          // ..translate
        else                             // drag-size:
            extent.set(anchorPt, p);     // change extent
        shp->setExtent(extent);          // move the shape
        XORShape(dc, shp);               // XOR (draw) at new location
        prevPt = p;
    }
    break;
```

First, the appropriate cursor is displayed, as per the standard Windows practice (see Section 5.3.2). Next (assuming we are dragging), the shape is XORed at it's old location (effectively un-drawing it), then again at its new spot. This makes the shape appear to move with the mouse. Note how easy the calculations are using the overloaded operators for *WPRect* and *WPPoint* that we implemented in Chapter 2. To move a shape, we simply "add" *p-prevPt* (a point) to *extent* (a rectangle).

Finally, when the user releases the mouse button, the shape is deposited, its original and new bounding rectangles are updated, and the cursor is unclipped and restored to its original shape:

```
case WM_LBUTTONUP:
    if (dragging) {
        shp = hilite->shape();              // get selected shape
        XORShape(dc, shp);                  // XOR (erase) old image

        if (p != orgPt) {                   // really moved:
            dc.LP2DP(orgBounds);            // original bounds in pixels
            invalidate(orgBounds, TRUE);    // old bounds need painting
            setHilite(NULL);                // un-hilite (old location)
            shp->invalidate(this);          // new bounds need painting too
            setHilite(shp);                 // re-hilite (new location)
        }
        Cursor = IDC_ARROW;                 // restore normal cursor
        Cursor.unClip();                    // free to move outside window
        dragging=NODRAG;                    // no longer dragging
    }
    break;
```

The select/drag logic is fairly nasty. We should look for some way to encapsulate it in our GPP library. I leave this task as an exercise for the reader.

8.4.4 Printing

If we were writing DRAW in DOS, this section would not appear in the book, because to make printing work would require another chapter. (DOS provides no support for graphics printing.) But in Windows, this is an area where GDI really shines. To print our shapes, all we have to do is "draw" them on a printer:

```
/////////////////////
// Print shapes. Pretty easy: just draw on printer DC!
//
BOOL DrawWin::filePrint(WPDlgPrint &pdlg)
{
    WPPrinter p = pdlg;
    p.mapMode(MM_LOMETRIC);      // set mapping mode
    p.doAbortDlg(this);          // do abort dialog
    p.startDoc("DRAW");          // start printing
    shapes.draw(p);              // draw on printer DC
    p.endPage();                 // end page
    p.endDoc();                  // end printing
    return TRUE;
}
```

So much for printing.

Of course, we haven't implemented *Windows++* support for printing yet (a minor detail). We'll do it in Section 8.5. As you'll see, it's not really as simple as *Windows++* makes it look.

Note, however, that just by using one of the logical mapping modes (MM_LOMETRIC), DRAW is automatically WYSIWYG (What You See Is What You Get):

the shapes are the same size when printed as they were when displayed in a window. This is another area where GDI excels: it lets programs deal in device-independent units. After all, a millimeter is a millimeter is a millimeter, on any device.

8.4.5 Miscellaneous Details

The rest of DRAW is straightforward, so I'll only provide the highlights:

- The Edit Front and Edit Back commands are handled by invoking the corresponding *GPShapeList* functions and updating the window.

- Edit Edge and Edit Fill are equally trivial: they invoke *edgeColor* or *fillColor* after converting the menu choice to the appropriate COLORREF. If Random is chosen as the color, a random RGB value is used (just like in RANDRECT).

- Edit Delete removes the selected shape from the list of shapes, then deletes it and its hilite.

- Edit Duplicate invokes a new virtual function, *GPShape::dup*, to create a copy of the selected shape, then adds it to the list.

- A *menuInit* function is provided to gray the various Edit commands appropriately. Edge, Fill, Front, etc. are only enabled if a shape is selected. The rest of the menu options are grayed by *WPMainWin*, as described in Section 6.3.7 (a virtual *anySelected* function tells whether a shape is selected).

- File New deletes all the shapes in the shape list, clears the window, and resets the state of the universe to its initial conditions (before the big bang).

- The mouse chords are implemented in the obvious manner. A new function, *constrainMouse*, adjusts the mouse point to meet the horizontal, vertical, or diagonal motion constraint; this function is then invoked as the first line in *mouse*. The details are a bit tedious, but straightforward.

As always, the full program is listed in Appendix A.

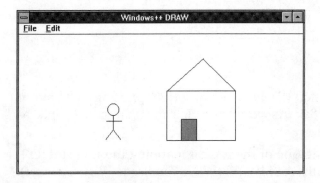

8.4.6 Evaluating DRAW: Issues for a Real System

The main purpose of the DRAW program is to show how object-oriented programming techniques, and C++ in particular, can be applied to solve the problems of graphics programming in Windows. As an educational example, DRAW serves its purpose well. However, as a drawing program it leaves much to be desired. Furthermore, the GPP library is not very robust, but somewhat idiosyncratic: it only provides the functions necessary to support DRAW.

Before leaving the subject, I thought I'd list some of these omissions, as well as some of the difficult problems that "real" graphics systems must deal with.

■ Lines, rectangles, and ellipses are not enough. A more complete system would include text, arcs, polygons, splines, and other shapes.

■ DRAW provides no *grid* or *rule* to guide the user when moving and sizing.

■ DRAW has no notion of *gravity* or *snapping*. In some drawing packages, when you move a shape near another one, the moving shape jumps or "snaps" onto the fixed one. This makes it easy to connect shapes to one another so they look connected even on high-resolution devices such as phototypesetters.

■ Cut, Copy and Paste are not implemented. Doing so requires writing shapes to the clipboard in an application-independent format, which raises the obvious question: what format?

■ GPP provides no way to change a shape's line width or dash pattern. (This would be trivial to add).

■ GPP provides no *load* or *save* function to save shapes to disk files; DRAW has no File Open nor Save command.

■ GPP does not support sophisticated geometric transformations such as rotation and shearing. These would be difficult to add, since GDI does not support them. We'd have to implement our own *Ellipse* and *Rectangle* primitives to use instead of the ones Windows provides.

■ GPP provides no way to *group* several shapes into a single shape. Such a feature is almost essential for drawing sophisticated illustrations. For example, you might want to draw a house from individual lines and rectangles, then group them so you can manipulate (duplicate, move, size) the house as single shape. If grouping were supported, it would raise another issue for DRAW: how to select more than one shape?

■ The use of integers for logical coordinates does not provide sufficient resolution for many graphics applications. While 32,768 logical coordinates may seem like plenty, it's not enough. Most graphics systems use floating point numbers and *RSUs* (ridiculously small units; e.g., .000001 inches) for geometric representations. This is not because any output device requires such high resolution, but because the precision is required to carry out some mathematical transformations. For example, while rotating a line, it's impossible to distinguish lines that intersect at shallow angles from ones that are truly parallel, without a high degree of precision.

There are many other issues, enough to fill an entire book. I just wanted to give you a taste for some of the difficulties that graphics programmers deal with.

8.5 Printing

OK, we've had our fun. Now it's time to address an important topic that everyone hates: printing. If you're allergic to printing, you may skip this section. (But you'll need a note from your doctor.)

Theoretically, "drawing" on a printer is no different from drawing on any other device. After all, the whole point of GDI is to provide a *device-independent* graphics interface. Whether the device is the screen or printer, you draw on it using the same GDI functions. Unfortunately, what sounds good in theory doesn't quite hold in practice. There are a number of special considerations that apply when printing in Windows:

- First, there are all those dreaded *Escape* functions. Windows provides a GDI function called *Escape* that lets you "access facilities of a particular device that are not directly available through GDI." In other words, to invoke device dependent functions. *Escape* is most commonly used for printing, and Windows programs are often full of calls like

  ```
  Escape(printDC, STARTDOC, len, "MYDOC", NULL); // start printing
  Escape(printDC, NEWFRAME, 0, NULL, NULL);      // new page.
  ```

  The *Escape* functions are identified by #*define* symbols in WINDOWS.H, and documented in the SDK *Reference, Volume 2.* The manual describes 58 pages of *Escape* functions! (Fortunately, most of them are rarely used.)

  Instead of having to remember the arguments to all these escape functions (most of which are NULL), we'd like to write

  ```
  printer.startDoc("myDOC");
  printer.endPage();
  ```

- Next, you have to write several lines of tedious code to set up an *abort procedure.* It's not considered friendly to leave the user waiting while your program goes merrily printing hundreds of pages of text. You're supposed to display a "Cancel" dialog that lets the user abort the print job. Of course, Windows doesn't do this for you; you have to create the dialog and write something called an *abort procedure* that you pass to the device using the *Escape* function SETABORTPROC. Everyone simply copies the code from the SDK manual, a favorite Windows programming book or some other program, so why not encapsulate it in a reusable subroutine?

As application programmers, we don't want to worry about all the mechanics of setting up the abort dialog, we simply want to tell the printer to use it:

```
printer.doAbortDlg();            // do abort dialog voodoo
```

■ Finally, Windows provides no support for simple things like printing ASCII text lines. If you want to print a series of text lines, you have to handle page ejection manually. You have to obtain the font height and divide it into the vertical resolution of the device to compute the number of lines that will fit on a page, then do a page eject (*Escape* function NEWFRAME) every time that many lines are printed. Application programmers sometimes find it convenient to print text as though the printer were a line printer:

```
WPLinePrinter p;
p.startDoc();
for (int i=o; i<nLines; i++)
    p.outLine(lines[i]);
p.endDoc();
```

Windows++ should take care of page ejects and all the other low-level stuff.

In the rest of this section, we'll proceed to fulfill this *Windows++* printing wish list.

8.5.1 *WPPrinter*

The first thing we need is a printer device context, which is naturally modeled as another kind of device context, that is, as a subclass of *WPDevContext:*

```
class WPPrinter : public WPDevContext {
public:
    WPPrinter(CSTR devname=NULL) : WPDevContext(devname);
};
```

The constructor simply passes the device name to *WPDevContext*, which creates the appropriate device context after looking up the driver and output file names in WIN.INI (see Section 8.2.3). For example, to get a device context for printer called "HP LaserJet III", all you have to do is write

```
WPPrinter p = "HP LaserJet III";       // create printer device context
```

Since *devname* defaults to NULL, we can also write

```
WPPrinter p;                           // create DC for default printer
```

to print to the default printer (the one specified as the *device* keyword in WIN.INI).

While this constructor works fine, it's not exactly what's needed to write applications in the easiest possible fashion. If you recall, back in Section 6.3.3 we added code to *WPMainWin* that automatically runs the print dialog and then invokes *file-Print* whenever the user invokes the File Print command from the main menu. To handle printing, an application simply provides a main window class with a *file-Print* function:

```
BOOL MyMainWin::filePrint(WPDlgPrint& pdlg)
{
    WPPrinter p = pdlg.getDeviceName();
    .
    .
}
```

Unfortunately, this won't work because there is no *getDeviceName* function for *WPDlgPrint*. The print dialog in COMMDLG (see Section 7.5.4) doesn't return the name of the selected printer; instead, it returns its HDC already loaded. No problem; all we have to do is invent another constructor for *WPPrinter*:

```
// Add new constructor
class WPPrinter : public WPDevContext {
public:
    WPPrinter(WPDlgPrint& pdlg) : WPDevContext(pdlg.getHDC());
};
```

This one simply gets *hdc* from the print dialog and passes it to *WPDevContext*. Now we have another problem. The destructor for *WPDlgPrint* deletes *hdc* when the print dialog is destroyed (*WPDlgPrint* created it, so it should delete it too). But the HDC is also deleted when the device context is destroyed, in ~*WPDevInfo*. As it stands, the HDC will get deleted twice! (A definite no-no.)

To fix this, we'll introduce a hidden flag that tells ~*WPPrinter* whether or not to delete the device context. Here are the modifications:

```
class WPPrinter : public WPDevContext {
    BOOL delDC;                         // Whether to delete DC
public:
    WPPrinter(CSTR devname=NULL) : WPDevCOntext(devname)
        { delDC=TRUE; }
    WPPrinter(WPDlgPrint& pdlg) : WPDevCOntext(pdlg.getHDC()
        { delDC=FALSE; }
    ~WPPrinter();
};
// Destroy printer device context: don't delete DC if flag says not to.
int WPPrinter::~WPPrinter()
{
    restoreSelection();                 // (always restore selected objects)
    if (!delDC)                         // Don't delete DC: set hdc to NULL..
        hdc=NULL;                       // ..so WPDevContext won't delete it!
}
```

If the device is obtained from the print dialog, *delDC* is set to FALSE, which causes the destructor to set *hdc* = NULL so ~*WPDevContext* won't delete it. The "normal" constructor (the one that creates the DC from a device name) sets *delDC* to TRUE, so the device context is deleted as normally happens.

This subterfuge may seem kludgy, but really it's Windows that's kludgy; all we're doing is cleaning up after it. Turning a mess into neatness necessarily requires kludginess! But we can hide it. The *delDC* flag is buried within the internals of *Windows++*, where applications need never know that there's any difference between an HDC that came from *CreateDC* and one that came from the print dialog.

Now applications can provide *filePrint* functions like this:

```
BOOL MyMainWin::filePrint(WPDlgPrint& pdlg)
{
    WPPrinter p = pdlg;            // get whatever printer the user
       .                           // selected in the print dialog
       .
       .
}
```

One of the advantages of building your own library is that you have the freedom to provide it with whatever functions you need to make programming easier. In this case, it's convenient to have a *WPPrinter* constructor that gets the device context from the print dialog, so we wrote one. This situation further illustrates the principle that library development and application development proceed hand-in-hand. You only really know what's required of the library when you try to write an application. (In this case, the application is WINEDIT, described in Section 6.3. In order to present a linear chapter organization, printing was put off until now, but in practice, and in fact, printing was implemented along with WINEDIT, when it was needed. In DRAW, we just reuse it again.)

There's another *Windows++* printer object, *WPPrinterInfo*, which gets an information context for a printer. You can use it to obtain information about the printer without drawing on it. This can sometimes be more efficient, since information contexts require less memory and CPU cycles to create than do full-blown device contexts. Applications that need special printer capabilities can use *WPPrinterInfo* to quickly check that they're supported by a particular device before actually printing.

8.5.2 *Escape* Functions

So much for creating and destroying printers (to be precise, printer device contexts). Now to actually print. As we observed earlier, what we want is a better interface to the dreaded *Escape* function. Instead of writing

```
HDC hdc;
Escape(hdc, STARTDOC, strlen(myDocName), myDocName, NULL);
...
Escape(hdc, NEWFRAME, 0, NULL, NULL);    // end page
Escape(hdc, ENDDOC, 0, NULL, NULL);      // end printing
```

we'd like to write:

```
WPPrinter p;
p.startDoc("myDOC");
.
.
p.endPage();                        // end page
p.endDoc();                         // end printing
```

This is exactly the sort of thing "brainless" functions were made for:

```
// Add escape function to device context (in WPGDI.H).
class WPDevContext : public WPDevInfo {
    int err;            // place to save error code
public:
    int escape(int func, int nbytes=0, LPSTR in=NULL, LPSTR out=NULL);
        { return err = Escape(hdc, func, nbytes, in, out); }
    int error()   { return err; }
};
// Add brainless Escape functions for printing (in WPGDI.H).
class WPPrinter : public WPDevContext {
public:
    int startDoc(CSTR name)
        { return escape(STARTDOC, strlen(name), (char*)name); }
    int endDoc()        { return escape(ENDDOC); }
    int endPage()       { return escape(NEWFRAME); }
};
```

I only bothered to implement the three functions shown above (the only ones needed for the WINEDIT program in Chapter 6). Feel free to add your own favorite *Escape* functions.[65]

Note once again the benefits of "brainless" repackaging: the arguments to each function are now self-documenting, and there's no need for superfluous zero and NULL arguments. More important, the printing functions are implemented in *WPPrinter,* where they belong; there's no way to invoke *startDoc* and the rest for some other kind of device context. More bulletproofing.

8.5.3 The Abort Dialog

The next item on our print agenda is the Abort dialog. We want to provide an easy way to do all the Windows mumbo-jumbo required to display an Abort dialog while the printer is printing. We'd like to simply write

```
printer.doAbortDlg();
```

and have the Abort dialog appear during printing. Of course, if the user actually presses

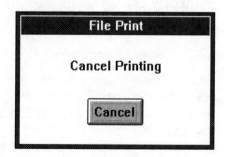

---

65 In version 3.1, Windows breaks *Escape* out into ordinary #*define* macros, which are not as good as inline functions. (They're not type-safe, and the argument declarations aren't self-documenting like they are with inline functions.)

the Cancel button, we want *Windows++* to abort the print job without the application having to do anything special. (Boy, application programmers sure are demanding!)

If you've ever seen what the normal Windows code for doing this looks like, you might be tempted to forget about Cancel, to heck with the user! But disgusting code is just the sort of thing that's perfect for encapsulation in a library—we only have to write it once, for future applications to reuse forever.

The Abort dialog voodoo is well-established. All we have to do is transliterate the Microsoft-approved code for how-to-do-print-abort from the SDK *Guide to Programming* or a handy text such as [Petzold 1990].

First, we add a few static class globals to store the dialog itself and an *Abort* flag:

```
// Add Abort, DlgAbort and pwin to WPPrinter class (in WPGDI.CPP)
class WPPrinter : public WPDevContext {
    static WPDlgPrintAbort *DlgAbort;      // new class: abort dialog
    static BOOL Abort;                     // abort flag
    WPWin *pwin;                           // parent window

    friend BOOL _export FAR PASCAL         // universal abort procedure
        WPPrintAbortProc(HDC hdcPrn, short nCode);
    friend WPDlgPrintAbort;
public:

    int doAbortDlg(WPWin *w);
    BOOL aborted()                         { return Abort; }
};
```

Unfortunately, the *Abort* flag and *DlgAbort* pointer must be globals, not data members, since Windows doesn't provide any way to pass application-specific information to the abort procedure. Another data member, *pwin*, identifies the window that owns the dialog.

The abort procedure looks like this:

```
///////////////////
// Universal print abort procedure.
// Signature (arguments and return value) is defined by Windows.
//
BOOL _export FAR PASCAL WPPrintAbortProc(HDC hdcPrn, short nCode)
{
    MSG msg;
    HWND hDlgAbort = WPWin::GetHwnd(WPPrinter::DlgAbort);
    while (!WPPrinter::Abort &&
            PeekMessage(&msg, NULL, 0, 0, PM_REMOVE)) {
        if (!hDlgAbort || !IsDialogMessage(hDlgAbort, &msg)) {
            TranslateMessage(&msg);
            DispatchMessage(&msg);
        }
    }
    return !WPPrinter::Abort;
}
```

The content is straight out of Petzold and should look familiar to Windows gurus. The procedure peeks to see whether there are any messages (i.e., whether the user pressed the Cancel button), and returns TRUE if printing should continue, or FALSE if it should be aborted. *WPPrintAbortProc* is exported so we don't have to bother with *MakeProcInstance*, and it's declared as a friend of *WPPrinter*, so it's allowed to access the private globals *Abort* and *DlgAbort*.

Finally, the Abort dialog itself:

```
//////////////////
// Standard Cancel dialog for printing: it's modeless
//
class WPDlgPrintAbort : public WPDialogModeless {
public:
    WPDlgPrintAbort(WPWin *pwin, CSTR resname="DLGPRINTABORT")
        : WPDialogModeless(resname, pwin) { createWin(); }
    BOOL command(int id, WORD msg);
};
```

The only non-inline function is *command*, which, if the user presses the Cancel button, simply sets the *WPPrinter::Abort* flag to TRUE:

```
BOOL WPDlgPrintAbort::command(int id, WORD msg)
{
    if (id==IDCANCEL) {
        WPPrinter::DlgAbort = NULL;    // clear pointer
        WPPrinter::Abort = TRUE;       // abort
    }
    return WPDialogModeless::command(id, msg);
}
```

Since *WPDlgPrintAbort* is also a friend of *WPPrinter*, it too is allowed to access *DlgAbort* and *Abort*. It also sets *DlgAbort* to NULL (the normal dialog *command* processing in *WPDialog* will destroy the dialog in response to IDCANCEL). The dialog itself is defined in a file called WPPRINT.DLG which applications must include in their resource files (or provide their own version):

```
DLGPRINTABORT DIALOG 76,48,102,57
STYLE DS_MODALFRAME | WS_POPUP | WS_CLIPSIBLINGS | WS_CAPTION |
WS_VISIBLE
CAPTION "File Print"
BEGIN
    CONTROL "Cancel",IDCANCEL,"Button",
        WS_TABSTOP | WS_CHILD | WS_VISIBLE | BS_PUSHBUTTON,36,33,30,14
    CONTROL "Cancel Printing",-1,"static",SS_CENTER | WS_CHILD,
        5,12,92,12
END
```

We can now glue all this code together in *WPPrinter::doAbortDlg*, which is the function we originally set out to write:

```
// First, instantiate static globals (In WPGDI.CPP)
BOOL WPPrinter::Abort;
WPDialogModeless *WPPrinter::DlgAbort=NULL;
```

```
/////////////////
// Tell printer to do abort dialog.
//
int WPPrinter::doAbortDlg(WPWin *w)
{
    pwin = w;
    Abort = FALSE;
    assert(DlgAbort==NULL);
    DlgAbort = new WPDlgPrintAbort(pwin);
    if (pwin)
        pwin->enableWin(FALSE);
    return escape(SETABORTPROC, 0, (LPSTR)WPPrintAbortProc);
}
```

All we do is initialize the *Abort* flag, create the dialog, and set the abort procedure using *escape* (since this is the only place SETABORTPROC is used, I didn't bother writing a brainless *setAbortProc* function). I've added a *WPWin** argument, so that *doAbortDlg* can disable the owning window while the job is printing. Of course, we have to re-enable it; the most convenient place to do so is in the destructor:

```
int WPPrinter::~WPPrinter()
{
    if (DlgAbort) {                      // dialog still exists (no cancel):
        DlgAbort->destroyWin();          // ..destroy it
        DlgAbort=NULL;                   // ..
    }
    if (pwin)
        pwin->enableWin(TRUE);           // enable parent (owner) window
    if (!delDC)
        hdc=NULL;
}
```

The result of all this is that applications need never again bother setting up abort dialogs and procedures—all they have to do is call *doAbortDlg.* (For an example, see the WINEDIT program described in Chapter 6.)

8.5.4 Line Printing

The last item on our agenda is implementing *WPLinePrinter,* the purpose of which is to make simple line printing easier. To print a sequence of ASCII text lines in Windows, you have to implement all the form-feed logic manually. This requires obtaining the font and page heights in order to calculate the number of lines that fit on a page, keeping track of how many lines have been printed, and invoking the *Escape* function NEWFRAME whenever a new page is required.

Ugh! All I want to do is print a few lines of ASCII text; why do I have to mess with fonts and do all that low-level stuff? (You ask, in disbelief.)

What we need is some specialized printer class that hides all this garbage so we can simply write

```
WPLinePrinter p;                    // create "line printer"
p.startDoc();                       // start printing
for (int i=o; i<nLines; i++)        // loop for each line:
    p.outLine(lines[i]);            // ..print the ith line
p.endDoc();                         // end printing
```

Since I expect you're getting the hang of things by now, I'll simply show you how *WPLinePrinter* is implemented:

```
class WPLinePrinter : public WPPrinter {
    int nLinesPage;                 // num lines per page
    int yChar;                      // height of char
    int curLine;                    // current line number
    void init();
public:
    WPLinePrinter(CSTR devname=NULL)  : WPPrinter(devname)     { init(); }
    WPLinePrinter(WPDlgPrint& pdlg)   : WPPrinter(pdlg)        { init(); }

    int outLine(char *buf, int len);
    int formFeed()                  { curLine=0; return endPage(); }
    int endDoc()
        { if (curLine>0) formFeed(); return WPPrinter::endDoc(); }
};

//////////////////////
// Common initializer for all line printer constructors.
// Get text character height, lines per page, etc.
//
void WPLinePrinter::init()
{
    TEXTMETRIC tm;
    getTextMetrics(tm);
    yChar = tm.tmHeight + tm.tmExternalLeading;
    nLinesPage = getVERTRES()/yChar-1;
    curLine = 0;
}

const char CONTROL_L = 12;

//////////////////////
// Print line. Automatically eject page properly.
//
int WPLinePrinter::outLine(char *buf, int len)
{
    if (buf[0]==CONTROL_L)          // do form-feed for Control-L
        return formFeed();
    if (curLine >= nLinesPage)
        formFeed();
    textOut(0, yChar*curLine, buf, len);
    curLine++;
    return error();
}
```

There's no magic here. All *WPLinePrinter* does is provide a few useful subroutines that bundle commonly used code sequences into single functions. Of course, the medium of C++ provides a powerful context to do it in, The notions of derived subclasses and inheritance are ideally suited for expressing a line printer as a kind of printer, one with added features. C++ makes it extremely easy to extend small systems into big ones, simply by deriving new classes.

> **C** *The various printing techniques described in this section could easily be adapted for C: the "brainless" Escape functions could be implemented as C macros like* PrStart-Doc, PrEndPage, *and so on; the rest could be implemented as functions (e.g.,* PrDoAbortDlg, PrLineOut).

WPLinePrinter is not strictly required to model Windows; it's just a little icing on the cake that makes programming easier without much effort. Of course, it's somewhat primitive; to be really useful, it needs more features like page headers and footers and a customizable page size (in *lines*). These would be fairly easy to add, so I won't do it; I primarily wanted to show you how you'd go about it. The basic idea is to encapsulate as much generic, low-level functionality as possible in high-level class methods (a fancy term for old-fashioned subroutines).

For a real-life example showing how printing works in practice, take a look at the WINEDIT program in Section 6.3 (or Appendix A).

8.6 Summary

I hope you've enjoyed this chapter. I have. (I've always liked graphics because it's so graphical). As is our custom, let's review what we've accomplished.

First, we repackaged GDI:

- We implemented a number of *Windows++* objects to model GDI objects such as device contexts, pens, brushes, and so on.

- In particular, we implemented a class hierarchy of device contexts. This hierarchy exposes the inherent differences implicit among different kinds of device contexts and hides the inconsistencies among them.

- We implemented three drawing objects: pens, brushes, and bitmaps. We did it in such a way that we encapsulated a number of GDI programming rules, so that the rules are automatically enforced by *Windows++*.

- We implemented two graphics programs: RANDRECT and MANDEL.

Then we built an object-oriented *Windows++* graphics library:

- The GPP library provides a C++ class hierarchy of *GPShapes*, which includes lines, rectangles, and ellipses.

- We used the GPP shape library to build a simple DRAW program.

Finally, we returned to GDI, to *Windows++*-ify printing, which is now much easier. Why, it's almost painless.

CHAPTER ■ 9

DLL-ing *Windows++*

In this chapter, we'll turn *Windows++* into the ultimate reusable code: a dynamic link library.

9.1 What's a DLL?

One of the truly wonderful features that Windows provides is the notion of dynamic link libraries (DLL). A DLL is essentially a library of subroutines that are "linked" at load or run time instead of at compile time.

To understand what this means, consider for a moment the familiar C library function *printf*. In DOS, every program that uses *printf* has a copy of it linked right in with the rest of the program. Just imagine how many programs are out there in the world with copies of *printf* compiled inside them! Not to mention numerous other library functions such as *strcpy* and *getc*. In a single-tasking operating system such as DOS, this is no cause for concern, but in multi-tasking operating systems such as Windows, a lot of memory is wasted when each program has its own copies of *printf* and all the other functions. Since the copies are 100 per cent identical for all programs, why not find some way to share them?

This is exactly what dynamic link libraries provide: a way to share subroutines among several programs running at the same time. Using DLLs, *printf* could be compiled into a special executable module—say, CLIB.DLL (dynamic link libraries usually have the suffix .DLL, but not always). This module would then be placed in a directory somewhere in the search path.

In addition to the DLL, which contains executable code, a special *import library* can be created. This library contains duplicate stub functions for each function in the DLL (actually, it contains "import-definition records," which are conceptually the same thing). These stubs are compiled and linked with applications, instead of with the real functions. The purpose of each stub is to make sure the proper DLL is loaded before calling the "real" function inside it.

The first time an application calls *printf*, Windows loads CLIB.DLL into memory; but when subsequent applications call it, Windows merely increments a reference counter instead of loading a second instance. Only one instance of CLIB.DLL is ever loaded, and all programs share it.

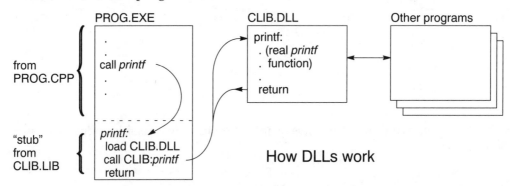

How DLLs work

While Windows doesn't use a DLL for the standard C library (*printf* and the rest are still compiled in, just like in DOS programs), it does use DLLs for the Windows API itself. Every Windows function (such as *CreateWindow, GetMessage*, etc.) resides in one of three DLLs: KERNEL.EXE, USER.EXE, or GDI.EXE. Each API function has only one incarnation, which all applications share.

DLLs provide other benefits besides sharing code. For example, by replacing a DLL, you can upgrade a code library without recompiling all the applications that use it. Microsoft can thus release a new GDI.EXE with bug fixes and enhancements, without requiring that existing applications be recompiled in order to use them. All users have to do is install GDI.EXE.[66]

DLLs can also be used to provide shareable resources such as dialog boxes and strings, not just code. For example, you could put all the dialog boxes and text messages for a text editor in a DLL, with separate versions for different languages. All a user would have to do to get a particular language is install the appropriate DLL. If someday you decide to support Swahili, all you'd have to do is translate the text, create a new SWAHILI.DLL, and ship it to your users.

Obviously, DLLs are neat stuff, and we want to use them for *Windows++*. Up until now, we've built *Windows++* as an ordinary old "static" link library. Each program we've built is linked with its own copy of *WPWin::createWin, ErrBox,* and all the other *Windows++* functions. This is why HELLO.EXE is over 58 kilobytes. If we ever expect to run more than one *Windows++* program at a time, this a waste of memory. If we convert *Windows++* into a dynamic link library, all our programs can share the same code. Even if we don't expect to run multiple *Windows++* appli-

---

66 Of course, this doesn't always work perfectly and can result in "versionitis" problems, where newer versions of the DLL don't always work with older applications.

cations, there are the still the other benefits mentioned. For example, we can provide enhancements and bug fixes to all *Windows++* applications simultaneously, simply by releasing a new DLL, without recompiling the applications.

So far, we've built reusable object modules. Dynamic link libraries let us build reusable executable modules.

Unfortunately, converting *Windows++* into a dynamic link library is easier said than done. As with so many things, it's easier to understand the basic idea than to implement the code. (Between the idea and the reality . . . falls the shadow.) Anyone who's ever attempted to create a dynamic link library knows that it can be a frustrating task—not because DLLs are difficult to understand, but because there are a few subtle restrictions they impose, as well as several magic compiler incantations that must be learned. On top of this, C++ creates additional DLL difficulties. But never fear, I'm here to serve as Virgil to your Dante; I'll do my best to guide you through the DLL inferno.

There's just one caveat: we'll take advantage of a number of special features provided by the Borland compiler that greatly simplify the creation of C++ DLLs. Unfortunately, the Zortech compiler does not provide analogous features (they no doubt will in a future release). For this reason, *Windows++* supports DLLs for Borland only. (Sorry, Zortech users.)[67]

As with all things, it's best to start small. Rather than attempt to convert the whole *Windows++* library in a single gigantic undertaking, we'll do it in three steps:

- First, we'll build a simple DLL that contains just one function, and a program that calls it.

- Next, we'll add C++ classes.

- Finally, we'll convert *Windows++* to a DLL.

The end result will be a dynamic link library WPP.DLL, which contains all our *Windows++* code in the form of executable subroutines, and a corresponding import library, WPP.LIB, with which to link applications.

9.2 DLL Basics

As our first task, we'll build a dynamic link library (ERRBOX.DLL) that contains just one function: *ErrBox*. This function displays a message box and accepts

---

67 It should be possible to build DLLs with Zortech, but difficult. You have to manually *_export* each member function, since Zortech doesn't support the shorthand for *_export*ing an entire class (see Section 9.3).

arguments in *printf* style (you may have noticed *ErrBox* throughout the code in earlier chapters):

```
#include <stdarg.h>

///////////////////
// This is a handy function for doing printf-style error boxes.
//
int ErrBox(CSTR format, ...)           // note variable argument list
{
    char buf[128];

    va_list argptr;                    // defined in <stdarg.h>
    va_start(argptr, format);          // ..
    vsprintf(buf, format, argptr);
    va_end(argptr);
    return MessageBox(NULL, buf, NULL, MB_OK | MB_ICONEXCLAMATION);
}
```

We'll also write a program that calls *ErrBox:*

```
// PROG.CPP
int PASCAL WinMain(HANDLE hinst, HANDLE pinst, LPSTR cmd, int show)
{
    time_t x = time(NULL) & 1;
    ErrBox("Something's rotten in %s\n", x ? "Denmark" : "Finland");
    return 0;
}
```

The purpose of ERRBOX and PROG is to review the basics of DLL programming. This will give us a chance to get warmed up before tackling the serious issues. Since most of the material is well-documented elsewhere, I'll simply review it here. If you're unfamiliar with DLLs, I encourage you to read either the SDK *Guide to Programming,* your compiler documentation, or a good Windows book.

9.2.1 Exporting DLL Functions

The first order of business when writing a DLL is to decide which functions you want to *export.* Only exported functions are callable from applications (DLLs may also contain internal, non-exported functions used only by the DLL). In our case the choice is easy, since there's just one: *ErrBox.*

There are two ways to export functions from a DLL:

- ■ You can declare the names of the exported functions in the EXPORTS section of the DLL's module definition (.DEF) file; or

- ■ you can use the *_export* modifier in the function declaration.

If you use the module definition file, you need to specify the mangled function names, which is extremely tedious unless you happen to be a C++ compiler: the only way to get the mangled names is from a .MAP file or other symbol listing. Using *_export* is much easier (almost essential in C++), so that's what we'll do:

```
// (In ERRBOX.H)
extern int _export ErrBox(const char* format, ...);
```

Actually, instead of writing *_export* directly in our source file, we'll introduce a macro, DLLFUNC, that's defined to *_export* if we're building a DLL and to an empty string otherwise:

```
// (In ERRBOX.H and WPPDEFS.H)
#if defined(__DLL__) || defined(USEDLL)
#define DLLFUNC _export
#else
#define DLLFUNC
#endif
```

__DLL__ is a built-in compiler symbol that's defined when building a DLL; USEDLL is a symbol that we'll define ourselves when we compile applications that use the DLL. Now instead of declaring exported functions with *_export*, we use DLLFUNC:

```
extern int DLLFUNC ErrBox(const char* format, ...);
```

The same macro must also be used in the function definition:

```
///////////////////
// Handy function for doing printf-style error boxes.
//
int DLLFUNC ErrBox(const char* format, ...)
{
    char buf[128];

    va_list argptr;
    va_start(argptr, format);
    vsprintf(buf, format, argptr);
    va_end(argptr);
    return MessageBox(NULL, buf, NULL, MB_OK | MB_ICONEXCLAMATION);
}
```

DLLFUNC is not required for ERRBOX, but don't forget that our ultimate goal is *Windows++*. We don't always want to build *Windows++* as a DLL; we still want to support ordinary static link libraries. (Why not?) DLLFUNC lets us do both. If we're building a DLL, all DLLFUNCs will get *_export*ed; otherwise, DLLFUNC has no effect. (Using *_export* in a static library is harmless, but inefficient.)

9.2.2 *LibMain* and *WEP*

Just as every Windows application must have a *WinMain* function, every DLL must have a *LibMain*. While a DLL doesn't "receive control" the same way an application does (it simply sits there, waiting to be called by some program), it must nevertheless provide a *LibMain* function. This function is called when the DLL is first loaded and provides an opportunity to perform any one-time initialization that may be required. Usually, *LibMain* unlocks the DLL's local heap (which starts out locked because Windows initializes it by calling *LocalInit* before *LibMain*). The typical vanilla *LibMain* function looks like this:

```
///////////////////
// DLL initialization routine,
// called by Windows when DLL is first loaded.
//
int FAR PASCAL
LibMain(HANDLE hinst, WORD ds, WORD heapsz, LPSTR cmdline)
{
    if (heapsz>0)
        UnlockData(0);
    return 1;
}
```

Windows passes four arguments to *LibMain:* the DLL's module instance handle, its data segment selector, the size of the DLL's local heap, and the command line string (to see how DLLs can get a command line, consult another reference). *LibMain* is expected to return an integer: 1 to indicate successful initialization or zero to indicate failure. If *LibMain* returns zero, Windows will unload the DLL.

With an application, when *WinMain* returns the program is "over," so Windows unloads it. With DLLs, however, the situation is different: when *LibMain* returns, the DLL remains loaded, waiting for an application to call it. The DLL stays resident in memory until Windows either shuts down entirely or decides to reclaim the memory that the DLL occupies (which it's guaranteed not to do as long as any program that uses the DLL is still running). Before actually killing the DLL, Windows calls another predefined function, *WEP* (Windows Exit Procedure), which every DLL must provide:

```
///////////////////
// DLL termination routine, called by Windows when DLL is unloaded.
// (In ERRBOX.CPP)
//
int FAR PASCAL WEP(int param)
{
    return 1;
}
```

Windows calls *WEP* with *param* set to either WEP_SYSTEMEXIT if Windows itself is shutting down, or WEP_FREE_DLL if only the DLL is being unloaded, so your *WEP* function can respond accordingly. (We won't have any occasion to use *param*.) *WEP* is supposed to return 1 to indicate success, but as with *WinMain*, Windows ignores the return value.

9.2.3 Choosing a Memory Model

Before compiling ERRBOX, we must choose a memory model. You can write DLLs for any memory model, but all exported functions in a DLL must necessarily be declared *far* since they reside in a different code segment from the applications that invoke them. All the problems associated with mixed model programming in C++

(see Section 4.1.2) still apply for DLLs, so we'll do the expedient thing: we'll compile the DLL using the large model.[68]

There's another reason for using the large model, which has to do with the infamous SS != DS problem. This problem is discussed at great length elsewhere (see [Petzold 1990] for a good explanation), but it's an important issue, and one that comes up again later, so let's review it briefly.

The problem arises from the fact that DLLs don't have their own stack but use the calling program's stack. In normal DOS and Windows programs, the stack (which includes automatic variables), static data, and the local heap are all allocated from the same data segment (called DGROUP). Under the Intel 80x86 architecture, the stack is addressed relative to the SS register, while static data is addressed relative to DS. Since both the stack and static data live in the same segment, SS = DS for "normal" programs.

In a DLL, however, the situation is different. A DLL has its own data segment, but has no stack. DLLs use the calling program's stack. This makes perfect sense if you think about it: DLL functions are supposed to act like ordinary subroutines, as if they had been linked with the application at compile time. Thus, in a DLL, SS should point to the calling program's stack. In fact, it does, but DS still points to the DLL's data segment. In short, SS != DS.

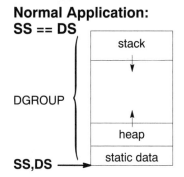

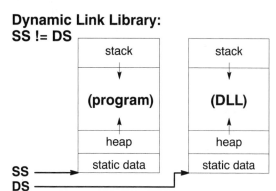

So why should you care that SS != DS? Because many functions implicitly assume that SS = DS. For example, consider the following situation in the medium model:

```
// In FOO.DLL
int len = strlen("Hello");

// strlen from standard C library, statically linked with FOO.DLL
int strlen(const char* s)
{
```

---

68 Note that, whereas with applications we have to worry about the large model multiple instance limitation (see Section 4.1.2), with DLLs we don't. The whole point of a DLL is that it has only one instance, regardless of how many programs use it.

```
    int len = 0;
    while (*s++)
        len++;
    return len;
}
```

Since "Hello" is a static string, it lives in the DLL's data segment and is addressed relative to DS. But the variable *s* in *strlen* is a stack variable, addressed relative to SS. For normal programs, this is OK since SS = DS; but in DLLs, SS != DS and the program won't work (*s* won't point to "Hello").

The SS != DS problem only arises in the medium and small models, where *near* pointers are used, and addresses are implicitly relative to SS or DS; in the large and compact models, all data pointers are *far* and explicitly contain their data segment selectors. While it's possible to circumvent the SS != DS problem even in the medium model, it's a lot simpler and more expedient to simply use the large model.

Which is the other reason for choosing the large model for our DLL.

9.2.4 Compiling ERRBOX

We're now ready to put the ERRBOX application together. We've written most of the code; all that remains are the compilation details. There are three files: ERR-BOX.H, ERRBOX.CPP and PROG.CPP. Here's the first:

```
//////////////////////////////////////////////////////////////
// WINDOWS++ CLASS LIBRARY.  Copyright 1992 Paul DiLascia.
// FILE: ERRBOX.H
//
// Declaration for only one DLL function: ErrBox

#include <windows.h>

#ifdef __DLL__
#define DLLFUNC _export
#else
#define DLLFUNC
#endif

extern int DLLFUNC ErrBox(const char* format, ...);
```

Here's ERRBOX.CPP:

```
//////////////////////////////////////////////////////////////
// WINDOWS++ CLASS LIBRARY.  Copyright 1992 Paul DiLascia.
// FILE: ERRBOX.CPP
//
// Simple DLL exports one function: ErrBox

#include "errbox.h"
#include <stdio.h>
#include <stdarg.h>
```

```
/////////////////
// DLL initialization routine, called by Windows when DLL is loaded.
//
int FAR PASCAL LibMain(HANDLE h, WORD ds, WORD heapsz, LPSTR cmd)
{
    if (heapsz>0)
        UnlockData(0);
    return 1;
}

/////////////////
// DLL termination routine, called by Windows when DLL is unloaded.
//
int FAR PASCAL WEP(int param)
{
    return 1;
}

/////////////////
// Handy function for doing printf-style error boxes.
//
int DLLFUNC ErrBox(const char* format, ...)
{
    char buf[128];

    va_list argptr;
    va_start(argptr, format);
    vsprintf(buf, format, argptr);
    va_end(argptr);
    return MessageBox(NULL, buf, NULL, MB_OK | MB_ICONEXCLAMATION);
}
```

The following command compiles ERRBOX:

```
bcc -ml -WDE -lC errbox.cpp
```

The Borland C++ compiler switch –WDE tells the compiler to produce a Windows DLL instead of a .EXE file, and to export all *exported* functions (–WD exports *all far* functions). Using –WDE also causes the compiler to define the special symbol __DLL__, which makes our DLLFUNC macro expand to _export. The –lC switch tells the linker to treat the exported DLL function names as case-sensitive. When the *bcc* command is executed, the compiler creates the DLL as a file called ERRBOX.DLL.

Next, we have to build the import library. Recall that this is an ordinary static link library that contains stubs for each exported DLL function. The stubs are linked with the application and, when called, perform the necessary magic to invoke the "real" DLL function. The import library is created by the special utility *implib*:

```
implib errbox.lib errbox.dll
```

This command creates ERRBOX.LIB from ERRBOX.DLL.

So much for ERRBOX; now let's compile PROG. Here's the full program:

```
//////////////////////////////////////////////////////////
// WINDOWS++ CLASS LIBRARY.  Copyright 1992 Paul DiLascia.
// FILE: PROG.CPP
//
// WinMain function calls ErrBox in DLL.
#include "errbox.h"
#include <time.h>
int PASCAL WinMain(HANDLE hinst, HANDLE pinst, LPSTR cmd, int show)
{
    time_t x = time(NULL) & 1;
    ErrBox("Something's rotten in %s\n", x ? "Denmark" : "Finland");
    return 0;
}
```

And here's the command to compile it:

```
bcc -ml -1C -WE -WS -DUSEDLL prog.cpp errbox.lib
```

This time we use –WE and –WS, since PROG is an application, not a DLL. The only thing new is that we define the symbol USEDLL. This is so that DLLFUNC will expand to _export. Since we don't use the –WD switch, __DLL__ is not defined. But we still want PROG to know that *ErrBox* is an exported function that resides in the DLL, so we define USEDLL. Finally, of course, we link PROG with the import library ERRBOX.LIB.

To invoke PROG, we can type

```
win prog
```

or create an icon for it and then double-click the icon in the usual Windows manner. The only requirement is that ERRBOX.DLL must reside somewhere in Windows' search path.

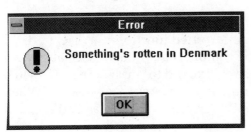

(Or perhaps something's rotten in Finland.)

9.3 Classes

Now that our minds are buzzing with thoughts of DLLs, we're ready to tackle the next problem: adding classes. This is complicated by the fact that classes may be split between the DLL and the application. For example, our HELLO program derives its main window (*HelloWin*) from *WPMainWin,* which we plan to put in the DLL. The inherited *HelloWin* functions (*WPWin::createWin,* etc.) reside in the

DLL, while the rest (*HelloWin::paint*, etc) reside in the application. As you'll see, this creates a slight problem, one that's easily overcome as long as you know the right compiler incantations.

In order to highlight the relevant details, we'll build another small application, a DLL that exports one class:

```
// (In DLL.H)
class Base {
    virtual void displayMsg();
public:
    void display();
};

// (In DLL.CPP)
void Base::displayMsg()
{
    MsgBox("Hello from DLL.");
}

void Base::display()
{
    displayMsg();
}
```

Then we'll write an application that derives a subclass from *Base:*

```
// (In APP.CPP)
class Derived : public Base {
    void displayMsg()                      { MsgBox("Hello from APP."); }
};

int PASCAL WinMain(HANDLE hinst, HANDLE pinst, LPSTR cmd, int show)
{
    Base     baseClassInstance;         // create instance of base class
    Derived  derivedClassInstance;      // create instance of derived class

    Base *p = &baseClassInstance;
    p->display();                       // should invoke DLL
    p = &derivedClassInstance;
    p->display();                       // should invoke APP

    return 0;
}
```

The purpose of DLL and APP is to illustrate the programming mechanics required to create DLLs with classes. You should think of *Base* as representing *Windows++* classes such as *WPMainWin*, and *Derived* as representing application-specific derived subclasses such as *HelloWin*.

9.3.1 Classes in the DLL

In theory, adding classes to a DLL is no big deal. Class member functions are just like any other functions that we might export, such as *ErrBox*. All we have to do is go through all our header files and _*export* every class member function using DLLFUNC. Ugh! That's a lot of typing. Moreover, we'd have to remember to do it every time we add a new library function. Fortunately, Borland provides a way to _export an entire class in one fell swoop:

```
class _export Base {
    .
    .
    .
};
```

This tells the compiler to export all class member functions for *Base*. (It also tells it to use *far* pointers for member functions and virtual function tables, but that's moot for us since we're using the large model.)[69] Instead of using *_export* directly, we'll pull the same trick that we used for functions:

```
// (In DLL.H and WPPDEFS.H)
#if defined(__DLL__) || defined(USEDLL)
#define DLLFUNC _export
#define DLLCLASS class _export
#else
#define DLLFUNC
#define DLLCLASS class
#endif
```

Now, instead of adding DLLFUNC everywhere, we only have to change every exported DLL class to DLLCLASS:

```
// (In DLL.H)
DLLCLASS Base {
    virtual void displayMsg();
public:
    void display();
};
```

Like DLLFUNC, DLLCLASS lets us use the same source files to build *Windows++* as either a dynamic or a static link library.

9.3.2 Classes in the Application

So much for exporting DLL classes; now let's tackle derived classes in the application. You might wonder why we have to do anything. Once the DLL classes are exported, why can't we just use them, the way we use *ErrBox* in PROG.CPP? Good question, but there is in fact a problem. It only arises when the class has virtual functions. To see just what it is, let's take a closer look at APP and DLL:

```
// (In DLL.H)
DLLCLASS Base {
    virtual void displayMsg();
public:
    void display();
};
```

---

69 Using *_export* for a class even exports static class data, such as *WPWin::createArgs*.

```
// (In DLL.CPP)
void Base::display()
{
    displayMsg();
}
// (In APP.CPP)
class Derived : public Base {
    void displayMsg()              { MsgBox("Hello from APP."); }
};
```

When *Base::display* (which resides in the DLL) invokes the virtual function *displayMsg*, it should invoke the version of *displayMsg* for whichever class the object (*this*) really is. If it's an instance of *Base, Base::displayMsg* should be invoked; if it's an instance of *Derived, Derived::displayMsg* should be invoked. But *Derived::displayMsg* lives in the application.

The problem is that if the DLL calls a virtual function that resides in the application, the call crosses a module boundary. When control passes to the application, DS will still point to the DLL's data segment, which is definitely bad news.

Here's another way to look at it: normally (that is, in C applications), DLLs only export functions to applications, but with virtual functions, it's as though the application were exporting functions to the DLL.

The situation is the same as that which arises when you use a callback function. Recall that any function whose address you pass to Windows in the expectation of having it called back (for example, a window procedure) must be have a special prolog. So far, we've handled such callback functions by _exporting them and using the –WE compiler switch to make the compiler generate the special Windows prolog, and by using –WS ("smart" callbacks) to load DS from SS.

This observation (that virtual functions are just like callback functions) points the way to a solution. All we have to do is _export the application class.[70] That way, the class member functions will get the "smart" prolog that loads DS from SS (which still works because in the DLL, SS = the application's SS = the application's DS.)

The upshot is that any application class derived from a DLL class must be exported. Since this is only necessary for applications that actually use the DLL, we'll introduce yet another macro (this is the last one):

```
// (In DLL.H and WPPDEFS.H)
#if defined(USEDLL)
#define APPCLASS class _export
#else
#define APPCLASS class
#endif
```

---

70 We really only need export the functions that are virtual, but it's easier and less error-prone to simply export the entire class.

APPCLASS expands to *class _export* if we're compiling an application for use with the DLL; otherwise it's just *class*. As mentioned before, we'll define USEDLL when compiling an application that uses the DLL (as opposed to the normal static link library). Now, everywhere our applications derive a class from a DLL class, we must use APPCLASS instead of *class*. For example

```
// (In APP.CPP)
APPCLASS Derived : public Base {
    void displayMsg()                    { MsgBox("Hello from APP."); }
};
```

And likewise in the HELLO program:

```
// (In HELLO.CPP)
APPCLASS HelloWin : public WPMainWin {
    .
    .
};
```

9.3.3 Compiling DLL and APP

The full DLL program is shown below:

```
///////////////////////////////////////////////////////////
// WINDOWS++ CLASS LIBRARY.  Copyright 1992 Paul DiLascia.
// FILE: DLL.H
//
// Sample DLL application using classes.

#include <windows.h>

#if defined(__DLL__) || defined(USEDLL)
#define DLLFUNC _export
#define DLLCLASS class _export
#else
#define DLLFUNC
#define DLLCLASS class
#endif

#if defined(USEDLL)
#define APPCLASS class _export
#else
#define APPCLASS class
#endif

DLLCLASS Base {
    virtual void displayMsg();
public:
    void display();
};
DLLFUNC MsgBox(LPSTR text, LPSTR caption="", int type=MB_OK);
```

Here's DLL.CPP:

```
///////////////////////////////////////////////////////////
// WINDOWS++ CLASS LIBRARY.  Copyright 1992 Paul DiLascia.
// FILE: DLL.CPP
//
// Sample program demonstrates how to build DLLs with classes.
```

```
#include "dll.h"
int DLLFUNC MsgBox(LPSTR text, LPSTR caption, int type)
{
    return MessageBox(NULL, text, caption, type);
}
void Base::displayMsg()
{
    MsgBox("Hello from DLL.");
}
void Base::display()
{
    displayMsg();
}
int FAR PASCAL LibMain(HANDLE h, WORD ds, WORD heapsz, LPSTR cmd)
{
    if (heapsz>0)
        UnlockData(0);
    return 1;
}
int FAR PASCAL WEP(int param)
{
    return 1;
}
```

And here's APP:

```
/////////////////////////////////////////////////////////
// WINDOWS++ CLASS LIBRARY.  Copyright 1992 Paul DiLascia.
// FILE: APP.CPP
//
// Sample program demonstrates how to build DLLs with classes.
#include "dll.h"
///////////////////////
// Class is derived from base class in DLL.
//
APPCLASS Derived : public Base {
    void displayMsg()                { MsgBox("Hello from APP."); }
};
int PASCAL WinMain(HANDLE hinst, HANDLE pinst, LPSTR cmd, int show)
{
    Base baseClassInstance;        // create instance of base class
    Derived derivedClassInstance;  // create instance of derived class

    Base *p = &baseClassInstance;
    p->display();                  // should invoke DLL
    p = &derivedClassInstance;
    p->display();                  // should invoke APP

    return 0;
}
```

Note that APP.CPP includes DLL.H, which contains the definitions and prototypes for classes and functions exported by the DLL.

The compilation details are the same as for ERRBOX. Here's the make file:

```
CL=bcc
DLLFLAGS= -ml -WDE
APPFLAGS= -ml -WE -WS -DUSEDLL

.cpp.obj:
    $(CL) -c $(DLLFLAGS) $*

app.exe: dll.lib app.cpp
    $(CL) -1C $(APPFLAGS) $*.cpp dll.lib

dll.lib: dll.dll
    implib dll.lib dll.dll

dll.dll: dll.cpp
    $(CL) -1C $(DLLFLAGS) $*.cpp
```

When you run APP, you'll see the following message boxes, in succession:

This proves that our virtual functions work correctly. If you're curious, you might try compiling APP without using APPCLASS and see what happens.

9.4 DLL-ing *Windows*++

So far, we've figured out how to export functions and classes from DLLs and how to use them in applications. This covers the mechanics of building DLLs, which you could have figured out yourself by reading your compiler manual. Now we're ready to deal with real issues.

From the preceding two sections, you might think all we had to do is write *LibMain* and *WEP*, add DLLFUNC, DLLCLASS, and APPCLASS macros everywhere, then simply recompile everything with the proper compiler switches.

You're right, we have to do all that, but that's not enough.

For example, where do we put *LibMain* and *WEP*? We need a new module, just like we have WINMAIN for *WinMain*. OK, consider it done: we'll put *LibMain* and *WEP* in LIBMAIN.CPP and link it with the DLL (we'll still link WINMAIN with the application).

That one was easy. The other problems are not so trivial. There are three in all; each is addressed in a separate section.

9.4.1 The Application Object

The first problem has to do with our application object. Recall that each of our *Windows++* programs contains a global *App* object that represents the application. This global object is used by several library functions. For example, *createWin* uses it to set *createArgs.wndcls.hInstance* to the module instance handle:

```
BOOL WPWin::createWin(...)
{
    .
    .
    createArgs.wndcls.hInstance = App();
    .
    .
}
```

Likewise, *WPMainWin* initializes the main window icon by loading the predefined application resource "AppIcon":

```
WPMainWin::WPMainWin() : WPWin("MAINWIN")
{
    .
    .
    createArgs.wndcls.hIcon = App.loadIcon("AppIcon");
    if (createArgs.wndcls.hIcon==NULL)
        createArgs.wndcls.hIcon = App.loadIcon(IDI_APPLICATION);
}
```

These functions now reside in the *Windows++* DLL, so where does *App* come from? *App* is instantiated in WINMAIN, which is not linked with the DLL. You might think the DLL should have its own *App* (after all, it's a module too). But if you think it through, you'll see that this doesn't work. When *WPWin* calls *App()* to get the module instance handle, we want the module instance handle for the application, not the DLL. Likewise, we want to load the icon from the application. In general, *App* everywhere represents the application, not the DLL. But there might be several *Windows++* applications running at once—HELLO, TOE, and MANDEL— how can the DLL know which *App* object to use?

Believe it or not, there is a way. The key is that a DLL always uses the stack from whichever program is calling it. When the DLL is running, the SS register points to the calling application's stack segment, which is the same as its data segment. The SS register thus provides a "hook" to identify the application using the DLL.

But how can we use it?

Instead of using a single *App* object, the DLL will maintain a list of *App* objects for all *Windows++* applications that are running. We'll store each application's data segment selector in its *App* object, so the DLL can look up the *App* whose data segment matches the value in SS. The details are fleshed out as follows.

First, we'll define a few more assembly language macros in WPHEAP.H:

```
#define GETDS(var)              asm { mov ax, ds; mov var, ax; }
#define GETSS(var)              asm { mov ax, ss; mov var, ax; }
#define GETAPPDS GETSS
```

GETDS and GETSS simply get the current value of the DS or SS register, respectively. For example, after executing

```
WORD dsval;
GETDS(dsval);
```

dsval contains the segment selector for the current data segment (DS register). GETSS does the same for SS. GETAPPDS is #*define*d to GETSS, because the application's data segment is always stored in SS, whether the application or the DLL has control: in the application, SS = DS = the application's data segment; whereas in a DLL, SS = the application's SS = the application's DS. (Amazing, isn't it?)

Next, we need a place to store the application's data segment in the *App* object:

```
// (In WPAPP.H)
DLLCLASS WPApp : public WPModule {
private:
    WORD dsval;                    // app's data segment
public:
    WPApp();
};
```

dsval is initialized in the constructor:

```
// (In WPAPP.CPP)
WPApp::WPApp()
{
    // store application's data segment
    WORD temp;
    GETAPPDS(temp);
    dsval = temp;
}
```

(The subterfuge with *temp* is required because the assembler knows nothing about C++. In particular, that *dsval* is really *this->dsval*. It can only parse *mov var, ax* if *var* is an ordinary stack or static variable.)

With the application's data segment safely tucked away inside *App* (automatically, without our programs having to do anything), we can now worry about how each application object can make itself "known" to the DLL. To do this, we'll have each *App* object automatically "register" itself when it's constructed, and unregister itself when it's destroyed. Here are the modifications to *WPApp*:

```
// (In WPAPP.H)
DLLCLASS WPApp : public WPModule {
private:
    static WPApp* registeredApps      // list of all registered apps
    WPApp *next;                      // next registered app
public:
    WPApp();
    ~WPApp();
};
```

```
// (In WPPAPP.CPP)
WPApp* WPApp::registeredApps = NULL;


/////////////////
// Construct new application object.
// Register the application in the global list "registeredApps".
//
WPApp::WPApp()
{
    // Store application's data segment (as before).
    WORD temp;
    GETAPPDS(temp);
    dsval = temp;

    // Register app with DLL: chain to list.
    next = registeredApps;
    registeredApps = this;
}


/////////////////
// Destroy application object: "unregister" the app.
//
WPApp::~WPApp()
{
    .
    . (as before)
    .
    // Unregister the app with the DLL.
    if (registeredApps == this)
        registeredApps = next;
    else {
        for (WPApp *app = registeredApps; app; app = app->next) {
            if (app->next == this) {
                app->next = next;
                break;
            }
        }
        assert(app);                    // Should always find it!
    }
}
```

The constructor adds the *App* object to the list of *registeredApps;* the destructor re-moves it. We're almost home. All that remains is to modify the DLL so that wher-ever it references *App,* it somehow invokes the calling application's *App.* Do to this, we'll need a function to retrieve the correct *App* object from the list:

```
// (In WPAPP.H)
DLLCLASS WPApp : public WPModule {
public:
    static WPApp* GetApp();             // get current app
};
```

```
/////////////////
// (In WPAPP.CPP)
// Get the application object for the calling application.
// We use the fact that SS==caller's DS.
//
WPApp* WPApp::GetApp()
{
    WORD dsval;
    GETAPPDS(dsval);                    // get application's data seg selector

    // Search list to find application
    for (WPApp *app = registeredApps; app; app = app->next) {
        if (app->dsval == dsval)
            return app;
    }
    assert(FALSE);                      // should always find it!
    return NULL;
}
```

GetApp simply searches the list of registered applications for the one whose DS value matches the caller's DS. Now, everywhere our code references *App.xxx,* we must change it to invoke *WPApp::GetApp()->xxx* instead. Rather than edit a lot of code, it's easier to simply redefine the symbol *App:*

```
// (In WPAPP.H)
#ifdef __DLL__
#define App (*WPApp::GetApp())
#else
extern WPApp App;
#endif
```

If we're compiling the DLL, *App* will expand to *(*WPApp::GetApp())*, which is precisely what we want; but if we're compiling an application, or *Windows++* as a static library, *App* is a static global just like it's been all along, before we started this whole DLL mess. In short, the symbol *App* always represents the application. (We could always define *App* to *(*WPApp::GetApp())*, but that would be inefficient; if we know there's only one *App*, why call a function to get it?)

To see how all this works in practice, let's examine a how typical application like HELLO now uses the DLL. When we compile HELLO, we'll link it with WIN-MAIN (like we've been doing all along), which contains the static object *App*.

- When Windows invokes HELLO, the C++ start-up code first calls the constructors for all static objects (before invoking *WinMain*). In particular, it calls the *WPApp* constructor to initialize *App.*[71]

---

71 Windows gurus will detect an analogy between the *WPApp* constructor and the *InitInstance* or *InitAppInstance* function that so many Windows programs provide to initialize each instance of the application. Exactly! What is the *WPApp* constructor, if not the function that initializes the application instance? *App* is an instance of an application! The nice thing about C++ is that static constructors are called automatically, so programmers don't have to remember to do it.

- The *WPApp* constructor lives in the DLL, so control passes there. The constructor first sets *dsval* to the application's data segment selector, which it gets from SS (via GETAPPDS), then adds *App* to the list of registered applications. HELLO's *App* object is now registered with the DLL.

- Now, whenever a DLL function like *createWin* or the *WPMainWin* constructor invokes *App*, it really invokes *GetApp*, which looks up the correct *App* object for whichever application is calling the DLL. (The look-up relies on the fact that, in a DLL, SS = the application's DS.)

- If an application function refers to *App*, it invokes the static global object itself (the instance in WINMAIN), not *GetApp* (but *App* is the same application object that *GetApp* would return).

- When HELLO terminates, the C++ exit code calls the *App* destructor (which also lives in the DLL); it removes *App* from the list of registered applications.

Every program's *App* object is automatically registered with the DLL as soon as the program starts (even before *WinMain* receives control), and unregistered when it terminates. In this way, our *Windows*++ DLL now supports many applications, each one with its very own *App* object. The DLL itself doesn't even have an *App* object, which makes perfect sense: the DLL is not an application, it's a DLL.

C *In C++, we use the* WPApp *constructor and destructor to initialize and terminate each application, and in particular, to register and unregister applications with the DLL. In C you'd do it in* AppInitInstance *and* AppTermInstance *functions, which you'd call from* WinMain *or some other suitable place. The DLL would still maintain a list of registered applications and have a function like* GetApp *to get the calling application's* App *object (which, in C, would be an ordinary* struct*).*

9.4.2 Object Ownership

The second problem we must worry about is *object ownership*. Whenever you write a DLL, you'd better have a clear understanding of who allocates and frees which objects, the application or the DLL. For example, if our DLL needs some storage, it calls *new*. But where does the storage come from? The application's local heap, the DLL's local heap, or global memory? What if the storage is allocated by the application but freed by the DLL, as is the case with window objects? (Remember, our programs create their windows by calling *new*; but the windows are destroyed automatically in *WPWndProc* when the window gets a WM_DESTROY message.)

The problem of object ownership can be troublesome but the way we've handled *App* makes it simply disappear! If you recall, our fancy memory allocation system (from Chapter 4) is based entirely on a handful of memory allocation functions (*farAlloc* and the rest), all of which belong to *WPApp*. You may have wondered at the time why this was done; I gave some feeble reason then, but the real reason is that by doing so, we automatically handle DLL object ownership correctly!

Back in Chapter 4, we implemented our own *new* and *delete* operators:

```
void * operator new(size_t size)        // (In WINMAIN.CPP)
{
#ifdef __LARGE__
    return App.farAlloc(size);
#else
    return App.localAlloc(size);
#endif
}

void operator delete(void *ptr)
{
#ifdef __LARGE__
    App.farFree(ptr);
#else
    App.localFree(ptr);
#endif
}
```

Since all memory is allocated from *App*, which always represents the application, all we have to is copy these functions to LIBMAIN.CPP. Since the DLL is always compiled under the large model, we don't even need *#ifdef*:

```
// (In LIBMAIN.CPP)
void * operator new(size_t size)
{
    return App.farAlloc(size);
}

void operator delete(void *ptr)
{
    if (ptr)
        App.farFree(ptr);
}
```

Now every time the DLL allocates storage, it allocates it from the application; and every time it frees an object, it returns it to the calling application. The DLL never owns any storage at all. It can only allocate and free storage from some application. This is the real reason for making *farAlloc* and the rest. member functions of *WPApp*. It makes sense: logically, every *Windows++* object belongs to some application, never to the DLL itself.[72]

---

72 It's conceivable that the DLL might want to own objects of its own. For example, it might create some sort of table or other data structure in *LibMain*, when the DLL is first loaded. This could be accommodated by giving the DLL an application object. For example, by declaring a global object *Dll*:

WPApp Dll; // in LIBMAIN.CPP

the DLL could then explicitly allocate storage from it using *Dll.farAlloc*, etc.

9.4.3 An Obscure Bug

The last DLL problem is an obscure flaw in our implementation of *new* and *delete*. I didn't discover it until I started using all this DLL stuff with the PEOPLE program described in Chapter 7 (at which point I had to add this section). If it's late, you're getting tired and impatient, and you hate memory management, skip this section; but if you love exploring the sublime nuances of C++ and Windows, read on.

In case anyone is still reading, the problem first surfaced when I wrote a DLL program that uses C++ stream i/o, though it has nothing particular to do with i/o *per se*. By writing our own *new* and *delete* operators, we replace the standard C++ operators for all modules that are linked with our programs. Any linked module that calls *new* will call our version. Now, this shouldn't cause a problem if we implement *new* and *delete* correctly. After all, these operators are well-documented and straightforward—*new* allocates a chunk of storage of a given size and returns a pointer to the storage; *delete* frees it.

But there is in fact a flaw with our *new* operator: it depends on the application object being initialized. To see why, consider what happens the first time *new* is invoked: *new* calls *App.farAlloc*, which resides in the DLL. The first time *farAlloc* is invoked, a new heap is required, so *farAlloc* invokes *MemHeap::new*, which in turn calls *App.localAlloc* (remember, the heaps themselves are always allocated from the local heap). But in the DLL, *App* is really a call to *GetApp*—which will fail to find the application object if it's not registered yet. Normally, this can't happen, because *App* is registered by its constructor, which is invoked by the C++ start-up code, even before *WinMain*. But what if the C++ start-up code itself were to call *new*? Then the *App* allocation functions would be invoked before *App* is registered.

This is precisely what happens with programs that use the C++ standard i/o library. This library contains initialization code that gets linked with our application. The initialization code calls *new* (our version), before *App* is initialized. *GetApp* fails to find the application object and crashes with an assertion failure. The problem only occurs in programs that use the DLL, because only in the DLL does *App* invoke *GetApp*; in the static version of the library, *App* is *App* (is *App)*.

Boy, life sure is tough.

Essentially, what we want is for our fancy memory management scheme to take effect when the application object is registered, and not before. The simplest way to do this is to allocate memory directly from the global heap until the application is initialized. The following modifications do the trick:

```
// (In WPAPP.H)
DLLCLASS WPApp : public WPModule {
private:
   BOOL   registered;              // Whether registered or not
};
```

```
// (In WPAPP.CPP)
WPApp::WPApp(FARPROC wndproc, FARPROC dlgproc)
{
    .
    .
    .
    registered = TRUE;
}
void FAR * WPApp::farAlloc(. . .)
{
    do {
        if (size >= HEAPSIZE || useGlobal || !registered) {

            .. (allocate from global heap as before) ..

        }
        .. (allocate from MemHeap before) ..
}
```

The *registered* flag marks whether the application object is registered or not; *farAlloc* uses it to allocate memory directly from the global heap if the application is not registered. This fixes the problem, since *farAlloc* can allocate memory without first "finding" the application to allocate it from, and *farFree* likewise "knows" how to free global memory correctly without looking for *App* (see Section 4.2.6).

Unfortunately, now our object bookkeeping is all screwed up, because when the destructor ~*WPApp* is called, some objects may legitimately remain. Objects allocated before the constructor haven't been freed yet. Fortunately, this is easy to fix: *App* simply records how many objects have already been allocated when it's initialized, and the destructor checks that no more than this number remain unfreed. The changes are straightforward, so I'll spare you the details (see Appendix A).

The same problem with *farAlloc* also exists with *localAlloc*: it depends on the *localHeap* having been initialized with the application's data segment, which is normally done by the constructor. Here's the fix:

```
void* WPApp::localAlloc(WORD size, BOOL useNoMemHandler)
{
    if (!registered) {
        // if start-up code calls new before App constructor,
        // initialize the local heap manually
        WORD temp;
        GETAPPDS(temp);
        localHeap.seg = temp;
    }
    .. (as before) ..
}
```

This bug illustrates two important points:

- While it's extremely useful to use static constructors to initialize your program before it even receives control, you must be careful about the order in which things happen, because it is possible that an object member function will be invoked before its constructor.

- You must be extremely careful when replacing *new* and *delete*, because you never know who else calls them. (The same holds for *malloc* and *free* in C programs.)

9.4.4 Miscellaneous Details

There are a few other minor modifications required to finish transforming *Windows*++ into a DLL. Most of them are the sort of thing that you only discover through trial and error, but are easy to fix once found. Rather than describe each one in gory detail, I'll simply list them:

- *WPWin::GetWin*, which now resides in the DLL, must be modified to use GETAPPDS instead of GETDS. Recall that this function recreates the 32-bit window object pointer from its 16-bit offset (which is stored in the window property list) by using DS as the segment. GETAPPDS ensures that it's the application's DS, not the DLL's.

- The universal window and dialog procedures (*WPWndProc* and *WPDlgProc*) are now moved to WINMAIN, which is linked with the application. This is required so we can continue to use the –WS (smart callbacks) compiler switch to avoid *MakeProcInstance*. –WS cannot be used for DLLs, since the "smart" prolog assumes SS = DS. Instead, we leave *WPWndProc* and *WPDlgProc* in the application. Since these functions are tiny, the slight increase in code size is worth the performance gained by avoiding *MakeProcInstance*. The addresses of *WPWndProc* and *WPDlgProc* are now stored in the *App* object, so the DLL can obtain them.

- We have the same problem with the global objects *Mouse, Keyboard,* etc. that we did with *App*. These objects are instantiated in WINMAIN, which is linked with the application. So how can the DLL access them? We could do the same thing that we did with *App*, but that's too much trouble. Since the global objects don't actually contain any data, but are merely syntactic placeholders, there's no harm in instantiating them twice: once in the application (in WINMAIN.CPP) and again in the DLL (in LIBMAIN.CPP).

- As an added feature, I changed the *showStats* function from Section 4.2.11 to display memory statistics for all applications registered with the DLL. (Formerly, it displayed the memory statistics for just the running application.) Since *showStats* is part of the DLL, why not run down the whole list of registered applications and display statistics for each one? To try it, just start up several *Windows*++ applications and type *Control–Z* at one of them.

The details can be found in the source listing in Appendix A.

9.4.5 Building the DLL

With all the problems out of the way, all that remains is to actually build the DLL. Here's the relevant fragment from the make file:

```
MODEL=1
WINFLAGS= -WDE

!ifdef USEDLL
DEFINES=$(DEFINES) -DUSEDLL
!endif

CL = bcc
CFLAGS = -a -c -w-par -m$(MODEL) $(WINFLAGS) $(DEFINES) $(ENVFLAGS)

WPPOBJ = WPAPP.obj WPCTRL.OBJ WPDLFILE.obj WPDLG.obj WPDLPRT.obj \
    WPDLSTR.obj WPGDI.obj WPGLOB.obj WPHEAP.obj WPMAIN.obj WPMDI.obj \
    WPMENU.obj WPODRAW.obj WPRECT.obj WPWIN.obj GPP.OBJ

.cpp.obj:
    $(CL) $(CFLAGS) $*

obj: $(WPPOBJ)

wpp.dll: $(WPPOBJ) libmain.obj
    tlink -Twd -C -c $(ENVFLAGS) c0dl -s @dll.rsp
    make USEDLL=1 MODEL=1 winmain.obj
    implib $*.lib $*.dll
    tlib $*.lib /C +WINMAIN,$*.1st
    del $*.bak

wpp.lib: $(WPPOBJ) winmain.obj
    del $*.lib
    tlib $*.lib/C @lib.rsp
```

Most of this should be familiar from APP and DLL. The main difference is that we have many more object modules, so the library and linker commands are bundled into separate response files LIB.RSP and DLL.RSP, which looks like this:

```
LIBMAIN WPAPP WPCTRL WPDLFILE WPDLG WPDLPRT WPDLSTR WPGDI WPGLOB+
WPHEAP WPMAIN WPMDI WPMENU WPODRAW WPRECT GPP+
WPWIN,wpp,wpp,cwl import commdlg,wpp.def
```

(LIB.RSP is in Appendix A). The only other trick is that, after building the import library WPP.LIB, we add WINMAIN.OBJ to it. The import library is no different from any other static link library, so we can add object modules to it. By putting WINMAIN in WPP.LIB, we link it with the application rather than the DLL. (It will get pulled in to resolve *WinMain, App, new,* and *delete.*)

9.5 Summary

It wasn't easy, but we've successfully converted *Windows++* to a DLL. Here's a quick review of what we did:

- In order to simplify things, we decided to build the DLL using the large model. We can still build *Windows++* as a medium or large model static link library.

■ A new module, LIBMAIN.CPP, contains *LibMain* and *WEP*, as well as copies of *new, delete,* and the global objects, such as *Mouse.*

■ DLL functions and classes are exported using the macros DLLFUNC and DLLCLASS. These macros give us the option of building *Windows*++ as a dynamic or static link library.

■ Application classes that are derived from library classes are also exported using a similar macro, APPCLASS, which expands to *class _export* when the symbol USEDLL is defined and remains just *class* otherwise. USEDLL is set when compiling applications that use the DLL; applications that use the static library are compiled with USEDLL undefined.

■ The major problem we had converting *Windows*++ to a DLL was dealing with the application object, *App.* To solve it, we modified the DLL to store a list of "registered" applications. Each application is registered when it starts up, and is unregistered when it terminates; the registration and unregistration are performed automatically by the static *App* constructor and destructor. The symbol *App* is redefined in the DLL so that instead of referring to a global object, it invokes a function that looks up the correct *App* object using the trick that SS = the application's DS.

■ Most importantly, we converted *Windows*++ to a DLL without modifying existing applications, except to change *class* to APPCLASS. The same applications can be used with either the dynamic or static library, simply by compling them with the symbol USEDLL defined or not.

While building DLLs is mostly a mechanical feat to get the proper function declarations and compiler switches, object-oriented programming helps out even here. By encapsulating memory management and other functionality in the application object, we've greatly simplified the task of writing DLLs. In particular, we have an elegant way to deal with object ownership. We've also made good use of the *App* constructor to perform a lot of initialization, automatically and invisibly to our programs.

Now we can go back and recompile all the programs we've written (HELLO, MKC, TOE, WINEDIT, MEDIT, MANDEL, DRAW, etc.) with USEDLL defined, so they can all share the same executable code in WPP.DLL. Here's a table showing the sizes before and after DLL-ing *Windows*++:

Program	Static	DLL
DRAW.EXE	78848	27648
HELLO.EXE	62464	14848
MANDEL.EXE	90624	48128
MEDIT.EXE	73216	22016
MEMTEST.EXE	54784	14336
MKC.EXE	62976	15872
PEOPLE.EXE	94720	51712
RANDRECT.EXE	62464	14848
TOE.EXE	70144	26112
WINEDIT.EXE	65536	18432
WPP.DLL		80538

The programs are significantly smaller, while the DLL is fairly large. Each statically linked program contains only those library modules it actually uses, but the DLL contains all *Windows++* modules. All in all, the savings are substantial.

That's reusability at the executable level!

CHAPTER · 10

Conclusion

Whew!

If you made it this far, congratulations, you're now a certified *Windows++* wizard!

It's been a long journey but, I hope, a rewarding one. Admittedly, much has been omitted (fonts, palettes, metafiles, OLE, C++ *templates*, and persistent objects, to name a few), but, as I stated at the outset, my aim was never to provide exhaustive treatments of Windows and C++, but rather to illustrate a *way* of programming Windows in C++. From this perspective, the journey has been, I believe, fruitful. Now that we've emerged from the trenches and reached the high ground, it's appropriate to cast a wayward glance back, examine the terrain we've crossed, and consider what we've learned along the way.

After rereading Section 1.2.2, I conclude that we've reached most of the goals we set out to achieve (the only place where *Windows++* falls a bit short is portability). Most important, *we've made Windows programming easier*. We did it using various specific tricks and techniques, most of which are fairly general and have applicability beyond Windows:

- Wherever possible, we've encapsulated generic behavior in subroutines. For example, we encapsulated the main message loop in *WPApp::run*, which we reuse in all our applications. We implemented a lot of GUI mechanics in subroutines, such as the details for graying menus and setting up a print Abort dialog. Using subroutines has little to do with C++ and OOP; it's an old and proven method of software engineering—but one that, as we've observed, seems to have been forgotten somewhere along the road to Windows. Forget about OOP—subroutines are the main vehicle for reusability. First, we figure out the correct Windows incantations required to perform some operation, then we encapsulate them in subroutines.

- While subroutines provide reusability, code isn't the only thing that we've reused. We also seen how to reuse other program elements, such as menu, icon, and accelerator table names, and command IDs. Even a simple macro can provide reusability: the resource macros we wrote in Section 6.3.9 encapsulate the proper CUA menu mnemonics and accelerator keys. The basic theme throughout all these examples is *only write it once.*

- We've used C++ to expose and clarify the implicit object-oriented nature of Windows. For example, we transformed the Windows notion of subclassing into the C++ notion of derived subclasses, and we made the WM_CREATE and WM_DESTROY messages correspond to C++ constructors and destructors. Doing this makes programming easier, since it's more straightforward to derive a subclass in C++ than in Windows. Furthermore, C++ offers richer object-oriented universe to play in.

- By using C++ subclasses to model different kinds of related Windows objects, we've made programming more foolproof. For example, by distinguishing *WPMultiEdit* from *WPEdit*, and implementing those functions that apply only to multi-line edit controls in *WPMultiEdit*, we ensure that no one incorrectly attempts to call them for an ordinary edit control. Where Windows lets you send any message to any window, *Windows++* groups functions with the classes that support them. More foolproof means more reliable, less bug-prone.

- While we sometimes use C++ to expose diversity in Windows, other times we use C++ to hide it. For example, we've hidden all the different ways Windows has to create and destroy different kinds of windows within the virtual functions *createWin* and *destroyWin*. Whether a window is just an ordinary window, a modal or modeless dialog, a common dialog, or an MDI window, the same functions, *createWin* and *destroyWin,* always work. We did a similar thing with drawing objects in Chapter 8. In general, where Windows has a half dozen or so different functions to perform the same operation, *Windows++* has one.

  A general guideline for when to expose and when to hide is to hide details that are circumstantial; expose differences that are fundamental.

- We've repackaged Windows using "brainless" functions, inline functions that do little more than pass their arguments directly to some Windows API function. Once again, the benefits are 1) that we use C++ default arguments to avoid typing unnecessary zeroes and NULLs; 2) that we use C++ function overloading to provide different flavors of the same function (for example, *clientToScren* for both points and rectangles); 3) that the arguments to brainless functions are self-documenting; 4) that, by making some functions private or protected, we can control their access; and finally, 5) that brainless functions define which operations are and are not supported by each *Windows++* class.

All these boil down to easier and more foolproof.

- We've used C++ operator overloading to good advantage. For example, we defined several arithmetic operators for points and rectangles that make geometric calculations a snap, as well as assignment operators to manipulate the *Mouse* and *Cursor,* which we modeled as C++ objects.

There are a few other tricks I could mention (for example, our trick of using constructors and destructors to encapsulate calling sequences), but the above list is adequate.

In the process of building *Windows++,* we've learned much about C++ and about OOP in general. In addition to all the C++ details (constructors, virtual functions, overloading, and so on), I hope readers will come away with a better understanding of object-oriented methodology. Here's my short list of OO lessons:

- To model a system using OOP techniques, the first thing one must do is identify the objects—or, to be precise, the classes of objects—that you want to model. Next, they must be classified according to their similar and different properties (data and functions). Whenever classes of objects share common properties, a base class is invented from which to derive them. As we've seen, it's sometimes desirable to expose the differences among different classes of objects; other times it's better to hide them.

- *Inheritance* is the primary vehicle for reusability in OOP. By deriving new classes from those provided by the library, *Windows++* applications simply inherit (reuse) the generic library behavior.

- *Virtual functions* provide a simple and easy, but extremely powerful, way to capture class-specific behavior in a generic fashion. Thus while every application has *fileOpen* and *paint* functions, each one implements them differently. Virtual functions provide *polymorphism:* different subclasses of objects perform the same operation differently. (In Windows, polymorphism is squeezed through a single function: the window procedure.)

I hope this book will persuade many programmers that C++ is a great language to program in, one that is for many reasons especially suited to deal with the challenges of Windows programming. Yet, as many observers have noted, "object-oriented" has become such an over-used buzzword that its meaning is more often lost than not. Rather than wave buzzwords, I've tried to simply show you how C++ can be useful, in real-life, down-to-earth Windows programs.

What is *Windows++?*

Before leaving, let's take a few moments to ponder a seemingly simple question: *What* is *Windows++?*

On the most straightforward level, *Windows++* is a reusable C++ class library. It provides a collection of C++ classes and functions that perform various Windows operations. These classes can be reused in applications to simplify programming.

But *Windows++* is more than a collection of subroutines; it's an application framework: it provides the form of an application, with no content. To write an application, *Windows++* programmers "fill in the blanks"—or, to be more precise, they fill in the virtual functions. The basic process goes something like this: derive application-specific subclasses from the built-in library classes, then write virtual functions to perform generic operations (such as File Open or *paint*) in an application-specific manner, as well as additional functions to perform application-specific processing, such as computing the Mandelbrot set or the next move in a tic-tac-toe game. *Windows++* takes care of the low-level details; application programmers are free to focus on applications.

While some programmers (for example, Windows developers) might scoff at the notion that programmers should "merely" fill in the blanks (*real* programmers don't need application frameworks) we needn't be distracted by this foolish view. Our system does not diminish programmers' skills, but rather liberates them. There are more interesting things to do than gray menus, register window classes, create printer Abort dialogs, and convert TABs to spaces. I ask you, which is more fun—figuring out how to create, select, and destroy a Windows *pen* object correctly, or figuring out the fastest algorithm to compute the Mandelbrot set?

Thus, in response to "what is *Windows++?*" we can also respond, "It's 'just' an approach to programming." The *Windows+* approach differs markedly from others, such as the copy-paste-edit, miles-of-open-code method espoused by Microsoft (and implicitly encouraged by most Windows programming books), and the push-a-button, automate-the-programmer philosophy adopted by commercial code generators. While *Windows++* is not for everyone, it offers many benefits over these approaches. It's more reliable and effective than copy-paste-editing, especially if you plan to write more than one application, and it offers more control than code generators. Besides, most programmers write better code than code generators. But more important, using your own library (one that you've written yourself) gives you the freedom to change it when you have some brilliant insight or realize that a slight change in the library can save you hours of effort writing your application (as we did when we added the *App.noQuit* flag for MDI child windows back in Section 6.4.4).

Windows++ embodies the view that applications precede systems. I don't mean to suggest that system software is unimportant; on the contrary, it's essential

(*Windows++* is system software). What I mean is that systems are the means and applications are the end. After all, the ultimate end of all programming (even operating systems) is some program that a person can use. From a design perspective, this means that applications should guide the development of systems. When designing a system, think first of how it will be used. I've tried to follow this principle throughout the book, by starting each chapter with some specific application as the goal. First, we imagine what the application code should look like, then we build the library to make it so. Perhaps our most successful application of this approach was in Chapter 7, where we imagined a dialog system that had no code, then proceeded to build it. This applications-oriented approach is nothing new, nothing fancy—it's not even object-oriented. Just good old-fashioned top-down design. It's the best way to ensure that you end up with a system that's useful.

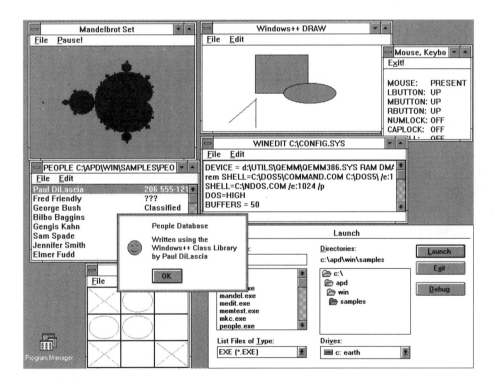

Finally, *Windows++* is the story of how I built a C++ class library to meet my programming needs. While some readers might take the *Windows++* source code verbatim from Appendix A and use it to build applications, I that most of you use the book as a guide to build your own library, one that meets *your* needs. Your efforts will be well-rewarded in the form of clearer, more reliable and concise code—not to mention the extra leisure time you may garner now that Windows programming is so easy!

Windows++ Source Code

This lengthy appendix contains the source code for the entire *Windows++* library, as well as the sample applications described in the book. The source code listed here differs from that shown in the main text, which has in many instances been cleaned up to improve legibility. Also, in the text, all classes are shown with the *class* designator, rather than the DLLCLASS and APPCLASS macros actually used in the source code (see Chapter 9). The code listed here also contains last-minute improvements and corrections that didn't make it into the main text. The code listed here should be considered as the final word.

If you don't want to type in a hundred pages of code, I'll sell you the source on diskette for only $25—there's a coupon at the back of the book. Believe me, this is a great deal!

A.1 Class Library

MAKEFILE.BCC

```
# Windows++ Makefile for BORLAND
# (C) Paul DiLascia 1992.
#
# To build Windows++, issue one of the following DOS commands.
#
#    make                make DLL and import lib (DLL is copied to $(WINDOWS))
#    make MODEL=l         make large model lbrary
#    make MODEL=m         make medium model library
#
#    If you want to make a new MODEL, make sure you first del *.obj
WINDOWS=C:\windows
MAKEFILE = -fmakefile.bcc
!ifndef MODEL
MODEL=l
ALL=wpp.dll commdlg.lib
WINFLAGS= -WDE
!else
ALL=wpp.lib commdlg.lib
WINFLAGS = -WE -WS
!endif
```

```
!ifdef USEDLL
DEFINES=$(DEFINES) -DUSEDLL
!endif
CL = bcc
CFLAGS = -a -c -w-par -m$(MODEL) $(WINFLAGS) $(DEFINES) $(ENVFLAGS)
WPPOBJ = WPAPP.obj WPCTRL.OBJ WPDLFILE.obj WPDLG.obj WPDLPRT.obj \
    WPDLSTR.obj WPGDI.obj WPGLOB.obj WPHEAP.obj WPMAIN.obj WPMDI.obj \
    WPMENU.obj WPODRAW.obj WPRECT.obj WPWIN.obj GPP.OBJ
.cpp.obj:
    $(CL) $(CFLAGS) $*
all: $(ALL)
obj: $(WPPOBJ)
commdlg.lib: commdlg.dll
    implib $*.lib $*.dll
wpp.lib: $(WPPOBJ) winmain.obj
    del $*.lib
    tlib $*.lib/C @lib.rsp
wpp.dll: $(WPPOBJ) libmain.obj
    tlink -Twd -C -c $(ENVFLAGS) c0dl -s @dll.rsp
    make $(MAKEFILE) USEDLL=1 MODEL=1 winmain.obj
    implib $*.lib $*.dll
    tlib $*.lib /C +WINMAIN,$*.lst
    del $*.bak
install: wpp.dll
    copy wpp.dll $(WINDOWS)
clean:
    del *.obj
    del *.map
    del *.lst
    del *.lib
    del *.dll
```

MAKEFILE.ZTC

```
# Windows++ Makefile for ZORTECH
# (C) Paul DiLascia 1992.
#
# To build Windows++, issue one of the following DOS commands.
#
#    make                make DLL library
#    make MODEL=l        make large model
#    make MODEL=m        make medium model
#
#    $(WINDOWS) is where DLL is copied to
CL = ztc
CFLAGS = -c -W2 -W3 -m$(MODEL) $(ENVFLAGS)
ALL=wpp.lib commdlg.lib
WPPOBJ = WPAPP.obj WPCTRL.OBJ WPDLFILE.obj WPDLG.obj WPDLPRT.obj \
    WPDLSTR.obj WPGDI.obj WPGLOB.obj WPHEAP.obj WPMAIN.obj WPMDI.obj \
    WPMENU.obj WPODRAW.obj WPRECT.obj WPWIN.obj GPP.OBJ
ZTCINC=d:\zortech\source\clib
ZTCASM= ztc -c -r -o+space -D_WINDOWS -m$(MODEL) -W1 -I$(ZTCINC)
ZTCOBJ = cw$(MODEL).obj cinit$(MODEL).obj setds.obj
.asm.obj:
    $(ZTCASM) $*.asm
.cpp.obj:
    $(CL) $(CFLAGS) $*
all: $(ALL)
obj: $(WPPOBJ)
commdlg.lib: commdlg.dll
    implib $*.lib $*.dll
wpp.lib: $(WPPOBJ) $(ZTCOBJ) winmain.obj
    del $*.lib
    zorlib $*.lib /c /n /b @lib.rsp
    zorlib $*.lib /n /b +cw$(MODEL)+cinit$(MODEL)+setds, $*.lst;
clean:
    del *.obj
    del *.map
```

```
        del *.lst
        del *.lib
        del *.dll
cinit$(MODEL).obj: cinit.asm
    $(ZTCASM) -ocinit$(MODEL).obj cinit.asm
cw$(MODEL).obj: cw.asm
    $(ZTCASM) -ocw$(MODEL).obj cw.asm
```

LIB.RSP

```
+WINMAIN.OBJ+WPAPP.OBJ+WPCTRL.OBJ+WPDLFILE.OBJ+WPDLG.OBJ &
+WPDLPRT.OBJ+WPDLSTR.OBJ+WPGDI.OBJ+WPGLOB.OBJ+WPHEAP.OBJ &
+WPMAIN.OBJ+WPMDI.OBJ+WPMENU.OBJ+WPODRAW.OBJ+WPRECT.OBJ &
+WPWIN.OBJ+GPP.OBJ WPP.LST;
```

DLL.RSP

```
LIBMAIN WPAPP WPCTRL WPDLFILE WPDLG WPDLPRT WPDLSTR WPGDI WPGLOB+
WPHEAP WPMAIN WPMDI WPMENU WPODRAW WPRECT GPP+
WPWIN,wpp,wpp,cwl import commdlg,wpp.def
```

WPP.DEF

```
LIBRARY WPP
DESCRIPTION 'Windows++ DLL library'
EXETYPE WINDOWS
CODE MOVEABLE
DATA MOVEABLE SINGLE
HEAPSIZE 5120
```

GPP.H

```
/////////////////////////////////////////////////////////
// WINDOWS++ CLASS LIBRARY.  Copyright 1992 Paul DiLascia.
// FILE: GPP.H
//
// Definitions for GPP (Graphics++) objects.
#ifndef GPP_H
#define GPP_H
#include "wpgdi.h"
DLLCLASS GPShapeList;
//////////////////
// Generic shape, an abstract class
//
DLLCLASS GPShape {
    GPShape *next;          // next shape in list
    COLORREF edge;          // edge color
    COLORREF fill;          // interior color
    void init()             { edge = COLOR_BLACK; fill = COLOR_NONE; }
protected:
    static WPRect ClipRect; // global clipping rectangle
    static BOOL DoClip;     // whether to clip
    WPRect extent;          // extent of shape
    friend GPShapeList;
public:
    GPShape()               { init(); }
    GPShape(WPRect& r)      { init(); setExtent(r); }
    virtual ~GPShape()      { }
    static void Clip(WPRect* r);     // set clipping rectangle
    // Data access
    COLORREF edgeColor()                { return edge; }
    COLORREF edgeColor(COLORREF c)      { return edge=c; }
    COLORREF fillColor()                { return fill; }
    COLORREF fillColor(COLORREF c)      { return fill=c; }
    void getExtent(WPRect& e)           { e = extent; }
    void setExtent(WPRect& e)           { extent = e; }
```

```
    // Virtual functions for specific shapes to implement
    virtual void getBounds(WPRect& r);
    virtual void draw(WPDevContext &dc);
    virtual void drawShape(WPDevContext &dc) = 0;
    virtual void invalidate(WPWin *w, BOOL erase=FALSE);
    virtual BOOL hitTest(WPPoint p, int radius);
    virtual int getHandles(WPPoint *buf);
    virtual GPShape* dup()      { GPShape *s = clone();
       if (s) memcpy(s,this,sizeof(GPShape)); return s; }
    virtual GPShape* clone()    { return NULL; }
};
/////////////////
// Line
//
DLLCLASS GPLine : public GPShape {
public:
    GPLine(WPRect& r) : GPShape(r)    { }
    void drawShape(WPDevContext &dc)
       { dc.line(extent.origin(), extent.endpt()); }
    int getHandles(WPPoint *buf);
    GPShape* clone()                  { return new GPLine(extent); }
};
/////////////////
// Rectangle
//
DLLCLASS GPRect : public GPShape {
public:
    GPRect(WPRect &r) : GPShape(r)    { }
    void drawShape(WPDevContext &dc) { dc.rectangle(extent); }
    GPShape* clone()                  { return new GPRect(extent); }
};
/////////////////
// Ellipse
//
DLLCLASS GPEllipse : public GPShape {
public:
    GPEllipse(WPRect &r) : GPShape(r)    { }
    void drawShape(WPDevContext &dc)     { dc.ellipse(extent); }
    GPShape* clone()                      { return new GPEllipse(extent); }
};
/////////////////
// "Hilite" shape.
//
DLLCLASS GPHilite : public GPShape {
    GPShape *hishape;       // hilighted shape
    WPPoint handles[4];     // size handles
    int nhandles;           // number of handles
    int radius;             // handle radius
public:
    GPHilite(GPShape *obj, int r);
    GPShape *shape()         { return hishape; }
    void drawShape(WPDevContext &dc);
    BOOL hitTest(WPPoint p, int radius);
    WPPoint anchor(WPPoint p);
    void invalidate(WPWin *w, BOOL erase=FALSE);
};
/////////////////
// List of shapes.  List is implicitly ordered from bottom to top,
// so drawing can be done by navigating the list.
//
DLLCLASS GPShapeList {
    GPShape *firstShape;    // first (bottom) in list
    GPShape *current;       // transient current for list navigation
public:
    GPShapeList()            { firstShape = current = NULL; }
    ~GPShapeList()           { deleteAll(); }
    void deleteAll();
```

```
      // Navigation methods
      GPShape *operator()()     { return current; }
      GPShape *next()           { return current ? current=current->next : NULL; }
      GPShape *first()          { return current=firstShape; }
      // Add/remove etc.
      GPShape *add(GPShape *obj);
      GPShape *remove(GPShape *obj);
      GPShape *front(GPShape *obj) { return add(remove(obj)); }
      GPShape *back(GPShape *obj)
         { remove(obj); obj->next = firstShape; return firstShape = obj; }
      // Miscellaneous
      void paint(WPPaintStruct& ps);
      void draw(WPDevContext& dc);
      GPShape* hitTest(WPPoint& p, int radius);
};
//////////////////
// Macro lets you write:
//
//     forEachGPShape(list, shape)
//        shape->doSomething();
//
#define forEachGPShape(list, s) \
   GPShape *s; \
   for (s = (list).first(); s; s=(list).next())
#endif
```

GPP.CPP

```
/////////////////////////////////////////////////////////
// WINDOWS++ CLASS LIBRARY.  Copyright 1992 Paul DiLascia.
// FILE: GPP.CPP
//
// Implementation of Windows++ Graphics system.
#include "gpp.h"
WPRect    GPShape::ClipRect;
BOOL      GPShape::DoClip=FALSE;
const     MINBOUNDS = 4;
//////////////////
// Set global clipping rectangle
//
void GPShape::Clip(WPRect *rect)
{
   DoClip = rect != NULL;
   if (rect) {
      ClipRect = *rect;
      ClipRect.normalize();
   }
}
//////////////////
// Get shape's bounding rectangle
//
void GPShape::getBounds(WPRect& r)
{
   r = extent;
   r.normalize();
   if (r.width()<MINBOUNDS || r.height() < MINBOUNDS)
      r += MINBOUNDS/2;
}
//////////////////
// Draw shape: do clip test, set pen, brush, etc., then call drawShape.
//
void GPShape::draw(WPDevContext &dc)
{
   if (DoClip) {
      WPRect temp;
      getBounds(temp);
      temp &= ClipRect;      // intersect w/clipping rectangle
      if (temp.isEmpty())
```

```
            return;
    }
    if (edgeColor()==COLOR_NONE)
        dc.setPen(NULL_PEN);
    else
        dc.setPen(edgeColor());
    if (fillColor()==COLOR_NONE)
        dc.setBrush(NULL_BRUSH);
    else
        dc.setBrush(fillColor());
    drawShape(dc);
}
/////////////////
// Test whether shape "touches" specified point.
// Algorithm:
//     First, try to eliminate by testing bounds; if can't eliminate,
//     render shape into little square and see if any pixels are on.
//
BOOL GPShape::hitTest(WPPoint p, int radius)
{
    WPSquare hit(p, radius);
    WPRect temp;
    getBounds(temp);
    temp &= hit;                // intersect them
    if (temp.isEmpty())         // point lies totally outside bounds:
        return FALSE;           // ..miss
    // Possible hit: explore further
    WPMemDC dc(NULL, hit);      // screen-compatible DC
    dc.whiteOut(hit);           // set all pixels white
    dc.setBrush(fillColor()==COLOR_NONE ? NULL_BRUSH : BLACK_BRUSH);
    drawShape(dc);              // render into square
    // See if any pixel is on.
    for (int x=hit.left(); x<hit.right(); x++) {
        for (int y=hit.top(); y<hit.bottom(); y++) {
            if (dc.pixel(x, y)==0)
                return TRUE;
        }
    }
    return FALSE;
}
/////////////////
// Invalidate shape in window: invalidate its bounding rectangle.
//
void GPShape::invalidate(WPWin *win, BOOL erase)
{
    WPRect rect;
    getBounds(rect);
    WPWinDC dc = win;
    dc.LP2DP(rect);
    win->invalidate(rect, erase);
}
/////////////////
// Get list of handles.
//
int GPShape::getHandles(WPPoint* pts)
{
    pts[0]=extent.origin();
    pts[1]=extent.topRight();
    pts[2]=extent.endpt();
    pts[3]=extent.bottomLeft();
    return 4;
}
int GPLine::getHandles(WPPoint* pts)
{
    pts[0]=extent.origin();
    pts[1]=extent.endpt();
    return 2;
}
```

```
////////////////
// Create "hilite" shape from given shape.
//
GPHilite::GPHilite(GPShape *shp, int r)
{
    assert(shp);
    hishape = shp;
    nhandles = shp->getHandles(handles);
    radius = r;
    shp->getExtent(extent);
}
////////////////
// Do hit test for hilite: TRUE if point lies within one of the handles.
//
BOOL GPHilite::hitTest(WPPoint p, int radius)
{
    for (int i=0; i<nhandles; i++) {
        WPSquare handle(handles[i], radius);
        if (handle.contains(p))
            return TRUE;
    }
    return FALSE;
}
////////////////
// Draw the hilite shape: draw each handle.
//
void GPHilite::drawShape(WPDevContext &dc)
{
    int oldrop = dc.rop2(R2_XORPEN);
    dc.setPen(WHITE_PEN);
    dc.setBrush(WHITE_BRUSH);
    for (int i=0; i<nhandles; i++) {
        WPPoint p = handles[i];
        dc.LP2DP(p);
        WPSquare handle(p, radius);
        int old = dc.mapMode(MM_TEXT);
        dc.rectangle(handle);
        dc.mapMode(old);
    }
    dc.rop2(oldrop);
}
////////////////
// Invalidate hilite: invalidate each size anchor
//
void GPHilite::invalidate(WPWin *win, BOOL erase)
{
    WPWinDC dc = win;
    for (int i=0; i<nhandles; i++) {
        WPPoint p = handles[i];
        dc.LP2DP(p);
        WPSquare handle(p, radius);
        win->invalidate(handle, erase);
    }
}
////////////////
// Determine size anchor given pt. Returns the anchor point.
// This is the handle farthest from the given point.
//
WPPoint GPHilite::anchor(WPPoint p)
{
    long distance=0;
    int anchor = 0;
    WPPoint delta;
    for (int i=0; i<nhandles; i++) {
        delta = handles[i] - p;
        long d = (long)delta.x*(long)delta.x + (long)delta.y*(long)delta.y;
        if (d > distance) {
            distance = d;
```

```
                anchor = i;
        }
    }
    return handles[anchor];
}
///////////////////
// Delete all shapes in list.
//
void GPShapeList::deleteAll()
{
    GPShape *sNext;
    for (GPShape *s = firstShape; s; s=sNext) {
        sNext = s->next;
        delete s;
    }
    firstShape=current=NULL;
}
///////////////////
// Add shape to end of list, which is front.
//
GPShape *GPShapeList::add(GPShape *shp)
{
    if (firstShape==NULL)
        firstShape=shp;
    else {
        GPShape *s;
        for (s = firstShape; s->next; s=s->next)
            ;  // (run to end of list)
        s->next = shp;
    }
    shp->next = NULL;
    return shp;
}
///////////////////
// Remove shape from list.
//
GPShape* GPShapeList::remove(GPShape *shp)
{
    if (firstShape==shp)
        firstShape = shp->next;
    else {
        forEachGPShape(*this, s) {
            if (s->next == shp) {
                s->next = shp->next;
                break;
            }
        }
    }
    shp->next=NULL;             // for safety
    return shp;
}
///////////////////
// Draw all shapes in list
//
void GPShapeList::draw(WPDevContext& dc)
{
    forEachGPShape(*this, s)
        s->draw(dc);
}
///////////////////
// Paint shapes in list. Like draw, but do clipping.
//
void GPShapeList::paint(WPPaintStruct& ps)
{
    ps.getPaintRect(GPShape::ClipRect);
    GPShape::ClipRect.normalize();
    BOOL save = GPShape::DoClip;
    GPShape::DoClip = TRUE;
```

```
        draw(ps);
        GPShape::DoClip = save;
}
///////////////////
// Do hit-detection for list of shapes: return topmost that hits.
//
GPShape* GPShapeList::hitTest(WPPoint& p, int radius)
{
    GPShape *shp = NULL;
    forEachGPShape(*this, s) {
        if (s->hitTest(p, radius))
            shp = s;
    }
    return shp;
}
```

LIBMAIN.CPP

```
/////////////////////////////////////////////////////////////
// WINDOWS++ CLASS LIBRARY.  Copyright 1992 Paul DiLascia.
// FILE: LIBMAIN.CPP
//
// Entry point for Windows++ DLL.
// Also contains "global" stuff that's in WINMAIN.CPP, such as
// new and delete, global objects and so on (but not WPWndProc and
// WPDlgProc, which are duplicated in each app in order to use smart
// callbacks instead of MakeProcInstance).
#include "wpapp.h"
#include "wpwin.h"
#include "wpglob.h"
WPMouse         Mouse;          // instantiate global objects
WPKeyboard      Keyboard;
WPCursor        Cursor;
WPWinIni        WinIni;
WPCaret         Caret;
WPClipboard     Clipboard;
int FAR PASCAL LibMain(HANDLE h, WORD ds, WORD heapsz, LPSTR cmd)
{
    if (heapsz>0)
        UnlockData(0);
    return 1;
}
int FAR PASCAL WEP(int param)
{
    return 1;
}
///////////////////
// Global new and delete operators.  DLL uses large model, so use
// far mem.  Note that the memory "belongs" to the calling application,
// since for the DLL, "App" is really a call to "GetApp()"!
//
void * operator new(size_t size)
{
    return App.farAlloc(size);
}
void operator delete(void *ptr)
{
    if (ptr)
        App.farFree(ptr);
}
```

WINMAIN.CPP

```
/////////////////////////////////////////////////////////////
// WINDOWS++ CLASS LIBRARY.  Copyright 1992 Paul DiLascia.
// FILE: WINMAIN.CPP
//
// WinMain function for Windows++ class library. Also contains other
```

```
// "global" stuff like the main window and dialog procs, global objects,
// new, delete, etc.
#include "wpapp.h"
#include "wpwin.h"
#include "wpdlg.h"
#include "wpctrl.h"
#include "wpglob.h"
// THE application object
WPApp App((FARPROC)WPWndProc,(FARPROC)WPDlgProc);
//////////////////
// Below are all the global objects.
//
WPMouse         Mouse;
WPKeyboard      Keyboard;
WPCursor        Cursor;
WPWinIni        WinIni;
WPCaret         Caret;
WPClipboard     Clipboard;
//////////////////
// WINMAIN function.  This is linked as part of the
// Windows++ library, so Windows++ programs should not
// supply WinMain.  Instead, they must supply WPApp::main.
//
int PASCAL WinMain(HANDLE hinst, HANDLE pinst, LPSTR cmd, int show)
{
    App.init(hinst, pinst, cmd, show);  // init application object
    App.main();                         // call user's entry-point
    return App.exitCode;                // (result from PostQuitMessage)
}
////////////////////////////////////////////////////////////////////
// This is THE Window Proc used for all Windows++ windows!
// The only message it actually handles is WM_DESTROY, to which it
// responds by destroying the linked Windows++ object.  Windows++
// programs should now NEVER DELETE WINDOWS OBJECTS, and window
// object must always be created with "new", not on the stack.
//
LONG _export FAR PASCAL WPWndProc(HWND hwnd, WORD msg, WORD wp, LONG lp)
{
    WPWin* win = WPWin::GetWin(hwnd);
    assert(win);
    if (msg==WM_DESTROY) {  // got WM_DESTROY:
        if (win->deletable)
            delete win;         // call virtual destructor
        else
            win->unLinkHwnd();
        return 0;
    }
    WPEvent event(msg, wp, lp);   // create an event object on the stack
    return win->msgProc(event);   // call virtual message proc
}
//////////////////
// This is THE dialog procedure used for all Windows++ dialog boxes
//
BOOL _export FAR PASCAL WPDlgProc(HWND hdlg, WORD msg, WORD wp, LONG lp)
{
    WPDialog *dlg;
    if (msg == WM_INITDIALOG) {
        dlg = WPDialog::NewDialog;      // dialog obj passed as global (ugh!)
        assert(dlg);                    // it better exist
        WPDialog::NewDialog = NULL;     // safety: don't re-init
        dlg->linkHwnd(hdlg);            // link to window
        return dlg->init();             // call init function
    } else {
        // Got some message other than WM_INITDIALOG
        dlg = (WPDialog*)WPWin::GetWin(hdlg);
        if (dlg==NULL)
            return FALSE;
    }
```

```
        WPEvent event(msg, wp, lp);
        return dlg->dispatchEvent(event);
}
//////////////////
// System-wide global new and delete operators.
// For large model, allocate objects from far (global) memory;
// for medium model, allocate all from the local heap.
//
void * operator new(size_t size)
{
#ifdef __LARGE__
        return App.farAlloc(size);
#else
        return App.localAlloc(size);
#endif
}
void operator delete(void *ptr)
{
    if (ptr)
#ifdef __LARGE__
        App.farFree(ptr);
#else
        App.localFree(ptr);
#endif
}
```

WPAPP.H

```
////////////////////////////////////////////////////////////
// WINDOWS++ CLASS LIBRARY.  Copyright 1992 Paul DiLascia.
// FILE: WPAPP.H
//
// Definitions for the application class, WPApp.
#ifndef WPAPP_H
#define WPAPP_H
#ifndef WPHEAP_H
#include "wpheap.h"
#endif
typedef BOOL (* NOMEMHANDLER)(WORD);
//////////////////
// Class used to represent a Windows module.
// Essentially, it's just a module instance handle.
//
DLLCLASS WPModule {
protected:
    char modname[16];       // module name
    HANDLE hinst;           // module handle
    LPCSTR cmdLine;         // windows command line
public:
    WPModule(HANDLE h=NULL) { hinst = h; modname[0]=0; }
    WPModule(CSTR nm)
        { strcpy(modname, nm); hinst = GetModuleHandle(modname); }
    ~WPModule() { }
    HANDLE getHinst()                 { return hinst; }
    HANDLE operator()()               { return hinst; }
    void getCmdLine(char *buf)        { lstrcpy(buf, (LPSTR)cmdLine); }
    int getUsage()                    { return GetModuleUsage(hinst); }
    CSTR getName();
    int getFileName(char *buf, int buflen)
        { return GetModuleFileName(hinst, (LPSTR)buf, buflen); }
    FARPROC getProcAddress(CSTR procname)
        { return GetProcAddress(hinst, (LPSTR)procname); }
    HMENU loadMenu(CSTR name)
        { return LoadMenu(hinst, (LPSTR)name); }
    HANDLE loadBitmap(CSTR name)
        { return LoadBitmap(hinst, (LPSTR)name); }
    HANDLE loadBitmap(int id)
        { return LoadBitmap(hinst, MAKEINTRESOURCE(id)); }
```

```
    HANDLE loadIcon(LPCSTR name)
        { return LoadIcon(HIWORD(name) ? hinst : NULL, (LPSTR)name); }
    HANDLE loadIcon(int id)
        { return LoadIcon(hinst, MAKEINTRESOURCE(id)); }
    HANDLE loadCursor(LPCSTR name)
        { return LoadCursor(HIWORD(name) ? hinst : NULL, (LPSTR)name); }
    HANDLE loadCursor(int id)
        { return LoadCursor(hinst, MAKEINTRESOURCE(id)); }
    int loadString(int id, LPSTR buf, int len=MAXSTRLEN)
        { return LoadString(hinst, id, buf, len); }
    HANDLE findResource(LPSTR name, LPSTR type)
        { return FindResource(hinst, name, type); }
    int loadResource(LPSTR name, LPSTR type, LPSTR buf, int len);
    int loadResource(int id, LPSTR type, LPSTR buf, int len)
        { return loadResource(MAKEINTRESOURCE(id), type, buf, len); }
};
///////////////////
// Used to represent a library module (e.g., a DLL).
//
DLLCLASS WPLibrary : public WPModule {
public:
    WPLibrary(CSTR libname);
    ~WPLibrary()    { if (hinst) FreeLibrary(hinst); }
};
///////////////////
// Application object.
// There is exactly one application for each Windows++ program.
// It stores the module instance handle.
// Each app must provide a "main" function.
// The application object also manages the application's memory.
//
DLLCLASS WPApp : public WPModule {
private:
    static WPApp* registeredApps;    // list of registered apps
    WPApp *next;                 // next registered app (DLL only)
    MemLocalHeap localHeap;      // THE local heap
    MemHeap * firstHeap;         // first heap in chain
    MemHeap * mruHeap;           // most recently used heap
    long   nBigObjBytes;         // number of bytes in "big" blocks
    int    nBigObj;              // number of "big" blocks allocated
    int    nStartObj;            // initial # "big" blocks
    BOOL   registered;           // Whether registered or not
    NOMEMHANDLER noMemHandler;
    int inNoMemHandler;
    BOOL callNoMemHandler(WORD size);
    MemHeap* addHeap(WORD size);    // add heap to chain
    MemHeap *findHeap(WORD seg);    // find heap w/given data segment
    void delHeap(MemHeap *heap);    // delete and remove heap from chain
    void freeAllHeaps();
    HANDLE pinst;               // previous instance handle
    int cmdShow;                // how to show window
    int exitCode;               // returned from WinMain
    WPMainWin *mainWin;         // main application window
    WORD dsval;                 // app's data segment
    FARPROC wndProc;            // ptr to app's window procedure
    FARPROC dlgProc;            // ptr to app's dialog procedure
    HWND mdiClientHwnd;         // MDI client win, if any
    WPDialogModeless *dialogs;  // list of modeless dialogs
    HANDLE accel;               // accelerator table, if any
    BOOL useWININI;             // use WIN.INI for profile
    void init(HANDLE h, HANDLE p, LPSTR cmd, int show);
    void main();
    void run();
    void makeIniFileName(char *buf);
    friend int PASCAL WinMain(HANDLE, HANDLE, LPSTR, int);
    friend WPMDIClient;
public:
    char scratch[1024];             // transient buffer anyone can use
```

```
    WPApp(FARPROC wndproc, FARPROC dlgproc);
    ~WPApp();
    // Access
    static WPApp* GetApp();       // get current running app if we're a DLL
    HANDLE getPrevInst()          { return pinst; }
    BOOL first()                  { return pinst==NULL; }
    FARPROC getWndProc()          { return wndProc; }
    FARPROC getDlgProc()          { return dlgProc; }
    // Memory allocation
    void *localAlloc(WORD size, BOOL useHandler=TRUE);
    void localFree(void* ptr);
    void FAR * farAlloc(DWORD size, BOOL useHandler=TRUE, BOOL global=FALSE);
    void farFree(void FAR* ptr);
    DWORD memSize(void FAR * ptr);
    // Miscellaneous
    NOMEMHANDLER setNoMemHandler(NOMEMHANDLER fn);
    static BOOL DfltNoMemHandler(WORD size);
    int showStats(BOOL cancel=FALSE);
    static void ShowAllStats();
    void quit(int ret=0)          { PostQuitMessage(ret); }
    void addDialog(WPDialogModeless *dlg);
    void removeDialog(WPDialogModeless *dlg);
    HANDLE loadAccel(CSTR acname)
        { return accel = LoadAccelerators(hinst, (LPSTR)acname); }
    // Application profile file
    int  getProfile(CSTR key,char *buf,int len,CSTR dflt="",CSTR app=NULL);
    int  getProfile(CSTR key, int dflt=0, CSTR app=NULL);
    BOOL setProfile(CSTR key, CSTR val, CSTR app=NULL);
    BOOL setProfile(CSTR key, int val,  CSTR app=NULL);
};
#ifdef __DLL__
// For a DLL, "App" calls GetApp to get calling program's App object.
#define App (*WPApp::GetApp())
#else
// For a normal program, "App" is a static global.
extern WPApp App;
#endif
#endif
```

WPAPP.CPP

```
/////////////////////////////////////////////////////////
// WINDOWS++ CLASS LIBRARY.  Copyright 1992 Paul DiLascia.
// FILE: WPAPP.CPP
//
// Implementation for module, library and application objects.
#include "wpapp.h"
#include "wpmain.h"
#include "wpglob.h"
#include "wpmdi.h"
#include "wpdlg.h"
#include <stdarg.h>
#include <sys\stat.h>
const char DFLTACCEL[] = "AppAccel";
WPApp* WPApp::registeredApps = NULL;
/////////////////////
// Get module's name.  Strip filename of path and extension.
//
CSTR WPModule::getName()
{
    if (modname[0] == 0 && hinst) {
        char buf[MAXFILENAMELEN];
        getFileName(buf, MAXFILENAMELEN);
        char *filename = NULL;
        for (char *next=strtok(buf,"\\"); next; next=strtok(NULL,"\\"))
            filename = next;
        strtok(filename,".");
        strcpy(modname, filename);
```

```
    }
    return modname;
}
/////////////////
// Load a user defined resource from the module file.
//
int WPModule::loadResource(LPSTR resname, LPSTR type, LPSTR buf, int len)
{
    int size = 0;
    HANDLE hres = findResource(resname, type);
    if (hres) {
        HANDLE hmem = LoadResource(hinst, hres);
        if (hmem) {
            size = SizeofResource(hinst, hres);
            LPSTR resPtr = LockResource(hmem);
            len = min(len, size);
            while (len-- > 0)
                *buf++ = *resPtr++;
            UnlockResource(hmem);
            FreeResource(hmem);
        }
    }
    return size;
}
/////////////////
// Create library object: load library module given name.
// Display error message if can't load it.
//
WPLibrary::WPLibrary(CSTR libname)
{
    hinst = LoadLibrary((LPSTR)libname);
    if (hinst < 32) {
        ErrBox("Error %d loading library %s", hinst, libname);
        hinst = NULL;
    }
}
/////////////////
// Init application object.
// Register the application in the global list "registeredApps".
//
WPApp::WPApp(FARPROC wndproc, FARPROC dlgproc)
{
    wndProc = wndproc;
    dlgProc = dlgproc;
    dialogs = NULL;
    noMemHandler = WPApp::DfltNoMemHandler;
    nStartObj = nBigObj + localHeap.numObj;
    // store application's data segment
    WORD temp;
    GETAPPDS(temp);
    dsval = temp;
    // Register app with DLL: chain to list
    next = registeredApps;
    registeredApps = this;
    registered = TRUE;
}
/////////////////
// Destroy application object: free all the app's memory (complain
// if there are unfreed objects remaining); then unregister the app.
//
WPApp::~WPApp()
{
    freeAllHeaps();
    // Unregister the app with the DLL.
    if (registeredApps == this)
        registeredApps = next;
    else {
        for (WPApp *app = registeredApps; app; app = app->next) {
```

```cpp
            if (app->next == this) {
                app->next = next;
                break;
            }
        }
        assert(app);
    }
    registered = FALSE;
}
///////////////////
// Initialize application object.  Called from WinMain.
//
void WPApp::init(HANDLE h, HANDLE p, LPSTR cmd, int show)
{
    hinst = h;
    pinst = p;
    cmdLine=cmd;
    cmdShow=show;
    // Load default accelerator table if it exists
    if (findResource((char*)DFLTACCEL, RT_ACCELERATOR))
        loadAccel((char*)DFLTACCEL);
}
///////////////////
// Run the message loop. This super-duper message loop handles a number of
// different situations, including: modeless dialogs, accelerators, MDI
// windows, PeekMessage, etc. It's the only one applications ever need.
//
void WPApp::run()
{
    assert(mainWin);
    mainWin->show(cmdShow);
    mainWin->update();
    HWND hwnd = (*mainWin)();
    MSG msg;
    BOOL peek=TRUE;
    while (peek || GetMessage(&msg, NULL, 0, 0)) {
        if (peek) {
            // We are doing peek message (app specified doIdle function)
            if (!PeekMessage(&msg, NULL, 0, 0, PM_REMOVE)) {
                peek = mainWin->doIdle();  // call app's doIdle function.
                continue;
            }
            if (msg.message==WM_QUIT)
                break;
        }
        // Check for MDI client message
        if (mdiClientHwnd && TranslateMDISysAccel(mdiClientHwnd, &msg))
            continue;
        // Check for modeless dialog message.
        BOOL dlgmsg = FALSE;
        for (WPDialogModeless *dlg=dialogs; dlg; dlg=dlg->next) {
            if (dlg->getHwnd() && IsDialogMessage(dlg->getHwnd(), &msg)) {
                dlgmsg=TRUE;
                break;
            }
        }
        if (dlgmsg)
            continue;
        // Check for accelerator key.
        if (accel && TranslateAccelerator(hwnd, accel, &msg))
            continue;
        // None of the above, so dispatch as normal.
        TranslateMessage(&msg);
        DispatchMessage(&msg);
    }
    exitCode = msg.wParam;
}
```

```
//////////////////
// Allocate far memory.
//
void FAR * WPApp::farAlloc(DWORD size, BOOL useHandler, BOOL useGlobal)
{
    do {
        if (size >= HEAPSIZE || useGlobal || !registered) {
            HANDLE h = GlobalAlloc(GMEM_MOVEABLE | GMEM_ZEROINIT, size);
            if (h) {
                nBigObj++;
                nBigObjBytes += GlobalSize(h);
                return (void FAR *)GlobalLock(h);
            }
        } else {
            void NEAR* np;
            // first try most recently used heap
            MemHeap *heap = mruHeap;
            if (heap && ((np = heap->alloc(size)) != NULL))
                return heap->makeFarPtr(np);
            // try other heaps
            for (heap = firstHeap; heap; heap=heap->next) {
                if (heap != mruHeap && (np = heap->alloc(size)) != NULL) {
                    mruHeap = heap;
                    return heap->makeFarPtr(np);
                }
            }
            // still no memory: try creating a new heap
            heap = addHeap(size);
            if (heap) {
                if ((np = heap->alloc(size))!=NULL)
                    return heap->makeFarPtr(np);
                delHeap(heap);
            }
            // We are really out of memory: try calling no-memory
            // handler to let app free some memory if possible.
        }
    } while (useHandler && callNoMemHandler(size));
    return NULL;    // all efforts failed (sob, sob): return NULL
}
//////////////////
// Allocate another heap.
//
MemHeap * WPApp::addHeap(WORD size)
{
    MemHeap *heap = new MemHeap(size);
    if (heap==NULL || heap->seg==0) {
        delete heap;
        return NULL;
    }
    heap->next = firstHeap;         // add heap to list
    firstHeap = mruHeap = heap;     // ...
    return heap;
}
//////////////////
// Find heap with given data segment.
// Uses MRU algorithm to improve performance.
//
MemHeap * WPApp::findHeap(WORD seg)
{
    if (mruHeap && mruHeap->seg==seg)
        return mruHeap;
    // Not MRU heap: search the list.
    //
    for (MemHeap *heap=firstHeap; heap; heap=heap->next) {
        if (heap->seg == seg)
            return mruHeap = heap;
    }
    assert(FALSE);      // should always find it!
```

```cpp
        return NULL;
}
///////////////////
// Free far memory.
//
void WPApp::farFree(void FAR* ptr)
{
    if (ptr==NULL)
        return;
    WORD seg = FP_SEG(ptr);                // get data segment..
    WORD off = FP_OFF(ptr);                // ..and seg-relative offset
    if (off==0) {                          // big block with no heap
        HANDLE h  = GlobalHandle(seg);
        nBigObj--;
        nBigObjBytes -= GlobalSize(h);
        GlobalUnlock(h);
        GlobalFree(h);
    } else {
        MemHeap *heap = findHeap(seg);     // find heap the mem belongs to
        heap->free((void NEAR*)off);       // free it
        if (heap->numObj==0)               // if that was the last object:
            delHeap(heap);                 // free the whole heap
    }
}
///////////////////
// Delete (free) a heap: remove from chain, and delete it.
//
void WPApp::delHeap(MemHeap *heap)
{
    if (heap==firstHeap)
        firstHeap = heap->next;
    else {
        for (MemHeap *h=firstHeap; h; h=h->next) {
            if (h->next == heap) {
                h->next = heap->next;
                break;
            }
        }
        assert(h!=NULL);        // should always find it!
    }
    if (heap==mruHeap)
        mruHeap = NULL;
    delete heap;
}
///////////////////
// Free all the app's memory heaps.
//
void WPApp::freeAllHeaps()
{
    long numObj = nBigObj + localHeap.numObj - nStartObj;
    while (firstHeap) {
        numObj += firstHeap->numObj;
        delHeap(firstHeap);
    }
    if (numObj != 0)
        ErrBox("%ld objects remaining!", numObj);
}
///////////////////
// Allocate memory from the application's local heap.
// Returns a pointer (either near or far, depending on the model).
//
void* WPApp::localAlloc(WORD size, BOOL useHandler)
{
    if (!registered) {
        // in case start-up code calls new before App constructor,
        // initialize the local heap manually
        WORD temp;
        GETAPPDS(temp);
```

```
        localHeap.seg = temp;
    }
    void NEAR *np;
    do {
        np = localHeap.alloc(size);
    } while (np==NULL && useHandler && callNoMemHandler(size));
#ifdef __LARGE__
    return localHeap.makeFarPtr(np);
#else
    return np;
#endif
}
/////////////////
// Free local memory.
//
void WPApp::localFree(void* ptr)
{
    if (ptr)
        localHeap.free((void NEAR*)ptr);
}
/////////////////
// Get size of memory block
//
DWORD WPApp::memSize(void FAR* ptr)
{
    WORD seg = FP_SEG(ptr);
    WORD off = FP_OFF(ptr);
    if (off==0)
        return GlobalSize(GlobalHandle(seg));
    MemHeap *heap = findHeap(seg);      // find heap the mem belongs to
    return heap->blockSize((void NEAR*)off);
}
/////////////////
// Set the "no memory" handler; returns old handler. Applications
// can use this to trap the "out of memory" condition.  The function
// should return TRUE if we're supposed to retry the allocation.
//
NOMEMHANDLER WPApp::setNoMemHandler(NOMEMHANDLER fn)
{
    NOMEMHANDLER oldFn = noMemHandler;
    noMemHandler = fn;
    return oldFn;
}
/////////////////
// Call the "no memory" handler, if any.  Returns BOOL indicating
// whether or not to retry the allocation that failed.
//
BOOL WPApp::callNoMemHandler(WORD size)
{
    BOOL ret = FALSE;
    if (noMemHandler && !inNoMemHandler) {
        inNoMemHandler++;                   // prevent infinite recursion
        ret = (*noMemHandler)(size);
        inNoMemHandler--;
    }
    return ret;
}
/////////////////
// Default no-memory handler just displays a message (which should really
// be a STRING resource).
//
BOOL WPApp::DfltNoMemHandler(WORD size)
{
    if (MsgBox("The system has run out of memory.  You may be able to reclaim
some memory by closing other applications; if so, close them now and then press
'Retry'; otherwise, press 'Cancel' to terminate this application", "ATTENTION",
MB_ICONSTOP|MB_RETRYCANCEL)==IDRETRY)
        return TRUE;
```

```
    App.freeAllHeaps();        // in case exit doesn't call ~WPApp
    exit(-1);                  // goodbye!
    return FALSE;              // to make compiler happy
}
///////////////////
// Display application statistics in a message box.
//
int WPApp::showStats(BOOL cancel)
{
    char *s=scratch;           // use scratch pad to build message string
    // Show number and size of "big" objects
    s += sprintf(s,"BIG OBJECTS:\t%d obj\t%ld bytes\n",nBigObj,nBigObjBytes);
    // First show stats for LOCAL heap
    long nObj = localHeap.numObj;
    long nBytes = localHeap.numBytes;
    s += sprintf(s, "LOCAL HEAP:\t%ld obj\t%ld bytes\n", nObj, nBytes);
    // Now show stats for other heaps, up to ten of them.
    MemHeap *h, *next;
    int nHeaps;
    for (h=firstHeap, nHeaps=0; h; h=h->next,nHeaps++) {
        if (nHeaps < 10)
            s += sprintf(s, "HEAP [%x]:\t%d obj\t%ld bytes\n",
                    h->seg, h->numObj, h->numBytes);
        else if (nHeaps==10)
            s += sprintf(s,". . .");
        nObj += h->numObj;
        nBytes += h->numBytes;
    }
    if (nHeaps)
        sprintf(s, "\nTotals: %d heaps, %ld objects, %ld bytes.",
            nHeaps, nObj, nBytes);
    return MsgBox(scratch, getName(), cancel ? MB_OKCANCEL : MB_OK);
}
///////////////////
// Show stats for all registered apps (if DLL).
//
void WPApp::ShowAllStats()
{
    WPApp *thisApp = &App;  // get current app
    thisApp->showStats();   // show current app's stats
    for (WPApp *app = registeredApps; app; app = app->next) {
        if (app != thisApp && app->showStats(TRUE)==IDCANCEL)
            break;
    }
}
///////////////////
// Get the application object for the calling application.
// We use the fact that SS==caller's data segment.
//
WPApp* WPApp::GetApp()
{
    WORD dsval;
    GETAPPDS(dsval); // get application's data segment selector
    // Search list to find application w/matching DS
    for (WPApp *app = registeredApps; app; app = app->next) {
        if (app->dsval == dsval)
            return app;
    }
    assert(FALSE);     // should always find it!
    return NULL;
}
///////////////////
// Add modeless dialog to application
//
void WPApp::addDialog(WPDialogModeless *dlg)
{
    dlg->next = dialogs;
```

```
    dialogs = dlg;
}
/////////////////
// Remove modeless dialog from application
//
void WPApp::removeDialog(WPDialogModeless *dlg)
{
    if (dlg==dialogs)
        dialogs=dlg->next;
    else {
        for (WPDialogModeless *d=dialogs; d; d=d->next) {
            if (d->next == dlg) {
                d->next = dlg->next;
                break;
            }
        }
        assert(d);
    }
}
/////////////////////////////////////////////////////////////////////////////
// The following functions access the Application's profile (.INI) file.
/////////////////////////////////////////////////////////////////////////////
//////////////////
// Make .INI filename from module name (appname.INI).
//
void WPApp::makeIniFileName(char *buf)
{
    strcpy(buf, getName());
    buf[8]=0;
    strcat(buf, ".ini");
}
//////////////////
// Get appliation profile string.  If no appname is specified,
// gets it from either WIN.INI or appname.INI, depending on
// value of flag useWININI.
//
int WPApp::getProfile(CSTR key, char *buf, int buflen, CSTR dflt, CSTR app)
{
    if (app==NULL)
        app=getName();
    if (useWININI)
        return WinIni.get(app, key, buf, buflen, dflt);
    makeIniFileName(scratch);
    return GetPrivateProfileString((LPSTR)app,
        (LPSTR)key, (LPSTR)dflt, buf, buflen, scratch);
}
/////////////////
// Same thing, only get integer instead of string.
//
int WPApp::getProfile(CSTR key, int dflt, CSTR app)
{
    if (app==NULL)
        app=getName();
    if (useWININI)
        return WinIni.get(app, key, dflt);
    makeIniFileName(scratch);
    return GetPrivateProfileInt((LPSTR)app, (LPSTR)key, dflt, scratch);
}
//////////////////
// Same thing, only set instead of get.
//
BOOL WPApp::setProfile(CSTR key, CSTR val, CSTR app)
{
    if (app==NULL)
        app=getName();
    if (useWININI)
        return WinIni.set(app, key, val);
```

```
    makeIniFileName(scratch);
    return WritePrivateProfileString((LPSTR)app,
        (LPSTR)key,(LPSTR)val,scratch);
}
/////////////////
// ...more of same
//
BOOL WPApp::setProfile(CSTR key, int val, CSTR app)
{
    if (app==NULL)
        app=getName();
    if (useWININI)
        return WinIni.set(app, key, val);
    makeIniFileName(scratch);
    char buf[16];
    itoa(val, buf, 10);
    return WritePrivateProfileString((LPSTR)app, (LPSTR)key, buf, scratch);
}
/////////////////////////////////////////////////////////////////
// Below are a few utility routines used throughout Windows++.
// This seems like as good a place as any to put them.
/////////////////////////////////////////////////////////////////
/////////////////
// This is a handy function for doing printf-style error boxes.
//
int DLLFUNC ErrBox(CSTR format, ...)
{
    char buf[128];
    va_list argptr;
    va_start(argptr, format);
    vsprintf(buf, format, argptr);
    va_end(argptr);
    return MessageBox(NULL, buf, NULL, MB_OK | MB_ICONEXCLAMATION);
}
/////////////////
// Utility function copies source string into caller's
// buffer, given buffer length.
//
int DLLFUNC StringCopy(char *dest, int buflen, CSTR src)
{
    int rlen = strlen(src);
    int len = min(buflen-1, rlen);
    if (len>0) {
        strncpy(dest, src, len);
        dest[len]=0;
    }
    return rlen;
}
/////////////////
// Assertion failure
//
void DLLFUNC DoAssert(CSTR msg, CSTR file, unsigned line)
{
    char buf[80];
    sprintf(buf,"at line %u in file %s: \"%s\"",line,file,msg);
    MsgBeep();
    if (MsgBox(buf,"ASSERTION FAILURE",
            MB_OKCANCEL|MB_ICONSTOP|MB_TASKMODAL)!=IDOK)
        exit(-1);
}
```

WPBUTN.H

```
/////////////////////////////////////////////////////////////
// WINDOWS++ CLASS LIBRARY.  Copyright 1992 Paul DiLascia.
// FILE: WPBUTN.H
//
// Button definitions.
```

```
#ifndef WPBUTN_H
#define WPBUTN_H
#ifndef WPCTRL_H
#include "wpctrl.h"
#endif
#ifndef WPODRAW_H
#include "wpodraw.h"
#endif
/////////////////
// Button object.  Underlying data is BOOL.
//
DLLCLASS WPButton : public WPControl {
public:
    WPButton(WPWin *pwin, int id, long sty=BS_PUSHBUTTON)
        : WPControl("Button", pwin, id, sty)   { }
    static WPControl* New(WPWin* pwin, int id)
        { return new WPButton(pwin, id); }
    // General control functions
    void updateScreen()             { if (object) setCheck(*((BOOL*)object)); }
    void updateObject()             { if (object) *((BOOL*)object)=getCheck(); }
    void linkObject(BOOL *pbool)   { object=pbool; }
    // "Brainless" Windows functions
    BOOL getCheck()                 { return sendMsg(BM_GETCHECK); }
    void setCheck(BOOL state)   { sendMsg(BM_SETCHECK, state); }
};
/////////////////
// Radiobutton group.  Underlying data is integer (enum).
//
DLLCLASS WPRBGroup : public WPControl {
public:
    WPRBGroup(WPWin *pwin, int id, long sty=BS_GROUPBOX)
        : WPControl("Button", pwin, id, sty) { }
    static WPControl* New(WPWin* pwin, int id)
        { return new WPRBGroup(pwin, id); }
    // General control functions
    void linkObject(int *pint, int nButtons)
        { object=pint; objsiz = nButtons; }
    void updateScreen()         { if (object) setSel(*((int*)object)); }
    void updateObject()         { if (object) *((int*)object) = getSel(); }
    // Get/set selection
    int getSel();
    void setSel(int sel);
};
/////////////////
// Checkbox group.  Underlying data is array of BOOLs.
//
DLLCLASS WPCBGroup : public WPControl {
public:
    WPCBGroup(WPWin *pwin, int id, long sty=BS_GROUPBOX)
        : WPControl("Button", pwin, id, sty) { }
    static WPControl* New(WPWin* pwin, int id)
        { return new WPCBGroup(pwin, id); }
    // General control functions
    void updateScreen()         { if (object) setSel((BOOL*)object); }
    void updateObject()         { if (object) getSel((BOOL*)object); }
    void linkObject(BOOL *array, int nButtons)
        { object=array; objsiz = nButtons; }
    // Get/set selection
    void setSel(BOOL *barray);
    void getSel(BOOL *barray);
    void setAll(BOOL val);
};
/////////////////
// Owner-draw button, multiply derived from button and owner-draw item.
//
DLLCLASS WPODButton : public WPButton, public WPOwnerDrawItem {
public:
    WPODButton(WPWin* pwin, int id) : WPButton(pwin, id, BS_OWNERDRAW),
```

```
            WPOwnerDrawItem(pwin, ODT_BUTTON) { }
    int getID() { return WPWin::getID(); }
};
#endif
```

WPCOMBO.H

```
/////////////////////////////////////////////////////////
// WINDOWS++ CLASS LIBRARY.  Copyright 1992 Paul DiLascia.
// FILE: WPCOMBO.H
//
// Combo box definitions.
#ifndef WPCOMBO_H
#define WPCOMBO_H
#ifndef WPLIST_H
#include "wplist.h"
#endif
#define CBS_DEFAULT   (WS_BORDER | CBS_AUTOHSCROLL | CBS_DROPDOWN)
#define CBS_DEFAULTOD (CBS_DEFAULT | CBS_OWNERDRAWVARIABLE)
/////////////////////
// Combo Box
//
DLLCLASS WPComboBox : public WPControl {
    WPListData *list;           // the list
public:
    WPComboBox(WPWin *pwin, int id, long sty=CBS_DEFAULT)
        : WPControl("ComboBox", pwin, id, sty) { }
    static WPControl* New(WPWin* pwin, int id)
        { return new WPComboBox(pwin, id); }
    void setList(WPListData *l, int sel=0, BOOL redraw=TRUE);
    // General control functions
    void linkObject(char* buf, int len)
        { object=buf; objsiz=len; }
    void updateObject()
        { if (object) getText((char*)object, objsiz); }
    void updateScreen()
        { if (object) { setText((char*)object); setMaxLen(objsiz-1); } }
    // List Box functions
    int count()                 { return sendMsg(CB_GETCOUNT); }
    void reset()                { sendMsg(CB_RESETCONTENT); }
    void append(CSTR text)      { sendMsg(CB_ADDSTRING, 0, text); }
    void insert(CSTR text, int i)
        { sendMsg(CB_INSERTSTRING, i, text); }
    void delItem(int index)     { sendMsg(CB_DELETESTRING, index); }
    // Get/set selection
    int getSel()                { return sendMsg(CB_GETCURSEL); }
    void setSel(int sel)        { sendMsg(CB_SETCURSEL, sel); }
    int setSel(CSTR text, int start=-1)
        { return sendMsg(CB_SELECTSTRING, start, text); }
    int getSel(char *buf)
        { return (int)sendMsg(CB_GETLBTEXT, getSel(), buf); }
    // Edit control functions
    LONG getTextSel() { return sendMsg(CB_GETEDITSEL); }
    LONG getTextSel(int& beg, int& end)
        { LONG x = getTextSel(); beg=LOWORD(x); end=HIWORD(x); return x; }
    void setTextSel(int beg=0, int end=MAXINT)
        { sendMsg(CB_SETEDITSEL, 0, MAKELONG(beg, end)); }
    BOOL setMaxLen(int len)
        { return sendMsg(CB_LIMITTEXT, len); }
    // Combo Box
    void showDropDown(BOOL show)        { sendMsg(CB_SHOWDROPDOWN, show); }
};
/////////////////////
// Owner-draw combo box, multiply derived from combo box and owner-draw item.
//
DLLCLASS WPODComboBox : public WPComboBox, public WPOwnerDrawItem {
public:
    WPODComboBox(WPWin* pwin, int id, long sty=CBS_DEFAULTOD)
```

```
        : WPComboBox(pwin, id, sty), WPOwnerDrawItem(pwin, ODT_COMBOBOX) { }
    int getID() { return WPWin::getID(); }
};
#endif
```

WPCTRL.H

```
//////////////////////////////////////////////////////////
// WINDOWS++ CLASS LIBRARY.  Copyright 1992 Paul DiLascia.
// FILE: WPCTRL.H
//
// Control class definitions.
#ifndef WPCTRL_H
#define WPCTRL_H
#ifndef WPWIN_H
#include "wpwin.h"
#endif
//////////////////////
// Generic control, an abstract class.
// Specifc controls are all derived from this class.
//
DLLCLASS WPControl : public WPWin {
private:
    void linkObject(void *obj, int siz) { object=obj; objsiz=siz; }
    BOOL tryLink();
    friend WPDialog;
protected:
    void *object;            // pointer to unknown object
    int objsiz;              // size of object
    WPControl(CSTR  classnm, WPWin *pwin, int id, long style=0);
public:
    // virtual functions defined by each specific control
    virtual void updateObject() = 0;
    virtual void updateScreen() = 0;
    BOOL createWin()
        { return tryLink() ? TRUE : WPWin::createWin(); }
};
#endif
```

WPCTRL.CPP

```
//////////////////////////////////////////////////////////
// WINDOWS++ CLASS LIBRARY.  Copyright 1992 Paul DiLascia.
// FILE: WPCTRL.CPP
//
// Implementation of control window classes.  To reduce compilation time,
// all control objects (edit, list box, etc.) are implemented here.
//
#include "wpctrl.h"
#include "wpbutn.h"
#include "wpcombo.h"
#include "wpedit.h"
#include "wplist.h"
#include "wpsbar.h"
#include "wpstatic.h"
#include "wpglob.h"
#include "wpgdi.h"
#include "wpapp.h"
#include <ctype.h>
#include <sys\stat.h>
//////////////////
// Create control object.
// Args like for WPWin: class name, parent win and id.
//
WPControl::WPControl(CSTR classnm, WPWin *pwin, int id, long style)
    : WPWin(classnm, pwin, id)
{
    createArgs.style |= style;
```

```
        object = NULL;
        objsiz = 0;
        tryLink();      // link if window already exists
}
/////////////////
// Try to link control to its window.
//
BOOL WPControl::tryLink()
{
    if (getHwnd())
        return TRUE;
    HWND hwndParent = GetHwnd(createArgs.parent);
    if (hwndParent) {
        HWND hwndChild = GetDlgItem(hwndParent, createArgs.id());
        if (hwndChild) {
            linkHwnd(hwndChild);
            return TRUE;
        }
    }
    return FALSE;
}
/////////////////
// Static helper function, used by button group objects to create
// button object for each button in the group if none exists.
//
static WPButton *GetButton(WPWin *pwin, int id)
{
    WPButton *butn = (WPButton*)pwin->getChild(id);
    if (butn==NULL)
        butn = new WPButton(pwin, id);
    assert(butn);
    return butn;
}
/////////////////
// Get selection of radiobutton group.  Returns integer: 0 if 1st
// button selected, 1 if second, and so on.  Assumes only one
// is selected.
//
int WPRBGroup::getSel()
{
    WPWin *parent = getParent();
    int id=getID();
    for (int count = 0; count < objsiz; count++) {
        if (GetButton(parent, ++id)->getCheck())
            return count;
    }
    return -1;
}
/////////////////
// Set radiobutton corresponding to enum: 0 sets first button,
// 1 sets second, etc.  All others are turned off.
//
void WPRBGroup::setSel(int sel)
{
    WPWin *parent = getParent();
    int id=getID();
    for (int count = 0; count < objsiz; count++)
        GetButton(parent, ++id)->setCheck(count==sel);
}
/////////////////
// Checkbox Button Group.
//
/////////////////
// Check buttons from arary of BOOLs.
//
void WPCBGroup::setSel(BOOL *barray)
{
    if (barray) {
```

```
            WPWin *parent = getParent();
            int id=getID();
            for (int count = objsiz; count > 0; count--)
                GetButton(parent, ++id)->setCheck(*barray++);
    }
}
/////////////////////
// Stuff array of BOOLs with current button states.
//
void WPCBGroup::getSel(BOOL *barray)
{
    if (barray) {
        WPWin *parent = getParent();
        int id=getID();
        for (int count = objsiz; count > 0; count--)
            *barray++ = GetButton(parent, ++id)->getCheck();
    }
}
/////////////////////
// Set all buttons in checkbox group on or off.
//
void WPCBGroup::setAll(BOOL val)
{
    WPWin *parent = getParent();
    int id=getID();
    for (int count = objsiz; count > 0; count--) {
        WPButton *butn = GetButton(parent, ++id);
        butn->setCheck(val);
    }
}
/////////////////////
// Edit Control
//
/////////////////////
// Filter keyboard char through "legalChars".
//
BOOL WPEdit::kbd(WPEvent& event)
{
    if (legalChars) {
        char c = event.key();
        if ( event.msg==WM_CHAR && ( isprint(c) && !strchr(legalChars,c)) ) {
            MsgBeep();
            return TRUE;
        }
    }
    return WPControl::kbd(event);
}
/////////////////////
// Paste text into edit control.
//
void WPEdit::paste(BOOL flush)
{
    int beg,end;
    getSel(beg, end);
    sendMsg(WM_PASTE);
    if (flush) {
        Clipboard.open(this);
        Clipboard.empty();
        Clipboard.close();
    }
    getSel(end, end);
    setSel(beg, end);
}
/////////////////////
// Load contents of file into edit control.
//
BOOL WPMultiEdit::load(CSTR fname)
```

```
{
    int ret = FALSE;
    struct stat temp;
    if (stat((char*)fname, &temp) >= 0) {
        DWORD len = temp.st_size;
        LPSTR buf = (LPSTR)App.farAlloc(len+1, FALSE);
        if (buf) {
            OFSTRUCT of;
            int fd = OpenFile((LPSTR)fname, (LPOFSTRUCT)&of, OF_READ);
            if (fd!=-1) {
                _lread(fd, buf, len);
                _lclose(fd);
                buf[len]=0;
                setText(buf);
                ret = TRUE;
            } else
                ErrBox("Unable to open file '%s'.", fname);
            App.farFree(buf);
        } else
            ErrBox("File too big.");
    }
    return ret;
}
/////////////////
// Write contents of edit control to file.
//
BOOL WPMultiEdit::save(CSTR fname)
{
    assert(*fname);
    DWORD len = getText();
    LPSTR buf = (LPSTR)App.farAlloc(len, FALSE);
    if (buf) {
        OFSTRUCT of;
        getText(buf, len);
        int fd = OpenFile((LPSTR)fname, (LPOFSTRUCT)&of, OF_CREATE);
        if (fd!=-1) {
            _lwrite(fd, buf, len);
            _lclose(fd);
        } else
            ErrBox("Unable to open file '%s'.", fname);
        App.farFree(buf);
        return TRUE;
    } else
        ErrBox("File too big.");
    return FALSE;
}
/////////////////
// List/Combo Box.
//
void WPListBox::setList(WPListData *l, int selected, BOOL redraw)
{
    if ((list = l) != NULL) {
        reset();                // erase contents
        if (list->firstItem()) {
            char buf[80];
            setReDraw(FALSE);
            // Add items 2 through N.
            while (list->nextItem()) {
                list->getItemText(buf, sizeof(buf));
                append(buf);
            }
            if (redraw)
                setReDraw(TRUE);
            // Now insert 1st item
            list->firstItem();
            list->getItemText(buf, sizeof(buf));
            insert(buf, 0);
        }
```

```
    }
    setSel(selected);
}
///////////////////
// Combo is same as for list box; they should really be derived from
// common base class to avoid duplicate code, but I was lazy.
//
void WPComboBox::setList(WPListData *l, int selected, BOOL redraw)
{
    if ((list = l) != NULL) {
        reset();                // erase contents
        if (list->firstItem()) {
            char buf[80];
            setReDraw(FALSE);
            // Add items 2 through N.
            while (list->nextItem()) {
                list->getItemText(buf, sizeof(buf));
                append(buf);
            }
            if (redraw)
                setReDraw(TRUE);
            // Now insert 1st item
            list->firstItem();
            list->getItemText(buf, sizeof(buf));
            insert(buf, 0);
        }
    }
    setSel(selected);
}
///////////////////
// Handle scrollbar message.
//
void WPScrollBar::handleMsg(int msg, int thumbPos)
{
    int pos = scrollPos();
    switch (msg) {
    case SB_LINEUP:
        pos -= lineIncr;
        break;
    case SB_LINEDOWN:
        pos += lineIncr;
        break;
    case SB_PAGEUP:
        pos -= pageIncr;
        break;
    case SB_PAGEDOWN:
        pos += pageIncr;
        break;
    case SB_THUMBPOSITION:
    case SB_THUMBTRACK:
        pos = thumbPos;
        break;
    }
    scrollPos(pos);
}
///////////////////
// Use GDI functions to update screen for a static icon.
//
void WPStaticIcon::updateScreen()
{
    if (object) {
        WPWinDC dc = this;
        dc.drawIcon(0, 0, (HICON)object);
    }
}
```

WPDLFILE.H

```
//////////////////////////////////////////////////////////
// WINDOWS++ CLASS LIBRARY.  Copyright 1992 Paul DiLascia.
// FILE: WPDLFILE.H
//
// File Dialog definitions.
#ifndef WPDLFILE_H
#define WPDLFILE_H
#ifndef WPDLG_H
#include "wpdlg.h"
#endif
extern "C" {
////////////////
// The following definitions come from COMMDLG.H,
// in the Micrsoft Windows 3.1 SDK.
//
struct OPENFILENAME {
    DWORD   lStructSize;        // size of this structure
    HWND    hwndOwner;         // owner window
    HANDLE  hInstance;         // module instance
    LPSTR   lpstrFilter;       // filename "filter" e.g., *.TXT
    LPSTR   lpstrCustomFilter; // custom filter
    DWORD   nMaxCustFilter;    // ..size
    DWORD   nFilterIndex;      // index of filter to display
    LPSTR   lpstrFile;         // filename
    DWORD   nMaxFile;          // ..
    LPSTR   lpstrFileTitle;    // file title
    DWORD   nMaxFileTitle;     // ..
    LPSTR   lpstrInitialDir;   // name of initial directory
    LPSTR   lpstrTitle;        // dialog title
    DWORD   Flags;             // see below
    WORD    nFileOffset;       // used internally ??
    WORD    nFileExtension;    // size of extension
    LPSTR   lpstrDefExt;       // default extension
    DWORD   lCustData;         // custom data
    FARPROC lpfnHook;          // dialog procedure, if hooked
    LPSTR   lpTemplateName;
};
typedef OPENFILENAME FAR * LPOPENFILENAME;
// DLL functions to run file dialogs.
BOOL  FAR PASCAL       GetOpenFileName(LPOPENFILENAME);
BOOL  FAR PASCAL       GetSaveFileName(LPOPENFILENAME);
short FAR PASCAL       GetFileTitle(LPSTR, LPSTR, WORD);
#define OFN_READONLY                 0x00000001
#define OFN_OVERWRITEPROMPT          0x00000002
#define OFN_HIDEREADONLY             0x00000004
#define OFN_NOCHANGEDIR              0x00000008
#define OFN_SHOWHELP                 0x00000010
#define OFN_ENABLEHOOK               0x00000020
#define OFN_ENABLETEMPLATE           0x00000040
#define OFN_ENABLETEMPLATEHANDLE     0x00000080
#define OFN_NOVALIDATE               0x00000100
#define OFN_ALLOWMULTISELECT         0x00000200
#define OFN_EXTENSIONDIFFERENT       0x00000400
#define OFN_PATHMUSTEXIST            0x00000800
#define OFN_FILEMUSTEXIST            0x00001000
#define OFN_CREATEPROMPT             0x00002000
#define OFN_SHAREAWARE               0x00004000
#define OFN_NOREADONLYRETURN         0x00008000
#define OFN_NOTESTFILECREATE         0x00010000
#define OFN_SHAREFALLTHROUGH   2
#define OFN_SHARENOWARN        1
#define OFN_SHAREWARN          0
#define SHARE_EXIST            (OF_EXIST | OF_SHARE_DENY_NONE)
} // end of extern "C"
////////////////
// File Open dialog.
```

```
//
DLLCLASS WPDlgFileOpen : public WPDialogModal {
protected:
    OPENFILENAME ofn;
    char tempbuf[MAXFILENAMELEN];
    char *filename;
public:
    WPDlgFileOpen(WPWin *pwin, char* fname, CSTR title=NULL);
    BOOL createWin();
    void destroyWin() { sendMsg(WM_COMMAND, IDABORT, result); }
    BOOL command(int id, WORD msg)    { return FALSE; }
    void setFilter(CSTR filt)
        { if (filt) ofn.lpstrFilter=(LPSTR)filt; }
    void setDir(CSTR dir)
        { ofn.lpstrInitialDir=(LPSTR)dir; }
};
/////////////////
// File Save As dialog.
// Like File Open, but uses different COMMDLG subroutine.
//
DLLCLASS WPDlgFileSaveAs : public WPDlgFileOpen {
public:
    WPDlgFileSaveAs(WPWin *pwin, char* fname, CSTR title=NULL);
    BOOL createWin();
};
#endif
```

WPDLFILE.CPP

```
/////////////////////////////////////////////////////////////
// WINDOWS++ CLASS LIBRARY.  Copyright 1992 Paul DiLascia.
// FILE: WPDLFILE.CPP
//
// Implementation of file dialogs.
#include "wpdlfile.h"
#include "wpapp.h"
#include "wpid.h"
const OFN_DEFAULT = OFN_ENABLEHOOK | OFN_PATHMUSTEXIST | OFN_HIDEREADONLY;
const OFN_OPENDEFAULT = OFN_DEFAULT | OFN_FILEMUSTEXIST;
const OFN_SAVEDEFAULT = OFN_DEFAULT | OFN_OVERWRITEPROMPT;
const char DEFAULTFILT[] = "Any File (*.*)\0*.*\0";
/////////////////
// Create File Open dialog.
//
WPDlgFileOpen::WPDlgFileOpen(WPWin *pwin, char* fname, CSTR title)
    : WPDialogModal(NULL, pwin)
{
    filename = fname;
    tempbuf[0]=0;
    memset(&ofn, 0, sizeof(ofn));
    ofn.lStructSize=sizeof(ofn);
    ofn.hwndOwner = GetHwnd(pwin);
    ofn.lpstrFile=tempbuf;
    ofn.nMaxFile=sizeof(tempbuf);
    ofn.lpstrTitle= (LPSTR)title;
    ofn.Flags= OFN_OPENDEFAULT;
    ofn.lpfnHook = App.getDlgProc();
    ofn.nFilterIndex=1;
    setFilter(DEFAULTFILT);
}
/////////////////
// Create window: just call COMMDLG.
//
BOOL WPDlgFileOpen::createWin()
{
    if ((result = GetOpenFileName(&ofn))!=0 && filename)
        strcpy(filename, tempbuf);
```

```
        return result != -1;
}
/////////////////////
// File Save As dialog.
//
WPDlgFileSaveAs::WPDlgFileSaveAs(WPWin *pwin, char* fname, CSTR title)
    : WPDlgFileOpen(pwin, fname, title)
{
    ofn.Flags= OFN_SAVEDEFAULT;
}
/////////////////////
// Create window: just call COMMDLG.
//
BOOL WPDlgFileSaveAs::createWin()
{
    if ((result = GetSaveFileName(&ofn))!=0 && filename)
        strcpy(filename, tempbuf);
    return result != -1;
}
```

WPDLG.H

```
/////////////////////////////////////////////////////////////
// WINDOWS++ CLASS LIBRARY.  Copyright 1992 Paul DiLascia.
// FILE: WPDLG.H
//
// Dialog box definitions.
#ifndef WPDLG_H
#define WPDLG_H
#ifndef WPCTRL_H
#include "wpctrl.h"
#endif
#ifndef WPODRAW_H
#include "wpodraw.h"
#endif
#ifndef WPID_H
#include "wpid.h"
#endif
typedef WPControl* pWPControl;
typedef pWPControl (*NEWCTLFN) (WPWin*, int);
/////////////////////
// Structure used to map controls to underlying data.
// Used to build table-driven dialogs.
//
struct WPControlMap {
    NEWCTLFN newfn;         // function to create instance of control
    int id;                 // control ID
    int offset;             // offset of data
    int len;                // length of data
    friend WPDialog;
};
/////////////////////
// Macros used to initialize static control maps
//
#ifndef offsetof
#define offsetof(typ,mbr)  ((size_t)((char *)&((typ *)0)->mbr - (char *)0))
#endif
#define cmCust(fn, id, typ, mbr) \
    { fn,id,offsetof(typ,mbr),sizeof(((typ *)0)->mbr) },
#define cmEdit(id, typ, mbr)    cmCust(WPEdit::New, id, typ, mbr)
#define cmButn(id, typ, mbr)    cmCust(WPButton::New, id, typ, mbr)
#define cmCmbo(id, typ, mbr)    cmCust(WPComboBox::New, id, typ, mbr)
#define cmList(id, typ, mbr)    cmCust(WPListBox::New, id, typ, mbr)
#define cmSbar(id, typ, mbr)    cmCust(WPScrollBar::New, id, typ, mbr)
#define cmRBgp(id, typ, mbr,n)  { WPRBGroup::New, id, offsetof(typ,mbr), n },
#define cmCBgp(id, typ, mbr,n)  { WPCBGroup::New, id, offsetof(typ,mbr), n },
#define cmPush(id)              { WPButton::New, id, NULL, 0 },
#define cmEnd(id)               { NULL, id }
```

```
/////////////////
// Base class used for all dialogs.
//
DLLCLASS WPDialog : public WPWin {
private:
    static WPDialog* NewDialog;      // global: dialog being initialized
    WPControlMap *ctlmap;            // control map links data to controls
    void *object;                    // underlying data object
    BOOL modified;                   // dialog modified
    WPODItemList odItems;            // owner-draw items, if any
    LONG msgProc(WPEvent &event) { return dfltMsgProc(event); }
    BOOL init();
    friend BOOL _export FAR PASCAL WPDlgProc(HWND, WORD, WORD, LONG);
protected:
    CSTR templateName;        // name of resource template
    int focusID;              // ID of control to receive initial focus
    int result;               // IDOK,IDCANCEL, etc.
    void endDlg(int code)     { result=code; destroyWin(); }
    void loadError();
public:
    WPDialog(CSTR resname, WPWin *pwin=NULL,
        WPControlMap *map=NULL, void* obj=NULL);
    void linkObject(void *obj, BOOL redisplay=TRUE);
    void* getObject()         { return object; }
    BOOL isModified()         { return modified; }
    void isModified(BOOL m) { modified=m; }
    // Virtual WPWin functions overridden for dialog boxes
    BOOL scrolled(int msg, int id, int thumbPos);
    BOOL command(int id, WORD msg);
    BOOL closed() { command(IDCANCEL, BN_CLICKED); return FALSE; }
    BOOL other(WPEvent &event);
    // New virtual functions defined for dialog boxes
    virtual void initDlg() { }
    virtual void updateObject();
    virtual void updateScreen();
    // Miscellaneous functions
    int run()                         { createWin(); return result; }
    void mapRect(WPRect& r)           { MapDialogRect(getHwnd(), (LPRECT)&r); }
    int returnCode()                  { return result; }
    WPControl *getControl(int id) { return (WPControl*)getChild(id); }
    int defaultID()                   { return LOWORD(sendMsg(DM_GETDEFID)); }
    void defaultID(int id)            { sendMsg(DM_SETDEFID, id); }
    void addODItem(WPOwnerDrawItem* od) { odItems.add(od); }
};
/////////////////
// Modal dialog box.
//
DLLCLASS WPDialogModal : public WPDialog {
public:
    WPDialogModal(CSTR resname, WPWin *pwin=NULL, WPControlMap *map=NULL,
        void* obj=NULL) : WPDialog(resname, pwin, map, obj) { }
    BOOL createWin();
    void destroyWin() { EndDialog(getHwnd(), result); }
};
/////////////////
// Modeless dialog box.
//
DLLCLASS WPDialogModeless : public WPDialog {
    WPDialogModeless* next; // next modeless dlg in app
    friend WPApp;
public:
    WPDialogModeless(CSTR resname, WPWin *pwin=NULL,
        WPControlMap *map=NULL, void *obj=NULL);
    ~WPDialogModeless();
    BOOL createWin();
};
#endif
```

WPDLG.CPP

```
/////////////////////////////////////////////////////////
// WINDOWS++ CLASS LIBRARY.  Copyright 1992 Paul DiLascia.
// FILE: WPDLG.CPP
//
// Dialog implementation.
#include "wpapp.h"
#include "wpdlg.h"
#include "wpsbar.h"
// This global is used to identify which dialog object should
// be linked when processing WM_INITDIALOG.
// Famous quote: "I can't program without globals." -BTB
//
WPDialog * WPDialog::NewDialog = NULL;
//////////////////
// Create dialog box.
//
WPDialog::WPDialog(CSTR resname, WPWin *pwin, WPControlMap *map, void *obj)
   : WPWin(NULL, pwin)
{
   NewDialog = this;       // set global so WPDlgProc knows to link me
   templateName = resname;
   ctlmap = map;
   object = obj;
   result = 0;
   focusID = 0;
}
//////////////////
// Initialize dialog.
// This private function is used interally by Windows++ only.
//
BOOL WPDialog::init()
{
   modified = FALSE;
   linkObject(object, FALSE); // link controls to underlying object
   initDlg();                 // call app-specific public virtual function
   updateScreen();            // copy object->screen
   return focusID==0;
}
//////////////////
// Link object to dialog. ctlmap specifies the structure of the object,
// and which controls are linked to which data members. The last entry
// in the table specifies the initial focus control ID.
//
void WPDialog::linkObject(void *obj, BOOL redisplay)
{
   object = obj;
   if (!ctlmap)
      return;
   // Loop over control map, linking each control one at a time.
   for (WPControlMap* map = ctlmap; map->newfn; map++) {
      int id = map->id;
      HWND chwnd = GetDlgItem(getHwnd(), id);
      if (chwnd==NULL) {
         // Control doesn't exist in dialog!
         ErrBox("Error: ID %d is in control map but not dialog!", id);
         continue;
      }
      WPControl *ctl = (WPControl*)GetWin(chwnd);
      if (ctl==NULL)                        // if control (W++ object) no exist:
         ctl = (*map->newfn)(this, id);     // create one.
      assert(ctl);
      // Now link the control to its data object.
      if (object && map->len > 0)
         ctl->linkObject((char*)object + map->offset, map->len);
      else
         ctl->linkObject(NULL, 0);
```

```
    }
    focusID = map->id;        // last id = initial focus
    if (redisplay)            // redisplay requested:
        updateScreen();       // update all the controls on screen
}
/////////////////
// Update the screen: just udpate each control.
//
void WPDialog::updateScreen()
{
    forEachChildWin(this, cwin) {
        ((WPControl*)cwin)->updateScreen();
        if (cwin->getID()==focusID)
            cwin->setFocus();
    }
}
/////////////////
// Update the data object: update from each control.
//
void WPDialog::updateObject()
{
    modified = TRUE;
    forEachChildWin(this, cwin)
        ((WPControl*)cwin)->updateObject();
}
/////////////////
// Handle menu command.
// Default behavior for modal dialog box:
// OK:      update the underlying object, then end the dialog.
// CANCEL:  end dialog, without updating.
//
BOOL WPDialog::command(int id, WORD msg)
{
    switch (id) {
    case IDCANCEL:
        if (queryEnd())
            endDlg(0);
        return TRUE;
    case IDOK:
        if (id==IDOK)          // if OK:
            updateObject();    // copy dialog box ==> data
        endDlg(id);            // and quit
        return TRUE;
    }
    return WPWin::command(id, msg);
}
/////////////////
// Handle scroll message: pass to scrollbar object.
//
BOOL WPDialog::scrolled(int msg, int id, int thumbPos)
{
    WPScrollBar *sb = (WPScrollBar *)getChild(id);
    if (sb)
        sb->handleMsg(msg, thumbPos);
    return sb!=NULL;
}
/////////////////
// Handle "rare" messages for dialogs.
// The only ones we do are those for owner-draw items.
//
BOOL WPDialog::other(WPEvent &event)
{
    if (odItems.dispatchEvent(event))
        return event.msg == WM_COMPAREITEM ? event.ret : TRUE;
    return WPWin::other(event);
}
void WPDialog::loadError()
{
```

```
        ErrBox("Couldn't load dialog: %s.", templateName);
        assert(FALSE);
}
/////////////////
// Create modal dialog box.
//
BOOL WPDialogModal::createWin()
{
    result = DialogBox(App(),
        (LPSTR)templateName,
        GetHwnd(createArgs.parent),
        App.getDlgProc());
    if (result==-1)
        loadError();
    return result != -1;
}
/////////////////
// Modeless dialog.
//
WPDialogModeless::WPDialogModeless(CSTR resname, WPWin *pwin,
    WPControlMap *map, void *obj) : WPDialog(resname, pwin, map, obj)
{
    App.addDialog(this);      // Tell App we exist!
}
WPDialogModeless::~WPDialogModeless()
{
    App.removeDialog(this); // Tell App we're gone now.
}
/////////////////
// Create modeless dialog box.
//
BOOL WPDialogModeless::createWin()
{
    HWND dlgHwnd = CreateDialog(App(),
        (LPSTR)templateName,
        GetHwnd(createArgs.parent),
        App.getDlgProc());
    if (dlgHwnd==NULL)
        loadError();
    return dlgHwnd != NULL;
}
```

WPDLPRT.H

```
/////////////////////////////////////////////////////////
// WINDOWS++ CLASS LIBRARY.  Copyright 1992 Paul DiLascia.
// FILE: WPDLPRT.H
//
// Printer dialog definitions.
#ifndef WPDLPRT_H
#define WPDLPRT_H
#ifndef WPDLG_H
#include "wpdlg.h"
#endif
extern "C" {
/////////////////
// The following definitions come from COMMDLG.H,
// in the Microsoft Windows 3.1 SDK.
//
struct PRINTDLG {
    DWORD    lStructSize;
    HWND     hwndOwner;
    HANDLE   hDevMode;
    HANDLE   hDevNames;
    HDC      hDC;
    DWORD    Flags;
    WORD     nFromPage;
    WORD     nToPage;
```

```
        WORD      nMinPage;
        WORD      nMaxPage;
        WORD      nCopies;
        HANDLE    hInstance;
        DWORD     lCustData;
        FARPROC   lpfnPrintHook;
        FARPROC   lpfnSetupHook;
        LPSTR     lpPrintTemplateName;
        LPSTR     lpSetupTemplateName;
        HANDLE    hPrintTemplate;
        HANDLE    hSetupTemplate;
};
typedef PRINTDLG FAR * LPPRINTDLG;
// DLL function to run print dialog.
BOOL  FAR PASCAL PrintDlg(LPPRINTDLG);
#define PD_ALLPAGES                       0x00000000
#define PD_SELECTION                      0x00000001
#define PD_PAGENUMS                       0x00000002
#define PD_NOSELECTION                    0x00000004
#define PD_NOPAGENUMS                     0x00000008
#define PD_COLLATE                        0x00000010
#define PD_PRINTTOFILE                    0x00000020
#define PD_PRINTSETUP                     0x00000040
#define PD_NOWARNING                      0x00000080
#define PD_RETURNDC                       0x00000100
#define PD_RETURNIC                       0x00000200
#define PD_RETURNDEFAULT                  0x00000400
#define PD_SHOWHELP                       0x00000800
#define PD_ENABLEPRINTHOOK                0x00001000
#define PD_ENABLESETUPHOOK                0x00002000
#define PD_ENABLEPRINTTEMPLATE            0x00004000
#define PD_ENABLESETUPTEMPLATE            0x00008000
#define PD_ENABLEPRINTTEMPLATEHANDLE      0x00010000
#define PD_ENABLESETUPTEMPLATEHANDLE      0x00020000
#define PD_USEDEVMODECOPIES               0x00040000
#define PD_DISABLEPRINTTOFILE             0x00080000
#define PD_HIDEPRINTTOFILE                0x00100000
// Default flags for COMMDLG print dialog: get printer DC.
const DWORD PD_DEFAULT = PD_RETURNDC;
struct DEVNAMES {
        WORD wDriverOffset;
        WORD wDeviceOffset;
        WORD wOutputOffset;
        WORD wDefault;
};
typedef DEVNAMES FAR * LPDEVNAMES;
#define DN_DEFAULTPRN       0x0001
} // end of extern "C"
/////////////////////
// Print dialog box.
//
DLLCLASS WPDlgPrint : public WPDialogModal {
        PRINTDLG pdlg;            // Windows COMMDLG structure
        HDC getHDC()              { return pdlg.hDC; }
        friend WPPrinter;
public:
        WPDlgPrint(WPWin *pwin);
        ~WPDlgPrint();
        void destroyWin()        { sendMsg(WM_COMMAND, IDABORT); }
        BOOL createWin()         { return result = PrintDlg(&pdlg); }
        // Functions to get results of print dialog from COMMDLG structure.
        DWORD flags()            { return pdlg.Flags; }
        void  flags(DWORD f)     { pdlg.Flags = f; }
        WORD  fromPage()         { return pdlg.nFromPage; }
        void  fromPage(WORD p)   { pdlg.nFromPage = p; }
        WORD  toPage()           { return pdlg.nToPage; }
        void  toPage(WORD p)     { pdlg.nToPage = p; }
        WORD  minPage()          { return pdlg.nMinPage; }
```

```
    void  minPage(WORD p)     { pdlg.nMinPage = p; }
    WORD  maxPage()           { return pdlg.nMaxPage; }
    void  maxPage(WORD p)     { pdlg.nMaxPage = p; }
    WORD  nCopies()           { return pdlg.nCopies; }
    void  nCopies(WORD n)     { pdlg.nCopies = n; }
};
/////////////////
// Print Abort dialog
//
DLLCLASS WPDlgPrintAbort : public WPDialogModeless {
public:
    WPDlgPrintAbort(WPWin *pwin, CSTR resname="DLGPRINTABORT")
      : WPDialogModeless(resname, pwin) { createWin(); }
    BOOL command(int id, WORD msg);
};
#endif
```

WPDLPRT.CPP

```
////////////////////////////////////////////////////////
// WINDOWS++ CLASS LIBRARY.  Copyright 1992 Paul DiLascia.
// FILE: WPDLPRT.CPP
//
// Print dialog implementation.
#include "wpdlprt.h"
#include "wpgdi.h"
/////////////////
// Create print dialog.
//
WPDlgPrint::WPDlgPrint(WPWin *pwin) : WPDialogModal(NULL, pwin)
{
    memset(&pdlg, 0, sizeof(pdlg));
    pdlg.lStructSize=sizeof(pdlg);
    pdlg.hwndOwner = GetHwnd(pwin);
    pdlg.Flags = PD_DEFAULT;
}
/////////////////
// Destroy print dialog.
// Destroy stuff as described in the SDK documentation.
//
WPDlgPrint::~WPDlgPrint()
{
    if (pdlg.hDevMode)
        GlobalFree(pdlg.hDevMode);
    if (pdlg.hDevNames)
        GlobalFree(pdlg.hDevNames);
    if (pdlg.hDC)
        DeleteDC(pdlg.hDC);
}
/////////////////
// Create print abort dialog. Works in conjunction w/WPPrinter.
//
BOOL WPDlgPrintAbort::command(int id, WORD msg)
{
    if (id==IDCANCEL) {
        WPPrinter::DlgAbort = NULL;
        WPPrinter::Abort = TRUE;
    }
    return WPDialogModeless::command(id, msg);
}
```

WPDLSTR.H

```
////////////////////////////////////////////////////////
// WINDOWS++ CLASS LIBRARY.  Copyright 1992 Paul DiLascia.
// FILE: WPDLSTR.H
//
// String dialog defnitions.
```

```
#ifndef WPDLSTR_H
#define WPDLSTR_H
#ifndef WPDLG_H
#include "wpdlg.h"
#endif
////////////////////
// Generic "string" dialog gets a string of text from user.
//
DLLCLASS WPDlgString : public WPDialogModal {
    LPSTR memTemplate;        // template for DialogBoxIndirect
    char *strBuf;             // caller's buffer
    int strLen;               // length
public:
    WPDlgString(WPWin *pwin, char *buf, int len, CSTR prompt, CSTR cap=NULL);
    WPDlgString(WPWin *pwin, char *buf, int len, CSTR resname)
        : WPDialogModal(resname, pwin) { memTemplate = NULL; createWin(); }
    ~WPDlgString();
    BOOL createWin();
    void initDlg();
};
#endif
```

WPDLSTR.CPP

```
/////////////////////////////////////////////////////////////
// WINDOWS++ CLASS LIBRARY.  Copyright 1992 Paul DiLascia.
// FILE: WPDLSTR.CPP
//
// String dialog implementation.
#include "wpdlstr.h"
#include "wpedit.h"
#include "wpapp.h"
///////////////////
// Use byte-alignment when compiling this
// module--required for DLGTEMPLATE & co.
//
#pragma option -a-        // works for Borland
#pragma ZTC align 1       // works for Zortech
////////////////
// Dialog template structure, from the SDK Reference Manual, Volume 2.
//
struct DLGTEMPLATE {
    long style;
    BYTE nItems;
    int x,y,cx,cy;
    char menuName[1];         // actual length is variable
    char className[1];        // ditto
    char caption[1];          // ditto
    struct DLGITEMTEMPLATE * setCaption(CSTR text);
};
//////////////////
// Set caption in dialog template, and return ptr to end
// of header, which is first item template structure.
//
DLGITEMTEMPLATE * DLGTEMPLATE::setCaption(CSTR text)
{
    if (text)
        strcpy(caption, text);
    else
        caption[0]=0;
    return (DLGITEMTEMPLATE *)(caption + strlen(caption)+1);
}
////////////////
// Dialog ITEM template structure, from the SDK Reference Manual, Volume 2.
//
struct DLGITEMTEMPLATE {
    int x,y,cx,cy;
    int id;
```

```cpp
    long style;
    char className[15];          // actual length is variable
// char text[1];                 // ditto
// BYTE extraBytes;              // by setText
    DLGITEMTEMPLATE * setText(CSTR text);
};
//////////////////
// Set item text.  Returns pointer to next item following this one.
//
DLGITEMTEMPLATE * DLGITEMTEMPLATE::setText(CSTR text)
{
    char *p = className + strlen(className)+1;
    if (text) {
        strcpy(p, text);         // append text to structure
        p += strlen(p)+1;        // ...
    } else
        *p++ = 0;
    *p++ = 0;                    // length of extra info = zero
    return (DLGITEMTEMPLATE *)p;
}
//////
// Static definition of dialog box.
// These structures are copied and filled in with
// the necessary variables, e.g., prompt and width, etc.
//
// First, a few constants to make the code more legible
const CXBUTTON = 30;         // width of button
const CXEDIT = 150;          // width of edit control
const CYITEM = 13;           // height of button or edit control
const CYSPACE = 5;           // interline space
const XMARGIN = 5;
//////////////////
// Here are the static structures.  Ugh!
//
static  DLGTEMPLATE DlgTemplate = {
    WS_POPUPWINDOW|DS_MODALFRAME|WS_DLGFRAME,4,40,80,0,55,0,0,0
};
static DLGITEMTEMPLATE ItemPrompt = {
    XMARGIN,CYSPACE,0,8,-1,
    WS_VISIBLE|WS_CHILD|SS_LEFT,"Static"
};
static DLGITEMTEMPLATE ItemInput = {
    XMARGIN,16,CXEDIT,CYITEM,WPIDED_STRING,
    WS_VISIBLE|WS_CHILD|WS_TABSTOP|WS_BORDER|ES_LEFT|ES_AUTOHSCROLL,"Edit"
};
static DLGITEMTEMPLATE ItemOK = {
    0,35,CXBUTTON,CYITEM,IDOK,
    WS_VISIBLE|WS_CHILD|WS_TABSTOP|BS_DEFPUSHBUTTON,"Button"
};
static DLGITEMTEMPLATE ItemCancel = {
    0,35,CXBUTTON,CYITEM,IDCANCEL,
    WS_VISIBLE|WS_CHILD|WS_TABSTOP|BS_PUSHBUTTON,"Button"
};
//////////////////
// Create string dialog and run it.
// caller's buffer will be stuffed w/user's input.
// Create dialog box on the fly (Probably the most disgusting
// function in all of Windows++!).
//
WPDlgString::WPDlgString(WPWin *pwin, char *buf, int len, CSTR pmt, CSTR cap)
    : WPDialogModal(NULL, pwin)
{
    assert(buf && pmt);
    strBuf = buf;
    strLen = len;
    if (cap==NULL)
        cap = "";
```

```
        // Create dialog template header.  Build it in App.scratch.
        DLGTEMPLATE *hdr = (DLGTEMPLATE *)App.scratch;
        *hdr = DlgTemplate;
        WPRect box = pmt;                 // get text dimensions of prompt
        int pmtHt = 8*box.height();     // convert height to dialog units
        // Compute size and position of dialog box.
        hdr->cx = max(4*box.width(), CXEDIT) + 2*XMARGIN;
        hdr->cy = 3*CYITEM + CYSPACE + pmtHt;
        // Center dialog box in parent window
        box = pwin;                 // dimensions of parent window
        hdr->x = (2*box.width())/LOWORD(GetDialogBaseUnits()) - (hdr->cx)/2;
        hdr->y = (4*box.height())/HIWORD(GetDialogBaseUnits()) - (hdr->cy)/2;
        // Create static text control for prompt.
        DLGITEMTEMPLATE *item = hdr->setCaption(cap);
        *item = ItemPrompt;
        item->cx = hdr->cx-XMARGIN;
        item->cy = pmtHt;
        item = item->setText(pmt);
        // Create edit control for input.
        *item = ItemInput;
        item->y = pmtHt + 2*CYSPACE;
        item = item->setText(NULL);
        // Create OK button.
        *item = ItemOK;
        int xOK = (hdr->cx - 3*CXBUTTON)/2;
        item->x = xOK;
        item->y = pmtHt + CYITEM + 3*CYSPACE;
        item = item->setText("&OK");
        // Create Cancel button.
        *item = ItemCancel;
        item->x = xOK + 2*CXBUTTON;
        item->y = pmtHt + CYITEM + 3*CYSPACE;
        item = item->setText("&Cancel");
        // Now we know how much storage is required; allocate it from
        // GLOBAL memory. This is required because DialogBoxIndirect
        // expects a handle to global memory.
        //
        int size = ((char*)item) - App.scratch;
        memTemplate = (LPSTR)App.farAlloc(size,TRUE,TRUE);
        char *src = App.scratch;          // copy from scratch..
        LPSTR dst = memTemplate;          // ..to global memory block
        while (size-->0)
            *dst++ = *src++;
        createWin();                 // run the dialog!
}
//////////////////
// Create string dialog.
// If we're doing it on-the-fly with DLGTEMPLATE, create using
// DialogBoxIndirect; otherwise invoke normal createWin function.
//
BOOL WPDlgString::createWin()
{
    if (memTemplate) {
        // Run the dialog.
        result = DialogBoxIndirect(App(),
            GlobalHandle(FP_SEG(memTemplate)),
            GetHwnd(createArgs.parent),
            App.getDlgProc());
        assert(result!=-1);
        return result != -1;
    }
    return WPDialogModal::createWin();
}
//////////////////
// Destroy string dialog: destory memory template
//
WPDlgString::~WPDlgString()
{
```

```
      App.farFree(memTemplate);
}
///////////////////
// Initialize dialog: link edit control to caller's string.
//
void WPDlgString::initDlg()
{
   WPEdit * ed = new WPEdit(this, WPIDED_STRING);
   ed->linkObject(strBuf, strLen);
}
```

WPEDIT.H

```
///////////////////////////////////////////////////////////
// WINDOWS++ CLASS LIBRARY.  Copyright 1992 Paul DiLascia.
// FILE: WPEDIT.H
//
// Edit control definitions.
#ifndef WPEDIT_H
#define WPEDIT_H
#ifndef WPCTRL_H
#include "wpctrl.h"
#endif
#ifndef WPID_H
#include "wpid.h"
#endif
#ifndef WPGLOB_H
#include "wpglob.h"
#endif
#define ES_DEFAULT      (WS_BORDER | ES_LEFT | ES_AUTOHSCROLL)
#define ES_DEFAULTMULTI (ES_DEFAULT | ES_MULTILINE | ES_AUTOVSCROLL)
///////////////////
// Your basic edit control.  Underlying data is string.
//
DLLCLASS WPEdit : public WPControl {
   CSTR legalChars;        // user can only type these chars
public:
   WPEdit(WPWin *pwin, int id, long style=ES_DEFAULT)
      : WPControl("Edit", pwin, id, style) { legalChars=NULL; }
   static WPControl* New(WPWin* pwin, int id)
      { return new WPEdit(pwin, id); }
   void setLegalChars(CSTR s)   { legalChars=s; }
   // Virtual WPWin functions overridden for edit controls
   BOOL gotFocus(WPWin *prev)
      { setSel(); return WPControl::gotFocus(prev); }
   BOOL kbd(WPEvent &event);
   // General control functions
   void linkObject(char* buf, int len)
      { object=buf; objsiz=len; }
   void updateObject()
      { if (object) getText((char*)object, objsiz); }
   void updateScreen()
      { if (object) { setText((char*)object); setMaxLen(objsiz-1); } }
   // Windows-related functions
   BOOL canUndo()           { return sendMsg(EM_CANUNDO); }
   BOOL undo()              { return sendMsg(EM_UNDO); }
   void emptyUndo()         { sendMsg(EM_EMPTYUNDOBUFFER); }
   BOOL isModified()        { return sendMsg(EM_GETMODIFY); }
   void setModified(BOOL m) { sendMsg(EM_SETMODIFY, m); }
   void getRect(WPRect &r)  { sendMsg(EM_GETRECT, 0, (LONG)&r); }
   // Set/get selection
   void setSel(int beg=0, int end=MAXINT)
      { sendMsg(EM_SETSEL, 0, MAKELONG(beg, end)); }
   BOOL getSel(int& beg, int& end)
      { LONG x=sendMsg(EM_GETSEL); beg=LOWORD(x);
        end=HIWORD(x); return beg!=end; }
   // Miscellaneous
   void setPasswordChar(char c)  { sendMsg(EM_SETPASSWORDCHAR, c); }
```

```
    void replaceSel(char *text)    { sendMsg(EM_REPLACESEL, 0, text); }
    void setMaxLen(int len)        { sendMsg(EM_LIMITTEXT, len); }
    // The following are used to simplify the Edit commands
    void cut()      { sendMsg(WM_CUT); }
    void copy()     { sendMsg(WM_COPY); }
    void clear()    { sendMsg(WM_CLEAR); }
    void paste(BOOL flush=TRUE);
};
/////////////////
// Multi-line edit control is subclass of generic edit control.
//
DLLCLASS WPMultiEdit : public WPEdit {
public:
    WPMultiEdit(WPWin *pwin, int id, long sty=ES_DEFAULTMULTI)
        : WPEdit(pwin, id, sty) { }
    static WPControl* New(WPWin* pwin, int id)
        { return new WPMultiEdit(pwin, id); }
    // Virtual WPWin functions overridden for multi edit
    BOOL gotFocus(WPWin *prev)     { return WPControl::gotFocus(prev); }
    // Windows functions for multi-edit controls only
    int numLines()                 { return sendMsg(EM_GETLINECOUNT); }
    int getLine(int nLine, char *buf, int len)
        { *((WORD*)buf) = len; return sendMsg(EM_GETLINE, nLine, buf); }
    int lineFromChar(int pos)      { return sendMsg(EM_LINEFROMCHAR, pos); }
    int linePos(int nLine)         { return sendMsg(EM_LINEINDEX, nLine); }
    int lineLenFromPos(int pos)    { return sendMsg(EM_LINELENGTH, pos); }
    int lineLen(int nLine)         { return lineLenFromPos(linePos(nLine)); }
    void lineScroll(int h, int v) { sendMsg(EM_LINESCROLL, 0, MAKELONG(v,h)); }
    void setRect(WPRect &rect, BOOL repaint=TRUE)
        { sendMsg(repaint ? EM_SETRECT : EM_SETRECTNP, 0, (LONG)&rect); }
    BOOL format(BOOL crlf)         { return sendMsg(EM_FMTLINES, crlf); }
    void setTabStops(int *tabs, int len)
        { sendMsg(EM_SETTABSTOPS, len, tabs); }
    // load/save operations
    BOOL load(CSTR fname);
    BOOL save(CSTR fname);
};
#endif
```

WPGDI.H

```
/////////////////////////////////////////////////////////////
// WINDOWS++ CLASS LIBRARY.  Copyright 1992 Paul DiLascia.
// FILE: WPGDI.H
//
// GDI (Graphics Device Interface) definitions.
#ifndef WPGDI_H
#define WPGDI_H
#ifndef WPRECT_H
#include "wprect.h"
#endif
#ifndef WPWIN_H
#include "wpwin.h"
#endif
#ifndef WPAPP_H
#include "wpapp.h"
#endif
const DWORD COLOR_RED   = RGB(0xFF,0,0);
const DWORD COLOR_GREEN = RGB(0,0xFF,0);
const DWORD COLOR_BLUE  = RGB(0,0,0xFF);
const DWORD COLOR_BLACK = 0;
const DWORD COLOR_WHITE = 0x00FFFFFF;
const DWORD COLOR_NONE  = 0xFFFFFFFF;
/////////////////
// This little structure is used to parse the driver and output names
// from WIN.INI, given a device name.  It makes it easier to create device
// contexts to printers and other devices.
//
```

```
struct WPDEVNAME {
   char namebuf[50];         // name buffer
   char* driverName;         // parsed driver name
   char* outputName;         // output file (e.g., LPT1:)
   WPDEVNAME(CSTR devname);
};
///////////////////
// Base class for all drawing objects (pen, brush, etc.)
//
DLLCLASS WPDrawObj {
protected:
   HANDLE hobj;                 // Windows handle
   BOOL del;                    // whether to delete
   void set(int h, BOOL d)      { hobj = h; del = d; }
   void destroy();
   WPDrawObj()                  { hobj=NULL; del=FALSE; }
   WPDrawObj(int h, BOOL d)     { set(h, d); }
   ~WPDrawObj()                 { destroy(); }
   friend WPDevContext;
public:
   HANDLE operator()()          { return hobj; }
};
///////////////////
// Pen object
//
DLLCLASS WPPen : public WPDrawObj {
public:
   // Constructors
   WPPen(int id) : WPDrawObj(GetStockObject(id), FALSE) { }
   WPPen(COLORREF color, int style=PS_SOLID, int wid=1 )
      : WPDrawObj(CreatePen(style, wid, color), TRUE) { }
   WPPen(LPLOGPEN data) : WPDrawObj(CreatePenIndirect(data), TRUE) { }
   void getObject(LOGPEN& data)
      { GetObject(hobj, sizeof(LOGPEN), (LPSTR)&data); }
};
///////////////////
// Brush object
//
DLLCLASS WPBrush : public WPDrawObj {
public:
   // Constructors
   WPBrush(int id) : WPDrawObj(GetStockObject(id), FALSE) { }
   WPBrush(COLORREF color) : WPDrawObj(CreateSolidBrush(color), TRUE)   { }
   WPBrush(COLORREF c, int h) : WPDrawObj(CreateHatchBrush(h, c), TRUE) { }
   WPBrush(LPLOGBRUSH data) : WPDrawObj(CreateBrushIndirect(data), TRUE) { }
   void getObject(LOGBRUSH& data)
      { GetObject(hobj, sizeof(LOGBRUSH), (LPSTR)&data); }
};
///////////////////
// Bitmap object.
//
DLLCLASS WPBitmap : public WPDrawObj {
public:
   WPBitmap(CSTR name) : WPDrawObj(App.loadBitmap(name), TRUE) { }
   WPBitmap(int id) : WPDrawObj(App.loadBitmap(id), TRUE) { }
   WPBitmap(WPDevContext* dc, int w, int h);
   DWORD getBits(LPSTR buf,int len) { return GetBitmapBits(hobj,len,buf); }
   LONG  setBits(LPSTR buf,int len) { return SetBitmapBits(hobj,len,buf); }
   DWORD extent()                   { return GetBitmapDimension(hobj); }
   DWORD extent(int w, int h)       { return SetBitmapDimension(hobj,w,h); }
   void getObject(BITMAP& data)
      { GetObject(hobj, sizeof(BITMAP), (LPSTR)&data); }
};
///////////////////
// Class to represent an information context
// is also the base class for all kinds of device contexts.
//
DLLCLASS WPDevInfo {
```

```
protected:
    HDC hdc;                    // Windows handle to DC
public:
    WPDevInfo() { hdc=NULL; }
    WPDevInfo(CSTR devname)
        {   WPDEVNAME dv = devname;     // parse device name
            hdc = CreateIC(dv.driverName, (LPSTR)devname, dv.outputName, NULL);
            assert(hdc); }
    WPDevInfo(CSTR devname, CSTR driver, CSTR output, CSTR init)
        { hdc = CreateIC((LPSTR)driver, (LPSTR)devname,
            (LPSTR)output, (LPSTR)init); assert(hdc); }
    virtual ~WPDevInfo()
        { if (hdc) { BOOL ret = DeleteDC(hdc); assert(ret); } }
    static HDC GetHDC(WPDevInfo *dc) { return dc ? dc->hdc : NULL; }
    HDC operator()()            { return hdc; }
    int getCap(int cap)         { return GetDeviceCaps(hdc, cap); }
    // Brainless fns for various device capabilities
    int getDRIVERVERSION()      { return getCap(DRIVERVERSION); }
    int getTECHNOLOGY()         { return getCap(TECHNOLOGY); }
    int getHORZSIZE()           { return getCap(HORZSIZE); }
    int getVERTSIZE()           { return getCap(VERTSIZE); }
    int getHORZRES()            { return getCap(HORZRES); }
    int getVERTRES()            { return getCap(VERTRES); }
    int getBITSPIXEL()          { return getCap(BITSPIXEL); }
    int getPLANES()             { return getCap(PLANES); }
    int getNUMBRUSHES()         { return getCap(NUMBRUSHES); }
    int getNUMPENS()            { return getCap(NUMPENS); }
    int getNUMMARKERS()         { return getCap(NUMMARKERS); }
    int getNUMFONTS()           { return getCap(NUMFONTS); }
    int getNUMCOLORS()          { return getCap(NUMCOLORS); }
    int getPDEVICESIZE()        { return getCap(PDEVICESIZE); }
    int getCURVECAPS()          { return getCap(CURVECAPS); }
    int getLINECAPS()           { return getCap(LINECAPS); }
    int getPOLYGONALCAPS()      { return getCap(POLYGONALCAPS); }
    int getTEXTCAPS()           { return getCap(TEXTCAPS); }
    int getCLIPCAPS()           { return getCap(CLIPCAPS); }
    int getRASTERCAPS()         { return getCap(RASTERCAPS); }
    int getASPECTX()            { return getCap(ASPECTX); }
    int getASPECTY()            { return getCap(ASPECTY); }
    int getASPECTXY()           { return getCap(ASPECTXY); }
    int getLOGPIXELSX()         { return getCap(LOGPIXELSX); }
    int getLOGPIXELSY()         { return getCap(LOGPIXELSY); }
    int getSIZEPALETTE()        { return getCap(SIZEPALETTE); }
    int getNUMRESERVED()        { return getCap(NUMRESERVED); }
    int getCOLORRES()           { return getCap(COLORRES); }
};
/////////////////////
// Information about the display
//
DLLCLASS WPDisplayInfo : public WPDevInfo {
public:
    WPDisplayInfo() : WPDevInfo("DISPLAY",NULL,NULL,NULL) { }
};
/////////////////////
// Information about the printer
//
DLLCLASS WPPrinterInfo : public WPDevInfo {
public:
    WPPrinterInfo(CSTR devname=NULL) : WPDevInfo(NULL) { }
};
/////////////////////
// Each type of drawing object has an ID, used as offset to store
// handle in a table.
//
enum WHICHOBJ { DPEN=0, DBRUSH, DBITMAP, DFONT, DRGN, DPALETTE,
    NDRAWOBJ };
/////////////////////
// Device context base class
```

```cpp
//
DLLCLASS WPDevContext : public WPDevInfo {
    WPDrawObj drawObj[NDRAWOBJ];  // current selected drawing objects
    HANDLE originalObj[NDRAWOBJ]; // original drawing objects
    const int* tabs;              // array of tab stops (logical x-coords)
    int ntabs;                    // number of tab stops
    int tabOrg;                   // relative x-origin of tabs
    int err;                      // last error code from Escape
    void init(HDC h)              // common initializer for all constructors
        { memset(this,0,sizeof(WPDevContext)); hdc = h; }
protected:
    BOOL anySelected;             // whether any new objects are selected
    WPDevContext(HDC h=NULL)      { init(h); }
    WPDrawObj* getDrawObj(WHICHOBJ which)   { return &drawObj[which]; }
    void restoreSelection();
    HANDLE select(WHICHOBJ which, int h, BOOL d);
    HANDLE select(WHICHOBJ which, WPDrawObj *obj)
        { return select(which, obj->hobj, FALSE); }
public:
    WPDevContext(CSTR devname)
        { WPDEVNAME dv = devname;
            init(CreateDC(dv.driverName, (LPSTR)devname, dv.outputName, NULL)); }
    WPDevContext(CSTR devname, CSTR driver, CSTR output, CSTR ini)
        { init(CreateDC((LPSTR)driver, (LPSTR)devname,
            (LPSTR)output, (LPSTR)ini)); }
    ~WPDevContext()
        { if (hdc && anySelected) restoreSelection(); }
    int error()                             { return err; }
    void setTabOrigin(int o)                { tabOrg = o; }
    void setTabs(int *tabArray, int len)    { tabs=tabArray; ntabs=len; }
    // Pen
    WPPen *getPen()                         { return (WPPen*)getDrawObj(DPEN); }
    HANDLE setPen(WPPen *pen)               { return select(DPEN, pen); }
    HANDLE setPen(int h)                    { return select(DPEN, h, FALSE); }
    HANDLE setPen(COLORREF color, int style=PS_SOLID, int wid=1)
        { return select(DPEN, CreatePen(style, wid, color), TRUE); }
    // Brush
    WPBrush *getBrush()                     { return (WPBrush*)getDrawObj(DBRUSH); }
    HANDLE setBrush(WPBrush* brush)         { return select(DBRUSH, brush); }
    HANDLE setBrush(int h)                  { return select(DBRUSH, h, FALSE); }
    HANDLE setBrush(COLORREF color)
        { return select(DBRUSH, CreateSolidBrush(color), TRUE); }
    HANDLE setBrushHatch(COLORREF color, int hatch)
        { return select(DBRUSH, CreateHatchBrush(hatch, color), TRUE); }
    // Logical/device coords
    BOOL DP2LP(WPPoint *pts, int n)         { return DPtoLP(hdc,(LPPOINT)pts,n); }
    BOOL LP2DP(WPPoint *pts, int n)         { return LPtoDP(hdc,(LPPOINT)pts,n); }
    BOOL DP2LP(WPPoint& p)                  { return DP2LP(&p, 1); }
    BOOL LP2DP(WPPoint& p)                  { return LP2DP(&p, 1); }
    BOOL DP2LP(WPRect& r)                   { return DP2LP((WPPoint*)&r, 2); }
    BOOL LP2DP(WPRect& r)                   { return LP2DP((WPPoint*)&r, 2); }
    // Brainless GDI functions
    BOOL arc(WPRect& box, WPPoint beg, WPPoint end)
        { return Arc(hdc, box.left(), box.top(), box.right(), box.bottom(),
            beg.x, beg.y, end.x, end.y); }
    BOOL bitBlt(WPRect& box, WPDevContext& srcDC,
        WPPoint srcPt, DWORD rop = SRCCOPY)
        { return BitBlt(hdc, box.left(), box.top(), box.width(), box.height(),
            srcDC.hdc, srcPt.x, srcPt.y, rop); }
    BOOL chord(WPRect& box, WPPoint p1, WPPoint p2)
        { return Chord(hdc,box.left(),box.top(),box.right(),box.bottom(),
            p1.x, p1.y, p2.x, p2.y); }
    void drawBitmap(int x, int y, WPBitmap* bm, DWORD rop = SRCCOPY);
    void drawIcon(int x, int y, HICON hicon)
        { DrawIcon(hdc, x, y, hicon); }
    int drawText(WPRect& rect, LPCSTR text, WORD format=0, int len=-1)
        { return DrawText(hdc, (LPSTR)text, len, (LPRECT)&rect, format); }
    BOOL grayString(WPRect& r, LPSTR text, WPBrush& brush)
```

```
            { return GrayString(hdc, brush(), NULL, NULL, lstrlen(text),
                r.left(),r.top(),r.width(),r.height()); }
void drawFocusRect(WPRect &rect)
            { DrawFocusRect(hdc, (LPRECT)&rect); }
BOOL ellipse(WPRect &box)
            { return Ellipse(hdc,box.left(),box.top(),box.right(),box.bottom()); }
int excludeClipRect(WPRect& box)
            { return ExcludeClipRect(hdc,box.left(),box.top(),
                box.right(),box.bottom()); }
int excludeUpdateRgn(WPWin *win)
            { return ExcludeUpdateRgn(hdc, (*win)()); }
int getClipBox(WPRect& box)      { return GetClipBox(hdc,((LPRECT)&box)); }
int intersectClipRect(WPRect& box)
            { return IntersectClipRect(hdc,box.left(),box.top(),
                box.right(),box.bottom()); }
int escape(int func, int nbytes=0, LPSTR in=NULL, LPSTR out=NULL)
            { return err = Escape(hdc, func, nbytes, in, out); }
BOOL charWidth(WORD c1, WORD c2, int *widths)
            { return GetCharWidth(hdc, c1, c2, (LPINT)widths); }
int offsetClipRgn(int x, int y)  { return OffsetClipRgn(hdc, x, y); }
int offsetClipRgn(WPPoint p)     { return OffsetClipRgn(hdc, p.x, p.y); }
BOOL fill(WPPoint p, COLORREF color, WORD how)
            { return ExtFloodFill(hdc, p.x, p.y, color, how); }
BOOL fill(WPPoint p, COLORREF color)
            { return FloodFill(hdc, p.x, p.y, color); }
BOOL fill(WPRect& rect, WPBrush& brush)
            { return FillRect(hdc, (LPRECT)&rect, brush()); }
int fillMode()                   { return GetPolyFillMode(hdc); }
int fillMode(int mode)           { return SetPolyFillMode(hdc, mode); }
DWORD getAspectRatio()           { return GetAspectRatioFilter(hdc); }
COLORREF bkColor()               { return GetBkColor(hdc); }
COLORREF bkColor(COLORREF c)     { return SetBkColor(hdc,c); }
int bkMode()                     { return GetBkMode(hdc); }
int bkMode(int mode)             { return SetBkMode(hdc,mode); }
DWORD brushOrg()                 { return GetBrushOrg(hdc); }
DWORD brushOrg(int x, int y)     { return SetBrushOrg(hdc, x, y); }
DWORD brushOrg(WPPoint p)        { return SetBrushOrg(hdc, p.x, p.y); }
int mapMode()                    { return GetMapMode(hdc); }
int mapMode(int m)               { return SetMapMode(hdc,m); }
COLORREF nearestColor(COLORREF color)
            { return GetNearestColor(hdc, color); }
DWORD getPos()                   { return GetCurrentPosition(hdc); }
DWORD getDCOrg()                 { return GetDCOrg(hdc); }
COLORREF pixel(int x, int y)     { return GetPixel(hdc, x, y); }
COLORREF pixel(WPPoint p)        { return GetPixel(hdc, p.x, p.y); }
COLORREF pixel(int x, int y, COLORREF color)
            { return SetPixel(hdc, x, y, color); }
COLORREF pixel(WPPoint p, COLORREF color)
            { return SetPixel(hdc, p.x, p.y, color); }
int rop2()                       { return GetROP2(hdc); }
int rop2(int rop)                { return SetROP2(hdc, rop); }
int stretchBltMode()             { return GetStretchBltMode(hdc); }
int stretchBltMode(int mode)     { return SetStretchBltMode(hdc, mode); }
WORD textAlign()                 { return GetTextAlign(hdc); }
WORD textAlign(WORD align)       { return SetTextAlign(hdc, align); }
int textCharExtra()              { return GetTextCharacterExtra(hdc); }
int textCharExtra(int e)         { return SetTextCharacterExtra(hdc, e); }
DWORD textColor()                { return GetTextColor(hdc); }
DWORD textColor(COLORREF c)      { return SetTextColor(hdc, c); }
DWORD textExtent(LPCSTR text, int len)
            { return GetTabbedTextExtent(hdc,(LPSTR)text,len,ntabs,(LPINT)tabs); }
DWORD textExtent(LPCSTR text)
            { return textExtent(text, lstrlen((LPSTR)text)); }
int textFace(char* buf, int len)
            { return GetTextFace(hdc, len, (LPSTR)buf); }
BOOL textMetrics(TEXTMETRIC &tm)
            { return GetTextMetrics(hdc, (LPTEXTMETRIC)&tm); }
```

```
    // Viewport and window
    void viewportOrg(WPPoint p)     { SetViewportOrg(hdc, p.x, p.y); }
    void viewportExt(WPPoint p)     { SetViewportExt(hdc, p.x, p.y); }
    void windowOrg(WPPoint p)       { SetWindowOrg(hdc, p.x, p.y); }
    void windowExt(WPPoint p)       { SetWindowExt(hdc, p.x, p.y); }
    WPPoint viewportOrg()
        { DWORD d=GetViewportOrg(hdc); return WPPoint(LOWORD(d),HIWORD(d)); }
    WPPoint viewportExt()
        { DWORD d=GetViewportExt(hdc); return WPPoint(LOWORD(d),HIWORD(d)); }
    WPPoint windowOrg()
        { DWORD d=GetWindowOrg(hdc); return WPPoint(LOWORD(d),HIWORD(d)); }
    WPPoint windowExt()
        { DWORD d=GetWindowExt(hdc); return WPPoint(LOWORD(d),HIWORD(d)); }
    void invert(WPRect &rect)       { InvertRect(hdc, (LPRECT)&rect); }
    BOOL lineTo(int x, int y)       { return LineTo(hdc, x, y); }
    DWORD moveTo(int x, int y)      { return MoveTo(hdc, x, y); }
    BOOL lineTo(WPPoint p)          { return lineTo(p.x, p.y); }
    DWORD moveTo(WPPoint p)         { return moveTo(p.x, p.y); }
    BOOL line(WPPoint a, WPPoint b) { moveTo(a); return lineTo(b); }
    BOOL frame(WPRect& rect, WPBrush& brush)
        { return FrameRect(hdc, (LPRECT)&rect, brush()); }
    BOOL patBlt(WPRect &box, DWORD rop=PATCOPY)
        { return PatBlt(hdc,box.left(),box.top(),box.width(),box.height(),rop);}
    BOOL pie(WPRect& box, WPPoint beg, WPPoint end)
        { return Pie(hdc, box.left(), box.top(), box.right(), box.bottom(),
          beg.x, beg.y, end.x, end.y); }
    BOOL polygon (WPPoint *pts, int n)
        { return Polygon (hdc, (LPPOINT)pts, n); }
    BOOL polyline(WPPoint *pts, int n)
        { return Polyline(hdc, (LPPOINT)pts, n); }
    BOOL polyPolygon(WPPoint *pts, int* counts, int nPoly)
        { return PolyPolygon(hdc, (LPPOINT)pts, (LPINT)counts, nPoly); }
    BOOL ptVisible(int x, int y)    { return PtVisible(hdc, x, y); }
    BOOL ptVisible(WPPoint p)       { return PtVisible(hdc, p.x, p.y); }
    BOOL rectangle(WPRect &box)
        { return Rectangle(hdc,box.left(),box.top(),box.right(),box.bottom()); }
    BOOL rectVisible(WPRect& rect)  { return RectVisible(hdc,(LPRECT)&rect); }
    BOOL restore(int saved=-1)      { return RestoreDC(hdc,saved); }
    BOOL roundRect(WPRect& box, int w, int h)
        { return RoundRect(hdc, box.left(), box.top(),
          box.right(), box.bottom(), w, h); }
    int save()                      { return SaveDC(hdc); }
    DWORD setMapperFlags(DWORD flags){ return SetMapperFlags(hdc, flags); }
    int setTextJustification(int nBreakExtra, int nBreakCount)
        { return SetTextJustification(hdc, nBreakExtra, nBreakCount); }
    BOOL stretchBlt(WPRect &d,
        WPDevContext& srcDC, WPRect &s, DWORD rop=SRCCOPY)
        { return StretchBlt(hdc, d.left(), d.top(), d.width(), d.height(),
          srcDC.hdc, s.left(), s.top(), s.width(), s.height(), rop); }
    long textOut(int x, int y, LPCSTR text, int len)
        { return TabbedTextOut(hdc,x,y,(LPSTR)text,len,
          ntabs,(LPINT)tabs,tabOrg); }
    long textOut(int x, int y, LPCSTR text)
        { return textOut(x, y, text, lstrlen((LPSTR)text)); }
    long printF(WPPoint p, CSTR format, ...);
    int updateColors() { return UpdateColors(hdc); }
    // Useful new functions
    void whiteOut(WPRect rect) { patBlt(rect, WHITENESS); }
    void blackOut(WPRect rect) { patBlt(rect, BLACKNESS); }
};
/////////////////
// Subclass for window device context
//
DLLCLASS WPWinDC : public WPDevContext {
protected:
    WPWin *win;                     // the window
    WPWinDC() { win = NULL; }        // no-arg constructor is private
public:
```

```
      WPWinDC(WPWin *);
      ~WPWinDC();
};
//////////////////
// Subclass for window DC, including non-client area.
//
DLLCLASS WPNCWinDC : public WPWinDC {
public:
   WPNCWinDC(WPWin *w);
};
//////////////////
// Memory device context
//
DLLCLASS WPMemDC : public WPDevContext {
public:
   WPMemDC(WPDevContext* dc, WPBitmap *bm);
   WPMemDC(WPDevContext* dc, WPRect &winRect, BOOL mono=FALSE);
   HANDLE setBitmap(WPBitmap *bm) { return select(DBITMAP, bm); }
   WPBitmap *getBitmap()          { return (WPBitmap*)getDrawObj(DBITMAP); }
};
//////////////////
// Paint structure, analogous to Windows' PAINTSTRUCT.
//
DLLCLASS WPPaintStruct : public WPDevContext {
   PAINTSTRUCT ps;             // Windows structure
   WPWin *win;                 // Windows++ window
public:
   WPPaintStruct(WPWin *win);
   ~WPPaintStruct();
   BOOL bkRedrawn()                    { return ps.fErase; }
   void getPaintRect(WPRect &box)   { box = ps.rcPaint; }
};
//////////////////
// The display DC
//
DLLCLASS WPDisplay : public WPDevContext {
public:
   WPDisplay() : WPDevContext("DISPLAY", NULL, NULL, NULL) {   }
};
//////////////////
// Printer device context.
//
DLLCLASS WPPrinter : public WPDevContext {
   static WPDlgPrintAbort *DlgAbort;    // abort dialog
   static BOOL Abort;                    // abort flag
   WPWin *pwin;                 // parent window
   BOOL delDC;                  // delete DC?
   friend BOOL _export FAR PASCAL WPPrintAbortProc(HDC hdcPrn, short nCode);
   friend WPDlgPrintAbort;
public:
   WPPrinter(CSTR devname=NULL);
   WPPrinter(WPDlgPrint& pdlg);
   ~WPPrinter();
   int doAbortDlg(WPWin *w);
   BOOL aborted()             { return Abort; }
   int startDoc(CSTR name)
      { return escape(STARTDOC, strlen(name), (char*)name); }
   int endDoc()               { return escape(ENDDOC); }
   int endPage()              { return escape(NEWFRAME); }
};
//////////////////
// Printer subclass to do simple line printing.
//
DLLCLASS WPLinePrinter : public WPPrinter {
   int nLinesPage;          // num lines per page
   int yChar;               // height of char
   int curLine;             // current line number
   void init();
```

```
public:
   WPLinePrinter(CSTR devname=NULL) : WPPrinter(devname) { init(); }
   WPLinePrinter(WPDlgPrint& pdlg)  : WPPrinter(pdlg)     { init(); }
   int outLine(char *buf, int len);
   int formFeed()          { curLine=0; return endPage(); }
   int endDoc()
      { if (curLine>0) formFeed(); return WPPrinter::endDoc(); }
};
///////////////////
// Device context for owner-draw controls and menus.
//
DLLCLASS WPOwnerDrawDC : public WPDevContext {
public:
   WPRect paintRect;
   WORD action;
   WORD state;
   WPOwnerDrawDC(LPDRAWITEMSTRUCT draw);
   ~WPOwnerDrawDC()  { restoreSelection(); hdc = NULL; }
};
#endif
```

WPGDI.CPP

```
////////////////////////////////////////////////////////////
// WINDOWS++ CLASS LIBRARY.  Copyright 1992 Paul DiLascia.
// FILE: WPGDI.CPP
//
// Implementation for Windows++ GDI functions.
#include <stdarg.h>
#include "wpgdi.h"
#include "wpglob.h"
#include "wpdlprt.h"
///////////////////
// Destroy drawing object, but only if delete flag says so.
// Internal protected function.
//
void WPDrawObj::destroy()
{
   if (hobj && del) {
      BOOL res=DeleteObject(hobj);
      assert(res);
   }
   hobj=NULL;
}
///////////////////
// Bitmap constructors
//
///////////////////
// Create w/specified dimensions
//
WPBitmap::WPBitmap(WPDevContext* dc, int w, int h)
{
   assert(dc);
   hobj = CreateCompatibleBitmap((*dc)(), w, h);
   assert(hobj);
   del = TRUE;
}
///////////////////
// Parse device name.  If devname is NULL, get printer info.
//
WPDEVNAME::WPDEVNAME(CSTR devname)
{
   char buf[50];
   if (devname==NULL) {
      WinIni.get("windows", "device", buf, sizeof(buf));
      devname = strtok(buf,",");
   }
   WinIni.get("devices", devname, namebuf, sizeof(namebuf));
```

```
        driverName = strtok(namebuf,",");
        outputName = strtok(NULL,",");
    }
const MAXSTOCKOBJ = 32;
//////////////////
// Private method to select a display object
// Destroys old selected object if required.
// "which" specifies whether object is a pen, brush, etc.
// "del" specifies whether to delete this object.
// If handle is small integer, assume stock object
//
HANDLE WPDevContext::select(WHICHOBJ which, int h, BOOL del)
{
    if ((HANDLE)h < MAXSTOCKOBJ) {
        h = GetStockObject(h);
        del = FALSE;              // never delete stock object!
    }
    assert(h);
    HANDLE old = SelectObject(hdc, (HANDLE)h);
    assert(old);
    WPDrawObj& obj = drawObj[which];
    assert(obj.hobj==NULL || obj.hobj==old);
    obj.destroy();
    obj.set((HANDLE)h, del);
    if (originalObj[which]==NULL)
        originalObj[which]=old;
    anySelected=TRUE;
    return old;
}
//////////////////
// Restore selected display objects (pens, brushes, etc.).
//
void WPDevContext::restoreSelection()
{
    assert(hdc);
    if (anySelected) {
        for (int i=0; i < NDRAWOBJ; i++) {
            if (originalObj[i]) {
                SelectObject(hdc, originalObj[i]);
                originalObj[i]=NULL;    // don't restore twice!
                drawObj[i].destroy();
            }
        }
    }
}
//////////////////
// printf-like function for device context.
//
long WPDevContext::printF(WPPoint p, CSTR format, ...)
{
    char buf[128];
    va_list argptr;
    va_start(argptr, format);
    int len = vsprintf(buf, format, argptr);
    va_end(argptr);
    return textOut(p.x, p.y, buf, len);
}
//////////////////
// Windows should have provided DrawBitmap, but didn't, so here it is.
// Code is from Petzold.
//
void WPDevContext::drawBitmap(int x, int y, WPBitmap* bitmap, DWORD rop)
{
    if (bitmap) {
        BITMAP bm;
        bitmap->getObject(bm);
        WPMemDC memdc(this, bitmap);
        WPRect dest;
```

```
          dest.origin(x, y);
          WPPoint p(bm.bmWidth, bm.bmHeight);
          DP2LP(&p, 1);
          dest.extent(p.x, p.y);
          p.x = p.y = 0;
          DP2LP(&p, 1);
          bitBlt(dest, memdc, p, rop);
     }

/////////////////
// Create Window DC
//
WPWinDC::WPWinDC(WPWin *w)
{
     assert(w);
     win = w;
     hdc = GetDC((*w)());
     assert(hdc);
}
/////////////////
// Destroy Window DC: use ReleaseDC instead of DeleteDC.
//
WPWinDC::~WPWinDC()
{
     if (anySelected)
        restoreSelection();
     BOOL ret = ReleaseDC((*win)(), hdc);
     assert(ret);
     hdc=NULL;
}
/////////////////
// Create window DC, including non-client area.
//
WPNCWinDC::WPNCWinDC(WPWin *w)
{
     assert(w);
     win = w;
     hdc = GetWindowDC((*win)());
     assert(hdc);
}
/////////////////
// Create memory DC from bitmap
//
WPMemDC::WPMemDC(WPDevContext *dc, WPBitmap *bm)
{
     hdc = CreateCompatibleDC(GetHDC(dc));
     assert(hdc);
     if (bm)
        setBitmap(bm);
     if (dc)
        mapMode(dc->mapMode());
}
/////////////////
// Create memory DC compatible w/existing DC.
// Rectangle says which window in primary DC to map;
// "mono" flags creates monochrome bitmap.
//
WPMemDC::WPMemDC(WPDevContext *dc, WPRect& winRect, BOOL mono)
{
     hdc = CreateCompatibleDC(GetHDC(dc));
     assert(hdc);
     // Get bitmap dimensions: convert window rect to device coords.
     WPPoint p = winRect.extent();
     if (dc) {
        dc->LP2DP(&p, 1);
        mapMode(dc->mapMode());
     }
     HBITMAP h =
```

```
        CreateCompatibleBitmap((dc && !mono) ? (*dc)() : hdc, p.x, p.y);
    assert(h);
    select(DBITMAP, h, TRUE);
    windowOrg(winRect.origin()); // window origin = top left corner of rect
}
/////////////////
// Create paint structure. Call Windows BeginPaint function.
//
WPPaintStruct::WPPaintStruct(WPWin *w)
{
    assert(w);
    hdc = BeginPaint((*w)(), &ps);
    assert(hdc);
    win = w;
}
/////////////////
// Destroy paint structure. Call Windows EndPaint function.
//
WPPaintStruct::~WPPaintStruct()
{
    if (anySelected)
        restoreSelection();
    EndPaint((*win)(), &ps);
    hdc = NULL;
}
WPOwnerDrawDC::WPOwnerDrawDC(LPDRAWITEMSTRUCT draw)
{
    paintRect = draw->rcItem;
    action = draw->itemAction;
    state = draw->itemState;
    hdc = draw->hDC;
    assert(hdc);
}
/////////////////
// Printing stuff
//
BOOL WPPrinter::Abort;
WPDlgPrintAbort *WPPrinter::DlgAbort=NULL;
/////////////////
// Create printer device context
//
WPPrinter::WPPrinter(CSTR devname) : WPDevContext(devname)
{
    assert(hdc);
    pwin = NULL;
    delDC=TRUE;
}
/////////////////
// Create printer from print dialog.
//
WPPrinter::WPPrinter(WPDlgPrint& pdlg) : WPDevContext(pdlg.getHDC())
{
    assert(hdc);
    pwin = NULL;
    delDC=FALSE;
}
/////////////////
// Do abort dialog
//
int WPPrinter::doAbortDlg(WPWin *w)
{
    pwin = w;
    Abort = FALSE;
    assert(DlgAbort==NULL);
    DlgAbort = new WPDlgPrintAbort(pwin);
    if (pwin)
        pwin->enableWin(FALSE);
```

```
        return escape(SETABORTPROC, 0, (LPSTR)WPPrintAbortProc);
}
/////////////////
// Destroy printer: destroy abort dialog if it's still there.
// Don't delete the DC if it came from print dialog.
//
int WPPrinter::~WPPrinter()
{
    if (DlgAbort) {
        DlgAbort->destroyWin();
        DlgAbort=NULL;
    }
    if (pwin)
        pwin->enableWin(TRUE);
    if (anySelected)
        restoreSelection();
    if (!delDC)
        hdc=NULL;                    // don't delete the DC
}
/////////////////
// Universal print abort procedure.
//
BOOL _export FAR PASCAL WPPrintAbortProc(HDC hdcPrn, short nCode)
{
    MSG msg;
    HWND hDlgAbort = WPWin::GetHwnd(WPPrinter::DlgAbort);
    while (!WPPrinter::Abort && PeekMessage(&msg, NULL, 0, 0, PM_REMOVE)) {
        if (!hDlgAbort || !IsDialogMessage(hDlgAbort, &msg)) {
            TranslateMessage(&msg);
            DispatchMessage(&msg);
        }
    }
    return !WPPrinter::Abort;
}
/////////////////
// Common initializer for all line printer constructors.
// Get text character height, lines per page, etc.
//
void WPLinePrinter::init()
{
    TEXTMETRIC tm;
    textMetrics(tm);
    yChar = tm.tmHeight + tm.tmExternalLeading;
    nLinesPage = getVERTRES()/yChar-1;
    curLine = 0;
}
const char CONTROL_L = 12;
/////////////////
// Do line output. Automatically eject page properly.
//
int WPLinePrinter::outLine(char *buf, int len)
{
    if (buf[0]==CONTROL_L)   // do form-feed for Control-L
        return formFeed();
    if (curLine >= nLinesPage)
        formFeed();
    textOut(0, yChar*curLine, buf, len);
    curLine++;
    return error();
}
```

WPGLOB.H

```
/////////////////////////////////////////////////////////
// WINDOWS++ CLASS LIBRARY.  Copyright 1992 Paul DiLascia.
// FILE: WPGLOB.H
//
```

```
// Windows++ global object definitions.
// Each global object is declared here and instantiated in WINMAIN.CPP.
#ifndef WPGLOB_H
#define WPGLOB_H
#ifndef WPPOINT_H
#include "wppoint.h"
#endif
#ifndef WPWIN_H
#include "wpwin.h"
#endif
#ifndef WPAPP_H
#include "wpapp.h"
#endif
/////////////////
// Global mouse object.  There's only one: Mouse.
// Use this object to get/set mouse parameters, capture the mouse, etc.
//
DLLCLASS WPMouse {
public:
    WPWin* capture()
        { return WPWin::GetWin(GetCapture()); }
    WPWin* capture(WPWin *win)
        { return WPWin::GetWin(SetCapture((*win)())); }
    void release()                     { ReleaseCapture(); }
    WORD getDoubleClickTime()          { return GetDoubleClickTime(); }
    void setDoubleClickTime(WORD msec) { SetDoubleClickTime(msec); }
    BOOL swapButtons(BOOL swap)        { return SwapMouseButton(swap); }
    BOOL swapButtons()         { return GetSystemMetrics(SM_SWAPBUTTON); }
    BOOL present()             { return GetSystemMetrics(SM_MOUSEPRESENT); }
};
extern WPMouse Mouse;
//////////////////
// Global Keyboard object, used to get info about the keyboard.
//
DLLCLASS WPKeyboard {
public:
    int codePage()                  { return GetKBCodePage(); }
    int type()                      { return GetKeyboardType(0); }
    int subType()                   { return GetKeyboardType(1); }
    int numFnKeys()                 { return GetKeyboardType(2); }
    int keyName(LONG lparam, char *buf, int buflen)
        { return GetKeyNameText(lparam, buf, buflen); }
    int state(int vkey)             { return GetKeyState(vkey); }
    void getState(BYTE* buf)        { GetKeyboardState(buf); }
    void setState(BYTE* buf)        { SetKeyboardState(buf); }
    BOOL isArrowKey(int key);
};
extern WPKeyboard Keyboard;
/////////////////
// Global Cursor.  Use it to move, hide, show, etc. the cursor.
//
DLLCLASS WPCursor {
public:
    HCURSOR operator= (HCURSOR hc)    { return SetCursor(hc); }
    HCURSOR operator= (LPCSTR name)   { return *this = App.loadCursor(name); }
    HCURSOR operator= (int id)        { return *this = App.loadCursor(id); }
    void setPos(int x, int y)         { SetCursorPos(x, y); }
    void getPos(WPPoint& p)           { GetCursorPos((LPPOINT)&p); }
    WPPoint operator()()              { WPPoint p; getPos(p); return p; }
    WPPoint operator= (WPPoint p)     { SetCursorPos(p.x, p.y); return p; }
    void clip(WPWin *win);
    void clip(WPRect &rect)           { ClipCursor((LPRECT)&rect); }
    void unClip()                     { ClipCursor(NULL); }
    void show(BOOL val)               { ShowCursor(val); }
    void operator++()    { show(TRUE); }
    void operator--()    { show(FALSE); }
};
extern WPCursor Cursor;
```

```
/////////////////
// This class encapsulates the wait (hourglass) cursor.
//
DLLCLASS WPWaitCursor {
   HCURSOR save;
public:
   WPWaitCursor(WPWin *win)
      { Mouse.capture(win); save = Cursor = IDC_WAIT; }
   ~WPWaitCursor()
      { Cursor = save; Mouse.release(); }
};
/////////////////
// Global Caret resource, similar to cursor.
//
DLLCLASS WPCaret {
public:
   void create(WPWin *win, WPBitmap& bm);
   void create(WPWin *win, int w, int h, BOOL gray=FALSE)
      { CreateCaret((*win)(), gray==TRUE, w, h); }
   void hide(WPWin *win)            { HideCaret((*win)()); }
   void show(WPWin *win)            { ShowCaret((*win)()); }
   void getPos(WPPoint& p)          { GetCaretPos((LPPOINT)&p); }
   void setPos(int x, int y)        { SetCaretPos(x, y); }
   void setBlinkTime(WORD msec)     { SetCaretBlinkTime(msec); }
   WORD getBlinkTime()              { return GetCaretBlinkTime(); }
   void destroy()                   { DestroyCaret(); }
   WPPoint operator()()             { WPPoint p; getPos(p); return p; }
   WPPoint operator= (WPPoint p)    { SetCaretPos(p.x, p.y); return p; }
};
extern WPCaret Caret;
/////////////////
// This global object represents the WIN.INI file.
// Use it to read/write from WIN.INI.
//
DLLCLASS WPWinIni {
public:
   int get(CSTR app, CSTR key, char *buf, int buflen, CSTR dflt="")
      { return GetProfileString((LPSTR)app,
         key ? (LPSTR)key : NULL, (LPSTR)dflt, (LPSTR)buf, buflen); }
   int get(CSTR app, CSTR key, int dflt=0)
      { return GetProfileInt((LPSTR)app, (LPSTR)key, dflt); }
   int getPrinterName(char* buf, int len);
   BOOL set(CSTR app, CSTR key, CSTR val)
      { return WriteProfileString((LPSTR)app, (LPSTR)key, (LPSTR)val); }
   BOOL set(CSTR app, CSTR key, int val)
      { char buf[16];
        itoa(val, buf, 10);
        return WriteProfileString((LPSTR)app, (LPSTR)key, (LPSTR)buf); }
   int getKeys(CSTR app, char *buf, int buflen)
      { return GetProfileString((LPSTR)app, NULL, "", (LPSTR)buf, buflen); }
};
extern WPWinIni WinIni;
/////////////////
// Clipboard. More of the same.
//
DLLCLASS WPClipboard {
public:
   BOOL open(WPWin *win)      { return OpenClipboard((*win)()); }
   BOOL close()              { return CloseClipboard(); }
   BOOL available(WORD fmt)   { return IsClipboardFormatAvailable(fmt); }
   int getData(WORD fmt, LPSTR buf, int buflen);
   int setData(WORD fmt, LPSTR buf, int buflen);
   BOOL empty()              { return EmptyClipboard(); }
   int numFormats()          { return CountClipboardFormats(); }
   int formatName(WORD fmt, char *buf, int buflen)
      { return GetClipboardFormatName(fmt, buf, buflen); }
   int getPriorityFormat(WORD *priorityList, int len)
      { return GetPriorityClipboardFormat(priorityList, len); }
```

```
      WORD registerFormat(CSTR name)
        { return RegisterClipboardFormat((LPSTR)name); }
};
extern WPClipboard Clipboard;
#endif
```

WPGLOB.CPP

```
/////////////////////////////////////////////////////////
// WINDOWS++ CLASS LIBRARY.  Copyright 1992 Paul DiLascia.
// FILE: WPGLOB.CPP
//
// Implementation of global objects.
#include "wpwin.h"
#include "wpglob.h"
#include "wpapp.h"
#include "wpgdi.h"
static char ArrowKeys[] = { VK_UP, VK_DOWN, VK_LEFT, VK_RIGHT, 0 };
BOOL WPKeyboard::isArrowKey(int key)
{
    return strchr(ArrowKeys, key) != NULL;
}
void WPCursor::clip(WPWin *win)
{
    assert(win);
    WPRect rect = win;
    win->clientToScreen(rect);
    clip(rect);
}
void WPCaret::create(WPWin *win, WPBitmap& bm)
{
    CreateCaret((*win)(), bm(), 0, 0);
}
int WPWinIni::getPrinterName(char* buf, int len)
{
    int ret = get("windows", "device", buf, len);
    strtok(buf,",");
    return ret;
}
int WPClipboard::getData(WORD fmt, LPSTR buf, int buflen)
{
    int len = 0;
    HANDLE hClipMem = GetClipboardData(fmt);
    if (hClipMem) {
        LPSTR lpClipMem = GlobalLock(hClipMem);
        if (lpClipMem) {
            len = GlobalSize(hClipMem);
            for (int i=len; i>0; i--)
                *buf++ = *lpClipMem++;
            GlobalUnlock(hClipMem);
        }
    }
    return len;
}
int WPClipboard::setData(WORD fmt, LPSTR buf, int buflen)
{
    int len = 0;
    HANDLE h = GlobalAlloc(GMEM_MOVEABLE, buflen);
    if (h) {
        LPSTR mem = GlobalLock(h);
        if (mem) {
            for (int i=buflen; i>0; i--)
                *mem++ = *buf++;
            SetClipboardData(fmt, h);
        }
    }
    return len;
}
```

WPHEAP.H

```
///////////////////////////////////////////////////////
// WINDOWS++ CLASS LIBRARY.  Copyright 1992 Paul DiLascia.
// FILE: WPHEAP.H
//
// Memory heap definitions.
#ifndef WPMEM_H
#define WPMEM_H
#ifndef WPPDEFS_H
#include "wppdefs.h"
#endif
#include <dos.h>
#ifdef __BORLANDC__
#define SWAPDS(val)     asm { push ds; mov ds, val; pop val; }
#define GETDS(var)      asm { mov ax, ds; mov var, ax; }
#define GETSS(var)      asm { mov ax, ss; mov var, ax; }
#elif __ZTC__
extern "C" WORD setDS(WORD seg);
#define SWAPDS(val)     (val = setDS(val))
#define GETDS(var)      (var = (unsigned short)asm(0x8C,0xD8))
#define GETSS(var)      (var = (unsigned short)asm(0x8C,0xD0))
#endif
#define GETAPPDS GETSS
const HEAPSIZE = 8192;  // smallest heap size
//////////////////
// Memory heap.  This class is used by the application object ONLY.
// It manages a chunk of windows global memory as a "local" heap.
// The heap is identified by its data segment.
//
class MemHeap {
protected:
    MemHeap* next;      // next heap in list
    long numBytes;      // total num bytes ever allocated from this heap
    int numObj;         // number of extant objects
    WORD seg;           // segment selector for this heap
    void *operator new(size_t size);
    void operator delete(void *heap);
    void NEAR * alloc(WORD size);
    void free (void NEAR* ptr);
    void FAR * makeFarPtr(void NEAR * np)
        { return (void FAR*) MK_FP(seg, (WORD)np); }
    WORD blockSize(void NEAR* ptr);
    MemHeap() { }               // for Local Heap
    MemHeap(WORD sz);
    ~MemHeap();
    friend WPApp;
};
//////////////////
// Special subclass models the application's "real" local heap.
// --I.e., the one whose data segment is the app's data segment.
//
class MemLocalHeap : public MemHeap {
public:
    MemLocalHeap();
};
#endif
```

WPHEAP.CPP

```
///////////////////////////////////////////////////////
// WINDOWS++ CLASS LIBRARY.  Copyright 1992 Paul DiLascia.
// FILE: WPHEAP.CPP
//
// Implementation of Windows++ memory heaps.
#include "wpapp.h"
//////////////////
// Overloaded new and delete operators always allocate storage
```

```
// for MemHeap objects from the application's local heap.
//
void *MemHeap::operator new(size_t size)
{
    return App.localAlloc(size);
}
void MemHeap::operator delete(void *heap)
{
    App.localFree((void NEAR*)heap);
}
/////////////////
// Initialize a new heap: allocate memory from Windows' global
// heap, and store its data segment.
//
MemHeap::MemHeap(WORD hpsz)
{
    assert(hpsz > 0);
    hpsz = max(hpsz, HEAPSIZE);
    HANDLE h = GlobalAlloc(GMEM_MOVEABLE|GMEM_ZEROINIT, hpsz);
    if (h) {
        void FAR* pGMem = GlobalLock(h);
        if (pGMem) {
            seg = FP_SEG(pGMem);
            if (LocalInit(seg, 0, hpsz-1)==0) {
                GlobalUnlock(h);
                GlobalFree(h);
                seg = 0;
            }
        } else
            GlobalFree(h);
    }
}
/////////////////
// Destroy local heap: return its global memory to
// windows, unless it happens to be the real local heap.
//
MemHeap::~MemHeap()
{
    WORD dsval;
    GETAPPDS(dsval);
    if (seg && dsval != seg) {
        HANDLE h = GlobalHandle(seg);
        GlobalUnlock(h);       // undo our lock
        GlobalUnlock(h);       // undo LocalInit's lock
        GlobalFree(h);         // free global memory
    }
}
/////////////////
// Allocate a block of memory from heap
// returns near pointer, relative to heap's data segment.
//
void NEAR* MemHeap::alloc(WORD size)
{
    WORD dsval = seg;
    SWAPDS(dsval);
    HANDLE h = LocalAlloc(LMEM_FIXED | LMEM_ZEROINIT, size);
    void NEAR *np = h ? (void NEAR*)LocalLock(h) : NULL;
    size = LocalSize((HANDLE)np);
    SWAPDS(dsval);
    if (np) {
        numObj++;
        numBytes+=size;
    }
    return np;
}
/////////////////
// Return a block of memory to heap.
// Complain if more objects freed than allocated.
```

```
//
void MemHeap::free(void NEAR* ptr)
{
    if (numObj-- > 0) {
        WORD dsval = seg;
        SWAPDS(dsval);
        WORD size = LocalSize((HANDLE)ptr);
        LocalUnlock((HANDLE)ptr);
        LocalFree((WORD)ptr);
        SWAPDS(dsval);
        numBytes -= size;
    } else
        ErrBox("Extra object freed!\nsegment: %x\toffset: %x.", seg, ptr);
}
/////////////////
// Get size of memory block.
//
WORD MemHeap::blockSize(void NEAR* ptr)
{
    WORD dsval = seg;
    SWAPDS(dsval);
    WORD size = LocalSize((WORD)ptr);
    SWAPDS(dsval);
    return size;
}
/////////////////
// Constructor for local heap, a subclass of the general heap.
// Instead of allocating global memory, the true local heap gets its
// segment from the application's data segment, which is always the
// current value of the stack pointer (SS), even if we are in a DLL.
//
MemLocalHeap::MemLocalHeap()
{
    WORD dsval;
    GETAPPDS(dsval);        // application's data segment
    seg = dsval;
}
```

WPID.H

```
///////////////////////////////////////////////////////////
// WINDOWS++ CLASS LIBRARY.  Copyright 1992 Paul DiLascia.
// FILE: WPID.H
//
#ifndef WPPID_H
#define WPPID_H
#define WPIDSB_VERT     -1 // "control ID" for vertical scroll bar
#define WPIDSB_HORZ     -2 // "control ID" for horizontal scroll bar
/////////////////
// Base dialog ID: after IDOK, IDCANCEL, etc.
// Applications should use control IDs starting here.
//
#define WPID_DLGBASE 10
/////////////////
// IDs for built-in commands and controls.
//
#define WPPIDBASE           512
#define WPIDM_EXIT          (WPPIDBASE + 0)
#define WPIDM_FILENEW       (WPPIDBASE + 1)
#define WPIDM_FILEOPEN      (WPPIDBASE + 2)
#define WPIDM_FILESAVE      (WPPIDBASE + 3)
#define WPIDM_FILESAVEAS    (WPPIDBASE + 4)
#define WPIDM_FILEPRINT     (WPPIDBASE + 5)
#define WPIDM_FILECLOSE     (WPPIDBASE + 6)
#define WPIDM_EDITCUT       (WPPIDBASE + 10)
#define WPIDM_EDITCOPY      (WPPIDBASE + 11)
#define WPIDM_EDITPASTE     (WPPIDBASE + 12)
```

```
#define WPIDM_EDITDELETE     (WPPIDBASE + 13)
#define WPIDM_EDITUNDO       (WPPIDBASE + 14)
#define WPIDM_ABOUT          (WPPIDBASE + 20)
#define WPIDM_DEBUG          (WPPIDBASE + 21)
#define WPIDM_MEMSTATS       (WPPIDBASE + 22)
#define WPIDM_WINTILE        (WPPIDBASE + 30)
#define WPIDM_WINCASCADE     (WPPIDBASE + 31)
#define WPIDM_WINARRANGE     (WPPIDBASE + 32)
#define WPIDM_WINCLOSEALL    (WPPIDBASE + 33)
#define WPIDM_WINNEXT        (WPPIDBASE + 34)
//////////////////
// IDs for built-in dialog controls
#define WPCTLBASE            (WPPIDBASE + 100)
#define WPIDED_STRING        (WPCTLBASE + 0)
//////////////////
// IDs for controls in COMMDLG.DLL.
//
#define IDOFN_EDFILENAME     1152
#define IDOFN_LBFILENAME     1120
#define IDOFN_SSPATHNAME     1088
#define IDOFN_PBHELP         1038
#define IDOFN_CBREADONLY     1040
#ifdef RC_INVOKED
//////////////////
// RC file macros to define CUA-compliant commands.
//
// File Menu
#define   FileNew       "&New\tCtrl-N",       WPIDM_FILENEW
#define   FileOpen      "&Open...\tCtrl-O",   WPIDM_FILEOPEN
#define   FileSave      "&Save\tCtrl-S",      WPIDM_FILESAVE
#define   FileSaveAs    "Save &As...",        WPIDM_FILESAVEAS
#define   FilePrint     "&Print...\tCtrl-P",  WPIDM_FILEPRINT
#define   FileClose     "&Close",             WPIDM_FILECLOSE
#define   FileExit      "E&xit",              WPIDM_EXIT
// Edit menu
#define   EditUndo      "&Undo\tAlt+Backspace",WPIDM_EDITUNDO
#define   EditCut       "Cu&t\tShift+Del",    WPIDM_EDITCUT
#define   EditCopy      "&Copy\tCtrl+Ins",    WPIDM_EDITCOPY
#define   EditPaste     "&Paste\tShift+Ins",  WPIDM_EDITPASTE
#define   EditDelete    "&Delete",            WPIDM_EDITDELETE
// Help menu
#define   HelpAbout     "&About...",    WPIDM_ABOUT
// Window
#define   WindowCascade  "&Cascade\tShift+F5",   WPIDM_WINCASCADE
#define   WindowTile     "&Tile\tShift+F4",      WPIDM_WINTILE
#define   WindowArrange  "Arrange &Icons",       WPIDM_WINARRANGE
#define   WindowCloseAll "Close &All",           WPIDM_WINCLOSEALL
// Accelerators
#define   AccFileNew     "^N",    WPIDM_FILENEW
#define   AccFileOpen    "^O",    WPIDM_FILEOPEN
#define   AccFilePrint   "^P",    WPIDM_FILEPRINT
#define   AccFileSave    "^S",    WPIDM_FILESAVE
#define   AccEditCut     VK_DELETE, WPIDM_EDITCUT, SHIFT, VIRTKEY
#define   AccEditCopy    VK_INSERT, WPIDM_EDITCOPY, CONTROL, VIRTKEY
#define   AccEditPaste   VK_INSERT, WPIDM_EDITPASTE, SHIFT, VIRTKEY
#define   AccEditUndo    VK_BACK, WPIDM_EDITUNDO, ALT, VIRTKEY
#define   AccWinCascade  VK_F5, WPIDM_WINCASCADE, SHIFT, VIRTKEY
#define   AccWinTile     VK_F4, WPIDM_WINTILE, SHIFT, VIRTKEY
#define   AccWinNext     VK_F6, WPIDM_WINNEXT, CONTROL, VIRTKEY
#define   AccMemStats    "^Z",    WPIDM_MEMSTATS
#endif // RC_INVOKED
#endif
```

WPLIST.H

```
//////////////////////////////////////////////////////
// WINDOWS++ CLASS LIBRARY.  Copyright 1992 Paul DiLascia.
// FILE: WPLIST.H
```

```
//
// List box definitions.
#ifndef WPLIST_H
#define WPLIST_H
#ifndef WPCTRL_H
#include "wpctrl.h"
#endif
#ifndef WPODRAW_H
#include "wpodraw.h"
#endif
/////////////////
// Generic list data.
//
DLLCLASS WPListData {
public:
   virtual BOOL firstItem() = 0;
   virtual BOOL nextItem() = 0;
   virtual void getItemText(char *buf, int len)=0;
};
#define LBS_DEFAULT    (WS_BORDER | LBS_NOTIFY | LBS_USETABSTOPS | WS_VSCROLL)
#define LBS_DEFAULTOD (LBS_DEFAULT | LBS_OWNERDRAWVARIABLE)
/////////////////
// List box.
//
DLLCLASS WPListBox : public WPControl {
   WPListData *list;        // the list
public:
   WPListBox(WPWin *pwin, int id, long sty=LBS_DEFAULT)
      : WPControl("ListBox", pwin, id, sty) { }
   static WPControl* New(WPWin* pwin, int id)
      { return new WPListBox(pwin, id); }
   void setList(WPListData *l, int sel=0, BOOL redraw=TRUE);
   // General control functions
   void linkObject(int *pint) { object=pint; }
   void updateScreen()        { if (object) setSel(*((int*)object)); }
   void updateObject()        { if (object) *((int*)object) = getSel(); }
   // Miscellaneous list box functions
   int count()                { return sendMsg(LB_GETCOUNT); }
   void reset()               { sendMsg(LB_RESETCONTENT); }
   void delItem(int index)    { sendMsg(LB_DELETESTRING, index); }
   void append(CSTR text)     { sendMsg(LB_ADDSTRING, 0, text); }
   void insert(CSTR text, int where)
      { sendMsg(LB_INSERTSTRING, where, text); }
   // Get/set selection
   int getSel()               { return sendMsg(LB_GETCURSEL); }
   void setSel(int sel)       { sendMsg(LB_SETCURSEL, sel); }
   int setSel(CSTR text, int start=-1)
      { return sendMsg(LB_SELECTSTRING, start, text); }
   int getSel(char *buf)
      { return (int)sendMsg(LB_GETTEXT, getSel(), buf); }
   void setTabStops(int *tabs, int len)
      { sendMsg(LB_SETTABSTOPS, len, tabs); }
};
/////////////////
// Owner-draw list box, multiply derived from list box and owner-draw item.
//
DLLCLASS WPODListBox : public WPListBox, public WPOwnerDrawItem {
public:
   WPODListBox(WPWin* pwin, int id, long sty=LBS_DEFAULTOD)
      : WPListBox(pwin, id, sty), WPOwnerDrawItem(pwin, ODT_LISTBOX) { }
   int getID() { return WPWin::getID(); }
};
#endif
```

WPMAIN.H

```
//////////////////////////////////////////////////////////
// WINDOWS++ CLASS LIBRARY.  Copyright 1992 Paul DiLascia.
```

```
// FILE: WPMAIN.H
//
// Definitions for WPMainWin, which represents a main window.
#ifndef WPMAIN_H
#define WPMAIN_H
#ifndef WPWIN_H
#include "wpwin.h"
#endif
#ifndef WPODRAW_H
#include "wpodraw.h"
#endif
const MAXPROMPTLEN = 80;
//////////////////
// Main application window. Each application has one.
//
DLLCLASS WPMainWin : public WPWin {
private:
    char filename[MAXFILENAMELEN];
    WPODItemList odItems;       // owner-draw items, if any
    int keyRepeat;              // key repeat for cursor movement
    BOOL noAppQuit;             // don't call app quit (for MDI);
    CSTR caption;               // window caption prefix
    CSTR fnFilter;              // filename filter
    BOOL modified;              // whether file modified
    BOOL fileKillConfirm();     // do file confirmation
    friend WPMDIChild;
protected:
    WPWin *promptWin;           // menu prompt window
public:
    WPMainWin(CSTR clsnm = "MAINWIN");
    ~WPMainWin();
    // Inline functions to access data members
    void fileNameFilter(CSTR filt)   { fnFilter = filt; }
    CSTR fileNameFilter()            { return fnFilter; }
    void fileCaption(CSTR cap)       { caption = cap; }
    void fileInit(CSTR fname, CSTR cap=NULL);
    // Miscellaneous
    void addODItem(WPOwnerDrawItem* od)    { odItems.add(od); }
    virtual BOOL doIdle()                  { return FALSE; }
    virtual int getMenuPrompt(char* buf, int id, WORD flags)
        { return 0; }
    // Virtual message functions for main window.
    BOOL command(int id, WORD msg);
    BOOL menuInit(WPMenu &menu);
    BOOL menuSelected(int id, WORD flags);
    BOOL kbd(WPEvent& event);
    BOOL activated(WORD state, BOOL minimized);
    BOOL closed();
    BOOL paint();
    BOOL queryEnd()    { return fileKillConfirm(); }
    virtual void paint(WPPaintStruct& ps) { }
    // Virtual functions to perform File commands.
    virtual void fileName(CSTR fn);
    virtual CSTR fileName()                 { return filename; }
    virtual BOOL fileIsModified()           { return modified; }
    virtual void fileIsModified(BOOL m)    { modified=m; }
    virtual BOOL fileNew()                  { return FALSE; }
    virtual BOOL fileOpen(CSTR fname)      { return FALSE; }
    virtual BOOL fileSave(CSTR fname)      { return FALSE; }
    virtual BOOL filePrint(WPDlgPrint &pdlg)   { return FALSE; }
    // Virtual functions to perform Edit commands.
    virtual BOOL editCut()                  { return FALSE; }
    virtual BOOL editCopy()                 { return FALSE; }
    virtual BOOL editPaste()                { return FALSE; }
    virtual BOOL editDelete()               { return FALSE; }
    virtual BOOL editUndo()                 { return FALSE; }
    virtual BOOL anySelected()              { return FALSE; }
    virtual BOOL canUndo()                  { return FALSE; }
```

```
    virtual BOOL canPaste()                    { return FALSE; }
};
#endif
```

WPMAIN.CPP

```
/////////////////////////////////////////////////////////
// WINDOWS++ CLASS LIBRARY.  Copyright 1992 Paul DiLascia.
// FILE: WPMAIN.CPP
//
// Implementation for WPMainWin.
#include "wpmain.h"
#include "wpapp.h"
#include "wpid.h"
#include "wpdlg.h"
#include "wpgdi.h"
#include "wpglob.h"
#include "wpdlfile.h"
#include "wpdlprt.h"
#include "wpmenu.h"
/////////////////
// Init Main Window object: set up default createArgs.
// Use module name as default main window class name
//
WPMainWin::WPMainWin(CSTR classnm) : WPWin(classnm)
{
    filename[0]=0;
    fnFilter=NULL;
    promptWin = NULL;
    noAppQuit = FALSE;         // only used by MDI Child
    caption = NULL;
    // Set default creation args
    createArgs.title = (CSTR)createArgs.wndcls.lpszClassName;
    createArgs.style = WS_OVERLAPPEDWINDOW;
    // Use "AppIcon" and "AppMenu" if any.
    createArgs.wndcls.lpszMenuName = "AppMenu";
    createArgs.wndcls.hIcon = App.loadIcon("AppIcon");
    if (createArgs.wndcls.hIcon==NULL)
        createArgs.wndcls.hIcon = App.loadIcon(IDI_APPLICATION);
}
/////////////////
// Destructor: post quit message to Windows.
// This happens automatically when the main window is destroyed!
//
WPMainWin::~WPMainWin()
{
    if (!noAppQuit)           // (if not MDI child):
        App.quit();           // quit
}
/////////////////
// Handle low-level commands for main app window, such as
// Exit, About and so on.
//
BOOL WPMainWin::command(int id, WORD msg)
{
    char temp[MAXFILENAMELEN];
    switch (id) {
    case WPIDM_EXIT:
    case WPIDM_FILECLOSE:
        close();
        return TRUE;
    case WPIDM_ABOUT:
        WPDialogModal aboutBox("DLGABOUT", this);
        if (aboutBox.run()==-1)
            MsgBeep();
        return TRUE;
```

```
        case WPIDM_MEMSTATS:
           WPApp::ShowAllStats();
           return TRUE;
        case WPIDM_FILENEW:
           if (fileKillConfirm() && fileNew())
               fileName("");
           return TRUE;
        case WPIDM_FILEOPEN:
           if (fileKillConfirm()) {
               WPDlgFileOpen openDlg(this, temp);
               openDlg.setFilter(fnFilter);
               if (openDlg.run() && fileOpen(temp))
                   fileName(temp);
           }
           return TRUE;
        case WPIDM_FILESAVE:
           if (fileName()[0]) {
               if (fileSave(fileName()))
                   fileIsModified(FALSE);
               return TRUE;
           }
           // no filename: fall through
        case WPIDM_FILESAVEAS:
           WPDlgFileSaveAs saveDlg(this, temp);
           saveDlg.setFilter(fnFilter);
           if (saveDlg.run() && fileSave(temp))
               fileName(temp);
           return TRUE;
        case WPIDM_FILEPRINT:
           WPDlgPrint pdlg = this;        // create print dialog
           if (pdlg.run())                // run dialog
               filePrint(pdlg);           // print!
           return TRUE;
        case WPIDM_EDITCUT:      return editCut();
        case WPIDM_EDITCOPY:     return editCopy();
        case WPIDM_EDITPASTE:    return editPaste();
        case WPIDM_EDITDELETE:   return editDelete();
        case WPIDM_EDITUNDO:     return editUndo();
        }
        return FALSE;
}
//////////////////
// Handle low-level keyboard messages: for now, all we do is
// translate arrow keys to cursor movement.  Note that all this
// is built-in, so applications never have to bother with it.
//
BOOL WPMainWin::kbd(WPEvent& event)
{
    switch (event.msg) {
    case WM_KEYDOWN:
        keyRepeat += event.keyRepeat();
        if (Keyboard.isArrowKey(event.key())) {
            // Got arrow key: move cursor
            WPPoint pt = Cursor();
            screenToClient(pt);
            switch (event.key()) {
            case VK_LEFT:  pt.x -= keyRepeat;    break;
            case VK_RIGHT: pt.x += keyRepeat;    break;
            case VK_UP:    pt.y -= keyRepeat;    break;
            case VK_DOWN:  pt.y += keyRepeat;    break;
            }
            // Don't move outside our window's client area
            WPRect rect = this;
            rect.capture(pt);
            clientToScreen(pt);
            Cursor = pt;
            return TRUE;
```

```
        }
        break;
    case WM_KEYUP:
        keyRepeat = 1;                          // Clear repeat count
        break;
    }
    return FALSE;
}
/////////////////
// Main window was activated: show the cursor if there's no mouse.
//
BOOL WPMainWin::activated(WORD state, BOOL minimized)
{
    if (!Mouse.present() && !minimized)
        Cursor.show(state);
    setFocus();
    return TRUE;
}
/////////////////
// Got WM_CLOSE message:
//
BOOL WPMainWin::closed()
{
    // automatically destroy window when close message received
    if (queryEnd())
        destroyWin();
    return TRUE;
}
/////////////////
// Handle pain message.
// Get paint struct and pass to app-specific virtual function.
//
BOOL WPMainWin::paint()
{
    WPPaintStruct ps = this;
    paint(ps);
    return TRUE;
}
/////////////////
// Initialize standard menu commands (File, Edit, etc)
//
BOOL WPMainWin::menuInit(WPMenu &menu)
{
    WPMenu mainMenu = this;
    if (menu==mainMenu) {
        // Initialize File menu
        BOOL gotFile = fileName()[0]!=0;
        menu.enableItem(WPIDM_FILESAVE, gotFile && fileIsModified());
        // Initialize Edit menu
        BOOL any = anySelected();
        menu.enableItem(WPIDM_EDITPASTE, canPaste());
        menu.enableItem(WPIDM_EDITCUT, any);
        menu.enableItem(WPIDM_EDITCOPY, any);
        menu.enableItem(WPIDM_EDITDELETE, any);
        menu.enableItem(WPIDM_EDITUNDO, canUndo());
        return TRUE;
    }
    return FALSE;
}
/////////////////
// Handle WM_MENUSELECT message.
// If there's a prompt window, invoke app to get the text, then
// display it in the prompt window.
//
BOOL WPMainWin::menuSelected(int id, WORD flags)
{
    if (promptWin) {
        char* buf = App.scratch;
```

```
            *buf=0;
            getMenuPrompt(buf, id, flags);
            promptWin->invalidate(TRUE);;
            promptWin->setText(buf);
        }
    return TRUE;
}
/////////////////
// Initialize filename.
//
void WPMainWin::fileInit(CSTR fname, CSTR cap)
{
    fileCaption(cap);
    if (fname && *fname)
        fileOpen(fname);
    fileName(fname);
}
/////////////////
// Set filename.
//
void WPMainWin::fileName(CSTR fname)
{
    if (fname && *fname)
        strcpy(filename, fname);
    else
        filename[0]=0;
    fileIsModified(FALSE);
    if (caption) {
        char *buf = App.scratch;
        sprintf(buf,"%s %s", caption, filename[0] ? filename : "(untitled)" );
        setText(buf);
    }
}
/////////////////
// Do confirmation before over-writing current file.
//
BOOL WPMainWin::fileKillConfirm()
{
    if (!fileIsModified())
        return TRUE;
    CSTR fname = fileName();
    char buf[MAXFILENAMELEN+40]="Save changes";
    if (fname[0]) {
        strcat(buf," to ");
        strcat(buf, fname);
    }
    strcat(buf,"?");
    MsgBeep();
    int answer = MsgBox(buf, caption, MB_YESNOCANCEL | MB_ICONQUESTION);
    if (answer==IDYES) {
        char temp[MAXFILENAMELEN];
        if (fname[0]==0) {
            WPDlgFileSaveAs saveDlg(this, temp);
            saveDlg.setFilter(fnFilter);
            if (!saveDlg.run())
                return FALSE;
            fname = temp;
        }
        return fileSave(fname);
    }
    return answer==IDNO;
}
```

WPMDI.H

```
/////////////////////////////////////////////////////////
// WINDOWS++ CLASS LIBRARY.  Copyright 1992 Paul DiLascia.
// FILE: WPMDI.H
```

```
//
// MDI (Multiple Document Interface) definitions.
#ifndef WPMDI_H
#define WPMDI_H
#ifndef WPMAIN_H
#include "wpmain.h"
#endif
#ifndef WPAPP_H
#include "wpapp.h"
#endif
/////////////////
// MDI client window.
//
DLLCLASS WPMDIClient : public WPWin {
private:
   WPMDIClient(WPMDIFrame *pwin);
   ~WPMDIClient()      { App.mdiClientHwnd = NULL; }
   WPMDIChild* activeWin()
      { return (WPMDIChild*)GetWin(LOWORD(sendMsg(WM_MDIGETACTIVE))); }
   friend WPMDIFrame;
};
/////////////////
// MDI Child window. It's derived from WPMainWin in order to inherit all
// the stuff for the File, Edit, etc. commands--even though the
// Frame window is really the main window.
//
DLLCLASS WPMDIChild : public WPMainWin {
   WPMDIClient* client;    // client window
public:
   WPMDIChild(CSTR classnm, WPMDIFrame *frame);
   BOOL createWin();
   void destroyWin()    { client->sendMsg(WM_MDIDESTROY, getHwnd()); }
   void maximize()      { client->sendMsg(WM_MDIMAXIMIZE, getHwnd()); }
   void restore()       { client->sendMsg(WM_MDIRESTORE, getHwnd()); }
   void activate()      { client->sendMsg(WM_MDIACTIVATE, getHwnd()); }
};
/////////////////
// MDI Frame window.
//
DLLCLASS WPMDIFrame : public WPMainWin {
   WPMDIClient *client;     // ptr to client window
   int winMenuPos;          // relative pos of "Window" menu
   friend WPMDIClient;
   friend WPMDIChild;
public:
   WPMDIFrame(int winMenu, CSTR classnm = "MDIFRAME");
   ~WPMDIFrame()          { closeAll(TRUE); }
   WPMDIClient* clientWin()    { return client; }
   WPMDIChild* activeWin()     { return client->activeWin(); }
   BOOL createWin();
   // Brainless functions
   void cascade()       { client->sendMsg(WM_MDICASCADE); }
   void tile()          { client->sendMsg(WM_MDITILE); }
   void arrangeIcons()  { client->sendMsg(WM_MDIICONARRANGE); }
   void nextWin()       { client->sendMsg(WM_MDINEXT); }
   BOOL closeAll(BOOL force=FALSE);
   // Virtual message functions
   BOOL menuInit(WPMenu &menu);
   BOOL command(int id, WORD msg);
   BOOL queryEnd();
};
#endif
```

WPMDI.CPP

```
//////////////////////////////////////////////////////
// WINDOWS++ CLASS LIBRARY.  Copyright 1992 Paul DiLascia.
// FILE: WPMDI.CPP
```

```
//
// Implementation of MDI window classes.
#include "wpapp.h"
#include "wpmdi.h"
#include "wpid.h"
#include "wpmenu.h"
/////////////////
// We need this window proc for frame windows because
// brain-damaged Microsoft uses one with non-standard arguments.
//
LONG _export FAR PASCAL WPDefFrameProc(HWND hwnd, WORD msg, WORD wp, LONG lp)
{
    HWND clientHwnd = GetWindow(hwnd, GW_CHILD);
    return DefFrameProc(hwnd, clientHwnd, msg, wp, lp);
}
/////////////////
// Initialize frame window.
// Argument is relative position in menu of "Window" popup.
//
WPMDIFrame::WPMDIFrame(int winMenu, CSTR classnm) : WPMainWin(classnm)
{
    createArgs.wndcls.lpfnWndProc = CASTWNDPROC WPDefFrameProc;
    createArgs.wndcls.hbrBackground = COLOR_APPWORKSPACE+1;
    createArgs.style |= WS_CLIPCHILDREN;
    client = NULL;
    winMenuPos = winMenu;
}
/////////////////
// Create frame window: create client window too.
//
BOOL WPMDIFrame::createWin()
{
    if (WPMainWin::createWin()) {        // create frame window
        client = new WPMDIClient(this);  // create client window
        assert(client);
        return TRUE;
    }
    return FALSE;
}
/////////////////
// Handle command:
//   MDI commands:    do it.
//   File commands:   do Open, New, Close, Exit; pass others to child.
//   Other:           pass to child.
//
BOOL WPMDIFrame::command(int id, WORD msg)
{
    WPMDIChild *active = activeWin();
    switch (id) {
    case WPIDM_WINCASCADE:   cascade();          return TRUE;
    case WPIDM_WINTILE:      tile();             return TRUE;
    case WPIDM_WINARRANGE:   arrangeIcons();     return TRUE;
    case WPIDM_WINNEXT:      nextWin();          return TRUE;
    case WPIDM_WINCLOSEALL:  closeAll();         return TRUE;
    case WPIDM_FILEOPEN:
    case WPIDM_FILENEW:
    case WPIDM_EXIT:
        break;
    case WPIDM_FILECLOSE:
        if (active)
            active->close();
        return TRUE;
    default:
        if (active && active->command(id, msg))
            return TRUE;
    }
    return WPMainWin::command(id, msg);
}
```

```
//////////////////
// Close all child windows.
//
BOOL WPMDIFrame::closeAll(BOOL force)
{
    WPChildWinList children = client;
    WPWin *nextwin;
    for (WPWin *cwin=children.first(); cwin; cwin=nextwin) {
        nextwin = children.next();
        if (force || cwin->queryEnd())
            cwin->destroyWin();
        else
            return FALSE;
    }
    return TRUE;
}
//////////////////
// Check if it's ok to kill the app: check each child window.
//
BOOL WPMDIFrame::queryEnd()
{
    forEachChildWin(client, cwin) {
        if (!cwin->queryEnd())
            return FALSE;
    }
    return TRUE;
}
//////////////////
// Initialize menu.
//
BOOL WPMDIFrame::menuInit(WPMenu &menu)
{
    WPMenu mainMenu = this;
    if (menu==mainMenu) {
        WPMDIChild *active = activeWin();
        // Initialize File menu
        BOOL gotFile = active && active->fileName()[0]!=0;
        menu.enableItem(WPIDM_FILESAVE, gotFile && active->fileIsModified());
        menu.enableItem(WPIDM_FILESAVEAS,active!=NULL);
        menu.enableItem(WPIDM_FILEPRINT, active!=NULL);
        menu.enableItem(WPIDM_FILECLOSE, active!=NULL);
        // Initialize Edit menu
        BOOL any = active && active->anySelected();
        menu.enableItem(WPIDM_EDITPASTE, active && active->canPaste());
        menu.enableItem(WPIDM_EDITCUT, any);
        menu.enableItem(WPIDM_EDITCOPY, any);
        menu.enableItem(WPIDM_EDITDELETE, any);
        menu.enableItem(WPIDM_EDITUNDO, active && active->canUndo());
        // Initialize Window menu
        for (int id = WPIDM_WINTILE; id <= WPIDM_WINCLOSEALL; id++)
            menu.enableItem(id, active!=NULL);
        return TRUE;
    }
    return FALSE;
}
//////////////////
// Initialize client window object.
// Note that the constructor actually creates the window too.
//
WPMDIClient::WPMDIClient(WPMDIFrame *frame) : WPWin("MDICLIENT", frame, 1)
{
    createArgs.style = WS_CHILD | WS_CLIPCHILDREN | WS_VISIBLE;
    // Get Window popup menu
    WPMenu menu=frame;
    WPSubMenu submenu(menu, frame->winMenuPos);
    // Set up weird windows structure.
    CLIENTCREATESTRUCT ccs;
    ccs.hWindowMenu = submenu();
```

```
    ccs.idFirstChild = 1;
    createArgs.lparam = (LPSTR)&ccs;
    createWin();                    // create window
    // Tell application object to translate accelerator keys.
    App.mdiClientHwnd = getHwnd();
}
/////////////////
// Initialize MDI child window.
//
WPMDIChild::WPMDIChild(CSTR classnm, WPMDIFrame *frame) : WPMainWin(classnm)
{
    createArgs.parent = frame->clientWin();
    createArgs.wndcls.lpfnWndProc = CASTWNDPROC DefMDIChildProc;
    createArgs.wndcls.lpszMenuName = NULL;
    createArgs.title = NULL;
    createArgs.style = 0;
    noAppQuit=TRUE;                 // hack so WPMainWin won't post WM_QUIT msg
}
/////////////////
// Create child window: do weird Windows incantations.
//
BOOL WPMDIChild::createWin()
{
    MDICREATESTRUCT cs;       // another unnecessary Windows structure
    cs.szClass = (char*)createArgs.wndcls.lpszClassName;
    cs.szTitle = (char*)createArgs.title;
    cs.hOwner = createArgs.wndcls.hInstance;
    cs.x  = createArgs.pos.left();
    cs.y  = createArgs.pos.top();
    cs.cx = createArgs.pos.width();
    cs.cy = createArgs.pos.height();
    cs.style = createArgs.style;
    cs.lParam = NULL;
    // Register window class if it ain't already registered!
    WNDCLASS temp;
    if (!GetClassInfo(cs.hOwner, cs.szClass, &temp)) {
        BOOL ret = RegisterClass(&createArgs.wndcls);
        assert(ret);
    }
    // Now create the child window.
    client = (WPMDIClient*)createArgs.parent;
    assert(client);
    HWND newhwnd = (HWND)(client->sendMsg(WM_MDICREATE, 0, &cs));
    linkHwnd(newhwnd);
    return hwnd!=NULL;
}
```

WPMENU.H

```
//////////////////////////////////////////////////////////
// WINDOWS++ CLASS LIBRARY.  Copyright 1992 Paul DiLascia.
// FILE: WPMENU.H
//
// Menu definitions.
#ifndef WPMENU_H
#define WPMENU_H
#ifndef WPPOINT_H
#include "wppoint.h"
#endif
#ifndef WPWIN_H
#include "wpwin.h"
#endif
// Default way to manipulate menu items is by command id, not position.
#define MF_DFLTPOS    MF_BYCOMMAND
/////////////////
// Menu class
//
DLLCLASS WPMenu {
```

```cpp
protected:
    HMENU hmenu;                    // Windows handle to menu
public:
    WPMenu()                        { hmenu = CreateMenu(); }
    WPMenu(HMENU h)                 { hmenu=h; }
    WPMenu(MENUITEMTEMPLATEHEADER& t)
        { hmenu=LoadMenuIndirect((LPSTR)&t); }
    WPMenu(WPWin *win)              { hmenu = GetMenu(win->getHwnd()); }
    void destroy()                  { DestroyMenu(hmenu); }
    HMENU operator()()              { return hmenu; }
    WPMenu& operator=(HMENU h)      { hmenu=h; return *this; }
    BOOL operator==(WPMenu &m)      { return hmenu==m.hmenu; }
    int count()                     { return GetMenuItemCount(hmenu); }
    int itemID(int pos)             { return GetMenuItemID(hmenu, pos); }
    WORD state(int id, WORD how=MF_DFLTPOS)
        { return GetMenuState(hmenu, id, how); }
    int getText(int id, char *buf, int buflen, WORD how=MF_DFLTPOS)
        { return GetMenuString(hmenu, id, (LPSTR)buf, buflen, how); }
    BOOL checkItem(int id, BOOL chk, WORD how=MF_DFLTPOS)
        { return CheckMenuItem(hmenu, id,
            chk  ? (how|MF_CHECKED) : (how|MF_UNCHECKED)); }
    BOOL enableItem(int id, BOOL enab, WORD how=MF_DFLTPOS)
        { return EnableMenuItem(hmenu, id,
            enab  ? (how|MF_ENABLED) : (how|MF_GRAYED)); }
    BOOL hiliteItem(WPWin *win, int id, BOOL hi, WORD how=MF_DFLTPOS)
        { return HiliteMenuItem((*win)(), hmenu, id,
            hi  ? (how|MF_HILITE) : (how|MF_UNHILITE)); }
    BOOL trackPopup(WPWin *win, WPPoint p)
        { return TrackPopupMenu(hmenu, 0, p.x, p.y, 0, (*win)(), NULL); }
    BOOL setBitmaps(int id, WPBitmap* bm0, WPBitmap* bm1,
        WORD how=MF_DFLTPOS);
    BOOL append(int id, CSTR text, WORD flags=0)
        { return AppendMenu(hmenu, MF_STRING|flags, id, (LPSTR)text); }
    BOOL append(WPMenu& popup, CSTR text)
        { return AppendMenu(hmenu, MF_POPUP, popup(), (LPSTR)text); }
    BOOL append(int id, WPBitmap& bm, WORD flags=0);
    BOOL appendSep()
        { return AppendMenu(hmenu, MF_SEPARATOR, 0, NULL); }
    HMENU appendPopup(CSTR text);
    BOOL insert(int pos, int id, CSTR text, WORD flags=MF_DFLTPOS)
        { return InsertMenu(hmenu, pos, MF_STRING|flags, id, (LPSTR)text); }
    BOOL insert(int pos, WPMenu& popup, CSTR text, WORD flags=MF_DFLTPOS)
        { return InsertMenu(hmenu, pos, MF_POPUP|flags, popup(), (LPSTR)text); }
    BOOL insert(int pos, int id, WPBitmap& bm, WORD flags=MF_DFLTPOS);
    BOOL insertSep(int pos, WORD flags=MF_DFLTPOS)
        { return InsertMenu(hmenu, pos, MF_SEPARATOR|flags, 0, NULL); }
    HMENU insertPopup(int pos, CSTR text, WORD flags=MF_DFLTPOS);
    BOOL modify(int pos, int id, CSTR text, WORD flags=MF_DFLTPOS)
        { return ModifyMenu(hmenu, pos, MF_STRING|flags, id, (LPSTR)text); }
    BOOL modify(int pos, WPMenu& popup, CSTR text, WORD flags=MF_DFLTPOS)
        { return ModifyMenu(hmenu, pos, MF_POPUP|flags, popup(), (LPSTR)text); }
    BOOL modify(int pos, int id, WPBitmap& bm, WORD flags=MF_DFLTPOS);
    BOOL remove(int pos, WORD flags=MF_DFLTPOS)
        { return RemoveMenu(hmenu, pos, flags); }
    BOOL deleteItem(int pos, WORD flags=MF_DFLTPOS)
        { return DeleteMenu(hmenu, pos, flags); }
};
/////////////////
// Submenu.
//
DLLCLASS WPSubMenu : public WPMenu {
public:
    WPSubMenu(WPMenu& menu, int pos) : WPMenu(GetSubMenu(menu(),pos)) { }
};
/////////////////
// Popup menu.
//
DLLCLASS WPPopupMenu : public WPMenu {
```

```
public:
   WPPopupMenu()   : WPMenu(CreatePopupMenu())   { }
};
////////////////
// System menu.
//
DLLCLASS WPSysMenu : public WPMenu {
   WPWin *win;
public:
   WPSysMenu(WPWin *w) : WPMenu(GetSystemMenu((*w)(), FALSE)) { }
   void revert(WPWin *w)   { hmenu = GetSystemMenu((*w)(), TRUE); }
};
#endif
```

WPMENU.CPP

```
/////////////////////////////////////////////////////////////
// WINDOWS++ CLASS LIBRARY.  Copyright 1992 Paul DiLascia.
// FILE: WPMENU.CPP
//
// Implementation of menu object.
// These functions are all pretty brainless.
#include "wpmenu.h"
#include "wpgdi.h"
BOOL WPMenu::setBitmaps(int id, WPBitmap* bm0, WPBitmap* bm1, WORD how)
{
   return SetMenuItemBitmaps(hmenu, id, how, (*bm0)(), (*bm1)());
}
BOOL WPMenu::append(int id, WPBitmap& bm, WORD flags)
{
   return AppendMenu(hmenu, MF_BITMAP|flags, id,
      (LPSTR)MAKELONG(bm(),0));
}
HMENU WPMenu::appendPopup(CSTR text)
{
   HMENU hPopup = CreateMenu();
   if (AppendMenu(hmenu, MF_POPUP, hPopup, (LPSTR)text) )
      return hPopup;
   DestroyMenu(hPopup);
   return NULL;
}
BOOL WPMenu::insert(int pos, int id, WPBitmap& bm, WORD flags)
{
   return InsertMenu(hmenu, pos, MF_BITMAP|flags, id,
      (LPSTR)MAKELONG(bm(), 0));
}
HMENU WPMenu::insertPopup(int pos, CSTR text, WORD flags)
{
   HMENU hPopup = CreateMenu();
   if (InsertMenu(hmenu, pos, MF_POPUP|flags, hPopup, (LPSTR)text) )
      return hPopup;
   DestroyMenu(hPopup);
   return NULL;
}
BOOL  WPMenu::modify(int pos, int id, WPBitmap& bm, WORD flags)
{
   return ModifyMenu(hmenu, pos, MF_BITMAP|flags, id,
      (LPSTR)MAKELONG(bm(), 0));
}
```

WPODRAW.H

```
/////////////////////////////////////////////////////////////
// WINDOWS++ CLASS LIBRARY.  Copyright 1992 Paul DiLascia.
// FILE: WPODRAW.H
//
// Definitions for owner-draw items.
```

```
#ifndef WPODRAW_H
#define WPODRAW_H
#ifndef WPPOINT_H
#include "wppoint.h"
#endif
/////////////////
// Generic header for all windows XXXXITEMSTRUCT's
//
struct ODITEMSTRUCT {
   WORD type;      // item type (ODT_BUTTON, etc.)
   WORD id;        // (control id)
};
typedef ODITEMSTRUCT FAR* LPODITEMSTRUCT;
typedef void FAR* ODDATA;               // any pointer for draw item
/////////////////
// Generic owner draw item used for list box, button, etc.
//
DLLCLASS WPOwnerDrawItem {
   WPOwnerDrawItem *next;
   WORD type;
   friend class WPODItemList;
public:
   WPOwnerDrawItem(WPWin *win, WORD t);
   WORD getType() { return type; }
   virtual int getID() = 0;
   virtual void paint(WPOwnerDrawDC &dc, ODDATA data) = 0;
   virtual WPPoint measure(ODDATA data) { return WPPoint(0,0); };
   virtual int compare(ODDATA data1, ODDATA data2) { return 0; };
   virtual void delItem(ODDATA data) { };
};
/////////////////
// Object to hold a list of owner draw items.
//
class WPODItemList {
private:
   WPOwnerDrawItem *first;
   WPOwnerDrawItem* getItem(LPODITEMSTRUCT &item);
public:
   WPODItemList() { first = NULL; }
   void add(WPOwnerDrawItem *od) { od->next = first; first = od; }
   BOOL dispatchEvent(WPEvent& event);
};
#endif
```

WPODRAW.CPP

```
/////////////////////////////////////////////////////////
// WINDOWS++ CLASS LIBRARY.  Copyright 1992 Paul DiLascia.
// FILE: WPODRAW.CPP
//
// Implementation of owner-draw objects.
#include "wpodraw.h"
#include "wpgdi.h"
#include "wpwin.h"
WPOwnerDrawItem::WPOwnerDrawItem(WPWin *win, WORD t)
{
   next = NULL;
   type = t;
   assert(win);
   win->addODItem(this);
}
WPOwnerDrawItem* WPODItemList::getItem(LPODITEMSTRUCT &item)
{
   WPOwnerDrawItem* od;
   for (od=first; od; od=od->next) {
      if (od->getType() == item->type && od->getID() == item->id)
         break;
   }
```

```
        return od;
}
BOOL WPODItemList::dispatchEvent(WPEvent& event)
{
    if (first==NULL)
        return FALSE;
    LPODITEMSTRUCT odi = (LPODITEMSTRUCT)event.lp;
    WPOwnerDrawItem *item;
    switch (event.msg) {
    case WM_DRAWITEM:
        item = getItem(odi);
        if (item) {
            LPDRAWITEMSTRUCT draw = (LPDRAWITEMSTRUCT)odi;
            WPOwnerDrawDC dc = draw;
            item->paint(dc, (ODDATA)draw->itemData);
            return TRUE;
        }
        break;
    case WM_MEASUREITEM:
        item = getItem(odi);
        if (item) {
            WPPoint dim =
                item->measure((ODDATA)((LPMEASUREITEMSTRUCT)odi)->itemData);
            ((LPMEASUREITEMSTRUCT)odi)->itemWidth  = dim.x;
            ((LPMEASUREITEMSTRUCT)odi)->itemHeight = dim.y;
            return TRUE;
        }
        break;
    case WM_DELETEITEM:
        item = getItem(odi);
        if (item==NULL) {
            item->delItem((ODDATA)((LPDELETEITEMSTRUCT)odi)->itemData);
            return TRUE;
        }
        break;
    case WM_COMPAREITEM:
        item = getItem(odi);
        if (item==NULL) {
            event.ret =
                item->compare((ODDATA)((LPCOMPAREITEMSTRUCT)odi)->itemData1,
                    (ODDATA)((LPCOMPAREITEMSTRUCT)odi)->itemData1);
            return TRUE;
        }
        break;
    case WM_VKEYTOITEM:
    case WM_CHARTOITEM:
        // Not supported yet
        break;
    }
    return FALSE;
}
```

WPP.H

```
////////////////////////////////////////////////////////////
// WINDOWS++ CLASS LIBRARY.  Copyright 1992 Paul DiLascia.
// FILE: WPP.H
//
// Main include file for Windows++ library.
// All it does is include all the other header files.
#ifndef WPP_H
#define WPP_H
#ifdef RC_INVOKED
#include "windows.h"
#include "wpid.h"
#else
#ifndef WPPDEFS_H
#include "wppdefs.h"
```

```
#endif
#ifndef WPID_H
#include "wpid.h"
#endif
#ifndef WPHEAP_H
#include "wpheap.h"
#endif
#ifndef WPRECT_H
#include "wprect.h"
#endif
#ifndef WPAPP_H
#include "wpapp.h"
#endif
#ifndef WPWIN_H
#include "wpwin.h"
#endif
#ifndef WPMAIN_H
#include "wpmain.h"
#endif
#ifndef WPCTRL_H
#include "wpctrl.h"
#endif
#ifndef WPBUTN_H
#include "wpbutn.h"
#endif
#ifndef WPCOMBO_H
#include "wpcombo.h"
#endif
#ifndef WPEDIT_H
#include "wpedit.h"
#endif
#ifndef WPLIST_H
#include "wplist.h"
#endif
#ifndef WPSBAR_H
#include "wpsbar.h"
#endif
#ifndef WPSTATIC_H
#include "wpstatic.h"
#endif
#ifndef WPDLG_H
#include "wpdlg.h"
#endif
#ifndef WPDLFILE_H
#include "wpdlfile.h"
#endif
#ifndef WPDLPRT_H
#include "wpdlprt.h"
#endif
#ifndef WPDLSTR_H
#include "wpdlstr.h"
#endif
#ifndef WPMENU_H
#include "wpmenu.h"
#endif
#ifndef WPGDI_H
#include "wpgdi.h"
#endif
#ifndef WPGLOB_H
#include "wpglob.h"
#endif
#ifndef WPMDI_H
#include "wpmdi.h"
#endif
#ifndef WPODRAW_H
#include "wpodraw.h"
#endif
#endif    // RC_INVOKED
```

```
#endif    // WPP_H
```

WPPDEFS.H

```
/////////////////////////////////////////////////////////
// WINDOWS++ CLASS LIBRARY.  Copyright 1992 Paul DiLascia.
// FILE: WPPDEFS.H
//
// Basic Windows++ type definitions, constants, etc.
#ifndef WPPDEFS_H
#define WPPDEFS_H
#ifndef RC_INVOKED
#include <string.h>
#include <stdlib.h>
#include <stdio.h>
#include <windows.h>
#endif
const MAXINT = 0x7fff;
const MAXFILENAMELEN = 128;
const MAXSTRLEN = 256;
typedef char*  STR;
typedef const  char* CSTR;
typedef const  char FAR* LPCSTR;
/////////////////////
// Roll our own assert macro for uniformity between compilers.
//
#undef assert
#ifdef NODEBUG
#  define assert(ignore)    ((void) 0)
#else
#  define assert(x)   ((void)((x) || (DoAssert(#x,__FILE__,__LINE__),1)))
#endif
#ifdef __BORLANDC__
#if defined(__DLL__) || defined(USEDLL)
#define DLLFUNC _export
#define DLLCLASS class _export
#else
#define DLLFUNC
#define DLLCLASS class
#endif
#if defined(USEDLL)
#define APPCLASS class _export
#else
#define APPCLASS class
#endif
// Define min, max: should use templates, but they don't work well
// with 'const' declarations.
#define max(a,b)   (((a) > (b)) ? (a) : (b))
#define min(a,b)   (((a) < (b)) ? (a) : (b))
// Put all FAR data in the DGROUP to avoid creating multiple data segments.
// Otherwise, Windows can't run multiple instances of our app.
#pragma option -zE_DATA -zHDGROUP -zFDATA
#elif __ZTC__
#define DLLFUNC
#define DLLCLASS class
#define APPCLASS class
#define strcmpi strcmpl
#endif
// To export object, use same syntax as for function
#define DLLOBJECT DLLFUNC
/////////////////////
// Global non-class-member functions
//
extern void DLLFUNC DoAssert(CSTR msg, CSTR file, unsigned line);
extern int  DLLFUNC StringCopy(char *dest, int buflen, CSTR src);
extern int  DLLFUNC ErrBox(CSTR format, ...);
/////////////////////
// Global new and delete operators used for ALL memory allocations.
```

```
//
extern void* operator new(size_t size);
extern void  operator delete(void * ptr);
/////////////////////
// Useful MsgBox and MsgBeep functions.
//
inline int MsgBox(CSTR text, CSTR caption="", int type=MB_OK)
{ return MessageBox(NULL, (LPSTR)text, (LPSTR)caption, type); }
inline void MsgBeep(WORD type=0)
{ MessageBeep(type); }
/////////////////////
// All the classes are declared below, without being defined.
// This is so we can make forward references to class types in
// function arguments, etc., (before the class is actually defined).
//
DLLCLASS WPApp;
DLLCLASS WPWin;
DLLCLASS WPMainWin;
DLLCLASS WPMenu;
DLLCLASS WPDialog;
DLLCLASS WPDialogModal;
DLLCLASS WPDialogModeless;
DLLCLASS WPDlgFileOpen;
DLLCLASS WPDlgPrint;
DLLCLASS WPDlgPrintAbort;
DLLCLASS WPDlgString;
DLLCLASS WPControl;
DLLCLASS WPButton;
DLLCLASS WPListBox;
DLLCLASS WPDevContext;
DLLCLASS WPPrinter;
DLLCLASS WPPaintStruct;
DLLCLASS WPOwnerDrawItem;
DLLCLASS WPOwnerDrawDC;
DLLCLASS WPMDIFrame;
DLLCLASS WPMDIClient;
DLLCLASS WPMDIChild;
DLLCLASS WPRegion;
DLLCLASS WPPen;
DLLCLASS WPBrush;
DLLCLASS WPBitmap;
struct   WPEvent;
#endif
```

WPPOINT.H

```
///////////////////////////////////////////////////////////
// WINDOWS++ CLASS LIBRARY.  Copyright 1992 Paul DiLascia.
// FILE: WPPOINT.H
//
// Declarations for WPPoint structure, the Windows++ analog of POINT.
#ifndef WPPOINT_H
#define WPPOINT_H
#ifndef WPPDEFS_H
#include "wppdefs.h"
#endif
/////////////////////
// Used in place of Windows POINT structure.
// Must be declared identically to POINT so we can cast.
//
struct WPPoint {
    int x,y;
    WPPoint(int xx=0, int yy=0)     { set(xx,yy); }
    WPPoint(POINT p)                { set(p); }
    void set(int xx=0, int yy=0)    { x=xx; y=yy; }
    void set(POINT p)               { set(p.x, p.y); }
    BOOL operator==(WPPoint p)      { return *((LONG*)this)==*((LONG*)&p); }
    BOOL operator!=(WPPoint p)      { return *((LONG*)this)!=*((LONG*)&p); }
```

```
    WPPoint& operator++ ()          { x++; y++; return *this; }
    WPPoint& operator-- ()          { x--; y--; return *this; }
    WPPoint operator+ (WPPoint p) { return WPPoint(x+p.x, y+p.y); }
    WPPoint operator- (WPPoint p) { return WPPoint(x-p.x, y-p.y); }
    WPPoint& operator+= (int n)     { x+=n; y+=n; return *this; }
    WPPoint& operator-= (int n)     { x-=n; y-=n; return *this; }
    WPPoint& operator+= (WPPoint p)  { x+=p.x; y+=p.y; return *this; }
    WPPoint& operator-= (WPPoint p)  { x-=p.x; y-=p.y; return *this; }
    WPPoint& operator*= (int m)    { x*=m; y*=m; return *this; }
    WPPoint& operator/= (int m)    { x/=m; y/=m; return *this; }
    WPPoint& operator*= (TEXTMETRIC &tm)
        { x*=tm.tmAveCharWidth; y*=tm.tmHeight; return *this; }
    WPPoint& operator= (POINT p)  { set(p); return *this; }
    WPPoint& operator= (LONG l)   { return *this = *((WPPoint*)&l); }
};
// Cast WPPoint to POINT
#define TOPOINT(p) (*((POINT*)&(p)))
#endif
```

WPRECT.H

```
/////////////////////////////////////////////////////////////
// WINDOWS++ CLASS LIBRARY.  Copyright 1992 Paul DiLascia.
// FILE: WPRECT.H
//
// Declarations for WPRect class, the Windows++ analog of RECT.
#ifndef WPRECT_H
#define WPRECT_H
#ifndef WPPOINT_H
#include "wppoint.h"
#endif
//////
// This class must be defined exactly as a Windows RECT, because
// we need to cast it to a RECT when calling Windows.
//
DLLCLASS WPRect {
    WPPoint org;    // origin of rectangle
    WPPoint end;    // endpoint of rectangle
public:
    WPRect() { }
    WPRect(WPPoint o, WPPoint e)          { set(o, e); }
    WPRect(int l, int t, int r, int b)    { set(l,t,r,b); }
    WPRect(RECT& rect)                    { *this = rect; }
    WPRect(WPWin *win)                    { *this = win; }
    WPRect(WPPaintStruct& ps)             { *this = ps; }
    WPRect(CSTR text)                     { *this = text; }
    void normalize();
    int left()          { return org.x; }
    int top()           { return org.y; }
    int right()         { return end.x; }
    int bottom()        { return end.y; }
    int left(int l)     { return org.x=l; }
    int top(int t)      { return org.y=t; }
    int right(int r)    { return end.x=r; }
    int bottom(int b)   { return end.y=b; }
    void set(WPPoint o, WPPoint e)        { origin(o); endpt(e); }
    void set(int l, int t, int r, int b)  { origin(l,t); endpt(r,b); }
    int width()         { return right()-left(); }
    int height()        { return bottom()-top(); }
    int width(int w)    { right(left()+w); return width(); }
    int height(int h)   { bottom(top()+h); return height(); }
    void origin(int x, int y)     { org.set(x,y); }
    void endpt(int x, int y)      { end.set(x,y); }
    void extent(int w, int h)     { width(w); height(h); }
    WPPoint& origin()             { return org; }
    WPPoint& endpt()              { return end; }
    WPPoint& origin(WPPoint p)    { return org=p; }
    WPPoint& endpt(WPPoint p)     { return end=p; }
```

```
    WPPoint extent()            { return WPPoint(width(), height()); }
    void extent(WPPoint p)      { width(p.x); height(p.y); }
    WPPoint topRight()          { return WPPoint(right(), top()); }
    WPPoint bottomLeft()        { return WPPoint(left(), bottom()); }
    void setEmpty()             { set(0,0,0,0); }
    BOOL isEmpty()              { return IsRectEmpty((LPRECT)this); }
    BOOL contains(WPPoint p)    { return PtInRect((LPRECT)this,*((POINT*)&p)); }
    void inflate(int w, int h)  { InflateRect((LPRECT)this, w, h); }
    void capture(WPPoint &p)
        {   p.x=min(max(p.x,left()),right()-1);
            p.y=min(max(p.y,top()),bottom()-1); }
    WPPoint center()
        { return WPPoint((end.x-org.x)/2,(end.y-org.y)/2); }
    void adjustWinRect(DWORD style, BOOL menu, DWORD exstyle=0)
        { AdjustWindowRectEx((LPRECT)this, style, menu, exstyle); }
    WPRect& operator= (WPWin *win);
    WPRect& operator= (CSTR text);
    WPRect& operator= (WPPaintStruct& ps);
    WPRect& operator= (RECT rect) { return *this = *((WPRect*)&rect); }
    BOOL operator==(WPRect& rect2)
        { return EqualRect((LPRECT)this, (LPRECT)&rect2); }
    WPRect& operator+= (WPPoint p)   { org+=p; end+=p; return *this; }
    WPRect& operator-= (WPPoint p)   { org-=p; end-=p; return *this; }
    WPRect& operator*= (int m)
        { width(width()*m); height(height()*m); return *this; }
    WPRect& operator/= (int m)
        { width(width()/m); height(height()/m); return *this; }
    WPRect& operator+= (int n) { org-=n; end+=n; return *this; }
    WPRect& operator-= (int n) { org+=n; end-=n; return *this; }
    WPRect& operator++ ()        { --org; ++end; return *this; }
    WPRect& operator-- ()        { ++org; --end; return *this; }
    WPRect& operator*= (TEXTMETRIC &tm) { org*=tm; end*=tm; return *this; }
    int operator&= (WPRect& rect2);
    int operator|= (WPRect& rect2);
};
/////////////////
// A square is a special kind of rectangle.
//
DLLCLASS WPSquare : public WPRect {
public:
    WPSquare(WPPoint p, int radius) { set(p, radius); }
    void set(WPPoint p, int r)
        { origin(p.x-r, p.y-r); endpt(p.x+r, p.y+r); }
};
/////////////////
// This subclass is identical to WPRect in all respects except that the
// constructor and assignment for a WPWin gets the entire window
// rectangle rather than just the client area.
//
DLLCLASS WPWindowRect : public WPRect {
public:
    WPWindowRect(WPWin *win)      { *this = win; }
    WPWindowRect& operator= (WPWin *win);
};
#endif
```

WPRECT.CPP

```
/////////////////////////////////////////////////////////////
// WINDOWS++ CLASS LIBRARY.  Copyright 1992 Paul DiLascia.
// FILE: WPRECT.CPP
//
// Implementation of rectangle object.
#include "wprect.h"
#include "wpwin.h"
/////////////////
// Make sure that left <= right and top <= bottom.
//
```

```
        void WPRect::normalize()
        {
            if (left() > right()) {
                int r = right();
                right(left());
                left(r);
            }
            if (top() > bottom()) {
                int b = bottom();
                bottom(top());
                top(b);
            }
        }
        ///////////////////
        // Assign WPRect to a Window: get the window rectangle.
        // If win ptr is NULL, get whole screen dimensions.
        //
        WPRect& WPRect::operator=(WPWin *win)
        {
            if (win)
                win->getClientRect(*this);
            else
                set(0, 0, GetSystemMetrics(SM_CXSCREEN),
                    GetSystemMetrics(SM_CYSCREEN));
            return *this;
        }
        ///////////////////
        // Intersect rectangle with another rectangle.
        //
        BOOL WPRect::operator&= (WPRect& rect2)
        {
            WPRect dest;
            BOOL nonempty = IntersectRect((LPRECT)&dest, (LPRECT)this, (LPRECT)&rect2);
            *this = dest;
            return nonempty;
        }
        ///////////////////
        // Union rectangle with another rectangle.
        //
        BOOL WPRect::operator|= (WPRect& rect2)
        {
            WPRect dest;
            BOOL nonempty = UnionRect((LPRECT)&dest, (LPRECT)this, (LPRECT)&rect2);
            *this = dest;
            return nonempty;
        }
        ///////////////////
        // WPWinRect: get window rectangle instead of client area.
        //
        WPWindowRect& WPWindowRect::operator=(WPWin *win)
        {
            win->getWindowRect(*this);
            return *this;
        }
        ///////////////////
        // Get dimensions of text string, in character units.
        // Sets origin=(0,0)
        // width  = num chars in longest line
        // height = num lines
        //
        WPRect& WPRect::operator=(CSTR text)
        {
            setEmpty();
            if (text && *text) {
                int nlines = 0;
                int maxwid = 0;
                for (;;) {
                    nlines++;
```

```
            CSTR end = strchr(text, '\n');
            if (end==NULL)
               break;
            maxwid = max(maxwid, end-text);
            text = end+1;
         }
         maxwid = max(maxwid, strlen(text));
         width(maxwid);
         height(nlines);
      }
      return *this;
}
```

WPSBAR.H

```
//////////////////////////////////////////////////////////
// WINDOWS++ CLASS LIBRARY.  Copyright 1992 Paul DiLascia.
// FILE: WPSBAR.H
//
// Scroll Bar definitions.
#ifndef WPSBAR_H
#define WPSBAR_H
#ifndef WPCTRL_H
#include "wpctrl.h"
#endif
/////////////////////
// Scroll bar, used for dialog controls.
// Underlying data is integer.
//
DLLCLASS WPScrollBar : public WPControl {
protected:
   int sbtype;
   int pageIncr;
   int lineIncr;
   HWND getScrollHwnd()        { return getHwnd(); }
public:
   WPScrollBar(WPWin *pwin, int id, long sty=0)
      : WPControl("ScrollBar", pwin, id, sty)
      { sbtype = SB_CTL; lineIncr = pageIncr = 1; }
   static WPControl* New(WPWin* pwin, int id)
      { return new WPScrollBar(pwin, id); }
   void pageSize(int n)        { pageIncr = n; }
   int pageSize()              { return pageIncr; }
   void lineSize(int n)        { lineIncr = n; }
   int lineSize()              { return lineIncr; }
   // General control functions
   void linkObject(int* pint) { object=pint; }
   void updateScreen()        { if (object) scrollPos(*((int*)object),TRUE); }
   void updateObject()        { if (object) *((int*)object) = scrollPos(); }
   // Windows-related scrollbar functions
   int scrollPos()
      { return GetScrollPos(getScrollHwnd(), sbtype); }
   int scrollPos(int pos, BOOL redraw=TRUE)
      { return SetScrollPos(getScrollHwnd(), sbtype, pos, redraw); }
   void getScrollRange(int& min, int& max)
      { GetScrollRange(getScrollHwnd(), sbtype, (LPINT)&min, (LPINT)&max); }
   void setScrollRange(int min, int max, BOOL redraw=TRUE)
      { SetScrollRange(getScrollHwnd(), sbtype, min, max, redraw); }
   void showScrollBar(BOOL show)
      { ShowScrollBar(getScrollHwnd(), sbtype, show); }
   void handleMsg(int msg, int thumbPos);
};
/////////////////////
// Vertical scroll bar, used for windows with scroll bars.
//
DLLCLASS WPVScrollBar : public WPScrollBar {
   HWND getScrollHwnd()     { return GetHwnd(getParent()); }
public:
```

```
        WPVScrollBar(WPWin *pwin, int id) : WPScrollBar(pwin, id, SBS_VERT)
            { sbtype = SB_VERT; }
    };
    //////////////////
    // Horizontal scroll bar, used for windows with scroll bars.
    //
    DLLCLASS WPHScrollBar : public WPScrollBar {
        HWND getScrollHwnd()      { return GetHwnd(getParent()); }
    public:
        WPHScrollBar(WPWin *pwin, int id) : WPScrollBar(pwin, id, SBS_HORZ)
            { sbtype = SB_HORZ; }
    };
    #endif
```

WPSTATIC.H

```
///////////////////////////////////////////////////////////
// WINDOWS++ CLASS LIBRARY.  Copyright 1992 Paul DiLascia.
// FILE: WPSTATIC.H
//
// Static control definitions.
#ifndef WPSTATIC_H
#define WPSTATIC_H
#ifndef WPCTRL_H
#include "wpctrl.h"
#endif
#define SS_DEFAULT       (SS_LEFT | SS_NOPREFIX)
#define SS_DEFAULTICON   (SS_ICON)
//////////////////
// Static control. Underlying data is string. A static has no
// updateObject operation, since the text can't be altered!
//
DLLCLASS WPStatic : public WPControl {
public:
    WPStatic(WPWin *pwin, int id, long sty=SS_DEFAULT)
        : WPControl("Static", pwin, id, sty) { }
    static WPControl* New(WPWin* pwin, int id)
        { return new WPStatic(pwin, id); }
    // General control functions
    void linkObject(char* buf) { object=buf; objsiz=strlen(buf); }
    void updateScreen()        { if (object) setText((char*)object); }
    void updateObject()        { /* static is read-only */ }
};
#ifdef __ZTC__ && __LARGE__
#define HANDLE2VOID(h)  ((void*)(long)h)
#else
#define HANDLE2VOID(h)  ((void*)h)
#endif
//////////////////
// Static icon. Like normal static control, but underlying data is HICON.
//
DLLCLASS WPStaticIcon : public WPStatic {
public:
    WPStaticIcon(WPWin *pwin, int id, long sty=SS_DEFAULTICON)
        : WPStatic(pwin, id, sty) { }
    static WPControl* New(WPWin* pwin, int id)
        { return new WPStaticIcon(pwin, id); }
    // General control functions
    void linkObject(HICON hicon)  { object = HANDLE2VOID(hicon); }
    void updateScreen();
};
#endif
```

WPWIN.H

```
///////////////////////////////////////////////////////////
// WINDOWS++ CLASS LIBRARY.  Copyright 1992 Paul DiLascia.
// FILE: WPWIN.H
```

```
//
// Defnitions for WPWin, THE base window class
// from which all window classes are derived.
#ifndef WPWIN_H
#define WPWIN_H
#ifndef WPRECT_H
#include "wprect.h"
#endif
#ifdef __BORLANDC__
#define CASTWNDPROC
#else
#define CASTWNDPROC (void*)
#endif
/////////////////
// Event object, used to pass msg, wParam, and lParam
//
struct WPEvent {
    WORD msg;    // the message
    WORD wp;     // word parameter
    LONG lp;     // long parameter
    LONG ret;    // return code
    WPEvent(WORD m, WORD w=0, LONG l=0) { msg=m; wp=w; lp=l; ret=0; }
    ~WPEvent() { }
    WORD cmd()          { return wp; }
    HMENU menu()        { return (HMENU)wp; }
    int childHwnd()     { return LOWORD(lp); }
    int childMsg()      { return HIWORD(lp); }
    int x()             { return LOWORD(lp); }
    int y()             { return HIWORD(lp); }
    int width()         { return LOWORD(lp); }
    int height()        { return HIWORD(lp); }
    LPSTR text()        { return (LPSTR)lp; }
    WPPoint point()     { return *((WPPoint *)&lp); }
    HWND focusHwnd()    { return (HWND)wp; }
    int key()           { return wp; }
    int keyRepeat()     { return LOWORD(lp); }
    int keyScan()       { return LOBYTE(HIWORD(lp)); }
    int keyFlags()      { return HIBYTE(HIWORD(lp)); }
    WPPoint screenPos() { return (WPPoint)GetMessagePos(); }
    DWORD time()        { return GetMessageTime(); }
};
/////////////////
// This structure is used to specify the Windows registration
// and creation arguments before creating an actual window.
//
struct WINCREATEARGS {
    WNDCLASS wndcls;      // Windows class registration struct
    CSTR title;           // window's title
    DWORD style;          // style (WS_OVERLAPPED, etc.)
    DWORD exstyle;        // extended style (Windows 3.0)
    WPRect pos;           // window position (x,y,w,h)
    HMENU hmenu;          // menu handle
    WPWin* parent;        // parent window
    LPSTR lparam;         // create parm
    int id()              { return (int)hmenu; }
};
/////////////////
// Used for getMinMaxInfo.
//
struct MINMAXINFO {
    WPPoint reserved;
    WPPoint maxSize;
    WPPoint maxPos;
    WPPoint minTrackSize;
    WPPoint maxTrackSize;
};
typedef MINMAXINFO FAR *LPMINMAXINFO;
```

```
//////////////////
// This is THE base window class, from which all window classes
// are derived.  It provides methods corresponding to most Windows
// functions that take a window handle (HWND).
//
DLLCLASS WPWin {
private:
    static WPWin* NewWin;     // window being created
    FARPROC oldProc;          // original window proc
    HWND hwnd;                // window handle
    BOOL deletable;           // window can be deleted
    void linkHwnd(HWND newhwnd);
    void unLinkHwnd();
    // Message procedure stuff
    LONG dfltMsgProc(WPEvent& e)
        { return CallWindowProc(oldProc, hwnd, e.msg, e.wp, e.lp); }
    virtual LONG msgProc(WPEvent& event);
    BOOL dispatchEvent(WPEvent& event);
    friend BOOL _export FAR PASCAL WPDlgProc(HWND, WORD, WORD, LONG);
    friend long _export FAR PASCAL WPWndProc(HWND, WORD, WORD, LONG);
    friend WPDialog;
    friend WPControl;
    friend WPMDIChild;
    friend WPMDIFrame;
public:
    WPWin(CSTR classnm, WPWin* pwin=NULL, int id=0);
    virtual ~WPWin();
    // Class-wide globals
    static WINCREATEARGS createArgs; // window creation args
    static TEXTMETRIC tm;            // text metrics for last created window
    // Overloaded new & delete
    void *operator new(size_t size);
    void operator delete(void *ptr);
    // Get handles/win ptr
    HWND getHwnd()                         { return hwnd; }
    HWND operator()()                      { return hwnd; }
    static HWND GetHwnd(WPWin* win)   { return win ? win->hwnd : NULL; }
    static WPWin* GetWin(HWND hwnd);
    // Create/destroy
    BOOL createWin(CSTR title)
        { createArgs.title = title; return createWin(); }
    virtual BOOL createWin();
    virtual void destroyWin()              { DestroyWindow(hwnd); }
    // Static (global) functions
    static WPWin* GetActiveWin()  { return GetWin(GetActiveWindow()); }
    static WPWin* GetFocusWin()   { return GetWin(GetFocus()); }
    static WPWin* FindWin(CSTR clsnm, CSTR winnm)
        { return GetWin(FindWindow((LPSTR)clsnm, (LPSTR)winnm)); }
    static WPWin* WinFromPoint(WPPoint p)
        { return GetWin(WindowFromPoint(TOPOINT(p))); }
    // Various flavors of SendMessage
    DWORD sendMsg(WPEvent& e)
        { return SendMessage(hwnd, e.msg, e.wp, e.lp); }
    DWORD sendMsg(WORD msg, WORD wp=0, LONG lp=0)
        { return SendMessage(hwnd, msg, wp, lp); }
    DWORD sendMsg(WORD msg, WORD wp, void FAR* lp)
        { return SendMessage(hwnd, msg, wp, (LONG)lp); }
    DWORD sendMsg(WORD msg, WORD wp, LPCSTR str)
        { return SendMessage(hwnd, msg, wp, (LONG)str); }
    // Properties
    HANDLE getProp(CSTR kwd)               { return GetProp(hwnd, (LPSTR)kwd); }
    void setProp(CSTR kwd, HANDLE val)  { SetProp(hwnd, (LPSTR)kwd, val); }
    void removeProp(CSTR kwd)            { RemoveProp(hwnd, (LPSTR)kwd); }
    // Parent/child stuff
    int getID()                     { return GetWindowWord(hwnd, GWW_ID); }
    WPWin* getParent()              { return GetWin(GetParent(hwnd)); }
    void setParent(WPWin* pwin){ SetParent(hwnd, pwin->hwnd); }
    BOOL childExists(int id)     { return GetDlgItem(hwnd, id)!=NULL; }
```

```
WPWin* getTopChild()        { return GetWin(GetTopWindow(hwnd)); }
WPWin* getChild(int id)     { return GetWin(GetDlgItem(hwnd, id)); }
WPWin* childFromPoint(WPPoint p)
    { return GetWin(ChildWindowFromPoint(hwnd, TOPOINT(p))); }
void notifyParent(int msg)
    { if (getParent())
        getParent()->sendMsg(WM_COMMAND, getID(), MAKELONG(hwnd, msg)); }
// Rectangles
void getClientRect(WPRect& rect)
    { GetClientRect(hwnd, (LPRECT)&rect); }
void getWindowRect(WPRect& rect)
    { GetWindowRect(hwnd, (LPRECT)&rect); }
BOOL getUpdateRect(WPRect& rect, BOOL erase=FALSE)
    { return GetUpdateRect(hwnd, (LPRECT)&rect, erase); }
// Validate/invalidate
void validate()
    { ValidateRect(hwnd, NULL); }
void validate(WPRect& rect)
    { rect.normalize(); ValidateRect(hwnd, (LPRECT)&rect); }
void invalidate(BOOL erase=FALSE)
    { InvalidateRect(hwnd, NULL, erase); }
void invalidate(WPRect& rect, BOOL erase=FALSE)
    { rect.normalize(); InvalidateRect(hwnd, (LPRECT)&rect, erase); }
// Position/size
void setPos(int x, int y)
    { SetWindowPos(hwnd, NULL, x, y, 0, 0, SWP_NOSIZE|SWP_NOZORDER); }
void setSize(int w, int h)
    { SetWindowPos(hwnd, NULL, 0, 0, w, h, SWP_NOMOVE|SWP_NOZORDER); }
void moveWin(WPRect& box, BOOL repaint=TRUE)
    { MoveWindow(hwnd,
        box.left(), box.top(), box.width(), box.height(), repaint); }
// Z-order
void setAfter(WPWin* after)
    { SetWindowPos(hwnd, GetHwnd(after),0,0,0,0,SWP_NOSIZE|SWP_NOMOVE); }
void bringToTop()     { BringWindowToTop(hwnd); }
void bringToBottom()
    { SetWindowPos(hwnd,1,0,0,0,0,SWP_NOSIZE|SWP_NOMOVE); }
// Timer
int setTimer(int id, int msec, FARPROC func=NULL)
    { return SetTimer(hwnd, id, msec, func); }
BOOL killTimer(int id)
    { return KillTimer(hwnd, id); }
int msgBox(LPCSTR text, LPCSTR caption="", WORD style=MB_OK)
    { return MessageBox(hwnd, (LPSTR)text, (LPSTR)caption, style); }
int warning(LPCSTR text, WORD style=MB_OK)
    { return msgBox(text, "Warning!", style|MB_ICONQUESTION); }
int errBox(LPCSTR text, LPCSTR caption=NULL,
    WORD style=MB_OK|MB_ICONEXCLAMATION)
    { return MessageBox(hwnd, (LPSTR)text, (LPSTR)caption, style); }
// Coordinates
void clientToScreen(WPPoint &point)
    { ClientToScreen(hwnd, (LPPOINT)&point); }
void clientToScreen(WPRect &box)
    { clientToScreen(box.origin()); clientToScreen(box.endpt()); }
void screenToClient(WPPoint &point)
    { ScreenToClient(hwnd, (LPPOINT)&point); }
void screenToClient(WPRect &box)
    { screenToClient(box.origin()); screenToClient(box.endpt()); }
void scrollWin(int x,int y)
    { ScrollWindow(hwnd, x, y, NULL, NULL); }
void scrollWin(int x,int y, WPRect* scrollRect=NULL, WPRect* clipRect=NULL)
    { ScrollWindow(hwnd, x, y, (LPRECT)scrollRect, (LPRECT)clipRect); }
// Miscellaneous
void setFocus()                 { SetFocus(hwnd); }
void setReDraw(BOOL val)        { sendMsg(WM_SETREDRAW,val); }
void update()                   { UpdateWindow(hwnd); }
BOOL show(int how=SW_SHOW)      { return ShowWindow(hwnd, how); }
```

```
    BOOL hide()                            { return ShowWindow(hwnd, SW_HIDE); }
    void showOwnedPopups(BOOL show)   { ShowOwnedPopups(hwnd, show); }
    void setText(LPCSTR text)   { SetWindowText(hwnd, (LPSTR)text); }
    int getText()                        { return GetWindowTextLength(hwnd); }
    int getText(LPSTR buf, int buflen)
        { return GetWindowText(hwnd, buf, buflen); }
    void close()             { sendMsg(WM_CLOSE); }
    void minimize()          { CloseWindow(hwnd); }
    void maximize()          { ShowWindow(hwnd, SW_SHOWMAXIMIZED); }
    BOOL isMinimized()       { return IsIconic(hwnd); }
    BOOL isMaximized()       { return IsZoomed(hwnd); }
    BOOL openIcon()          { return OpenIcon(hwnd); }
    BOOL isIconic()          { return IsIconic(hwnd); }
    BOOL enableWin(BOOL b)   { return EnableWindow(hwnd, b); }
    BOOL isEnabled()         { return IsWindowEnabled(hwnd); }
    BOOL isVisible()         { return IsWindowVisible(hwnd); }
    BOOL isZoomed()          { return IsZoomed(hwnd); }
    BOOL flash(BOOL invert=TRUE)
        { return FlashWindow(hwnd, invert); }
    int getClassName(LPSTR buf, int buflen)
        { return GetClassName(hwnd, buf, buflen); }
    LONG style()             { return GetWindowLong(hwnd, GWL_STYLE); }
    LONG style(LONG style)   { return SetWindowLong(hwnd, GWL_STYLE, style);}
    void setMenu(HMENU hmenu)   { SetMenu(hwnd, hmenu); }
    void drawMenu()             { DrawMenuBar(hwnd); }
    // Add owner-draw item
    virtual void addODItem(WPOwnerDrawItem* od)   { assert(FALSE); }
    // Virtual message functions corresponding to WM_ messages.
    virtual BOOL activated(WORD state, BOOL iconic) { return FALSE; }
    virtual BOOL closed()                          { return FALSE; }
    virtual BOOL command(int id, WORD msg)         { return FALSE; }
    virtual BOOL enabled(BOOL state)               { return FALSE; }
    virtual BOOL getMinMaxInfo(LPMINMAXINFO mmi)   { return FALSE; }
    virtual BOOL gotFocus(WPWin *prev)             { return FALSE; }
    virtual BOOL kbd(WPEvent& event)               { return FALSE; }
    virtual BOOL killedFocus(WPWin *next)          { return FALSE; }
    virtual BOOL menuInit(WPMenu &menu)            { return FALSE; }
    virtual BOOL menuSelected(int id, WORD flags)  { return FALSE; }
    virtual BOOL mouse(int msg, WPPoint p, WORD flags)
        { return FALSE; }
    virtual BOOL moved(int x, int y)               { return FALSE; }
    virtual BOOL paint()                           { return FALSE; }
    virtual BOOL queryEnd()                        { return TRUE; }
    virtual BOOL queryMaximize()                   { return TRUE; }
    virtual BOOL scrolled(int msg, int id, int thumbPos) { return FALSE; }
    virtual BOOL sized(WPRect &box, WORD how)      { return FALSE; }
    virtual BOOL timer(int id)                     { return FALSE; }
    virtual BOOL other(WPEvent &event)             { return FALSE; }
};
/////////////////
// Class used to navigate the child windows of a window.
//
DLLCLASS WPChildWinList {
private:
    WPWin *pwin;    // parent window;
    WPWin *cwin;    // current child
    WPWin *nextWPWin(HWND hwnd);
public:
    WPChildWinList(WPWin *p)    { pwin=p; cwin=NULL; }
    WPWin * first();
    WPWin * next()
        { return cwin = nextWPWin(WPWin::GetHwnd(cwin)); }
};
/////////////////
// Clever little macro lets you write:
//
//     forEachChildWin(parent, child)
//         child->doSomething();
```

```
//
#define forEachChildWin(pwin, cwin) \
    WPChildWinList _children = pwin; \
    for (WPWin *cwin=_children.first(); cwin; cwin=_children.next())

////////////////
// This class handles deferred window positioning.
//
DLLCLASS WPDeferWinPos {
    HANDLE posInfo;
public:
    WPDeferWinPos(int nWins)    { posInfo = BeginDeferWindowPos(nWins); }
    ~WPDeferWinPos()            { EndDeferWindowPos(posInfo); }
    void move(WPWin* win, WPRect& pos,
        WORD flags=SWP_NOREDRAW|SWP_NOZORDER, WPWin* after=NULL)
        { posInfo = DeferWindowPos(posInfo, (*win)(),
                WPWin::GetHwnd(after),
                pos.left(), pos.top(), pos.width(), pos.height(), flags); }
};
#endif
```

WPWIN.CPP

```
//////////////////////////////////////////////////////////
// WINDOWS++ CLASS LIBRARY.  Copyright 1992 Paul DiLascia.
// FILE: WPWIN.CPP
//
// Implementation of base window class for all window objects.
#include "wpapp.h"
#include "wpwin.h"
#include "wpid.h"
#include "wpmenu.h"
#include "wpgdi.h"
// this property links a window to its object
char WP_WINPTR[] =  "w+";
WINCREATEARGS WPWin::createArgs;
TEXTMETRIC WPWin::tm;
WPWin *WPWin::NewWin = NULL;
////////////////
// Always allocate from local heap so we can store
// 16-bit offset in window property list.
// Also, store ptr in NewWin so constructor can mark as deletable.
//
void* WPWin::operator new(size_t size)
{
    return NewWin = (WPWin*)App.localAlloc(size);
}
void WPWin::operator delete(void* ptr)
{
    assert(((WPWin*)ptr)->deletable);
    App.localFree(ptr);
}
////////////////
// Initialize WPWin instance.
//
WPWin::WPWin(CSTR classnm, WPWin* pwin, int id)
{
    oldProc = NULL;
    hwnd = NULL;
    deletable = this==NewWin;
    NewWin=NULL;
    // set default registration args
    createArgs.wndcls.lpszClassName = (LPSTR)classnm;
    createArgs.wndcls.style = CS_HREDRAW | CS_VREDRAW;
    createArgs.wndcls.lpfnWndProc = CASTWNDPROC DefWindowProc;
    createArgs.wndcls.cbClsExtra = 0;
    createArgs.wndcls.cbWndExtra = 0;
    createArgs.wndcls.hInstance = App.getHinst();
```

```
    createArgs.wndcls.hIcon = NULL;
    createArgs.wndcls.hCursor = LoadCursor(NULL, IDC_ARROW);
    createArgs.wndcls.hbrBackground = GetStockObject(WHITE_BRUSH);
    createArgs.wndcls.lpszMenuName = NULL;
    // set default creation args
    createArgs.title = NULL;
    createArgs.style = createArgs.exstyle = 0;
    createArgs.pos.origin(CW_USEDEFAULT, CW_USEDEFAULT);
    createArgs.pos.extent(CW_USEDEFAULT, CW_USEDEFAULT);
    createArgs.hmenu = (HMENU)id;
    createArgs.parent = pwin;
    createArgs.lparam = NULL;
    if (pwin)
        // child window: set style and chain to list
        createArgs.style = WS_CHILDWINDOW | WS_VISIBLE;
}
/////////////////
// Link object to a real (Windows) window.
//
void WPWin::linkHwnd(HWND newhwnd)
{
    assert(hwnd==NULL);                      // better not be already linked!
    assert(IsWindow(newhwnd));               // better have a real HWND!
    hwnd = newhwnd;                          // store Window handle
    setProp(WP_WINPTR, (HANDLE)this);        // store ourself in window prop
    //////
    // Now "hook" the window's window proc--i.e., subclass it, saving
    // the original window procedure.
    //
    oldProc = (FARPROC)GetWindowLong(hwnd, GWL_WNDPROC);
    SetWindowLong(hwnd, GWL_WNDPROC, (LONG)App.getWndProc());
    if (hwnd) {
        WPWinDC dc = this;
        dc.textMetrics(tm);
    }
}
/////////////////
// Get window object from window handle (HWND)
//
WPWin* WPWin::GetWin(HWND hwnd)
{
    if (hwnd==NULL)
        return NULL;
    assert(IsWindow(hwnd));
    HANDLE winptr = GetProp(hwnd, WP_WINPTR);
    if (winptr==NULL)
        return NULL;
#ifdef __MEDIUM__
    return (WPWin*)winptr;  // in medium model, just cast to ptr
#else
    WORD appds;
    GETAPPDS(appds);                    // get application's data segment
    return (WPWin*)MK_FP(appds, winptr);
#endif
}
/////////////////
// Destroy window: unlink it.
//
WPWin::~WPWin()
{
    unLinkHwnd();
}
/////////////////
// Unlink a window.
//
void WPWin::unLinkHwnd()
{
    if (hwnd) {                              // if linked:
```

```
            if (oldProc) {
                // restore old window proc
                SetWindowLong(hwnd, GWL_WNDPROC, (LONG)oldProc);
                oldProc = NULL;                  // just to be safe!
            }
            assert(GetWin(hwnd)==this);      // double-check for safety
            removeProp(WP_WINPTR);           // free up window property
            hwnd = NULL;                     // goodbye window handle!
        }
}
//////////////////
// Create window using current values in createArgs.
//
BOOL WPWin::createWin()
{
    // Note: window (HWND) might already exist if attached to a dialog control
    //
    if (hwnd==NULL) {
        LPSTR classnm = createArgs.wndcls.lpszClassName;
        assert(classnm);
        HANDLE hinst = createArgs.wndcls.hInstance;
        assert(hinst);
        WNDCLASS temp;
        // Register window class if it ain't already registered!
        if (!GetClassInfo(hinst, classnm, &temp) &&   // try module..
            !GetClassInfo(NULL, classnm, &temp)) {     // ..and built-in
            BOOL ret = RegisterClass(&createArgs.wndcls);
            assert(ret);
        }
        HWND newhwnd = CreateWindowEx(createArgs.exstyle,
            classnm,
            (LPSTR)createArgs.title,
            createArgs.style,
            createArgs.pos.left(),
            createArgs.pos.top(),
            createArgs.pos.width(),
            createArgs.pos.height(),
            GetHwnd(createArgs.parent),
            createArgs.hmenu,
            hinst,
            createArgs.lparam);
        linkHwnd(newhwnd);
    }
    return hwnd!=NULL;
}
//////////////////
// Virtual message procedure handles messages sent from Windows.
//
LONG WPWin::msgProc(WPEvent &event)
{
    switch (event.msg) {
    case WM_QUERYENDSESSION:
        return queryEnd();
    case WM_QUERYOPEN:
        return queryMaximize();
    }
    return dispatchEvent(event) ? event.ret : dfltMsgProc(event);
}
//////////////////
// Dispatch message to appropriate virtual function
//
BOOL WPWin::dispatchEvent(WPEvent &event)
{
    switch (event.msg) {
    case WM_PAINT:
        return paint();
    case WM_GETMINMAXINFO:
        return getMinMaxInfo((LPMINMAXINFO)event.lp);
```

```
      case WM_ACTIVATE:
         return activated(event.wp, HIWORD(event.lp));
      case WM_ENABLE:
         return enabled(event.wp);
      case WM_SETFOCUS:
         return gotFocus(GetWin(event.focusHwnd()));
      case WM_KILLFOCUS:
         return killedFocus(GetWin(event.focusHwnd()));
      case WM_HSCROLL:
      case WM_VSCROLL:
         HWND sbhwnd = HIWORD(event.lp);
         int id = sbhwnd ? GetDlgCtrlID(sbhwnd) :
             event.msg==WM_VSCROLL ? WPIDSB_VERT : WPIDSB_HORZ;
         return scrolled(event.wp, id, LOWORD(event.lp));
      case WM_KEYDOWN:  case WM_KEYUP:  case WM_CHAR:   case WM_DEADCHAR:
         return kbd(event);
      case WM_LBUTTONDOWN: case WM_LBUTTONUP: case WM_LBUTTONDBLCLK:
      case WM_RBUTTONDOWN: case WM_RBUTTONUP: case WM_RBUTTONDBLCLK:
      case WM_MBUTTONDOWN: case WM_MBUTTONUP: case WM_MBUTTONDBLCLK:
      case WM_MOUSEMOVE:
         return mouse(event.msg, event.point(), event.wp);
      case WM_MOVE:
         return moved(event.x(), event.y());
      case WM_SIZE:
         WPRect box = this;
         box.extent(event.width(), event.height());
         return sized(box, event.wp);
      case WM_COMMAND:
         return command(event.cmd(), event.childMsg());
      case WM_SYSCOMMAND:
         return command(event.cmd(), 0);
      case WM_INITMENU:
         WPMenu menu = (HMENU)event.wp;
         return menuInit(menu);
      case WM_MENUSELECT:
         return menuSelected(event.wp, LOWORD(event.lp));
      case WM_CLOSE:
         return closed();
      case WM_TIMER:
         return timer(event.wp);
      }
      return other(event);
}
/////////////////
// Move iterator to first child window.
//
WPWin * WPChildWinList::first()
{
   HWND hwnd = GetWindow((*pwin)(), GW_CHILD);
   cwin = WPWin::GetWin(hwnd);
   return cwin ? cwin : nextWPWin(hwnd);
}
/////////////////
// Get next Windows++ sibling window.
// (Skip windows w/no WPWin object.)
//
WPWin * WPChildWinList::nextWPWin(HWND hwnd)
{
   while (hwnd) {
      hwnd = GetWindow(hwnd, GW_HWNDNEXT);
      if ((cwin = WPWin::GetWin(hwnd))!=NULL)
         return cwin;
   }
   return NULL;
}
```

A.2 Sample Programs

Below is the source code for the sample programs described in the main text. Since all the module definition files (.DEF) are the same, only HELLO.DEF is shown. Just change HELLO to your favorite name.

MAKEFILE.BCC

```
#
# Windows++ Makefile for Borland.
# (C) Paul DiLascia 1992.  All rights reserved.
#
# Contains all build instructions for Windows++ sample programs
#
# To build sample programs, issue one of the following DOS commands.
#
#   make                make using DLL
#   make MODEL=l        make using large model
#   make MODEL=m        make using medium model
WPPDIR = ..
!ifndef MODEL
MODEL=l
DEFINES=-DUSEDLL
!endif
LIBS= $(WPPDIR)\wpp.lib $(WPPDIR)\commdlg.lib
CL = bcc
FLAGS= -WE -WS -w-par -I$(WPPDIR) -m$(MODEL) $(DEFINES) $(ENVFLAGS)
LFLAGS= -lC -M $(FLAGS)
RC = rc
RCFLAGS = -I $(WPPDIR)
.cpp.exe:
    $(CL) $(LFLAGS) $*.cpp $(LIBS)
    $(RC) -t $(RCFLAGS) $*
all: DRAW.EXE HELLO.EXE LAUNCH.EXE MANDEL.EXE MEDIT.EXE MEMTEST.EXE \
    MKC.EXE PEOPLE.EXE RANDRECT.EXE TOE.EXE WINEDIT.EXE
clean:
    del *.obj
    del *.exe
    del *.map
```

MAKEFILE.ZTC

```
# Windows++ Makefile for Zortech.
# (C) Paul DiLascia 1992.  All rights reserved.
#
# Contains all build instructions for Windows++ sample programs
# Requires Zoretch Version 3.0r4 or greater.
#
# To build sample programs, issue one of the following DOS commands.
#
#   make MODEL=l        to make using large model
#   make MODEL=m        to make using medium model
#
WPPDIR = ..
CL = ztc
LFLAGS= -W2 -W3 -DDEBUG -m$(MODEL) -I.. $(ENVFLAGS)
LIBS= $(WPPDIR)\wpp.lib $(WPPDIR)\commdlg.lib
# Microsoft RC compiler is required; this comes with Zortech.
# RC has problems with some files unless -K is specified.
#
RC = rc
RCFLAGS = -K -I $(WPPDIR)
```

```
.cpp.exe:
    $(CL) $(LFLAGS) $*.cpp $(LIBS)
    $(RC) -t $(RCFLAGS) $*
all: DRAW.EXE HELLO.EXE LAUNCH.EXE MANDEL.EXE MEDIT.EXE MEMTEST.EXE \
    MKC.EXE PEOPLE.EXE RANDRECT.EXE TOE.EXE WINEDIT.EXE
clean:
    del *.obj
    del *.exe
    del *.map
```

DRAW.H

```
/////////////////////////////////////////////////////////
// WINDOWS++ CLASS LIBRARY.  Copyright 1992 Paul DiLascia.
// FILE: DRAW.H
//
// Command IDs for DRAW
//
#define ID_EDITDUP        11
#define ID_NEWLINE        12
#define ID_NEWRECT        13
#define ID_NEWELLIPSE     14
#define ID_FRONT          15
#define ID_BACK           16
#define ID_TOGGLEBUF      17
// Base IDs for edge and fill commands
#define ID_EDGE           20
#define ID_FILL           30
// Below are added to ID_EDGE or ID_FILL
#define ID_COLORBLACK     0
#define ID_COLORWHITE     1
#define ID_COLORRED       2
#define ID_COLORGREEN     3
#define ID_COLORBLUE      4
#define ID_COLORNONE      5
#define ID_COLORRANDOM    6
#define ID_COLORLAST      7
#define NEDITCOMMANDS     9       // Number of items in Edit menu
#define POS_NEW           0       // relative pos in Edit menu of New command
```

DRAW.CPP

```
/////////////////////////////////////////////////////////
// WINDOWS++ CLASS LIBRARY.  Copyright 1992 Paul DiLascia.
// FILE: DRAW.CPP
//
// Sample Object-Oriented Graphics Editor using GPP Graphics.
#include <wpp.h>
#include <gpp.h>
#include "draw.h"
const HIT_RADIUS = 7;       // radius for hit test
const HANDLE_RADIUS = 3;    // radius for size handles
enum DRAGSTATE    { NODRAG=0, DRAGMOVE, DRAGSIZE };
enum MOVESTATE    { MOVEALL=0, MOVEFIRST, MOVEX, MOVEY, MOVEDIAG };
/////////////////////
// Main DRAW window class.
//
APPCLASS DrawWin : public WPMainWin {
    static WPRect DfltSize; // default size for new shapes
    GPShapeList shapes;     // list of shapes
    GPHilite* hilite;       // current hilite (selected) shape
    GPShape* newShape;      // pending new shape
    // Dragging stuff
    DRAGSTATE dragging;     // drag mode (move/size)
    WPPoint orgPt;          // pt where started dragging
    WPPoint prevPt;         // previous point in drag
    WPPoint anchorPt;       // size anchor point
    WPRect  orgBounds;      // original bounds of shape
```

```
        // Mouse constraint stuff
        WPPoint orgMousePt;
        MOVESTATE motion;
        long ax, ay;
        // Internal methods
        GPShape* setNewShape(GPShape *shp);
        GPHilite* setHilite(GPShape *shp);
        void XORShape(WPDevContext& dc, GPShape *shp);
        void constrainMouse(WORD msg, WPPoint& p, WORD flags);
public:
        DrawWin();
        ~DrawWin() { delete newShape; }
        // Virtual message functions
        void paint(WPPaintStruct &ps)        { shapes.paint(ps); }
        BOOL anySelected()                   { return hilite!=NULL; }
        BOOL menuInit(WPMenu &menu);
        BOOL mouse(int msg, WPPoint p, WORD flags);
        BOOL command(int id, WORD msg);
        BOOL fileNew();
        BOOL filePrint(WPDlgPrint &pdlg);
};
// Default size for new shapes: sqaure
WPRect DrawWin::DfltSize(0,0,10,-10);
/////////////////
// Program entry point
//
void WPApp::main()
{
        mainWin = new DrawWin;
        run();
}
DrawWin::DrawWin() : WPMainWin("DRAWWIN")
{
        createArgs.wndcls.hCursor = NULL;       // I'll set cursor myself
        createArgs.wndcls.style |= CS_OWNDC;    // create my own DC
        createWin("Windows++ DRAW");            // create main window
        WPWinDC dc = this;
        dc.mapMode(MM_LOMETRIC);                // (1 logical unit = .1 mm)
        fileNew();
}
/////////////////
// Draw shape in XOR mode.
//
void DrawWin::XORShape(WPDevContext& dc, GPShape *shp)
{
        dc.setPen(WHITE_PEN);
        dc.setBrush(NULL_BRUSH);
        dc.rop2(R2_XORPEN);
        shp->drawShape(dc);
        dc.rop2(R2_COPYPEN);
}
/////////////////
// Set the new shape: destroy old one, change cursor.
//
GPShape* DrawWin::setNewShape(GPShape *shp)
{
        delete newShape;
        if (shp)
           Cursor = "CrsNew";
        return newShape = shp;
}
/////////////////
// Select new shape. De-select previous one, if any.
//
GPHilite* DrawWin::setHilite(GPShape *shp)
{
        if (shp != hilite) {
           if (hilite) {
```

```
                if (hilite->shape()==shp)
                    return hilite;
                // Un-hilite previous shape
                hilite->invalidate(this,TRUE);
                delete shapes.remove(hilite);
                hilite = NULL;
                update();
            }
            if (shp) {
                // Hilite new shape
                hilite = new GPHilite(shp, HANDLE_RADIUS);
                hilite->invalidate(this);
                shapes.add(hilite);
                update();
            }
        }
    }
    return hilite;
}
//////////////////
// Handle mouse action.
//
BOOL DrawWin::mouse(int msg, WPPoint p, WORD flags)
{
    constrainMouse(msg, p, flags);
    GPShape *shp;
    WPWinDC dc = this;          // get window DC..
    dc.DP2LP(p);                // convert mouse to logical coords
    switch(msg) {
    case WM_LBUTTONDOWN:
        if (newShape) {
            // New shape pending: drop it at mouse location
            WPRect extent;
            shp = newShape;                 // New shape:
            shp->getExtent(extent);         // get its extent
            extent += p-extent.endpt();     // move to mouse location
            shp->setExtent(extent);         // ..and set
            shapes.add(shp);                // add to shape list..
            shp->draw(dc);                  // ..and draw.
        } else
            shp = shapes.hitTest(p, HIT_RADIUS);
        if (setHilite(shp)) {
            if (newShape) {
                shp = hilite;               // so we'll do drag size mode
                newShape=NULL;              // clear
            }
            // If there's a hilited shape, set up drag state
            Cursor = "CrsDrag";
            Cursor.clip(this);
            prevPt = orgPt = p;
            shp->getBounds(orgBounds);
            anchorPt = hilite->anchor(p);
            // Now go into appropriate mode and XOR shape.
            if (shp==hilite) {
                dragging = DRAGSIZE;
                shp=hilite->shape();
            } else
                dragging = DRAGMOVE;
            XORShape(dc, shp);
        }
        break;
    case WM_MOUSEMOVE:
        Cursor = newShape ? "CrsNew" : (dragging ? "CrsDrag" : IDC_ARROW);
        if (dragging && p != prevPt) {
            shp = hilite->shape();          // selected shape
            XORShape(dc,shp);               // XOR (erase) at old location
            WPRect extent;
            shp->getExtent(extent);
            if (dragging==DRAGMOVE)         // drag move:
```

```
                    extent += p-prevPt;          //    move extent
                else                             // drag size:
                    extent.set(anchorPt, p);     //    size extent
                shp->setExtent(extent);          // move the shape
                XORShape(dc, shp);               // XOR (draw) at new location
                prevPt = p;
            }
            break;
        case WM_LBUTTONUP:
            if (dragging) {
                shp = hilite->shape();           // selected shape
                XORShape(dc, shp);               // erase prev location
                if (p != orgPt) {
                    dc.LP2DP(orgBounds);
                    invalidate(orgBounds, TRUE);
                    setHilite(NULL);             // un-hilite (old location)
                    shp->invalidate(this);       // repaint
                    setHilite(shp);              // re-hilite (new location)
                }
                Cursor = IDC_ARROW;
                Cursor.unClip();
                dragging=NODRAG;
            }
            break;
    }
    return TRUE;
}
///////////////////
// This function implements the mouse chords.
//
void DrawWin::constrainMouse(WORD msg, WPPoint& p, WORD flags)
{
    switch (msg) {
    case WM_LBUTTONDOWN:
        orgMousePt=p;                         // save original mouse pos
        motion = MOVEFIRST;                   // this is first motion
        break;
    case WM_MOUSEMOVE:
        if (!dragging || motion==MOVEALL)
            break;
        WPPoint delta = p - orgMousePt;
        if (motion==MOVEFIRST) {
            // This is first mouse motion: determine constraint, if any.
            if (flags & MK_SHIFT)
                motion = (abs(delta.x) > abs(delta.y)) ? MOVEX : MOVEY;
            else if (flags & MK_CONTROL && dragging==DRAGSIZE) {
                WPRect aspect(anchorPt, hilite->anchor(anchorPt));
                if (aspect.width()==0)
                    motion = MOVEY;
                else if (aspect.height()==0)
                    motion = MOVEX;
                else {
                    motion = MOVEDIAG;
                    WPWinDC dc = this;
                    dc.LP2DP(aspect);
                    ax = aspect.width();
                    ay = aspect.height();
                }
            } else
                motion = MOVEALL;
        }
        WPPoint newPt = p;
        if (motion==MOVEX)
            newPt.y = orgMousePt.y;        // do horizontal constraint
        else if (motion==MOVEY)
            newPt.x = orgMousePt.x;        // do vertical constraint
        else if (motion==MOVEDIAG) {
            // do diagonal (aspect ratio) constraint
```

```
                if (abs(delta.x) > abs(delta.y))
                    delta.y = (ay * (long)delta.x) / ax;
                else
                    delta.x = (ax * (long)delta.y) / ay;
                newPt = orgMousePt + delta;
            }
        if (newPt != p) {                  // if point was constrained:
            p = newPt;
            clientToScreen(newPt);         // convert to screen coords
            Cursor = newPt;                // ..and udpate real cursor
        }
        break;
    }
}
/////////////////
// Function to convert Menu ID to COLORREF.
//
static COLORREF MenuColor(int id)
{
    static COLORREF colorMap[] = {
        COLOR_BLACK,    COLOR_WHITE,    COLOR_RED,
        COLOR_GREEN,    COLOR_BLUE,     COLOR_NONE
    };
    if (id<0 || id>=ID_COLORLAST)
        return COLOR_NONE;
    return id==ID_COLORRANDOM ? RGB(rand()&255, rand()&255, rand()&255)
        : colorMap[id];
}
/////////////////
// Handle menu command.
//
BOOL DrawWin::command(int id, WORD msg)
{
    switch (id) {
    case ID_NEWLINE:
        setNewShape(new GPLine(DfltSize));
        return TRUE;
    case ID_NEWRECT:
        setNewShape(new GPRect(DfltSize));
        return TRUE;
    case ID_NEWELLIPSE:
        setNewShape(new GPEllipse(DfltSize));
        return TRUE;
    case WPIDM_EDITDELETE:
        if (hilite) {
            hilite->shape()->invalidate(this);
            delete shapes.remove(hilite->shape());
            setHilite(NULL);
        }
        return TRUE;
    case ID_EDITDUP:
        if (hilite) {
            GPShape *shp = hilite->shape();
            shapes.add(shp->dup());
            setHilite(shp);
        }
        return TRUE;
    case ID_FRONT:
    case ID_BACK:
        if (hilite) {
            GPShape *shp = hilite->shape();
            if (id==ID_FRONT) {
                shapes.front(shp);        // move to front
                shapes.front(hilite);     // ..but not ahead of hilite
            } else
                shapes.back(hilite->shape());
            shp->invalidate(this);
            update();
```

```
            }
            return TRUE;
        default:
            if (id >= ID_EDGE && id<ID_FILL+ID_COLORLAST) {
                if (hilite) {
                    GPShape *shp = hilite->shape();
                    if (id >= ID_FILL)
                        shp->fillColor(MenuColor(id-ID_FILL));
                    else
                        shp->edgeColor(MenuColor(id-ID_EDGE));
                    shp->invalidate(this);
                    update();
                }
                return TRUE;
            }
            break;
    }
    return WPMainWin::command(id, msg);
}
/////////////////
// Handle File New command. Set everything to initial state.
//
BOOL DrawWin::fileNew()
{
    shapes.deleteAll();
    setNewShape(NULL);
    hilite = NULL;
    dragging = NODRAG;
    invalidate(TRUE);
    update();
    return TRUE;
}
/////////////////
// Print shapes. Pretty easy: just draw on printer DC!
//
BOOL DrawWin::filePrint(WPDlgPrint &pdlg)
{
    WPPrinter p = pdlg;
    p.mapMode(MM_LOMETRIC);
    p.doAbortDlg(this);
    p.startDoc("DRAW");
    shapes.draw(p);
    p.endPage();
    p.endDoc();
    return TRUE;
}
/////////////////
// Initialize menu.
// Do DRAW-specific commands, then pass to WPMainWin.
//
BOOL DrawWin::menuInit(WPMenu &menu)
{
    WPMenu mainMenu = this;
    if (menu==mainMenu) {
        WPSubMenu editMenu(menu, 1);
        BOOL any = anySelected();
        for (int i=0; i<NEDITCOMMANDS; i++)
            editMenu.enableItem(i, any, MF_BYPOSITION);
        editMenu.enableItem(POS_NEW, TRUE, MF_BYPOSITION);
    }
    return WPMainWin::menuInit(menu);        // pass along to main win!
}
```

DRAW.DLG

```
DLGABOUT DIALOG  72,21,122,54
STYLE DS_MODALFRAME | WS_POPUP | WS_CLIPSIBLINGS
BEGIN
```

```
    CONTROL "OK",IDOK,"Button",BS_DEFPUSHBUTTON | WS_TABSTOP | WS_CHILD |
WS_VISIBLE,31,35,30,14
    CONTROL "GPP Draw Program",-1,"static",WS_CHILD | SS_LEFT,31,4,82,9
    CONTROL "(C) 1992 Paul DiLascia",-1,"static",WS_CHILD | SS_LEFT,31,12,85,8
    CONTROL "appicon",-1,"static",SS_ICON | WS_CHILD,8,4,16,16
    CONTROL "Implemented using Windows++",-1,"static",WS_CHILD |
SS_LEFT,8,22,108,8
END
```

DRAW.RC

```
//////////////////////////////////////////////////////////
// WINDOWS++ CLASS LIBRARY.  Copyright 1992 Paul DiLascia.
// FILE: DRAW.RC
//
#include "wpp.h"
#include "draw.h"
AppIcon  ICON draw.ico
CrsDrag  CURSOR drag.cur
CrsNew   CURSOR new.cur
AppMenu MENU {
    POPUP "&File" {
        MENUITEM FileNew
        MENUITEM FilePrint
        MENUITEM HelpAbout
        MENUITEM SEPARATOR
        MENUITEM FileExit
    }
    POPUP "&Edit" {
        POPUP "&New" {
            MENUITEM "Line\tCtrl-L",       ID_NEWLINE
            MENUITEM "Rectangle\tCtrl-R",  ID_NEWRECT
            MENUITEM "Ellipse\tCtrl-E",    ID_NEWELLIPSE
        }
        MENUITEM EditDelete
        MENUITEM "D&uplicate\tCtrl-U",     ID_EDITDUP
        MENUITEM SEPARATOR
        POPUP "&Edge Color" {
            MENUITEM "Black",        ID_EDGE+ID_COLORBLACK
            MENUITEM "White",        ID_EDGE+ID_COLORWHITE
            MENUITEM "Red",          ID_EDGE+ID_COLORRED
            MENUITEM "Green",        ID_EDGE+ID_COLORGREEN
            MENUITEM "Blue",         ID_EDGE+ID_COLORBLUE
            MENUITEM SEPARATOR
            MENUITEM "Random",       ID_EDGE+ID_COLORRANDOM
            MENUITEM "None",         ID_EDGE+ID_COLORNONE
        }
        POPUP "F&ill Color" {
            MENUITEM "Black",        ID_FILL+ID_COLORBLACK
            MENUITEM "White",        ID_FILL+ID_COLORWHITE
            MENUITEM "Red",          ID_FILL+ID_COLORRED
            MENUITEM "Green",        ID_FILL+ID_COLORGREEN
            MENUITEM "Blue",         ID_FILL+ID_COLORBLUE
            MENUITEM SEPARATOR
            MENUITEM "Random",       ID_FILL+ID_COLORRANDOM
            MENUITEM "None",         ID_FILL+ID_COLORNONE
        }
        MENUITEM SEPARATOR
        MENUITEM "&Front\tCtrl-F", ID_FRONT
        MENUITEM "&Back\tCtrl-B",  ID_BACK
    }
}
AppAccel ACCELERATORS
BEGIN
    "^L", ID_NEWLINE
    "^R", ID_NEWRECT
    "^E", ID_NEWELLIPSE
    "^U", ID_EDITDUP
```

```
    "^F", ID_FRONT
    "^B", ID_BACK
    "^A", ID_TOGGLEBUF
    AccFileNew
    AccFilePrint
    AccMemStats
END
#include "wpprint.dlg"
#include "draw.dlg"
```

HELLO.CPP

```
//////////////////////////////////////////////////////////
// WINDOWS++ CLASS LIBRARY.  Copyright 1992 Paul DiLascia.
// FILE: HELLO.CPP
//
#include <wpp.h>
APPCLASS HelloWin : public WPMainWin {
public:
    HelloWin() { createWin("Hello"); }
    void paint(WPPaintStruct &ps) {
        WPRect clientArea = this;
        ps.drawText(clientArea, "Hello, Windows++.",
            DT_SINGLELINE | DT_CENTER | DT_VCENTER);
    }
};
void WPApp::main()
{
    mainWin = new HelloWin;
    run();
}
```

HELLO.DEF

```
NAME HELLO
EXETYPE WINDOWS
STUB 'WINSTUB.EXE'
CODE PRELOAD MOVEABLE DISCARDABLE
DATA PRELOAD MOVEABLE MULTIPLE
HEAPSIZE  5000
STACKSIZE 5120
```

HELLO.DLG

```
DLGABOUT DIALOG  72,26,124,56
STYLE DS_MODALFRAME | WS_POPUP | WS_CLIPSIBLINGS
BEGIN
    CONTROL "OK",IDOK,"Button",BS_DEFPUSHBUTTON | WS_TABSTOP | WS_CHILD |
WS_VISIBLE,30,33,30,14
    CONTROL "AppIcon",-1,"static",SS_ICON | WS_CHILD,7,8,16,16
    CONTROL "Windows++ HELLO Program",-1,"static",WS_CHILD | SS_LEFT,30,8,80,17
END
```

HELLO.RC

```
//////////////////////////////////////////////////////////
// WINDOWS++ CLASS LIBRARY.  Copyright 1992 Paul DiLascia.
// FILE: HELLO.RC
//
#include "wpp.h"
AppIcon  ICON hello.ico
AppMenu MENU {
    MENUITEM "E&xit!", WPIDM_EXIT
}
DLGABOUT DIALOG  72,13,124,70
STYLE DS_MODALFRAME | WS_POPUP | WS_CLIPSIBLINGS
BEGIN
```

```
    CONTROL "OK",IDOK,"Button",BS_DEFPUSHBUTTON | WS_TABSTOP | WS_CHILD |
WS_VISIBLE,32,50,30,14
    CONTROL "Written using the Windows++ Class Library by Paul
DiLascia",-1,"static",WS_CHILD | SS_LEFT,32,18,88,28
    CONTROL "AppIcon",-1,"static",SS_ICON | WS_CHILD,7,22,16,16
    CONTROL "Windows++ HELLO Program",-1,"static",WS_CHILD | SS_LEFT,32,5,80,8
END
APPACCEL ACCELERATORS
BEGIN
    "^X", WPIDM_EXIT
    "^Z",  WPIDM_MEMSTATS
END
```

LAUNCH.CPP

```
///////////////////////////////////////////////////////
// WINDOWS++ CLASS LIBRARY.  Copyright 1992 Paul DiLascia.
// FILE: LAUNCH.CPP
//
// This program never registers a window class nor displays a window;
// it just goes right into the dialog.  Demonstrates how to subclass
// the File Open dialog box.  Also shows how to access WIN.INI.
#include <stdio.h>
#include <direct.h>
#include <wpp.h>
const IDM_SETDEBUGGER = 10;
// These keys are used to save stuff in WIN.INI
//
CSTR KEYDIR= "Path";
CSTR KEYDEBUGSTR  = "DebugString";
CSTR KEYSCREENPOSX= "ScreenXPos";
CSTR KEYSCREENPOSY= "ScreenYPos";
/////////////////
// The Launch dialog is a special case of the file open dialog.
//
APPCLASS Launch : public WPDlgFileOpen {
    char dirname[MAXFILENAMELEN];
    char filename[MAXFILENAMELEN];
    char debugString[30];     // debugger program; e.g., "ZDBW /2"
    WPEdit *edFileName;        // edit control for filename
    WPListBox *lbFileName;     // list box for filename
    WPStatic *ssPathName;      // static text of path name
public:
    void initDlg();            // called for WM_INITDIALOG
    BOOL command(int id, WORD msg);
    Launch();
};
void WPApp::main()
{
    useWININI=TRUE;           // use WIN.INI for profile
    Launch dlg;               // create dialog
    dlg.run();                // ..run it
}
Launch::Launch() : WPDlgFileOpen(NULL, filename, "Launch")
{
    // Read stuff from WIN.INI
    App.getProfile(KEYDEBUGSTR, debugString, sizeof(debugString));
    App.getProfile(KEYDIR, dirname, sizeof(dirname));
    // Override default OFN data
    ofn.Flags |= OFN_SHOWHELP;
    ofn.lpstrInitialDir = dirname;    // start w/dir from WIN.INI
    ofn.lpstrTitle= "Launch";
    setFilter("EXE (*.EXE)\0*.exe\0COM (*.COM)\0*.com\0");
}
/////////////////
// Initialize the dialog box.  Use screen position from WIN.INI,
// set filespec to *.exe, add command to ventilator (system) menu.
//
```

```
void Launch::initDlg()
{
    setPos(App.getProfile(KEYSCREENPOSX), App.getProfile(KEYSCREENPOSY));
    edFileName = new WPEdit      (this, IDOFN_EDFILENAME);
    lbFileName = new WPListBox    (this, IDOFN_LBFILENAME);
    ssPathName = new WPStatic     (this, IDOFN_SSPATHNAME);
    // Change names of buttons
    WPButton *butn = new WPButton(this, IDOFN_PBHELP);
    butn->setText("&Debug");
    butn = new WPButton(this, IDOK);
    butn->setText("&Launch");
    butn = new WPButton(this, IDCANCEL);
    butn->setText("E&xit");
    // Add "Set Debugger" command to system menu
    WPSysMenu sm = this;
    sm.appendSep();
    sm.append(IDM_SETDEBUGGER, "Set Debugger...");
}
BOOL Launch::command(int id, WORD msg)
{
    switch (id) {
    case IDOK:
    case IDOFN_PBHELP:
        edFileName->getText(filename, sizeof(filename));
        if (filename[0] == 0)                    // no filename:
            lbFileName->getSel(filename);        // ..try list box
        // Execute program. Pre-pend debugger string if requested.
        char wincmd[80]="";
        if (id == IDOFN_PBHELP) {
            // pre-pend debugger string to executable filename
            strcat(wincmd, debugString);
            strcat(wincmd, " ");
        }
        strcat(wincmd, filename);
        int err = WinExec(wincmd, SW_SHOWNORMAL);
        if (err==2)
            ErrBox("Can't find program \"%s\".", wincmd);
        else if (err <= 32)
            ErrBox("Error %d from WinExec",err);
        return TRUE;              // ( DON'T exit dialog )
    case IDCANCEL:
        // Exit: save stuff in profile
        WPWindowRect pos = this;
        App.setProfile(KEYSCREENPOSX, pos.left());   // screen position
        App.setProfile(KEYSCREENPOSY, pos.top());    // ..
        App.setProfile(KEYDEBUGSTR,   debugString);  // debugger command
        ssPathName->getText(dirname, sizeof(dirname));
        App.setProfile(KEYDIR, dirname);
        endDlg(0);
        return TRUE;
    case IDM_SETDEBUGGER:
        WPDlgString dlg(this, debugString, sizeof(debugString),
            "Enter debug command:","Set Debugger");
        return TRUE;
    }
    return WPDlgFileOpen::command(id, msg);
}
```

LAUNCH.RC

```
/////////////////////////////////////////////////////////
// WINDOWS++ CLASS LIBRARY.  Copyright 1992 Paul DiLascia.
// FILE: LAUNCH.RC
//
AppIcon ICON launch.ico
```

MANDEL.H

```
/////////////////////////////////////////////////////////
// WINDOWS++ CLASS LIBRARY.  Copyright 1992 Paul DiLascia.
// FILE: MANDEL.H
//
#define ID_BITMAP 10
#define IDM_PAUSE 11
```

COMPLEX.H

```
/////////////////////////////////////////////////////////
// WINDOWS++ CLASS LIBRARY.  Copyright 1992 Paul DiLascia.
// FILE: COMPLEX.H
//
#ifndef COMPLEX_H
#define COMPLEX_H
typedef float REAL;        // could be float
class complex
{
private:
   REAL re;
   REAL im;
public:
   complex()    { re=0; im=0; }
   complex(REAL r, REAL i) { set(r,i); }
   void set(REAL r, REAL i) { re=r; im=i; }
   REAL& real()    { return re; }
   REAL& imag()    { return im; }
   void real(REAL r) { re=r; }
   void imag(REAL i) { im=i; }
   REAL abs2() { return re*re + im*im; }
   friend complex operator+ (const complex &c1, const complex &c2)
      { return complex(c1.re + c2.re, c1.im + c2.im); }
   friend complex operator- (const complex &c1, const complex &c2)
      { return  complex( c1.re - c2.re, c1.im - c2.im ); }
   friend complex operator* (const complex &c1, const complex &c2)
      { return  complex( c1.re*c2.re - c1.im*c2.im,
         c1.re*c2.im + c1.im*c2.re ); }
   friend int operator== (const complex &c1, const complex &c2)
      { return c1.re == c2.re && c1.im==c2.im; }
   friend int operator!= (const complex &c1, const complex & c2)
      { return c1==c2 ? 0 : 1; }
};
#endif
```

MANDEL.CPP

```
/////////////////////////////////////////////////////////
// WINDOWS++ CLASS LIBRARY.  Copyright 1992 Paul DiLascia.
// FILE: MANDEL.CPP
//
// Sample program to generate and display the Mandelbrot Set
#include <time.h>
#include <wpp.h>
#include "mandel.h"
#include "complex.h"
const MAXITERATIONS = 128; // max number of iterations
const DIVERGE = 4;          // sequence diverges if abs value greater than 4
const MAXNCOLORS = 64;      // maximum number of colors to use
const NSUBDIVISIONS = 20;   // subdivision of little rectangles
//////////////////
// The main window
//
APPCLASS Mandelbrot : public WPMainWin {
   COLORREF *colors;        // array of colors used to paint
   WPMemDC *memdc;          // memory bitmap
   int ncolors;             // number of colors
```

```
    WPRect clientBox;        // client area rectangle
    WPRect magnifyBox;       // box to magnify
    WPRect drawBox;          // current box we're drawing
    WPPoint moveRight, moveDown;      // used to translate drawBox
    complex cmin, cmax;      // rectangle in complex plane
    complex delta;           // complex increment
    BOOL dragging;           // we are dragging mouse
    BOOL pause;              // we are paused
    BOOL done;               // we are done painting the screen
    void init();             // initialize bitmap and calculation
    COLORREF computePixel(WPPoint p, complex& c);
public:
    Mandelbrot();
    ~Mandelbrot();
    // Virtual message functions
    void paint(WPPaintStruct& ps);
    BOOL command(int id, WORD msg);
    BOOL mouse(int msg, WPPoint p, WORD flags);
    BOOL sized(WPRect &box, WORD how);
    BOOL doIdle();
    BOOL fileNew();
};
//////////////////
// This class is used to draw the bitmap in the About dialog box.
//
APPCLASS BitmapButton : public WPODButton {
    WPBitmap *bitmap;
public:
    BitmapButton(WPWin *pwin, int id, CSTR bitmapname)
        : WPODButton(pwin, id)  { bitmap = new WPBitmap(bitmapname); }
    ~BitmapButton()            { delete bitmap; }
    void paint(WPOwnerDrawDC &dc, ODDATA data)
        { if ((dc.action & ODA_DRAWENTIRE) && bitmap)
          dc.drawBitmap(0, 0, bitmap); }
    BOOL gotFocus(WPWin *prev)
        { if (prev) prev->setFocus(); return TRUE; }
};
//////////////////
// Abouf dialog box: the only thing special is an owner-draw button
//
APPCLASS AboutMandel : public WPDialogModal {
public:
    AboutMandel(WPWin *pwin) : WPDialogModal("DLGABOUT",pwin) { run(); }
    void initDlg() { new BitmapButton(this, ID_BITMAP, "AboutBitmap"); }
};
void WPApp::main()
{
    mainWin = new Mandelbrot;
    run();
}
//////////////////
// Create main window
//
Mandelbrot::Mandelbrot()
{
    createArgs.wndcls.hCursor = NULL;    // we will set our own cursor
    createWin("Mandelbrot Set");   // create window
    time_t ntime;                  // seed for random num generator
    srand(time(&ntime));           // ..
    // Allocate array of colors
    WPWinDC dc = this;
    ncolors = min(dc.getNUMCOLORS(), MAXNCOLORS);
    colors = new COLORREF [ncolors];
    fileNew();
}
//////////////////
// Destroy window: destroy bitmap and color array
//
```

```
Mandelbrot::~Mandelbrot()
{
    delete memdc;
    delete colors;
}
/////////////////
// File New command: restore default plane region, pick random colors.
//
BOOL Mandelbrot::fileNew()
{
    WPWinDC dc = this;
    for (int i=0; i<ncolors; i++)
        colors[i] =
            dc.nearestColor(RGB(5+rand()%250, 5+rand()%250, 5+rand()%250));
    cmin.set(-2.0, -1.2);    // default region in complex plane
    cmax.set(1.2, 1.2);      // ..to show
    init();
    return TRUE;
}
/////////////////
// Initialize plane region.
//
void Mandelbrot::init()
{
    clientBox = this;
    // compute delta value to increment complex number "c"
    //
    delta.real((cmax.real()-cmin.real())/clientBox.width());
    delta.imag((cmax.imag()-cmin.imag())/clientBox.height());
    //////
    // Compute logical y-origin for window.  If the plane region spans
    // both positive and negative y (imaginary) values, we want to
    // take advantage of symmetry by setting the window coords with a
    // negative y-origin.
    //
    if (cmin.imag() < 0 && cmax.imag() > 0)
        clientBox += WPPoint(0, ( cmin.imag() / delta.imag()));
    // Create memory bitmap and initialize it to all white.
    WPWinDC dc = this;
    delete memdc;
    memdc = new WPMemDC(&dc, clientBox);
    memdc->whiteOut(clientBox);
    done = FALSE;
    // Compute size of incremental "draw" box.
    drawBox = clientBox;
    int w = ((drawBox.width() +(NSUBDIVISIONS-1))/NSUBDIVISIONS) | 1;
    int h = ((drawBox.height()+(NSUBDIVISIONS-1))/NSUBDIVISIONS) | 1;
    drawBox.extent(w, h);
    moveRight.set(w, 0);     // moves box right
    moveDown.set(0,h);       // moves box down
    invalidate(TRUE);        // clear screen
}
/////////////////
// Paint: just blast the bitmap to the screen.
//
void Mandelbrot::paint(WPPaintStruct& ps)
{
    WPRect dst = this;
    ps.stretchBlt(dst, *memdc, clientBox);
}
/////////////////
// User re-sized the window.
// If we're done, just re-paint; otherwise re-initialize bitmap.
//
BOOL Mandelbrot::sized(WPRect &box, WORD how)
{
    if (!done)               // not done drawing:
        init();              // ..start all over
```

```
        return TRUE;
}
////////////////////
// Handle menu command.
//
BOOL Mandelbrot::command(int id, WORD msg)
{
    switch (id) {
    case WPIDM_ABOUT:
        AboutMandel(this);    // do special "About" dialog
        return TRUE;
    case IDM_PAUSE:
        pause = !pause;
        WPMenu menu = this;
        menu.modify(IDM_PAUSE, IDM_PAUSE, pause ? "&Continue!" : "&Pause!");
        drawMenu();
        return TRUE;
    }
    return WPMainWin::command(id, msg);
}
////////////////////
// Handle mouse message.
// This implements the drag-select-magnify-region function.
//
BOOL Mandelbrot::mouse(int msg, WPPoint p, WORD flags)
{
    switch(msg) {
    case WM_LBUTTONDOWN:
        if (!dragging) {
            dragging=TRUE;
            Cursor.clip(this);
            Cursor = IDC_CROSS;
            magnifyBox.origin(p);
            magnifyBox.endpt(p);
        }
        break;
    case WM_MOUSEMOVE:
        Cursor = dragging ? IDC_CROSS : IDC_ARROW;
        if (dragging) {
            if (p != magnifyBox.endpt()) {
                WPWinDC dc = this;
                dc.drawFocusRect(magnifyBox); // erase old focus rect
                magnifyBox.endpt(p);
                dc.drawFocusRect(magnifyBox); // draw new one
            }
        }
        break;
    case WM_LBUTTONUP:
        if (!magnifyBox.isEmpty()) {
            magnifyBox.normalize();
            WPRect rect = this;
            REAL xscale = (cmax.real()-cmin.real())/rect.width();
            REAL yscale = (cmax.imag()-cmin.imag())/rect.height();
            cmax.set(cmin.real() + xscale * magnifyBox.right(),
                     cmin.imag() + yscale * magnifyBox.bottom());
            cmin.set(cmin.real() + xscale * magnifyBox.left(),
                     cmin.imag() + yscale * magnifyBox.top());
            init();
        }
        Cursor = IDC_ARROW;
        Cursor.unClip();
        dragging = FALSE;
        break;
    }
    return TRUE;
}
////////////////////
// Compute color of pixel and set it in the bitmap. Returns color.
```

```
//
COLORREF Mandelbrot::computePixel(WPPoint p, complex &c)
{
    COLORREF color = memdc->pixel(p);
    if (color == COLOR_WHITE) {
        complex z;
        for (int n = 0; n<MAXITERATIONS; n++) {
            REAL zrr = z.real() * z.real();
            REAL zii = z.imag() * z.imag();
            REAL zir2 = 2 * z.real() * z.imag();
            if (zrr + zii >= DIVERGE)
                break;
            z.real(zrr-zii + c.real());
            z.imag(zir2 + c.imag());
        }
        color = n>=MAXITERATIONS ? COLOR_BLACK : colors[n % ncolors];
        memdc->pixel(p, color);
        if (clientBox.top() != 0) {
            p.y = -p.y;                    // use symmetry
            memdc->pixel(p, color);
        }
    }
    return color;
}
/////////////////////
// Compute next little rectangle of pixels. We take advantage of the fact
// that each colored region is connected: if all the boundary points of a
// box are the same color, we can fill the box with that color and be done
// with it.
//
BOOL Mandelbrot::doIdle()
{
    if (done || dragging || pause)
        return TRUE;
    for (WPRect box = drawBox; !box.isEmpty(); --box) {
        // Each iteration of this loop paints the boundary of the box,
        // then shrinks the box one pixel.
        COLORREF color1, color;
        BOOL first = TRUE;
        BOOL allSameColor = TRUE;       // assume boundary points are same color
        // do top edge
        WPPoint p = box.origin();
        REAL creal = cmin.real() + (p.x * delta.real());
        REAL cimag = cmin.imag() + ((p.y-clientBox.top()) * delta.imag());
        complex c (creal, cimag);
        for (p.x=box.left(); p.x <= box.right(); p.x++) {
            color = computePixel(p, c);
            if (first)
                color1 = color;
            else if (color != color1)
                allSameColor = FALSE;
            first = FALSE;
            c.real() += delta.real();
        }
        // do bottom edge
        p.y = box.bottom();
        c.real(creal);
        c.imag(cmin.imag() + ((p.y-clientBox.top()) * delta.imag()));
        for (p.x=box.left(); p.x <= box.right(); p.x++) {
            if (computePixel(p, c) != color1)
                allSameColor = FALSE;
            c.real() += delta.real();
        }
        // do left edge
        p.x = box.left();
        c.real(creal);
        c.imag(cimag);
        for (p.y=box.top(); p.y<=box.bottom(); p.y++) {
```

```
            if (computePixel(p, c) != color1)
                allSameColor = FALSE;
            c.imag() += delta.imag();
        }
        // do right side
        p.x = box.right();
        c.real(cmin.real() + (p.x * delta.real()));
        c.imag(cimag);
        for (p.y=box.top(); p.y<=box.bottom(); p.y++) {
            if (computePixel(p, c) != color1)
                allSameColor = FALSE;
            c.imag() += delta.imag();
        }
        if (allSameColor) {
            // All boundary points are the same color:
            // fill the box and quit loop.
            if (color==COLOR_BLACK) {
                memdc->blackOut(box);
                if (clientBox.top() != 0) {
                    // use symmetry
                    box.top(1-box.top());
                    box.bottom(1-box.bottom());
                    memdc->blackOut(box);
                }
            } else {
                WPBrush brush(color);
                memdc->fill(box, brush);
                if (clientBox.top() != 0) {
                    // use symmetry
                    box.top(1-box.top());
                    box.bottom(1-box.bottom());
                    memdc->fill(box, brush);
                }
            }
            break;
        }
    }
    // Now blast the result to window
    WPWinDC dc = this;
    dc.windowOrg(clientBox.origin());
    box = drawBox;
    dc.bitBlt(box, *memdc, box.origin());
    if (clientBox.top() != 0) {
        box.top(1-box.top());                          // use symmetry
        box.bottom(1-box.bottom());
        dc.bitBlt(box, *memdc, box.origin());
    }
    // Move box right; if at edge, move down to start of next row
    //
    drawBox += moveRight;
    if (drawBox.left() >= clientBox.right()) {
        drawBox.left(0);
        drawBox.right(moveRight.x);
        drawBox += moveDown;
        if (clientBox.top() !=0 && drawBox.top() >= 1) {
            while (drawBox.bottom() <= -clientBox.top())
                drawBox += moveDown;
        }
        if (drawBox.top() >= clientBox.bottom())
            done = TRUE;
    }
    return TRUE;
}
```

MANDEL.DLG

```
DLGABOUT DIALOG  20,13,181,92
STYLE DS_MODALFRAME | WS_POPUP | WS_CLIPSIBLINGS
```

```
BEGIN
    CONTROL "&OK",IDOK,"Button",BS_DEFPUSHBUTTON | WS_TABSTOP | WS_CHILD |
WS_VISIBLE,89,60,30,14
    CONTROL "Written using Windows++ (C) 1992 Paul
DiLascia",-1,"static",WS_CHILD | SS_LEFT,89,33,84,20
    CONTROL "MANDEL",-1,"static",WS_CHILD | SS_LEFT,89,15,80,8
    CONTROL "ABOUTBITMAP",ID_BITMAP,"button",BS_OWNERDRAW | WS_CHILD |
WS_VISIBLE,5,8,74,75
END
```

MANDEL.RC

```
/////////////////////////////////////////////////////
// WINDOWS++ CLASS LIBRARY.  Copyright 1992 Paul DiLascia.
// FILE: MANDEL.RC
//
#include "wpp.h"
#include "mandel.h"
AboutBitmap BITMAP "mandel.bmp"
AppMenu MENU {
    POPUP "&File" {
        MENUITEM FileNew
        MENUITEM HelpAbout
        MENUITEM FileExit
    }
    MENUITEM "&Pause!",       IDM_PAUSE
}
AppAccel ACCELERATORS
BEGIN
    AccFileNew
    AccMemStats
END
#include "mandel.dlg"
```

MEDIT.CPP

```
/////////////////////////////////////////////////////
// WINDOWS++ CLASS LIBRARY.  Copyright 1992 Paul DiLascia.
// FILE: MEDIT.CPP
//
// Multi-file editor.
#include <wpp.h>
/////////////////////
// Main edit window class--almost identical to WINEDIT.
//
APPCLASS EditWin : public WPMDIChild {
    static BOOL first;       // first edit window created?
    WPMultiEdit *editCtl;    // main edit window
protected:
    BOOL gotFocus(WPWin *prev)
        { editCtl->setFocus(); return FALSE; }
public:
    EditWin(WPMDIFrame *frame, CSTR fname=NULL);
    BOOL sized(WPRect &box, WORD how)
        { editCtl->moveWin(box); return FALSE; }
    // File command functions
    BOOL fileIsModified()          { return editCtl->isModified(); }
    void fileIsModified(BOOL m)    { editCtl->setModified(m); }
    BOOL fileOpen(CSTR fname)      { return editCtl->load(fname); }
    BOOL fileSave(CSTR fname)      { return editCtl->save(fname); }
    BOOL filePrint(WPDlgPrint &pdlg);
    BOOL fileNew()
        { editCtl->setSel(); editCtl->clear(); return TRUE; }
    // Edit command functions
    BOOL editCut()      { editCtl->cut(); return TRUE; }
    BOOL editCopy()     { editCtl->copy(); return TRUE; }
    BOOL editPaste()    { editCtl->paste(); return TRUE; }
    BOOL editDelete()   { editCtl->clear(); return TRUE; }
```

```
    BOOL editUndo()        { editCtl->undo(); return TRUE; }
    BOOL canPaste()        { return Clipboard.available(CF_TEXT); }
    BOOL canUndo()         { return editCtl->canUndo(); }
    BOOL anySelected()
        { int beg,end; return editCtl->getSel(beg, end); }
};
BOOL EditWin::first = TRUE;
//////////////////
// Create new edit window (as MDI child).
//
EditWin::EditWin(WPMDIFrame *pwin, CSTR fname) : WPMDIChild("EDITWIN", pwin)
{
    createWin();              // create this window
    // Create multi-line edit control
    editCtl = new WPMultiEdit(this, -1);
    createArgs.pos = this;
    createArgs.style |=
        ES_AUTOVSCROLL | ES_AUTOHSCROLL | WS_VSCROLL | WS_HSCROLL;
    editCtl->createWin();
    fileInit(fname,"");
    setFocus();
    if (first) {
        maximize();
        first = FALSE;
    }
}
//////////////////
// Print the file. Should really check pdlg for num copies, etc.
//
BOOL EditWin::filePrint(WPDlgPrint &pdlg)
{
    char *line = App.scratch;
    int nlines = editCtl->numLines();
    WPLinePrinter p = pdlg;
    p.doAbortDlg(this);
    p.startDoc(fileName());
    for (int i=0; i < nlines && !p.aborted(); i++) {
        int len = editCtl->getLine(i, line, 256);
        p.outLine(line, len);
    }
    p.endDoc();
    return TRUE;
}
//////////////////
// Main (MDI Frame) window class.
//
APPCLASS EditFrame : public WPMDIFrame {
    int pmtHeight;            // height of prompt line
public:
    EditFrame(CSTR fname=NULL);
    BOOL sized(WPRect &box, WORD how);
    BOOL fileOpen(CSTR fname)  { new EditWin(this, fname); return TRUE; }
    BOOL fileNew()             { new EditWin(this); return TRUE; }
    int getMenuPrompt(char* buf, int id, WORD flags)
        { return id ? App.loadString(id, buf, MAXPROMPTLEN) : 0; }
};
//////////////////
// Initialize main window.
//
EditFrame::EditFrame(CSTR fname) : WPMDIFrame(2 /* "Window" menu pos*/ )
{
    createArgs.style |= CS_DBLCLKS;
    WPWin::createWin("MEDIT"); // create main window
    // Create prompt line
    promptWin = new WPStatic(this, -1);
    createArgs.style |= WS_BORDER;
    promptWin->createWin();
    pmtHeight = tm.tmHeight;
```

```
    if (fname && *fname)
        fileOpen(fname);
}
//////////////////
// Main window was re-sized
//
BOOL EditFrame::sized(WPRect &box, WORD how)
{
    // Adjust client window
    box.height(box.height()-pmtHeight);
    clientWin()->moveWin(box);
    // Adjust prompt line
    WPRect pmtbox;
    pmtbox.origin(0, box.height());
    pmtbox.extent(box.width(), pmtHeight);
    promptWin->moveWin(pmtbox);
    return TRUE;
}
//////////////////
// Main entry point.  Command line argument is name of file to open
//
void WPApp::main()
{
    char fname[80];
    getCmdLine(fname);
    mainWin = new EditFrame(fname);
    run();
}
```

MEDIT.RC

```
//////////////////////////////////////////////////////////
// WINDOWS++ CLASS LIBRARY.  Copyright 1992 Paul DiLascia.
// FILE: MEDIT.RC
//
#include "wpp.h"
AppMenu MENU {
    POPUP "&File" {
        MENUITEM FileNew
        MENUITEM FileOpen
        MENUITEM SEPARATOR
        MENUITEM FileSave
        MENUITEM FileSaveAs
        MENUITEM FileClose
        MENUITEM SEPARATOR
        MENUITEM FilePrint
        MENUITEM SEPARATOR
        MENUITEM FileExit
    }
    POPUP "&Edit" {
        MENUITEM EditUndo
        MENUITEM SEPARATOR
        MENUITEM EditCut
        MENUITEM EditCopy
        MENUITEM EditPaste
        MENUITEM SEPARATOR
        MENUITEM EditDelete
    }
    POPUP "&Window" {
        MENUITEM WindowCascade
        MENUITEM WindowTile
        MENUITEM WindowArrange
        MENUITEM WindowCloseAll
    }
}
AppAccel ACCELERATORS
BEGIN
    AccFileNew
```

```
            AccFileOpen
            AccFilePrint
            AccFileSave
            AccEditUndo
            AccEditCut
            AccEditCopy
            AccEditPaste
            AccWinCascade
            AccWinTile
            AccWinNext
            AccMemStats
END
STRINGTABLE {
    WPIDM_EXIT, "Exit from program."
    WPIDM_FILENEW, "Create a new file."
    WPIDM_FILEOPEN, "Open an existing file."
    WPIDM_FILESAVE, "Save current file on disk."
    WPIDM_FILESAVEAS, "Save current file with a different name."
    WPIDM_FILEPRINT, "Print current file."
    WPIDM_FILECLOSE, "Close current file."
    WPIDM_EDITUNDO, "Undo previous edit operation."
    WPIDM_EDITCUT, "Delete selected text and transfer it to the clipboard."
    WPIDM_EDITCOPY, "Copy selected text to the clipboard."
    WPIDM_EDITPASTE, "Insert contents of clipboard at current location."
    WPIDM_EDITDELETE, "Delete selected text without transferring it to the
clipboard."
    WPIDM_WINCASCADE, "Arrange windows like a card file."
    WPIDM_WINTILE,    "Arrange windows like bathroom tiles."
    WPIDM_WINARRANGE, "Arrange icons neatly."
    WPIDM_WINCLOSEALL,"Close all windows."
}
#include "wpprint.dlg"
```

MEMTEST.CPP

See Section 4.3, page 150.

MKC.CPP

```
//////////////////////////////////////////////////////////
// WINDOWS++ CLASS LIBRARY. Copyright 1992 Paul DiLascia.
// FILE: MKC.CPP
//
// Sample program to demonstrate use of keyboard, mouse and cursor.
// Shows status of [NUM CAP SCROLL] LOCK, mouse buttons and cursor pos.
// Also moves the cursor using arrow keys.
#include <wpp.h>
int TABS[] = { 12, 25 };            // tab-stops (in text coords)
const int NTABS = sizeof(TABS)/sizeof(TABS[0]);
const VK_SCROLLLOCK = 0x91;         // code for scroll lock
APPCLASS MKCWin : public WPMainWin {
    TEXTMETRIC tm;             // text metrics
    int button[3];            // button states
    int repeat;               // keyboard repeat count
public:
    MKCWin();
    void paint(WPPaintStruct &ps);
    BOOL kbd(WPEvent& event);
    BOOL mouse(int msg, WPPoint p, WORD flags);
    BOOL activated(WORD state, BOOL minimized);
};
void WPApp::main()
{
    mainWin = new MKCWin;
    run();
}
```

```
/////////////////
// Create main window.  Use cursor from resource file.
//
MKCWin::MKCWin()
{
    createArgs.wndcls.hCursor = App.loadCursor("XCURSOR");
    createWin("Mouse, Keyboard, Cursor");
    // Convert tab stops from text to pixel coordinates
    WPWinDC dc = this;
    dc.textMetrics(tm);
    TABS[0] *= tm.tmAveCharWidth;
    TABS[1] *= tm.tmAveCharWidth;
}
/////////////////
// Paint status of CAPSLOCK, etc. Uses Windows 3.0 tabbed text.
//
void MKCWin::paint(WPPaintStruct &ps)
{
    ps.setTabs(TABS, NTABS);
    WPPoint pt(tm.tmAveCharWidth, tm.tmHeight);
    ps.printF(pt, "MOUSE:\t%sPRESENT\t",
        Mouse.present() ? "" : "NOT ");
    pt.y += tm.tmHeight;
    for (int i=0; i<3; i++) {
        ps.printF(pt, "%cBUTTON:\t%s\t", "LMR"[i], button[i] ? "DOWN" : "UP");
        pt.y += tm.tmHeight;
    }
    ps.printF(pt,"NUMLOCK:\t%s\t", Keyboard.state(VK_NUMLOCK) ? "ON" : "OFF");
    pt.y += tm.tmHeight;
    ps.printF(pt,"CAPLOCK:\t%s\t", Keyboard.state(VK_CAPITAL) ? "ON" : "OFF");
    pt.y += tm.tmHeight;
    ps.printF(pt,"SCROLL:\t%s\t", Keyboard.state(VK_SCROLLLOCK) ? "ON":"OFF");
    pt.y += tm.tmHeight;
    WPPoint crs= Cursor();
    screenToClient(crs);
    ps.printF(pt, "CURSOR:\t(%d,%d)\t", crs.x, crs.y);
}
/////////////////
// Handle mouse message.
// Record button state and always invalidate the client area.
//
BOOL MKCWin::mouse(int msg, WPPoint p, WORD flags)
{
    switch(msg) {
    case WM_LBUTTONDOWN:
    case WM_LBUTTONUP:
        button[0] = (msg==WM_LBUTTONDOWN);
        break;
    case WM_MBUTTONDOWN:
    case WM_MBUTTONUP:
        button[1] = (msg==WM_MBUTTONDOWN);
        break;
    case WM_RBUTTONDOWN:
    case WM_RBUTTONUP:
        button[2] = (msg==WM_RBUTTONDOWN);
    }
    invalidate();
    return TRUE;
}
BOOL MKCWin::activated(WORD state, BOOL minimized)
{
    if (!Mouse.present() && !minimized)
        Cursor.show(state);
    setFocus();
    return TRUE;
}
/////////////////
// Handle keyboard message
```

```
//
BOOL MKCWin::kbd(WPEvent& event)
{
    switch (event.key()) {
    case VK_NUMLOCK:                        // for any of these...
    case VK_CAPITAL:
    case VK_SCROLLLOCK:
        invalidate();                       // repaint window
        return TRUE;
    }
    switch (event.msg) {
    case WM_KEYDOWN:
        if (Keyboard.isArrowKey(event.key())) {
            // Got arrow key: move cursor
            WPPoint pt = Cursor();
            screenToClient(pt);
            repeat += event.keyRepeat();
            switch (event.key()) {
            case VK_LEFT:  pt.x -= repeat;    break;
            case VK_RIGHT: pt.x += repeat;    break;
            case VK_UP:    pt.y -= repeat;    break;
            case VK_DOWN:  pt.y += repeat;    break;
            }
            // Don't move outside our window's client area
            WPRect rect = this;
            rect.capture(pt);
            clientToScreen(pt);
            Cursor = pt;
            return TRUE;
        }
        break;
    case WM_KEYUP:
        repeat = 1;                          // Clear repeat count
        return TRUE;
    }
    return WPMainWin::kbd(event);
}
```

MKC.RC

```
/////////////////////////////////////////////////////////
// WINDOWS++ CLASS LIBRARY.  Copyright 1992 Paul DiLascia.
// FILE: MKC.RC
//
#include "wpp.h"
xcursor CURSOR mkc.cur
AppMenu MENU {
    MENUITEM "E&xit!",           WPIDM_EXIT
}
AppAccel ACCELERATORS
BEGIN
    "^X", WPIDM_EXIT
    "^Z", WPIDM_MEMSTATS
END
```

PEOPLE.H

```
/////////////////////////////////////////////////////////
// WINDOWS++ CLASS LIBRARY.  Copyright 1992 Paul DiLascia.
// FILE: PEOPLE.H
//
#ifndef PEOPLE_H
#define PEOPLE_H
#include <wpp.h>
#define IDLB_PEOPLE      (WPID_DLGBASE + 0)
#define IDM_EDIT         (WPID_DLGBASE + 1)
#define IDM_EDITNEW      (WPID_DLGBASE + 2)
```

```
#define IDM_OKNEXT        (WPID_DLGBASE + 3)
#define IDM_OKPREV        (WPID_DLGBASE + 4)
#define IDSI_ABOUTICON    (WPID_DLGBASE + 9)
#define IDED_NAME         (WPID_DLGBASE + 10)
#define IDED_ADDR         (WPID_DLGBASE + 11)
#define IDED_CITY         (WPID_DLGBASE + 12)
#define IDCB_STATE        (WPID_DLGBASE + 13)
#define IDED_ZIP          (WPID_DLGBASE + 14)
#define IDED_PHONE        (WPID_DLGBASE + 15)
#define IDB_SELECTED      (WPID_DLGBASE + 16)
// The following must be consecutive
#define IDRBG_STATUS      (WPID_DLGBASE + 20)
#define IDB_FRIEND        (WPID_DLGBASE + 21)
#define IDB_BUSINESS      (WPID_DLGBASE + 22)
#define IDB_OTHER         (WPID_DLGBASE + 23)

#endif
```

PEOPLE.CPP

```
/////////////////////////////////////////////////////////
// WINDOWS++ CLASS LIBRARY.  Copyright 1992 Paul DiLascia.
// FILE: PEOPLE.CPP
//
#include "people.h"
#ifdef __ZTC__
#include <fstream.hpp>
#include <iomanip.hpp>
#else
#include <fstream.h>
#include <iomanip.h>
#endif
APPCLASS CBUSStates : public WPComboBox, public WPListData {
    static CSTR States[];
    int curState;
public:
    CBUSStates(WPWin *pwin, int id) : WPComboBox(pwin, id)
        { setList(this); createWin(); }
    static WPControl* New(WPWin* pwin, int id)
        { return new CBUSStates(pwin, id); }
    BOOL firstItem()    { return curState = 1; }
    BOOL nextItem()     { return States[curState] ? ++curState : 0; }
    void getItemText(char *buf, int len)
        { strcpy(buf, States[curState-1]); }
};
CSTR CBUSStates::States[] = {
    "AL","AK","AZ","AR","CA","CO","CN","DC","DE","FL","GA","HI","ID",
    "IL","IN","IA","KS","KY","LA","ME","MD","MA","MI","MN","MO","MS",
    "MT","NE","NV","NH","NJ","NM","NY","NC","ND","OH","OK","OR","PA",
    "RI","SC","SD","TN","TX","UT","VT","VA","WA","WV","WI","WY",NULL
};
//////////////////
// Special kind of edit control lets user type digits only.
//
DLLCLASS EditZip : public WPEdit {
public:
    EditZip(WPWin *pwin, int id) : WPEdit(pwin, id)
        { setLegalChars("0123456789-"); createWin(); }
    static WPControl* New(WPWin* pwin, int id)
        { return new EditZip(pwin, id); }
};
enum STATUS { STFRIEND=0, STBUSINESS, STOTHER, NSTATUS };
class Person {
#ifdef __ZTC__                  // Bcause Zortech can't handle static
public:                         // initialization of ControlMap correctly.
#endif                          // ztc thinks these fields are private.
    char    name[50];           // name, etc
    char    addr[50];
```

```
       char      city[30];
       char      zip[10];
       char      phone[15];
       char      state[3];
       STATUS    status;
       BOOL      selected;
public:
       Person() { clear(); }
       Person    *next;           // next person in list
       Person    *prev;           // previous person in list
       int format(char *buf, int len)
           { return sprintf(buf,"%s\t%s", name, phone); }
       void clear()
           { memset(this, 0, sizeof(Person)); }
       friend istream& operator>>(istream& is, Person& p);
       friend ostream& operator<<(ostream& os, Person& p);
       friend APPCLASS DlgEditPerson;
};
APPCLASS DlgEditPerson : public WPDialogModal {
       static WPControlMap ControlMap[];
public:
       DlgEditPerson(WPWin *pwin, Person *p)
           : WPDialogModal("DLGEDITPERSON", pwin, ControlMap, p) { createWin(); }
       BOOL command(int id, WORD msg);
       void updateScreen();
};
WPControlMap DlgEditPerson::ControlMap[] = {
       cmEdit( IDED_NAME,         Person,  name )
       cmEdit( IDED_ADDR,         Person,  addr )
       cmEdit( IDED_CITY,         Person,  city )
       cmCust( CBUSStates::New,IDCB_STATE, Person,  state )
       cmEdit( IDED_PHONE,        Person,  phone )
       cmRBgp( IDRBG_STATUS,      Person,  status,      NSTATUS )
       cmCust( EditZip::New,    IDED_ZIP,   Person,  zip )
       cmButn( IDB_SELECTED,      Person,  selected )
       cmPush( IDM_OKNEXT)
       cmPush( IDM_OKPREV)
       cmEnd(IDED_NAME)
};
BOOL DlgEditPerson::command(int id, WORD msg)
{
       switch (id) {
       case IDM_OKNEXT:
       case IDM_OKPREV:
          updateObject();
          Person *p = (Person*)getObject();
          p = id==IDM_OKNEXT ? p->next : p->prev;
          assert(p);
          linkObject(p);
          return TRUE;
       }
       return WPDialogModal::command(id, msg);
}
void DlgEditPerson::updateScreen()
{
       Person *p = (Person*)getObject();
       getChild(IDM_OKNEXT)->enableWin(p->next != NULL);
       getChild(IDM_OKPREV)->enableWin(p->prev != NULL);
       WPDialogModal::updateScreen();
}
const char DELIM = 1;
const char NL = '\n';
istream& operator>>(istream& is, Person& p)
{
       char delim;
       is.get(p.name, sizeof(p.name), DELIM); is >> delim;
       is.get(p.addr, sizeof(p.addr), DELIM); is >> delim;
       is.get(p.city, sizeof(p.city), DELIM); is >> delim;
```

```
      is.get(p.state,sizeof(p.state),DELIM); is >> delim;
      is.get(p.zip,  sizeof(p.zip),  DELIM); is >> delim;
      is.get(p.phone,sizeof(p.phone),DELIM); is >> delim;
      is >> (int)p.status >> delim;
      is >> p.selected >> delim;
      is.get();               // eat newline
      return is;
}
ostream& operator<<(ostream& os, Person& p)
{
   if (p.name[0]) {
      os << p.name << DELIM;
      os << p.addr << DELIM;
      os << p.city << DELIM;
      os << p.state << DELIM;
      os << p.zip << DELIM;
      os << p.phone << DELIM;
      os << (int)p.status << DELIM;
      os << p.selected << DELIM;
      os << NL;
   }
   return os;
}
//////////////////
// Alternating icon is special kind of static icon.
//
APPCLASS AltIcon : public WPStaticIcon {
   HICON icon1;
   HICON icon2;
   HICON whichIcon;
   int nclicks;
protected:
   BOOL timer(int id);
public:
   AltIcon(WPWin *pwin, int id, CSTR name1, CSTR name2);
   ~AltIcon() { killTimer(1); }
};
//////////////////
// Create alternating icon
//
AltIcon::AltIcon(WPWin *pwin, int id, CSTR name1, CSTR name2)
   : WPStaticIcon(pwin, id)
{
   whichIcon = icon1 = App.loadIcon(name1);
   icon2 = App.loadIcon(name2);
   nclicks=0;
   setTimer(1, 200);
   createWin();
}
//////////////////
// Handle timer message: swap icons
//
BOOL AltIcon::timer(int id)
{
   if (++nclicks > 5) {
      linkObject(whichIcon = whichIcon==icon1 ? icon2 : icon1);
      updateScreen();
      if (nclicks > 6)
         nclicks=0;
   }
   return TRUE;
}
//////////////////
// Special About dialog box w/animated icon.
//
APPCLASS AboutPeople : public WPDialogModal {
public:
   AboutPeople(WPWin *pwin) : WPDialogModal("DLGABOUT",pwin)
```

```
            { createWin(); }
        void initDlg()
            { new AltIcon(this, IDSI_ABOUTICON, "Hello1","Hello2"); }
};
// tab stops for main list window
static int TABS[] = { 100, 150, 200 };
const NTABS = sizeof(TABS)/sizeof(TABS[0]);
APPCLASS PeopleWin : public WPMainWin, public WPListData {
    WPListBox *lbPeople;
    Person *firstPerson;
    Person *curPerson;
    int nPerson;
    int nPeople;
public:
    PeopleWin(CSTR fname);
    ~PeopleWin() { fileNew(); }    // delete all the people
    BOOL command(int id, WORD msg);
    BOOL menuInit(WPMenu &menu);
    void editPerson();
    BOOL fileOpen(CSTR fname);
    BOOL fileSave(CSTR fname);
    BOOL fileNew();
    BOOL sized(WPRect &box,WORD how) { lbPeople->moveWin(box); return TRUE; }
    BOOL gotFocus(WPWin *prev)       { lbPeople->setFocus(); return TRUE; }
    BOOL anySelected()               { return lbPeople->getSel()!=-1; }
    Person* getSelectedPerson();
    int getIndex(Person *p);
    // These are the ListData methods.
    BOOL firstItem()
        { return (curPerson=firstPerson) != NULL; }
    BOOL nextItem()
        { if (curPerson) curPerson=curPerson->next; return curPerson!=NULL; }
    void getItemText(char *buf, int len)
        { if (curPerson) curPerson->format(buf, len); else *buf = 0; }
};
void WPApp::main()
{
    char fname[80];
    getCmdLine(fname);
    mainWin = new PeopleWin(fname);
    run();
}
PeopleWin::PeopleWin(CSTR fname)
{
    createWin();
    lbPeople = new WPListBox(this, IDLB_PEOPLE);
    createArgs.pos = this;
    createArgs.style &= ~WS_BORDER;
    lbPeople->createWin();
    lbPeople->setList(this);
    lbPeople->setTabStops(TABS, NTABS);
    fileInit(fname, "PEOPLE");
    fileNameFilter("People Files (*.PPL)\0*.PPL\0");
}
Person *PeopleWin::getSelectedPerson()
{
    int index = lbPeople->getSel();
    Person *p = NULL;
    if (index >= 0) {
        for (p=firstPerson; p && index-->0; p=p->next)
            ;
    }
    return p;
}
int PeopleWin::getIndex(Person *person)
{
    int index = 0;
    for (Person *p=firstPerson; p; p=p->next, index++)
```

```
         if (p==person)
             break;
      return index;
}
void PeopleWin::editPerson()
{
    Person *p = getSelectedPerson();
    assert(p);
    WPDialog *dlg = new DlgEditPerson(this, p);
    if (dlg->isModified()) {
        fileIsModified(TRUE);
        lbPeople->setList(this, getIndex((Person*)dlg->getObject()));
    }
}
BOOL PeopleWin::command(int id, WORD msg)
{
    switch (id) {
    case WPIDM_ABOUT:
        AboutPeople about(this);
        return TRUE;
    case IDM_EDIT:
        editPerson();
        return TRUE;
    case IDM_EDITNEW:
    case WPIDM_EDITDELETE:
        ErrBox("Not implemented yet.");
        return TRUE;
    case IDLB_PEOPLE:
        if (msg==LBN_DBLCLK)
            editPerson();
        return TRUE;
    }
    return WPMainWin::command(id, msg);
}
BOOL PeopleWin::menuInit(WPMenu &menu)
{
    WPMenu mainMenu = this;
    if (menu==mainMenu) {
        Person *p = getSelectedPerson();
        menu.enableItem(IDM_EDIT, p!=NULL);
        menu.enableItem(WPIDM_EDITDELETE, p!=NULL);
    }
    return WPMainWin::menuInit(menu);
}
/////////////////
// File Open command
//
BOOL PeopleWin::fileOpen(CSTR fname)
{
    ifstream inf(fname);
    if (!inf)
        return FALSE;
    nPeople = 0;
    fileNew();
    Person *prev = NULL;
    for (Person *p = firstPerson; !inf.eof(); p = p->next) {
        nPeople++;
        p = new Person;
        inf >> *p;
        p->prev = prev;
        if (prev)
            prev->next = p;
        else
            firstPerson = p;
        prev = p;
    }
    lbPeople->setList(this);
```

```
    return TRUE;
}
/////////////////
// File Save command
//
BOOL PeopleWin::fileSave(CSTR fname)
{
    ofstream fout(fname);
    if (fout) {
        for (Person* p = firstPerson; p; p=p->next)
            fout << *p;
        return TRUE;
    }
    return FALSE;
}
/////////////////
// New file: delete all the people
//
BOOL PeopleWin::fileNew()
{
    while (firstPerson) {
        Person *p = firstPerson->next;
        delete firstPerson;
        firstPerson = p;
    }
    lbPeople->setList(this);
    return TRUE;
}
```

PEOPLE.DLG

```
DLGABOUT DIALOG  72,13,124,70
STYLE DS_MODALFRAME | WS_POPUP | WS_CLIPSIBLINGS
BEGIN
    CONTROL "OK",IDOK,"Button",BS_DEFPUSHBUTTON | WS_TABSTOP | WS_CHILD |
WS_VISIBLE,32,50,30,14
    CONTROL "Written using the Windows++ Class Library by Paul
DiLascia",-1,"static",WS_CHILD | SS_LEFT,32,18,88,28
    CONTROL "AppIcon",IDSI_ABOUTICON,"static",SS_ICON | WS_CHILD,7,22,16,16
    CONTROL "People Database",-1,"static",WS_CHILD | SS_LEFT,32,5,80,8
END
DLGEDITPERSON DIALOG  28,32,221,109
STYLE WS_POPUPWINDOW | DS_MODALFRAME | WS_CLIPSIBLINGS | WS_DLGFRAME
CAPTION "Edit Person"
BEGIN
    CONTROL "",IDED_NAME,"edit",WS_TABSTOP | WS_CHILD | WS_BORDER |
ES_LEFT,38,8,109,12
    CONTROL "",IDED_ADDR,"edit",WS_TABSTOP | WS_CHILD | WS_BORDER |
ES_LEFT,38,22,109,12
    CONTROL "",IDED_CITY,"edit",WS_TABSTOP | WS_CHILD | WS_BORDER |
ES_LEFT,38,36,74,12
    CONTROL "",IDCB_STATE,"combobox",CBS_DROPDOWN | WS_TABSTOP | WS_CHILD |
WS_VSCROLL,116,36,31,70
    CONTROL "",IDED_ZIP,"edit",WS_TABSTOP | WS_CHILD | WS_BORDER |
ES_LEFT,38,50,50,12
    CONTROL "",IDED_PHONE,"edit",WS_TABSTOP | WS_CHILD | WS_BORDER |
ES_LEFT,38,64,50,12
    CONTROL "&Relation",IDRBG_STATUS,"button",BS_GROUPBOX | WS_TABSTOP |
WS_CHILD,159,5,56,53
    CONTROL "&Friend",IDB_FRIEND,"button",BS_AUTORADIOBUTTON | WS_TABSTOP |
WS_CHILD,170,16,42,11
    CONTROL "&Business",IDB_BUSINESS,"button",BS_AUTORADIOBUTTON | WS_TABSTOP |
WS_CHILD,170,29,42,11
    CONTROL "&Other",IDB_OTHER,"button",BS_AUTORADIOBUTTON | WS_TABSTOP |
WS_CHILD,170,42,42,11
    CONTROL "&Selected",IDB_SELECTED,"button",BS_AUTOCHECKBOX | WS_TABSTOP |
WS_CHILD,106,65,42,11
    CONTROL "&OK",IDOK,"Button",BS_DEFPUSHBUTTON | WS_TABSTOP | WS_CHILD |
```

```
WS_VISIBLE,170,67,41,14
    CONTROL "OK&&Next",IDM_OKNEXT,"Button",WS_TABSTOP | WS_CHILD | WS_VISIBLE |
BS_PUSHBUTTON,106,86,41,14
    CONTROL "&Cancel",IDCANCEL,"Button",WS_TABSTOP | WS_CHILD | WS_VISIBLE |
BS_PUSHBUTTON,170,86,41,14
    CONTROL "Zip",-1,"static",WS_CHILD | SS_LEFT,4,52,29,9
    CONTROL "Phone",-1,"static",WS_CHILD | SS_LEFT,4,66,29,9
    CONTROL "Name",-1,"static",WS_CHILD | SS_LEFT,4,9,29,9
    CONTROL "Address",-1,"static",WS_CHILD | SS_LEFT,4,24,29,9
    CONTROL "City/St",-1,"static",WS_CHILD | SS_LEFT,4,38,29,9
    CONTROL "OK&&Prev",IDM_OKPREV,"Button",WS_TABSTOP | WS_CHILD | WS_VISIBLE |
BS_PUSHBUTTON,38,86,41,14
END
```

PEOPLE.RC

```
///////////////////////////////////////////////////////
// WINDOWS++ CLASS LIBRARY.  Copyright 1992 Paul DiLascia.
// FILE: PEOPLE.RC
//
#include "people.h"
AppIcon   ICON hello.ico
Hello1    ICON hello1.ico
Hello2    ICON hello2.ico
AppMenu MENU {
    POPUP "&File" {
        MENUITEM FileNew
        MENUITEM FileOpen
        MENUITEM SEPARATOR
        MENUITEM FileSave
        MENUITEM FileSaveAs
        MENUITEM SEPARATOR
        MENUITEM HelpAbout
        MENUITEM FileExit
    }
    POPUP "&Edit" {
        MENUITEM EditDelete
        MENUITEM SEPARATOR
        MENUITEM "&New Person...", IDM_EDITNEW
        MENUITEM "&Person...",  IDM_EDIT
    }
}
AppAccel ACCELERATORS
BEGIN
    AccFileNew
    AccFileOpen
    AccFileSave
    AccMemStats
END
#include "people.dlg"
```

RANDRECT.CPP

```
///////////////////////////////////////////////////////
// WINDOWS++ CLASS LIBRARY.  Copyright 1992 Paul DiLascia.
// FILE: RANDRECT.CPP
//
// RANDRECT adapted for Windows++ from orignal program by
// Charles Petzold in "Programming Windows" Chapter 12.
#include <wpp.h>
APPCLASS RandRect : public WPMainWin {
public:
    RandRect()                  { createWin("Windows++ Random Rectangles"); }
    BOOL doIdle();              // virtual function called during idle loop
};
void WPApp::main()
{
    mainWin = new RandRect;
```

```
    run();
}
BOOL RandRect::doIdle()
{
    WPRect win = this;
    WPRect box(rand() % win.width(), rand() % win.height(),
        rand() % win.width(), rand() % win.height());
    box.normalize();       // normalize (no negative width, ht)
    WPWinDC dc = this;
    dc.setBrush( RGB(rand()&255, rand()&255, rand()&255) );
    dc.rectangle(box);
    return TRUE;           // tell Windows++ to do idle loop
}
```

RANDRECT.RC

```
/////////////////////////////////////////////////////////
// WINDOWS++ CLASS LIBRARY.  Copyright 1992 Paul DiLascia.
// FILE: RANDRECT.RC
//
#include "wpp.h"
AppIcon  ICON randrect.ico
AppMenu MENU {
    MENUITEM "E&xit!", WPIDM_EXIT
}
AppAccel ACCELERATORS
BEGIN
    AccMemStats
END
```

TOE.CPP

```
/////////////////////////////////////////////////////////
// WINDOWS++ CLASS LIBRARY.  Copyright 1992 Paul DiLascia.
// FILE: TOE.CPP
//
// This program "learns" to play tic-tac-toe by recording a history of all
// its games and choosing moves that prove historically to win.
#include <wpp.h>
#include <time.h>
const SQM_CHECKED = 1;                   // message sent to parent
enum SQSTATE {
    SQFREE= 1,                           // square is free
    SQOOO = 3,                           // square is O
    SQXXX = 5,                           // square is X
};
/////////////////
// Window class for a board square
//
APPCLASS Square : public WPWin {
    SQSTATE state;                       // state of square: free, X or O
public:
    BOOL paint();
    BOOL mouse(int msg, WPPoint p, WORD flags);
    Square(WPWin *pwin, int id);
    SQSTATE operator()()       { return state; }
    void set(SQSTATE newstate);
};
/////////////////
// This structure is used to save the result of a game.
//
struct GAME {
    char moves[9];                       // the game
    int nmoves;                          // number of moves
    int result;                          // whether I won, lost or drew
};
const NHISTORY = 50;                     // save this many games
```

```
const NSQUARES = 9;                    // nine squares in board
enum RESULT { LOSE=-1, DRAW=0, WIN=2 };
//////////////////
// This is the main tic-tac-toe window.
//
APPCLASS ToeBoard : public WPMainWin {
    Square *squares[NSQUARES];         // the board = 9 child squares
    GAME history[NHISTORY];            // history of past games
    int histLen;                       // number of games played
    int curGame;                       // current game number
    int curMove;                       // current nove number
    int win,block;                     // hint: move to win or block
    // these are all special toe functions
    SQSTATE operator[](int x)  { return (*squares[x%NSQUARES])(); }
    BOOL tictactoe();                  // test if tic-tac-toe
    BOOL tictactoe(int i, int j, int k); // ditto
    BOOL computeValue(int move);       // compute value of move
    void newGame(int result);          // start a new game
    int computeMove();                 // figure out next move
    void think();                      // pretend to "think"
    void setSquare(int move, SQSTATE which);
    // Here are the virtual message functions
    BOOL command(int id, WORD msg);    // handle child message
    BOOL sized(WPRect &pos, WORD how); // re-size window
    BOOL kbd(WPEvent& event);
public:
    ToeBoard();
};
//////////////////
// Entry point
//
void WPApp::main()
{
    mainWin = new ToeBoard;     // create tic-tac-toe board
    run();                      // run message loop
}
//////////////////
// Initialize board square.
//
Square::Square(WPWin *pwin, int id) : WPWin("square", pwin, id)
{
    state = SQFREE;                    // square is free to start
    createArgs.wndcls.hCursor = NULL;  // we will set cursor in real-time
    createArgs.style |= WS_BORDER;     // draw a border around it
    createWin();                       // create the window
}
//////////////////
// Paint X or O depending on state of square.
//
BOOL Square::paint()
{
    WPPaintStruct ps = this;
    WPRect box = this;
    box -= 2;                // shrink 2 pixels
    switch (state) {
    case SQOOO:
        ps.setPen(COLOR_BLUE);
        ps.ellipse(box);
        break;
    case SQXXX:
        ps.setPen(COLOR_RED);
        ps.line( box.origin(),  box.endpt() );
        ps.line( box.topRight(),box.bottomLeft() );
        break;
    }
    return TRUE;
}
```

```
/////////////////
// Change state of square.
//
void Square::set(SQSTATE newstate)
{
    state = newstate;
    invalidate(TRUE);
    Cursor = state==SQFREE ? "XCURSOR" : IDC_ARROW;
}
/////////////////
// Handle mouse event.
//
BOOL Square::mouse(int msg, WPPoint p, WORD flags)
{
    switch (msg) {
    case WM_LBUTTONDOWN:
        if (state!=SQFREE)
            MsgBeep();                          // square is taken: beep
        else
            notifyParent(SQM_CHECKED);     // tell main window
        break;
    case WM_MOUSEMOVE:
        Cursor = state==SQFREE ? "XCURSOR" : IDC_ARROW;
        break;
    }
    return TRUE;
}
/////////////////
// Create tic-tac-toe board
//
ToeBoard::ToeBoard()
{
    // compute default size of toe board from screen size
    int cx = GetSystemMetrics(SM_CXSCREEN);
    int cy = GetSystemMetrics(SM_CYSCREEN);
    int side = min(cx,cy)/2;
    createArgs.pos.origin((cx-side)/2, (cy-side)/2);
    createArgs.pos.extent(side, side);
    createWin("TOE");                       // create window
    histLen = curGame = 0;                  // no games played yet
    // create child window for each square
    for (int i=0; i<NSQUARES; i++)
        squares[i] = new Square(this, i);
}
/////////////////
// Resize all the squares to fit the window.
//
BOOL ToeBoard::sized(WPRect &pos, WORD how)
{
    pos /= 3;                               // shrink by 1/3
    WPPoint moveRight(pos.width());      // moves rectangle right one square
    WPPoint moveDown(0, pos.height());  // moves rectangle down one square
    // Now reposition each square (child window)
    int s = 0;
    WPDeferWinPos defer = NSQUARES;
    for (int i=0; i<3; i++) {
        WPRect box = pos;                    // box = position of 1st square in row
        for (int j=0; j<3; j++) {
            defer.move(squares[s++], box); // move the window
            box += moveRight;                // move box right one
        }
        pos += moveDown;                    // move down one row
    }
    return TRUE;
}
/////////////////
// Hande keyboard event.
//
```

```
BOOL ToeBoard::kbd(WPEvent& event)
{
    Square *sq;
    switch (event.msg) {
    case WM_CHAR:
        if (event.key() == ' ' || event.key() == '\r') {
            sq = (Square*)WinFromPoint(Cursor());
            assert(sq);
            sq->mouse(WM_LBUTTONDOWN, Cursor(), 0);
        }
        return TRUE;
    case WM_KEYDOWN:
        if (Keyboard.isArrowKey(event.key())) {
            // Got arrow key: move cursor
            sq = (Square*)WinFromPoint(Cursor());
            assert(sq);
            WPRect winRect = sq;
            int id = sq->getID();
            switch (event.key()) {
            case VK_LEFT:    id--;    break;
            case VK_RIGHT:   id++;    break;
            case VK_UP:      id-=3;   break;
            case VK_DOWN:    id+=3;   break;
            }
            id = (id+NSQUARES) % NSQUARES;      // new square
            winRect = squares[id];              // new square's rectangle
            winRect /= 2;                       // ..halve it
            Cursor = winRect.endpt();           // put cursor in center of square
            return TRUE;
        }
        break;
    }
    return WPMainWin::kbd(event);
}
/////////////////
// Process message from child square.
//
BOOL ToeBoard::command(int id, WORD msg)
{
    if (id<0 || id>=NSQUARES)
        return WPMainWin::command(id, msg);
    switch (msg) {
    case SQM_CHECKED:
        setSquare(id, SQXXX);     // put X where user clicked
        if (tictactoe())          // user got three in a row?
            newGame(LOSE);        // too bad, I lose
        else {
            int mymove = computeMove();      // figure out my move
            if (mymove >= 0) {               // got a move:
                think();                     // pretend to think
                setSquare(mymove, SQOOO);    // put O in my square
                if (tictactoe())             // three in a row?
                    newGame(WIN);            // hooray, I win!
            } else
                newGame(DRAW);               // no possible move: draw
        }
        break;
    }
    return TRUE;
}
/////////////////
// Simulate thinking by waiting 2 seconds.
//
void ToeBoard::think()
{
    WPWaitCursor wait = this;  // change cursor to wait icon
    time_t t;
    t = time(NULL)+2;
```

```
    while (time(NULL) < t)
        ;
}
///////////////////
// Record a move.  Store it in current game, change square and clear hints.
//
void ToeBoard::setSquare(int move, SQSTATE which)
{
    history[curGame].moves[curMove++] = move;      // record move in history
    squares[move]->set(which);              // set square
    win = block = -1;                       // clear hints
    update();                               // force move to be displayed
}
///////////////////
// Clear all squares.  First display message.
//
void ToeBoard::newGame(int result)
{
    MsgBox(result==WIN ? "I Win!" : result==LOSE ? "You Win!" : "Draw!");
    // save game result in history buffer
    history[curGame].result = result;
    history[curGame].nmoves = curMove;
    if (++histLen < NHISTORY)
        curGame++;
    // reset move num to zero and all squares to free
    curMove=0;
    for (int i=0; i<NSQUARES; i++)
        squares[i]->set(SQFREE);
}
///////////////////
// Check for tic-tac-toe.  i,j,k are three squares in a row.
// Returns TRUE if all the squares are X's or O's, otherwise FALSE.
// If two out of three are X or O, set "block" or "win" to the move that
// either blocks user from tic-tac-toe or wins for me.
//
int ToeBoard::tictactoe(int i, int j, int k)
{
    ToeBoard &board = *this;                // board is now reference to this.
    int prod = board[i] * board[j] * board[k];
    if (prod==SQXXX*SQXXX)
        block = board[i]==SQFREE ? i : board[j]==SQFREE ? j : k;
    else if (prod==SQOOO*SQOOO)
        win = board[i]==SQFREE ? i : board[j]==SQFREE ? j : k;
    return prod==(SQXXX*SQXXX*SQXXX) || prod==(SQOOO*SQOOO*SQOOO);
}
///////////////////
// Determine if there's a tic-tac-toe.  Returns TRUE if there are
// three X's or O's in a row.  Check up-down, left-right and diagonals.
//
BOOL ToeBoard::tictactoe()
{
    for (int i=0; i<3; i++) {
        if (tictactoe(i, i+3, i+6))          // up-down
            return TRUE;
        if (tictactoe(3*i, 3*i+1, 3*i+2)) // left-right
            return TRUE;
    }
    if (tictactoe(0, 4, 8))                  // diagonal
        return TRUE;
    return tictactoe(2, 4, 6);               // other diagonal
}
///////////////////
// Compute "value" of a possible move: start with 1000, then subtract 1
// for each game where the same move caused a loss; add one for each win.
// history.result is +1 (win), -1 (loss), or 0 (draw).
//
int ToeBoard::computeValue(int move)
{
```

```
        history[curGame].moves[curMove] = move;
        int val = 1000;
        for (int h=0; h<min(NHISTORY,histLen); h++) {
            if (history[h].nmoves >= curMove &&
                    memcmp(history[curGame].moves, history[h].moves, curMove+1)==0)
                val += history[h].result;
        }
        return val;
}
//////////////////
// Compute next move.
// First check hints: look first for winner, then block.
// Otherwise, compute value of all possible moves and select the best one.
// Returns the square number of move, or -1 if no squares free (draw).
//
int ToeBoard::computeMove()
{
    ToeBoard &board = *this;
    if (win>=0)
        return win;                      // I can win
    else if (block>=0)
        return block;                    // I can block
    // compute values of all legal moves
    int moveVal[NSQUARES];
    for (int move=0; move<NSQUARES; move++)
        moveVal[move] = board[move]==SQFREE ? computeValue(move) : -1;
    // moveVal array now has value of each move or -1 if square is taken.
    // Choose the best one.
    //
    int which = 0;
    for (int i=0; i<NSQUARES; i++) {
        if (moveVal[i] > moveVal[which])
            which = i;
    }
    return moveVal[which] >= 0 ? which : -1;
}
```

TOE.DLG

```
DLGABOUT DIALOG  8,20,143,56
STYLE DS_MODALFRAME | WS_POPUP | WS_CLIPSIBLINGS
BEGIN
    CONTROL "&OK",IDOK,"Button",BS_DEFPUSHBUTTON | WS_TABSTOP | WS_CHILD |
WS_VISIBLE,56,35,30,14
    CONTROL "TOE written using Windows++",-1,"static",SS_CENTER |
WS_CHILD,17,10,119,9
    CONTROL "by Paul DiLascia (C) 1992",-1,"static",SS_CENTER |
WS_CHILD,34,20,85,8
    CONTROL "appicon",-1,"static",SS_ICON | WS_CHILD,5,10,16,16
END
```

TOE.RC

```
//////////////////////////////////////////////////////////
// WINDOWS++ CLASS LIBRARY.  Copyright 1992 Paul DiLascia.
// FILE: TOE.RC
//
#include "wpp.h"
xcursor CURSOR toe.cur
AppIcon ICON toe.ico
AppMenu MENU {
    POPUP "&File" {
        MENUITEM HelpAbout
        MENUITEM FileExit
    }
}
AppAccel ACCELERATORS
BEGIN
```

```
        AccMemStats
END
#include "toe.dlg"
```

WINEDIT.CPP

```cpp
/////////////////////////////////////////////////////////
// WINDOWS++ CLASS LIBRARY.   Copyright 1992 Paul DiLascia.
// FILE: WINEDIT.CPP
//
// Single file editor.
#include <wpp.h>
/////////////////////
// Main edit window class.
//
APPCLASS EditWin : public WPMainWin {
    WPMultiEdit *editCtl;    // main edit window
    int pmtHeight;           // height of prompt line font
public:
    EditWin(CSTR fname=NULL);
    // Virtual message functions
    BOOL sized(WPRect &box, WORD how);
    BOOL gotFocus(WPWin *prev)     { editCtl->setFocus(); return FALSE; }
    int getMenuPrompt(char* buf, int id, WORD flags)
        { return id ? App.loadString(id, buf, MAXPROMPTLEN) : 0; }
    // File command functions
    BOOL fileIsModified()          { return editCtl->isModified(); }
    void fileIsModified(BOOL m)    { editCtl->setModified(m); }
    BOOL fileOpen(CSTR fname)      { return editCtl->load(fname); }
    BOOL fileSave(CSTR fname)      { return editCtl->save(fname); }
    BOOL fileNew()
        { editCtl->setSel(); editCtl->clear(); return TRUE; }
    BOOL filePrint(WPDlgPrint &pdlg);
    // Edit command functions
    BOOL editCut()        { editCtl->cut(); return TRUE; }
    BOOL editCopy()       { editCtl->copy(); return TRUE; }
    BOOL editPaste()      { editCtl->paste(); return TRUE; }
    BOOL editDelete()     { editCtl->clear(); return TRUE; }
    BOOL editUndo()       { editCtl->undo(); return TRUE; }
    BOOL canPaste()       { return Clipboard.available(CF_TEXT); }
    BOOL canUndo()        { return editCtl->canUndo(); }
    BOOL anySelected()
        { int beg,end; return editCtl->getSel(beg, end); }
};
/////////////////////
// Main entry point.   Command line argument is name of file to open
//
void WPApp::main()
{
    char fname[80];
    getCmdLine(fname);
    mainWin = new EditWin(fname);
    run();
}
/////////////////////
// Initialize main window.
//
EditWin::EditWin(CSTR fname)
{
    createWin();              // create main window
    // Create edit control
    editCtl = new WPMultiEdit(this, 1);
    createArgs.style |= WS_VSCROLL;
    editCtl->createWin();
    // Create prompt line
    promptWin = new WPStatic(this, 2);
    promptWin->createWin();
    pmtHeight = tm.tmHeight;
```

```
    fileInit(fname, "WINEDIT");
}
//////////////////
// Main window was re-sized
//
BOOL EditWin::sized(WPRect &box, WORD how)
{
    // Adjust edit control
    box.height(box.height()-pmtHeight);
    editCtl->moveWin(box);
    // Adjust prompt line
    WPRect pmtbox;
    pmtbox.origin(0, box.height());
    pmtbox.extent(box.width(), pmtHeight);
    promptWin->moveWin(pmtbox);
    return TRUE;
}
//////////////////
// Print the file. Should really check pdlg for num copies, etc.
//
BOOL EditWin::filePrint(WPDlgPrint &pdlg)
{
    char *line = App.scratch;
    int nlines = editCtl->numLines();
    WPLinePrinter p = pdlg;
    p.doAbortDlg(this);
    p.startDoc(fileName());
    for (int i=0; i < nlines && !p.aborted(); i++) {
        int len = editCtl->getLine(i, line, 256);
        p.outLine(line, len);
    }
    p.endDoc();
    return TRUE;
}
```

WINEDIT.DLG

```
DLGSEARCH DIALOG  10,17,132,27
STYLE WS_POPUPWINDOW | WS_VISIBLE | WS_CLIPSIBLINGS | WS_DLGFRAME
CAPTION "Search"
BEGIN
    CONTROL "",WPIDED_STRING,"edit",ES_AUTOHSCROLL | WS_TABSTOP | WS_CHILD |
WS_BORDER | ES_LEFT,31,7,96,12
    CONTROL "Search:",-1,"static",WS_CHILD | SS_LEFT,3,8,26,10
END
```

WINEDIT.RC

```
/////////////////////////////////////////////////////////
// WINDOWS++ CLASS LIBRARY.  Copyright 1992 Paul DiLascia.
// FILE: WINEDIT.RC
//
#include "wpp.h"
AppMenu MENU {
    POPUP "&File" {
        MENUITEM FileNew
        MENUITEM FileOpen
        MENUITEM SEPARATOR
        MENUITEM FileSave
        MENUITEM FileSaveAs
        MENUITEM SEPARATOR
        MENUITEM FilePrint
        MENUITEM SEPARATOR
        MENUITEM FileExit
    }
    POPUP "&Edit" {
        MENUITEM EditUndo
        MENUITEM SEPARATOR
```

```
                MENUITEM EditCut
                MENUITEM EditCopy
                MENUITEM EditPaste
                MENUITEM SEPARATOR
                MENUITEM EditDelete
        }
}
AppAccel ACCELERATORS
BEGIN
        AccFileNew
        AccFileOpen
        AccFilePrint
        AccFileSave
        AccEditUndo
        AccEditCut
        AccEditCopy
        AccEditPaste
        AccMemStats
END
STRINGTABLE {
    WPIDM_FILENEW, "Create a new file."
    WPIDM_FILEOPEN, "Open an existing file."
    WPIDM_FILESAVE, "Save current file on disk."
    WPIDM_FILESAVEAS, "Save current file with a different name."
    WPIDM_FILEPRINT, "Print current file."
    WPIDM_EXIT, "Exit from program."
    WPIDM_EDITUNDO, "Undo previous edit operation."
    WPIDM_EDITCUT, "Delete selected text and transfer it to the clipboard."
    WPIDM_EDITCOPY, "Copy selected text to the clipboard."
    WPIDM_EDITPASTE, "Insert contents of clipboard at current location."
    WPIDM_EDITDELETE, "Delete selected text without transferring it to the
clipboard."
}
#include "wpprint.dlg"
```

A.3 Zortech Files

This section describes changes to the *Zortech* Windows start-up code that are required to make static initialization work correctly. Essentially, this involves changing the Zortech code to call *_doctors* ("do constructors"), which invokes the static constructors, just before invoking *WinMain,* instead of earlier, when Windows isn't initialized yet. Two files must be changed: CINIT.ASM and CW.ASM. Once compiled, these modules are added to the *Windows++* library, so that they're linked instead of the versions in the Zortech libraries.

Note: you must use the Microsoft MASM assembler to compile the files shown here. If you don't have MASM, you can purchase the *Windows++* diskette, which comes with pre-compiled .OBJ files.

CINIT.ASM

Below are the changes for CINIT.ASM:

Line 21: Add *_doctors* as public function. Original line:

```
    public __dos,__dodtors
```

Change to:

```
    public __dos,__dodtors,_doctors    ; added _doctors 12/9/91 PD
```

Line 194: Don't call _doctors here. Original line:

```
    call    doctors                     ;perform static constructors
```

Change to:

```
    ;; Modified Paul DiLascia 12/9/91
    ;; for Windows, don't call constructors here
    ;; --do it just before WinMain
    ifndef _WINDOWS                 ;; mod PD
    call    _doctors                ;perform static constructors
    endif                           ;; mod PD
```

Line 224: Add Windows prolog. Original line:

```
doctors    proc    near
```

Change to:

```
func    _doctors                    ;; mod PD: export as func
        WINENTER_NF                 ;; mod PD: add Windows prolog
```

Line 268: Add Windows epilog. Original lines:

```
CT4:    ret
doctors    endp
```

Change to:

```
CT4:    WINLEAVE_NF                 ;; mod PD
    ret                             ;; mod PD
c_endp _doctors endp                ;; mod PD
```

CW.ASM

Below are the changes for CW.ASM:

Line 25: add __doctors as extern symbol. Original line:

```
    extrn _exit     : far
```

Change to:

```
    extrn _exit     : far
    extrn __doctors : far           ;; mod PD
```

Line 32: Same reason as above. Original line:

```
    extrn _exit       : near
```

Change to:

```
    extrn _exit       : near
    extrn __doctors                 : near ;; mod PD
```

Line 213: Add call to static constructors just before WinMain. Original lines:

```
st4:
    ;Call the application's entry point
    push   hInstance
```

Change to:

```
st4:
    call    __doctors                       ;; mod PD
    ;Call the application's entry point
    push   hInstance
```

SETDS.ASM

This tiny function implements SETDS for Zortech: *setDS* sets the DS register to the value of its argument, and returns the old value.

```
; ds.asm
; Copyright (C) 1991 Paul DiLascia
; Get/Set DS register for Zortech
include macros.asm
    begcode    ds
    c_public setDS,
; set DS register from argument passed
; returns old DS
func    setDS
    push BP
    mov BP,SP
    mov AX,DS
    mov DS,P[BP]
    pop BP
    ret
c_endp setDS
    endcode ds
    end
```

A.4 Class Hierarchy Map

The following diagrams show the inheritance relationships among the various window and GDI classes.

Window Classes

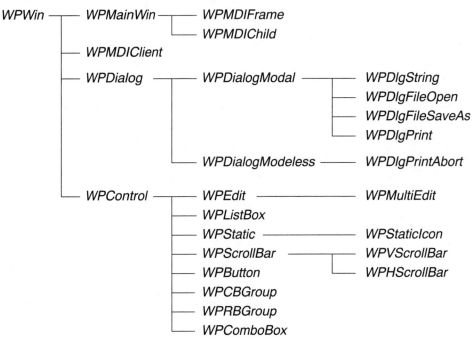

GDI Classes

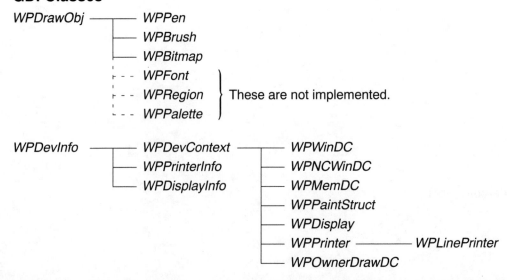

BIBLIOGRAPHY ∎

Coad 1990.
> Peter Coad & Edward Yourdon, *Object-Oriented Analysis*
> Prentice Hall, 1990.

Foley & Van Dam 1990.
> James D. Foley, Andries Van Dam, Steven K. Fiener, and John F. Hughes,
> *Computer Graphics: Principles and Practice*, Second Edition
> Addison-Wesley, 1990.

IBM 1989.
> *Common User Access Advanced Interface Design Guide*, First Edition
> International Business Machines, 1989.

Lippman 1991.
> Stanley B. Lippman, AT&T Bell Labs,
> *C++ Primer*, Second Edition
> Addison-Wesley, 1991.

Mandelbrot 1982.
> Benoit Mandelbrot, *The Fractal Geometry of Nature*
> W. H. Freeman, 1982.

Meyer 1988.
> Bertrand Meyer, *Object-oriented Software Construction*
> Prentice Hall, 1988.

Petzold 1990.
> Charles Petzold, *Programming Windows (Version 3)*, Second Edition
> Microsoft Press, 1990.

Schulman 1991a.

> Andrew Schulman, "Windows 3.0: All That Memory, All Those Modes"
> *PC Magazine,* June 11, 1991.

Schulman 1991b.

> Andrew Schulman, "Porting DOS Programs to Protected-Mode Windows
> with the WINDOS Library"
> *Microsoft Systems Journal,* September, 1991.

Schulman 1992.

> Andrew Schulman, David Maxey, and Matt Pietrek, *Undocumented Windows*
> Addison-Wesley, 1992.

R. Stevens 1989.

> Roger Stevens, *Fractal Programming in C*
> M&T Books, 1989.

Stroustrup 1991.

> Bjarne Stroustrup, *The C++ Programming Language,* Second Edition
> Addison-Wesley, 1991.

Yao 1990.

> Paul Yao, "Windows 3.0 Memory Management: Supporting Disparate
> 80x86 Architectures"
> *Microsoft Systems Journal,* November, 1990.

INDEX

Windows++
SOURCE DISK

To receive a disk containing the source code for *Windows++* and the sample programs described in the book, please fill in the coupon below (or a copy thereof) and mail it with a check or money order, payable to *Paul DiLascia*, to:

Paul DiLascia
PO Box 391632
Cambridge, MA 02139

The disk contains the following items:

- Source code for the entire *Windows++* library, including changes to the Zortech start-up code (.OBJ files included, in case you don't have MASM).

- Source code for all sample programs, including DRAW, HELLO, LAUNCH, MANDEL, MEDIT, MEMTEST, MKC, PEOPLE, RANDRECT, TOE, and WINEDIT, plus the sample DLLs from Chapter 9.

- MAKEFILEs, .RC, and .ICO files, and so on—everything you need to build the programs in the book.

- Program and library source code for HELLO programs 1, 2, and 3.

- Last-minute enhancements and bug fixes not covered in the book.

The software compiles using the Borland 3.0 or Zortech 3.0r4 C++ compilers. *Windows++* comes without support, nor with any guarantee except that it's what's shown in the book. You may use the library to build applications that you resell to others, but you may not redistribute the source code itself.

- -

Please send me the companion disk for *Windows++*.

Name: _____

Address: _____

_____

City: _____ State: _____ Zip: _____

☐ 5.25 inch (default)   ☐ 3.5 inch

Send me _____ copies at $25 each: _____

Shipping outside USA add $5/disk: _____

TOTAL: _____